INDIAN FOOD

A HISTORICAL COMPANION

The publisher is grateful to the Indian National Science Academy for permission to print this monograph, completed under the auspices of Indian National Commission for History of Science. The Academy is not responsible for the views expressed in the book.

INDIAN FOOD

A HISTORICAL COMPANION

K. T. ACHAYA

DELHI
OXFORD UNIVERSITY PRESS
CALCUTTA CHENNAI MUMBAI
1998

Oxford University Press, Great Clarendon Street, Oxford OX2 6DP

Oxford New York
Athens Auckland Bangkok Calcutta
Cape Town Chennai Dar es Salaam Delhi
Florence Hong Kong Istanbul Karachi
Kuala Lumpur Madrid Melbourne Mexico City
Mumbai Nairobi Paris Singapore
Taipei Tokyo Toronto

and associates in

Berlin Ibadan

First published 1994
Oxford India Paperbacks 1998

ISBN 0 19 564416 6

Printed at Pauls Press, New Delhi 110 020
and published by Manzar Khan, Oxford University Press
YMCA Library Building, Jai Singh Road, New Delhi 110 001

PREFACE

The present volume is the outcome of a research project on the history of Science in India, funded generously by the Indian National Science Academy, New Delhi. The Centre for the History and Philosophy of Science, Bangalore provided the administrative support. I am grateful to Dr. A. K. Bag of the former organization and Dr. B. V. Subbarayappa of the latter.

The book deals with the food materials and food practices of the Indian subcontinent. The arrangement of the first thirteen chapters is broadly historical, ending with the period of British food ambience in India. A few regional cuisines have been considered, again within a historical context wherever possible; there will still be room for exploration by scholars of local literatures and cultural mores. The fourteenth and fifteenth chapters describe the origins of Indian food materials in botanical and genetic terms. The last chapter is concerned with the food plants that were brought into India from South America and Mexico after the 15th century AD.

Each chapter carries one or more boxed items. This essentially journalistic device enables the inclusion and highlighting of relevant material which might otherwise interrupt the narrative flow of the text. References are numbered chapterwise, and listed together at the end of the book, to avoid distractions caused by footnotes, or even end-of-chapter notes. The four indexes should be helpful in locating various types of specific information without difficulty.

Italicizing Indian words in a text dealing with Indian food would have made for uncomfortable reading, and has therefore been avoided. I have attempted to use English spellings as close as possible to the Indian pronunciation. This has meant some simplification of the several sh, th, ch, t, l and n sounds of Sanskrit, Tamil and other Indian languages. Except for indicating lengthened vowels, diacritical marks have been avoided. Thus thavā represents the Indian griddle pan, shāli winter rice, shāstra knowledge and Charaka and Sushrutha the two medical writers.

Particular assistance in regard to the historical foods was rendered by Smt. Visalakshi and Dr. (Smt.) Radha Krishnamurthy (for Karnataka), by the late Dr. Saradha S. Srinivasan (for Gujarat), and by Smt. Bunny Gupta and Smt. Jaya Chaliha (for Bengal), to all of whom I owe a debt of thanks. Illustrations have come from many hands, each of which has been individually credited. I am grateful to the Oxford University Press, and to Mukul Mangalik for seeing the book through the press.

Bangalore
February 1992

K. T. ACHAYA

CONTENTS

LIST OF ILLUSTRATIONS AND ACKNOWLEDGEMENTS

Every effort has been made to trace the sources of illustrative material used in this book. The publishers would be happy to hear from copyright owners of material hitherto untraced.

Line Drawings

Black and White Plates

Chapter 1

ANCESTRAL LEGACIES

The world, man and his food

Three hundred million years ago the earth is believed to have consisted of one large land mass, Pangaea, which broke up in course of time into fragments.[1,2,3] The largest of these, called Gondwana, then further fragmented about 10 million years ago to yield the huge land masses of Africa, India, Australia and Antarctica. Once India had separated, it moved northwards rather rapidly to collide with what is now Tibet, thrusting upwards the towering Himālayan ranges. At this time India was still connected by land with Africa, but rising ocean levels, as a result of the warming of the planet and the melting of glacial icy layers, eventually submerged this bridge.[4] Still left above water were the islands of Madagascar, Mauritius, the Maldives and the Laccadives. Evidence for this scenario comes from common geological formations and pollen fossils that now exist in these once-connected land areas.

Over the last 100,000 years, glacial ages have alternated with warmer epochs.[4a] Following the last warm period, about 15,000 years ago, man came into his own, starting off as a food gatherer and then becoming a food cultivator.

During the long hominid phase of man, fruits appeared to have been his main dietary item.[5] After the divergence thereafter of the human and ape lines, meat began to enter the meal of *Homo stabilis*. When *Homo erectus* appeared some 1.8 million years ago, crude tools had just begun to be made. Using them, larger quantities of meat were to be had, and the accumulations of animal bones at human abodes suggest that meat formed at least half the total diet. As hunting skills improved, so did the reliance on meat, though, alongside, an ever-widening range of wild vegetable foods was also being gathered by foraging. The development of agriculture after about 10,000 BC rapidly changed the dependence on constant hunting for animal food. In the course of a few millennia meat declined even further, and vegetable foods came to dominate the diet.[5]

At every place where man has evolved, a similar evolutionary pattern has characterized the kind of food that he consumed. This can be deduced from the evidence that he left behind by way of tools, cave paintings and surviving words.

Tools of early man in India

Some thirty sites dating from about half a million years ago have been uncovered. These occur all over India, except for the western coastal strip which is a later geological formation. Early palaeolithic tools, some 250,000 years old, take the form of heavy clubs, technically termed cleavers and hand axes. These were used to club down animals.[6,7] Gujarāt is especially rich in them, perhaps because there was a land bridge with Africa before the sea level rose during the last warm period. Even as recently as 10,000 years ago, the sea levels were lower than they are today.[4b] Tools of the Middle Stone Age, 50,000 to 40,000 years ago, mostly consist of pointed oval-shaped stones of various kinds. These were used as axes, spears, scrapers and knives, all of which suggest again a mainly meat diet.[8] With time these tools grow more finished and polished, and by the New Stone Age or neolithic times distinct types can be discerned.[9] Pebble implements are frequently of quartzite, retaining part of the crust of the pebble from which they had been struck. Flakes were either struck off singly from a rock to give a single sharp edge, or repeatedly, to leave a serrated one. Handaxes were pear-shaped or oval, even up to an arm in length, and cleavers were similar but oblong in shape, with a long chisel edge. Such tools have been found all over the country and again con-

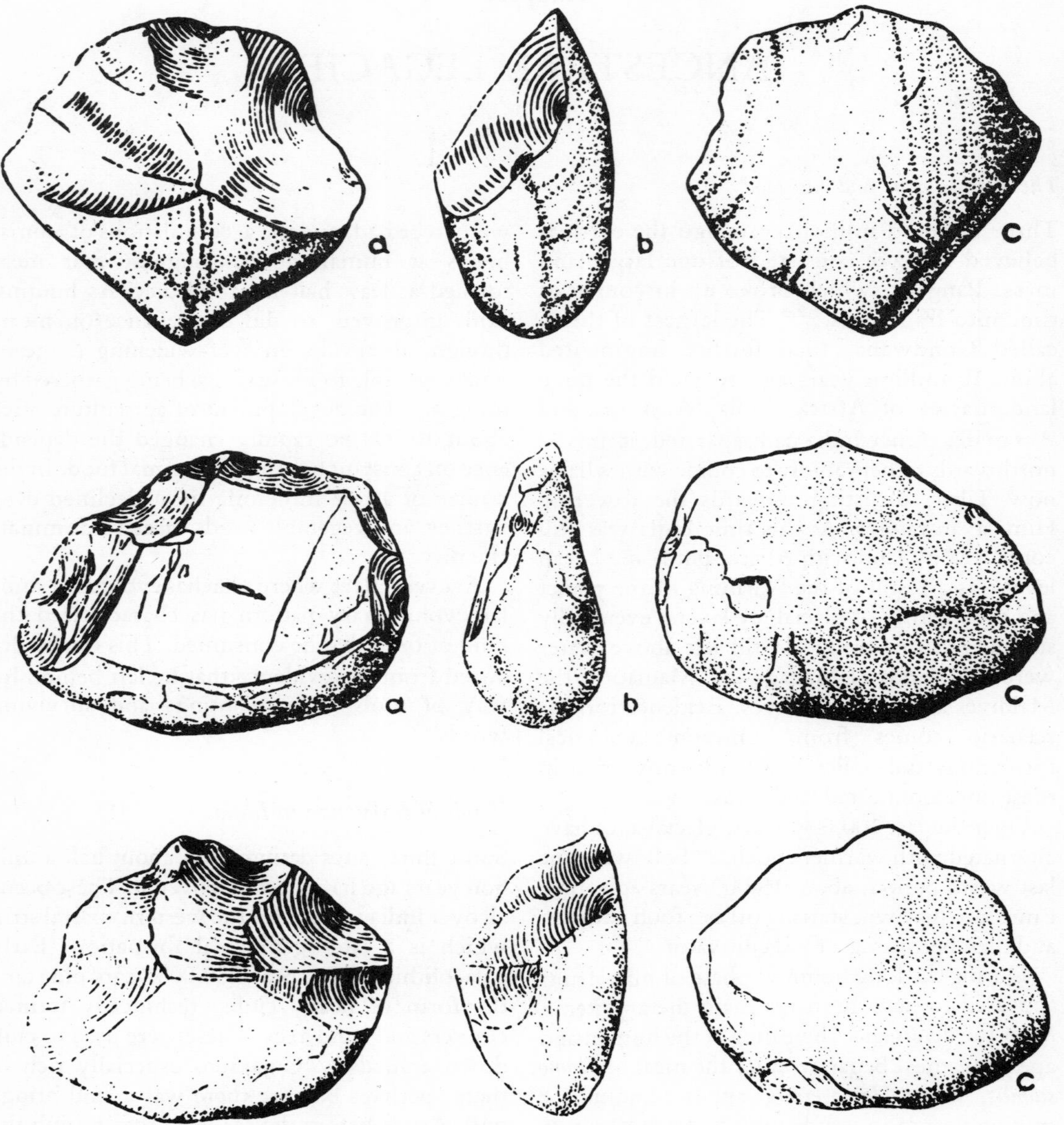

Chopping tools, the earliest type of human implements.

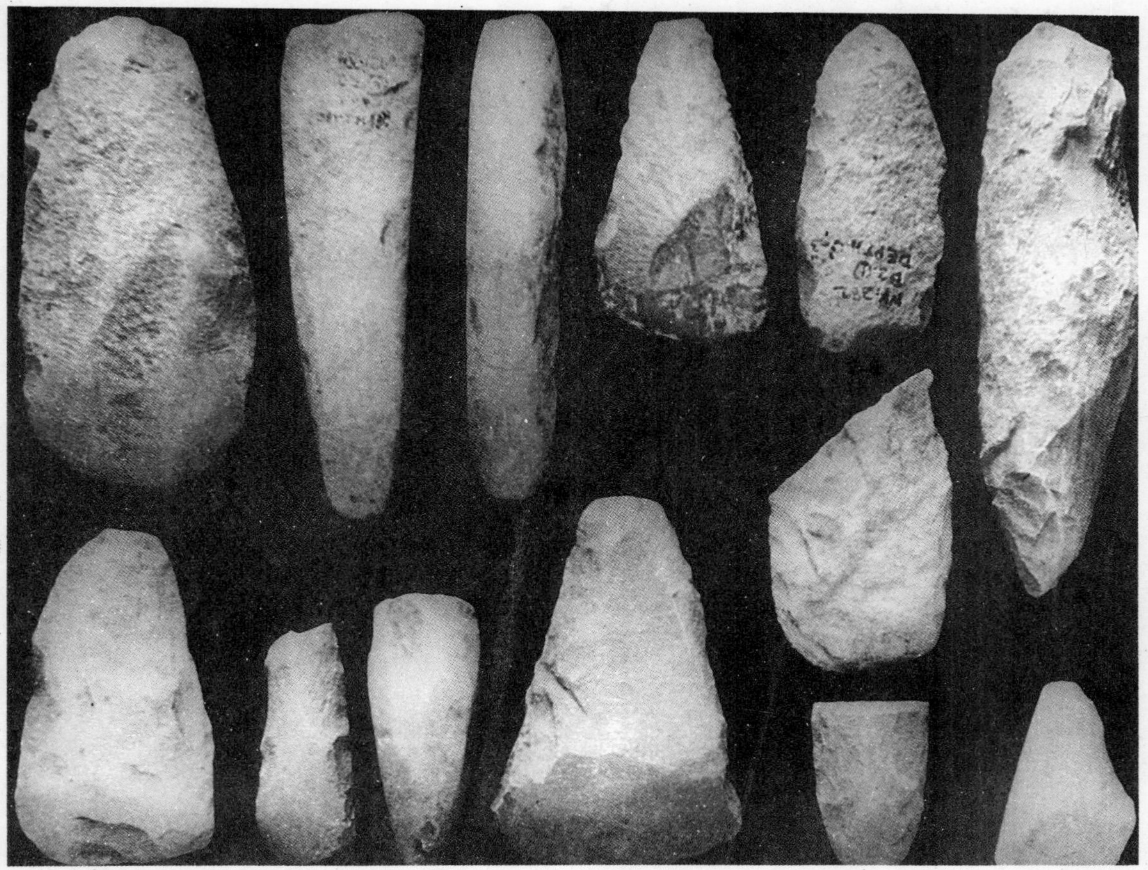

Pointed ovals, used by man at the food-collecting stage.

note an essentially meat diet. Some tools are clearly of the digging type, so the meat must have been complemented with natural foods like honey, berries, fruits, roots, herbs and nuts.

The next step in tool evolution took the form of small, sharp stone flakes called microliths, which have been found in very large numbers in southern and western coastal India. These were fine chips, struck off from rocks or fine-grained stones like jasper, agate, flint and crystal.[10] Microliths could be affixed to an arrow to greatly widen the scope and range of man's hunting activity, and several microliths could be fixed to a lance to give it a rasping character useful in dealing with animals. Affixed to wooden handles, microliths yielded scrapers, scythes and knives, which of course enlarged the possibilities of using vegetable foods, and gave food-gathering a new dimension. Thus the tools that we now unearth give us a good idea of the foods that our ancestors ate.

Analyses of human bones correlate well with other evidence.[11] Skeletons from central India, about 15,000 years old, show excessive development of the bones of the right forearms, presumably from throwing spears and slings, while the customary squatting posture resulted in irregular facets and grooves in the hip, near the knee, and at the base of the shinbone.

When and where the use of fire originated is not known. Suspending an animal high above fire is still practised by primitive peoples, not to cook meat, but to prevent it from putrefying too quickly.[12] Sparks from spontaneous friction, or even forest fires could have led man to the con-

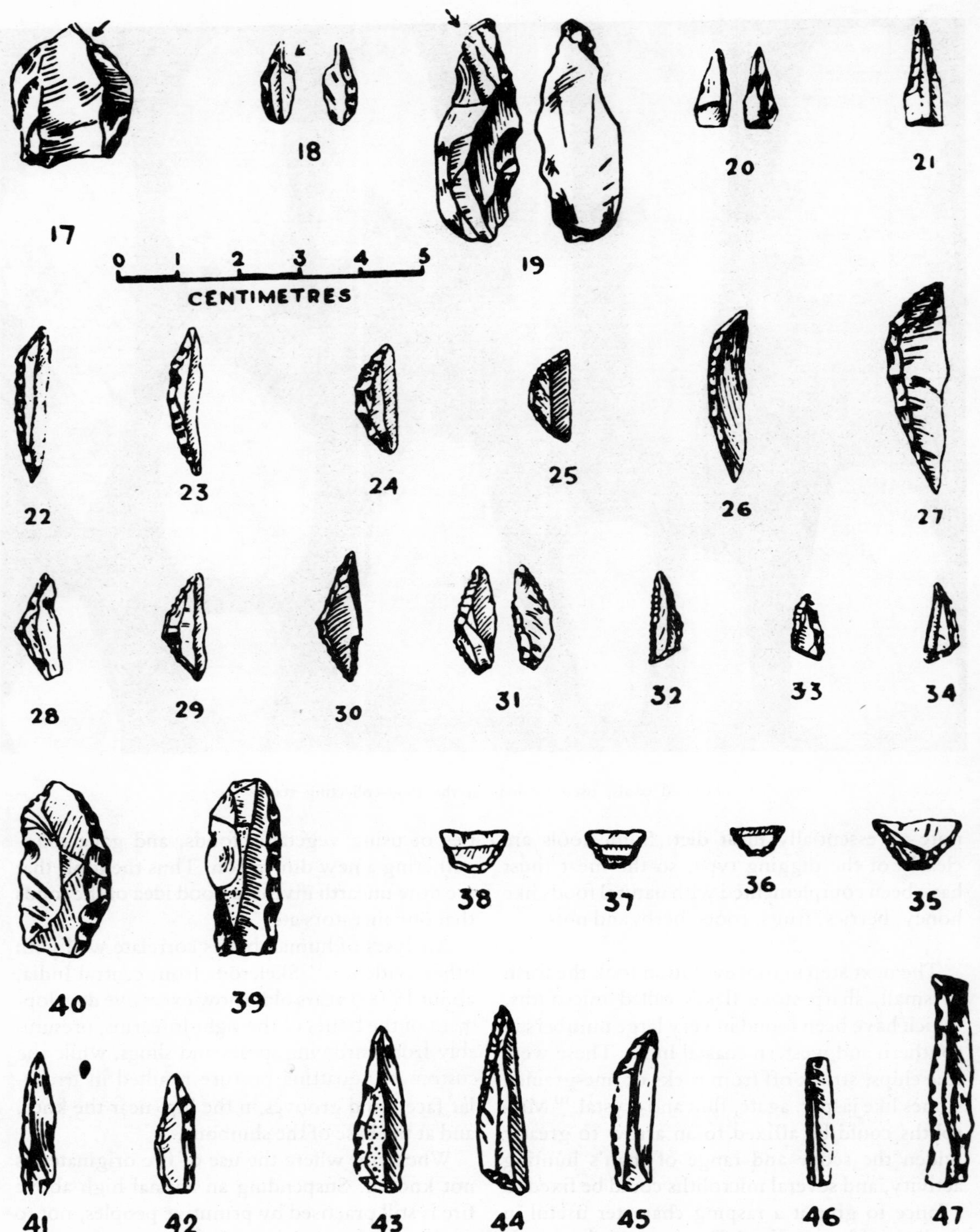

Microliths, developed as man took to agriculture.

cept of roasting meat directly on a flame, or on hot ashes or embers. The Peking cave in China, which was in use 500,000 years ago, shows evidence of the use of fire for roasting and cooking meat.[13] The concept of boiling came much later. It is in fact unknown even now to some African bushmen and Australian Aboriginals, since it implies the use of a fired pot to hold water. Originally a skin-lined hole in the ground may have served for cooking, and then perhaps a clay-lined basket which when burnt left behind the clay form. About 7,000 years ago the first true clay boiling pot was discovered.[13] From the shape, colour and decoration of such pots found in India, whether these are painted grey ware, black-and-red pottery, northern black painted and polished ware, or rouletted grey and black ware, archaeologists draw important conclusions about the origin and movement of various cultures that existed in the past.

We have wandered away from the stone tools of early man. From about 5000 BC neolithic tools emerge in India, reflecting an important shift from the food-gathering to the food-cultivation stage, from a nomadic to a settled life. Chisels, axes, adzes, choppers, scrapers, knives and hammers all grow more sophisticated.[14] The stones chosen to make them also become diversified. Dolerite, basalt and archaen schist are employed in the south-east; and sandstone, dolerite, gneiss and igneous rock in the eastern states.[15,16] A big step forward is taken with the advent of saddle querns for grinding grain or spices. These come in a variety of designs, flat or concave or convex, shallow or deep. With these were paired separate stone grinders that were either cylindrical or round, and used either horizontally or upright.[3] Deep mortars and long pestles for the pounding of grains appear later. In the south of India the mortars are made from black-coloured trap that is much harder than the quartzite used in earlier times indicating that fabrication technology had improved sharply in a few thousand years.[3] Drills to raise fire have been found, marking a new dimension in cooking.[8] The plethora of net-sinkers, both in coastal and riverine sites, is evidence of considerable fishing activity, as are the fish hooks found in many neolithic sites.[3] The use of fish comes at a rather late stage in the diet of man, since it needs a more sophisticated technology.

The first paintings

When did man become an artist and begin giving concrete form and shape to what he felt? The earliest bone sculptures and drawings appear in France and Spain in the palaeolithic era about 25,000 years ago. As yet India has revealed few if any rock paintings which are as old as that. Caves at Bhimbetka in Madhya Pradesh, about 40 kilometres south of Bhopāl, show an unbroken record of the artistic activity of our forefathers.[17,18,19] The earliest, dating from upper palaeolithic times or about 8,000 BC, are in green with a black wash, and have neither an outline nor human figures. As time advances, humans appear, and there are double and single outlines without filling; by neolithic times, say about 3000 BC, outline figures with fill-in shading occur in abundance.

Of particular interest to us is that many of the drawings deal with one of man's major concerns, that of finding food. Hunting with spears, trapping deer, stalking game with bows and arrows (which are sometimes shown clearly serrated with attached microliths), and spearing fish or catching them in nets are all portrayed with energy and realism, and an economical use of line, wash and hatch-lines which compel admiration. The animals shown being hunted are equally of interest. In addition to the bison, gaur, peacock, tiger, and rhinoceros are animals like the giraffe and ostrich which no longer exist in India. A number of engraved ostrich eggs have been discovered at Patne in the Dhūlē district of Mahārāshtra, radio-carbon dated to 40,000 years ago. Obviously ostriches were common then. Indeed, though today confined to the African continent, they are known to have roamed all over southern Europe, Asia, Africa and the Mongolian desert. Women are shown gathering fruit, with long baskets slung on their backs. Particularly interesting are drawings of kneeling or squatting women kneading balls (of dough?) in querns shaped like a wide and shallow letter W (p. 99). What these were made of, we can only speculate.

Paintings during this phase in the Bhimbetka caves, as well as those at Singhanpūr near Rāigarh, and Benekar near Hampi in Karnātaka, show groups of linked dancers performing what appear to be magic rituals, aimed perhaps at gaining control over the desired prey. Elaborate masks and head-dresses suggest that they tried to imitate or emulate animals and birds. Enormous bows appear, as tall as the hunter himself, and traps made of pliant materials like reeds and ropes. The quest for food was an arduous and incessant activity which the artistry of early man has recorded for us with vigour and grace.

About 3000 BC, as the metal age draws in, such hunting scenes become surprisingly rare. What now appear are animal processions, bullock carts with yoked oxen, cows, a humped bull with lyre-shaped horns, fowls and dogs, and the first depiction of a man riding a horse. Indian nomad man had by now become a settled food cultivator.

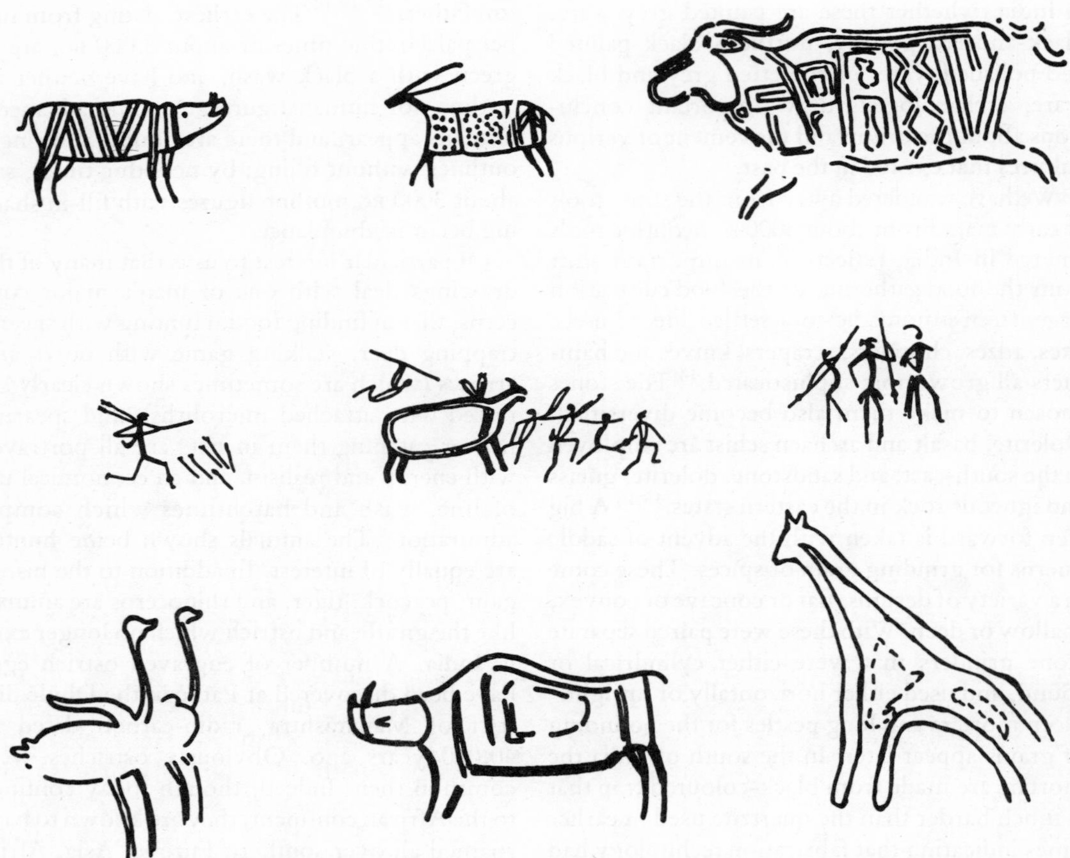

Drawings of animals, from the Bhimbetka caves in Madhya Pradesh.

Language and food

Broadly, three groups of languages are to be found in India. The forerunner of one group, found in the north, is Sanskrit, which is itself believed to share a common ancestry with the European romance languages, and even more closely with old Persian. The *Rigveda*, composed in old Sanskrit about 1500 BC, is the oldest representative of this tongue. In the south, present-day Tamil is the successor of a language which is surmised to have been spoken at one time over a very wide area in Asia, Africa and America. Some trace it to Uralic, spoken once by people resident in Central Asia. This is thought to have developed on the one hand into Finnish, Estonian and Samoyedic by migrant races, and into Dravidian languages by other groups moving into the southern hemisphere. These deductions are based on remarkable similarities in morphology, one of which is common suffixes for past, present, and present-future case-endings. A third group of languages consists of those spoken by the even older inhabitants of India, who are generally called Mundas or Austrics. They were once widely spread over the country, but now live mostly in Bihār, Orissa, West Bengal, Madhya Pradesh and Tripura, with a particularly high concentration in the Ranchi district of Bihār. Persisting words from ancient tongues can provide interesting clues to the origin or movement of food materials.

Vrntāka, for brinjal, is a pre-Sanskrit word.

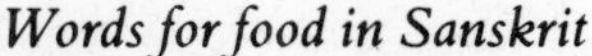

Words for food in Sanskrit

Words in Sanskrit that have a distinctly foreign flavour have frequently been traced to an earlier Munda inheritance. From jom, to eat, is thought to have arisen chom-la and thence chāval, the Hindi word for rice.[20] The cereal *Eleusine coracana* is commonly called rāgi (from rāgā, red in Sanskrit), but has innumerable names in various parts of India, such as marua, mandwa, nāngli, nāchui, kōday, kōdra, kayur, kevar, kupra, kurakan, rotka, tamidelu, taindulu and bavto.[21a] All these have a distinctly Munda provenance. Even the Sanskrit names of three common pulses, māsha (math), mudga (mung) and masūra (masoor) have an aboriginal ring to them.[22] The oilseed sarshapa (sarson) has a pre-Sanskrit sound to it, as does tila for sesame seed; both are known to have existed in the Indus Valley before the Aryan advent. The common generic term for tuber in Sanskrit is āluka, but there is an array of distinctive aboriginal names for several edible *Dioscorea* species, like ato sang, bengo-nari, bir sang, gun, genasu, kalangu, kullu, kniss, kris, myauk, piska, taguna, tar and tarar.[21b] Old vegetables show up in Sanskrit carrying their Munda names, such as vatingana, vārtāka and vrntāka for the brinjal, alābu for the pumpkin, tundi for the tinda, and patōla for the parwal, while the flower of the lotus plant, many parts of which are edible, was pundarika.[22] Names of certain ancient fruits

Sculptural representation of a Jataka tale, Bharhut. Banana plant (*left*). Cat stealing fish (*right*).

show their lineage: kadalī for the banana, panasa for the luscious jackfruit, jāmbu for the roseapple (*Syzygium jambos*) and jāmbula for the succulent purple jāmoon (*Syzygium cumini*). The lime, numbaka (now nimbu, Sanskrit nimbuka), is yet another article with an old name tag, as is nāgarangā (nārangi) for the orange.

The word for coconut, nārikela (now nāriyal) seems to have entered the aboriginal Indian tongue from two words, both from south-east Asia. These are the nasal terms niu, ngai and niyor, meaning essence or oil, and kolai for nut, merged to give nārikela or the oily nut.[23] Indeed the word nai became the generic word in Tamil for any semi-solid fat, like ghee (nai) and butter (vennai). The cautious suggestion that nai may derive from the Sanskrit snēha, meaning oil, does not seem to stand up to scrutiny.[24a] A related ancestry attaches to the present Tamil word for oil, which is ennai. In old Tamil the sesame was called ell or enn, and the essence or oil from it was ennai. In time the latter beame a generic term for all liquid oils, with a prefix attached: thus ellu-ennai was sesame oil, thēngā-ennai coconut oil, and nall-ennai groundnut oil. A similar sequence occurred in Sanskrit with the word thaila, originally the oil of tila (sesame), but later a common term for vegetable oils as a class. There are other examples too in both languages of the particular word becoming the

Box 1
A WORD PUZZLE

Brevity may be the soul of wit, but it can also mislead. About the year 486 BC, Gautama Buddha died at the age of eighty in Kushinagara after eating a meal served to him by his disciple, the blacksmith Chunda.[45] This meal was described as shukaramaddava, and the earliest commentary by Buddhagōsa explains this as the first flesh of an excellent boar, neither too young nor too old, soft, oily and wellcooked under Chunda's own instructions. The next commentator, Dhammapāla, concisely repeats this interpretation, adding that it comes from the *Mahāathakathaka*, an older commentary now lost.

It seemed unlikely to anyone familiar with the Buddha's teaching that meat was only to be taken when there was no alternative, that he would have eaten such a dish. Dhammapāla suggested that the food was either a sprout of bamboo softened by boars, or a mushroom grown in a place softened by boars. Old Chinese sources have confirmed the latter interpretation. The actual Chinese words used for the main ingredient of the dish are those for the sandalwood mushroom.[45] This agrees closely with the term ahichattaka, literally snake-unbrella and hence possibly a mushroom, that was employed by Dhammapāla himself. The Pāli scholar Rhys Davids translated the word as truffles, and there are several medicinal plant names in the *Rajanighantu* compounded with shukara, like shukarakanda, shukarapadika and shukareshta.[46] Nowhere else is maddava associated with meat, and pork is designated in Buddhist scriptures by the term sukaramāmsa.

The meal served by Chunda is supposed to have brought on a relapse of dysentery, which actually caused the Buddha's death.[47] Could the poisonous principles known to reside in certain mushrooms have been responsible for this?

general: madhu for honey and later for sweetness in Sanskrit, and puli for the tamarind and later for sourness in Tamil.

In the area of spicing and flavouring materials, the Sanskrit word chinchā for the tamarind has aboriginal moorings. The word for ginger is srngavēra, from inji (still used in Tamil for the commodity) and vēr or root, reflecting the southern origin of ginger. Haridrā (haldi) for turmeric likewise has a Munda air to it. Vedic literature mentions the community of Nishādas, literally meaning turmeric eaters (nishā = turmeric, ad = to eat).[25] Among the Nishāda types described in the *Yajurveda* are svānin (dog-keepers), chandāla (dog-eaters) and punjistha (fowlers), which implies that both dogs and fowls had been domesticated before the Aryans arrived. This is confirmed by Harappan archaeological evidence, and by the fact that kukkuta, the Sanskrit term for fowl, is pre-

Uprooted rhizomes of turmeric.

Turmeric plant.

Aryan.[25] Dogs and sacrificial fowls are important even now among tribes like the Mundas, Santhāls, Hos and Kharias.[25] Asura was a pejorative term used for the non-Aryan peoples. This was perhaps because they imbibed the distilled drink surā,[26] which would imply that alcohol distillation was known. Both the betel leaf, tāmbūla, and the areca nut which has long accompanied it, guvāka, have distinctly Munda names, showing the ancient lineage of these masticants.[27] Pān, the current term, is from parna, Sanskrit for leaf.[27]

A few words from Tamil also entered Sanskrit as the Aryans moved South. Conspicuous among such food-related words is milagu or miriyam (pepper) which occurs as maricha (mirchi in Hindi).[29a] Later, noting the desire of the Greeks and Romans for it, pepper is termed yavanapriya—here indeed is history in a name![29b] Thuvarika, the pulse, is from the Tamil thuvarai, though it has another Sanskrit name ādhakī, now arhar. The Sanskrit terms for the mango, āmra or āmbāh (now ām), appear in rather late literature, lending some support to their possible derivation from the Tamil mā or mānggā (mān-kāy). Possibly the bhendi (Hindi for lady's finger, there being no Sanskrit name) is also from the Tamil vendekayi. The southern fried snack vatai became vataka on adoption by the north. The Tamil meen (fish) became

'Mango' derived from the Tamil 'mānggā'.

meenam, neer (water) niram, and the pearl, muthu, became mukta.[29c,29d] Both Persian and Arabic are credited with the term pilav, pulāo or pallāo for the well-known dish of rice cooked with spiced meat. Yet both Sanskrit (in the *Yāgnavalkya Smriti*)[30] and Tamil[29e] call the product pallāo or pulāo long before the Muslim advent.

Sanskrit also absorbed, though somewhat later, foods and goods of Chinese origin, giving them the pre-fix chīnī. The peach was chīnāni, the cultivated pear chīnarājaputra[31,32,33] (the hillpear of Kashmir has a Sanskrit name, nāshpāti), and lettuce, the *Pisonia alba*, became chīnasālit.[34a] Sometimes, especially in Bengal, the prefix could simply imply a foreign origin, not necessarily Chinese. Thus the *Panicum millet* sānwa or shāma is chīna, camphor is chīnakarpūra, vermilion chīnapistha (Hindi sindoor), and the groundnut chīnībādām. The word chīnī itself is commonly used for granulated white sugar. This commodity may once have been made in and imported from China especially to our eastern and southern ports, but there is fair evidence that a Chinese emperor about AD 627 sent a delegation to the Emperor Harsha to learn the technique of making crystal sugar.[21c] Certainly the processing of the sugarcane, and perhaps even earlier of toddy sap from the palmyra palm, to brown sugar (gur or jaggery from the Sanskrit guda), rock sugar (khand) and crystal sugar (sharkarā, originally meaning simply gritty) was known in India at a very early date. This is borne out by the literary usage of these words even in the *Sūtra* literature from 800 BC,[36] and their more explicit usage with reference to specific commodities in the *Arthashāstra* of Kautilya about 300 BC.[35]

Indian words in foreign tongues

The commerce of south India with Arabia, Greece and Rome can be traced in words that also made the journey. The Greek word oryza for rice (also now the Latin designation of the botanical genus) is believed to have been derived from the Tamil arisi (which itself seems to have stemmed from the Sanskrit or old Persian varisi). Peperi, or peperi makron, was from the Tamil pippali, and the Greek karphea (meaning twigs) for cinnamon stemmed from karuva or karappa-pattai. From Greek these words passed in turn into many modern European languages.

With English, of course, there were intimate contacts during the long presence of the British in India for nearly 350 years. Some Indian words, however, had entered English even before, having travelled with various commodities. Pepper, sugar (from the Sanskrit sharkarā), camphor (Sanskrit karpūra), mango (Tamil mānggā) and orange (Sanskrit nāgarangā) are examples of these.[37a] After the European arrival here, there were many other adoptions into English, often through Portuguese and usually with some Anglicization. Among words for several fruits and trees were the jack (from Malayalam chekka),[37b] jāmbu and jamoon, [37c] the palmyra palm, and the tamarind (from the Arabic thamar-i-Hindi or fruit of India, rather than tamar-i-Hind or date of India).[37d] Other words that made the passage were the betel leaf (from the Malayalam vettilē, itself meaning veru-ila or mere leaf),[37e] the areca nut (from the Malayalam adakka, itself meaning a close arrangement, adai, of the nut, kāy),[37f] and jaggery (like sugar, a corruption of the Sanskrit sharkarā and the Malayalam chakkara).[37g] Among prepared foods adopted by English were curry (from the Tamil kari meaning a pepper-spiced dish),[37h] chutney (identical with the Hindi word for a ground relish),[37i] kedgeree (an adaptation of the Sanskrit/Hindi khichri for a mixed rice-pulse dish),[37j] hopper (from the Tamil rice-cake āppam,[37k] itself believed to derive from the Sanskrit fried dainty, apūpa),[38] pilāu (from both Sanskrit and Tamil, as has earlier been mentioned), and the soup mulligatawny (literally pepper-water in Tamil).[37k] Names of two drinks now widely used have an Indian origin: one is toddy (tāri, fermented palmyra sap)[37l] and the other is punch (from five, pānch in Hindi),[37m] which is made up of the five components lime juice, sugar, spice, water and arrack. The last of these is a distilled spirit, whose name in English was derived from the arāk of Arabic.[37n]

Resemblances have been pointed out between words in Sanskrit and in the Quichua tongue of the South American Indians of Peru, suggesting a link between the Aryan and American Indian cultures in bygone times. In listing such words relating to food, the Quichua term will be given first, then the English word in brackets, and finally the Sanskrit: chupe (soup) sūpa; muti (pounded corn) mut (to pound); pirhua (granary) pūra; pisi (small) pīs (to fragment); rupani (to burn) ru (fire); sacha (tree) saccha; sapi (root) sappa (foot of a tree); soro (corn liquor) surā (liquor); and uira (corn stalk), vīra (stalk).[39, 40]

South India shares some 300 words in common with Africa, perhaps in consequence of both an ancient racial connection and considerable commercial intercourse in the last few thousand years.[41] Some of these words are: neew (oil) nai; suuna (millet) souna; cub (rice) sooru; owuru (mortar) ural; ānd (pot) andā; and kuman (pot) kuunai.[41]

Resemblances between old Dravidian and the Sumerian/Akkadian languages of about 3000 BC have also been noted. Two words for sesame oil were in common: ell and enn,[42] and there is a further resemblance between ell, sesame oil, and the elaion and oleum of Greek and Latin.[28] The word payaru, once used for all leguminous plants, and, by a narrowing of the sense, for the green gram (pesaru in Telugu, hesaru in Kannada) is believed to have given rise to the Greek term phaseolus. This was later used as the botanical name in Latin for an important genus of legumes, and payaru itself may have originated from a common east-Mediterranean word, now lost.[28] And whence comes the word gram used for pulses only in India? From the Portuguese graō, originally a term for all grain. Somehow this was appropriated first by the Bengal gram, *Cicer arietinum*, and by extension applied to all pulses in India.[37o]

Language may have originated about 25,000 years ago somewhere in the Central European land mass.[43] This primeval language has been termed nostratic, from the Latin noster meaning our. As groups moved outwards, a tongue called Indo-European came to be spoken in parts of the Middle East and around the Caspian Sea. This gave rise to Sanskrit about 1500 BC or earlier, and to Greek about a hundred years later. Contemporary with it were nine other root proto-languages, including Uralic which gave rise both to the Dravidian mother language and to Finnish and Hungarian. If ultimately all languages were once related, some resemblances between them are perhaps only to be expected. Yet even Tamil is plagued with controversy. Some linguists assert that it is a distinctive language group; others derive it squarely from old Indo-Aryan, much as were derived, considerably later, the modern languages of both north and south India.[44]

Whatever be the case, language certainly carries clues to food movements and adoptions wherever cultures have come into contact, right from very ancient times (exemplified by Munda words in Sanskrit) to later historical periods.

Chapter 2

HARAPPAN SPREAD

Origins

Settlements that predate the great Indus Valley civilization, both in time and cultural evolution, occur at many places in the north and northwest of the country. The existence of stone age cultures in Ladākh and at Burzahom in Kāshmīr suggest links with Central Asia through the easily negotiable Ladākh route.[1] Rāwat, in the Pothohor plateau near Islamabad, has recently been excavated,[2] and a dozen other sites, dating back to around 5000 BC and suggestive of great prosperity, have been identified in and around Mekrān in the valley of the river Kech in Baluchistān.[2] At Mehrgarh, along the Bolār river, an emerging culture could be traced layer by layer over a period of three thousand years.[3] Dating back to around 6000 BC were found both two-rowed and six-rowed hulled barley, and four varieties of wheat, along with small flat blades with which to harvest these grains, and small grinding stones to process them. Bēr (*Ziziphus* spp.) and date fruits were known, and several wild animals were used as food. By 5000 BC, domestic sheep and goats outnumber wild animals, and the first wild buffalo bones to be found outside China appear. Over the next millennium only domestic animal bones occur, suggesting that apart from food, these beasts were probably employed for agriculture and dairying. Accompanying these bones are charred grains of wheat, barley and cotton, and storage jars for foodgrains.

The millennium after 4000 BC shows large settlements, with plenty of animal food, a new cereal, oats, a new variety of barley (*Hordeum hexastichum*), two new varieties of bread wheat (*Triticum sphaerococcum* and *T. compactum*) and a new wine grape, *Vitis vinifera*. Numerous querns occur, and grain is stored in jars in rooms meant for the purpose, just a metre high and on the ground floor. Artistic endeavour takes the

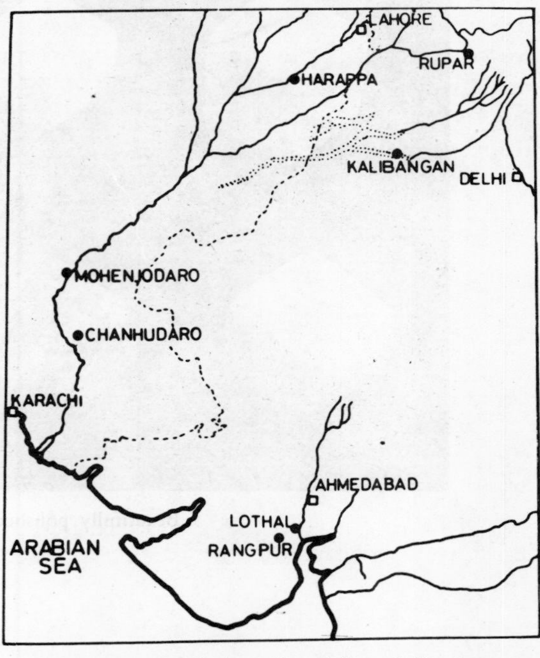

Some towns of the Indus Valley civilization.

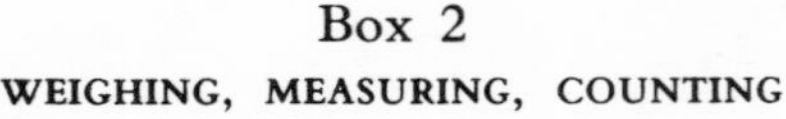

Box 2

WEIGHING, MEASURING, COUNTING

Beautifully-polished, accurate, cubical weights occur all over the Indus Valley.[9c,48] These were once thought to belong to two series, one decimal and the other binary. Recently both series have been connected to the weight of the tiny red seed with a black spot, *Abrus precatorius*, called rati, gunji or krsnala, which averages 109 milligrams in weight.[4e] One series of weights had a base of 12 ratis or 1.2184 grams, and the other of 8 ratis or 0.871 gram, and each had multiples of the series 1, 2, 5, 10, 20, 50, 100, 200, 500 etc. The famous series of weights clearly set down fifteen hundred years later in the *Arthashāstra* starts from rati seeds (see Box 29), and goldsmiths use them even now to weigh gold and diamonds in tiny balances with brass pans.

Another series of weights in the form of truncated prisms was also found at Lothal. While still related to a basic weight of 1.2184 grams, these were in the ratios 7/2, 7, 14 and 28. They appear to have been related to the Assyrian shekel of the time, and were perhaps employed in the sea trade.[4e] The largest weight found in the Indus Valley had a mass of 10.97 kg.[9c]

Gold discs found in a burial pot in Lothal were in a definitely decimal progression. Again, the gold coins of the *Arthashātra*, the dhānya, gunja and māshaka, bear a 1 : 2 : 5 relationship.[48] India's earliest silver coins weigh 32 ratis, [10e] a binary multiple, and the pala, in use till recent times, was 320 ratis (34.88 grams), a binary-decimal combination.[49] The historical Indian system of weighing is thus of Harappan origin.

The Harappans used a bronze bar ba-

Beautifully polished weights from Lothal.

Box 2 (*contd.*)

lance with suspended pans,[50] and for heavier weights wooden ones with rope-suspended pans. The word tula for a light balance first occurs in the *Vājanaseyi Samhitā*, and the *Arthashāstra* describes sixteen balances, of which ten were light ones with double pans, and the rest heavier ones for weighing upto 53 palas (about 1.85 kg). The king's balance, the āyamāni, weighed out 5, 10 and 17 per cent more of produce respectively than the public balance, the servant's balance and the harem balance, the difference constituting the royal margin of profit taken right at source.

An ivory scale found at Lothal showed linear markings measuring 1.704 millimeters. The angula of the *Arthashāstra*, measuring 17.78 mm, would therefore constitute ten of these, and longer lengths would follow.[4e,48] Bricks of the Harappan system were always in the ratio 4 : 2 : 1, the present English Bond system of masonry.[51] Actual constructions show that the value of *pi*,[51] and of the square root of 2 divided by 5, as well as the relationship between the hypotenuse and the other sides of a right-angled triangle were known to the Harappans.[6]

Some 2900 seals have been recovered from the Valley, and most carry animal, tree and human figures. All have pictographic signs on the top; usually these consist of five signs, the longest one showing seventeen signs arranged in three lines.[9c] These have been variously deciphered as a tantric language,[52] as a pre-Sanskrit, pre-Brahmi language,[48] as a Dravidian language,[53] and as a numerical system.[54] According to the last of these, the symbols for 1, 2 and 3 are simple strokes, and thereafter symbols are used in decimal, additive and multiplicative combinations. Even a figure of 22,000 can be shown with just five symbols. The Chinese, Egyptians and Greeks used these symbols in modified form. There is even a suggestion that the pictographs found on old wooden tablets in Easter Island bear a resemblance to those of the Indus Valley.[55, 56]

The zero, shunya, and the decimal place-value system originated later in India, but the seeds may have been laid by Harappan computations. Of these achievements it has been said that 'no single mathematical creation has been more potent for the general go-on of intelligence and power.'[57]

South India originally employed a numbering system based on eight.[58a] When Brahmi numerals brought in the unit of ten, the system was modified. As a relic of that period, even the current Tamil term for nine is en-patthu, a defective ten, and ten itself, patthu, is probably from the Sanskrit pankti.[58a]

form of terracotta figures of humped bulls, a ram, wild boar and several birds. Brick kilns fired with straw and dung are in use, and square brick buildings and community granaries have developed. Perhaps the onager, an early form of the horse, or the horse itself, had been domesticated. The resemblance, in so many respects, between Mekran and the Indus Valley civilization is indeed quite striking. During the succeeding millennium, from about 3200 BC,[4a] a thousand settlements constituting this civilization were to blossom over an enormous area in northwest India.

Foods raised in the Indus Valley

At Harappā, in the Montgomery district of Pākistān, the common staples were wheat and barley. This was also true of Mohenjodaro and Chanhudaro further south, and of Kālibangan in Rājasthān. However, Banawāli in Rājasthān yielded only wheat.[12a] Several kinds of wheat were found, all being varieties of the bread wheat species *Triticum aestivum*. The varieties prevalent in Harappa were the *sphaerococcum* and *compactum*, at Mohenjodaro and Navdatoli-

Carbonized rice grains from Hastinapur, Uttar Pradesh. (*c.* 1000BC).

Maheshwar the *aestivum* and *compactum*, and at Mundigak only the *compactum*.[9b] Thus at least four varieties of wheat were raised. The barley found at all places was of both the two-rowed and six-rowed cultivated types, *Hordeum vulgare*, var. *distichum* and var. *hexastichum*, mostly the latter.[9b] Barley was also picked up at late-Harappan sites like Daimabād in Mahārāshtra[12a] and Atranjikhera in Uttar Pradesh.[14] Rice spikelets or their imprints showed up at the Gujarāt sites of Lothal and Rangpūr, and at Hulās in the Saharānpūr district of Uttar Pradesh, representing probably the easternmost point of the Harappan civilization.[12a,13] The charred grains from Surkotada in Kutch were found to be mostly wild forms, tentatively identified as the *Setaria* species (to which belongs kāngni or Italian millet), rāgi (*Eleusine coracana*) and the grain amaranths.[12a] Stems of a *Sorghum* species, *S. halapense* were found at Nageshwar, near Dwārka.[15] Thus agro-climatic conditions, then as now, governed the choice of the cereal staple; and the choice was quite wide even 4500 years ago in northwest India.

Pulses have always been important as foods in India. Peas were found in Harappā, Kālibangan and Daimabād, and the chickpea (chana, Bengal gram, *Cicer arietinum*) at Kālibangan and Daiṃabād.[12a] Masūr dhāl (*Lens culinaris*) occurs at Daimabād even from an early phase. At Navdatoli-Maheshwar it is likewise found early. The horsegram (kulthi, *Dolichos uniflorus*) and mung (greengram, *Vigna radiata*), are found in a later phase though even this is before 1500 BC.[7b, 12a]

Oilseeds were also raised. At Harappā an unmistakable 'lump of charred sesame',[16] was found at a depth of about two metres, and at Chanhudaro carbonized seeds of rāi, *Brassica juncea* subsp. *juncea*.[17a] Carbonized linseed has been

Carbonized wheat found in the excavations of Mohenjodaro.

Carbonized rāi seeds excavated at Chanhudaro

unearthed at Navdatoli in Madhya Pradesh in 1600–1450 BC strata,[17a] and a piece of flax string, also a linseed plant product, from Chandōli (1400–1200 BC) nearby. The plant is very ancient in the Middle East, and is likely to have been known all along to the Harappans as well. Perhaps the coconut was known, too, judging from a piece of jewellery[18] and an earthenware bowl, both resembling the nut,[19a] found in Harappā. Cottonseeds from about 4500 BC[3] have been found even in Mehrgarh, cotton fabrics and thread in Mohenjodaro and Nevāsa,[20a] and light cotton spindles all over the Valley. Knowledge of oilseeds implied, in all likelihood, knowledge of their oils. Besides, since numerous animals were consumed, their fats, for cooking purposes, were probably also obtained easily enough, simply by boiling.

The fruits to be had can be inferred mostly from representations. At Harappā

> Two tiny faience sealings shaped like a date seed. . . an earthenware jar with porous earth which contained a few seeds of the melon species which unfortunately were too brittle to be lifted up . . . a well-made pendant in the form of a lemon leaf of burnt steatite, two polychrome earthenware vases, the former shaped like a pomegranate and the latter like a coconut . . . a representation of a lotus fruit in faience.

were excavated.[16] There is some reason to believe that bananas were also known.[21]

To judge from the quantity of bones left behind, animal foods were consumed in abundance: beef, buffalo, mutton, turtles, tortoises, gharials, and river and sea fish.[11,21] A plethora of fish hooks made from bone and copper testify to the latter. Harappan seals show both the characteristic hump-backed and the dew-lapped zēbu cattle of India that closely resembled the modern Kānkrej breed,[19b] as well as the flat-backed urus type with forward-pointing horns. The wild buffalo is depicted on a seal in the act of throwing its hunters, but the Harappans had definitely tamed the animal, and there are naturalistic representations of it in clay.[22] Certainly the buffalo appeared much earlier in China than it did in the Indus Valley,[23a] both wild and tame, not to speak of its even earlier appearance at Mehrgarh. It is known to have played a big part in the cultivation of the swampy Gangetic plain.[10b] The Harappans knew the domestic fowl, but its remains are few, and it is not depicted on any seals. Even though domestication may have occurred outside the orbit of the Harappan civilization, perhaps in the Gangetic valley,[23b] the Indian jungle fowl *Gallus gallus* is considered to have been the progenitor of all domestic poultry in the world. Poultry entered China about 1500 BC,[23b] and Europe used fowls for purposes of food, eggs, divination and cock-fighting only after 600 BC.[24] The domesticated dog was

Pomegranates were known in Harappan times.

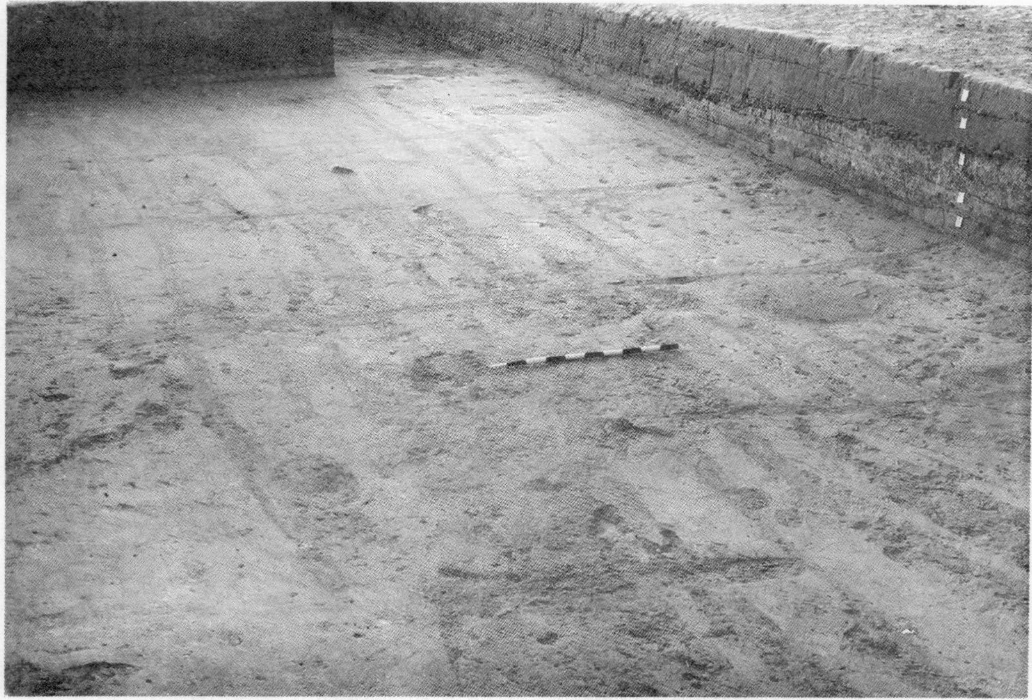

Earliest known ploughed field, Kālibangan, Rājasthān. Furrows at right angles can be clearly seen.

known in Harappā, as were the elephant (domesticated even earlier by the Mundas), the camel and the ass. There are no representations of the horse, and no horse saddles, and the bone-remains suggest the small, country-bred animals of today rather than the powerful equine that the Aryans later rode and harnessed to their chariots.[23c,25a]

Raising crops

At Kālibangan in Rājasthān, on the rolling sand-dunes of the now-dry river Ghaggar (the ancient Saraswathi), excavations disclosed a ploughed and abandoned field. This dates back to before 2800 BC, and certainly represents the earliest ploughed field to have been found anywhere in

Modern ploughed field in Rājasthān. Long furrows held tall bajra plants at right angles to shorter mustard plants.

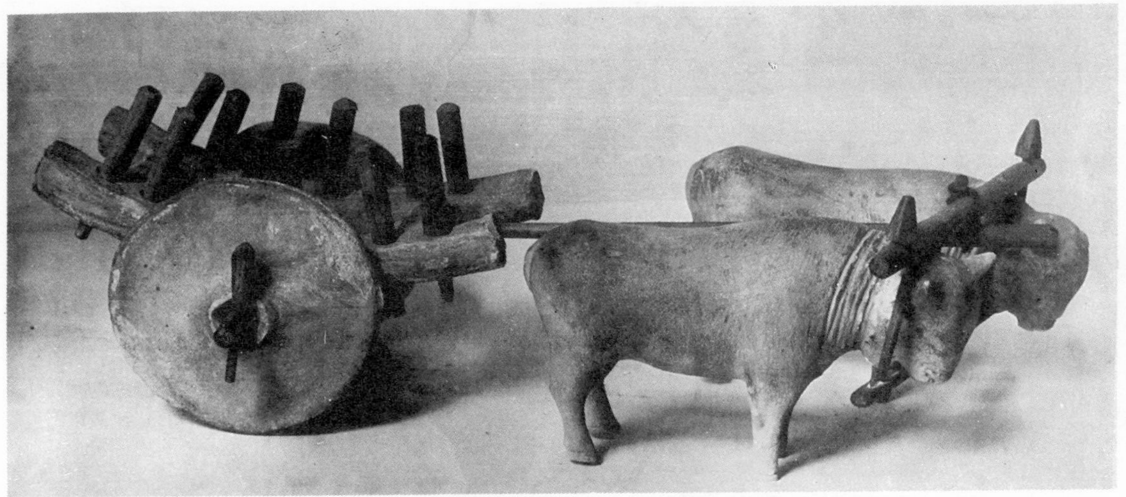

Clay model of a bullock cart carrying produce, Indus Valley.

the world.[26] North-south furrows were spaced fairly wide apart, and at right angles to these were closer-spaced east-west furrows. Even today in the Rājasthān area, horsegram is grown on wide furrows so as not to cast shadows on the shorter mustard plants at right angles to them, a remarkable persistence of agricultural practice. Obviously ploughs were known,[27] and beautiful clay models of ploughs have been recovered in Harappā.[19c] Agricultural tools have nowhere been found in the valley; iron was not known, and implements made of wood have perished. Possibly agriculture was not a complex operation. Annual flood inundation along natural channels was employed, as in the Indus Valley system; bullocks for ploughing were readily available; and tilling was not really essential for growing wheat, being necessary only for weed control.[12a]

Roughly-made pottery jars with deep grooves round the middle, found in vast numbers at Mohenjodaro, are surmised to be the remains of pots fixed on water wheels for raising water from rivers.[28] Such devices were later called ashmanchakra and araghatta by the Aryans. The ghatayantra of later Vedic times seems to have designated pots mounted on long ropes slung from a pulley mounted over a well.[29] The true Persian wheel with a bucket chain and pin-driven gear came to India much later,[30a] in the 4th century AD according to some,[31a] and the 10th century AD according to others.[32a]

Opinions differ too on whether any striking climatic changes have occurred, over five thousand years, in the Indus Valley and elsewhere in India. The enormous numbers of bricks that were baked would have required vast amounts of wood for firing the kilns, yet today the area is almost bare of forests. The elephant and the rhinoceros, both swamp animals, are shown on Harappan seals.[33a] The discovery of rice as the only staple in 1300 BC layers at Hastinapura near Meerut suggests much more annual rainfall than the present 80 cm:[34] rice needs at least100 cms, or irrigation, and was grown later in many Aryan areas which today can only support wheat. The Mathura sculptures which span the period 500 BC to AD 650 reveal that two thousand years ago the Braj districts of Uttar Pradesh, which today bear a desert vegetation, had wet tropical forests with evergreen trees.[33a] The beautiful ashoka tree with scarlet flowers, *Saraca indica*, sculpted with loving familiarity in Mathura, is today restricted to the lower Himālayas and to hilly terrain elsewhere.[33a] Travellers in much later times describe passing through thick forests where none now exist. Xuan Zang (7th century AD) passed through them before reaching both Kalinga (Orissa) and Vārānasi,[35] and Edward Terry (AD 1616) declared that the whole country 'is as it were a Forrest, for a man can travell no way but he shall see them'.[36] It would appear from literary evidence that forest cover, even a few hundred years ago, was considerably more extensive than in more recent times. While the above evidence would suggest that the climate earlier was wetter than it is today, pollen analysis indicates that any change in vegetation has been caused not by climatic but by biotic factors.[37a] Further, the presence in the Indus Valley of drought-resistant varieties of bread wheat like *var. sphacrococcum* point to a dry climate even then[12a] while at Kālibangan in Rājasthān, the harsh climate may account for the predominance of barley, since the alkaline saline soil is unsuited to wheat.[37a] In any case, whether the more extensive forest cover contributed to greater precipitation seems doubtful at best.

Methods of storing food

Among the marvels of the larger Indus Valley cities were the elaborate arrangements for mass storage of foodgrains.[7,16,18,23d,25a,27a] The largest granary was found at Harappā in the shape of a mud platform, 52 by 42 metres in size and 1.2 metres high, on which stood two identical granary blocks 17 by 6 metres, placed 7 metres apart, and with 3 metre thick walls. Each block had six chambers, with corridors between them, opening only on the outside and approached by a short flight of steps. Each chamber was divided into four storage spaces by full-length walls. The floor rested on sleepers, and air could circulate in the void below and enter the chamber for aeration through small triangular vents. The granary faced the river, along which grain possibly arrived. Some form of state authority appeared likely from the sheer size of the granary.

At Mohenjodaro the massive brick platform, raised high with steep sloping walls, was all that remained, with the bases of some twenty-seven storage blocks arranged crosswise to facilitate air-circulation. The granary itself was probably of wood and has disappeared. Halfway up the brick platform was an unloading platform with

Reconstruction of the granary at Harappā. The design permitted free air circulation through the grain.

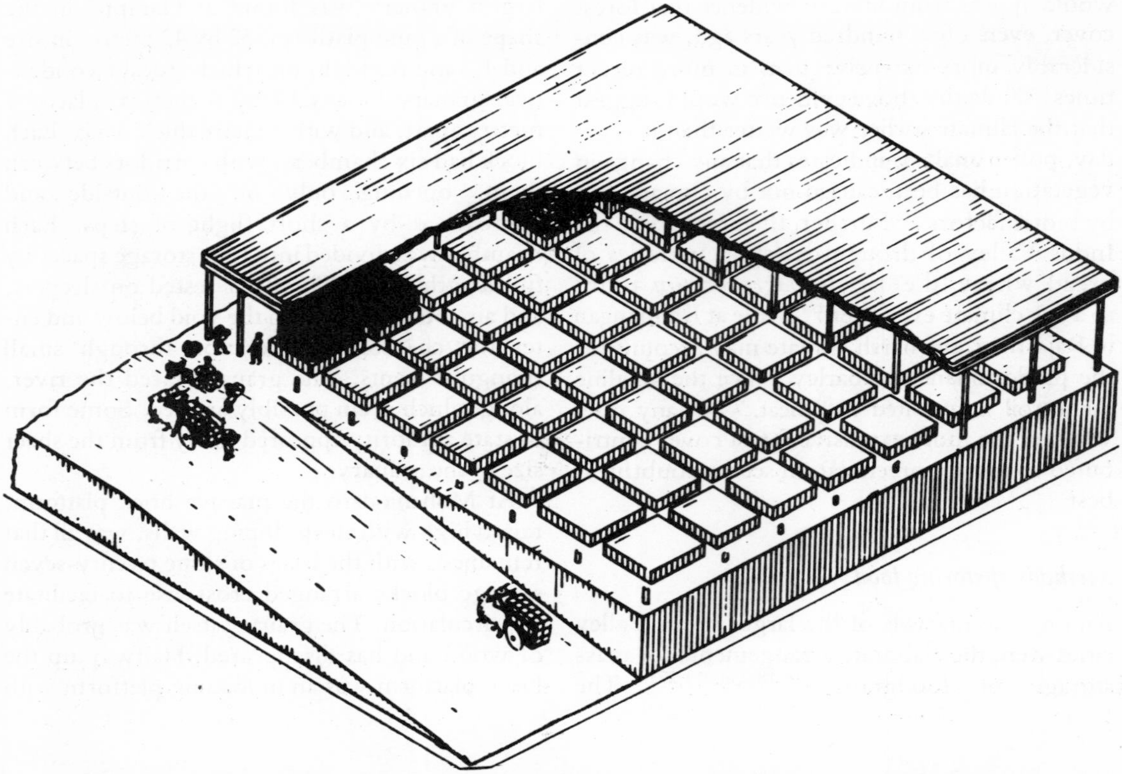

Reconstruction of the warehouse at Lothal with storage chambers built on square brick platforms.

niches in which carts bringing grain from the adjacent river must have stood. Possibly through such a situation and arrangement, the precious food supply in the elevated granary could be defended from attack. At Lothal the corresponding structure was more in the nature of a warehouse, overlooking the dock, and standing on an enormous mud platform, 3.5 metres high and 51 by 45 metres each way. On this rested twelve square brick pallets, 3.7 metres each way and a metre high. A great deal of melted material was found inside, suggesting that the original wooden chambers had burnt down.

Clay jars for storing grain.

A row of circular platforms each 3 metres across, and constructed of bricks placed on edge and fanning outwards were found near the granaries at Harappa and Mohenjodaro. Fragments of husk, barley and burnt wheat were lodged in the crevices, and there was a central hole where the pounding operations must have been carried out using wooden pestles, which is the practice in Kashmir to this day. A special class of workers probably performed the operation.[10c]

In homes, grains were stored in pottery jars resembling the kothis of the present, some quite large, fixed in the floor with only their rims

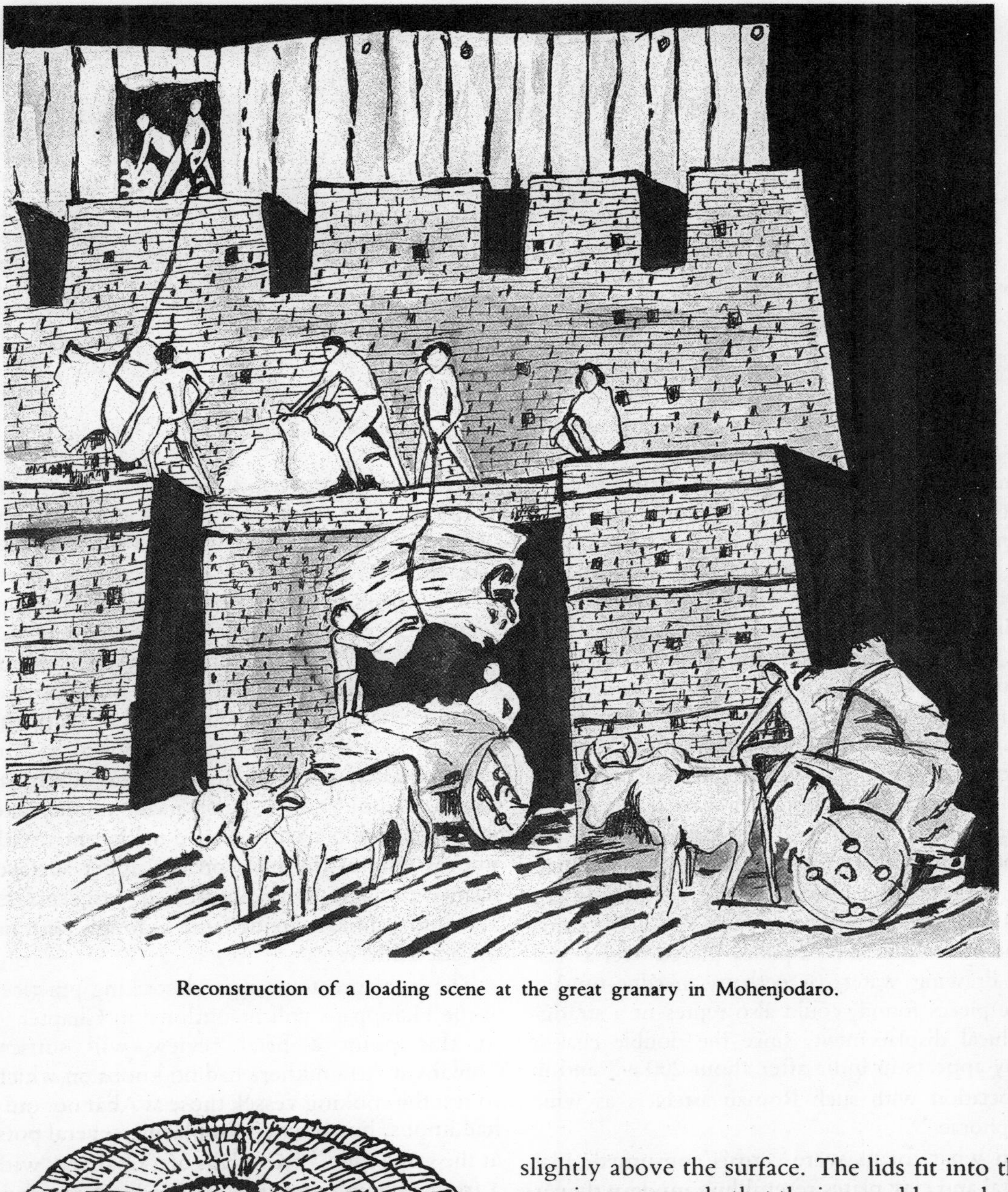

Reconstruction of a loading scene at the great granary in Mohenjodaro.

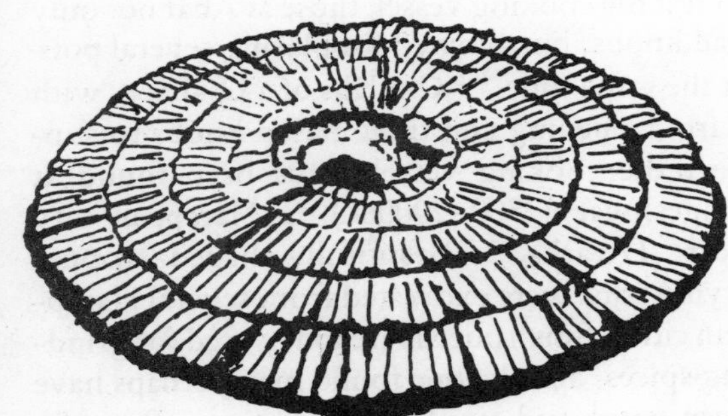

Brick platform for pounding grain.

slightly above the surface. The lids fit into the openings so snugly that the jars could even have been insect-proof[7,21]

Ways of preparing and eating food

While the pounding platforms were used for large-scale operations by the state, smaller pounders were employed in homes. Their sizes were frequently 53 by 19 centimetres, they were

Small saddle quern from Mohenjodaro, perhaps for grinding spices.

made of sand-stone or even of quartzite, and fixed firmly in the ground.[18] Some had even been worn down to 12 centimetres by constant use. Domestic grinding stones were essentially of two kinds. Smaller saddle querns had ends pointing upwards, with a small cylindrical roller, used with both hands and in a kneeling position. A variation was a flat, squarish stone and a cylindrical roller. The second type had a small circular depression in the centre, and a round biconcave grinder, well-suited for crushing soaked grains.[27a] A heavy circular stone with a central hole was found at Mohenjodaro and another at Lothal. Though strongly resembling the two-part unit now in use for grinding grain, and originally identified as such, the single stone is now thought to be a pulley placed over a well for drawing water, or perhaps an edge-runner. The pieces found could also represent a stratigraphical displacement, since the double chakki only appears in India after about 200 BC, and in association with such Roman artefacts as wine amphorae.[38]

In what forms were cereals consumed? Flat metal and clay plates resembling modern thavās have been found in plenty at Harappan sites, suggesting that the baked chapāti may have been known. The shapes of numerous clay vessels were well-suited to boiling barley and rice. Many circular ovens have been found at Indus Valley sites. Some, like those discovered at Mohenjodaro,[27a] Chanhudaro[4b] and Lothal,[39] are extremely large and have a firing section placed below the ground; these were almost certainly used for firing and glazing large clay objects, for bead-making, or even for metallurgy (see Box 3). Smaller mud-plastered ovens with a side opening are in evidence at Kālibangan, 'very closely resembling the present-day tandoors'.[9c,40a] Till very recently, the tandoor style of baking was confined to the extreme northwestern part of greater India. Perhaps the greatest variety of naan breads cooked in tandoors is today available in the capital of Afghanistān, Kābul:[41] thick, crisp naan; thinner and longer parakki-naan; naan-e-nakhooni, with impressions of the nails on the upper surface; naan-e-panjagi, with impressed fingerprints; and roghani naan, made from a dough with fat kneaded into it.

The implements, tools and cooking practices of the Harappans will be outlined in Chapter 9. At this point a brief review will suffice. Chūlāhs at Atranjikhera had no knobs on which to rest the cooking vessel; those at Ahār not only had knobs, but allowed for placing several pots at the same time.[40b] Chūlāhs of a U-shape, with a front opening and three raised knobs to support the cooking vessel, have been found at Nageshwar (2500–2000BC), a Harappan city near Dwārka.[15] Beautifully-shaped copper frying pans were excavated from several Harappan cities. Small querns are today used for grinding spices, and the one found may perhaps have been employed similarly. A variety of mostly clay and some metal vessels were available for

Box 3

EXTRACTING METALS, AND USING THEM

The Indus Valley knew four metals, silver, gold, copper and tin.[4f] A silver vessel found at Mohenjodaro had been wrapped in a madder-dyed piece of cotton cloth, which was preserved by the action of the silver salts and could even be identified as *Gossypium arboreum*. A series of gold discs was found at Lothal (see Box 2), and elsewhere gold jewellery in various shapes was found. Gold may have been either indigenous or imported,[43] and this was true all through Indian history, to meet the insatiable demands for adornment of both Indian women and men.

Copper was in extensive use in the Valley perhaps after a chance initial discovery.[59] The ore was roasted before smelting, and silica then added as a flux.[60a] Huge chūlāhs for the purpose were discovered at Ahār, which was a major smelting centre.[60a] Another was Chanhudaro, where an immense quantity of blade axes, chisels, spearheads, and dishes and vessels of various shapes and sizes were found.[45] Axes were apparently cast, and knives and chisels wrought.[60a] Mohenjodaro was not a production centre, but obtained its utensils from Chanhudaro about 150 km away. Copper and bronze articles in about equal number have been found at Mohenjodaro, but the paucity of tin, of which 10 to 20 per cent must be alloyed with copper to yield bronze, probably restricted production of the latter despite its superior qualities.[60a] Inclusion of tin was deliberate in the Indus Valley, but in later times this was more often simply a consequence of its presence in the copper ore itself.[27a] The famous dancing girl figure from Mohenjodaro, heavily bangled, is cast in bronze, a technique that would reach its pinnacle three thousand years later in south India.

Copper ore for the Ahār smelting centre was drawn from the Aravalli range in Rājasthān. One source was Khetri, perhaps by way of Gāneshwar just 75 km away, where a trove of a thousand objects was found in strata that even preceded the Indus Valley culture.[4g] Other sites of copper-bronze technology were Langhnaj, Jorwe, Nevāsa, Utnūr, Tellakotta, Paiyampalli and Hallūr in central and south India, and, in the northeast, after 1300 BC, Chirand, Hastinapura and Atranjikhera.[27a] Copper has always had pride of place in the Indian kitchen, both for cooking after suitable tin plating, and for storing drinking water, which the copper ions render sterile.

Iron is found occasionally between 1300 and 1000 BC in Ahār and Pirak in western India, and in many south Indian sites. In the next two hundred years, finds in these areas increase, and central India also enters the picture. In the Gangetic valley iron shows up about 800 to 500 BC, and thereafter iron objects are to be found all over India.[30b] There is abundant evidence of smelting activity in the valley of the Tapti about 800 BC.[60a] The implements found analyse to 99.76 per cent iron, and were made by forging thin layers of red-hot sheets, joining them by forge welding, and then shaping the implement again by forging.[60a] Deliberate carburation of iron to steel begins about 200 BC[60b] and an array of armaments and some agricultural implements appear. The famous Damascene swords were made from Indian steel. The south of India skipped the usual stage of copper (which is scarce there); instead, since iron ore abounds in the Deccan, the south discovered that metal early in history. The vast ash mounds found at numerous sites in the Krishna valley were attributed to the burning of accumulated

Box 3 (*contd.*)

cattle dung from large pens in neolithic times.[62] There is now an alternative suggestion that these ash heaps represent the sites where iron was smelted using dung as fuel.[29b] Numerous weapons dating back even to 1000 BC in the south show that tempering and quenching were known, and that carburation was achieved by the Wootz method of hammering iron in clay vessels at a temperature below its melting point.[62]

Brass is an alloy of copper with 10 to 18 per cent zinc. Brass vessels of excellent quality have been found at Takshasila at 4th century BC levels, and elsewhere even earlier.[63] An excellent zinc distillation unit going back to the first century BC and in continuous use till AD 1825 has been discovered at Zawar in Rājasthān about 50 km from Udaipūr.[63] Zinc was sublimated in domed furnaces, and condensed in a series of funnels placed in some of the perforations at the mid-floor level, to be delivered to receptacles placed on the floor below. A temperature of 900 to 950°C was probably achieved by burning cowdung cakes, a light but efficient fuel.[63]

cooking and dining, even a serving-dish with a fitted cover.[8] Shell was crafted to give cups, dippers and ladles, and kitchen knives were made of chert. All the accoutrements of varied and tasty cooking and eating were at hand.

Copper frying pan from Mohenjodaro.

Trade

Commerce was a vital component of the essentially urban Harappan civilization, and the range of trading seems to have been wide. It is now well-established that trade flowed between the valleys of the Indus in India and the Euphrates in Mesopotamia. There are numerous references in Akkadian cuneiform tablets to Meluha, to the sons of Meluha, to Meluhan ships docking at Akkad city, to a Meluhan interpreter, and even to a Meluhan village situated in the city of Lagash. Meluha has now been identified with the Indus Valley civilization, and the term is even thought to persist in the later Aryan usage of mleccha for an undesirable alien.[43] Akkadian cylinder seals, distinct from the square ones of the Harappans, have been found at very early levels (late 4th to middle 3rd millennium BC) in northern Indus Valley settlements.[4c] Harappan seals, and etched carnelian beads (a distinctive Indus Valley manufacture)[4d] have been found in many foreign towns: at Kish in Sumer[10d] and at Tepe Hissar, Shah Tepe II, Susa, Kallah Nisar and Mughal Ghundai in Irān and Mesopotamia.[4d] Both land and sea routes were in use.

This trade seems to have been very much to India's advantage.[43] Cotton and cotton goods were important items then and later, and these were of sufficient volume to balance the imports of even an expensive item like gold. Barley, and sesame and linseed oils (the se-gis-i and i-gis of Sumerian tablets) were exported, besides cane and other woods like teak, deodhar, cedar, ebony, sisham and fir; ivory; a variety of gems and stones; pigments; and copper. The primary imports appear to have been silver and gold.[43]

Decline of the Harappan civilization

Corrected radiocarbon dates indicate that early Indus Valley settlements like Amri, Kot Diji and Kālibangan originated about 3200 BC and had a span of about a thousand years.[4a,12b] Later cities like Mohenjodaro and Lothal came into existence about 200 to 500 years later, but declined within a century of the earlier ones.[4a,12b]

While the cities of the Indus Valley faded away, its culture did not die.[46] Residents moved outwards to such later settlements as Rangpūr, Alamgīr and Hulās.[11] Even today the small settlement of Nirmand, about 150 km upstream from Ropār on the right bank of the river Sutlej, has Harappan features, by way of a citadel, sacred wells used for special religious purposes, and a dominant priestly heirarchy.[47] In south India, Harappan ceramic forms yielded to a fine red lustrous pottery which was sometimes painted in the Harappan tradition.[5] Much practical and theoretical Harappan knowledge was inherited by the Aryans. But the whole ethos changed, from the practical, mechanical and commercial outlook that characterized the Harappan civilization to one in which trade was despised, and the inner, contemplative life exalted.

Chapter 3

FOODS OF THE GODS

Aryans

Broadly speaking the Aryan civilization followed the Harappan, but what actually transpired is shrouded in uncertainty. The view that long prevailed was based on the linguistic affinity between Sanskrit, Persian and the Indo-European languages. Nomadic tribes living in the steppe grasslands near the Ural mountains,[1] and calling themselves Āryās, were postulated to have fanned out following climatic changes to reach as far west as Ireland (Eire is a cognate form of Āryā) and as far east as India.[2a] Based on a study of the *Purānas*, Pargiter argued that this entry was not from the northwest into Punjāb, but mainly from the north into the area around Allahabād. Three tribes formed the chief migrant groups. One of these were the Ailas or Aryans, who eventually came to dominate the whole of north India; the second were the Dhaityas, who practised an early form of brahminism replete with magic rituals; and the third consisted of the Manva or Dravidians, an even earlier ethnic stock.[3] Another group with affiliations to Central Europe and Iran did enter India from the northwest to settle in the land of the seven rivers, Saptasindhu, but this was a small one. The interaction between these two groups of migrants was one major determinant of the Vedic and later Hindu culture of the country.[4a]

The Harappan civilization was subsumed by the Vedic.[6] Although it lived on in many ways in the culture that replaced it, it needs to be emphasized that the Harappan civilization was an essentially urban one, whereas the Vedic was agricultural, pastoral and philosophical, keenly alive to forces within and without that affect man's equanimity and comfort. A prayer from the *Yajurveda*, composed about 800 BC, reads like a litany of foods:

'May for me prosper, through the sacrifice, milk, sap, ghee, honey, eating and drinking at the common table, ploughing, rains, conquest, victory, wealth, riches. May for me prosper, through the sacrifice, low-grade food, freedom from hunger, rice, barley sesame, kidney beans, vetches, wheat, lentils, millets, panicum grains and wild rice. May for me prosper, through the sacrifice, trees, plants, that which grows in ploughed land, and that which grows in unploughed land.'[5b]

Vedic agriculture

The Aryans set the agricultural pattern of food production that still persists in India. Fields were ploughed with two oxen drawing a plough made of khadira wood, attached to the yoke by a harness made of hemp or leather.[7] Castrated bulls were used for ploughing, with their ears marked to indicate ownership.[8a] A light wooden plough was used. This suits Indian conditions even now because it does not turn up and desiccate the soil below. No wonder that iron ploughs, known since about 800 BC, have never become popular in India. The very act of ploughing later achieved ritual significance.

When the first Buddhist monastery was consecrated in Sri Lanka by Mahindra, the son of the emperor Ashōka, its boundaries were outlined by the reigning king employing a golden plough.[10]

Water was raised from rivers directly, or by deflecting them into man-made channels and building weirs across them to flood the fields.[11a] Water was raised with the ashmanchakra, consisting of clay pots attached to wheels.[7] These methods could raise water by nearly 10 metres (20 cubits) to the river brim, and a further 10 metres to inundate the fields, to the surprise of later Greek writers like Megasthenes (*c.* 300 BC). In the *Rāmāyana*, the land of Kosala is eulogized by Rāma as adhsvamātrakah, that is, as relying on irrigation rather than rainfall for its fecundity. The *Arthashāstra* of Kautilya (*c.* 300 BC) has many references to an extensive system of irrigation.[12a]

The *Kashyapa Samhitā* (*c.* 200 BC) has detailed accounts of every aspect of rice cultivation:[12b] sowing, irrigation, seed transplanting, weeding, watering, protection from birds like parrots (using buffalo skeletons as scarecrows),[11b] defence against vermin like rats, locusts and borer insects, reaping and finally threshing. Even the conditions needed to take a second crop are elaborated.[12b] The collection of cowdung (sarishaka or sakrit) is noted in the *Rigveda*, and both the *Atharvaveda* and the *Taittirīya Samhitā* note the use of animal refuse as fertiliser.[13a] Such use was also recorded by Kautilya in the *Arthashāstra* while Bāna in the *Harshacharita* (7th century AD) describes graphically the use of cowdung for manuring fields;[13a] in earlier times it was perhaps mainly employed for horticultural produce. Kashyapa (*c.* 150 BC) shows a minute knowledge of many fertilisers, including oilcakes, with detailed prescriptions for their use.[12c] Fodder crops were silaged as early as the *Rigveda*, the process being called sujavas.[12d] In the *Parasāra Samhitā* (*c.* AD 500) it was enjoined that a dung heap be left undisturbed for ten

Ashmanchakra, the Aryan water wheel with clay pots.

The neem tree; its bark was used to bring sick plants back to health.

months before use. This practice is now known to reduce active ammonia and increase humus.[12d]

Apart from mantras, charms and amulets to ward off pests, use of the ashes of cowdung, and of sesame seed, honey and ghee is prescribed. Fumigation with oilseeds like karanja and those of terminalia species is recommended.[12f] Elaborate seed dressings had developed by AD 500.[14] One consisted of successively soaking the seeds in milk, smearing with ghee, rolling in cowdung, and fumigation with animal flesh and then with animal manure. Extracts and pastes of various materials are prescribed for nursing sick trees back to health. These include oilcakes, animal dung, bone marrow, the barks of several trees like the neem, soapnut, arpana, udumbara, cinnamon, and *Solanum indicum*, mustard seed and linseed, and asafoetida. As in humans, plant diseases too were traced to imbalances between the three dōshas, namely bile, phlegm and wind (see Chapter 7), and treated accordingly.[12f]

There was an early appreciation of such practices as land fallowing, crop rotation and seasonal sowing. The *Rigveda* has only one reference to it, but the *Yajurveda* is explicit. The *Taittirīya Samhitā*, roughly contemporary with the latter, mentions two crops from a field in a year, the different seasons for ripening various crops, and the proper times for harvesting them.[12g] Three clear crop seasons, and the produce to be grown during each, are defined in the *Arthashāstra*.[15a] Rice was raised in the rainy season and harvested with the onset of winter; dhāls, lentils, beans and peas were harvested in spring; and barley, wheat, linseed and hemp (cannabis) were sown in winter and reaped early next summer. Later, finer gradations into six seasons (pre-spring,

spring, hot, rainy, autumn and winter) were in vogue.[16]

The *Rigveda* mentions neither rice nor wheat but only barley (yava); the *Yajurveda* has all three, besides a panicum cereal, an oilseed (tila, sesame) and several pulses, such as māsha (uṛad), masūra (masoor), mudga (mung), and kalāya (peas or mattar). The *Brhadāranyaka Samhitā* states that there are ten foodgrains.[17] These were rice, barley, sesame, kidney beans (masha), millet, panic seed (priyangu), wheat, lentils (khalva) and horsegram (khalakhulá, later kulattha, now kulthi). The *Arthashāstra* lists sugarcane and mustard (both known from much earlier, but not mentioned in ritual lists), linseed (atasī), safflower (kusumbha), and kōdhrava (kōdhra, varagu, *Paspalum scrobiculatum*). About a century later the *Mārkandeya Purāna* and *Vishnu Purāna* refer to gavēdhuka (coix, Job's tears), shyāmaka (*Echinochloa frumantacea*), aman rice, wild rice (nīvarā), a new 'flute barley' (vēnuyava, bamboo grains) and chickpeas (chana, Bengal gram). This of course is only the literary record. Some archaeological findings have already been mentioned in Chapter 2, and further details of such finds of major staples, as well as the botanical and genetic story, find their place in Chapter 14.

After the crops had ripened, they were reaped using sickles, and bundled. Three sheaves were left in the field to propitiate the goblin gandharvas who guarded them, and four were brought home and hung there to propitiate its goddess. Grain was threshed on the ground in the field or village, winnowed, and dried in the sun. The grain was measured out by volume, and sheaves set aside for the gods, the king, the family priest and servants. The rest was stored for family use in various ways; in receptacles (kathinya), in well-baked clay pots, in woven rope containers plastered with mud, or in underground pits protected against thieves, rodents and insects.[12b] Spells were additionally invoked to exorcise these predators.[7]

Supplementary foods were raised on village outskirts. Banks of rivers 'beaten by foam' were considered suitable for growing pumpkins and gourds, and lands that were frequently flooded for long pepper (pippali), grapes and sugarcane. Vegetables and root crops were raised in the

Grapes were grown by Aryans in lands which were frequently flooded.

Box 4

SANSKRIT SOURCES

While certain hymns of the *Rigveda* show internal evidence of having been formulated in some earlier homeland of the Aryans, they appear to have been set to verse from perhaps about 1700 BC. These earlier verses could therefore mirror prior observations, such as the reference to the abundance of the river Saraswathi mentioned in this chapter. Thus references to food in the *Rigveda* must be viewed with some caution. The same is true of the *Mahābhārata*. While the great Kurukshetra battle has been placed from many considerations at 1424 BC, the core of the epic itself was written down only a thousand years later from oral tradition, and would reflect prevailing food habits at the time of its composition. Let us look at some primary Sanskrit sources in approximately historical order.

Period 1700 BC to 1500 BC

Rigveda: A collection of 1017 hymns plus 11 others, totalling 1028 suktas.[35a] Each is further sub-divided into 8 ashtakas (octaves) or khandas (sections), and each of these have 8 further divisions called adhyāyas (chapters). Further dissection yields 2006 vargas (classes), 10,417 riks (verses; hence the name) and 153,826 padas (words). Another division yields 10 mandalas (circles or classes) and 8 anuvakas (sections). Of these ten, mandala numbers 2 to 7 are attributed to single families,[8a] and are probably the oldest nucleus.[36] Mandala 9, carrying the soma hymns (see Box 5), was probably introduced into the collection later.

Period 1500 BC to 800 BC

Sāmaveda: A song book with 1547 stanzas, all but 75 of which occur in the *Rigveda*.

Yajurveda: A prayer book of mantras for a priest to recite at sacrifices. There are two texts, the black and the white. The latter is attributed to the sage Yāgnavalkya Vājasaneya, and consists of 40 chapters, of which 15 are of later date than the rest.

Atharvaveda: This is in two recensions or samhitās. This veda consists of 20 books carrying 731 hymns, many drawn from the *Rigveda*. These hymns consist of charms and spells against maladies, accompanied by the use of herbs and dietary injunctions. The hymns are attributed to the first physician, Dhanvantari (see Box 12).[18b]

Brāhmanas and *Āranyakas*: These are books of prayer designed to relate the ritual to the sacred text. Each *Veda* has its own *Brāhmanas*, such as the *Aitareya* and *Kaushika Brāhmanas* of the *Rigveda*, the *Taittiriya Brāhmana* for the *Yajurveda*, and the *Gopatha Brāhmana* for the *Atharvaveda*. At the end of each *Brāhmana* are placed the *Āranyakas* or forest books, explaining the symbolism of the sacrifice.

Upanishads: These are philosophical writings attached to the *Vedas*, and the source of Vedānta philosophy. The *Rigveda* has the *Aitareya* and *Kaushītaki Upanishads*, and the white *Yajurveda* has the *Brhadāranyaka* and *Īsha Upanishads*. Authorship of the Upanishads is obviously not uniform.[34]

Period 800 BC to 350 BC

Sūtras: These consist of 8 vedāngas or manuals of instruction in phonetics, grammar, metrics, astronomy, astrology and ritual (kalpasūtra).

Purānas: Eighteen later non-religious works which record ancient Aryan ruling dynasties. Parts of these are thought to be very old.

Pāninīyam: The great grammar of Pānini, which has been described as a 'natural history of the Sanskrit language.'[35a]

Box 4 (*contd.*)

Nighantu: A treatise on medicine by a later Dhanvantari,[18b] perhaps a ruler of Vārānasi.[37a]

Buddhist canon: These consist of three pitakas written in Pāli, a provincial dialect of Sanskrit, and are termed *Vināyaka, Sutta* and *Abhidamma*. Also of value are the *Dhammapada*, 423 verses expounding Buddhist ethics, and the *Jātakas*, consisting of some 500 tales relating to previous birth of the Buddha which yield information on social customs of the time.

Period 350 BC to AD 1

Indica: The memoirs of Megasthenes written about 330 BC. He was the Greek ambassador to the court of Chandragupta Maurya.

Arthashāstra: A manual of statecraft by Kautilya, also called Chānakya, who lived around 300 BC in the court of Chandragupta Maurya.

Mahābhāshya: A commentary by Patanjali (about 200 BC) on the grammar of Pānini, defending it against the criticisms of Katyāyana.

Rāmāyana: One of the great epics originally written by Vālmiki about 400 BC, with later accretions over many centuries.

Mahābhārata: The other great epic. It consists of 18 parvas (books), being accretions over several centuries on the original tale of Vyāsa (about 400 BC).

Manusmriti: The Institutes or Codes of Manu, in Sanskrit *Mānava Dharma Sūtra*, a digest in 2685 verses of the creeds and laws of behaviour current at the time (about 200 BC).

vicinity of wells; and low grounds, like the moist beds of lakes, were suitable for leafy crops. Marginal furrows between rows of other crops were recommended for planting fragrant plants and medicinal herbs.[18a] The sugarcane crop was watched over by overseers, and the canes after cutting were stored for crushing when convenient. Fruits were ripened on the tree, or artificially in several ways: by burying them in sand or in respiring grain, by using the heat of a fire of dung cakes, or by mixing ripe with green fruit.[14] Some spices were cultivated in Aryan times, like turmeric, fenugreek (mēthi), ginger and garlic. Others like pepper and cardamom came from south India, and asafoetida from Afghanistan.

Cereals and pulses

What were the foods actually eaten between 1500 and 350 BC by the Aryans, who called themselves devas or gods? Deductions about the food the Harappans ate are based on archaeological artefacts (Chapter 2). Regarding food eaten by the Aryans, the literary works which they produced, starting with the *Rigveda* of about 1500 BC, are excellent if indirect sources of information. Some of the more important of these are listed in Box 4, and a well-documented book has appeared on the foods and drinks that occur in these Sanskrit works, chronologically listed from the earliest times to about AD 1200.[19]

To begin with, barley was the major grain eaten by the Aryans. It was fried and consumed in the form of cakes dipped in ghee, or as sweet cakes called apūpa fashioned out of the flour, boiled in water or fried in ghee, and then dipped in honey. The modern Bengali sweets pua and mālpua preserve both the name and the essentials of this preparation. Barley was also parched to give lājāh, which was powdered, and the flour mixed with water, ghee, milk or curds (to give karambha) or even with soma juice (see Box 5). Rice, which is first mentioned slightly later but thereafter dominates the Aryan food system, was cooked with water (odana, later called bhātka and still later bāth), or milk (kshīra), or sesame seed and milk (krsāra), perhaps a forerunner of the later khichdī made from rice and dhāl. Boiled rice was eaten as such or accompanied by a variety of materials like curds, ghee, sesame seeds, mudga (mung), beans (māsha, urad) or meat preparations.[27] Lājāh, parched rice, was the ritually-pure form of rice that a bride had to throw into the fire,[20] and it was also a regular food item, either soaked in milk, or perhaps mixed with some seasoning. Chipita was flattened rice (the modern chivda or chidva), also known as prthuka.[21] It was made then, as now, by moistening rice, parching it slightly, and then beating the grains flat in a mortar using a pestle. The terms missita and dhānidhaka, though not explicit, could refer in their context to puffed paddy or rice, the modern kheel or muri.

Wheat is not mentioned in the *Rigveda*, only in the *Yajurveda* and the *Brāhmanas*. The word dhāna is ambiguous, and simply means food, which was probably rice. The word for wheat, godhūma, is clearly the same as the old Persian term gandum.[22a] It is contemptuously described as food for the mlecchas (outcasts),[12h] and this could mean the vanquished Harappans who certainly used wheat extensively (Chapter 2). A number of minor grains also figure between 1500 and 800 BC. These include shyāmāka (*Echinochloa frumantacea*), priyangu (*Setaria italica*) and anu (*Panicum miliaceum*); wild rice, nīvarā; Job's tears, gavēdhukā; and ambāh or nambāh (whose identity is not clear).[19] A dish of several cereals cooked together was appropriately called chitrānna.[23]

From the *Yajurveda* onwards the three pulses māsha (urad), mudga (mung) and masūra (masoor) are constantly in evidence as the most commonly-used grain legumes, and māsha occurs even in the *Rigveda*. The dish kulmāsha, which appears to have been māsha dressed with guda and oil, has the connotation of a poor man's food in the Vedic period. It may have resembled the ghugri of the present, a slightly dressed parched gram. In the *Sūtra* period, from about 800 to 350 BC, thin and thick barley gruels (yavāsu) appear, as well as polished or pearl barley boiled in milk (yavaka). Rice becomes the major staple, and is eaten after boiling with water (ōdana) or milk, or along with curds, honey or meat (mamsaudana). Rice cakes are termed pishtakas. Sweet fried apūpas shaped like figs are popular, made of the flours of rice, barley or parched rice. Forest dwellers are stated to consume the minor cereals. Like the three major pulses, kulattha (kulthi) or the horsegram is extracted to yield a soup. The vataka (vadā) is made of soaked, coarsely-ground and fermented dhal (especially māsha), fashioned into different shapes and fried.[19]

The early canonical literature of the Buddhists and Jains (*c.* 400 BC) again reveals extensive use of fine rice (shāli) or ordinary rice (vrīhi), either boiled, or cooked with til seeds, or made into gruel (yāgu). Sweetened dishes using jaggery are made with broken rice, or with rice mixed with oilcakes and fried (shaskuli). Barley and wheat are less popular than rice, but wheat cakes do get fair mention. New pulses that now appear in literature are kalāya (mattar, peas), ādhakī (arhar, tuvar), chanaka (chana), alisandaga (perhaps Kābūli or large chana, stated to come from Alexandria), and nishpāva (hyacinth bean). Pulses are eaten as soups (sūpa or yūsa), vatakas (vadās) and parpatas (pāpads).[27]

Parpata, crisp pulse-based pāpad.

After 350 BC, many new varieties of rice and barley find mention. Parched barley is termed dhānāh, and its gruel vātya. Wheat receives more frequent mention. Pea soup is very popular. The rājmāsha makes its appearance, and before the millennium ends and the Christian era begins, a taboo against māsha (urad) is aired.[19]

Milk products

Cattle were an integral part of the Vedic culture, and the literature before 800 BC is full of references to the milk of the cow, though that of the buffalo and the goat also finds mention. This is used fresh (warm milk issuing from the udder was considered as already having been cooked by Indra),[24] boiled, mixed with soma juice, or as cream. The colostrum of the first ten days after calving was discarded.[27] Already the cow was being called vara or a blessing. The cow is referred to 700 times in the *Rigveda* alone, as frequently as Indra himself, and is a symbol of endless bounty in numerous contexts.[24] Milk was curdled with a starter from an early run, or with pieces of various green materials like the putika creeper, the palāsha (palash) bark, or the fruit of the kuvala (bēr, *Ziziphus*). Curds (dadhi, the present dahi) were eaten with rice, barley or soma juice. Curds folded into fresh milk constituted a popular drink, the solid and liquid portions of this being termed amishka and vajina respectively. Curd after dilution and churning, carrying butter globules in the liquid mass, was termed prasādjya. Two forms, with and without holes, of dadhanwat are noted; these may be paneer and ripened cheese respectively. Ghee was ghrta, prepared by melting down and desiccating butter, and a commodity of enormous prestige (see Chapter 6). It was used for frying (for example of apūpas), for mixing with soma juice, and as a dip to add relish to other foods.[19]

After 800 BC, the taboo on the use of colostrum was extended to include the use of the milk of a cow in heat, a pregnant cow, or a cow suckling another's calf. A favourite curd preparation was pāyasya (different from pāyasa), in which the solid part of curds, presumably after straining them away, was mixed with boiled milk, crystal sugar and fragrant herbs. Shikarinī, the modern shrīkhand, also employed strained curds, crystal sugar and spices. The solid part of cow ghee was called manda. Buttermilk was in wide use, and it was turned into a seasoned dish called sāga. The Buddha allowed his followers milk and its products. Jains soaked cloth in milk, then dried the cloth, and used it with water to yield a reconstituted product called kholas.[27]

After the third century BC, the *Arthashāstra* describes how commercial milking (dōhaka) and churning (manthaka) were in charge of a state official. Dadhi (curd) could be bought from a mathitikā. Preferred uses of various milk products were also listed. The solid part of thickened milk, called kurchikā, was allotted to soldiers with their rations, the liquid part (kilasa or skim milk) to cows with their fodder, and the residual buttermilk (udhasvit) from churning butter was fed to dogs and pigs. All this is singularly like modern practice. Sugared and spiced curd, called rasala, was a popular home item. Further taboos faced the brahmin: he was forbidden milk of the sheep, mare, ass, camel, deer and woman![19]

Animal foods of the Aryans will be separately considered in Chapter 5.

Fruits and vegetables

Though several fruits and vegetables were known even before the Aryan efflorescence, as we have seen in Chapter 2, it is only as late as the *Yajurveda* and its *Brāhmanas* that fruits come to be mentioned. The date (khajūra), bilva (bael, *Aegle mermelos*) and three varieties of the bēr (*Zizyphus* spp.) find mention. The mango or āmra first appears in the *Shatapatha Brāhmanà*, and āmalaka, the āmla, in the *Jaiminīya Upanishad Brāhmana*, both dating back to about 1000 BC. Vegetables start in the *Rigveda* with the lotus stem (visa) and cucumber (urvāruka), followed in the later *Vedas* by lotus roots (shāluka), bottle gourd (alābu), the singhāda (mulāli; saphāka), two other aquatic plants (avaka and andika), the bitter gourd (karivrnta, later karavella, now karēla), and several flavouring materials: ashvabāla (a variety of methi), madhuka flowers (mahua), and maduga (perhaps the fragrant southern herb marugu).[19]

The Indian fig (udumbara) and the purple jāmoon figure in the literature of the later Vedic period. The radish and ginger were munched after a heavy meal, but onions, garlic and leeks were avoided by fastidious people. Uncooked vegetables, collectively termed shāka in Sanskrit and tharkārī in Hindi, were cooked to give bhāji or shrāna.[19]

New fruits that find mention around 400 BC in Buddhist and Jain literature are the coconut, banana, jackfruit (panasa), palm, tendu (tindu-

Lotus roots, a delicacy since Aryan times.

ka), grapes, phālsa (pārusaka), karaunda (karamoda) and several citrus species. Vegetables noted in this literature include yams (āluka), two convolvulus roots (etāluka and kadambu), spinach (pālaka or pālankya), and two leafy vegetables (savastika and manduki).[19]

Around 300 BC, Kautilya mentions rājādana or ksiri (now kauki, *Manilkara kauki*) and cucumber (as chidbhita), while Patanjali writes of bimba (*Momordica balsamina*) and grapes (drākshaka). The *Rāmāyana* has a list of forest fruits used by hermits, which include the bēr, bhilāwan (bhallātaka), pīlu (*Salvadora* spp.), plāksha (*Ficus lucescens*), asvatta (*Fiscus religiosa*), kasmarya (perhaps a *Berberis* species) and inguda (*Balanites aegyptica*). Vegetables that are recorded are the sūran or elephant yam (vajrakanda), the pindāluka (possibly the sweet potato), the long bottle gourd (kalāsaka), the lasora (*Cordia sebestana*) and sleshmātaka (*Cordia dichotoma*), sudarshanā or vrsapani, bamboo leaves, and karīra (*Capparis decidua*).[19]

Oilseeds and oils

The pala of the *Rigveda* may be the sesame, which is the meaning it bears in later compound forms.[25] From the *Atharvaveda* onwards, frequent references occur both to tila, the sesame seed, and to its oil, thaila, the term later becoming a generic word for all vegetable oils. The sesame seed constituted one of the nine sacred grains (navadhānya), with great importance in many rituals.[25] As a food it was cooked with rice to give tilaudana, and with rice and milk to give krsāra.[19] It was fashioned with jaggery syrup into a laddukā, cooked with vegetables, and roasted, pounded and worked up with water to give a rolled-out parpata (pāpad).[19] A wild sesame seed, jartila, permitted as food to ascetics, is recorded in the *Taittiriya Samhitā*.[19] Ṡesame oilcake or sesame powder compounded with coarse rice flour and jaggery gave the tasty fried dish shaskuli,[26,27] the tilkut of today.

The common black mustard seed of today, called rāi, was then rājika, and yellow sarson was shvēta-sarshapa, gaura-sarshapa or siddhārtha.[19] Mustard seeds were seen as powerful agents in warding off evil spirits during illness or at an accouchement.[19] The Buddhist canon notes their use as spices. Their first notice as a source of oil is in the *Sūtra* literature after 800 BC,[19] though the indigenous population had doubtless used mustard oil from very early times (Chapter 2).

Use of pungent brassica leaves as a tasty relish, still consumed as sarson-ka-saag, is first noted around 500 BC in the *Acaranga Sūtra*,[28] and may well be older. The safflower seed, kusumbha, is referred to as a source of oil in early Buddhist canon; the *Arthashāstra* lists it among a number of oilseeds that were crushed, the others being the linseed (atasī), castorseed (eranda), mahua (madhuka), ingudi (*Balanites aegyptiaca*), neem (nimbuka) and kusāmra, of unknown identity.[15b]

The prevalence of frying even in the *Rigveda* period may be inferred from the use of the term ghrtavantam (cooked in ghee) for the apūpa, while the *Dharma Sūtras* (600–300 BC) mention vatakas fried in ghee.[19] The Aryans used only ghee for frying. The general populace must have used vegetable oils all along, though this first finds mention only in the *Sūtras*. The *Arthashāstra* has forty references to frying, [5d] particular mention being made of mustard oil, a practice still widely prevalent in the Ganges valley. Much later the physician Charaka recommends ghee for frying in autumn, animal body fats in spring, and oil (with special commendation of sesame oil) in the rainy season. A note of caution is sounded against daily use of oil.[29] About the same time Sushrutha also warns that fried foods are hard to digest. The animal fats in use were those of the fish, pig, alligator, bear and ass. These fats were permitted even by the Buddha if a monk fell ill, suggesting a medical connotation.

Salt, spices and condiments

In early Vedic times, salt was a rarity; it does not find mention in the *Rigveda*, though the later Vedas do cite it frequently.[19] Salt quickly assumes ritual significance,[19] and in the *Sūtras* its use in food is not permitted to students, widows and newly-married couples for the first three days. Salt was obtained from river, lake, sea, swamp and mine, according to Buddhist canon, and its production was a state monopoly under a salt supervisor in Mauryan times (see Chapter 10).[15c] It was also an expensive commodity, inviting no less than six taxes, four to be paid by the seller and two by the buyer.[15c] It featured frequently in barter transactions between urban folk and tribal people with no access to salt. Black or vida salt was interdicted in the two great Epics in ceremonies for the ancestors (shrāddha).

The earliest spices recorded were mustard (baja), a sour citrus (jambīra), turmeric (haridrā) and long pepper (pippali).[19] As the Aryans settle down we read of black pepper (maricha) and asafoetida (hingu). The list is scant: probably the Aryans looked down on spice use, and the rest of the population of course left no records. By the Buddhist era ginger, cumin, cloves, a sour myrobalan and vinegar are in use. Spicy relishes begin to figure either during a meal (vyanjana) or after it (uttaribhāga). Sādava connotes either a spiced fruit dish or a spiced fruit drink. The period of the Epics and the *Manusmṛiti* sees mention of coriander, cardamoms of four kinds (of which the green variety was much esteemed), cinnamon, spikenard (jatamanshi), nutmeg (jaiphal) and aloes. Vinegar was made from a variety of sugary materials, like sugarcane juice, jaggery, honey, jackfruit and jāmoon. Fruits like the mango, āmla and cucumber were preserved in vinegar or sour rice gruel (kānjika). Two spicy concoctions, sūpa and nisthāna, popular in Ayodhya in Rāma's time, were made by cooking pork and mutton in fruit juices. A pepper-flavoured decoction of a tree bark, mesashringi, is mentioned in the *Manusmriti*.[19]

Sweet foods

Honey must have been the earliest sweetener, and the *Rigveda* is of the opinion that the product from small bees was better than that from large ones.[19] It was used to sweeten apūpas, and was forbidden to students and women. Guests were welcomed to a household with madhuparka, a honey-sweetened concoction of curd and ghee. By the Buddhist period honey recedes, and guda (jaggery) and sugar take over as common sweetening agents.

The sugarcane is not mentioned in the *Rigveda*, but occurs frequently in all the *Samhitās*, and its chewing is mentioned in the *Atharvaveda*. Thickened sugarcane juice was phanita, and further concentration yielded guda. Rock sugar (khand) may have been known by 800 BC. Guda was the base for numerous sweet preparations. Mixed with it, sesame seeds were shaped to give palāla; wheat flour, fried in ghee and with milk

Box 5
THE MYSTERIOUS SOMA

Common to the priestly practices both of the ancient Iranian Aryans and the early Vedic Aryans was an exhilarating drink called hoama in Iran and soma in India. The drink was offered to the gods, and imbibed by the priests and proponents of the sacrifice. It was clearly distinguished from a mere alcoholic stimulant. In course of time Soma had become the moon goddess, and almost the entire ninth mandala of the *Rigveda*, consisting of 114 hymns, is addressed both to the libation and to the goddess.[35c] An individual who imbibed soma was exhilarated beyond his natural powers, and the juice itself was described as being 'primeval, all-powerful, healing all diseases, bestower of riches, loved by the gods, even the supreme being.' Indra was exhorted to destroy enemy strongholds after fortifying himself with soma juice. In elaborate rituals, the soma plant was sprinkled with water and ground (using a stone) on other stones placed above holes connected underground, which yielded a resonant sound likened to the bellowing of bulls. The ground mass was collected on a cowhide, strained through a cloth of sheep's wool, and the sparkling tawny filtered liquid mixed for consumption with milk, curds or flour.

Several attempts have been made to identify the soma plant. One guess was *Sarcostemma acidum*, a leafless shrub, still called somalata in several Indian languages and carrying a constituent toxic to white ants and man.[38a] Another was *Asclepias acida*, the American milkweed, not indigenous to India, which contains a poisonous glucoside; the leaf juice is used against worms and to combat bleeding, and the roots to induce vomiting.[38b] A third candidate is *Ephedra*, a genus which carries an adrenalin-like alkaloid called ephedrine; two species, *E. gerardiana* and *E.major*, are densely-branched but almost leafless shrubs, the dried stems of which are employed in allergic conditions and as a cardiac stimulant.[38c] A fourth claimant is the Indian bhang plant, *Cannabis sativa*, whose leaves are chewed, or extracted to yield bhang, or compressed to constitute gānjā. No identification seems really satisfactory.[39]

A strong case has been made out for the fly agaric mushroom, of a deep red colour with white spots, which is *Amanita muscarita*.[40] It exerts hallucinogenic effects of the kind described in the *Vedas*, and contains the principles muscimol and muscarine.[41] Much of the poetic if rather cryptic imagery of the texts seems to fit the mushroom. Thus it is red, udder-like and powerful; has a head like a cap, and a single, seeing eye, like a stud or a knob; is betrayed by a fly; has a hide of wool, and the dress of a sheep, is by day red, by night silvery, like Agni and like Surya. The Amanita mushroom is an Old World species, quite different from the hallucinogenic mushrooms of Central America with principles of a different nature, namely psilocybin and psilocin.[41]

---

then added, yielded samyāva, often flavoured with cardamom, pepper or ginger; and ground barley or wheat mixed with jaggery yielded abhyūsa. Some of these confections were artistically shaped. The rice-flour sweet preparation, mōdaka or madhugōlaka, looked like a fig, and the barley flour confection, shastika, was cone-shaped and had delicate surface markings.

By late Buddhist times, some sophisticated sweets are mentioned. The mandaka, now called mandē, was a large parāta stuffed with a sweetened pulse paste, which was then (as now) baked on an inverted pot; madhusarika was a sweet cake; morendaka, made from khoa, was shaped like the eggs of a mōra (peacock); gulala-lāvaniya was perhaps the modern gōle-pāpadi, a tiny, fully-expanded pūri, perhaps both sweetened and salted; and hayapunna was the modern ghevara and the earlier ghrtapūra, a fried wheat-ghee dough confection coated with fine sugar.[30] Rice cooked in milk and sugar was pāyasa, a popular sweet even now.

Water and other beverages

The *Vedas* list rivers, wells, springs and rain as sources of potable water. The *Sūtras* recommend the filtration of drinking water. Jains were obliged to boil water every few hours and to strain it through a cloth before drinking, and Buddhist texts enjoin the use of pure rain water for consumption. Water meant for drinking had to be 'clear, cool, shining like silver, health-giving and with the fragrance of the lotus'. In fact, the lotus was frequently grown in tanks to purify the sorrounding water.[7] The danger of drinking any kind of water indiscriminately was well recognized: one injunction goes so far as to say that water is for animals to drink, and only fit for man to bathe in![31]

Fruit beverages developed at a very early stage of Aryan life as refreshing drinks, and the eight kinds allowed to Buddhist monks are a good sampler.[19] These were juices of the ripe mango, jāmoon, banana, grapes, phālsa, coconut and edible waterlily roots, besides diluted honey. A surprising omission is sugarcane juice; this is added to the list in the *Rāmāyana,* which however interdicts extracts of the liquorice leaf.[22b] Buddhist monks took no meals in the evening, but were permitted beverages. Jain monks had a similar list, but the fruits permitted also included the date, pomegranate, bēr, myrobalan and tamarind; the extract of green bamboo stem was allowed, but sour fermented gruel (kānjika) was banned.[32] The *Arthashāstra* mentions other drinks like curd (dahi), buttermilk, a gruel soured with the āmla (dhanyāmla) and a syrup of molasses (gadōdhaka). The sweetened juice of sour fruits had a generic name, rāga, and thickened fruit juices were termed sādhava.[19]

Alcoholic beverages will be considered in Chapter 5. Soma juice, the intriguing Vedic Aryan drink, is described in Box 5.

Lotus flowers were used to purify and scent drinking water.

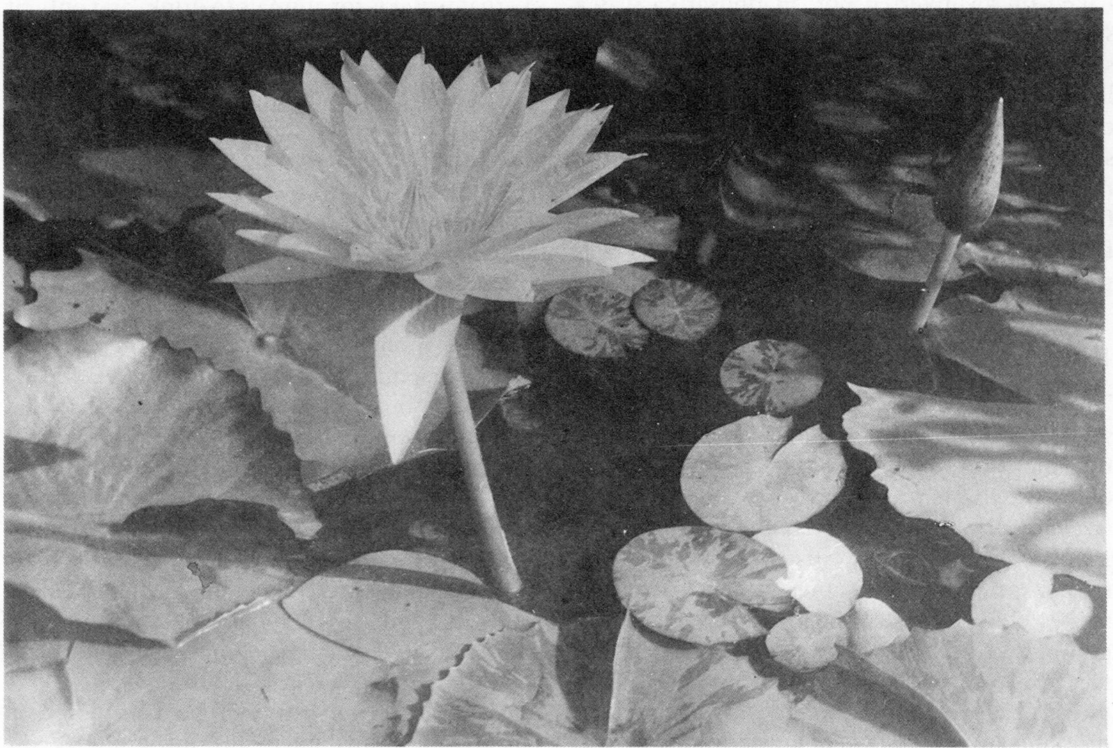

Roots of the waterlily were used to prepare a refreshing drink.

The expansion of the Aryans

Slowly, the Aryans expanded their influence all over India. Great rishis constituted the advance guard.[8b] Agasthya went to the south, Gōtama Rāhūguna to the east, Rāma Jamadagnya to the extreme west, and a rishi of the Kashyapa-gōtra, perhaps Chandradeva, to Kashmir. The far south and its west coast were probably discovered by the sea route, since the Vindhya mountains offered a considerable obstacle to access overland.[33] The route to the east coast from the Indo-Gangetic plain was across the central land mass, and then down along the coast. The easternmost areas, Bengal and Assam, felt the breath of Aryanism much later than the rest of the country, perhaps only after Buddhism had appeared. Eventually the whole of India came under the sway of the Aryan ethos in matters both spiritual and temporal. Food was a part of both.

Chapter 4

THE FOODS OF SOUTH INDIA

The south of India represents a very ancient land area, made up essentially of the solidified mass of liquid outflows of iron-rich lava which spread out 50 million years ago. Eruptions of gases from fissures gave rise to numerous straight ridges, and eventually swampy marshes with dinosaurs appeared.[1a] The pattern of tools that have been found is identical to those found elsewhere that mark the evolution of man (Chapter 1). Renigunta, Vemula and Yerragondapālam in Āndhra Pradesh show typical choppers, cleavers and thin pointed ovals,[2] and this is followed by fine microliths found in abundance all over the south.[1a] A special development in the south around 4000 BC was the tērī or sand-dune fishing culture of the sea-coasts, which used microliths extensively.[3a,4] Yet another unusual feature of south India was the megalithic phase of about 750 BC; this lasted for about a century, when huge stone structures were put up, and tools made of iron (for which there are numerous Tamil words) were in wide use. Rice was grown,[5] and around 500 BC King Vijayā may have carried a knowledge of irrigation with him to Sri Lanka where it flowered in the elaborate irrigation systems of Dambulla and Anurādhapūra.[6]

Influences on the food culture of the south

South India was exposed to a variety of enriching influences during its development. There was a connection with Africa through Gujarāt when the seas were at a considerably lower level than now and a land bridge existed. This influence is reflected in the great similarity of the tools in use in both places some 250 thousand years ago. Pottery head-rests found at T. Narsipūr and Hallūr, dated about 1800 BC, suggest a possible connection with Egypt.[7a] So does the discovery, by Flinders-Petrie, of Indian figures among moulded clay heads showing various racial types in an Egyptian tomb from 500 BC.[8a] Equally old finds of ragi (*Eleusine coracana*), bājra and jowār at sites in upper and central Deccan are strongly suggestive of communication between the two areas. Animals now extinct in India, like the giraffe, bison, antelope and ostrich are depicted in stone age paintings (Chapter 1); their bones also show up in excavations, all of which strongly suggests that a land connection with Africa must have existed. Affinities in cultural traits, artefacts and linguistic features further

Jowār was found in upper and central Deccan sites.

underline the connection from prehistoric to more recent times.[9] Transfer of food plants (like those noted above) besides certain *Hibiscus* species like the lady's finger and the ambādi, some gourds, and the tamarind can all be traced to this connection.

Food is also one means of tracing a link between south India and south-east Asia. The coconut is from New Guinea, and the banana, betel leaf, arecanut, sagopalm and certain yams have certainly flowed into south India from the same direction. Words for these foods in Tamil appear to be assimilated ones. Australian Aboriginals strongly resemble certain ethnic groups in south India, who were once called Nāgās;[10] there may have been a proto-Caucasoid centre in the interior of Asia, from which migrants moved southwards to India, south-east to Asia and Australia, and eastwards to constitute the Ainu of Japan.[11a]

There is a likelihood too that long before the Aryans came south, about 600 BC, the Harappan people had already found their way there. Pottery from megalithic tombs carry decorative markings that remarkably resemble those of the Indus Valley of a millennium earlier.[3b] Early Tamil script resembles early Gujarāthi (before its Aryanization).[3a] Possibly some food materials may have come too. Could irrigation, and dam building, both of which were known in the Indus Valley, have also come at that time to south India, to give impetus to the raising of rice?

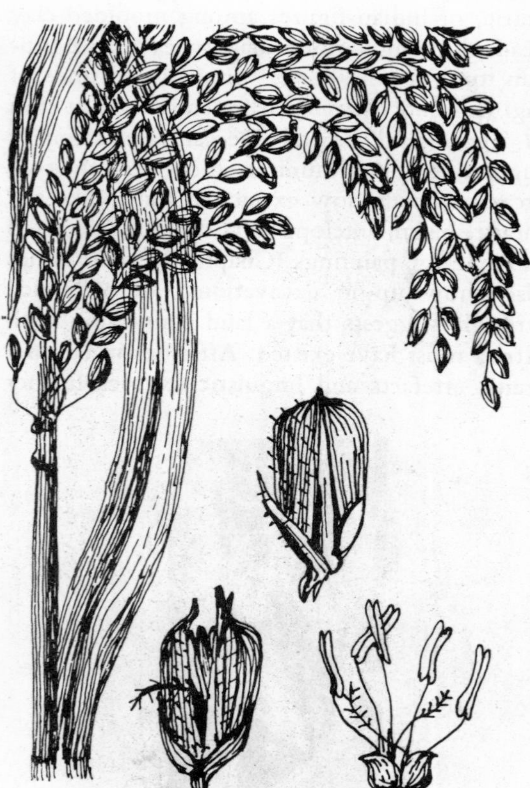

The graceful and prolific rice plant.

Archaeological food finds in south India

Brahmagirī in Karnātaka provides evidence of food production by 2300 BC.[3a] About 2100 BC, by radiocarbon dating, there existed in many places in south India professional cattle-keepers who herded up to a thousand animals in pens, in which the accumulated dung was periodically burnt, leaving behind great mounds of ash that have been recently excavated.[12] Meat and milk must therefore have been food items in wide use. Nagarjunakonda, even by 2000 BC, shows evidence of some food cultivation, and by 1500 BC there are plenty of charred animal and fish bones, and hoeing implements and quartz microliths that generally reflect agricultural pursuits. In fact, by about 1800 BC, excavations at several places show cultures that are fully agricultural: Utnūr, Narsipūr, Tekkalakota, Paiyampalli, Ādichanallūr, Cuddapah and Hallūr. The cereals found were rāgi, the panicum samāi, bājra, jowār and kōdhra (varagu), while pulses included horsegram (kulthi) and mung.[13a,14] Probably these neolithic cultures of the south had also developed cotton, and its weaving into cloth.[14]

By 750 BC the megalithic culture is in evidence all over south India. The use of iron was known, and the horse was in regular service.[5] The staple food was rice, but grains that could be rāgi were found in a megalithic site in Kodagu. Cattle, sheep, goats and the domestic fowl were used as sources of meat. Huge tanks were built by bunding to supply both domestic and irrigation water that made possible the growing of rice.

In the upper Deccan, south of the Vindhyas, a

Rāgi plants, whose purplish grains were a staple food even in early times.

series of metal-using settlements have been explored dating from almost 2500 BC. Everywhere animal foods were in plentiful use (beef, mutton, pork, venison, fowl and fish). At Inamgaon, 85 km east of Pūnē, barley, wheat, jowār, rice, lentils, peas and kulthi were cultivated between 1600 and 700 BC.[15] At Navdatoli, on the banks of the Narmada river 96 km south of Indore, wheat was raised about 2000 BC, to yield place about two centuries later to rice, masoor, mung, kesari, peas and two unidentified grains. The linseed was grown, perhaps as a source of oil. Evidence indicates that Jorwe, in Maharāshtra, raised wheat, barley, possibly jowār, lentils and peas around 750 BC.[15]

It would thus appear that rāgi, bājra and jowār were the important cereals of the early south, supplemented doubtless with other grains like the panicums (varagu, panivaragu) and Italian millet (thennai). Rice shows up archaeologically in rather late finds, between 1600 and 1300 BC in the upper Deccan, and only around 1000 BC in the more southern sites. But once it came in, rice took a strong hold. Certainly it dominates the Tamil literature that appeared from about the start of the Christian era (Box 6).

Food in Tamil literature

From the very beginning, the foods of the Tamil country were always portrayed in regional and occupational terms. The earliest tribes were the villavar or bowmen who lived by the chase in jungles and hilly tracts, and the meenavar or fisher folk who dwelt by sea or river.[16] After the Aryans arrived, six occupational classes evolved in course of time. The arivar were sages who sought solitude, the villavar constituted the landed gentry, and the āiyar or vedduvar were shepherds and huntsmen. Artisans like goldsmiths, blacksmiths, carpenters and potters con-

Box 6
TAMIL LITERATURE

In ancient times, Tamil poets were believed to have gathered at three Sangams to recite their works, which were then put together in collections. There is much dispute about the dates of these three academies of letters, but periods of 300 to 100 BC, 100 BC to AD 300, and AD 300 to AD 700 are now commonly accepted on grounds of both internal and external evidence.[3b, 19a,22,51,52]

No works of the First Sangam have survived. From the Second, only fragments have survived, of the *Tholkāppiyam*, a grammatical treatise in the form of sūtras that is attributed to the sage Agasthya. From the Third Sangam a mass of material has come down by way of both collections of works, and of stories. The nature of these is tabulated below.

ANTHOLOGIES

(a) *Ettuthokai* (Eight Collections): Some of these may be of the 2nd and 3rd centuries AD, others later.

(b) *Patthupāttu* (Ten Idylls): The first four of these are dated to the 3rd and 4th centuries AD, and the last six to the 6th century AD. These ten idylls included the *Pattinapālai, Porunarāru, Perumpānūru*, and the long poem of 782 lines, *Mathuraikkānchi*, dated about AD 450.

(c) *Pathinēndru-Kīllkannaku* (Eighteen Minor Didactic Poems): These are placed in the 6th and 7th centuries AD.

INDIVIDUAL POEMS

(a) *Nedunalvadal*, by Nākkirar.

(b) *Thirukkural*, by Thiruvalluvar.

COLLECTIONS

(a) *Aganānūru* or *Akam-nānūru*: Some of these pieces may be older, but most are of the 4th to 6th centuries AD.

(b) *Puranānūru*: A collection of the works of 150 poets, including Kapilar, Avvaiyār and Korur-Kilar. The earliest of these stem from before the 5th century AD, the others being later.

EPICS

(a) *Silapaddikāram* (Story of the Anklet): This is by Ilango Atikal, and is dated about the 6th century AD.

(b) *Manimekhalai*: This is by Seetalai Sattanār, and is contemporary with the above epic.

(c) Five other epics have survived while three more have been lost.

LATER LITERATURE

(a) Nāyanār mystics: These works date from the 7th to the 12th centuries AD, and include the *Thiruvāchchakam, Thevāram* and *Periyapurānam*.

(b) Ālwār mystics: There is a collection of 4000 stanzas, of the same period as the above, by poet-mystics like Nammālwar, Thirumangai, Kulasekarā and others.

The references to food in the text of this chapter thus belong mostly to the 4th, 5th and 6th centuries AD.

---

stituted the fourth group, and armed men the fifth. The valayar or pulayar consisted of scavengers and fishermen.[16] A passage from the *Perumpānūru* (about the 3rd century AD) describes the food served to a wandering minstrel in these terms:

The hunters served him, on the broad leaf of a teak tree, with coarse rice of a red colour (was this hand-pounded rice, or a naturally red variety?) and the flesh of the iguana. The shepherds gave him chōlam (jowār) and beans and millet boiled in milk. In the agricultural tracts, the labourers invited him to a meal of white rice and the roasted flesh of the fowl. On the sea coast, the fishermen fed him with rice and fried fish in dishes made of palmyra leaves. The brahmin gave him fine rice with mango pickle and the tender fruit of the pomegranate cooked with butter and fragrant curry leaves. The farmers feasted him with sweetmeats, the fruit of the jack and the banana, and the cooling waters of the coconut.[16]

Projecting from local experience, all land on the earth's surface was believed to consist of five types.[17a] Desert and sandy land was termed pālai, mountainous country kurinji, forest tracts mullai, agricultural river valleys marudam, and the coastal littoral neydal. Each area grew distinctive foods.[17b] Desert land could grow nothing, and the inhabitants obtained what they could by pilferage! Mountain areas grew two mountain rices (āivanam and thōrai), and thennai (Italian millet). Bamboo rice (mungilarisi) is mentioned, but since the bamboo flowers only twice or thrice in a century, this must have been a rare product. The mullai forest areas raised varagu, sāmai, horsegram, beans and lentils, while the mountain valleys raised red rice (chennel), white rice (vennel) and a refined variety, pudunel.

Rice in the southern diet

Food was rich and varied in south India in the first few centuries AD. As observed above, there were at least five varieties of rice.[18a] Rice was of course mostly eaten boiled, but sometimes fried aromatics were sprinkled on it.[19a] Dressing with tamarind gave puli-kari (puli-sādam),[20a] and further with sesame seeds and sugar yielded chitrannam.[20b] Rice could be cooked with a pulse (the present pongal),[21] or cooked with 'fatted meat',[22] or 'well-cooked with ghee'.[23a] There is a poetic description of 'rice which looked like jasmine buds, the grains elongated like fingers, and separate from one another'.[22] A Sanskrit work of the 6th century AD, the *Dasakumāracharita* of Dandin,[24] relates the tale by which Gomini, a lass of the Dravidian country, found a husband by the economical way in which she dealt with a quantity of paddy. All the steps in the processing of paddy are elegantly and lovingly described: grinding, drying, removing the husk, and then polishing with a pounder (whose end is covered with iron plates), followed by winnowing the grains, and then washing them before cooking in boiling water.[24] Rice kept for three years was considered healthy.[17b] Pulangalarisi was paddy parboiled by immersion in hot water, drying and pounding. Both ageing and parboiling could have been means based on experience for hardening rice, and the latter gave, on milling, a higher yield of whole grains, and of a better nutritive quality, than did raw rice. Aval was rice that was soaked, and roasted in sand until about to puff, followed by flattening in a pounder. Soaked rice was puffed to pori by throwing it on hot sand. Both aval and pori were eaten after soaking in milk.[25] Cooked rice was kept in cold water overnight, and the rice and water consumed as the first meal of the next day.[20c] Even rice gruel was soured overnight to yield a beverage. These practices were tantamount to eating stale food in the Aryan view, and according to the *Baudhāyana Dharma Sūtra*, a work of the south, they were very specific to southern Brahmins.[26] In the home of an Āndanār or Aryan brahmin, 'rice which bears a bird's name (rājannan) was eaten with chips of the green fruit of the kommatimalūla shrub, peppered and spread with curry leaf and fried in fresh cow butter . . . with excellent sliced tender mango pickle'.[22]

Rice was converted into many appetizing foods. The āppam, mentioned in the *Perumpānūru*, was a pancake baked on a concave circular

Pounding, to dehusk paddy or to flatten rice.

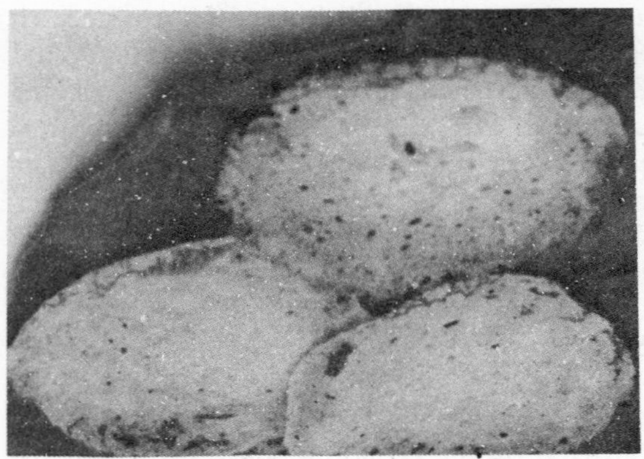

Āppam, made from fermented rice batter.

clay vessel and a favoured food, taken soaked in milk.[27] So was the idi-āppam, thread-like extrusions of a dough of boiled and mashed rice, which in Chōlā times (say the 10th century AD) was eaten with sweetened coconut milk.[20a] Other forms of shallow pan-fried snacks were the dōsai and adai, both based on rice.[27] The dōsai is now made by fermenting a mixture of rice and urad dhāl overnight before frying, and the adai is a mixture of almost equal parts of rice and no less than four pulses, ground together before shallow frying. The moodagam of the *Mathuraikkanchi* may be the deep-fried mōdagam (mōdak) of the present. The idli had not yet made its appearance, and will be considered in Chapter 8. In slightly later Chōlā times the athirasam appeared, a deep-fried patty of sweetened rice flour,[20a] which is called naiāppam in Kerala today (Chapter 10).

Other cereals find occasional mention. There is a description in the *Karuntogai*[18b] of 'kēlvaragu (red ragi) spread on the broad surface of a rock to dry', and a reference in the *Puranānūru* to 'husking and cooking the rāgi grain'.[19a] In another context, we read of poets (who were always treated with great respect by kings) being plied 'morning and evening with food made by boiling in milk mixed with honey the grain of rāgi, which grows on dry land and resembles the eggs of pigeons'[19b] (this seems inaccurate; perhaps the dough was shaped into balls, as is the practice today). The fat meat of a roasted rabbit served as a side-dish.[19b] Varagu (*Paspalum scrobiculatum*) was sown along with kollu (horsegram), and one poet describes habitations in mountainous country thatched with varagu straw.[22] The grain itself was made into 'a savoury food that is a mixture of the small-boiled grains of varagu and good boiled pulse'.[22] The grain thennai (Italian millet, *Setaria italica*) when cooked was accurately likened to 'a swarm of the tiny young of crabs' in the *Perumpānūru*.[22] Sāmai (*Panicum miliare*) has been recovered from burials at Adichanallur,[23b] though it seems to have escaped mention in Tamil literature.

Other foods of the south

Among the several pulses, kadalai (chickpea, Bengal gram) is described as the 'bean which grows on stout creepers' and which is 'fried in sweet-smelling oil'.[19a] The kollu or mudhira (horsegram) is mentioned as growing in forest tracts (mullai) along with beans and lentils.[17b] Rather surprisingly ulundu (urad), which is today so vital an ingredient in making dōsai, adai and idli, does not appear in literature. Nor does thuvarai (arhar), the common pulse of the present in south India. Pastoral people are described as imbibing an aromatic tamarind soup,[25] perhaps akin to the thuvar-based rasam of the present day.

Oils of the sesame and coconut were in use.

Foam on the surface of chekku-crushed sesame oil.

In the hill country, the sesame pod was stated to be ripe for picking when it turned dark. The oil from the seeds was obtained, as noted in the *Nāladiyar* and *Nālāyira Thivya Prabantham* of the 7th and 8th centuries AD, using a chekku or oil press, and the characteristic foam (nurai) noted in the much earlier *Puranānūru* in respect of sesame oil suggests that the chekku was even then in use.[28] Sesame oil was exported,[25] and the *Periplus* (described later in this Chapter) testifies to coconut oil export even in the 1st century AD. Ghee, called butyron, was sent in leather skins from south India to Rome,[19c] and was used domestically by the wealthy, both for cooking and in sacrifices.[18b]

For many vegetables, there were specific names for every part and stage of growth. Brinjals and pāgal (bitter gourd) were in use.[17b] We read of a dish of 'vegetables cooked in milk',[22] not a practice at present. Certain types of unripe bananas were used as vegetables, as they still are. Tubers were treated as vegetables in the kitchen, and there were many of them with a variety of generic names: kandam, mūlam, vēm, shadai, shivai and thuri.[17b] Specifically noted were the underground parts of the palmyra tree, water lily, and yams.[18b] Tubers of the sweet potato are described in the *Puranānūru* as 'descending from the creeper'.[19a] The leaves of the chembu (*Colocasia esculenta*, arvi) were cooked along with ripe yams,[22] and 'large tubers' were also cooked with meat.[17b] Several green leafy vegetables are mentioned as foods of the poor. These were the kuppu-keerai (*Amaranthus viridis*), vallai, munnai (*Meyna laxiflora*, syn. *Vangueria spinosa*) and vellai (*Cleome viscosa*), which were eaten with rice and a sweet-and-sour preparation of nellikāi (*Emblica officinalis,* the āmla).

There were a fair variety of fruits. The jackfruit grew in marudam or mountainous regions. Fruits grew along the bark, and there were some of fine flavour which grew underground (*Karuntogai*).[29a] A young man waiting to be married is told that his betrothed is as delicate as the 'tender stalk which holds the large jackfruit, though her love for you is immense'.[29b] The mango was also found in marudam. Again there is a charming analogy: the eye of a woman is compared to a very tender mango cut horizontally in two with a rusty knife, the stone resembling the pupil surrounded by the white of the eye.[29b] The woodapple (*Limonia acidissima*) was the principal fruit of desert areas.[25] Among the other fruits noted are the banana, nellikāi (āmla), jāmoon (called naval), Indian fig, jujube (bēr, *Ziziphus* spp.), lemon and pomegranate, and those of trees like the coconut, palmyra, and iron-wood tree (*Memecylon umbellatum*).[17b] Pomegranate sprinkled with pepper was fried in ghee to give a spicy relish.[18b] Two sour fruits, the tamarind and nellikāi, were combined in making a drink.[18b]

Pepper was of course the prized spice of the south, sought all over India and even overseas. It grew in the Chera country (now called Kērala). Other flavouring agents were turmeric, ginger, cloves, cardamom, tamarind and lemon; mustard is mentioned along with pepper for spicing meat, but does not seem to have been widely used.[17b] There is frequent mention of pickle (urukāi), made for example from the tender mango.[22] Chewing the betel leaf was initially a southern custom (Box 7).

Herds of cattle, as we have seen, were kept even in 2160 BC, and by the period of classical Tamil literature most milk products find mention: cream (edu or perugu), curds (thayiru), buttermilk (which had five names), butter (vennai) and ghee (nai). There is a curious reference in the *Nachchinārkkiniyar* to the removal of all fat from milk using a 'medicine'; such de-fatted milk was sold, but is stated to be 'worthless'.[30] Curds were spiced with pepper, cinnamon and ginger, and buttermik was drunk with a meal.[24] The buffalo was not merely a draught animal, but a source of milk, unlike in south-east Asia where the water buffalo is never milked. Even today the Todas of the Nilgiri hills in south India milk buffaloes and prepare ghee as an indispensable part of their daily ritual.[23c]

Pre-Aryan southerners had no inhibitions about eating flesh. Even thereafter, Kapilar, the famous Brahmin priest of the Sangam epoch, speaks with relish,[18b] and without fear of social ostracism[21] of the use of meat and drink. There

Box 7

CHEWING THE BETEL LEAF

The leaf of the betel vine (*Piper betle*) is usually chewed along with grits of the areca nut (*Areca catechu*), a dab of slaked lime and a smear of katthā paste (the extract of the heartwood of *Acacia catechu*). It is recognized even in Sanskrit literature as being a south Indian practice. The earliest northern reference to chewing the leaf is in the Buddhist *Jātaka* tales,[53] then in the famous Mandasor silk weavers' inscription of about AD 473, in Varāhamihira's *Brhat Samhitā* of about AD 530, and in Charaka, Sushrutha and Kashyapa.[54] Kālidāsa in his *Raghuvamsa* definitely associates it with southern India (then called Malaya), and the *Mrcchakatika* of Shudraka describes betel leaves being eaten with camphor in the mansion of Vasantasena.[53]

In the Tamil *Silapaddikāram* of about the 6th century AD, the heroine Kannagi gives her husband Kōvalan betel leaves and areca nuts to eat at the end of his last meal, before he departs on his fatal mission of selling her anklet at Madurai.[32] This is not a really early date, and words for the various components used in chewing are extremely old. A Vietnamese book, *The Life-Story of Tan and Lang*, dated before 2000 BC, is said to mention betel leaf chewing.[54,55] The practice is common and extremely ancient (see Chapter 8) over a very large part of southeast Asia and the islands beyond,[55] The name for the nut is arec in the Talinga dialect of the Sunda Islands, though the word areca now in use in English is believed to have emerged in south India, by way of the Portuguese, from the Malayālam adakka, itself derived by combining adai (a close cluster) with kāi (nut).[56] The term betel for the leaf comes, again *via* the Portuguese, from the Malayālam and Tamil vetrilai or vetthilē, meaning truly-a-leaf, and likewise the Hindi pān is from the Sanskrit parna meaning a leaf. Even in AD 1560 Garcia da Orta mentioned the word pāk used by common people in Kerala for the quid, and the addition of camphor to it by grandees.[57] The Sanskrit words thāmbūla for the leaf and guvāka for the nut, and even the vetr stem of the Tamil word vetrilai, all have structural correspondences with words like blu, balu and mlu which are used for the betel leaf in some Munda dialects of Indian aboriginal peoples.[58]

The use of the leaf and the nut seem to have entered south India simultaneously. The use of astringent katthā as an accompaniment is noted by all the medical authorities, Charaka, Sushrutha and Vāghbhata, and that of lime by Varāhamihira. Addition of aphrodisiacs yields a quid with the bed-breaking connotation of palangtōd![59] The betel quid in India is regarded as an auspicious item and a symbol of hospitality, and is offered as a moral and even legal commitment when an agreement is drawn up.[38b] It is of interest that coca leaves are also chewed along with slaked lime in South America as a means of releasing the stimulant alkaloid cocaine.[60]

A whole technology has developed round the practice of chewing.[59] Containers of brass, copper and silver to hold the various ingredients are called pāndān. These are usually artistically perforated to allow for circulation of air, and come in a variety of floral, bird and animal motifs. Nut crackers for splitting and shredding consist of hinged blades which are fashioned after parrots, peacocks, horse riders, celestial figures and amorous couples. Containers of lime paste, called chunadāni, take the shape of mangoes, leaves, swans and elephants, and even the spittoons for discarding saliva or solids are beautifully made of silver, brass and black bidari metal.[59] Distinctive types of betel leaves now grown in the country go by such popular names as Banglā, Mithā, Sānchi, Kapoori, Desavari and Ambari.[61]

were four names for beef (vallūram, shuttiraic-chi, shūshiyam and padittiram) showing that it was in wide use, and the *Perumpānūru* (one of the Ten Songs) talks of a fat bull being slaughtered in the open.[22] Even buffalo meat was consumed. There were fifteen names for the domestic pig, and even wives of the rich traders living in the coastal neydal regions relished pork.[18b] The wild boar is described as being hunted using dogs and nets, a practice also for the rabbit and hare.[22] Captured boars were fattened with rice flour and kept away from the female to improve the taste of the flesh.[16] Even meat from an elephant either killed in battle or hunted down was dried and stored for consumption.[18b] The Kuravars liked deer and porcupine, the Mallar fried snails, and fishermen the tortoise.[18b] A dish of 'iguana red meat big with ova resembling chank shell beads' is set down with obvious relish.[18b] There was no taboo, such as prevailed in the north of India, on eating the domestic fowl (called karugu or kōzhi). Another bird frequently mentioned is the peafowl,[31a] and both the quail and parrot were used as food. A king is described as feeding his labourers with choice dishes like the rich roast flesh of lampreys, and the fat of turtles.[31b] Fish was relished, quite naturally, by the folk of the littoral, and several kinds are mentioned: the aral,[27] varal and horned vālai, besides prawns, caught by such fishing communities as the Meenavar.[18] In fact, the Tamil word meen for fish even entered the Sanskrit language. At a meal, white rice was served with curried crabs and vegetables.[22]

There were many ways in which animal foods were cooked: One word for black pepper was kari, and it was an important ingredient in meat dressing. Centuries later the word was to be anglicized to curry, with the much wider connotation of any seasoned dish (Chapter 16). Meat that was first marinated with ground spices like pepper and mustard seeds, and then fried in oil, yielded thāllitakari, or kuy. Fried meat had three names, one of which was pori-kari. Meat that was boiled with flavourants like pepper and tamarind was termed pulingari or tuvai.[17b] Tuvai could be further ground down and spiced to give a pasty relish.[18b] Hare meat is described as being fried,[22] and naturally also was fish, whether fresh, dried[18b] or salted,[22] sometimes with a dousing of tamarind sauce.[18b] Roasting was also much in favour then, apparently much more so than at present in south India. We read about 'hot meat, roasted on the points of spits',[32] and 'fine large pieces of fat meat roasted on iron spikes' (*Porunarāru*).[22] There is a poetic description of basting a roast:

> Like drops of rain that fall in the full lake:
> Drips down the fat from the meat served up.[31c]

The same verse continues with the line: 'roasted flesh is carved and eaten', which suggests that large joints, or whole animals, were roasted; elsewhere we learn that whole roasted animals were valued for their taste.[27] Even semi-dried fish was relished after roasting.[22]

There were two sources of sugar in the south, the sugarcane and the palmyra. The poet describes the river 'Kāvēri, along whose banks the sweet cane's white flowers wave, like pennoned spears rising from the plain',[31d] and indeed the sugarcane was associated with river valleys.[18b] We learn from the *Aganānūru* that when carts got stuck in the mud, stalks of sugarcane were heaped beneath the wheels to provide a grip.[19a] Sugarcane juice was a popular drink, especially among women, along with tender coconut water and fresh palmyra sap, and in fact a mixture of the three called munnīr is noted in the *Puranānūru*.[21,25] The juice was extracted and boiled down to the coarse brown sugar, jaggery, which was the common sweetening agent.[17b] The names for this product both in Tamil (ayir) and Sanskrit (sharkarā) were mere extensions in the use of these words, which originally meant sandy or gritty.[17b] White sugar seems to have been imported into south India from China,[17b] even though it was then being manufactured in the north of the country. Sweetmeats of many shapes sold by vendors are described in the *Mathuraikkānchi*.[29b] Surprisingly, jaggery made from sweet palmyra sap does not appear to be mentioned by any poet. Honey was a prized product especially of the Kurinji area, and there

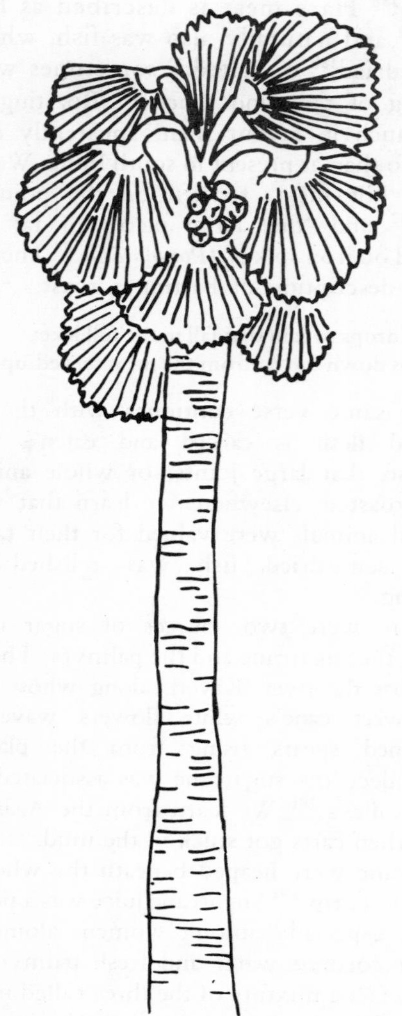

Palmyra palm, from Buddhist sculpture.

were as many as seven names for it. Honey was employed in barter, for example for fish oil and toddy from the littoral,[18b] and there is mention of liquor brewed from honey by the mountain-dwelling Kuruvar, which was matured in bamboo cylinders.[17b]

Being surrounded by the sea, salt in south India was a well-known commodity, manufactured in many places (see Chapter 9), and an important item of trade.[27] Entire families moved around selling salt in carts.[27] These were called vandichattu, and the *Pattinapālai* notes that as a pastime young girls kept count of the numbers of such carts that passed along the highway. Salt was, of course, used in cooking, and for salting and preserving dried meat and fish.

Alcoholic beverages were in common use at all levels of society. Even women drank, especially in the company of their lovers. The poorer classes imbibed toddy made by fermenting the sap of the palmyra palm (*Borassus flabellifer*).[16] Poets wrote of sturdy sailors who lived a dangerous life and were fond of strong liquor.[19a] Wine brewed from germinated grains in pots is mentioned more than once, and was drunk for example by soldiers.[22] Liquor shops in Madurai floated gay streamers, and a piece of raw ginger chewed while drinking was recommended as an antidote to the heavy imbiber.[19a] Another antidote was a concoction of the overripe seeds of the jackfruit, buttermilk, tamarind and the gruel resulting from boiling aged rice.[17b] During the 1st and 2nd centuries AD, when trade with Rome was at its peak, southern kings had access to 'cool, green and fragrant (Italian) wine, served in golden goblets held by bright-bangled girls'.[22] After the Aryans had established themselves, old habits died hard, and even brahmins were not reticent in using either meat or liquor.[18b,33]

Trade in food in ancient south India

With produce in south India being so strongly regional, trade in commodities between regions was quite natural. This frequently took the form of barter. Thus paddy could be bartered for fish, or for curd, and fish oil for honey or edible roots.[18b,27] The herdsman's wife 'feeds all her relations with the rice received in exchange of buttermilk; for ghee supplied she accepts, not a piece of fine gold, but instead a she-buffalo, a cow, or a black-heifer worth its value' (*Perumpānūru*).[22] Venison or arrack might be bartered for sugarcane or beaten rice.[18b] Salt was widely vended slung in two bags across the backs of oxen,[18b] or by 'salt sellers who enter villages crying out the price of salt',[22] or in rows of carts creaking along.[27] Indeed paddy and salt were the principal measures of value.[18b] Pepper moved in caravans of asses to the big cities.[27] A picture of the town of Madurai in the *Mathuraikkānchi* written by Mankudi Maruthanar conveys the excitement of the market place:

> Sacks of pepper and the sixteen kinds of grains such as paddy, millet, gram, peas and sesame seeds are heaped in the grain merchant's street; the brokers move to and fro with steelyards and measures in their hands, weighing and measuring the pepper and grams purchased by the people . . . The hotels and restaurants are now, in the cool of the evening, crowded by visitors who feast upon luscious fruit such as the jack, mango and banana, and on sugar candies, tender greens, edible yams, sweetened rice or savoury preparations of meat.[16]

Other Tamil poems of the 1st and 2nd centuries AD speak of Yavanas (Greeks) of fine physique and strange speech, whose well-built ships rode the waves of foaming rivers.

Evidence from the Roman side fully corroborates Tamil writings. In AD 40 a Greek sailor, Hippalos, discovered, for the west, the monsoon winds to and from India, briskly fanning the trade that had already developed between south India and Rome. A remarkable book, the *Periplus Maris Erythraei* (Circumnavigation of the Erythrean Sea), written in the 1st century AD by a Greek sailor posted in Alexandria, describes the trade from south Indian ports based on obvious personal knowledge.[34] Ptolemy, about 50 years later, lists 11 ports on the coasts of India, and 30 walled towns. Many ports have since been identified.[34A,36,37,38c,39,40] Starting from Kanyākumāri (Kōmar, perhaps the port of Saliyur, now called Alangakulam) and going up the east coast lay the following ports: Sasikonrai (Tuticorin), Korkai (Comari, the pearl harbour in Thirunelveli), Kolkai (Colchi), Nikama (Nagapattinam), Tondi (Tyndis), Puhar (Camara or Khaberis, where the Greeks had an emporium), Veerai (Pouduke, Puducherry or Arikamedu), Soppatinam (Sopatina, perhaps Vāyalur, which had a lighthouse), Macchilipatnam (Maisolia), Dantapūra (Palour, perhaps

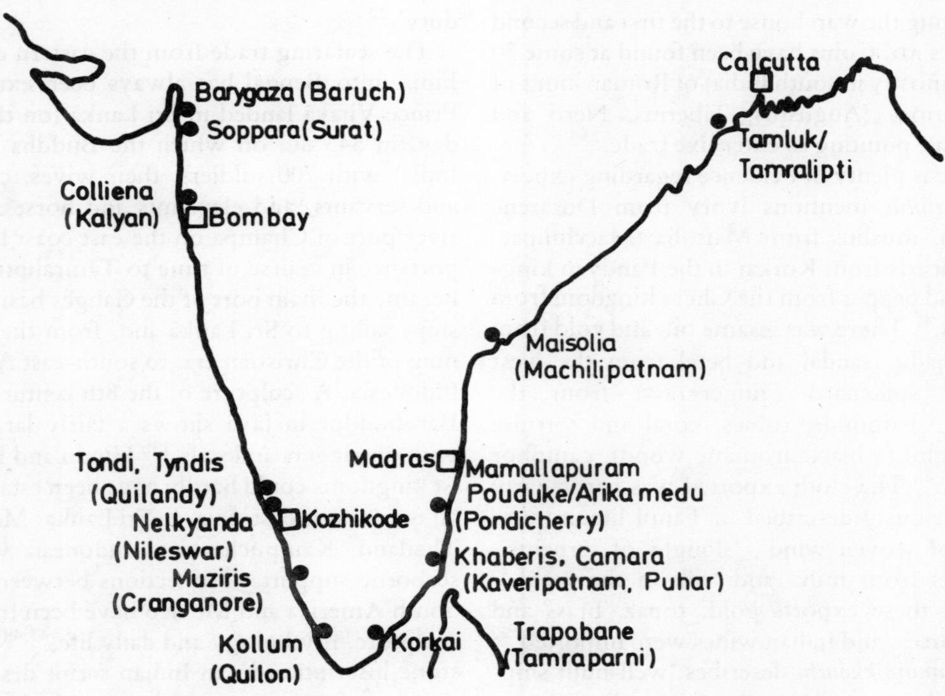

Ports of South India when trade with Rome was at its height.

Pūri) and Tāmluk (Tāmralipti). Starting again from Kanyākumāri and going up the west coast the following were the ports to be encountered: Nakkita (Nalcynda, on the river Pampa near Pārakkal), Paralia (near Quilon), Muziris (near Cranganore), Tyndis (near Kozhikode), Naura (Cannanore), Champāvati (Symalla) and Colliena (Kalyān), both near Bombay, Soppara (Ophir, 40 km north of Bombay), Bharukkacha (Broach) and Lothal. Two names for pepper listed in the *Amarakōsha* are derived from the names of ports: kollaka from the port of Korkai, and dhāmmapattana from Dharmarad on the eastern coast of Malaysia.[41] At Arikamedu near Pondicherry (the Pouduké of early Roman writers) was excavated a Roman warehouse fifty metres long, with a ramp running from it perhaps to the quay.[43, 44] Roman amphorae with two handles at the top, in which wine was transported, were found in the warehouse in large numbers; some bore the marks of known Roman potters, like VIBII, CAMURI and ITTA, thus dating the warehouse to the first and second centuries AD. Coins have been found at some 30 places (mostly in south India) of Roman kings of that period, (Augustus, Tiberius, Nero and Caligula), pointing to extensive trade.[23d]

There is plenty of evidence regarding export. The *Periplus* mentions ivory from Dosarene (Orissa), muslins from Maisolia (Macchilipatnam), pearls from Korkai in the Pandyan kingdom, and pepper from the Chēra kingdom from Muziris.[41] There was sesame oil, and gold from Kongunādu, sandal and betel from the west coast,[25] spikenard (gingergrass) from the Ganges, diamonds, rubies, coral and tortoise shell, aghil (a black aromatic wood), camphor and salt.[45] The cloth exported was particularly fine, variously described in Tamil literature as 'webs of woven wind', 'sloughs of serpents', 'vapours from milk' and 'silk in the web'.[45] Against these exports gold, topaz, brass and lead, horses, and Italian wines were imported.[22] The *Mathuraikkānchi* describes 'well-built ships loaded (among other things) with different kinds of grain, white salt, sweetened tamarind, and salted fish', and the *Pattinapālai* talks of 'well-weighed goods in abundance being exported with the Tiger mark (of the ruling kings) impressed on them so as to recover customs duty'.[22]

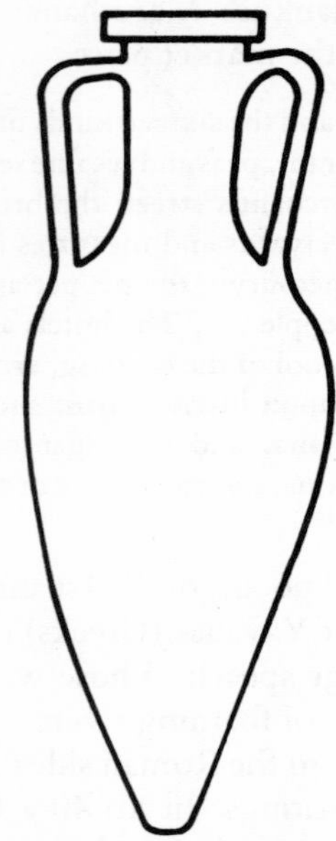

Roman wine amphora found in Pondicherry.

The seafaring trade from the eastern coast of India upto Bengal has always been extensive. Prince Vijayā landed in Sri Lankā (on the very day, in 543 BC, on which the Buddha died in India) with 700 soldiers, their wives, children and servants, and elephants and horses.[46] The river port of Champa on the east coast lost importance in course of time to Tāmralipti which became the main port of the Ganges basin, with ships sailing to Sri Lankā and, from the beginning of the Christian era, to south-east Asia and Indonesia. A sculpture of the 8th century AD in Baroboddūr in Jāvā shows a fairly large ship with outriggers and sails.[13b] Hindu and Buddhist kingdoms could hardly have been established all over south-east Asia, in Sri Lanka, Malaysia, Thailand, Kampuchea and Indonesia without seaborne support. Connections between India, South America and Mexico have been traced in sculpture, mythology and daily life.[47,48] Even a stone inscription in an Indian script describing the visit of a merchant ship to the Mexican coast in AD 923 has recently been found,[49,50] as will be described in Chapter 16, Box 33. These voyages perhaps have a bearing on the movement of plants, which will also be commented upon later.

Chapter 5

MEAT AND DRINKS

It is clear from earlier chapters that the Harappans, the Vedic Aryans and the residents of south India, like their contemporaries elsewhere in the world, enjoyed eating animal food and drinking alcoholic liquors. Yet it is only in India that concepts of vegetarianism and abstinence emerged as strong ethical doctrines and a way of life among considerable sections of the population. Let us now examine how this came to pass.

The prevalence of meat-eating

No less than 250 animals are referred to in the Vedas, and 50 of these were deemed fit for sacrifice, and by inference for eating.[1a] Some of these were raised domestically, like cattle of all kinds, and swine. Professional hunters who lived near the jungles, which were widespread in those days, regularly captured game for the market using bows, arrows, poisoned darts, spears, javelins and blowpipes. Ruses were used to capture animals, alive or dead. Fowlers waited at the edges of a lake or pool and trapped birds, with nets or with their feet, using bird calls and decoys to lure their prey.[1a] Fishermen captured both fish and turtles (whose flesh and eggs were much esteemed) using hooks, nets and basket traps.[1a] The market-place had different stalls for the vendors of the meats of various animals: gōgataka (cattle), arabika (sheep), shukharika (swine), nagarika (deer), shakuntika (fowl) and gidhabuddaka (alligator and tortoise).[2] The abattoirs for domestic animals had specific names, like garaghatanam (beef) and shukarasanam (swine).[2] Neither ducks, nor the eggs of poultry find mention in these transactions.

In the *Rigveda*, horses, bulls, buffaloes, rams and goats were all described as being sacrificed for food.[3] In the elaborate Aja-Panchandam rite of the *Rigveda*, a male goat was seized, his feet carefully washed, and his joints cut up neatly with 'the grey knife' (ayas). The meat was then cooked in cauldrons, while the sacrificed animal was simultaneously bidden to go to the third heaven, where the righteous dwell.[3] The 162nd hymn of the *Rigveda* describes in detail the ritual steps to be followed in sacrificing a horse, then in roasting it whole, in collecting the oozing fat, and in performing the subsequent carving. Knowledge of its anatomy is excellent.[4] Each carved portion had a specified recipient: for example, the right thigh went to the brahmin who chanted the mantras, and the two jawbones and tongue to the prastota priest.[5] Bulls and barren cows were favoured by Agni, a dwarf ox by Vishnu, a drooping-horned bull with a blaze on the forehead by Indra, a black cow by Pushan, and a red cow by Rudra.[6] Indra is exhorted to cut down his adversaries 'just as cows are butchered at the place of sacrifice'.[5] The *Shatapatha Brāhmana* and the *Yājnavalkya Samhitā* both enjoin that for a special guest, a big ox (mahoksha) or a big goat (mahāja) should be sacrificed.[6] According to Pānini, a new word, gōghna, was coined compounding the words for bull and kill to signify a guest so honoured.[6] The *Taittirīya Brāhmana* praised Agasthya for his sacrifice of one hundred bulls.

These practices continue even after AD 800 in

Box 8

THE DRESSING OF MEAT

Food was the bedrock of healing in the Indian system of medicine, and the *Sushrutha Samhitā* is in large measure a cookery book. It describes seven types of meat preparations.[27]

Sour meat was prepared using ghee, curd, rice gruel soured by fermentation, acid fruits and pungent and aromatic ingredients. Dried meat, when thereafter roasted, yielded parisukamāmsam, and the third type was minced meat, ulluplamāmsam. Fresh meat when fried was termed bharjita, and meat that had been ground and shaped into patties or balls was termed pishtha. Roasting meat over a charcoal fire while basting it with ghee gave pratāpta. The seventh type was vesavāra, and it was frequently used for stuffing; to make it, boneless meat was first boiled, then ground fine, and cooked with such ingredients as ghee, molasses, black pepper and ginger in variations of taste and flavour. Thus even at an early period items like shaped meat roasted on skewers, and ground, shaped meats were in general use.[27]

About the 2nd century, meat cooked with rice is referred to in the *Yāgnavalkya Smriti* as pallāo-mevach,[27] and the word palāo also occurs in early Tamil literature of a slightly later period.[3]

The *Rāmāyana* and *Mahābhārata* mirror the lives of kshatriya princes who consumed rich dishes of meat. Rāma and Lakshmana while in exile in the Dandakāranya forest hunted animals for the pot, and a favourite dish of Sītā was rice cooked with deer meat, vegetables and spices, called māmsabhutadana.[28] At the sacrificial fire of King Dasharatha, countless dishes of meat of all kinds (mutton, pork, chicken, peacock) were served; these had been cooked in fruit juices, or fried in butter, or had cloves, carraway seeds and lentils simmering in them.[29] Even the special feast arranged in honour of so good a saint as Bharadwāja lists pig and fowl among the appetizing dishes served.[26] Elsewhere the hare, hedgehog, porcupine, tortoise and iguana are mentioned.[19]

The *Mahābhārata* mentions pishthaudana, a dish of rice cooked with mince meat.[28] The Pāndavas while in the Kaniyaka forest ate many kinds of deer, and Duryōdhana liked rice cooked with meat. King Yudhisthira fed ten thousand brahmins with pork and venison, besides preparations of milk and rice mixed with ghee and honey, and with fruits and roots.[29] Elsewhere in the epic, besides roasted birds, are mentioned the swine, cow, donkey, camel and sheep.[30] Capping them all is a graphic description in the *Mahābhārata* of the food served at a picnic:

> Clean cooks, under the supervision of diligent stewards, served large pieces of meat roasted on spits; meat cooked as curries and sauces made of tamarind and pomegranate; young buffalo calves roasted on spits with ghee dropping on them; the same fried in ghee, seasoned with acids, rocksalt and fragrant leaves; large haunches of venison boiled in different ways with spices and mangoes, and sprinkled over with condiments; shoulders and rounds of animals dressed in ghee, sprinkled over with seasalt and powdered black pepper, and garnished with radishes, pomegranates, lemons, fragrant herbs, asafoetida and ginger.[31]

The cooking of meat along with sourish fruits is particularly noteworthy; it runs through all the historic literature, and yet has all but disappeared at the present time, except for the use of tamarind.

the later Vedic literature. The *Grhya Sūtras* prescribe that at the annaprāsana ceremony, at which a child is first given food other than milk, the kind of meat that it is served will influence its subsequent nature: ram's meat would confer physical strength, partridge meat saintliness, fish a gentle disposition, and rice and ghee glory.[1,7a] Use of rhinoceros flesh (khadga) at a shrāddha (death anniversary), and even of vessels made from rhinoceros bones, had a special sanctity in the *Āpasthamba* and *Baudhāyana Dharma Sūtras*.[8a] The *Jātaka* tales list the flesh of the pigeon, partridge, monkey and elephant as edible. To this, the *Brhat Samhitā* (6th century) adds buffaloes and lizards.[9] At a shrāddha ceremony, use of meat was very meritorious according to the *Vishnu Purāna* (3rd or 4th century), and the meats listed are those of the hare, hog, goat, antelope, deer, gāyal and sheep; both priest and performer partook of the meal.[9]

The *Arthashāstra* of Kautilya, of about 300 BC, makes reference to a Superintendent of Slaughter Houses, implying state supervision of animal slaughter. Cooked meat seemed to have been sold in shops, because Kautilya gives the proportions of ingredients that would be required by a cook for dressing 20 palas (about 700 grams) of fresh meat; these were one kuduba (250 grams) of oil, two-thirds of a kuduba (175 grams) of curds, one pala (35 grams) of salt, and one-fifth of a pala (7 grams) of pungent spices. Venison cooked with rice was a popular dish, the sāranga deer being particularly favoured. The *Charaka Samhitā* has a formidable list of edible meats, the more unusual of which are those of the alligator, tortoise, jackal and porcupine. Box 8 describes how meat was dressed before consumption.

The emergence of prohibitions and the spread of vegetarianism

Despite the huge variety of meat, and its wide range of consumption, the thoughtful Aryan, right from the start, had begun to question the taking of life for food, with particular reference to the bounteous and gentle cow. The sacrificial cow had always been a barren one; according to the *Atharvaveda*, it was destined 'for the gods and brahmins'.[6] The funeral ceremonies of the *Asvalāyana Grhyasūtra* demand the sacrifice of a cow. Yet even the *Rigveda* has a whole hymn to nutrition (pīlu) in which only vegetable foods are listed, and carries two verses in praise of 'the cow, Aditi, the sinless'. The word gau is used for the cow, and the term aghnyā ('not to be eaten, inviolable') is employed no less than sixteen times, in contrast to three references to the bull, using the masculine form aghnya with a short terminal 'a'.[5] Some composers of the Rigvedic verses at any rate considered the whole bovine species as inviolable. Yet in the *Shatapatha Brāhmana* when the eating of beef is declared a sin, the imposing Upanishadic sage Yāgnavalkya bluntly states: 'That may well be; but I shall eat of it nevertheless if the flesh be tender (amshala).'[4]

In the later Dharma literature, starting with the *Dharma Sūtras*, various ingenious prohibitions begin to appear.[5] Vasishta excludes milch cows and draught oxen, but considers them fit for religious sacrifice, and Gautama and Āpasthamba have similar injunctions. Baudhāyana exacts penances for killing even an ordinary cow, and stricter ones for a milch cow or draught ox. There is a clear thread here of utilitarian needs rather than just humanitarian ones. The *Manu Smriti* in no less than 54 verses has a very long list of forbidden meats, including all carnivorous birds, birds which strike with their beaks or scratch with their toes, web-footed birds, those which dive, and those which live on fish.[11] Both the village cock and the village pig are not allowed, yet nowhere is beef expressly prohibited; in fact the slaying of bovines (gōhatyā) is a lesser sin (upapātaka) than the drinking of spirituous liquor (mahāpātaka). Yet it is clear that the injunctions against killing the milch cow or draught bull, which were originally economic in origin, have grown into a larger concern for the taking of animal life.

The battle of the Vedic sacrifice, it has been said, was really won by the Buddhists and the Jains. Buddha himself favoured non-injury and was strongly opposed to ritual sacrifice, yet even he permitted his followers animal flesh on occasion if the killing had been unintentional (see Chapter 6). The emperor Ashoka in his edicts not only preached non-killing powerfully but himself prac-

Buddha, the proponent of non-killing.

tised it.[12] The very first edict on the Girnar stones in Gujarāt states: 'No living being may be slaughtered for sacrifice; no festive gatherings may be held. Formerly slaughter in the kiṇg's kitchen was great: now it has almost been stopped.'[13] Strong condemnation for the taking of life for food also came from Jainism, which goes to extraordinary lengths to avoid injury even to living forms that cannot be seen, let alone to large animals (see Chapter 6). From being simply one virtue of a priest, these powerful forces pushed the concept of ahimsā or non-killing, and its corollary of a totally vegetarian diet, into common consciousness.[14] Each of the three Vedic schools, those of Shankara, Mādhva and Rāmānuja, thrust the ritual sacrifice aside in its own way, Mādhva declaring that only an animal made of flour should be used if a sacrifice was needed.[23] Vegetable substitutes were found, such as the round pumpkin or the coconut smeared with vermilion powder to replace the bloody head.

Visitors to India comment on its vegetarian habits. Both Fa Xian in the 5th century [15] and Xuan Zang in the 7th[15A] remark on the widespread, almost universal, vegetarianism but probably erred in seeing the world through Buddhist glasses. Al-Biruni, in the middle of the 11th century, records his observations more carefully.[16]

Part of an edict of Emperor Ashoka.

The rule prohibiting the killing of animals, he says,

applies in particular only to Brahmins, because they are the guardians of the religion, and because it forbids them to give way to their lusts. It is allowed to kill animals only by strangulation, but only certain animals, others being excluded ... those which are forbidden are cows, horses, mules, asses, camels, elephants, tame poultry, crows, parrots, nightingales, all kinds of eggs, and wine. The last is allowed to a Sūdra; he may drink it, but dare not sell it, just as he is not allowed to sell meat.

He goes on to give reasons why cow eating, which had prevailed earlier, was not allowed later. It had been forbidden

on account of the weaknesses of men, who were too weak to fulfil their duties, as also the Veda ... This theory however is very little substantiated. Other Hindus told one that the Brahmins used to suffer from the eating of cow's meat ... as it is essentially thick and cold ... the power of digestion is so weak that they must strengthen it by eating the leaves of the betel after dinner, and by chewing the betel nut. I for my part am uncertain and hesitate between two different views ... (here there is a lacuna in the original manuscript) ... As for the economic reason, we must keep in mind that the cow is the animal which serves man in travelling by carrying his load, in agriculture in the works of ploughing and sowing, and in the household by the milk and the products made from it. Further man makes use of its dung, and even of its breath. Therefore it was forbidden to eat cow's meat.[16]

Another circumstance relevant to the development of vegetarianism in India was the sheer abundance and wide range of foodstuffs available even from Harappan times, by way of cereals, pulses, oilseeds, vegetables, fruit and milk, and the spices, condiments and sweetening agents that could fashion vegetarian meals of high nutritional quality, and gustatory and aesthetic appeal. It is perhaps no exaggeration to say that nowhere else in the world except in India would it have even been possible to be a vegetarian in 1000 BC.

South India, as we have seen in Chapter 4, relished a great variety of meat dishes at all levels of society. The coming of the Aryans by about 500 BC, and even more so of Buddhists and Jains, brought the vegetarian ethos into the south. Even so, among the early brahmins, the eating of meat died hard. Eventually vegetarianism prevailed, and spread as a symbol of prestige or piety even to a few other non-brahmin sections of south Indian society.

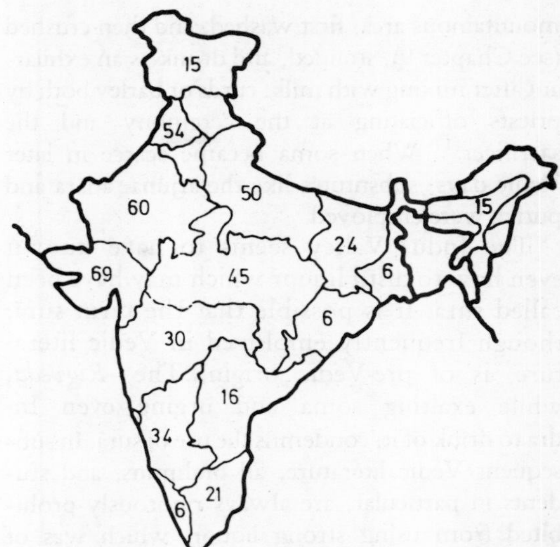

Percentages of vegetarians in different states.

At the present time, census reports reveal that about 25 to 30 per cent of the Indian population as a whole are total vegetarians. States with a high proportion of vegetarians (shown as a percentage of the total population) are Gujarat 69, Rājasthān 60, Punjāb–Haryāna 54 and Uttar Pradesh 50. At medium levels stand Madhya Pradesh 45, Karnātaka 34, Maharāshtra 30 and Bihār 24. Low-vegetarian states are Tamil Nādu 21, Āndhra Pradesh 16, Assam 15, and Kerala, Orissa and West Bengal 6 each. Coastal states tend to have a low proportion of vegetarians, since fish is available as a comparatively inexpensive food material. Gujarāt constitutes a notable exception, for reasons which will be considered in Chapter 10.

Alcoholic beverages

The juice of the soma plant was not an alcoholic beverage, and was indeed carefully distinguished from the alcoholic surā. It had moreover an important place in the rituals of the early Aryans. The identity of soma has been discussed in Box 5. The material was brought from a mountainous area, first washed, and then crushed (see Chapter 9), strained, and drunk as an exhilarant after mixing with milk, curds or barley both by priests officiating at the ceremony and the sacrificer.[17] When soma became scarce in later Vedic days, substitutes like the arjuna, ādara and putika were employed.

The Indus Valley seems to have known even how to distil liquor which may have been called surā. It is possible that the term surā, though frequently employed in Vedic literature, is of pre-Vedic origin. The *Rigveda*, while exalting soma and urging even Indra to drink of it, condemns the use of surā. In subsequent Vedic literature, all brahmins, and students in particular, are always rigorously prohibited from using strong liquor, which was of course always available. A wide range of raw materials, ferments and flavouring agents were used to produce a large number of alcoholic drinks (see Box 9). Kshatriyas and vaishyas were permitted liquors made from honey, mahua flowers and jaggery, but not spirits distilled from fermented flour.[18a] Yet even the *Sūtras* enjoin that strong liquor should be served to guests as they enter a new house, to women at the time when a bride comes into her husband's home, and to women who dance at weddings.[18a] The *Manusmriti* states that there is no turpitude in drinking wine, but that a virtuous abstention from it produces a signal compensation.[31] Incidents in the Buddhist *Jātaka* tales suggest that drinking was by no means uncommon, and that women and even hermits imbibed liquor. Buddhist monks were permitted wine when they were ill, but Jain monks could not even stay in a place where jars of wine were stored.

Among kshatriyas drinking was the accepted norm. Sītā promises the river Gangā a thousand jars of wine if her exiled party were to return home safe.[19] After they do so, Rāma feeds her with his own hands with maireya, a spiced wine.[19] Meanwhile the happy public in the city outside indulge in drunken orgies, and even the atmosphere of Ayodhyā reeked of wine.[19] In the *Mahābhārata*, Krishna enjoys drinking freely with Arjuna, and the Yādavas are finally killed in a drunken brawl. Even a virtuous lady, Sudeshnā, is shown as being drunk on wine. Drinking scenes are depicted in sculpture on the Sānchi stūpa,[19] in the Kushāna temples at Mathura,[10] and in the Chālukyan temples at Pattadakal in south India.[20] The man-about-town (nagaraka) of the *Kāmasūtra* sips drinks from a chasuka, while nibbling at sweet, bitter and acidic snacks.[21] In the plays of Kālidāsa, both citizen and constable are shown drinking liquor in *Shakuntala*; in *Raghuvamsa*, the whole of Raghu's army is shown as drinking coconut wine (perhaps toddy), and an intoxicated Irāvathi is unable even to move about properly.[22]

Public taverns and drinking areas are frequently described in Sanskrit literature, as shaundikas and pānabhūmis. In Mauryan times,

> every village had at least one tavern, identifiable by the flag that it flew. The towns contained many taverns, grouped in the same district but sufficiently spaced out to prevent their being side by side. They were often furnished and decorated in style, and contained several courtyards, rooms filled with seats and couches, and also counters where perfumes, flowers and garlands could be bought. It was a lucrative business, for the sale of fermented and alcoholic drinks continued throughout the day and well into the night. The customers ate salt with their drinks to encourage their thirst.[1b]

Both in the literature of the north and south, it was customary to depict liquor as enhancing the charm of a woman by heightening her amorous disposition and the rosiness of her complexion.[8b,20]

Drinking couple, from a Chālukyan temple.

Box 9

A CHOICE OF LIQUORS

The following is a list, in roughly historical order, of alcoholic drinks as they appear in Sanskrit literature, put together from various sources.

Surā: The earliest-mentioned liquor made from barley or rice flour by fermentation, mentioned frequently, though derogatorily, in the Vedas. Later a generic word for a strong drink

Māsara: A fermented mixture of barley gruel, or later of rice gruel (kānjika), and spices, which was then filtered. Also perhaps pre-Aryan

Parisruta: Fermented flowers with added aromatic grasses

Kilāla: Fermented, sweetened cereal drink

Kalika: A kind of wine

Avadatika: A kind of wine, different from kalika

Maireya: A liquor, probably distilled, flavoured with the tree bark of mesashringi (*Gymnema sylvestre*), with guda (or sugar), pepper, triphalā and spices added to it

Kashāya: A fermented extract of rice meal and flowers

Madhya: A general term for a strong liquor

Vāruni̅: Distillate of fermented mahua (*Madhuca indica*) flowers. Later also employed for the distilled ferment from dates and palm fruits, and perhaps for any strong drink

Madīrā: A general term for wine of high quality

Prasannā: Fermented rice flour, flavoured with spices, bark and fruit. The name may be suggestive of the clarity of the drink

Shīdhu: Fermented and distilled sugarcane juice with dhātaki flowers (*Woodfordia fruticosa*). The red flowers contributed colour, astringent tannins and an alcoholic ferment. Amlashīdhu may have had āmla fruit (*Emblica officianalis*) in addition

Kādambarī: A distilled liquor based on kadamba flowers (*Anthocephalus cadamba*)

Thāllaka: Wine from palm fruit juice

Jāthi: Wine flavoured with jasmine flowers

Khajūrāsava: Wine from dates

Jāmbu-āsava: Wine from the jāmbu fruit (*Syzygium cumini*)

Mēdhaka: Wine or distilled liquor made from rice and spices. The name may suggest the fattening property of the drink.

Shahakārasurā: Wine brewed from mango juice

Mahāsurā: Mango juice wine with a high proportion of fruit extract, perhaps modified with spices

Kaula: Wine from the ber fruit (*Zizyphus* species)

Svetāsurā: A clear drink, achieved by adding katasharkarā (either granulated sugar, or a plant of some kind) and liquorice decoction, to prasannā

Sambhāriki̅: a heavily-spiced liquor

Divya: A liquor flavoured with kadamba tree bark

Āsava: A generic class of distilled liquor, named after the source: pushpa-, phala-, madhvika-, sharkarā-, surā- and nārikela-, and later sweetened and flavoured

Arishta: Wines of medical connotation, as the name (meaning absence of injury) suggests

Kohala: Distilled liquor based on parched barley flour

Kashya: A strong intoxicant

Kāpisāyani: Wine made from white grapes, imported from Kāpisī, Afghanistan

Hārahūraka: Wine made from black grapes, imported from Hārahūr, Afghanistan

Ancient Indian medical authorities take a view of drinking which strikes one as being thoroughly balanced and modern. Charaka counselled moderation, since alcohol increases pittha (the mental principle) while lessening both kapha (the physical principle) and vātha (the vitality principle).[24] It was particularly to be avoided in the summer and rainy seasons when the digestion is weak. Sushrutha is more cautious, and specifically recommends liquor only as a medical aid before a surgical operation to induce slumber.[24] Vāghbhata, slightly later, advises a man to drink unvitiated liquor like rum and wine, and mead mixed with mango juice 'together with friends'.[25]

Visitors to India down the ages testify to the prevalence of drinking mostly among the nobility, and to the sobriety of the general population. Thus Al-Masūdi in AD 947 says: 'The Indians abstain from drinking wine, and censure those who consume it; not because their religion forbids it, but in the dread of its clouding their reason and depriving them of its powers.'[26]

Chapter 6

INDIAN FOOD ETHOS

Every community that lives in India has a distinct food ethos. Most of these, however, have been influenced by Aryan beliefs and practices. Originally starting from the north and northwest of India, Aryan ideas gradually expanded all over the country subsuming earlier practices and exerting a strong influence even on those cultural beliefs that appeared later, whether from within or without. A discussion of Aryan practices would, therefore, make a good beginning to this chapter.

Aryan Food Beliefs

The idea of food

Food in Aryan belief was not simply a means of bodily sustenance; it was part of a cosmic moral cycle.[1,2] The *Taittirīya Upanishad* states:

> From earth sprang herbs, from herbs food, from food seed, from seed man. Man thus consists of the essence of food. . . From food are all creatures produced, by food do they grow. . . The self consists of food, of breath, of mind, of understanding, of bliss.

And the *Bhagavad Gīta* says: 'From food do all creatures come into being.' In the great Aryan cosmic cycle, the eater, the food he eats and the universe must all be in harmony. All food on being ingested was believed to give rise to three products. The densest of these is faeces which gets excreted; the product of intermediate density is transmuted into flesh, and the third product, the finest and rarest, is manas, which is thought or mind. Prasād, which is the left-over of food that has been offered to the gods, is thought to be pure rasa or essence that leaves no residue and maintains man's spirituality. Built on such exalted premises, the Hindu ethos of food has indeed a unique range and depth.[1,2]

The classification of food

Food materials were classified into various vargas, which correspond fairly closely to the divisions in use today: sukhadhānya (cereals), samidhānya (pulses), shākna (vegetables), phala (fruit), sūpyam (spices), pāyovarga (milk products), māmsavarga (animal meats) and madhyavarga (alcoholic beverages).[3] However, in ritual terms a different concept prevailed. Rice, wheat, barley and lentils were all raised with the help of the plough, and were therefore termed anna or kristapachya. Food materials that grew without cultivation (akristapachya) like wild grains, vegetables, and fruit, were broadly termed phala and fell into a different category. At certain auspicious ceremonies, or for men who had taken sannyās, only the latter category of foods was permitted. Thus the starchy yam or water-chestnut (singhādā) would qualify not as anna but as phala, permitted during a fast. So would flowers (pushpa), roots (mūla), bulbous tubers (kanda), leaves (patra), fruits (themselves also called phala) and some pods or legumes (shimbi). Lentils (masūr), as we have seen, qualify as anna, not so chana (the chickpea), which is not classed as an auspicious grain. Milk and ghee are ritually pure, especially auspicious and therefore extremely flexible in use as food ingredients. Ghee is quite different ritually from a cooking oil: frying in the former constitutes a superior ritual act, not comparable to frying in vegetable oil. An outcome of these ritual distinctions is the two major classes into which cooked foods fall, namely kaccha and pucca.

Kaccha and pucca foods

Orthodox sects such as the Kānyakubjas of Kannauj in Uttar Pradesh have been carefully studied because they still observe these distinctions with particular care.[1,2] Even elsewhere, however, they are fairly universal, if slightly blurred. Literally kaccha means imperfectly cooked and pucca the opposite, but ritual usage goes beyond this. Both are of course fully-cooked foods in a modern sense.

Kaccha foods are basically foods cooked in water, like rice, khichdī and dhāl. These items of food are considered both exclusive and pure, and the rules governing their preparation are designed to ensure this. Boiling with water tends to render any anna or its flour pure, and when this is done within the restricted cooking area and in a ritual cooking pot, the sthāli, a kaccha product results. Once the cooking of a kaccha food starts, usually by setting the rice or dhāl to boil, the cook cannot leave the food area till the meal has been prepared, served and eaten following ritual rules. Should he do so, he will have lost his own purity, and another bath, fresh clothes and fresh cooking will be called for. A kaccha food item can be cheap or expensive, plain or festive, of average or superior nutritive quality. Even a marriage feast could consist entirely of kaccha foods like sweet rice, pallāo, chana dhāl, urad dhāl and dahi-vadā. Wheat breads like roti and chapati were not in vogue in Vedic times, and therefore escaped ritual classification; since they do not involve boiling, such items would not therefore strictly qualify as kaccha foods, even though eaten now at every meal. Kaccha food had to be cooked afresh for every meal; left-over or stale food, termed bāsi or jūtha, was likely to have become polluted.[1,2]

Pucca foods are essentially those cooked with fat, meaning of course ghee. They are destined, primarily, for use outside the domestic food area. A pucca food is one in which the first contact is with ghee. Thus in preparing halwa, the ghee must first be added to the pan and only then should the anna or the phala follow. Sometimes use of the same ingredients in a different sequence will determine the ritual classification. Thus to make kshīrikā (kheer), a pucca food, the rice must first come into contact with ghee, before milk, fire and sugar enter the picture. If this

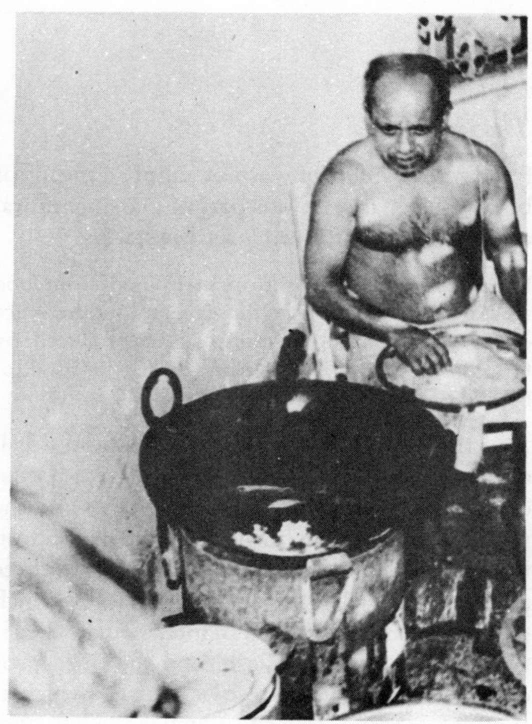

A brahmin cook.

Krishna and Balaram at a picnic, using cups and plates made of palāsh leaves.

sequence is not followed, and the rice is added say to boiling milk, with ghee and sugar added later, the dish will be called doodhbāth, and is a restrictive kaccha food. Common daily dishes are most affected by such sequences. Pucca foods suffer less restrictions, are less liable to pollution, and can be shared outside the family by those of either lower or higher levels of purity.[1,2]

Pollution and food

Concepts of pollution are intimately woven into cooking and eating practices. It would be unthinkable for a cook or housewife to taste any dish during the course of its preparation. Water must never be sipped from a tumbler, but poured into the mouth from above, since one's own saliva is polluting. Water used for rinsing the mouth must be cast out, never swallowed.[6a] In many rituals, sprinkling with water has a strong connotation of purification: on the leaf before eating, or during a penance, or a temple ritual, or over a corpse. Even a bath should be taken in flowing water, or by pouring water over oneself, never in a small quantity of still water, let alone in a tub. Eating on plates and cups made of banana leaves, or disposable leaves of palāsh and banyan stitched together with slivers of hay or cane was intended to prevent cross-pollution.

All lower castes could receive cooked food or water from a brahmin, but higher castes would on no account receive cooked food from lower ones. The pecking order among numerous sub-castes was extremely complex, and zealously observed. Patanjali remarks that while food vessels used by carpenters, blacksmiths, washermen and weavers could be used by others after certain specified and rigorous methods of cleaning, no known method of cleaning was adequate to purify the food-vessels used by very low classes like the Chandālas and Mritapas. These communities were even obliged to live outside the towns and villages for fear that they would pollute others.[4]

Domestic cooking practices

The domestic hearth in a Hindu home was considered an area of high purity, even of sanctity.[1,2] In fact it was set up adjacent to the area of worship, on some auspicious forenoon of a bright fortnight during the northern course of the sun (uttarāyana). The domestic hearth had to be located far away from waste-disposal areas of all kinds, and demarcated from sitting, sleeping and visitor-receiving areas. Nor could pure and impure areas face each other. Before entering the cooking area, the cook was obliged to take a bath, and don unstitched washed clothes. Even now, a stitched shirt or jibba will commonly be removed for fear of pollution before cooking commences.

The objective of cooking is not simply to produce materials suitable for eating, but to conjoin the cultural properties of the food with those of the eater. Cooking on fire, or without it (see Box 10), has many complexities. For example, even though milk is always boiled prior to setting it to curds, the resulting curd does not have the connotation of a fire-prepared food. On the other hand, milk as it emerges hot from the udder is already a cooked food in ritual terms, having been cooked within the animal by the divine power of Indra.[5] The use of milk as an ingredient usually results in a food with the greatest transactional restrictions. Foods altered by fire are not culturally neutral; yet milk and ghee, though considered to have already been cooked, are taken to be neutral. Various pulses like mung dhāl, urad dhāl and whole chana grains are all roasted by professional grain parchers; but in the Hindu belief this operation does not constitute ritual cooking, and these parched grains can therefore be bought and used equally by a brahmin and shūdra. Yet rice or dhāl, if treated at the domestic hearth with fire, become highly restrictive kaccha foods that are unfit for consumption outside the family. Fruits like the banana, mango and melon can be traded and bought by all in the market place; but when taken home and peeled, scraped or broken in the kitchen, they become restricted foods in terms of purity.

Vegetables almost always need the application of fire to make them edible. Cooking them means that they be ritually washed in the home to render them of sufficient rank to be permitted to enter the food area. Certain highly-ranked dishes could be made without the use of fire. The two auspicious libations, madhuparka and panchagavya (see Box 11) are both of this kind, being simply mixed together from their ingredients. Pickling using the heat of the sun was not ritually the same thing as the use of fire.

Despite these ritual restrictions, the organoleptic qualities of prepared foods were not neglected. Food could have six tastes, namely sweet, sour, salty, bitter, pungent and astringent. Each food, according to its taste, was thought to exert a specific action on the three body humours (Chapter 7), and a meal needed to contain all six if it was to be balanced and healthy.[66] Regional cuisines, while still maintaining this basic concept of six tastes, have put them into practice in various ways (Chapter 10). Texture was also important, and finished foods could be of five types. Charvya denoted foods to be chewed, bhōjya foods that needed no chewing, lehya were foods to be licked, chushya those to be sucked, and peya those that were drunk. Buddhist monks later divided food into two classes: Panchabhōjaniyas, wet and soft foods (like rice, boiled barley and peas, baked cakes) that could be swallowed, and panchakhādaniyas, hard and solid foods (like roots, stalks, leaves, and fruit) that had to be chewed; doubtless there were five of each kind.

Types of cooking will be considered in Chapter 9.

Eating rituals and ceremonies

Food was never to be eaten standing up, lying down, moving about or from the lap. One had

Box 10
HINDU FOOD TAXONOMY

The purpose of all cooking of course is to convert potentially edible material into palatable form, āhāra. In the Hindu ethos there is the added requirement that it should be both auspicious and ritually pure for those who are to eat it. Given this basis, cooking in the Hindu concept can occur even without the use of heat. The tabular statement of food taxonomy that follows shows the nature of the cooking gradations that still exist among very orthodox brahmin communities such as the Kānyakubja of Uttar Pradesh.[1, 2]

1. WITHOUT FIRE
   - 1.1 With water and/or manual techniques
   - 1.2 With milk products
   - 1.3 With air and sun
2. WITH FIRE
   - 2.1 With ghee
     - 2.1.1. With anna (cultivated grains)
       - a) With water and/or salt
       - b) Without water and/or salt
     - 2.1.2 Without anna (to yield phalahār)
       - a) With milk and milk products
       - b) With fruit or vegetables
   - 2.2 Without ghee

The ritual importance of four elements, namely fire, ghee, cultivated grains (anna) and non-cultivated materials (phala) is the basis of the entire scheme. Another key concept is that milk and ghee are considered as being already fully cooked; no change occurs in ritual terms on further cooking, whatever the physical evidence to the contrary. The mere presence of these confers ritual purity on the dish.

The simple washing of vegetables or soaking of dhāls fall into category 1.1, besides such operations (all of which are considered as cooking) as peeling, grating, cutting, sifting and grinding. Under category 1.2, involving the use of milk or its products but no heat, would fall the preparation of a panchāmrita or madhuparka, or of a dish of freshly-cut fruits dressed with milk or curd. Under category 1.3, the classical Indian example is the pickling of vegetables or unripe fruit using the heat of the sun, or the dehydration of vegetables for preservation by sun-drying. The legendary king, Nala, is believed to have excelled in cooking without fire or water, and food termed Nala-pāka is still cooked in the Jagannāth temple in Pūri.

The second major division of the system is cooking with fire, which is the more conventional concept of cooking. Cooking with ghee is of course a very familiar operation, but there is a fine ritualistic distinction with regard to when ghee makes contact with the material being cooked. The text gives an example by way of kshīrika and doodhbāth. Shallow-fried, sautéed vegetables would fall into the category of phalāhār. Cooking without ghee but on the fire would embrace such operations as boiling and stewing.

to eat sitting on the ground, alone, facing east or north, and in total silence. Morsels of the meal were to be cast into the fire as an oblation, and prayers offered to various deities and one's ancestors. Portions of food were reserved for brahmins, serpents, dogs and insects, and laid outside for crows, who were believed to be messengers to the world of the spirits. The householder was expected to see to the feeding of his guests (see Box 11) and of any pregnant women, infants and aged persons in his household before he himself sat down to eat.

Prior to eating, a few drops of water would be sprinkled on the leaf for purity, and, on the rice

Box 11
GOOD HOST AND HONOURED GUEST

In the *Mānava Dharma Shāstra*, also known as the *Manusmriti*, the following exhortation is directed to a model host:[11]

Let him, being pure and attentive, place on the ground the seasoning for the rice, such as broth and pot herbs, sweet and sour honey; as well as various kinds of hard foods that require mastication, and soft foods, roots, fruits and savoury and fragrant drinks.

'All these he shall present, and being pure and attentive, successively invite them to partake of each, proclaiming its qualities; cause them to partake gradually and slowly of each, and repeatedly urge them to eat by offering the food and extolling its qualities.'

'All the food shall be very hot, and the guests shall eat in silence.' 'Having addressed them with the question: 'Have you dined well?, let him give them water to sip, and bid farewell to them with the words: 'now rest.'

Guests had an honoured rank in Vedic society, only below that of father, mother and teacher. On arrival, a guest was ceremoniously received, given water for washing, and then offered the ambrosial beverage madhuparka.[7] This consisted of the five ingredients ghee, curd, milk, honey and sugar. In early Vedic times, if the guest was an honoured brahmin or a king, a large bull or goat would be sacrificed in his honour, even if the host himself did not eat meat. Later this ritual became symbolic, and the guest was given a knife as a token of sacrifice, which he returned after a prayer. During the meal, the host was expected to be solicitous, either eating later or finishing his own meal quickly so as to rise first and look after his guests.[7] These practices continue to be observed.

Madhuparka was an auspicious ritual beverage.[7] Apart from its use to welcome a guest, it was given to women after five months of pregnancy. At birth, the lips of the first son, were moistened with it. The student was offered madhuparka when he left home for his apprenticeship, the suitor when he went to the girl's home, and the bridegroom when he arrived at the bride's home for the wedding.[7]

Another ritual concoction called panchagavya was a mix of five products of the sacred cow, namely milk, curds, ghee, urine and dung. This was considered the supreme purificatory material, and was either drunk during a ritual, or rubbed on the face and body (as when taking sannyās), or sprinkled on a corpse during the last rites.

---

that had been served, a few drops of ghee. Every item placed on the leaf had its exact position and ritual eating order. Today these practices have become region-specific, as we shall see in Chapter 10. The higher male principle resided on the right: only the right hand was therefore to be used for eating, reserving the left for baser functions outside the meal.

A traveller made obeisance to the domestic fire before leaving home, prayed, drank a consecrated beverage, and set off right foot first in a cart smeared with ghee from the ritual offering.[7]

A student would leave his home to live for many years with the teacher in apprenticeship, during which he abided by numerous restrictions on the use of foods that might sharpen his baser appetites. At an advanced stage, he would even be obliged to beg for his food from citizens of the town. Some of these restrictions persisted even after he had returned home.

Marriage was a major event in life, and foodgrains played an important part in the ceremony. Among the orthodox Kānyakubjas of Uttar Pradesh, rice stained with turmeric is tied atop the sacred sthambha outside, and at its foot wheat grains are sown a few days ahead to sprout. Grains of barley are used to decorate a ritually-important earthen pot (kalash) with a lighted lamp on it.[1,2] The evening feast consists of kaccha foods like rice bāth and vegetable curry. The priests worship the Sun and Mars with red, uncooked masoor dhāl, the silvery Moon with white rice, Venus with yellow-green mung, Jupiter with yellow turmeric or chickpea, and Saturn with black sesame seeds. At the marriage ceremony described in Vedic literature, parched grains (lājāh) are thrown by the bride with joined hands into the sacred fire,[8a] and after the rite of the seven steps (saptapadi) which the couple take together, they are showered with rice grains as a fertility symbol.[92] In her new home, the bride first touches the cooking utensils, and then sets about cooking ceremonial food for her new family.

Pregnancy invited a whole host of Vedic injunctions. Certain foods had to be especially eaten, and other foods to be especially avoided, such as those which are too spicy or too 'cold'. Several rituals had to be undergone, including an offering of madhuparka from the husband in the fifth month. Following the birth of a child, the household was considered to be under ritual pollution for twelve days, and no outsiders were entertained. The new mother was given specialized herbal foods and rich preparations, including, on the sixth day, a variety of festive preparations. After the twelfth day, a semblance of normalcy prevailed. The mother was not ritually pure enough to enter the cooking area for another five months, but was permitted to undertake some peeling and cutting of phala for further cooking, elsewhere in the house.

The child's annaprāsana was held on an auspicious day when it was about six months old. It was then given its first solid food in the way of a paramānna of boiled rice, milk, sugar and honey, a little of which was put gently into its mouth after the ceremony.[10] In early Vedic days, even some meat was included, as described in Chapter 5.

Death was a traumatic event. The family stopped all eating and drinking till the cremation was over. During the subsequent mourning period, the auspicious baghārna or frying of spices could not be performed in the house, and the family was fed on food sent by relatives. Use of auspicious foods like milk and its products, urad dhāl, chana dhāl and its flour (besan), and turmeric

Brass rattles, shaped like coconuts, used in a Naṭangu marriage ceremony in Tamil Nadu.

(highly auspicious) was all abandoned. Frequently the old hearth was demolished, and a new one put up after the mourning period had elapsed. Numerous ceremonies followed during the rest of the year. At the annual shrāddha ceremony only certain foods like apūpas (sweet fried cakes of rice or barley), boiled mung or horsegram dhāl as a sweet gruel, black sesame seeds, green bananas and so on would be permitted, and many others prohibited.[8a,11] Only the sweet potato is allowed even today in the food offered to the deity at the Jagannātha temple in Pūri, though in the surrounding area it has been all but displaced in household use by the potato.

Festival and temple foods

At several feasts specific foods are made. Even in 200 BC, Patanjali notes that only vatakas (vadās) are eaten on vatakini Paurnamāsi day.[13] Deepāvali, the festival of the victory of good over evil, is an occasion for sweetmeats, which take the form of moulded animals and toys made of pure sugar, or of a sweet-stuffed parāta called pōli. At Vināyaka Chaturthi, a sweet puff called mōdaka, a favourite of the god Ganesha, is made, while in south India a salted preparation of whole soaked chickpea called sundal is necessary for this festival. Rāma favours a soaked raw dhāl preparation called kosumalli consisting of diced cucumber and coconut tossed in lemon juice. Panaka, a jaggery drink with ginger and cardamom, and mēva, which has a mixed fruit base, are also his favourites. The south Indian new year is celebrated with a boiled rice preparation sweetened with jaggery called sakkarai pongal.

Temples have their own special foods, and even the prasād offered to the presiding deities in different temples can be quite distinctive. In the south the Padmanābhaswami temple in Trivandrum has a special aviyal that uses traditional vegetables, fresh coconut and coconut oil, and no mustard seeds. The Ganesha temples of Kerala have the unni-āppam, which are spongy-brown fried pieces made of a melange of rice powder, banana, jackfruit and jaggery. The Muruga temple of the Palani hills has its own panchamrita of crystal sugar, honey, ghee, cardamom and fruits (bananas, dates and raisins), which does not go rancid for even six weeks.[11] The great Vishnu temple of Devarājaswami in Kānchipuram makes a giant idli weighing a kilo and a half; this is spiced with pepper, jeera, ginger and asafoetida, fermented with curd, and then steamed.[11] The Vishnu temple at Srīmushnam has a sweet prepared from korai, which are held to be dear to Varāha, the boar incarnation of Vishnu.[14]

In the great Thirupati temple dedicated to Lord Venkatēshwarā, laddus are given as prasādam to the pilgrims after first having been offered to the diety. As many as 70,000 of these are made every day in the inner kitchen by thirty cooks who use up 3 tonnes of urad dhāl, 6 tonnes of sugar and 2.5 tonnes of ghee, besides large amounts of raisins, cashewnuts and cardamom. Smaller quantities of other sweets are also made, besides 3000 each of vadā, dōsai and rava-āppam. In the inner kitchen, some 400 kg each of various rice-based dishes like savoury and sweet pongal, sour rice, curd rice and sweet pāyasam are cooked every day to be served to pilgrims who eat in the dining halls.[15] At the Dharmasthalā temple in Karnātaka, food is served every day to 30 to 50 thousand people.

Some of the most elaborate preparations of temple food are perhaps those at the Jagannātha Temple in Orissa,[16, 17] where every day a thousand persons manning 750 chūlahs and ovens turn out a hundred varieties of dishes using rice, wheat and their flours, grits, urad dhāl, indigenous vegetables, jaggery and spices, with cow ghee as the cooking medium. The gods are served ritually five times a day, and pilgrims can eat at the spacious bhōga mandapa, or buy mahāprasād at a huge market within the temple walls.

Fasts

Fasts or vratas make special demands on the orthodox Hindu. They are of five kinds.[18] Vara fasts are on weekdays, the Adityavarāvrata to Surya being an example. The Tithivratas occur on certain days of the lunar months; there are very many of these, Durgāshtami and Krishnajanmāshtami being examples. On certain days

The god Ganesha holding his favourite sweet, the stuffed mōdaka.

of the lunar stations occur the Nakshatra fasts. Māsavratas are fasts that occur in certain months like Kārthika, while Samvatsara fasts with restrictive eating could even spread out from one ekādashi to the same one a whole year later. Fasts commonly observed among Hindus are Rāma Navami, Shivarāthri, Sankrānthi and the ekādashi, which is the eleventh day of the lunar fortnight.

Fasts do not usually involve complete abstention from food, but only varying degrees of restrictions. Sometimes use of pure ghee is mandatory to induce sāttvika thoughts, and rocksalt may replace seasalt in domestic cooking. In some fasts, plough-grown rice is abjured in favour of wild rice or other wild grains. In others, only restrictive kaccha foods are permitted, in yet others only food left over from the previous day. 'Fruits only' is a common form of observance; others take the form of eating only before moonrise, or perhaps only after sunset. Modern practices, like fasting on a Friday, or missing the night meal on one day of the week, may tend to be dietetic in intention, but do have a ritualistic origin.

Buddhist Food Concepts

Buddhism, Jainism and Sikhism crystallized out of a Hindu matrix. In terms of food practices they have naturally many features in common with the Hindu ethos, but also some distinct elements.

In the *Lankavatāra Sūtra*, Buddha is recorded as saying:

> I enjoin the taking of food made out of rice, barley, wheat, mudga, māsha, masūra and other grains, ghee, oil of sesamum, honey, molasses, sugar, fish, eggs and others, which are full of soul qualities but devoid of faults; they were consumed by the Āryas and by the rishis of yore.[19]

On many occasions he counselled moderation in order to guard the doors of the organs of sensation, meaning lack of self control, or excessive enjoyment of the pleasures of the table.[20] Monks were advised to eat solid foods only between sunrise and noon, and nothing between noon and sunrise; this would subdue passions and lead to spiritual strength. Anything that was offered, whether coarse food, fine food or no food, should be accepted without attachment or craving.[20] A begging bowl (pātra) and a water-strainer (parishrāvana) were essential items in a monk's equipment.

The desire not to distress the giver of food, and to avoid the extreme austerities of certain brāhmanas and shramanas, led the Buddha to turn down suggestions that meat and fish consumption be prohibited for Buddhist monks.[21a] However the flesh eaten had to be 'blameless' in three ways: the killing should not have been either seen or heard or suspected by the monks (adrastam, asrutam, aparivirtakam), it being the responsibility of the person giving the food to ensure such blamelessness. The Mahāyāna *Sūtras*, in particular the *Lankavatāra*, stress total ahimsā, which Ashoka also strongly enjoined. The Chinese *Agamas* omit all references to meat and fish eating, and both the Hīnayāna Monks of China and southeast Asia, and the tantric Buddhists of Tibet, have always eaten flesh foods.

It has been pointed out that the Buddha spoke in Magadhi while all records are in Pāli.[22] What he actually said cannot be known with certainty, and can be interpreted according to the bias of the writer.

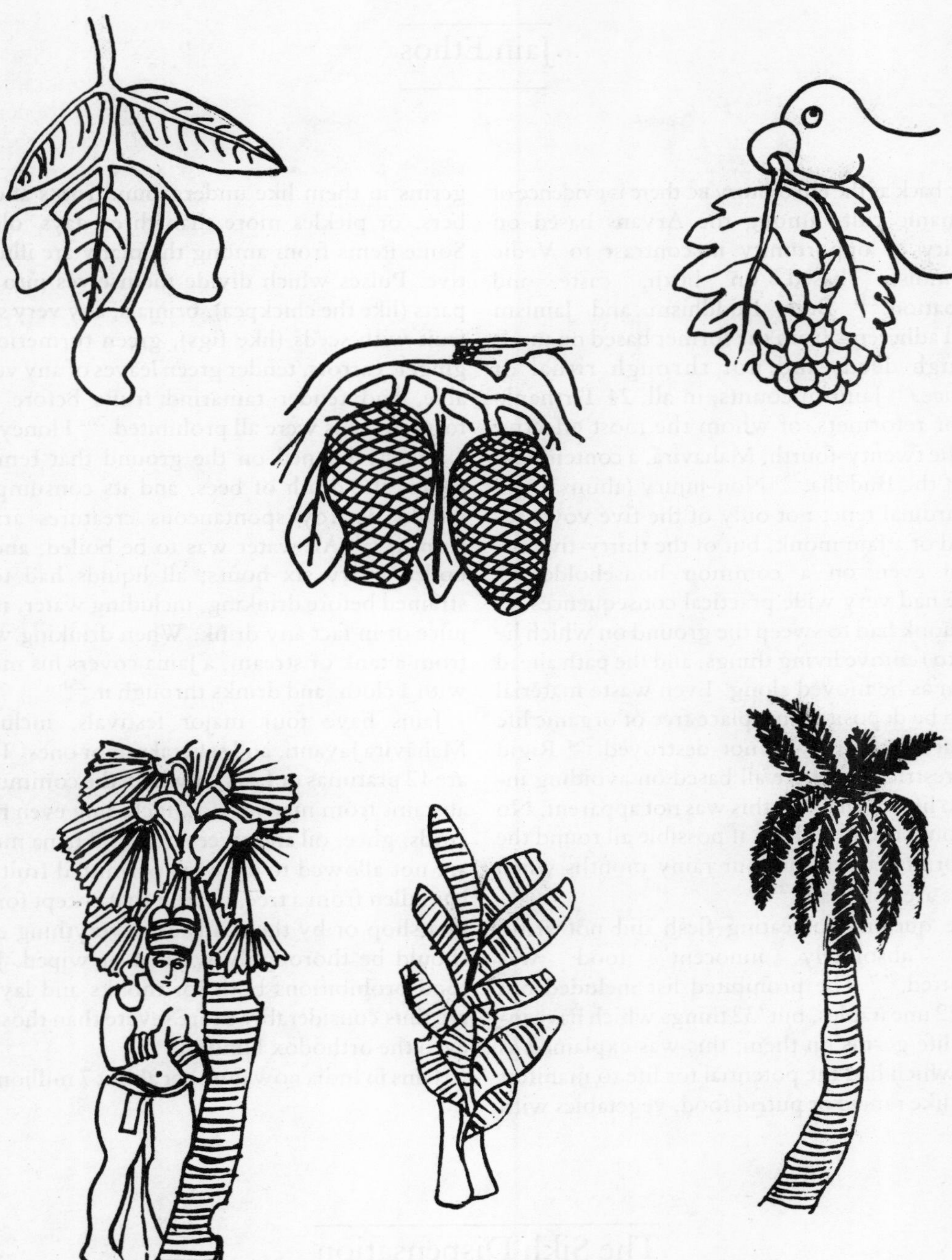

Representation of selected flora depicted in Buddhist sculptures.

Jain Ethos

As far back as the 8th century BC there is evidence of shramanic cults among the Aryans based on equality of opportunity in contrast to Vedic brahminism based on birth, caste and occupation.[23a] Both Buddhism and Jainism found adherents from the former based on merit through deeds and not through ritual or sacrifice.[24a] Jainism counts, in all, 24 Tīrthankaras or reformers, of whom the most effective was the twenty-fourth, Mahāvīra, a contemporary of the Buddha.[25a] Non-injury (ahimsā) was the cardinal tenet not only of the five vows required of a Jain monk, but of the thirty-five enjoined even on a common householder.[23b] These had very wide practical consequences. A Jain monk had to sweep the ground on which he slept to remove living things, and the path ahead of him as he moved along. Even waste material had to be deposited in a place free of organic life so that the latter was not destroyed.[26a] Rigid food restrictions were all based on avoiding injury to life, even when this was not apparent. No one could eat after dark, if possible all round the year or at least in the four rainy months when insects are abundant.[25b]

The question of eating flesh did not arise. Only 'absolutely innocent' food was permitted.[26b] The prohibited list included not only 22 uneatables, but '32 things which have infinite life germs' in them; this was explained as food which had the potential for life to manifest itself, like rancid or putrid food, vegetables with germs in them like underground roots and tubers, or pickles more than three days old.[26b] Some items from among the many are illustrative. Pulses which divide themselves into two parts (like the chickpea), brinjals, any very small fruit with seeds (like figs), green turmeric and ginger, carrots, tender green leaves of any vegetable, and tender tamarind fruits before they formed seeds were all prohibited.[26a] Honey was expressly banned on the ground that removal meant the death of bees, and its consumption would destroy spontaneous creatures arising from it.[25b] All water was to be boiled, and reboiled every six hours; all liquids had to be strained before drinking, including water, milk, juice or in fact any drink. When drinking water from a tank or stream, a Jaina covers his mouth with a cloth, and drinks through it.[25b]

Jains have four major festivals, including Mahāvīra Jayanti, and several minor ones. There are 12 pratimas or fasts, at which the community abstains from many foods, including even milk, curds, ghee, oil and sweetmeats.[26a] Jaina monks are not allowed to eat even permitted fruit that has fallen from a tree, or fruit that is kept for sale in a shop or by the roadside. Everything eaten should be thoroughly washed or wiped. Jaina food prohibitions both for monks and laymen are thus considerably more severe than those for even the orthodox Hindu.

Jains in India now number about 7 million.

The Sikh Dispensation

The holy book, the *Ādi Granth* or *Granth Sāhib,* was compiled by Guru Arjan, the fifth guru of the Sikhs, and the tenth Guru declared that the Book itself was hereafter the Guru that would provide leadership to the community. This is a collection of writings by twenty authors who span six centuries, with those of six Gurus forming the bulk. It has many exhortations to high principles of conduct, but does not concern itself with laying down ceremonies or rituals or any earthly code of laws, though in practice some have emerged.[27] Khālsā tradition is also embodied in the *Rahatnāmās* or Codes of Conduct compiled by several contemporaries of Gurú Gobind Singh. Thus after a child is born the Guru administers a few drops of water and sugar on its lips, and at baptism the candidate has to accept 16 conditions among which are abstinence from all intoxicants and from tobacco in any form. At the engagement ceremony of a couple, sacred food or kaval prasād is prepared. This is a special wheat halwā, which also figures in ceremonies after a cremation.[27]

Food figures in some of the selections in the *Ādi Granth*, but even these offer advice more than laying down definite rules.[28] 'Cursed is such a living which induces one to eat and fatten his belly.' 'Even the dry grains of saints are treasured by all; but the 36 kinds of food prepared in the house of a follower of Mammon are like poison.' 'Which place can be considered pure, where I can sit and take my food?' In practice alcohol is forbidden, and so is beef, but not pork. Slaughter is performed by cutting the jugular vein at the throat.

Sikhs now constitute 15 million, or about 2 per cent of the population, largely centred in Punjab, Haryana and around Delhi.

Buddhism, Jainism and Sikhism were indigenous faiths. Four others were exotic. In historical order these were Judaism, Christianity, Zoroastrianism and Islam.

Jewish Food Laws

Four distinct groups of Jews made India their home. The Bene-Israel community believe that they belong to the tribe of Reuben, one of the ten tribes of Israel[29] who came to India following persecution by the Greek overlord Antiochus Epiphanes. The band arrived at Navagaon port in the Konkan after a shipwreck that left only seven couples alive. They completely adapted to local custom, and after many centuries eventually made their mark in Bombay as distinguished professionals, now numbering about 900.[29]

The Cochin Jews arrived originally in the port of Cranganore in Kerala in the 1st century AD after their second temple in Palestine was destroyed by the Romans.[30] They prospered there for ten centuries, until the community was subjected to persecution first by the Muslims and then by the Portuguese. The group fled to Cochin, where they were well received and allowed to build a synagogue in 1567. Today their numbers are sadly depleted by emigration to Israel, and only five families are said to remain.[30]

The third group are Baghdad Jews, numbering about a thousand, who came in much later and now do business in Bombay, Pūnē and Calcutta. The fourth consist of European Jews recently arrived following Nazi persecution.[31]

By and large Jews in India follow the dietary laws set out in the Old Testament (especially in Leviticus and Deuteronomy), and in the rabbinical regulations that are known as the rules of Kashruth.[32] Two strictures that are universally followed are the ban on the eating of pork, and the injunction that the kosher system of animal slaughter be followed; this consists in cutting the jugular vein and allowing the blood (considered to be a part of life) to drain out thoroughly. Meat is usually not eaten by orthodox Jews at the same meal as dairy products, and even separate dishes and vessels are used for each type of food. Fish without scales are not permitted, meaning shell-fish and sea food.[32]

The Christian Ethic

Christianity came into India in two phases. In the state of Kērala, the first Christians were believed to have been converted by the Apostle St. Thomas himself within a few years of the death of Jesus. The Apostle is believed to have met his death near Madrās sixteen years after landing in India, having been stabbed in the back with a lance.[33] Since their scriptures are in Syriac, a dialect of Aramaic, members of the community are called the Syrian Christians of India. They were for long almost totally engaged in trade, and for a while even had their own king at Velyārvattam. There are few food taboos, but in the course of years some preferences have arisen from among local foods. These will be described in Chapter 10 as part of the regional foods of India.

The second wave of Christianity was the rather brutal Catholicism that came with Portuguese colonialism first into Kērala and shortly thereafter into Goa. Use of only fish on Fridays was part of the creed, and of ritual bread and wine in the Church services. The fusion of Portuguese cuisine with the raw materials of Goa created a distinctive Goanese cuisine which, being essentially regional, will be described in Chapter 10.

The presence of Portuguese Christian communities in Bengal markedly influenced the making of sweets there, as we shall see in Chapter 10.

In Pondicherry, which was subject to French influence for four centuries, three French-inspired breads are available: the crisp pain sec, the stick-like baguette, and the soft, crescent-shaped croissant.[34] The boudin and saucisse are spicy pork-based sausages. Paté is made by steaming a spiced paste of pork liver which is laced with some cognac, while jambon is pork cooked in beer and then smoked. Beef is used to make a roasted filet, and a ragout stew with mixed vegetables. Tomate farcie is tomato stuffed with spiced minced beef, and fried meat balls constitute boulette. Steamed fish is served with mayonnaise and garlic paste (to yield poisson capitaine), and fish croquettes are baked after rolling in an egg-breadcrumb mix. Desserts with a French flavour are gateau mocha (a sponge cake with coffee, cream and rum), creme caramel custard, and flanc, another custard with grated nutmeg.[34]

Christians now constitute about 3 per cent of the population of India. Most share the prevailing regional cuisine.

Food Among The Pārsis

Islam was established in Iran after the fall of the Sassanian empire; Zoroastrian sacred fire temples were destroyed and religious persecution drove its followers first into the mountains and then to the port town of Hormuz.[35] Around AD 850, a group seeking a new home set out in seven junks, arriving first at the island of Diu, off Gujarāt, and then entering the mainland.[36] After a couple of decades, the small migrant community again took sail, and after a violent thunderstorm reached Sanjan port in the Thānā Kingdom of Jādi Rāna (Vajjadeva). He welcomed them, and allowed the first fire temple in India to be set up.[29] Persecution from the invader Sultan Mahmūd Bagda once again drove the Pārsis with their sacred fire into the mountains. Later they were able to settle in Navsāri and Udwēda, and to thrive as a mercantile community with a strong religious and social ethic based on 'good thought, good word and good deed'. Today Pārsis are to be found all over India, though totalling only about 100,000.

There are few food restrictions in the Pārsi ethos, but some Hindu customs have been adopted voluntarily, such as the prohibition on beef. The dishes themselves are a blend reflecting both an Iranian ancestry in its strong non-vegetarian component, and local Gujarāthi cuisine.[37] The Iranian influence shows itself also in the free use of nuts, raisins and sultānās. Pārsis love the distinctive sweet fried noodle dish called sēv, the rich drink falooda made from sago granules, the mutton-barbecued shoojan, a distinctive pallāo (there must be at least twenty forms of it in India), and the dhansākh: this is rice cooked with pulses, which have taken the place of the rājmāh beans and spinach used in Iran. At least three dhāls, and even up to nine, are cooked together to give dhansākh, but into it go also pieces of fatty meat, tripe and vegetables.[38] From the local ūndhiu, a mixed vegetable dish baked underground, has blossomed the Pārsi oberu, to which quail meat is sometimes added. Chutnies, morabbas and snacks have been freely borrowed and adapted. The coconut with a dab of vermilion is an auspicious symbol among both Gujarāthis and Pārsis, and its soft pulp goes extensively into cooking. Fish, freely available in Gujarāt, is baked with spices in a banana leaf packet to give the delicious patra. Patia is pomfret in a dark vinegar sauce, and there are several dry fish preparations besides. Eggs are a great favourite; they are baked on a green layer of pot herbs, with added ingredients like potatoes, tomatoes, almonds, raisins, cream and butter, to yield akuris with various names like akeedar, tharkāri or Bhāruchi.[37] The sources may be diverse, but the unifying Pārsi touch is distinctive.

Food and Islam

The Muslim impact on north India started with numerous raids mainly for booty and plunder by the Arab Mahmud Ghaznavi between AD 998 and 1030. This was followed by the conquest of Sindh and Punjāb by Mohammad Ghōri in the decade after AD 1182, and the establishment in AD 1206 of the Slave dynasty in Delhi under Sultan Qutb-ud-din Aibek. The Moghul dynasty was set up in Delhi by the Afghan Babar in AD 1526, and was to blaze in splendour for two centuries.

In south India, Arab traders had been active for centuries even before the coming of Islam. After its advent they married local women, and the Māpillahs or Moplahs (literally mahā-pillā, or esteemed bridegroom) proliferated by conversion from the surrounding community. About AD 1292, Father Menetillus says there were 12,000 Muslims in Calicut alone 'who are for the greater part natives of the country'. Elsewhere conversion to Islam was particularly notable along the route of the invaders in the northwest (in what is now Pākistān), in the east in the Bengal area (now Bānglādesh), in Hyderabād city, and in pockets in Uttar Pradesh and elsewhere in India. Today Muslims constitute about 12 per cent of the total population.

Dietary injunctions are derived both from the Qurān and the Sunnah, which are the recorded words of the prophet Muhammad.[39] Swine flesh is prohibited, but seafood is allowed. Except for fish, it is mandatory to slaughter an animal by cutting the jugular vein, or by piercing the hollow of the throat using a sharpened knife, while uttering the name of Allāh, a procedure termed halāl. Alcohol is forbidden, along with games of chance since 'in both there is great sin and harm.'[40a] Wine is referred to indirectly elsewhere as Khamar (which means to cover up), since it clouds the brain.[40b] Incidentally the Qurān itself has four words derived from Sanskrit, all connected with food: kafūr (karpūra, camphor), zenjabid (srngavēra, ginger), mushk (kastūri, musk) and ambar (a resin).[41a] The Arabic language has, of course, many more from centuries of trade contacts. Islam enjoins that no food be wasted, even left-overs being saved and eaten; it also stresses zakat, the necessity to share food with others. Fasting is enjoined on all the faithful during Ramzān, the ninth month of the Muslim lunar year, with a meal before sunrise (fatoor) and one after sunset (sahoor or suhoor), which should preferably commence by eating some dates. Indeed, dates, honey, figs, olives, milk and buttermilk are items specially recommended as food in the Qurān.[42]

In India, while these injunctions are mostly observed, in practice the foods actually consumed and the social dietary ritual are influenced by the practices of the surrounding regions. Numerous studies from every part of India exemplify this.[42] Commensality means interdining, a cardinal concept in Islam. Yet in Bihār, Rājasthān, the Laccadive Islands and rural West Bengal, while the higher castes may kneel in prayer alongside the lower, they draw the line at interdining, receiving food, and invitations to social feasts, rationalizing these practices on grounds of social hygiene and personal cleanliness.[42]

Examples of regional influences may be cited from three areas. Observations made nearly a century ago in the extreme northwest state that after a funeral no meat or flesh is eaten; loaves of bread accompany the corpse to the grave, and no food is eaten from the house of mourning for forty days thereafter.[43] A woman seven months pregnant receives vegetables, dried fruit and cakes on her lap. In the Islamic tradition, dates and sugar are distributed to the boy's party after an engagement, and later, at the wedding, the bride and her kinswoman will eat off the same plate,[43] a practice that would be almost unthinkable in the Hindu ethos. In rural West Bengal, a black dot is applied to a child's forehead to ward off evil spirits, and the mother is given 'hot' foods for the first five days.[44a] For forty days both mother and child are considered polluted, and she can neither touch the Qurān nor offer namāz. In exact parallel with the Hindu annaprāsana, the child is given its first solid food at the Mammar bath ceremony in its seventh month. Islamic festivals like Bakrīd, Īd and Moharram are of course all performed, and fish is an important part of both regular and ceremonial diets.[44a] In the far south at Nellore, turmeric is applied on the face of a bride (an auspicious Hindu custom), and astrology is extensively used in fixing up a match or in going on a journey.[45] However, the actual foods used by the community have a strong Islamic connotation. Maleeda, consisting of broken bread with sugar and ghee, is a common ritual offering among Muslims all over India, including those at Nellore. So are palāo, biriyāni, shola (khichrī with meat) and haleem (a ground wheat and meat porridge) that is eaten with rōti. Two breads are distinctive: sheermāl, a sweet, baked, bun-like type, and khajūr, a sweetened crisp bread with poppy seeds and copra shavings. Kababs of many kinds are much more common among Nellore Muslims than among their meat-eating Hindu neighbours, and they are called by such names as sheekh, shammi, husseni and tikkā. Distinctive sweet concoctions include fruit juices and sherbets, phirnī (wheat sūji first boiled with sugar, milk and spices, and later fried in ghee) and sēviyan. Other sweets shared in common with their Hindu neighbours are kheer, laddu, jilēbi, halwā, sohan halwā and burfi. So are the many rāyatas, chutnies, morabbas and pickles eaten as food relishes in the area, and indeed all over the country.[45]

The historical etiquette and food habits of mainstream Muslims in the seat of empire, Delhi, will be considered in Chapter 12.

Chapter 7

FOOD AND THE INDIAN DOCTORS

The writings of three giants of medicine named Charaka, Sushrutha and Vāghbhata (see Box 12), and of some lesser lights, codified Hindu ideas as they existed about the start of the Christian era. Illnesses were believed to arise primarily because of disharmony between the bodily humours, which were, in the Hindu view, also connected with cosmic factors. Good health represented a balance between various forces, and dietary injunctions were just as important as medication in its maintenance. In fact some medical preparations were simply regular cooked food items. Thus vatikā and gutikā were pills and balls, mōdaka was a sweet uncooked pill, and yavāgu a grain gruel with added medicinal herbs. Thaila was an oil-based decoction both for external and internal use, arishta and āsava were medicated fermented liquors, and kānjika was a rice gruel soured by fermentation. All these constituted items of prescription to restore the health balance.

Hot and cold foods

The basic belief was that the five states of matter, loosely translated as earth (prthvi), water (ap), fire (tējas), air or mind (vāyu), and sky, ether or space (ākāsha) combined in the body to engender three dhātus, which are kapha (earth plus water), pittha (fire) and vatha (air plus sky). These three dhātus are expressive of the three gunās or attributes of matter. Kapha represents the gunā tamas, which, is linked with courage and valour, but is in practice expressed in an indifferent, ignorant or mechanical response. Pittha relates to sattva, which is expressed by way of intelligence and sobriety, and of pleasure attained through knowledge and regulated action. Vātha is connected with the guna rajas, manifested in enthusiasm and energy, and in a love of gain through excited action but uncertain judgement.[1]

Foods possess the same gunas, and engender them when ingested. According to the *Bhagavad Gītā*,[2] tāmasic foods are cold, stale and highly-spiced, rendering the eater dull and slothful. Examples of such foods are pork, beef, non-scaly fish and strong brews. Sāttvika foods are savoury, nutritive and agreeable, conducive to serenity and spirituality. Examples are milk and its products, jaggery, honey, fruits, goat and sheep meat, chicken, eggs and wine.[3] Rājasic foods are bitter, sour, salty, pungent, dry and burning; they stimulate a person and make him restless. Eating foods that clash with any ingrained temperament, or seasonal contra-indications, can bring about imbalances among the three dōshas, which are expressed in ill-health and disease.

People of hot, rājasic nature are assisted to better harmony by eating cold, sāttvika foods. Tāmasic foods would help a sāttvika-type person in winter. Frequent consumption of hot, spicy, sour and bitter foods can permanently affect one's disposition, making it fickle and restless. The numerous food prohibitions, espe-

Box 12
FATHERS OF INDIAN MEDICAL SCIENCE

According to mythology, the creator of the universe Brahmā imparted medical knowledge to a creative sage, Prajāpati, who instructed the two ashvins, twin Vedic deities. This knowledge passed to Indra, the leader of the gods, who parcelled out general and internal medicine to Ātreya and Bharadwāja, pediatrics to Kashyapa, and surgery to Dhanvantari, all these being great rishis and teachers.[15] Ātreya's exposition was recorded by his pupil Agnivēsha, and about the 5th century BC it seems to have been refined and redacted by Charaka. The term charaka has the connotation of roving, [26] and Charaka may have been one person, or several persons who adopted a descriptive name, or even a school or tradition,[24] which may have built upon the original text over the span of a few centuries.

The *Charaka Samhitā* consists of eight major sections divided into 120 chapters. Special emphasis is given to fundamentals (*Sūtra Sthāna*, 30 chapters) and to therapeutic treatments (*Cikitsa*, 30 chapters). The former section describes basic concepts, physiological processes, and food and drink groups, and the latter is a systematic account of how a doctor should diagnose and remedy ailments using an integrated approach. Drugs are divided according to their pharmacological action into fifty groups, and their action on the body is interpreted on a rational basis based on actual observation. There are details of 341 medicinal plants and their products, 177 drugs of animal origin and 64 drugs of mineral origin. Referring to the science of dietetics as āhāratattva, the effects of foods on bodily health are viewed in relation to physiological effect, temperament, cooking and season.[24] The work, it has been said, represents a 'momentous step forward from magico-religious therapeutics to rational therapeutics with perceptible results'.[26]

Sushrutha is again of doubtful historicity.[5b] The *Sushrutha Samhitā* now available to us is the recension of Nāgārjuna of about the 3rd or 4th centuries AD, which probably retained material going back several centuries. Dalhana's commentary on the work of about AD 1100 is a further source of information. The *Sushrutha Samhitā* is in six sections, all of which relate to different aspects of surgery.[7] Again various foods are reviewed in relation to their effect on health, and specific dietary items are prescribed for health conditions like fever, debility, dysentery, jaundice, asthma, tuberculosis, dyspepsia and intestinal worms.[14]

Vāghbhata was a Buddhist physician of the mid-seventh century AD who wrote two distinct works.[9] *Ashtāngahrdayasamhitā* or Compendium of Science, is of greater value then *Ashtāngasamgraha* or Collection of the Essence of Science. The former is an Ayurvedic text, much respected and quoted by later writers, and is particularly good on food injunctions related to season.

Another source is Jīvaka, the personal physician of Buddha. Buddhism places much emphasis on healing as a compassionate science.

The Bower manuscript was discovered in the twentieth century in a monastery. It is essentially a copy of the *Charaka Samhitā* by four Buddhist monks of Kashmir who had migrated to Kuchar. One part deals with snakebite and appears to have been copied from a source other than Charaka.[5c] A major topic in the text is the medicinal value of garlic, lasuna.[27]

Unāni medical lore first came to India with Arab traders, and later with the

Box 12 (*contd.*)

Moghuls, absorbing the while a great deal of ayūrvedic lore.[25] Among the earlier great figures of Arab medicine were Al-Rāzi, who dealt in detail with smallpox and measles; Al-Majusi, who specialized in dietetics and materia medica; and Ibn-Sina (Latinized to Avicenna), who analysed in depth both pathological and psychological phenomena.[25]

The southern Buddhist doctor-monk Nāgārjuna lived about the 7th or 8th century AD.[5b] He pioneered the use of metals for rejuvenation, and invented black sulphide of mercury for the purpose, as set down in his *Rasaratnākara*. Ayurvedic dietetic injunctions were soon incorporated into south Indian cognisance. Thus Thiruvalluvar in the *Thirukkural* has a chapter on medicine. Medical science involves four components, the patient, physician, medicine and the compounder.[28] The physician was enjoined to ascertain the condition of the patient, the nature of his disease and the season of the year before proceeding with the treatment. 'There is no disaster in life', the adult is admonished, 'if one eats in moderation food that is not disagreeable. As pleasure dwells with him who eats moderately, so disease is the lot of the glutton who eats voraciously.'[28] Moderation in Ayūrvedic terms is designated tripti, literally satisfaction, but here connoting the appeasement of hunger and thirst. In contrast is atisauhitya, meaning overeating to satiety.[12]

cially for students, widows and those under vow, are based on the perceived effects of certain tāmasic or rājasic foods in enhancing restlessness and eroticism. A food like garlic may help a person with a sluggish digestion, but overexcite a naturally rājasic temperament. A basic postulate was that there was a direct relationship between the taste of a substance and its physiological action. There were six 'pure' tastes; but no less than 63 mixed tastes were noted by Charaka.[4] Much more apparent in the choice of foods for medication or daily use are seasonal factors. The Aryan hot-cold food theory based on humoural imbalances spread in course of time to many parts of the world (see Box 13).

Recommended amounts and kinds of food

The sensible physician was advised to first take into account the regulation of digestion, and only then turn to the treatment of disease. The quantity of food, the doctors advised, should be adjusted to the digestive capacity. Normally only two meals were to be eaten daily.[5a] The *Arthashāstra* of Kautilya, no doubt drawing upon Ayūrvedic practice, recommended that a 'gentleman's meal' should consist of one prastha of pure unbroken rice, one-fourth of a prastha of pulses, one-sixth of a prastha of ghee or oil, and one-sixtyfourth of a prastha of salt.[6a] While the weight of a prastha is uncertain (454 grams is one suggestion), the relative proportions, except for a rather high level of fat, are remarkably in accord with a modern Indian balanced diet. Thin people were advised to use liquor after a meal to put on weight, and fat people could reduce by imbibing honey and water.[5a] Parched foods were stated to be more easily digested than fried foods, and unspiced soups more easily than spiced ones.

The stomach was visualized as consisting of four parts; two parts could be filled with solid food and one with liquid, leaving one part empty for the movement of wind.[6b] Sushrutha recommended a definite meal order.[7] First came sweet foods, such as fruits or confectionery or pāyas, then acid foods, next saline foods followed by pungent foods, and finally other foods. Frequently a beverage was offered after a meal; this could vary widely in nature, from simple cold or warm water to a thin cereal decoction, meat soup, a sour gruel, fruit juice or milk, according to temperament. Some of these drinks will be described later in this Chapter.

Box 13
A WIDESPREAD FOOD THEORY

The hot-cold food concept so elaborately developed by the Indo-Aryans and integrated with the theory of ill-health through humoural imbalance made its way round the world in course of time. Arabic translations of Indian medical texts were made, and two Indian doctors, Manka and Saleh,[16] were body physicians to the great Haroun al-Raschīd. When these translations reached western Europe, they were absorbed by Greek physicians.[17] They became the prevalent medical belief of the time, to be carried in the course of 16th century colonial expansion all over the world. The Spaniards taught humoural medicine when they established medical teaching at the University of Mexico in 1580,[18] and also elsewhere in South America, from where it was carried to the Philippines. Indian medical principles also travelled all over southeast Asia from about the start of the Christian era when Hindu and Buddhist kingdoms developed there.

Even now foods are chosen in India on the basis of these beliefs, especially in the north of the country where seasonal variations in climate are much more extreme, and hot-cold food beliefs are more strongly entrenched. During spring, heavy and cold foods are avoided and pungent foods preferred.[19] Cold and sweet foods are the choice of the summer months, while the monsoon season calls for hot foods in the conceptual sense. In winter, hot foods are the rule, such as dry fruits and their confections, coconut and copra-based items, almond-based delicacies like bādām milk and bādām halwā, and sweets like laddus rich in fat.[20]

Perceptions of what constitutes a hot or a cold food vary with availability, common usage and region. Wheat is considered a hot food in south India, where traditionally it was not common, but only as a moderately hot food in the north, where it is the everyday staple.[21] In Gujarāt, the common grain bājra is regarded as a hot food, but rice, maize and jowār are cold. All pulses, except for masoor, had a common cold-food connotation in a survey made in western India, [21] but in the north they are considered hot, in particular the rājmāh, kulthi (horsegram) and mattar (green peas). Green leafy vegetables are mostly accepted as being cold. So are most fruits, with the exception of the mango, jackfruit and papaya, all hot fruits. The majority of spices, and especially mustard seeds,[18] are regarded as hot, but even certain astringent condiments like kothmīr, jeera and saunf (fennel, *Foeniculum vulgare*) are frequently regarded as cold. Jaggery is a hot food, but sugarcane juice and honey are cold ones. Strangely, ghee and hydrogenated fats rate as hot foods, whereas oils like mustard and sesame are considered cold. Eggs are hot foods in Bangladesh but cold ones in Thailand.[18] Meats get their rating in terms of season. Fatty meats are for winter, game birds are the choice for summer, the flesh of marshy and watery animals is preferred in spring, while deer meat can be eaten all the year round.

In practice, 'hot' mangoes, which are summer fruits, must be accompanied by milk. Pregnant women avoid hot foods, particularly the papaya, but newborn infants in Bengal are given 'hot' honey and mustard oil to furnish strength and ward off colds.[18] Buttermilk quenches the fires of diarrhoea, and hot foods like pepper, ginger and turmeric counteract colds and cough.

In a modern scientific experiment, lists

Box 13 (*contd.*)

of hot and cold foods were first drawn up based on extensive questioning of individuals in the Hyderabad area.[22] The 'hot' list included wheat, horsegram, drumstick, bittergourd, garlic, carrot, potato, radish, vegetable oil, jaggery, dates and skim milk powder, The 'cold' list had dry maize, green gram, pumpkin, large onions, brinjal, green peas, green tomatoes, certain oils, sugar, bananas and skim milk. Two diets identical in terms of nutrients, like calories, proteins, fats and vitamins were fashioned using items from each list. These items were then fed for ten days to four adult men, after which the subjects were examined. On the 'hot' food diet, a burning sensation while passing urine was noted; the urine itself showed a high acidity, indicating that the important acid–base balance of the body had altered. In normal good health, a basic reaction is essential, with at least a 4:1 ratio in favour of alkalinity. Though the intake of sulphur on both diets had been the same, its excretion on the 'hot' diet was much higher. Again, though the protein content of both diets was the same, less nitrogen was retained in the body on the 'cold' diet. There seems to be more to the hot-cold food theory than meets the eye.

Many dried fruits like figs, apricots, raisins and dates are now known to be highly alkaline. Less so are tubers and green leafy vegetables, and still less so fruits like citrus, peaches, grapes, bananas and water-melons.[23] Acid-formers include most seafoods, meats, fish, many whole grains, and most nuts.[23]

The hands were smeared with sandal paste after a meal to remove grease, washed thoroughly, and then dried. Finally fragrant toothpicks were offered.[9]

Chewing thāmbūla, a betel quid, had become a common practice in north India by about 500 AD. This could consist simply of the leaves, arecanut grits, a dab of slaked lime (chunām) and a smear of katthā paste (the heartwood extract of *Acacia catechu*), or additionally, in more elite society, of flavourants like camphor, cardamom, cinnamon and cloves.[6d] A fragrant cigar might end the meal; this was made by smearing a reed with a paste of sandalwood powder containing spices like nutmeg and cardamom, allowing it to dry, and withdrawing the reed to leave a tubular cigar.

For everyday consumption, Sushrutha recommended the shāli rice shāstika, barley, mudga (mung), venison, butter, āmlaka, rock salt, honey and rainwater.[7] Great stress was laid on suiting foods to the season, of which six were distinguished: pre-spring, spring itself, summer, the rainy season, autumn and winter.[9] Strength and the digestive fire are strongest in winter, least during the summer and monsoon periods, and intermediate in the three other seasons: food choices had to be made accordingly. During hemantha from mid-November to mid January and shishira, from mid-January to mid-March man was at his peak strength. He could then digest sour and salty meat dishes of goat mutton, or of watery or marsh animals like the iguana roasted on a spit, or of birds and beasts of prey, besides new rice, milk preparations, sweets and hot water to drink. During spring (vasantha), from mid-March to mid-May, heavy, sour, oily and sweet foods were to be avoided; barley, wheat and the flesh of the stag, antelope, hare, quail and partridge, along with certain kinds of liquor, were advised, and sleeping during the day was warned against.

With the advent of summer (grīshma) lasting from mid-May to mid-July, cold, oily and fluid foods, such as cold preparations of barley with milk and sugar, milk itself, rice, ghee and deer meat were the proper foods. Salty, sour and pungent foods were taboo; as was daytime napping in cool places. Spirituous liquors were to be heavily diluted with water, or better still avoided altogether. In the rainy season or varshā, from mid-July to mid-September, digest ion was weak, and strong meat was banned. Venison with a boiled sauce, barley, wheat and old rice, and a medicinal type of liquor in small doses with honey or water were recommended. Autumn (sharad), from mid-September to mid-November, was the time to avoid ghee and other fats, and bitter drinks, and to eat moderately of foods that were light, cold and bitter so as to avoid biliousness (pittha).

Few of the ritualistic interdictions so common in Vedic literature can be discerned in these meals. Animal food of wide variety, liquor in moderation, and a balance of dishes are everywhere in evidence. In fact it has been pointed out that there is no diet specified at all for a strict vegetarian! Rather strangely, the use of turmeric (haridrā) is not mentioned anywhere, as one might have expected from the rationalism in evidence. As regards the use of alcohol, Charaka listed seven sources of wine and 84 alcoholic liquors, and was all for moderate drinking as a source of pleasure, apart from its digestive, nourishing and stimulating consequences.[6b] Sushrutha was of the view that alcohol induces pittha, but nevertheless listed 30 types of wine. Vāghbhata urged the moderate use of liquor in winter: 'Together with friends, drink unvitiated (undiluted?) āsava and aristha liquor, rum, wine and mead mixed with mango juice,' he advises, while recommending abstinence from liquor in summer.[9]

Charaka classifies vegetable food materials into six vargas or types.[8] Dhānya represent grains with husks, and these are further subdivided into eleven classes, e.g. shāli, vrīhi, yava, godhuma, etc., all being cereals. Shāmidhānya represent twelve kinds of pulses, like mudga, māsha, etc., shāka are made up of eighteen kinds of vegetables, phala represent fruits. Harid are exemplified by ginger, garlic, onion and radish, and āhārayōgi-varga (though literally meaning the food of ascetics) has the oils of sesame, mustard, and the like. In each class, the most beneficial and the least beneficial items are noted. The *Charaka Samhitā* catalogues the digestibility, nutritive value and medicinal action of several hundred edible and potable substances, and there are lists also of compatible combinations, and of those foods that are considered unwholesome in particular seasons.

Sushrutha's classification is fifteen-fold, and includes shāli, shāstika and vrīhi (all rices) as three of the classes, and yava (barley), shimbi (horsegram) and tila (sesame) as separate classes. Also in a separate class is thaila-varga (vegetable oils), as also are ikshu (sugarcane), kanda (tubers), pushpa (flowers) and udbhid (salt). Phala and shāka vargas make up the list.[8]

Let us look at some of these comestibles through the eyes of these doctors.

Foodgrains

By the start of the Christian era, rice reigned supreme, with barley a distant second, and wheat barely mentioned except as a winter food.[9] A great many rice varieties are noted by the doctors. Pride of place always lay with shāli or winter rice, and in particular raktashāli or red rice to which disease-curing effects were attributed. The quick-ripening, 60-day variety was shāshtika, which grew in summer in the plains and was considered nourishing, while the poorest of all was the monsoon rice vrīhi. Old rice was more easily digested than new, and raw rice least easily of all.

Barley continues as a foodgrain, and two new wheat varieties, madhūlika and nandimukhi, are mentioned, the former as wholesome, and the latter as good for health. The identity of another grain, kudhānya (literally, poor grain), is uncertain. The three Aryan pulses of long standing continue (mudga, masūra and māsha), the last being described as difficult to digest. Kulthi (horsegram) is recommended to increase the flow of breast milk. Vātāma (mattar, indigenous peas) and rājmāsha (perhaps the lobia and not the rājmāh of the present, which is the kidney bean) are both in use.

In what ways were these materials eaten? Rice was mostly boiled in water, or sometimes in milk, and was accompanied by ghee, pulses, meat, fruits or tubers. A tasty rice soup was made using long pepper (pippali), dry ginger and pomegranate juice. Sushrutha mentions vishyandaha, ghee-fried rice or wheat flour into which milk and molasses were added to give a fluid of medium thickness. Svāstika is described as a conical cake of barley flour, with some sort of surface markings. Samitāh is a preparation of wheat flour stuffed with ground boiled mung, perhaps like the modern pōli. Sprouted grains, virūdhaka, were used uncooked or made into sweets.[6e]

No less than twenty-four kinds of pulse extracts, termed yūsa, are listed, made mostly from mung and kulthi. Whole grains of mung and chana were puffed to yield ulumbāh. Pāpads, called parpatas, were made from various pulses.

Oilseeds and oils

The initial Aryan preference for ghee as a cooking medium shows appreciable softening by the early years of the Christian era. Charaka recommended the use of ghee only in the autumn; in the spring it was animal body fats for cooking, and in the rainy season vegetable oils. Sesame oil was highly regarded both as a base for medication and for frying and cooking, though not for use every day. Charaka even ponders over the fact that using vegetable oils, the non-Aryan (dhaitya) kings remained healthy, did not feel tired, fought bravely in battle, and conquered old age. Sushrutha was of the opinion that fried foods are difficult to digest, and urged moderation in the use of oil in the kitchen.

No less than sixty oilseeds are noted by Sushrutha.[7] These include the tila (sesame), sarshapa (sarson, mustard), kusumbha (safflower), atasī (linseed), eranda (castor); priyala (the chirōnji, *Buchanania angustifolia*), bilva (bael, *Aegle marmelos*), vibhītaka (baheda, *Terminalia bellirica*, karanja (*Pongamia pinnata*), kola (*Ziziphus* species) and ingudi (*Balanites aegyptiaca*). The Kautilya *Arthashāstra* mentions, in addition, neem (nimba, *Azadirachta indica*), kapittha (*Limonia acidissima*), madhuka (mahua, *Madhuca indica*) and kusāmra (whose identity is uncertain).[13] Numerous animal fats are listed including tallow from fatty tissues (meda), lard (vasā) and even majjā (bone marrow).[7] The effects of each oil and fat on health are ingeniously catalogued.

Vegetables and fruit

The *Bhela Samhitā* of approximately the same period commends the use of the āmlā, haritakī (*Terminalia chebula*) and vibhītaka (*Terminalia bellirica*), these being the three common myrobalans.[6b] The patōla (parwal) and vārtāka (brinjal) are praised as good vegetables, but by and large the medical trio are strangely silent on the subject of the fruit-type vegetables. A very large number of green leafy vegetables, on the other hand, were in use, among them those of the satina (a kind of pea), vasthuka (bethusāg, *Chenopodium album*), watercress (chanchū, chandrasūr, *Nasturtium officinale*), chilli (chilla, badābaṭhua, perhaps *Casearia tomentosa*), green radish (moolee-ka-sāg), mandukaparni (brāhmi, *Centella asiatica*) and jīvanti (sarsaparilla).[6b] A soup called khada was made from tender green leaves. Sushrutha states that in the Suhma country (Bengal), tender leaves were boiled, the water squeezed out, and jeera and black seeds of rāi added before shaping the mass into a delicacy called sindhaki.[7]

Charaka lists sixty-one fruits, most of which have been noted in earlier chapters.[6b] New items mentioned by him are the lakūcha (*Artocarpus lakoocha*, barhal or dahua in Hindi, the monkey jack), which is classed as a mediocre fruit, tuda (mulberry), sinchītika (the apple, with a Chinese prefix to its name), mōcha (banana, distinguished from the earlier kadali, or cooking plantain), vātāma (the almond, bādām), abhīsikha (the pistachio nut), aksōta (the walnut, akrōt), asvattha (peepal fig, *Ficus religiosa*) and nyagrōdha (banyan fig, *Ficus benghalensis*). Three varieties of the bēr or jujube earlier recorded (badari, karkhandu and vatari) are now joined by a fourth, sauvira.[4] Two varieties each are noted of the grape and the pomegranate, and of the pārusaka (the phālsa fruit), one sweet and the other sour.[7] Fruits mentioned in literature for the first time by Charaka are the nāgarangā (nārangi, orange), bhavya (or kāmarangā, Hindi kāmrākh, *Averrhoea carambola*), and pāravata, a kind of apple called pālevat that is still grown in Assam.[6b]

Milk and its products

Sushrutha mentions human milk, and the milk of the cow, buffalo, goat and sheep, describing the distinct qualities of each.[7] For instance, cow milk had a stabilizing effect on body secretions, and buffalo milk was fat-rich and more cooling, but impaired digestion. Human milk was recommended in eye diseases. Evening milk was more easily digested than morning, and milk freshly-drawn and warm from the udder was wholesome. Milk, in general terms, was a cold food, mild in action, and useful both in normal and disturbed bodily conditions.[7]

Cream of milk, santanika, had many beneficial effects on health. The use of curds in autumn, summer and spring was not recommended, nor its inclusion in a night meal.[10a] Distinctions were made between sweet, slightly acid and strongly acid curds.[7] Diluted curd made from skimmed milk, āsaradadhi, was heat-producing and digestive; that from whole milk was called ghola.[7] Mixing spices like pieces of cloves and sour pomegranate seeds with curds, and adding camphor for fragrance, gave sattaka.[6b] Rasāla or marjikā consisted of three parts of curds whisked with one part of sugar and seasoned with dry ginger and rock salt. Shikharinī was derived from curds, and seems to have resembled the shrīkhand of the present.[9]

Ghee made from the milk of the cow was rated highest, that of the sheep lowest. Special curative properties were associated with ghee made from thickened milk, ghee that had been preserved from 11 to 100 years in a vessel, called kumbhaghrta, and ghee matured for more than a century, termed mahāghrta.[7]

Flesh foods

Charaka considered meat a nourishing food, and prescribed its use for the weak, for convalescents, for those subject to very hard physical work, and for men addicted to the debilitating pleasures of wine and women. Deer meat (jangalavāsa) and its sauce were considered particularly nourishing, and other meats rated highly

Deer, a favourite of Sītā.

were those of the goat, hare, rōhita fish, tortoise, parrot, quail, partridge, peacock and alligator (gōdha).[14] Other animals whose flesh was eaten included the sheep, goose, cock, porcupine, pigeon and jackal, besides fish and certain birds.[14] Beef was described by Sushrutha and in the *Brhadāranyaka Upanishad* as pavitra or pure.[14] In winter, when the digestion was strong, or in all seasons for those with naturally-strong digestive systems, Charaka recommended the flesh of those creatures which dart suddenly on their prey, or those which live underground, in marshy places or in water, or those which walk on water.[6b] Vāghbhata commends fat meat and rich broths as winter-season foods.[9]

Sushrutha describes seven types of cooked meat. These were sour meat, roast dried meat, minced meat, fried meat, ground meat, grilled meat and meat for stuffing,[6b] and they have been described in Chapter 5. Meat was also used in other ways. A meat soup or broth that used vida salt, jeera and asafoetida was highly rated. Meat was cooked in an oven (kandu) after marinating it in spices like black mustard (rāi) powder and fragrant spices. Vesavāra or meat stuffing could be either spiced with long pepper (pippali), round pepper (maricha) and ginger, or sweetened with guda and ghee. Consumption of seasoned meat every day was not considered conducive to good health.[6b]

Fish are stated to be sweetish, carminative and heavy. Fresh-water fish are fattening and leave little residue, while sea fish are muscle builders.

An exotic preparation described by Charaka as an aphrodisiac was a large omelette, vrsyapūpalika, made of crocodile eggs and rice flour, fried in ghee.

Sweet items

Honey was recommended by the doctors for consumption primarily in the rainy season.[6b] Eight varieties of honey were recorded by Charaka and Sushrutha. The first is maksika from small bees, the next brahmara from large ones, and there were six others (see Chapter 9). Honey was considered by Sushrutha as cold, palatable and antitoxic, of use in deranged humours, ulcers and obesity.[7]

No less than twelve varieties of sugarcane are noted by Sushrutha, and Vāghbhata lists five. The best kind was vamshaka, with thin reeds, and next the paundra variety from the Pundra area of Bengal.[5a] Sugarcane was frequently eaten raw, but special medical effects were attributed to its pressed juice, unboiled as well as boiled, to its syrup and to sugar itself. The juice extracted using rollers was poorly rated in nutritive terms, presumably compared to chewing the cane itself. Sushrutha's observations suggest that as sugar products became purer and whiter, they also became 'cooler' but more difficult to digest. A new sugar product that finds mention in this period (apart from the much earlier phanita, guda and khand) was matsyandika; it is described as having a globular appearance, rather like fishroe, which would certainly suggest crystal sugar. Sugar was also made from honey (perhaps this was the portion that crystallizes out), and from mahua flowers. It also came from something called yavasa; this term is likely to imply the plant of a foodgrain (yava and yavaka are terms for barley), and could be jowār (*Sorghum vulgare*), which has an exceptionally sweet stalk.

A number of new names of sweetmeats appear in these medical works. Samyava was a blend of fried wheat flour, milk, ghee and sugar, flavoured with cardamom, pepper and ginger; if coconut shreds were added, the confection was called ghrtapūra. Madhushirsaka or madhukrōda was, as its name implies, a sweet confection, perhaps of the stuffed wheat flour type. Pūpalika was a cake of rice or wheat flour, centred with honey, and cooked in ghee; sometimes a stuffing of mung paste could also be used. Utkarika was a preparation of rice flour with molasses and ghee, which was rolled up to yield vartika. Details are usually insufficient to describe these preparations with any accuracy.

Apart from beverages of a medicated kind, which we shall shortly consider, several sweetened liquids were in contemporary use. Panaka or pana was the general term for a juice or syrup of sweet fruits like the mango, grape, woodapple, date, palm, bēr, banana, apricot, jackfruit, pomegranate, kadamba, bilva, rājādana and madanaphala, and of sourish ones like the

Kapittha fruit, used to acidify curds.

āmalaka, tamarind, jāmoon and phālsa. Three of these fruit juices mixed with honey and water constituted panchamrutha, while a fruit juice thickened by boiling down was termed yūsa. Rasa was an extract of sugarcane or even of cereals, and kānjika was rice or barley water soured by acetic fermentation. Barley water itself was yavōdaka; with five spices added to it, it gave panchasēvapanaka, a refreshing drink.

Rāga was a sweet liquid preparation (also incorporating rice grits) made from sour fruits like the tamarind, jāmoon, pārusaka (phālsa) and nimbuka (lime), sweetened with sugar-candy and spiced with black mustard.[9] Sādhava was a class of sour fruit juices thickened on a fire; rāga-sādhava seemed to connote the product from a boiled and softened mango, to which was added oil, dry ginger, salt and spices. From curds came khada (perhaps resembling the khadi of the present) by acidification with kapittha (the wood apple fruit) and changeri (the Indian sorrel leaf, amrul in Hindi, *Oxalis corniculata*), followed by seasoning with pepper and jeera. The same product with oil, sesame seeds and urad pulse added to it was termed kambalika by Sushrutha.

Salt, vinegar and asafoetida

Charaka lists five types of salt: rock salt, sea salt, vida, audvida, and sauvarchala. Sushrutha adds nine others, but both give nutritional pride of place to sea salt.

Vinegar, a product of acetic fermentation (Sanskrit shukta or chukra, Hindi shirka) was well-known but of no importance as a cooking aid. Buttermilk containing added sugar or honey was fermented by keeping the pot in a heap of grain (which is warm through respiration), and Dalhana mentions that vinegar was made from jaggery, sugarcane juice and honey. Sushrutha describes a class of preparations called āsuta, comprising vegetables like radish and gourd preserved in vinegar.

Asafoetida (hingu) had long been in use. It is called bāhlika in the *Bhela Samhitā* indicating its origin from Afghanistān, both then and even now.

Water

Water boiled with nine spices in equal amounts gave chūrnādīvāsin, while a certain digestive drink, perhaps spiced with pepper, went by the name of pratipana.

Water for drinking was given careful attention. It had to be boiled, exposed to sunlight and then filtered through charcoal.[9] Either a piece of hot copper was placed in it, or the water was stored in copper vessels.[11] The germicidal property of copper ions had obviously been recognized. Water for drinking was sometimes perfumed, e.g. with flowers of the pātala (*Stereospermum sauveolens*).[9] Condensed atmospheric water was the best of all drinks, and next best was that obtained from porous soil. Cleanly-collected rain water was filtered and stored in a container of gold or silver, or a boiled clay pot.[7]

Tender-coconut water was used in therapy.

Therapeutic diets

Certain specific items of food suggested for various conditions by Sushṛutha may be briefly recorded.[7] Coconut water was recommended for biliousness (deranged pittha), and barley water for fever, thirst and indigestion. In convalescence or slight fever, boiled rice with lightly-seasoned meat was recommended, and during fever, the juices of tender radish, parwal and neem. Loss of appetite, debility and thirst could be counteracted with a suspension of parched barley or rice in water, sweetened with honey or jaggery, or with buttermilk containing bitter juices. In dysentery, milk was as valuable as ambrosia. For tuberculosis, it was animal meat all the way; the flesh of the crow, vulture, mongoose, cat, cormorant or beasts of prey fried in mustard oil, or, as an alternative, the flesh of the camel, ass, elephant, mule, horse or forest-dwelling herbivores. Vomiting called for milk, or soups of meat, or light cereals, and tender vegetables. Asthma needed extracts of chicken, pigeons and wild fowl, cooked with large quantities of acid juices, salt and ghee. When intestinal worms were present, milk, meat, ghee, green leafy vegetables, curds and sweet or acid substances were all forbidden. Dyspepsia called for fruits, cooked roots, tasty beverages, and sweetmeats made with acid juices.[7] These injunctions can hardly be faulted even in the light of present hindsight.

The accent was always on the preservation of good health through a well-adjusted diet. 'Without proper diet, medicines are of no use; with proper diet, medicines are unnecessary' sums up this attitude very pithily.

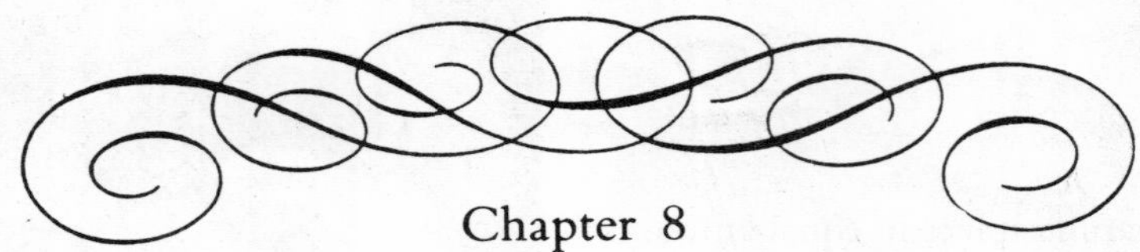

Chapter 8

ROYAL FARE

Our story of food in India, both in the north and the south, has so far advanced to about the end of the first millennium of the Christian era. In picking up the tale during the next millennium, two royal authors have a great deal to contribute. King Someshwara of Kalyānā in Central India in his *Mānasollāsa* written about AD 1130, deals with all the duties and recreations of a ruler, among which are included matters relating to food and its preparation in the royal kitchen.[1,2] King Basavarāja of the Keladi Kingdom flourished around AD 1700 in what is now western Karnātaka, and his *Shivatattvaratnākara* is a monumental work that takes all knowledge as its province, and this includes food, one of the 64 arts or shāstras.[3] Box 14 describes these two kings.

Apart from their writings, feasts either given by royalty or served to them are described in literary works that emanate from several regions in India, either in Sanskrit or in the regional languages that were establishing themselves between AD 1000 and 1500. Regional foods will themselves be described in Chapter 10, and will serve to add to the list of foods depicted by imperial writers.

Mānasollāsa[4a–7]

Rice, wheat, and imagination

Rice and wheat were both staple foods of the time. Wheat had staged a come-back to the popularity that it had enjoyed in Harappan times after having been all but displaced by rice during the Vedic period. Both staples were utilized in a variety of ingenious ways. King Someshwara informs us that mandakas were made from wheat flour, which was obtained by washing wheat, drying it in the sun, grinding, and then sifting on a sieve. The flour was mixed with ghee and salt and made into balls, which were flattened out either between the palms, or using a roller on a flat piece of stone. The circles were first cooked on a potsherd, and then roasted on live coals before eating. These are of course the parātas or more accurately the māndēs of the present, and one could stuff them, as is still done, with various fillings. Sweet materials like honey would yield what were called madhumestaka or madhushīrshaka; jaggery and mashed dhals would give pahalikas or pōlikas; and savoury stuffings yielded angarapōlikas. Kasara was a wheat flour preparation fried in ghee, with milk, sugar and spices added (probably to the dough), and suhālī is described as consisting of hard cakes of wheat flour that had

Box 14

ROYAL AUTHORS

The later Western Chalukyas ruled from their capital Kalyānā in today's Bidar district, about 160 km west of Hyderabād.[1,2] King Someshwara III reigned from AD 1126 to 1138 and overcame, after a long fight, the Hoysala king Vishnuvardhana who had sought to invade his kingdom. According to an inscription, Someshwara is credited with having 'placed his feet on the heads of the kings of Āndhra, Dravida, Magadha and Napāla (Nepal), and being lauded by all learned men'. In inscriptions he is referred to as bhūlōkamalla (wrestler of the earth) and sarvajnachakravarthi (omniscient emperor).

To Someshwara is attributed the Sanskrit work *Abhilashitarthachintāmani*, which is better known by its alternative title *Mānasollāsa*, meaning refresher of the mind.[5] The contents suggest that only a king could have written the work. It consists of 100 chapters grouped into 5 equal books, of which the third describes the pleasures of royalty.

The book can be accurately dated from internal evidence. In the section on astronomy, King Someshwara elects to give the dhruvankas for calculation of the planetary positions for the first Friday of the year Chaitra Shāka 1051, corresponding to the year AD 1129–30, some three years after he had ascended the throne. It was perhaps the very day, or one near it, on which he had made the calculation.

The chapter entitled Annabhōga occupies about twenty pages.[5] It gives recipes, some fairly detailed and others less so, for the preparation of a variety of dishes that are even now current in the Kannada, Marathi and Tamil areas, like the idli, dōsai, vadai, dahi-vadā, pōli, wadian, shrīkhand, phēni and laddu (see text). However the king deals with these vegetarian dishes rather tersely, and devotes more attention to non-vegetarian food preparations. The flourish is imperial; we are told that 'even though food preparations served in earthen vessels taste well, kings must be served in vessels made of gold'.

Another ruler who was also a poet was Keladi Basavarāja.[3] From AD 1696 to 1714 he ruled the kingdom of Keladi, which from being a small feudatory of the mighty Vijayanagar empire grew into a powerful kingdom extending from Goa to Cannanore. Basavarāja was a devoted Veerashaivite who worshipped both Shiva and Veerabhadra, and his encyclopaedic work in Sanskrit is appropriately called *Shivatattvaratnākara* and deals with the whole range of human knowledge.[14] The preparation and serving of food form part of the section devoted to Society and Amusements. Like the *Mānasollāsa* of King Someshwara, it amalgamates personal knowledge and observation with a mass of material on an immense variety of subjects drawn from earlier literature.

been fried in very hot oil and then coated with sugar, perhaps similar to the modern kalkhand or bālushāhi. Patrikas were round cakes of wheat flour piled one over the other prior to frying, and samitah was a preparation of wheat flour stuffed with boiled and ground mung dhal. Pūrana appear to have been both by name and description the pūranpōli of today, being described as cakes stuffed with a mix of jaggery and boiled and ground mung dhal paste. Sēvika was the sēv of the present day, but murmura, which now signifies just puffed rice in Maharāshtra, referred then to a more elaborate sweet preparation of wheat flour, guda and certain aromatic spices. Another snack, veshtikā, now called bedavi in Hindi, is described as a cake of wheat flour stuffed with chana paste and spices.

The above list does include some items in which cereals and pulses are employed together, but pulses themselves were the base of many preparations. Vidalapāka was made from a mixture of five pulse flours: chana, rājmāsha, masoor, mung and parched thuvar, seasoned with rock salt, turmeric and asafoetida, and cooked on a slow fire. Could this have been an ancestor of the pesarattu of the Āndhra country? Vatakas were the fermented urad vadās of today; these were soaked in milk to give kshīravata, and in sour rice water or kānji (and later in sour curd) to give the modern dahi-vadā. The *Mānasollāsa* mentions, without description, another variety of vadā known as manāhvataka. Yet another variation was ghārika, which survives in the present garagé of Maharāshtra: this was an urad vadā with five or seven holes in it, fried very crisp in oil to a dark brown colour. Katakarna was a fried delicacy: a paste of pre-soaked peas was salted and lightly fried, cowpea (lōbia or nishpava) powder was mixed in, the mixture was shaped into patties, and fried in ghee. Vatikā was the wadian or vadi of today, shaped pieces of fermented urad dhāl paste. Pūrika were small fried cakes of gram flour: not the pūri of the present, but the pāpadi. Pārika appear to have resembled the bonda of today, being described as cakes of besan powder or ground boiled pulses, spiced with salt, pepper, asafoetida and sugar, and fried in oil. Blending of pulses along with vegetables and meat to give curries was practised; thus mung dhāl, pieces of lotus stalk, and chirōnji (priyala) seeds were seasoned with asafoetida and green ginger pieces, fried in oil, and boiled to a curry, to which might have been added fried brinjal pieces, mutton, jackal meat or even animal marrow, the dish being finished with black pepper and dry ginger: an elaborate concoction truly fit for a king.[4–7]

The *Mānasollāsa* also describes the dhōsaka (dōsai) and the idarikā (idli), in making both of which only pulses and no rice appear to have been used. Box 19 in Chapter 10 describes these essentially southern snacks.

Meat for a King[4a,5,6,7]

King Someshwara was obviously no vegetarian, and meat items have pride of place in his chapter on food. Liver was carved into the globular shape of betel nuts, which were first roasted on charcoal, and then fried with spices, eventually to be placed in curds, or in a decoction of black mustard. Roasted tortoise, seasoned fish and fried crabs were other dishes that were relished. It is rather interesting that the roasting of a whole pig, and subsequent charcoal broiling of pieces carved out of the roast, is still carried out among the royalty of Rājasthān to give what are now called shūlas.[8]

The best cuts of meat are described by the king. In one recipe, pieces of meat were mixed with a paste of gram pounded with spices, and fried; to this were added tender hyacinth beans (nishpava), certain berries, onion and garlic, and the whole mass was taken up in some sour juice and flavoured. A less acidic preparation was kavachandi, in which plum-shaped pieces of sheep mutton, mixed with grams or sprouted mung and powdered spices, were fried along with garlic, onions, and vegetables like the brinjal and radish. Another dish, puryala, specifies meat shaped into āmla-like pieces which were cooked with spices (probably bagaar frying is what is meant), the resulting liquid preparation being again cooked with certain acid fruits, sunthakas (roasted pork pieces), spices and rock salt, flavoured with garlic and asafoetida. To make krishnapāka, the use of sheep mutton in the shape of betel nuts, along with some blood, was specified. It would be interesting to know how these globular shapes, each resembling some natural fruit, were actually carved out from hunks of various meats: there must have been high wastage!

Bhaditraka was the kabāb of today, in which pieces of meat were bored, stuffed with spices, roasted on spits, and then spiced again; sometimes, after cooking, the roasted bhaditrakas were allowed to dry out, and later fried in ghee. Ground meat was also used to stuff brinjals, followed by frying, to give pūrabhattāka, a common item even of the present. Included by King

Someshwara as a non-vegetarian food material were 'peculiar mice that lived in the fields near rivers'; a modern Indian sociologist has noticed exactly this item as an off-season food of the villagers of the Mandya district of Karnātaka.[9] To make a rōhitaka (rōhu) fish preparation, another source, the *Samaraichchakaha* (12th century), directs that the skin be peeled off, the fish marinated in asafoetida and salt, then dipped in turmeric water, and finally fried.[10]

Relishes gave piquancy to a meal. Pickles are referred to as sandān in Somadeva's *Yasastilakā*, written about AD 959.[10] The *Mānasollāsa* describes pralēhakas, acidic relishes made from sūrana (yam), curds and fruit juices by cooking them down with spices and some oil over a slow fire.[6] Even rice in its gruel was soured by fermentation (kānjika), and consumed as a relish after seasoning. This once very common dish of the south seems to have been all but given up now. Betel leaves finished the meal; five aromatic ingredients went into a special folded pān, the panchasugandhika-thāmbūla, namely the cardamom, clove, nutmeg, mace and camphor.

The many wonders of milk

Milk and curds were the basis of several refreshing drinks. Whey was prepared by adding acid fruit juices to boiled milk to precipitate the solids, which were then strained away; sugar and cardamom were put into the liquid, followed by a second straining, after which either fruits or roasted tamarind seeds were blended in to give a beverage. Two other common beverages were coconut water, and phanita, which consisted of diluted molasses sprinkled with pepper.[10] Majjika, the majjigé of today's Karnataka, was prepared by mixing churned buttermilk with sugar and spices. Curd itself, made pungent with seeds of rāi (black mustard), was called rājikaraddha, and themana was a soup of curds. Buttermilk, with tamarind, sugar, cardamom, ginger and asafoetida added, was used to flavour the water resulting from the washing of rice, and yield a beverage termed vyanjana.[10] It looks as though nothing was wasted. Another milk product mentioned is rāyata, the modern rāita.

Curds also lent themselves to sweet preparations. Most simply, they were flavoured with sugar and camphor. Shrīkhand, then called shikharinī or rasāla, was made exactly as it is now by beating up sugar and aromatic spices with de-watered curds. Sweet preparations from milk included kshīravata and kshīrayastika, the nature of which is not described.

Satisfying a sweet tooth

Many sweets were based on milk. For the making of what is today called chhana, the *Mānasollāsa* recommends the addition of some sour substance (even sour curds from a previous operation) to boiled milk, after which the precipitate was separated. It was mixed with rice flour, fashioned into various shapes, fried in ghee and coated with sugar to give kshīraprakāra. Shaping it into the likeness of the eggs of a peacock (mora) gave the delicacy morendaka. These two sweets may be considered starting points for the whole range of modern Bengali milk sweets (Chapter 10).

Sweets based on wheat flour are also described by King Someshwara. Kasāra was a blend of wheat flour, milk, ghee, crystal sugar, cardamom and black pepper, and this mix, stuffed in a wheaten envelope, gave what was termed udumbara. A mix of wheat flour, guda, black pepper and cardamom yielded murmura. Varsapālagōlakas are likened to hailstones, and the ingredients were rice flour, sugar and aromatic spices like cardamom and camphor. Ghrtapūra (also called havispura) seemed to have been the ghevara of today, a pressed mass of fine wheat flour mixed with milk, fried in ghee and coated with sugar. Khajjaka, plain or sweet, was a wheat flour preparation fried in ghee, the khāja of today, and phēnaka was the strand-like phēni of the present. Sweet balls prepared with rice or pulse flours and sugar were termed laddukas or mōdakas, of very ancient lineage and still going strong. Sharkari-putrika were moulded dolls made of sugar, a great festival favourite with children then as now.

Foods of a Royal Couple

The *Padmāvat* of the 16th century originates from Gujarat, and is the tale of Kisar Khān and his Hindu wife Padmāvati.[11] Foods served at a feast given by them were wheat based rōtis like the lucchahi, pūri, sōhāri and mānda, a liquid dhāl dish jhalar, many pickles (sandān), sugar syrup (kadohi) and sweet confections like kandarā (sweetened milk solids, the present shakarapāka), kheer of jowār, and moranda (dewatered dahi solids sweetened and shaped to resemble peacock eggs). The dinner, the poet tells us, went off excellently.

Karnātaka

Royal feasts

Here is a feast for kings, as described in Kannada verse by Terekanambi Bommarasa, written about 1485.[12] 'The Kings', he says, 'are relishing the kadubu made of black gram: it looked like a full moon; like a mass of mist set together; as if heavenly nectar had solidified into circles; or as if a drop of moonlight had hardened. The kadubu was attractive to the eye and pleasing to the mind.' Next we read that

> the women served an unfried brinjal bāji, which contained coconut shreds, curry leaves and cardamom, mixed well, and flavoured with citrus juice and a little camphor... The tamarind side-dish and the pickle were consumed with great relish; the pāpads were broken into pieces and the pacchadi eaten with delight. The meal was laid on broad banana leaves spread on the floor, and the kingly lords of the earth ate slowly until their appetites were satiated'.

Several other kingly feasts appear in Kannada literature down the centuries.[12] Nemichandra, in his *Lilāvati* of about AD 1170 (almost exactly contemporary with King Someshwara), mentions serving to the king, Nīlāpati, on a lotus leaf, a large number of pickles made from fruits, vegetables and roots, all flavoured with camphor. Another feast, for King Kanteerava Narasa Rājēndra, was served by women whose charms are described at considerable length by Gōvinda Vaidya in 1648 and again by Mallarasā in 1680. These ladies had faces like the full moon, collyrium in their eyes, turmeric on their faces, ladies of all the four classical types with bells round their waists, bangles on their hands, anklets which made music on their feet, wide of hip and slender of waist. In the *Jaimini Bhāratā* of Lakshmeesha (perhaps *c.*1700), it is Krishna himself who is served, rather curiously, by both Dēvaki and Yasōdha. The foods served in these feasts are listed in Box 18 of Chapter 10, and described also in the same Chapter.

Dining together

Two more meals, one to a group of Brahmins and the other a domestic meal, have both culinary and human interest.[12] The poet Mangarasā gives an enthusiastic description of a Hindu din-

Sweet sesame laddus.

ner from the time of sitting down to the final appreciation.

The brāhmins sat before the ornate chowka squares, on which the banana leaves and leaf cups had been laid out. They threw their sacred threads over their shoulders, loosened their garments, completed their rituals and dined heartily, stroking their beards and moustaches in anticipation. Bring on the cooked rice, serve the thogay relishes and the ghee in the leaf cups! Are they tasty? Place before them the spiced palidya curd, and the idli and dōsai, with milk and sugar! Oh pundit: please savour the pāyasams, are they not tasty? Oh priest: help yourself to the dosai and the fried karajiggē sweet dish! Oh jois; is this oil-fried puri soft enough? Oh dikshit: do not these sugary burudegallu balls satisfy amply your tastes? In these terms was the food praised.[12]

Finally let us listen as Annāji, writing about 1600 in Kannada, describes a domestic meal:

There was mixed rice, kattōgara and kalasōgara; a sweet pāyasam; freshly-made ghee that flashed in cups like amber; solid ghee; milk thickened by boiling till it fell in flakes; a pickle of tender mangoes, the stalks of which had not even lost their fresh green colour; and vegetables delicately acid and salt. All these were served at the meal.[12]

He also describes the following scene in a sweetmeat shop, listing, by name, several items:

For those who cannot command these delicacies at home the sweetmeat shop offers a variety of delights. There is karajjigē, a sweet made from maida flour; athirasā fried in ghee; urad-based vadai; idlis as fair as the moon; sweet sesame balls; obattu garigē, round as the earth, made of wheat or rice flour and jaggery, flavoured with lemon and fried in ghee; chakli; delicious strands of phēni; jilabīya, looking like plant stems, and resembling rods of nectar; manōharada, fried globes held together with jaggery; and hālundigē, cakes of fine rice powder with milk and sugar.

Sivatattvaratnākara

The Royal kitchen and cooking accoutrements

The royal kitchen, according to king Basavarāja of Keladi, author of the encyclopaedic work, had to be 32 feet long and 8 feet wide, and provided with a chimney.[13] On the east side of the kitchen should be kept conical ovens made of iron, with nine top openings to hold vessels of different shapes and sizes, and also the cooking vessels. To the southeast should be placed the embers for use in the ovens, to the south firewood, to the west the waterpots, and to the north the winnowing basket and brooms. The northwest was the place for the mortar and pestle, the pounding mortar, and for cutting vegetables; and the southwest the kalpana (working area). The kitchen utensils in use are listed, and are described in Chapter 9. The darvi or scraper had to be made of wood or coconut shell, a foot long, one end as broad as a palm, the other banded with three inches of gold, silver or iron. The pounding mortar, ulūkhala, was 4 feet long, 3 feet wide, with a rim 4 inches wide, and a central cavity 7 inches wide and 16 inches deep. The shūrpa was shaped like an elephant's ear.

The material of which a cooking vessel is made influenced the food cooked in it, and the effect that it exerted on the body. Taking rice as an example, cooking it in a copper vessel des-

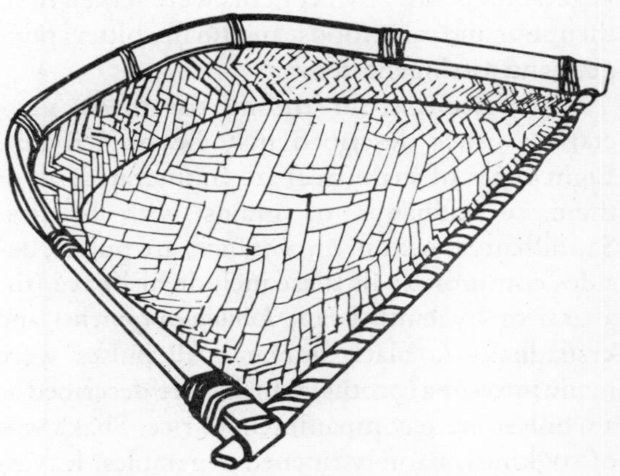

The plaited shūrpa or winnowing basket.

troys gas (vātha), removes spleen disease and was recommended for yōgins. Cooking in bronze destroys all the three dōshas, in gold alleviates poison (perhaps a king had to be careful here), wards off indigestion, jaundice, consumption and the diseases caused by vātha (wind), besides enhancing vigour, vitality and eroticism. Rice cooked in a silver vessel removes phlegm, biliousness and indigestion; made in tinned vessels, the cooked rice rendered the body cool, and in earthenware put down biliousness. Much was made of earthenware. When the pot was made from the earth from dry land (jangalā), the dish cooked was good for the blood, skin diseases, itches and wound-healing. Earthenware from watery land (anupa) yielded food that conduced to digestion, strength and pleasure, and that from wild and marshy land (sadhārana) to the alleviation of blood derangements caused by bile, of phlegm, and of cold, while enhancing complexion and strength.[13]

Kinds of food

Food was served to the king seated on a special pedestal, the bhōjana-pīta, wide, square, made of wood and decorated with gold.[13] If this faced east, it conduced to long life, if south to fame, if west to health and wealth, and if north to truthfulness. Making a choice must have been difficult! Of course only gold vessels were used by the king for eating. Drinks and bhakshyas (chewed items, like rōtis) were placed on the left of the plate, rice in the middle, and greens and vegetables below. Sweet items were served first, then sour and salty foods, and finally bitter, pungent and astringent items.

Some items from among the many vegetarian dishes described may be singled out. Eight types of shāli (rice) are enumerated, all of them sukhadhānya or grains with bristles. Samidhānya, next in importance, are pulses; besides common dhāls these include nishpava (the avarai or hyacinth bean, *Lablab purpureus*) and krsnādhaka (a black thuvar). All pulses were made into sūpa (broths) which were described as a wholesome accompaniment to rice. Shāka was of six kinds, namely ripened vegetables, leaves, tubers, roots, flowers and pods (shimbi). Milk could be boiled down to different degrees to yield pānapāka (to half), lehyapāka (to one-third), ghutipāka (to one-sixth) and sharkarapāka (to one-eighth, a solid product now called khoa). These were all consumed after flavouring with fragrant flowers or with fruit. Similarly there were four sugar syrups of different consistencies, termed mrdu, madhyama, khara and sarika. To the khara syrup adding milk, cardamom, kēsar, and camphor yielded the sweet confection varselapāka. Relishes, called upadamsha, could be made in five ways: without cooking, by boiling in water, by mixing and heating in oil, by direct heating without water or oil, and by cooking in a vessel. Water was classified into nine types depending on source. Three methods for its fumigation were recommended: treatment with earth and fragrant materials (pindavāsa), with mango juice or flowers (pushpavāsa), or by adding various powders (chūrnādivāsa). An intriguing remark is that drinking water could be cooled in 'machines made of pūgapatta' (bark of the areca), then filtered and perfumed.

Accompaniments

The best arecanuts in the kingdom came, according to the king, from Vēlavarna, Īsvarapūra, Kōtikapūra, Vanavāsa and Rāstrarājā; the best betel leaves also came from the last two of these places, the very best being called karpūravalli and nāgavalli. Lakshmi was believed to reside in the forepart of the betel leaf, Jyestha at the back, the Lord of Speech at the right, Pārvati at the left, Vishnu inside, the Moon outside, Shiva at all the edges, and Cupid everywhere. Yama, the lord of death, resided at the root (stalk), which explains why the stalk is always pinched away before the leaf is eaten. Small toothpicks called vati and ghutikā were made from picchumanī wood, or from bamboo, grass or metals. To make scented toothpicks, the slivers were marinated in bovine urine mixed with haritakī powder (*Terminalia chebula*) for a week, then immersed in scented water, smeared with spices and flavours, and dried.[13]

About the same period (1700–50) prized varieties of betel leaf in the Maharāshtra area were Gangeri and Rām-teki, and of the areca nut

Betel leaves, in each part of which resided specific dieties.

Chīkani, Shrīvardhan Rōtha and Fulabharda; the quid kulapi-vīda, made up of 10–12 leaves, had a filling of betel nuts, katthā and chunnā to which were added cardamom, nutmeg, almond, pista and coconut shreds.[14]

Additional royal recipes are featured in Box 15.

North India

Epic feasts

Both the *Rāmāyana* and the *Mahābhārata* describe sumptuous dinners which reflect the foods of the kshatriyas at about the beginning of the Christian era (Chapter 5, Box 8). A century later things seem more restrained, and flesh foods are less in evidence even among these warriors.

Three royal meals

Summaries of the following three accounts pertain to the period around AD 1000.[4b] The first, taken from the *Bhavisayattakaha*, is an account of the occasion when Bhavissa got back his wife, and the king was a guest. The first course served to King Shrenika consisted of fruits such as the

Oranges were relished by royalty.

Box 15
ROYAL RECIPES

Though practical details are lacking, both the *Mānasollāsa* and the *Shivatattvaratnākara* do give some indication of how individual food dishes were made. The dōsa, idli and vadā are all mentioned, and will be dealt with in Box 19 of Chapter 10. Certain others will now be described.[6,7]

The patrikā, at present termed the chirotti, drew its name from thin writing sheets placed in a heap, since the confection consisted of discs of wheat that were placed one over the other, fried in ghee and then dusted with ground sugar. The Mānasollāsa has some interesting items derived from pulses. Veshta in Sanskrit means to encircle or surround, and the veshtikā (today called vedhami in Gujarat and Maharashtra) was a circlet of spiced besan paste with some sugar added and then rolled in wheat flour before being baked on an earthen plate. Vatikā was the vati or warri of the present, a ball of spiced and ground urad paste fermented for a few days and then deep-fried. From the two terms vidala meaning cooking, baking or dressing, and dālana for splitting, grinding or crushing, originated the name vidalapāka for a slowly-cooked dish of spiced mixed pulses like masūra, rājmāsha and ādhakī.

The preparation and the dressing of meat are carefully described. Detailed instructions are furnished for dehairing a pig by one of two methods. The first of these was to cover the body with a white cloth, and then pour boiling water on it till the bristles loosened sufficiently to be pulled out by hand. The other was to smear the animal with clay and then burn the skin away with a fire made of grass. To prepare tasty sunthakas, a whole pig was first roasted on an open fire. After this pieces of the roast were carved out, broiled on live charcoal, and eaten after seasoning with rock salt and black pepper, or sour lemon juice, a dish called chakkalika. Alternatively, the sunthakas were carved out of the roast in the form of long strips 'resembling palm leaves' and the pieces were placed in spiced curds. Something akin to modern bacon is suggested by the injunction that in preparing the 'khanda of vapā', the latter should be kept in the form of a roll 'like a panchānga'. The term sunthakas seems to be a generic one for items drawn from a roasted pig. Thus it is applied also to a preparation from the entrails, mixed with marrow and spices, and again broiled on a charcoal fire to give a dish specifically termed mandaliya. Rajput royalty has always been partial to dishes of pork (see Chapter 10).

Among the numerous items of the Karnātaka area in the *Shivatattvaratnākara* are some specially described as being 'fit for kings'.[13] Bamboo rice, which is rare and only available about once in fifty years (see Chapter 14) is naturally enough one of them, and is even called rājanna-akkī or the rice of kings. This could be boiled like rice, or boiled in the kanji of ordinary rice to yield shudōdana, which is described as resembling thumbē flowers. Tamarind cooked in oil with a dash of asafoetida was recommended for pouring over rice as a 'finish'. Ordinary boiled rice could be exalted to a feast dish by dressing with pāpads, pumpkin crisps, coconut gratings, lime juice, roasted urad and the like to give various katta-yōgaras. A crisp relish was suppani, wheat and rice grits deep-fried to crispness and brownness, stated to be used by kings. Items served to kings or by them have been described in the text. Generally they are no different from normal festive foods but some are worthy of mention. A crisp relish was pūri-vilangāyi, to make

Box 15 (*contd.*)

which the grits of rice and of mung dhāl were roasted together, spiced and flavoured with camphor, made into marbles of the size of areca nuts using rice powder paste as a binder, and then deep-fried. Yet another crispy was made from chopped jackfruit cooked in ghee with spices, then made into balls with curds and deep-fried to crispness. Pudé was a generic term for mixed fried vegetables folded into a turmeric leaf and then steamed: one example of the filling was bṛinjal fried with rice grits and chopped onion. Bāji, a bartha, was another brinjal dish. Bamboo shoots, steeped in salt water to remove astringency and then fried, were a great delicacy. Pālidhya was a class of spiced vegetables cooked in curd and finished with a baghār seasoning.

A very popular dessert consisted of ripe fruit mixtures mashed together, called seekharanē. Mātulunga fruit (*Citrus medica*) was stewed to remove its acidity and then boiled in buffalo milk with sugar and cardamom. Laddus made of urad were termed manōharada, and those from fermented rice-urad mixtures piyasha-pinda. Crescent-shaped stuffed sweet puffs were termed karajikāyi or karajigē, and sweet rice balls, deep-fried till brown, were hālugarigé. Clotted cream flakes (rabbri) in sugared milk was kenē-payasa. Two unusual sweets were bhōjanādhika-rōti and madhunālā. The former was a mix of broken pieces of mandigē (a sweet pōli) with buffalo milk, mango juice and sugar fashioned into balls which were sealed in coveṛs of dough, perfumed with flower petals, baked on glowing coals and eaten with sugar and ghee. Madhunālā, the honied tube, was made by first mixing equal parts of rice flour, wheat flour and besan with well-ripened mashed bananas and butter; the resulting paste was then smeared to dry on a bamboo stem, which was then withdrawn to leave a tube. This was filled with sugar, sealed and deep-fried in ghee.

pomegranate, grape and bēr, which could be chewed. Next came fruits for sucking, such as sugarcane pieces, dates, oranges and mangoes. The third course comprised preparations that could be licked, and the fourth sweets like sēvaka, mōdaka, phēnaka, and ghrtapūra. The fifth course was boiled rice, anḍ the sixth consisted of broths prepared by mixing many foodstuffs. Then the king washed his hands, the dishes and cups were removed, and curd preparations, constituting the seventh course, were served. Once again, the dishes were removed, hands washed, and some half-boiled milk (warm, or boiled down to half?) containing sugar, honey and saffron was served. After the king had cleaned his teeth with toothsticks and a fragrant powder, he again washed his hands with warm water and fragrant powder.

In the second feast, drawn from the *Apabrahmsatrāyi*, the items served are pickles prepared with karīra fruit (*Capparis decidua*) and karamarda fruit (*Carissa carandas*), vatakas (vadās) of many kinds in milk and curds, and vegetables such as karavella (karēla or bitter gourd).

The third marriage feast comes from *Naishadha Charita*, and is written by a poet who was clearly also a gourmet. There was boiled rice served hot, unbroken, fragrant and well-cooked, with each grain separate. Milk rice was served with ghee, and the mustard-flavoured curd was so pungent that the feasters were obliged to scratch their heads! There were tasty broths of venison and fish. So skilful was the cooking that the party could not tell vegetarian and meat dishes apart. There was wheat dressed like the bimbi fruit (*Cephalandīa indica*), vatakas floating in milk, laddukas white as hailstones, sugar dolls, and sweet cakes. The betel leaves served at the end, we are told, 'had the sting of a scorpion'.[4b]

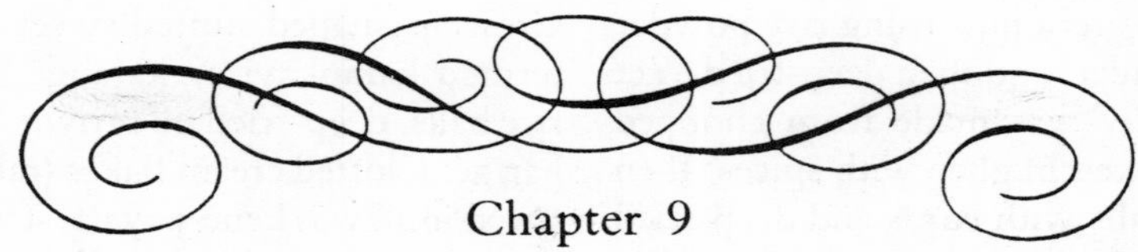

Chapter 9

UTENSILS AND FOOD PREPARATION

The edible ingredients produced in India over the centuries, actual recipes and dishes, and the cooking ethos have been reviewed in earlier chapters. It remains to consider the ways in which cooked foods were produced and the utensils employed to produce them. Many of these were obviously used at a domestic level. Yet there have always been food preparation operations carried out on a larger community scale, frequently by professionals. Both the archaeological evidence for these tools and techniques and references to them in literature will be drawn upon.

Domestic Operations

Grinding and pounding

The prehistoric Bhimbetka cave paintings (Chapter 1) show women on their knees, or standing up, mixing something in a device that is drawn like a very shallow letter 'w'. Saddle querns for grinding grain or spices go back roughly to neolithic times. Simple units with a slight inward or outward curvature were paired with a muller (grinding stone) which progressed from a simple rounded pebble to dressed concave or convex stones.[1,2] The Indus Valley had two types. One was more or less flat and with it went a cylindrical muller rolled with both hands, a common pairing even today. The other had a small circular depression and was used for crushing grains, rather than grinding them, with a rounded stone held in one hand. A flat four-legged quern of the latter type is depicted in Sānchi sculpture about 250 BC.[3a] A later type consisted of a solid cylindrical stone base, on which revolved a heavy domed stone worked by two women making use of a pole passing through two holes opposite each other.[3c,4] Later, about the early Christian era, the upper domed stone was replaced by the now-familiar heavy circular stone with a single wooden peg on its periphery.[5] Though the heavy lower stone with a hole at its centre has been found at Lothal[5] and Mohenjodaro,[6a] this may not be a grindstone at all but a stone pulley for drawing water from wells, since the upper part of the pair has never been found.[7]

Mortars fixed firmly in the ground for dehusking grain were discovered at Harappā[1] and Mohenjodaro.[4] An hour-glass type mortar with a woman wielding a long pounder is sculpted at

Drawings from the Bhimbetka caves in MP depicting women pounding, rolling, and grinding.

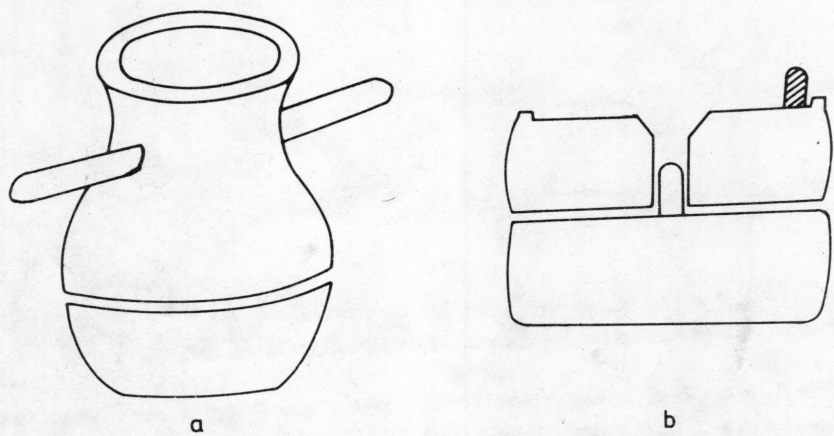

Querns consisting of two heavy stones employing two women (*left*), one woman (*right*).

A panel from the great stūpa at Sānchi (2nd century BC) showing rolling, pounding, and winnowing operations.

Stone pulley found in Mohenjodaro and in Lothal.

Sānchi.[8] The *Dasakumāracharita* (6th-7th centuries AD) graphically describes the pounding of grain in a mortar of arjuna wood using a heavy pestle of khadira wood, with an iron-ringed tip,[9] and a Tamil work of about the 3rd century AD describes 'white rice, well-cleaned in pounders set in iron rings'.[10] Sanskrit terms for the flat grinding quern (drshad), mortar (ulūkhala) and pestle (musāla) are suspected to be borrowings from even earlier Munda usage.[11] In south India also, grain crushers, milling stones, mortars and pestles have been found in several neolithic sites of the 2nd millennium BC[12]. Information is scarce on the historicity of the wooden dhenki or foot-pounder of Bengal and the Indo-Gangetic plain; since it is the vehicle of Nārada,[13] the dhenki itself must be fairly old. After pounding paddy, the chaff was removed by winnowing in a shūrpa (again perhaps a borrowed word), the winnowing tray that is still in use. Large quantities of pounded grain, such as would result from dhenki operation, were poured from a height in a slight draft in the open to separate a lighter heap of bran from the heavier grains. Sieves for sifting were termed chalani and thithau in Vedic Sanskrit.[14]

Ways of cooking

Several cooking operations were in use since very early times. These were thālanam (drying), kvāthanam (parboiling), pachanam (cooking in water), svēdanam (steaming), bhavita (seasoning), apakva (frying), bharjanam (dry roasting), thandūram (grilling) and putapāka (baking). Devices for these operations developed in parallel.

Both above-ground and underground mud hearths were found in Kālibangan, an Indus Valley settlement.[15a] Chulahs carrying knobs, with one to three openings and of round and square shapes, have been unearthed at several sites. Those at Ahār, Navdatoli and Jorwē were dated 1500–1000 BC[16] and at Atranjikhera 600 BC.[15b] The Ajantā frescoes of the 7th century AD show a kitchen with knobbed chūlāhs.[17]

Baking, called putapāka, is not a common style of Indian cooking, but ovens of different sizes have been found at Mohenjodaro and other Indus Valley sites. Some of these are not for cooking, but are very large kilns for firing pottery (see Chapter 1, Box 3).[18a]

Roasting meat on spits was even part of the Vedic sacrifice,[19a] as described later in this Chapter. Meat roasted on a spit (shūla) is graphically described in the *Mahābhārata* (Chapter 5) and in

Scene from rural Bengal showing the dhenki.

south Indian literature (Chapter 4). The modern kabāb has therefore a long history in India.

Though a thavā for indirect grilling has not been specifically identified among the Indus Valley finds, a typical dough-kneading plate with sides sloping outwards was discovered at Mohenjodaro,[6b] besides rolling pins exactly like those of the present.[20a] The preparation of flat cakes on a broken earthenware plate (kapāla) is mentioned in *Sūtra* literature, and the purodāsha offering of the *Grhya Sūtra* sacrifice, the apūpa, was open-baked in a pan with a varying number of hollows resembling dishes, imparting a variety of shapes to the cake itself.[21] The south Indian kuzhi- or kuzhal-āppam made of rice is still baked on a stone with depressions in it. Other variations employ a covered concave grill, called a battalā in Karnātaka, or a hot tile (kenchu).[22a] Cooking between two plates with live coals both below and above was also employed; or the material was placed directly on coals, and the outer charred crust discarded before eating.

Steaming was termed svinnabhaksya or svēdanam.[23] The statement of the Chinese pilgrim Xuan Zang in the 7th century AD that 'India does not know the use of the steamer',[24] does not really deny the use of techniques to achieve steaming in simpler ways in which India has always excelled. One was to place the material, in lumps tied in thin cloth or in wicker baskets, over a wide mouthed vessel in which water was boiled,[22] or in trays or leaves supported inside a larger vessel. A wide bamboo tube with a pierced disc at the lower end, fixed tightly on the spout of a vessel in which water is boiled, has long been used in Kerala to steam the rice-coconut puttū. A tall earthen cylinder with many perforations all over it has been found in neolithic and Indus Valley sites. One use suggested for this, among others, is that it is a steam-cooking vessel.[15c]

Cooking for a prolonged period over a slow fire was known to have several virtues. In later times, the effect was enhanced by sealing the lid on the cooking vessel with a plastic dough. The style was called dumpukht in the north, and kanika in Kannada, in which it first finds literary mention in AD 1606, though it could have been in use even earlier. It is essential for making palāo by slow cooking of rice and meat using internally-generated steam under slight pressure, and may have received impetus as a Muslim refinement in cooking palaō and biriyāni.

Other cooking methods at present in use in the Indian kitchen can be briefly mentioned.[25] Bhunāo is the term used for an initial roasting of vegetables or meat to dry it down before boiling it into a wet or dry curry. The initial frying of spices in hot fat, not together but one after the other, before adding the vegetables or meat, constitutes baghār; sometimes the spices after the baghār operation may simply be used to dress the finished dish, say one of dhāl. Tālna has today come to mean deep-fat frying in a kadhāi, and bhunāna signifies tandoor-grilling. Fumigation, now termed dhuanār, is frequently alluded to even in early literature. It consists of rendering a dish fragrant with the aroma (of say ghee or cloves) by placing in the cooked dish a hot tile, or a small katōri of hot embers, or even a cup of onion skin, dropping the ghee or spice on this, and covering the dish to fumigate its contents.

A domestic operation of long standing is that of setting milk to curds, and of churning curds to butter. The Indus Valley almost certainly knew dairy operations, as witness the seals of the magnificant Kankrej bull still with us (Chapter 2). The *Rigveda* has several references to the churning of curds with a corrugated stick, the mixture after the operation being called prasādjya.[19b] Freshly-prepared butter was later called navaneetha, a favourite of the boy Krishna; butter prepared from fresh milk was called phanta (by Pānini) and kshīrotana-vaneetha (by Sushrutha), and the ghee made from it pāyasarpis (by Varāhamihira). Churning in an earthen pot with a stick, which is rotated by a woman using a stout rope wound round it, is shown at the Lakshmanā temple in Khajuraho.[8] The sound made is poetically compared to the 'growl of a tiger' in a Tamil poem of the 4th century AD;[10] to seed the milk, a pat of curd, poetically described as resembling a 'white mushroom' was employed. To sell her butter, the poet recalls, the cowherd's wife sets off 'placing the pot, with its speckled mouth, on her head, supported by a circlet of flowers'.[10] The Tamil literature of the first few centuries of the

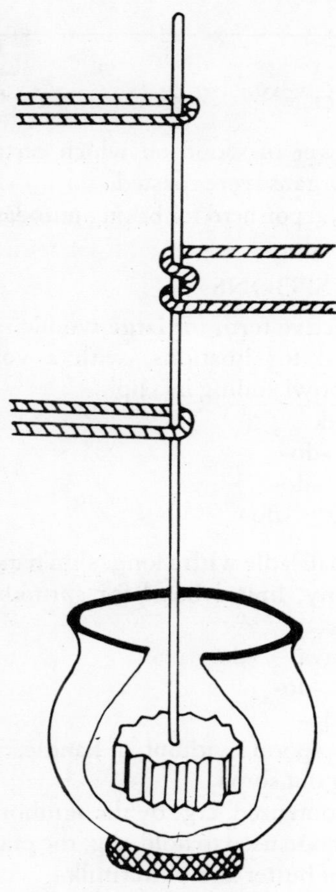
Curd churner.

Christian era is replete with references to cream (edu, perugu), curds, buttermilk, butter and ghee.[26] Herds of cattle in very large numbers were kept even by 2000 BC (see Chapter 4).[27]

Kitchen and table utensils

Among the numerous metal vessels actually found in the Indus Valley can be discerned a thāli-like pan; a kneading pan, a thavā-like plate, a copper frying pan with a turned-in handle,[6,20b] a heavy copper kumbha for fetching water,[5] and a lōtā-shaped vessel with a long spout rising from near the base.[28] At Chanhudaro were also found in abundance kitchen knives fashioned out of sharp chert flakes.[28] Nearly a thousand copper objects were found at Gāneshwar, which was probably the point of manufacture for supply to nearby towns like Kālibangan, Mohenjodaro and Harappā.[29a]

In Aryan times, even the *Rigveda* mentions numerous utensils.[9b,30] These were made of copper in the beginning, first termed simply āyas and later red āyas, to distinguish it from white āyas, or iron,[31a] when this metal came into common use about the end of the *Sūtra* period. Storage vessels for soma juice were the amatra, ahāra, kōsa, dru, kalasa, chamu and drōna, and to hold other liquids were the kumbha, āchechana, a gold kalasam, a water bucket udanchana, nested vessels called dhishana, and a milk bag (dhrti). There were drinking cups, cooking pots, a covered cauldron, spoons and ladles, strainers and knives. Larger utensils were the grinding stones (grāvan, adhri), mortar and pestle, roasting spit (shūla), bellows (dhmātr), winnowing basket, and leather storage bags for water, liquor and curds.[30] The Vedic sacrifices enshrined in the *Sūtras* employed an enormous number of utensils of rigidly-specified design and structure (see Box 16). The Soma rites, performed three times a day, employed twelve main vessels, including the sthālipāka (cooking in a pot) and the shūlagrāva (cooking on a spit).[32] For the pravargya rite, the ajamēdha (goat) sacrifice and the ashvamēdha (horse) sacrifice, special cauldrons for cooking, each with a different name (mahāvīra, gharma and ukha) had to be fashioned by hand (even though the potter's wheel was well-known) and fired afresh each time.[33] For making the ashtaka cake, exactly four shāravas of rice had to be used, while the purodāsha cake was baked in different shapes.[21] Not surprisingly, several of these vessels later became volume measures, like the drōna, kumbha, kalasha, ghata, sharāva and sthāli.[34]

Many of these objects from Vedic times are still with us, like the chulli (chūlāh), the spit or shūla (now the name of a roast pork dish of the Rājputs), the drshad (flat grinding stone), and the deep grinder with a plump upright stone (an essential item for idli and dōsa grinding in south India). Others are the kalasha, kumbha, pātra, bharjanapātra (now called kadāhi or kadhāi, from the later Prakrit word kataha which occurs in the *Rāmāyana* and *Sushrutha Samhitā*),[35,36] ājyasthāl (now thava), and small kitchen mortars. Some old utensils have altered, notably the sthāli, once a cooking pot, but now an eating

Box 16

UTENSILS OF THE VEDIC SACRIFICE[32,33]

CONTAINERS

pātra: sacrificial wooden vessels, placed in pairs on the sacrificial grass, and of five kinds (upamsu-, urdhva-, rtu-, sukra- and manthi-) for different uses

sambharanī: wooden vessel in which are placed the wet, pounded soma stalks

dronakalasa: bucket-type vessel covered with a filter to receive strained soma juice

pūtabhrt: clay trough to hold prepared soma juice

chamasa: oblong tub with handle, of ten types, for use by different priests for various purposes such as holding soma, drinking soma (by the priest), holding sacred water and holding sacred food in the vow rite

agrāyanasthāli: a vessel to receive strained soma juice in the agricultural rite when new fruits are eaten

sharāva: earthen dish holding water with which a new mother is sprinkled

pinvana: two milk vessels

sarpirdhana: bowl for butter

idapātra: a deep, oblong container with a flat rim to hold ghee

pranītāpranayana: -do-

nināhya: earthen waterpot buried in the ground to keep its contents cool

LARGE EARTHEN COOKING POTS

ukhā: square pot used to boil flesh

mahāvīra: wide-mouthed pot in which milk and ghee are heated

gharma: large earthen pot in which milk is boiled

kumbha: cooking vessel for boiling rice

shrāpana: cooking vessel

OVENS, BAKING, ROASTING

chulli: clay oven

kuplū: -do-

bhrāstra: -do-

shūla: skewer of wood on which certain animal organs were roasted

gārhyapatya: potsherd for baking purodāsha

kapālas: -do-

LADLES, SPOONS

sruk: collective term for large wooden ladles used for libations, with a yoni-shaped bowl ending in a lip

jūhu : a sruk

dhruvā: -do-

upabhrt: -do-

pracharani: -do-

darvī: a small ladle with a long, slim handle and a tiny, lipless bowl for sprinkling libations

sruvi *or* sruva: -do-

tragbila: -do-

vitasi: -do-

pariplava: spoon without a handle, for drawing out soma

havani: spoon used, e.g. by the agnihotr

grahani: spoon used to hold, e.g. the prasādādjya of butter and buttermilk

pariplupātra: a ladle

antardhāna: -do-

prasaka: a decanting vessel with a long handle and a large, cup-like bowl

OFFERING VESSELS

vāyavya: waisted, spouted cylinder used to make offerings to twelve deities

urdhvapātra: waisted, spouted cylinder

anvahāryasthāli: -do-

agrayanasthāli: -do-

akaraphālika: snake-shaped board, one-arm long, on which sesame seeds are offered in the sacrifice

STIRRERS, SCRAPERS

pārshra: stirrer-spoon for the marrow

meksana: wooden scraper with a square, flat head for stirring the flour and boiling water used in making purodāsha; dis-

Box 16 (*Contd.*)

carded after use

CUTTERS

svadhiti: knife to dissect sacrificed animal
sāsa: kitchen knife
sphya: wide, dagger-shaped wooden implement used for several purposes during the sacrifice

FIRE UTENSILS

arani: a spindle (worked with a length of string) and a wooden board carrying a friction hole used for raising fire
satā: two large vessels for carrying embers
parīshasa: tongs to lift the gharma from the fire
upavesana: wooden poker for stirring the fire, and for removing embers
dhrshti: a pair of pokers used for stirring the fire and for removing embers

STRAINERS

pavitrā: strainer made out of sheep's wool used for filtering soma juice
karōtara: a strainer

POUNDERS, GRINDERS

ulūkhala: a wooden mortar
musāla: wooden pestle for the ulūkhala
drshad: lower flat grinding stone
drshadputra: upper milling stone
upalā: -do-
peshanī: the two parts of the milling outfit taken together

BASKETS

palva: winnowing basket holding sacrificial grain
shūrpa: winnowing tray of bamboo or reed

LEAF UTENSILS

patravali: plate or cup made of leaves stapled together with splinters
purnaputa: a funnel of folded palāsha leaf, in which a lump of boiled rice is hung on a tree

plate, thāli.

Further utensils appear in later times. The Sānchi stūpa has a small goblet with crossed straps,[8] perhaps the bhrngāra or water jar allowed to a Buddhist monk as one of eight personal items.[19c] Patanjali (mid 2nd century BC) has a tiny water jug, kundikā, for student use,[37] and the *Rāmāyana* mentions three drinking goblets, an iron pan (aluhi) and a boiler (pitara).[19e] Among the items of interest in the *Amarakōsha* compilation of the 5th century AD are a deep frying vessel (rjisha), roasting plate (bhrāsta, perhaps the modern thavā), straminers (karkari and galantika) and leather bottles (kutuh and kutup) for storing oil.[14] At three places in Bānā's *Harshacharita* occur a tangle of various utensils forming part of the kitchen entourage of the king while camping.[38,39] These defy sorting-out, but appear to be water pots, small pots, jars, a cup, and a molasses-pot (phanita-sthāli), also baking trays (thalaka and sakatika), a simmering pan (thapika, Hindi tai), saucepan (charu), thavā (thapaka) and spit (hasthaka).

In south India, the archaeological record is of course much older than the earliest Tamil literature. The latter belongs to the first few centuries of the Christian era, when utensils had obviously developed a good deal.[26,40,41] Mortars of wood and stone used to pound paddy and rice were called ural and ulukhal, words resembling the Sanskrit ulūkhala. Grinding stones, frequently shaped to resemble animals (for example, the tortoise), were called ammi, tiruvai, āttukal and kulavi, and the stone mullers puttil and vatigai. Pots were made either of clay or stone, and had a variety of names. Liquor was served in a bowl called mandai.[42] The kalam and kundam were versatile pots, the kallu-kundam being a toddy pot. Pots could be suspended from the roof in a rope sling (shimili), or kept in stands called pattadai, shumudu or shummadu. There were three types of agappai spoons, thattai-sanda- and shirra-, and many other ladles called sattuvam, karandi, muttai, thaduppu, maravai, thotti, kinnam, marakkal (or abanam) and vattil, a flat ladle of stone, wood or metal. Wood fric-

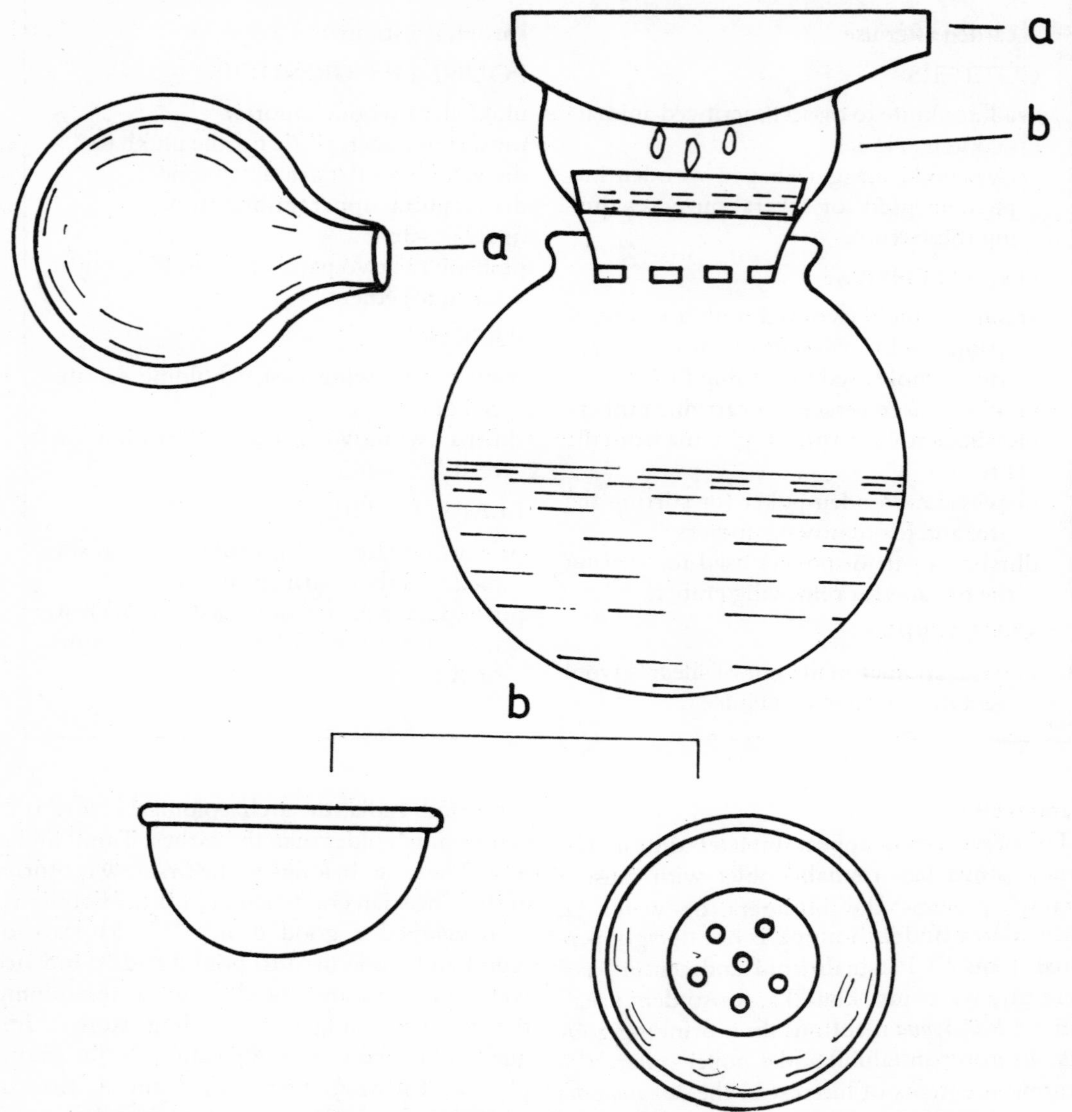

Distillation outfit, reconstructed by assembling clay articles found in several Indus Valley sites.

tion devices were used to raise a fire, censers (tadavu, indalam) to hold embers, and pokers (nelikōl) for raking the fire. In a pot called kumpatti a perpetual fire was kept going, into which was poked a stick called sulundu, sometimes tipped with sulphur.[26] The winnowing pan was murram, the sieve salladai, and plates for various uses went by such names as sinnam, sulagu, thattu and murrul. The kūdu was a bamboo coop to protect food from flies. Kitchens had mats (pāī) to sit on and lofts for storage (paran, idanam, kaludu, padagam and panavai). Leaf plates made of the ambal (lotus), banyan and teak are described in earlier literature, but by the 8th century AD, banana leaves were in common use for dining.[43a] Practically all these objects, and the words describing them, persist to this day. In the south also, as in the north, some vessels evolved into measures of volume, like kalam, padi, nāli and uri.[34] Lacking copper ore, this stage was largely skipped in favour of iron utensils from abundant raw material.[18b]

So similar were the utensils used in the north and the south, that a book written in Sanskrit about AD 1700 by a south Indian king, Basavarāja of Keladi (see Box 14), uses Sanskrit terms to denote many utensils in the southern kitchen, like gharatta for the grinding stone, pravani for the frying pan, and kharpava for the griddle.[44] Of course there are specifically regional utensils. Punjab has the distinctive tandoori baking oven. Kāshmīr has items with Central Asian affiliations, like the large trāem with its cover, the sarpōsh (on which is served wazwan food cooked by professionals), the khandakari (samovar) used for brewing the aromatic kāhwāh tea, and certain distinctive ladles used in cooking and serving.

Current Indian utensils: The thavā (*top left*), the thāli (*top right*), the kadhāi (*bottom right*) and the parāt (*bottom left*).

Large-Scale Operations

The large-scale pounding of grain in the bigger Indus Valley cities on circular brick platforms with a central depression, and its storage in very large granaries, has been described in Chapter 2. Hardly ever in later Indian history till present times was grain ever procured and stored by the state on such a scale. About AD 1300 Alauddin Khilji attempted to hold the price-line for food grains by procuring and storing them in granaries in Delhi.[45a] About AD 1350, Ibn Battūta describes grain that had been stored in granaries in the walls surrounding Delhi for ninety years: 'I have seen the rice brought out of one of these stores, and although it had gone black in colour it was still good to the taste.'[45] None of these were really large or sustained operations.

Professional cooking and dining

The king's kitchen was called rasavati or mahānasa,[46a] and is depicted in Cave 17 of the Ajanta frescoes as an open thatched hut.[47] Apart from food variety, the cook had also to ensure freedom from poison, for which an official food taster was usually in attendance.[46b] The cook went by many names, such as alarika, sūpakāra, ōdanika, bhōjanadatr, and sudas.[48] There were also specialists, like the avalika (who regulated the spicing and flavouring of dishes), apūpika (for baking) and kandavika (for frying).[14] In pre-Aryan south India, poets in particular expected lavish hospitality from royalty; one of them was fed with 'the soft boiled legs of sheep fed on sweet grass, and large chops of hot meat roasted on the points of spits . . . (besides) sweets of excellent taste in varied shapes', and of course strong liquor, sometimes scented and flavoured.[49]

Eating in public was not permitted to austere brahmins during Vedic and even later times,[50] but there were no such inhibitions on others. Eating houses were a common feature of town-life, and in the commercial areas of the city were shops, piled with 'cooked rice and prepared food ready for eating, whose pungent odours assailed the nostrils.'[46c] In south India, eating out was much in vogue, and hotels and restaurants in the cool of the evening vended sweetened rice, fruits, sugar candies, tender greens, edible yams, and savoury meat preparations.[51] On the seashore were kaazhiyar and kuuviyar, vendors of snacks like the āppam, idi-āppam, adai and moodagam.[52] Doubtless these catering establishments used normal domestic cooking practices and utensils, as they still do, only on a larger and more intensive scale.

Alcoholic drinks

Soma juice, as we have seen (Box 5 and Chapter 5) was not an alcoholic drink but an exhilarant prepared in an elaborate ritualistic fashion by crushing the raw material in a mortar and pestle, or between two stones, followed by filtration into special ritual tubs and jars (Box 16). Soma was drunk, both by priest and devotee, after mixing with water, milk, curds, ghee, honey or grains.

Was liquor made in the Indus Valley? Apparently not merely brewed but even distilled. A distillation assembly has been put together using clay objects commonly found at Harappan sites.[53] A circular basin, with a wide hole at the bottom, was fitted snugly on the mouth of a water pot. In the hole was cradled a smaller basin with several perforations in its base. Alcohol boiled in the lower pot rose through the holes; it condensed on the underbelly of a handled receptacle, holding cold water, placed on top of the assembly, to fall in drops into the annular space of the fitted basin. The only special vessel required was the small perforated basin; this repeatedly turns up at Indus Valley sites, with no satisfactory use yet assigned to it.

Surā in the *Rigveda* represents an intoxicating liquor distilled after fermentation of barley or wild paddy. While the use of soma is praised, that of surā is mostly condemned (Chapter 5).

Later Vedic literature has kilāla (a sweetened drink made from fermented cereals), māsara (a filtered rice gruel liquor) and parisruta (a fermented product from certain flowers and grass). Subsequently numerous liquors find mention. The *Rāmāyana* has four,[54] Kautilya names twelve, and Charaka lists no less than 84 kinds of alcoholic liquor. In Box 9, these beverages have been listed in roughly chronological order.

According to Charaka, nine sources were employed for fermentation. These were sugarcane juice, guda, molasses, honey, coconut water, sweet palmyra sap and mahua flowers. The fruits used included the grape, mango, woodapple, date palm, bēr, banana, apricot, jackfruit, the rose-apple or jāmbu, the purple jamoon, the pomegranate, bilva, rājādana (chironji) and mādanaphala (*Mimusops elengi,* Hindi maulsari). Flavouring materials employed were fragrant flowers like the kadamba, pātala, jāthi and dhātaki, and spices like the haridrā (haldi), black pepper and elaichi. Astringent materials utilized are given as the areca nut (pūgaphala), and barks of trees like the kapittha, mesashringi and kadamba.

The method of production of various liquors receives some attention only in the *Arthashāstra* of Kautilya, yet even this description is couched in such terse language that any interpretation is rather subjective, and each translator gives his own version.[55,56,57] The ferment (kinva) consisted of a mix of one drona of māsha (urad) pulse, a third more of rice, and a karsha portion of morata (*Alangium salviifolium*). To this could optionally be added a mix of one karsha each of six spices that included cinnamon, cardamom and three peppers. These spices seemed to have acted both as flavourants and as a source of enzymes, as they do for example in the preparation of the fermented pulse patty, warri or wadian. Some ambiguity arises because these same spices could also be added at the end for flavouring, and the same is true of astringents, and of sweeteners like jaggery, phanita, honey, mahua flowers and liquorice (which can also function of course as fermentable raw materials). Periods of fermentation are never specified, nor is the important question of whether the product is used as a wine or after distillation.

Prasannā is made using 12 ādhakas of (probably rice) flour, 8 parts of water and 5 prasthas of ferment. Since the latter contains flavourants, the final product must have carried some flavour, and no additives are mentioned. Medhaka was made from rice using a much higher proportion of ferment; if svetasurā was indeed the same as medhaka, as one commentator assumes,[56] then it was probably a distilled drink. Maireya was a drink of the nobility. Kshatriyas were not permitted drinks brewed from cereal flours,[19b] and maireya was apparently a guda-or sugar-based, flower-flavoured, distilled product, to which was further added a sweetener, astringents and pepper; sweetening could be done either with expensive honey, cheaper guda or even cheaper phanita (molasses).[29] Āsava, according to one interpretation, was merely an infusion of phanita, kapittha and honey, which could be strong or light depending on the quantity of ingredients employed.[56] Yet the *Rāmāyana* describes an āsava as a strong drink,[19e] and this seems to find support in the long list of sweeteners, spices and astrginents prescribed as additives for it even in the *Arthashāstra*. Undoubtedly a strong drink was shīdhu, which was fermented sugarcane juice distilled over fragrant red dhātaki flowers. It was stated to be a favourite of the non-Aryan population.[19e]

Fruits and certain flowers were also fermented to give distinctive products, which must have also been expensive. A mango-based wine called sahakārasurā yielded the spiced product mahāsurā. From the jāmbu fruit and from dates came āsavas with the parent names, while the ber fruit yielded kaula, and fruits of the palmyra palm thālakka. From jasmine flowers came jāthi, madhuka flowers yielded the strong distilled drink vārunī, and kadamba flowers the wine called kādambarī.

In south India, toddy was brewed in pots tied below incisions made in the spathes of the palmyra palm; the intensely sweet juice (now called neera) was collected overnight, and fermented during the heat of the day. 'Toddy', we read in the *Puranānūru*, 'flows like water' in the port town of Muziris.[40] The practice of smearing the pots with lime to prevent fermentation, if the juice was needed for drinking or to make jaggery, is an ancient one, as such pots turn up in excavations. The sweetest toddy was claimed to be produced in Kuttanād, now in Kērala.[58] Arrack, distilled from toddy, was a favourite of sailors.[41] Liquor was also brewed in strong-mouthed jars from paddy and from rice; pounded germinated paddy mixed with a porridge of rice was stated to yield 'after two days and two nights a high-flavoured wine'.[10] The flavour of wine was enhanced by burying it underground, filled in the hollows of stout bamboo stems.[26] Thoppi was a home-brewed rice liquor,[26] and richer people fermented rice in the presence of fragrant flowers such as the dhātaki.[51] In mountainous areas, wine was brewed from honey, and again matured underground before use.[26] During the first two centuries of the Christian era, when trade with the Roman empire was at its height, Italian wine was imported by royalty in two-handled amphorae, large numbers of which have been found in a warehouse of the times excavated at Arikamedu, near Pondicherry. A favourite drink of women was munnīr (triple-liquid), a mixture of tender coconut juice, sugarcane juice and palmyra juice (probably unfermented)[40] Liquor was very widely consumed, and there are as many as 60 pure Tamil names for it to be found in early literature.[26]

Parched, puffed and parboiled rice

Even the *Rigveda* mentions dhānāh, which is beaten or parched barley, as well as saktu (the present sattu), the gritty flour derived from parched grains of barley, and later of rice.[19b] Charaka lists not only parched barley but also parched pulses like mung, masoor and mattar under the generic name bhrstadhānya. Other Sanskrit words for parched grains are ulumbāh, lājāh, prthuka and chipita, the last of which survives in chivda or chidva, the fried, spiced snack made from parched rice.[59] Chura is the current term for parched and beaten rice.

In south India, the *Karuntogai* (*c.* 6th century AD) described the manufacture of aval (still the term for beaten rice) by flattening out wet paddy using a pestle of black heartwood.[41] The *Perumpānūrrupadai*, one of the *Patthupāttu*, also mentions aval by name.

Though a commercial product both in the north and south, the method of manufacture of parched or beaten rice was the same as by the domestic process, namely to moisten the grains with water, then flatten them, and finally to parch them afterwards on hot sand. Professional parchers, pāpad makers (kāgal kutas), oil-crushers (ghānchis) and distillers of wine even accompanied the armies of kings in the past.[60]

Puffed grains may have been denoted by the Sanskrit terms missita and dhānidhaka, but this is not certain. The term pori occurs in Tamil in the 6th century AD.[26] Its production was probably effected by the simple method in use at present, that of throwing handfuls of rice on very hot sand. The chickpea was subject to puffing to give a porous, crunchy product; this is used as such as a snack food, or is ground into a flour called besan (kadalai-māu in Tamil), which is the batter of choice all over India for making a variety of deep-fried snacks. The term pori for puffed rice in south India occurs in early Sangam literature. In the *Karuntogai*, it finds mention as a favourite food eaten with milk or as a sweet confection.

Parboiled rice, pulungalarisi in Tamil, first occurs in the *Sirupān-arrupudai* of slightly later Sangam literature.[26] The method of production is not described but could have been the same as the one later in use, of soaking paddy in cold water for a few days, then boiling the grain till soft, drying in the sun and dehusking the paddy either by pounding in a mortar, or by grinding between stones.

Oilseed processing

At least two oil-bearing seeds, sesame and mustard, were known to the Harappans; they had copper frying pans with a lip, and small stone querns on which to grind spices. Body fats of various animals and that of milk were available (Chapter 2). All the elements of frying were therefore present. How the oil was obtained is not known, but boiling the ground fatty material with water is a simple enough procedure.

The *Rigveda* mentions two devices for crushing soma juice, the grinding stones (grā-

Sculpture showing an oilpress in the 12th century AD temple at Darāsuram in Tamilnadu.

van) and the mortar-and-pestle, ulūkhala-musala.[61] Associations with grāvan in several spoken Prakrit languages (ghavan in Marāthi for a stone mortar, ghatani for a mill in Gujarāthi, and ghatanika for a heavy club in the *Rāmāyana*) seem to have yielded the colloquial word ghana, later ghani, for the oilpress. From ulūkhala, and ulūkhalika for grinding, came khali (oilcake), ukhli and okhli for small mortars, and kolhu for the press. The Tamil chekku for an oilpress is clearly from chakra, a wheel, by way of the Pāli chakka, from which also derives the grinding stone chakki. Tamil works of the 7th and 8th centuries AD use the term chekku. Thus the three terms ghani, kolhu and chekku for the oilpress all seem to stem from early Sanskrit words for crushing devices.[62]

The device itself now takes the form of an animal drawing a loadbeam to which is attached a pestle rotating in a mortar to achieve oilseed

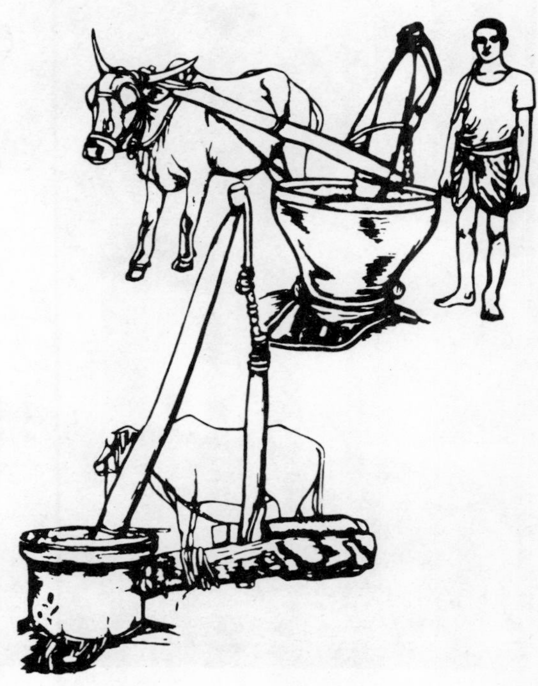

Two designs of the ghani.

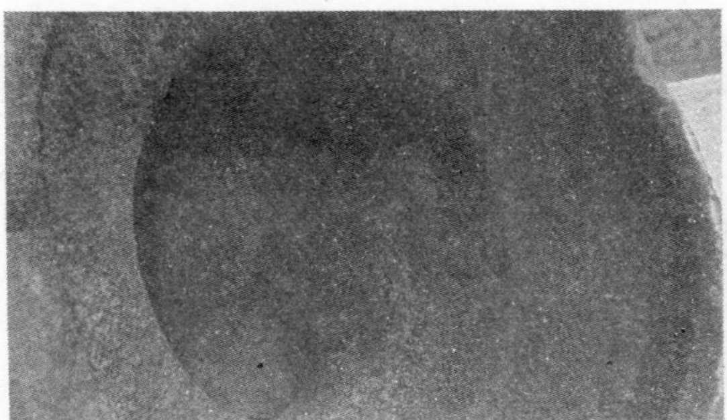

Crushing devices assembled at Dwārkā, Gujarāt (also *below*)

crushing. Sanskrit words for an oil mill (*thaila-peshana-yantra*) and for an oilmiller (*thailika, thēlika*) occur from Pānini (6th century BC) onwards. The use of animal power is never mentioned, and perhaps the miller (called chakrin in the *Amarakōsha*)[14] walked round in a circle himself. Numerous oilseeds are listed as being crushed in the *Manusmriti* and the *Arthashāstra*.

Few old oilpresses have survived. A number of crushing units have been assembled at Dwārka in western Gujarāt; though labelled soma crushers, these appear to be typical ghanis, and have been dated by one authority to the first two centuries AD.[62] A century ago, 400–500 thousand ghanis served to crush all the vegetable oil needed for the use of Indians throughout the country. Thereafter modern machinery began to displace these ancient devices.

Sugarcane pressing and juice processing

Sugarcane crushers of the barrel type closely resemble the oilpress, both the principle of liquid expulsion, and the means of doing so, being the same. Usually the sugarcane press is larger in size. The Sanskrit word ikshu for sugarcane gave rise to the later terms ikh and ukh, and to

Sugarcane crushing in a kolhu, from a Jain manuscript, AD 1540.

ukhli or okhli for a small mortar.[63] The terms kolhu and ghani are both used also for the sugarcane press, and in Marāthi the term khali or khalli denotes solid substances derived from crushing, even when as dissimilar as oilcake and sugar.[64] The Buddhist literature refers to sugarcane juice being extracted with a machine (yantra),[19c] and in the Kushāna period (*c.* AD 200), machine-extracted juice is declared inferior,[19b] presumably to the hand-extracted product.

The other device for crushing sugarcane is the roller mill with rotating cylinders. This seems to have originated from a similar mangle device for removing seeds from cotton,[65] but perhaps only as late as AD 1500.

Harappan cities have yielded charcoal derived from some *Saccharum* species, which may or may not be the sugarcane.[66] The *Rigveda* has kushāra, which seems to stand for the sugarcane.[19a] The *Atharvaveda* alludes to the chewing of ikshu, and later literature has frequent references to it.[19a] The *Sūtra* literature,[19a] 800–300 BC, notes the thickening of sugarcane juice to give first phanita, and then solid guda (jaggery). The next stage, that of rock sugar or khand, is first described by Alexander's party (326 BC), who describe 'stones the colour of frankincense, sweeter than figs or honey'.[66] Charaka refers to a sugarcane variety paundraka from Pundra, or north Bengal, and even derives the word guda from Gauda (Bengal).[19g] Kautilya (300 BC) describes all forms of sugar, upto sharkara or granulated sugar, as does Patanjali (mid-2nd century BC).[19d] In the time of Harsha (7th century AD) a delegation from China visited him to learn the technique of sugar production in India. A method, now lost, used in Bengal, was to cover gur with a moss called pata, which devoured the reddish-brown impurities to leave granules of cystal sugar.[66a]

Jaggery in south India was also derived from the sweet juice of the palmyra palm spathe, and in Bengal from the trunk of the date palm, slaked lime being smeared on the pot to prevent fermentation.[10] The juice is simply boiled down and poured into coconut shell halves to set to jaggery or vellam, a word found in the earliest Tamil literature. Sugarcane was also processed in the south, and cane sugar crystals were termed ayir, meaning gravel, which is exactly the meaning of the Sanskrit sharkarā as well. The modern Tamil term sakkarai is clearly of Sanskrit origin.

Honey

The prehistoric cave paintings at Bhimbetka (Chapter 1) show men despoiling beehives built on rocks, perhaps about 6000 BC.[67] Later three kinds of honey were commonly recognized:[67] māksika from the common honey bee (*Apis cerana indica*), also called by the same Sanskrit name; bhramara honey from a large black rock bee (*Apis dorsata*) of the same name; and ksaudra from the dwarf ksudra bee (*Apis florea*).[68] Charaka and Sushrutha mention several others: pauttika honey from the tiny puttika bee; and chātra, arghya, auddhālika and dāla, all of which have been identified in modern terms.[68]

Even as early as the *Rigveda* the Rbhu brothers are credited with building artificial hives of reeds and straw, in which were fixed sections from a natural hive;[67] a year later, four sections were removed and the rest left in. In later times hives were kept in logs or pots in a horizontal position, or on four-legged stools (perhaps to prevent ants from entering), or in a hole in the wall; this procedure is still in use in Kashmir, both ends of the hole being detachable.[69] When ready, the bees are smoked out and a few combs removed; when the ends are replaced, the swarm soon returns.

The *Mahābhārata* has references to bee gardens, apiary keepers and pollen-yielding plants, suggesting some degree of commercialization by then.[68] Generally, honey was collected, both in the north and south of India, by forest dwellers for sale or barter (Chapter 4). The *Mahāvamsa* tells a tale of three brothers, two of whom collected honey for sale by the third.[68] Beeswax is called by the expressive term madhucchishta (honey-residues) in the *Harshacharita* of Bāna.[68]

Salt

Certain pottery moulds with convolutions inside found in the Indus Valley were probably salt moulds of a kind still used in India.[20a] The *Rigveda* does not mention salt, but thereafter many types of salt are noted. Five of the more important types are first mentioned in the *Vinaya Pitaka*,[19c] and later by Charaka.[19f] These are rock salt, sea salt, vida, aubhida (perhaps also the udhedaga of Kautilya) and sauvarchala. Sushrutha has nine others, most of which appear to be mineral salts of both sodium and potassium, [19f] and Kautilya mentions 'salt from the Sindhu country'.

Sea salt production is described, but not that of any other kind. Sea water was evaporated in long, shallow beds, and salt simply raked off. In Kautilya's account, the lavanadhyāksha (Superintendent of Salt) scrutinized salt manufacturing practices and regulated trade, employing a system of licences for which either a fixed fee was paid, or a share of output retained.[70] The Superintendent also sold salt received by Government (one-sixth of produce) as its share, profit being ensured by the five per cent difference between the king's measure and the common measure (see Box 2), and differences also between buying and selling prices.

The activities of salt vendors living in the coastal littoral of south India are frequently described in literature: 'hearths of stones left by the salt vendors', and 'white salt manufactured in clayey beds'.[10,41] Five names are recorded for salt beds (nannugupalam, alkkar, uvarkkalam, uvalagam and kazhi),[26] and places at which sea salt was manufactured were Markanam, Kanyakumāri, Variyūr, Aythurai and Bāpatla.[26] Salt was vended as head loads, and transported in carts across the peninsula by the producer moving with his family. Salt and honey were principal measures of value, being exchanged for food commodities like rice.

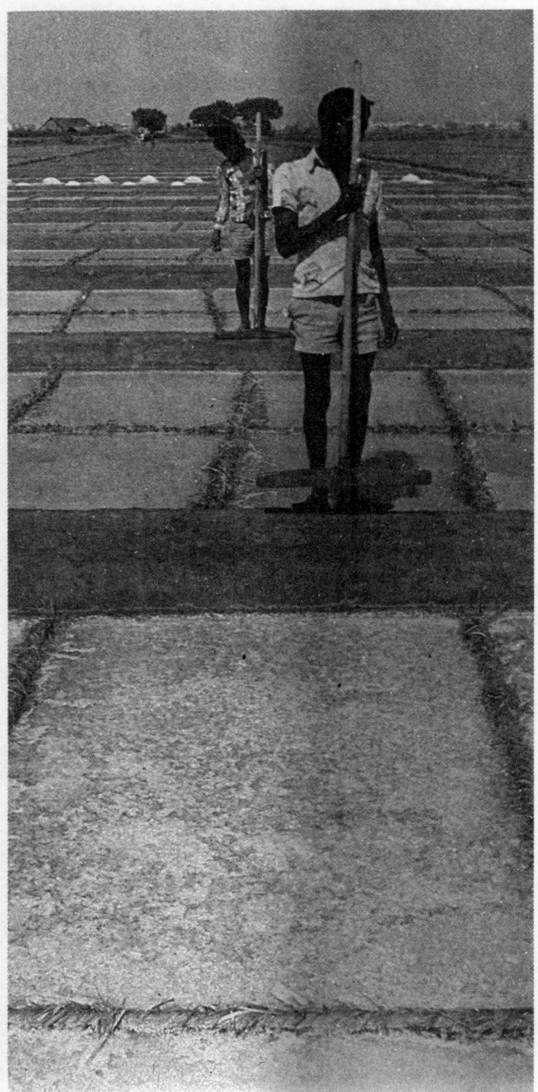

Evaporation of sea water to yield salt.

Cold water and ice

Evaporative cooling in really porous clay jars was the time-honoured technique of cooling water. In the *Harshacharita* of the 7th century AD,[39] whey to be used as a gargle by the king's dying father is kept 'in a new vessel besmeared with wet clay', and later 'buttermilk was kept very cold [shishira-kriyā] in pails packed with ice', which may have been brought, as it was in much later Moghul times, from the Himalayan heights by river and then overland.

In 1775, an English judge recorded a description of ice-making in Allāhabād by overnight cooling of water during the three winter months, when the temperature was close to freezing, but never below it.[71] Boiled water was poured a couple of centimetres deep into small shallow porous vessels and the latter placed in shallow pits, well insulated at the bottom and sides, that had been scooped out in the ground in quiet and windless surroundings. Overnight ice would form, sometimes all the way through, and this was collected and kept in insulated pits. The British expanded the technique, and a century later were making 23–29 tonnes in one night and storing it for use all the year round.[72]

The Moghuls, according to the *Ain-i-Akbari* (AD 1590) used post-carriages and bearers to transport ice to Delhi. 'Out of the ten boats employed for the transport of ice, one arrives daily at the capital (then Lahore), each being manned by four boatmen. . . twelve pieces of ten to four seers (a seer is about a kilogram) arrive daily . . . All ranks use ice in summer; the nobles use it throughout the whole year.'[73] One of the closest sources to Delhi was the mountain near Kasauli called Choori Chandni-ki-Dhar, which is perennially covered with snow.[74]

According to Abul-Fazl, it was Akbar who introduced saltpetre for cooling water in India. The French traveller Francois Bernier (1665) says that the 'higher sorts of people' cooled Ganges water by pouring it into tiny flagons, which for the space of seven or eight minutes were placed in water into which three or four handfuls of saltpetre had been thrown.[75] In the 18th century in British India, 'every family had its abdar, the servant who stayed up all night constantly moving an earthenware jug of water in a larger vessel containing saltpetre and water which produced a chilled liquid by morning'.[76]

About 150 years ago, a persevering American, Frederic Tudor, after 28 years of experimenting with shipping ice to the West Indies, succeeded in transporting huge chunks of the frozen water of Wenham Lake from Massachusetts to South America and beyond using 'felt and sweet-smelling pine sawdust' as packing materials.[77]

On 6 September 1833 the ship *Tuscany* arrived in Calcutta from Boston with 180 tons of its ice-cargo (two thirds of that loaded) still intact, and ice houses for storage of the precious commodity were built in Calcutta, Madras and Bombay.[69] Referring to this, Thoreau in his *Walden* poetically remarks that 'soon the waters of my beloved Walden will blend with the sacred waters of the Ganges'.[78] In fact the massive imports of ice between 1830 and 1870 from New England to India led to the appointment of the first American Consul-General in Bombay in 1838, and even stimulated the industrial development of New England.

In 1874, the International Ice Company started manufacturing ice in Madras by the 'steam process',[77] and in 1878 Calcutta followed suit.[72] Alongside, for domestic cooling and preservation, newspapers advertised cabinet refrigerators of polished oak in which a block of ice was held in a galvanized iron tray at the top, and items placed in the lined cold cabinet below.[79] Box 17 describes how ice-cream developed as a consequence of ice production.

Box 17

WATER-ICES AND ICE-CREAMS

Marco Polo is credited with having brought back to Italy, in the 13th century AD, recipes for various water-ices that had long been consumed in China.[79] French and English cookbooks of the 18th century mention butter ices and cream ices, and the term ice-cream first appears in America in May 1777 in the *New York Gazette*. The author was Philip Lenzi who described himself as a confectioner from London. In 1797 a public announcement for the sale and supply of ice-cream to the citizens of Baltimore was made in a newspaper,[80] and in 1809 Dolly Madison, wife of the President of the United States, served it to state guests with considerable attendant publicity. The same Frederic Tudor who brought ice from America to India (see text) made ice-cream in the West Indies using milk, cream and fruit juices in 1810 in an effort to establish a trade in ice that would help to render 'a beverage . . . or tepid water . . . palatable' in a hot climate,[77] and he had an enormous success in selling both ice and ice cream in South America, Iran and India.[80] Ice cream was first manufactured commercially in 1851 by one Fussel in Baltimore,[80] and soon afterwards in Washington D.C., Boston and New York.[79] To make the product in the home using a freezing mixture of ice and salt, churning pails cranked by hand became popular soon after the turn of the century in Europe, England and the colonial empires.

Long before all this happened a frozen dessert had been developed in Ḍelhi, either brought by the Moghuls from Kābūl or originated by them in India. This was the kulfi, which derived its name from the conical metal device in which it was made.[80] The *Ain-i-Akbari* of 1590 describes its preparation in Emperor Akbar's royal kitchens by freezing a mixture of khoa, pistachio nuts and kēsar (zaffrān) essence in conical metal receptacles after sealing the contents with dough, exactly as it is made today.

Chapter 10

REGIONAL CUISINES

So far, through archaeological and literary evidence, we have followed the foods of north India and the Gangetic plain on the one hand, and those of the Tamil country on the other. For central and western India, only archaeological evidence could be considered, and without the evidence of contemporary literature, regional cuisines can hardly be discerned.

In the south, Kannada and Telugu writing assumed a distinctive shape about the 6th century AD, and Malayālam some four centuries later. Bengali took form about the 10th century and Gujarāthi in the west at the same time. Poets living in Gujarāt and Kāshmir had, however, written in Sanskrit in earlier times. Consequently certain regional eating habits do find mention.

In this chapter, an attempt will be made to trace the patterns of food in Karnātaka and Gujarāt from historical literary works, and, though to a more limited extent, in Bengal and Kāshmir. At the same time we will also look at the distinctive cuisines that have developed in various areas of the country among groups with a distinct ethnic or religious affinity.

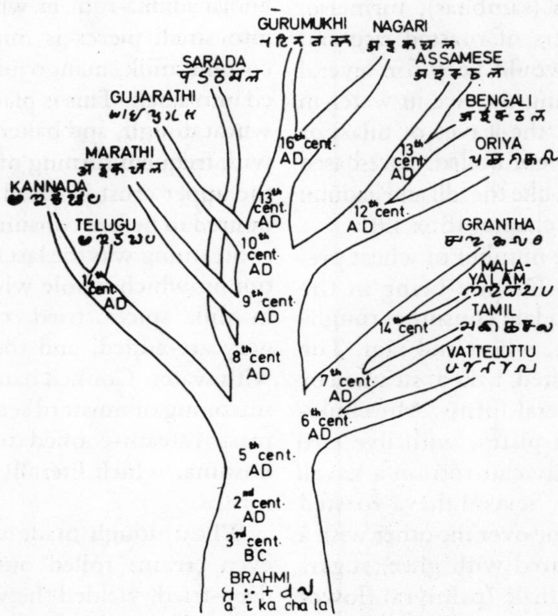

The evolution of the scripts of various Indian languages.

South India

Karnātaka

Sources: The *Sūpa Shāstra* of Mangarasā (AD 1516) is an exhaustive work on cooking,[1] and the published version also carries an Appendix with a number of extracts of earlier and later writers spanning the period AD 920 to 1700.[2] The *Lokōpakāra (*AD 1025) of the Jain poet Chāvundarāya is also of particular interest in that it has an entire chapter devoted to cooking.[3] Names of dishes mentioned for the first time over a period of eight centuries are recorded in Box 18. Some of these foods will now be described.

Food dishes: Rice had pride of place after the 10th century AD in Karnātaka.[1,2,3] Four varieties of a cooked rice-ghee combination flavoured with garlic and salt, called kattōgara, are illustrative. Crushed pāpad was mixed in to yield one variation, crisp-fried sandigēs made of the ash gourd another, and various cooked greens gave rise to yet others. A mung dhāl khichadi is mentioned by this name. Further flavour changes were rung by mixing in lime, hulī (sāmbhār), turmeric, tamarind, or the powders of roasted rice and chana.[3] Curd rice that would keep for several days was made by cooking the rice in water in which, as a preliminary, the leaves of tulasi or mādala (*Citrus medica*) were boiled. Rice-based preparations of Karnātaka like the idli and kadubu are described later in this chapter (Box 19).

An exceptionally large number of wheat preparations are described. Despite being in the south, Karnātaka, even today, consumes roughly equal amounts of rice, wheat and rāgi. The wheat items could be roasted, baked, steamed or fried. Roasting took several forms. Mucchula-rōti was baked between plates, with live coal above and below, and kivichu-rōti on a kavali (thavā) with a little ghee. Several thavā-roasted rōtis could be mounted one over the other with a pierced stick, and flavoured with ghee, sugar, edible camphor and the thalē (palmyra) flower to yield the chucchu-rōti. A stack of ghee-smeared circles mounted one over the other, savadu-rōti, was baked on a griddle under cover of a cup. A cup cover above, live coals below, and a ball of dough within yielded uduru-rōti, from which the blackened crust was peeled off before consumption. Mandigē or mandagē was a delicate baked product; when baked on a heated tile (kenchu) it was called white-mandigē, and when over-heated but still very soft it was ushnavarta-mandigē, which when exposed to air became vāyuputa-mandigē. The stuffing could be varied. Sugar and ghee yielded khanda-mandigē; use of multi-layered fillings of cooked chana, coconut shreds, dates and raisins yielded a mandigē variation called pēranē-hūrigē. Today the mandigē or māndē of Belgaum is a very large and fine parāta stuffed with finely-ground sugar containing cardamom powder, baked on an upturned clay pot, and folded into a moderately stiff rectangle.

True baking within a seal of wheat dough, called kanika in Kannada, is used to make the bhōjanadhika-rōti, in which mandigē broken up into small pieces is mixed with milk, cream, coconut milk, mango juice and sugar, and pressed into a ball. This is placed within a covering of wheat dough, and baked under seal on a hot tile with frequent turning of the vessel. When done, the upper crust is sliced off and ghee and sugar poured in before consumption.

Steaming was the last step in a complex operation in which whole wheat flour is first cooked in milk; spices, fried coconut grating and jaggery are added, and the mass is cooked again with water. Cooked banana flowers are put in, a seasoning of mustard seeds given, and the whole mass is steam-cooked to yield gōdhuma-rambakusuma, which literally means wheat-flowers-mix.

Wheat dough made with sweetened milk or even cream, rolled out into circles and then deep-fried, yielded the yeriappa and the babara. Balls of dough made with wheat flour, curds and sweetened cream were deep-fried to produce pavuda. A less viscous wheat batter prepared with

Box 18

KARNĀTAKA FOOD PROGRESSION

Writings on food in Kannada go back about a thousand years, in the form either of whole books, or of long chapters, or of detailed descriptions of religious or secular feasts. These have all been brought together in one volume,[1] with an appendix.[2] Food preparations from these accounts have been described in the text. In this Box are listed the names of food items in the order in which they are first mentioned in these books, along with the year in which the book appeared. The names of the authors and the titles of their works will be found in the reference list to this chapter.

Year AD	*New food item mentioned*
920	iddaligē, pūrigē, sōdhigē, lāvangē, ghratapūran, mandagē
1025[3]	pālundē (synonym hālundē), melōgara, several leaf-based relishes, chana vadās, pālidhya (a curd-based relish), sandigē (crisp relishes), shikarinī (shrīkhand)
1068	bamboo shoots in curds, undigē, pearl-like padaligē (a dessert), 'frothy and milk-like' madakangalu, very fragrant hayanga
1165	various boiled rices (ōgara), melōgara (vegetable savouries), bisumbōrigē
1200	happalā (pāpads), balaka (vegetable pieces soaked in curd, dried, spiced and fried)
1222	hōlige, saravaligeya-pāyasa (from vermicelli)
1235	shāli-anna (kēsari-bāth), a bead-like pāyasam (sago-based?)
1430	nuchin-undē (steamed tuvar dhāl patties) eaten with curds, kadubu
1485	kajāyya (sweet-stuffed pakodas), brinjal-bāji (bhartha), rāita, pacchadi and pālidhya (curd and buttermilk relishes), paramana (sweet rice pāyasa)
1560	sēvigē-dōsai (of vermicelli), chakkali
1584	seekaranē (thick fruit pulp concotion, eaten with milk)
1594	shrīkhand (called by this name), various types of kadubu, eaten in different ways (see Box 19), rice or chana cooked with soma (wine?) and salt, various styles of cooking several vegetables (eight kinds of field bean are listed), thambittu (a wheat flour preparation)
1600	athirasā (fried rice-jaggery patties), obattu (sweet stuffed parāta, usually termed pūrigē or hūrigē till now), mañoharada-undē, sweet burudē, jilābi (called by this name, and described as 'looking like a creeper'), wheat pāyasa
1606	sandigēs (of sesame seeds, ash gourd peels and onions), pacchadi of radish and cucumber, chakōta (grapefruit), rice-banana sukhivadē, mixed rice-wheat pāyasa
1614	numerous vegetable preparations, cooked with a complex fried masāla
1648	thuvar dhal cooked with vegetables (huli, the modern sāmbhār of Tamil Nadu), two sweet rōtis sanjeevani and kilasāgara, thambālu (colostrum), paneer, nālikera (banana)
1700[2q]	kacchadi (milk blended with curds)
1700[2]	kosamri of chana, vadē of colocasia leaves, hōligē (so far termed hūrigē)

Thus both the persistence of food items and their gradual evolution are well documented, down the centuries, in a regional language.

sweetened milk was forced through a hole made at the base of a coconut shell cup (the usual extrusion device) directly into hot ghee to give the rope-like chilumuri.

As would be expected of vegetarian poets, descriptions of vegetable preparations are plentiful. Chāvundarāya, even in his one chapter, mentions 31 vegetables,[3] and Mangarasā has a long chapter on the cooking of vegetables.[1] Chapter 8 of the *Lingapurāna* of Gurulinga Dēsika (AD 1594) is a long one, and various ways of cooking, each of nearly a dozen vegetables, are outlined.[21] Thus brinjals could be seasoned with ghee, salt, methi, urad and cream before boiling. They could be roasted in ghee; spiced; placed on live coals and made into bāji (bhartha); cut into small pieces and cooked with jaggery—there were so many kinds of brinjals to do all this with! The bittergourd had first to be debittered with salt water and washed. Thereafter many ways of cooking were open. It could be stuffed with a favourite masāla, tied with string and cooked; ghee-fried; cooked with jaggery syrup; cut into rounds and cooked with salt; cooked whole, stuffed or flavoured; and cooked with masāla in a spicy juice in which the fruit would float. An unusual method that now seems to have been given up, was to cook roots and greens in milk.[3] Some preparations are frequently mentioned down the centuries. Melōgara was a dish of pulses and greens in which tamarind was eschewed, and coconut gratings figured prominently. Eating pleasure, we are told, comes from various kinds of melōgara.[21] To make it, mung dhāl, avarai beans, urad dhāl, fresh chana or tuvar dhāl were first cooked with sesame seeds, then cooked again with greens, drumsticks, chakōta (grapefruit), salt and coconut gratings, and finally mixed with ghee and tempered with asafoetida and thick milk. Even wheat dough pieces rolled into thin strands and fried could go into melōgara. Several vegetables destined for a melōgara needed to be pre-treated, each one differently. Certain leaves were first washed in lime water before cooking, other greens were washed in turmeric water, and yet others with common salt or alkaline ashes. The sūrana root was first boiled with betel leaves, or soaked in rice water and then cooked with tamarind leaves. A melōgara dish of dhāl and beans could be sweet, sour or spicy.[3]

Relishes were of many kinds. The bālaka (pronounced with a hard 'l') is now made by soaking large chillis in salt water, drying them, and frying them in oil when needed as a crisp and spicy accompaniment to food. Historically, some twenty kinds of bālaka were prepared using various vegetables and their peels.[21] The same work mentions five kinds of happalā (pāpad) and fifty kinds of pickle (uppinkāyi).[21] Deep-fried items eaten as crisp and crunchy accompaniments to a meal were the chakkali (called murukku in Tamil Nādu), a circle built up of continuous widening rings extruded from a thick rice-urad batter, and numerous sandigē, irregular lumps of spiced rice-urad batter, or sesame powder, or onion, or even vegetable skins like those of the ashgourd, deep-fried to crispness in very hot fat. Curd-based relishes with greens and raw vegetables were called by various names, such as pacchadi, kacchadi, krasāra-kacchadi (this had milk with the curds), pālidya (one variety was called kajja), thambuli (with greens and coconut gratings) and rāyita (a word in common use today). Kosamris were uncooked relishes made from chana or mung, which were soaked in salt water to soften and swell, and then garnished with salt, mustard seeds and fresh coriander.

There was a vast variety of sweet items and they alter little over a millennium. Sweet boiled rice, rice pāyasam in milk (of which paramana was a prized kind that is repeatedly extolled), a rice-derived vermicelli pāyasam, mixed rice-wheat pāyasams, rice kadubu with a sweet filling, and deep-fried delicacies of rice flour and jaggery (now called athirasa) were all based on rice. Wheat was amenable to sweet use, especially in the form of ravā grits, from which came shāli-annā (now called kēsari-bāth, flavoured with the fragrant stamens of saffron called kēsar), a fried ball (ghrtapūra), a pāyasam (kajjāya), and a laddugē. Wheat vermicelli from hard wheat doughs was extruded really fine as phēni, and usually eaten with sugared milk. Sweet wheat rōtis, stuffed with a mash of boiled chana, jaggery and coconut, constituted pūrigē or hūrigē, or the later hōligē; a thinner,

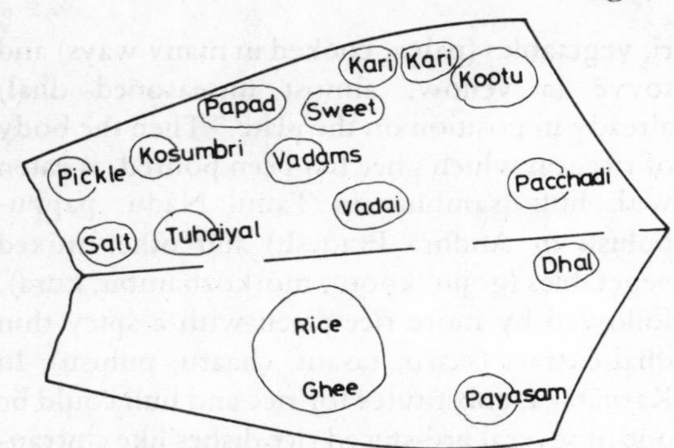

Arrangement of food on a banana leaf, Tamil Nadu.

drier form was the obattu, and there was a rolled-up, cylindrical form called surali-hōligē. Rolled-out pieces of dough were fried in various forms and then dusted with castor sugar to give several phēnis and chirottis; madhunālā was a small tube of dough (of wheat, rice and chana, with added mashed banana) filled with sugar, sealed at both ends and then deep-fried.[1] Karaji-kāyi was a half-moon puff with a sweet stuffing; if only sugar constituted the stuffing, the result was sakkaré-burudē. Pulse flours of chana and black gram were also used to make sweetmeats. Boondi grains made using them were shaped with sugar syrup into laddugé, pinda, mōti-chūr and manōhara-undé. The jil-ābi, 'like a creeper, tasty as nectar' was made of chana flour; it was first mentioned by this name in AD 1600, [2m] and as jilébi later (Chapter 12, Box 24). Milk was the major ingredient for sweet pāyasa, as also for hāl-undé (balls of sweetened khoa) and hālaugu (the hālubai of today). Shikharinī consisted of curd solids lightly spiced and sweetened, the modern term shrīkhand first being used for the dish in Kannada in AD 1700.[2r] Fruit juices, called rasāyasa, appear through the centuries. Chāvundarāya gives elaborate directions for extracting the juice from each of several fruits by exposure to the sun.[3] Another popular mix of ripe fruits or their mashes was seekaranē, of which there were numerous variations in choice and combination of fruits.

No non-vegetarian food finds mention in these texts.

One can easily trace in these preparations and their names many that are now current. The majjigé-huli is the historical pālidya, the kootu is melōgara, and chitranna, puliyōdarē and bisibélé-huli-anna are all forms of kattōgara. Amvadé or ambodé, a vadé of mixed dhāls, is less frequent, but other vadās, and the new bonda, are still here, as are all the forms of pāyasa, hōligé, obattu and chirotti. Old sweets like the kajáyya and the sukhin-undé are disappearing, but Mysore pāk is still a favourite. Did it get its name from the city or state of Mysore? Or is it named after masoor dhāl flour? The latter is sometimes used to make it in the north, but in Karnātaka itself only chana flour (besan) would ever be employed.

Food distinctions: The twenty accounts pertaining to food in Kannada literature,[2] from which the present account has drawn, span a thousand years and reflect a variety of situations during which the foods described were served. Certain of them pertain to kingly repasts and have been recounted in Chapter 8. Some describe dinners eaten by Veerashaivite worshippers of Shiva,[2c,2f,2l,2j,2t] and others describe feasts given to gurus or mystics like Allama Prabhu.[2g,2h,2k] Yet others are public feasts,[2d,2l] and some are simply dinners[2d,2l] served by wives to their husbands.[2r,2s] Two are accounts by Jain poets describing foods with which they are familiar,[2l,3] and one purports to describe a meal served to rich people.[2b] Yet this divergence of occasion can hardly be inferred from the nature of the food dishes served at each meal, which show little difference between one and another.

Slight sociological distinctions occasionally do surface. In one account, three levels of Shiva

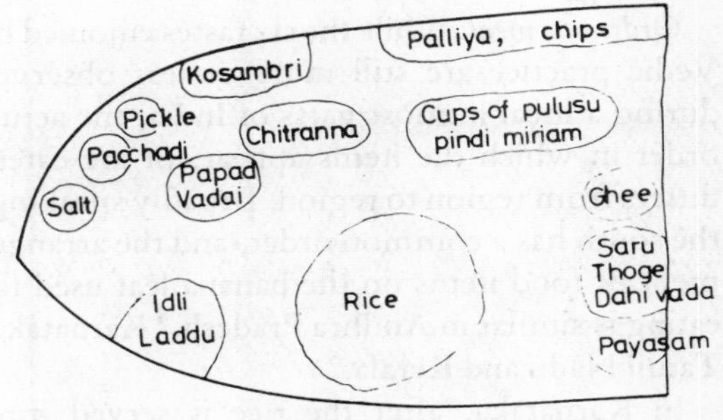

Arrangement of food on a banana leaf, Andhra Pradesh.

devotees are assigned different foods. Thus gnānalingā (novitiate) devotees are given sugared milk, creamy milk with cardamom and ghee, and lots of pāyasa. Stauncher devotees get bajja (a kind of curd-based pālidhya), kajjāya (a fried, sweet-stuffed pakodas, like the sweet puffs of today), and five kinds of flavoured milk to help digestion. The advanced devotees, pushkārākēshavu, get sannigé (perhaps this was a sago pāyasa, since it is described as being cool and white like the moon and like a sparkling necklace of stars), sēmiya (vermicelli) pāyasa which is like 'the eye of the moon' and is flavoured with sandalwood, milk of rare quality, and butter. Everything offered is white and pure, spiritual and sāttvika: even the ghee-fried vegetables have sugar added to them, and white salt is employed. In another poem, the choice foods for richer people are various sweet fried dishes (hōligé, māndigé, hūrigé, athirasā), pāyasas of wheat, vermicelli and chana, kadubu, and ghee; the lesser lights get a spicy huli (sāmbhār) with banana pith in it, and hōligé cooked in oil.[2u]

The ambience of public feasts was one of great good cheer and sheer exuberance in the enjoyment of food. 'How can I,' asks one poet, 'describe the beauty, generosity and nobility of food served so lavishly?'[2k] At another meal,[2u], the diners enquire: 'who made this sweet potato dish? It is Mallamma's handiwork. Who created this kosamri of chana dhāl? The neighbour's wife Gangamma,' and so on for a long list of dishes.[2u] In fact sometimes the food becomes secondary to descriptions of the assorted charms of the ladies serving it, as described in Chapter 8. And the diners eat to excess, bursting their waist-strings, getting up with difficulty but exclaiming with satisfaction.[2u]

Order of a meal: While the six tastes enjoined by Vedic practice are still more or less observed during a meal in most parts of India, the actual order in which the items appear, or are eaten, differs from region to region. Broadly speaking, the south has a common order, and the arrangement of food items on the banana leaf used for eating is similar in Āndhra Pradesh,[4] Karnātaka, Tamil Nādu and Kērala.[5]

In Karnātaka, after the rice is served, tiny mouthfuls of it are tasted mixed with the kosamri, vegetables (palya, cooked in many ways) and tovvé (a yellow, almost unseasoned dhāl) already in position on the plate.[6] Then the body of rice, on which ghee has been poured, is eaten with huli (sāmbhār in Tamil Nādu, pappupulusu in Āndhra Pradesh) and other mixed vegetables (gojju, kootu, mōrkozhambu, kura), followed by more rice eaten with a spicy thin dhal extract (saaru, rasam, chaaru, pulusu). In Karnātaka, substitutes for rice and huli could be one of several pre-spiced rice dishes like chitranna (lime rice) or bisibélé-huli-anna (in Tamil, sāmbhār-sādham). Now comes the sweet, which could be a pāyasam, or kēsaribāth (a sweet, flavoured wheat or rice), or a solid sweet like Mysore-pāk or jilēbi. Meanwhile bits will be pinched off the salty snacks, vadē, bōnda or even idli, and munched. And finally to soothe the palate will come rice with curds or buttermilk served either separately or sometimes as a pre-mixed preparation (mosaru-annā, thayirsādham).

The Kodavās

Perched on the highlands of southern Karnātaka in Kodagu district are a warlike and distinctive people with a unique cuisine. Rice is eaten boiled, or as a distinctive ghee-coated product (nai-kūlu) or as a palāo with the meat chunks firm and every grain coated evenly with masālā. Rice is also transformed in numerous ways, and each has a distinct non-vegetarian accompaniment. The rōti (akki-otti) is based on a rice dough rolled out on a wet cloth, roasted and eaten with a spicy sesame chutney, or a red pumpkin (kumbla) curry, or with a dry and salty dish of bamboo shoot chiplets (these shoots are also pickled). With the palāo goes a pasty relish of ripe wild mangoes in a curd base called māngaypajji. A paper-thin, soft handkerchief of rice (neer-dōsai) is accompanied by a chicken curry into which goes a lot of fresh coconut. The nūputtu of Kodagu is the strand-like idi-appam of south India, once eaten with jaggery water, but now with any liquid curry. Steamed balls of mashed and cooked rice constitute kadambuttu, which is paired with a pork dish with a very thick masāla in which an essential component is the black, sun-drawn extract of the kokum fruit (*Garcinia indica*) locally called kāchampuli, the acidity of which serves to keep the fat on the meat firm and springy. A breakfast dish consists of a sweetish thick steamed batter of broken rice (thari) liberally sprinkled with fresh coconut called pāputtu, which is often eaten with ghee and the honey so plentifully found in Kodagu. Another is thaliya-puttu, the kadubu of Karnātaka, steamed on a metal plate (thaliya). Two fish are in use. One is the sardine, matthi-meen, and the other the tiny whitebait (koylé-meen), cooked and eaten bones and all. Two popular desserts are both based on the banana. Well-ripened fruits are mashed with the powder of roasted rice, to which a little mēthi is added, to give uncooked thambuttu, eaten with ghee, fresh coconut scrapings and whole roasted sesame seed. To make koālé-puttu, a banana mash with small wedges of mature coconut is steamed in a banana leaf packet, which is opened to give a brown slab, eaten either hot or cold with fresh butter. The name is a corruption of koovalé-puttu, originally made with the soft, weepy variety of jackfruit called koovalé.

Hyderābād

The city of Hyderābād was founded in 1589 by Mohammad Quli Qutbshah, and Muslim royalty there created a whole cuisine of very distinctive foods.[7,8] Among the leavened, oven-baked breads are kulcha, a square product often marked with two cross-lines, and sheermāl, which are described in this chapter in Box 21. Both are eaten early in the morning with gelatinous narahari, which are lamb trotters and tongue that have been cooking slowly all night. Qābooli is a khichadī of rice and kābūli chana, in contrast to mung dhāl which is the usual pulse in a khichadī that is eaten with kheema. In making Hyderābād kacchi-biriyāni, the meat almost disintegrates while the rice remains firm; there is no overall coating of gravy or ghee, only irregular saffron staining. Accompanying this light, dry biriyāni is the rather watery onion rāita called boorani. Biriyani is said to differ from palāo when the meat takes precedence over rice in the mix.

Haleem is a finely-ground paste of both wheat and meat, delicately spiced. Full-boiled eggs in a minced meat coating constitute nārgisi-kōfta; when broken open, the golden yolk surrounded by egg white against an earth-brown meat background recalls the narcissus flower nārgis sprouting from the bare earth.[9] Chakna is a dish of offal, and dālchā is lamb stewed with beans and tamarind. Lukmi is like the Italian ravioli, small squares of soft pastry filled with spiced meat and fried. Mutton or chicken can be baked in a seal of dum. Long large chillis are cooked as a vegetable into the fiery mirchi-ka-sālan, and the famous baghāra-baingan consists of whole slit brinjals with the stalks left on, which have been cooked with a thick masāla of copra, groundnuts and sesame seeds in a tart tamarind base, with distinctive *fines herbes*. A handi of vegetables is cooked in an earthen pot. Quarters of hard-boiled eggs frequently garnish a thick sweet-sour sauce of tomato. The very sweet, ghee-rich fried bread pudding laced with almonds, which elsewhere is called shāhi-tukdā, is in Hyderābād termed double-ka-meeta, the name stemming from the double-rōti (bread loaf) that is used to make it. Badām-ki-jāli are latticed sweets of ground almonds, and andon-ki-peosi a baked mix of eggs, khoa, kēsar and sugar. The cuisine of Hyderābād represents a superb example of the imaginative use of local ingredients to create totally new concoctions.

Kērala

Five distinct groups live in the state of Kērala, and each has a distinctive food list. Let us take the ancient community of Syrian Christians first (see Chapter 6).[10, 11, 12]

The rice āppam, a pancake also called vella-āppam, is common to all Kēralites, eaten with a meat stew by *Syrians*, and with an aviyal of vegetables by Nampoothiris and Nairs. Syrians favour the kal-āppam, baked on a stone griddle rather than a clay one. The kuzhal-āppam, as its name implies, is a fried crisp curled up like a tube, and is typical of Syrians. There are two other Syrian āppams, very different in character, and both sweet. The acch-āppam is a deep-fried rose-cookie made of rice, the name coming from the frame (accha) needed to make it; this is dipped in batter, drained, and then immersed in hot oil. The nai-āppam, called athirasam in Tamil Nadu, is a deep-fried, chewy, dark doughnut. fashioned from toddy-fermented rice and jaggery. There are two other breakfast items common to all Kēralites. The idi-āppam is a dish of cooked rice noodles, eaten with sweetened coconut milk or with a meat or chicken curry. The puttu consists of rice grits and coconut shreds, which are alternately layered in a bamboo tube. The latter is then affixed to the spout of a vessel in which water is boiled. The mass is pushed through after it has been steamed. Being rather dry, puttu is commonly eaten with bananas, or with a spicy dry chanā. Another rice-coconut combination uses fried rice, and is called avalose, a Syrian speciality. It can be moulded into an unda (ball) with sugar syrup. The churutta (literally cigar) is rice-based again, and has a crisp, translucent outer case, filled with rice grits and sweet, thickened palmyra juice (called pāni). The unniāppam, eaten by all Kēralites, consists of a mash of ripe jackfruit, roasted rice flour and jaggery, folded in the form of a triangle in a vazhana leaf and steamed. Jackfruit cooked with jaggery and cardamom constitutes chakka-varattiyathu.

The Syrians eat beef, and eracchi-olathiyathu (fried meat) is a wedding special, a dry dish of beef chunks and coconut pieces fried in its own fat. To make eracchi-thōran, cubed beef is first boiled with vinegar and salt, then shredded on a grinding stone, lightly fried with spices, a coconut-masālā mixture added, and the whole briefly steamed.[10] Kappa-kari has pieces of tapioca in the beef, and is finished by frying in oil. Most curries, including meat, always have a lot of coconut milk. Meen-vevicchadhu (cooked fish) is cooked differently in different areas even by Syrians. Both in Kōttayam and Trichūr, river fish is used; this is cooked in Kōttayam with the sour kokum fruit rind, called kodampuli, and is very red in colour with added chillies and even colouring matter; in Trichūr, tender mango as the souring agent and coconut milk are used. Meen-pattichadhu uses very small fish like oil sardines, or even prawns, with coconut gratings. For Christmas there may be a wild duck, cooked as mappas, or roasted with stuffing. Wild boar cooked with a strong masālā, or pickled in oil, is also a Syrian speciality.

For pouring on dry dishes, buttermilk mixed with turmeric and spices is used, called kacchiamōru. Some sweet items have been mentioned earlier. A wedding special is thayirum-pazhampāni, in which sweet palmyra juice is thickened by boiling down and poured on ripe bananas, mashed together, and eaten with curd. As a deep-fried savoury snack there is pakku-vadā, a version of pakōda.

The Muslims of Kērala are called *Mōplāhs,* a corruption of mahāpillā or māpillai, meaning bridegroom or a person held in high esteem.[11] They are descendants of Arab traders who married local Kērala women, later expanding their ranks by conversion. Though the Kērala usage of rice, coconut and jaggery is evident, there is Arab influence to be seen in the biriyānis and the ground wheat-and-meat porridge aleesa, elsewhere called harīsa.

The rōti is the distinctive podi-patthiri, a flat thin rice chapāti made from a boiled mash of rice baked on a thavā and dipped in coconut milk. The ari-patthiri is a thicker version made from parboiled rice and flattened out on a cloth or banana leaf to prevent it sticking. Nai-patthiri is a deep-fried pūri of raw rice powder with some coconut, fried to a golden brown. All these patthiris are eaten at breakfast with a mutton curry. Steamed puttus, eaten with small bananas, would figure also at the morning repast. A wedding-eve feast could include the nai-chōru, rice fried lightly in ghee with onions, cloves, cinnamon and cardamom to taste, and finally boiled to a finish. A wedding dinner would necessarily mean a biriyāni of mutton, chicken, fish or prawn which is finally finished by arranging the separately cooked flesh and the cooked rice in layers and baking with live coals above and below. Several flavoured soups are made from both rice and wheat, with added coconut or coconut milk, and spices. A whole-wheat porridge with minced mutton cooked in coconut milk is called kiskiya. A distinctive and unusual sweet is mutta-māla (egg garlands), chainlike strings of egg yolk cooked in sugar syrup but later removed from it, and frequently served with a snow-like pudding called pinnanthappam made from the separated egg whites which have been whisked up with the remaining sugar syrup, steamed, and cut into diamond shapes.[11]

The *Thīyas* are a community that formerly tapped toddy but have now entered many other professions.[7] Āppam and stew are the breakfast fare, the stew being varied: fish in coconut sauce with tiny pieces of mango, mutton in coconut milk, or simply a sugared thick coconut milk. A bread speciality is nai-patthal, in the shape of a starfish. The curd pacchadi may be of pumpkin, and the sweet dessert may be a prathaman, which is mung dhāl boiled in coconut milk and flavoured with palm jaggery, cardamom and ginger powder, and laced with fried cashewnuts, raisins and coconut chips.

The *Nāirs* are the Nākar, the original warrior class of Kērala, whose cooking skills have carried them as professionals to non-vegetarian families all over the south.[13] Breakfast again is either the vella-āppam or the bamboo-steamed puttu, eaten with sweetened milk and tiny bananas. Certain vegetable specialities, though eaten by all Kēralites, have special Nāir associations. The sāmbhār of tuvar dhāl with added vegetables is a regular item. Aviyal is a mix of vegetables like green bananas, drumsticks, various beans and green cashewnuts (this is distinctive to the Nāirs) cooked in coconut milk and then tossed with some coconut oil in spiced sour curd. Kālan is the same dish that uses green bananas alone, and ōlan is a dish of white pumpkin and dried beans cooked in coconut milk and coconut oil. A wedding feast of the Nāirs will include several types of pacchadis, pickles, chips and pāyasams based on milk, coconut milk, rice, dhāl and bananas. No meat is served at a wedding, though normally meat is eaten. Such domestic meat and chicken cooking, though spiced, uses a great deal of fresh coconut and coconut milk which tempers the dish to mildness. Small pieces of ashgourd or raw mango cooked with coconut, curds and chilli paste,[14] is pulissēri, and puli-inji is fried sliced ginger.

The *Nampoothiris* are the brahmins of Kērala who may have first arrived there about the 3rd century BC.[13] They are strict vegetarians who favour the idli, dōsai and puttu for breakfast with a coconut or curd accompaniment, and eat their rice with kootu, kālan and ōlan. Use of garlic in cooking is avoided. The thōran is usually made from the pods of green payaru (lōbia) cut into small bits, stir-fried in oil and finally finished by cooking with a little water. Green bananas, spinach, cabbage and peas can all be made into thōran, and eaten with rice. Aviyal and erissēri, a pumpkin curry, are in use. All Kērala groups eat yellow banana chips fried in coconut oil and lightly salted. The best ones are reputed to be made in Kōzhikode, which also boasts of a special sweet halwā made of bananas. The pāyasam of Kērala uses rice and milk, but the prathamans have milk with fruit or dhāl, or with paper-thin shreds of a rice roll, cooked separately and added to the sweetened milk to give pālada-prathaman.[14] Chātha pulissēri is a shrāddha speciality, a sour buttermilk preparation with pepper, salt and coconut paste, thickened by boiling down. Southern snack items are featured in Box 19.

Box 19

SNACKS OF THE SOUTH

The idli, kadubu, dōsai, āppam and vadai of southern India have each had a long history, though not every detail can be clearly traced.

The idli seems to be first mentioned in writing in Shivakōtyācharya's *Vaddarādhané*, a Kannada work of AD 920, as one of eighteen items served when a lady offers refreshments to a brahmachāri who visits her home.[2a] Thereafter it is frequently mentioned, and in AD 1025 the poet Chāvundarāya describes it unequivocally as urad dhāl soaked in buttermilk, ground to a fine paste, mixed with the clear water of

Box 19 (*Contd.*)

curds, jeera, coriander, pepper and asafoetida, and then shaped.[3] The *Mānasollāsa* of about AD 1130 written in Sanskrit describes the iddarika as made of fine urad flour, fashioned into small balls, fried in ghee and then spiced with pepper powder, jeera powder and asafoetida.[64] In Karnātaka, the idli in AD 1235 is described as being 'light, like coins of high value',[2f] which is not suggestive of a rice base. In Tamil literature the ittali is first mentioned only as late as the *Maccapurānam* of the 17th century AD.[65] The steaming vessel in Kannada is alagé (with a hard 'l'), and the iddaligé has the same hard 'l'.[1a] In all these references, three elements of the modern idli are missing. One is the use of rice grits (in the proportion of two parts to one of urad). The next is the long process of grinding and the overnight fermentation of the mix. The last is the steaming of the batter. The literature offers no certain answers as to when in the last few centuries these elements entered the picture.

In AD 1485 and AD 1600[2k,2m] the idli is compared to the moon, which might suggest that rice was in use; yet there are references to other moon-like products made only from urad flour. The Indonesians ferment many materials (soyabeans, groundnuts, fish), and have a similar fermented and steamed item called kedli. Steaming is a very ancient form of food preparation in the Chinese ethos, referred to by Xuan Zang when he says that in the 7th century AD India did not have a steaming vessel.[15b] It has been suggested that the cooks who accompanied the Hindu kings of Indonesia during their visits home (often enough, looking for brides) during the 8th to 12th centuries AD brought fermentation techniques back with them to their homeland.[67] Perhaps the use of rice along with the pulse was necessary as a source of the mixed natural microflora needed for an effective fermentation. Yeasts have enzymes which break down starch to simpler sugar forms, and bacteria which dominate the idli fermentation carry enzymes for souring and leavening through carbon dioxide production.[68] Even Czechoslovakia has a similar steamed product called the knedlik (pronounced needleek).[69] Steaming can of course be achieved by very simple means, merely by tying a thin cloth over a wide-mouthed vessel in which water is boiled, and its antiquity would be impossible to establish. It is not unlikely that the name of the idli persisted even though its character changed with time.

The kadubu and idli are very similar. Tharagu-kadubu, which is kadubu steamed on leaves, is first mentioned in Kannada in AD 1430.[2g] Urad-kadubu is noted in 1485,[2h] kadubu made from tiny sévagé (vermicelli) in AD 1560,[2j] and in AD 1594, kadubu made from ravā or chanā or vermicelli, and containing bamboo shoots besides.[21] The kadubu must have differed from the idli to have been mentioned separately all along. As now made, the kadubu is steamed as a slab held on a leaf or a metal tray. Such inward steaming leads to a denser and less porous texture than for the idli, which is through-steamed on a piece of thin cloth or in the perforated hollows of a metal tray supported half-way within a steaming vessel. Stuffings both sweet and savoury can be placed between layers of kadubu and the resulting sandwich cut into smaller pieces for consumption. The denser kadubu is also amenable to further breaking up, followed by frying,[2p] or fashioning into a kheer in milk, or reshaping with jaggery into a ball or disc,[21] or even roasting further to crispness to yield a product called uduru.[21] The Kānchipūram idli also seems to have changed its character. Once a spongy product made entirely of urad dhāl, it now denotes an idli or kadubu with added seasoning and nuts, rather like the rava idli of the present time.

The tōsai (dōsai) is first noted in the

Box 19 (*Contd.*)

Tamil Sangam literature (see Box 6) of about the 6th century AD.[70] It was then perhaps a pure rice product, shallow-fried in a pan, while the āppam of similar vintage was heated without fat on a shallow clay chatti. Today both idli and dōsai use the same fermented batter, slightly thinner in case of the latter. Did the idli operation precede that of the dōsai, or was it the other way round? The dōsai of Tamil Nadu is a soft, thick product while that of Karnātaka is thin, crisp and large.[71] It is frequently stuffed in modern times with a spiced potato mash to yield the popular masālā-dōsai.

The circular āppam is mentioned in the *Perumpānūru* of about the 5th century AD along with the idi-āppam which consists of the soft extruded noodles of a mash of steamed rice. Both products seem to have remained unchanged to this day. The āppam batter is fermented overnight using toddy and baked in a clay pan to yield a product with a thick, soft, spongy centre and a lacy crisp brown edge. Heating on a metal plate held over boiling water yields kal-āppam. Steaming in a banana leaf packet, with jaggery, grated coconut and jackfruit pulp added to the rice batter, yields yellé-āppam (leaf-āppam).

Vatā and vataka make their first appearance in the *Sūtra* literature of about 500 BC,[72a,72b] and regularly thereafter. Tamil literature does not seem to carry it till quite late. The modern vadai connotes a deep-fried shaped snack in which urad (yielding the meddhu-vadá) and chanā (the ám-badá) pulse flours are generally employed and occasionally tuvar and masūr. A Kannada work of AD 1430[2g] describes both a roasted vadē and a steamed nuchin-undē made of ground tuvar eaten with spiced curds. The urad vataka was once also placed in milk, buttermilk and curds (Chapter 3), but at present only the dahi (thayir) vadai steeped in spiced curds seems to have survived.

The vadé of Maddūr, a small town midway between Bangalore and Mysore has become somewhat of a local speciality. It goes back about eight decades, and is made of ravā with plenty of fried onion shreds, which give it a sweet taste, some chopped cashewnuts, and sprinklings of roasted ravā.[73]

The bajji consists of slices of vegetables dipped in besan batter and deep-fried to crispness. This may have originated in south India, though now popular all over the country. The identical product tempurā considered typical of Japan, seems to have been introduced into that country from India by Portuguese missionaries, merchants and seamen accustomed to eating fried fish on meatless days.[74]

The dahi-vadā or thayir-vadē.

Eastern India

Bengal

Fertility of the land: The Dakārnava (a tāntric Buddhist work), the *Dāker-Vachana*, and the *Khanār Vachana*, all works of the earliest Bengali literature of the 10th and 11th centuries AD, are full of aphorisms and wise sayings which show the abundance of produce derived from good agriculture.[15a] 'The millet chinakaon (*Panicum miliaceum*) grows abundantly if it rains in Phālgun (February-March)'... 'plant patōl (parwal) in a sandy soil' ... 'sow the seeds of mustard close' ... 'on the north of your land plant a fruit orchard, on the east have a pond with ducks, on the west an avenue of bamboos, and leave the south open ...' A medieval text, the *Shunya Purāna*, states that fifty kinds of rice were grown in Bengal.[16a]

Later European travellers to Bengal in the 16th and 17th centuries, like Varthema, Barbosa, Caesar Fredrick and Ralph Fitch testify to the abundance of Bengal.[17] 'The country abounds in grain of every kind, sugar, ginger, the best place in the world to live in (Varthema, *c.* AD 1505).' And Bernier (c. AD 1600) is no less enthusiastic : 'Bengal abounds with every necessity of life . . . rice . . . wheat . . . three or four sorts of vegetables . . . geese and ducks . . . goats and sheep . . . pigs . . . fish of every species, whether fresh or salt, in the same profusion . . . this is a fertile kingdom'.[18a] The Portugese came in large numbers in the 16th century. They intermarried with the locals, and also introduced a variety of new crops, like tobacco, potato, cashewnut, papaya (pēpē) and guava (peyārā).[19a]

The use of fish: Even from early times, the brahmins of Bengal defended their eating of fish. After quoting the views of earlier authorities like Yāgnavalkya, Manu and Vyāsa, the politician and scholar Bhatta Bhavadēva (11th/12th century AD) says: 'All this prohibition is meant for the prohibited days like Chaturdasi and others . . . so it is understood that there is no crime (dōsha) in eating fish and meat.'[20] The *Brhaddharma Purāna* recommends for consumption the rohita, shakula, saphara and other fish which are white and have no scales, Srīnāthāchārya also allowed Bengali brahmins the use of fish and meat except on some parvan days, and hilsā fish was particularly popular. Only raw and dried meat was disallowed to brahmins, as were onions, garlic and mushrooms.[20] Even the great Bengali spiritual leaders of recent times used animal food. Rāmakrishna Paramahamsa said in 1822: 'I love to eat fish in any form,' and Swami Vivekānanda is recorded as having enjoyed a rice meal that included fish shukto, machhēr jhōl, sour fish curry, sweet curd and sandesh.[21,22] Even the Gowda-Sāraswath brahmins of Karnātaka eat fish, possibly a carryover from their original home in Bengal (Gauda).

Vegetarianism in Bengal: The Vaishnavites of Bengal, largely centred in Navadvīp, are strict vegetarians who take no meat or fish. Even 'hot'

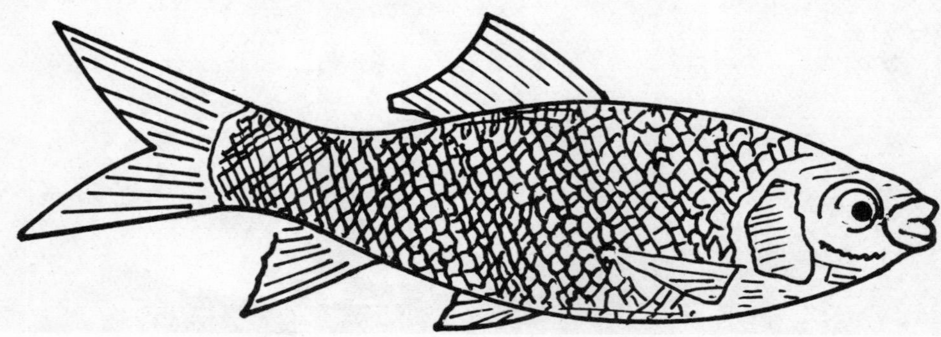

Rohu, a fish of the carp family, is a common preference among Bengalis.

foods like onions and masūr dhāl are not permitted and up until about 1900, they eschewed new foods like potatoes and tomatoes in favour of traditional sweet potatoes and colocasia (arvi). In fact the adoption of the potato was slow in general, only gaining acceptance about the middle of the nineteenth century. The evangelism of Chaitanya (1486–1533), who was born in Navadvīp, gave a strong fillip to Vaishnavism and thus to vegetarian eating. A feast given to Chaitanya at the house of the advaita Sārvabhauma consisted of shāli rice drenched in yellow ghee, surrounded by leaf cups of dhāl, sāg, and vegetables like the parwal, pumpkin and brinjal, several tubers and banana flowers.[23a] Fried bōdās of mung and urad, deep-fried puffs or singhādās stuffed with coconut, sweet-sour relishes like ambal and tauk, sweet rice-milk pāyesh, thickened milk, small sweet bananas (chāpāl), dahi and sandesh also figured. The *Krishnamangal* of Krishnadās written about AD 1525 has a list of items cooked by the gopīs and gopas of Brindāvan, at Krishna's request, for worship.[18] These included various sūpas (soups), greens (some cooked in honey), baramānkachu (a large arum tuber), bananas with paneer, brinjals with mānkachu, fried green bananas, fried horseradish and chutney, and, as dessert, kheer, bananas, laddu and other sweets. Various sāgs are described in works of this period, like bethua, kalar, kacchu, gima and kumra, while vegetables noted are achyuta, patōl, basthuk, kōl, salincha and hilanchā.[24a,24b,24c]

Styles of food: There are two distinct styles of Bengali cooking, though rice is the staple in both.[25] East Bengali food, which is exemplified by the cuisines of Chittagong and Dhākā, lays less emphasis on dhāl and is strong on fish. The food of West Bengal, as in Calcutta or the Parganās, is distinguished by the liberal use of poppy seeds (posto). East and west Bengali cooking differ both in the choice of spices and the way in which dishes are prepared. Both employ mustard in three different ways — fried in oil, carefully crushed to yield a pungent paste, and as a cooking medium. Fish and prawns are common to both cuisines, but regional preferences have developed on the basis of availability. East Bengalis prefer fish from big rivers, and West Bengalis fish bred in tanks or from estuaries, like mangor and tapsee, but the river fish hilsā is a universal favourite. West Bengali food is strong on milk-based sweets,[25] and on fried snacks like kachuri and singhādā.

The procession of tastes at a meal run from a bitter start to a sweet finish. To start with, especially at lunch, is shukto. This is a dish that is essentially bitter, made up of neem or other bitter leaves, bittergourd, brinjals, potatoes, radish and green bananas, with spices like turmeric, ginger, mustard and rādhuni (celery seed) pastes. Rice is first savoured with ghee, salt and green chillies; then comes dhāl, accompanied by fried vegetables (bhājā), or boiled vegetables (bhātē), followed by spiced vegetables like dālnā or ghonto. Then come fish preparations, first lightly-spiced ones like mācchēr jhōl, then those more heavily spiced, after which would follow a sweet-sour ambal or tauk (chutney) and fried pāpads. A dessert of mishti-dōi (sweet curds), accompanied by dry sweets, or of pāyesh, accompanied by fruits like the mango, will end

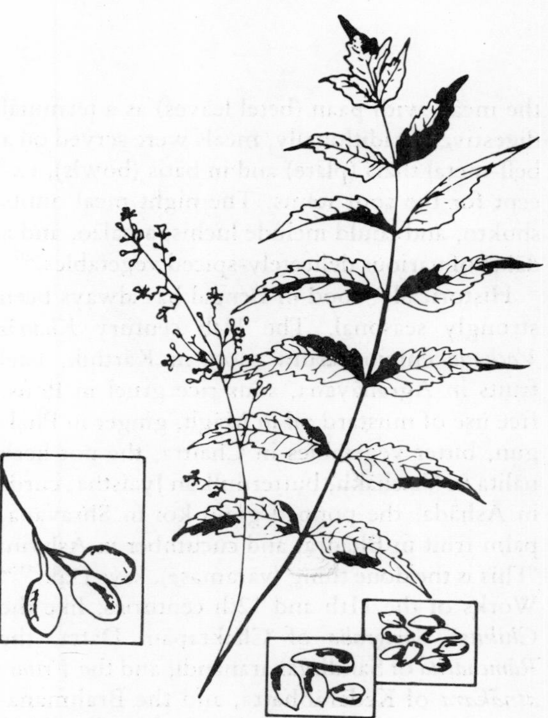

Neem leaves are used in making shukto.

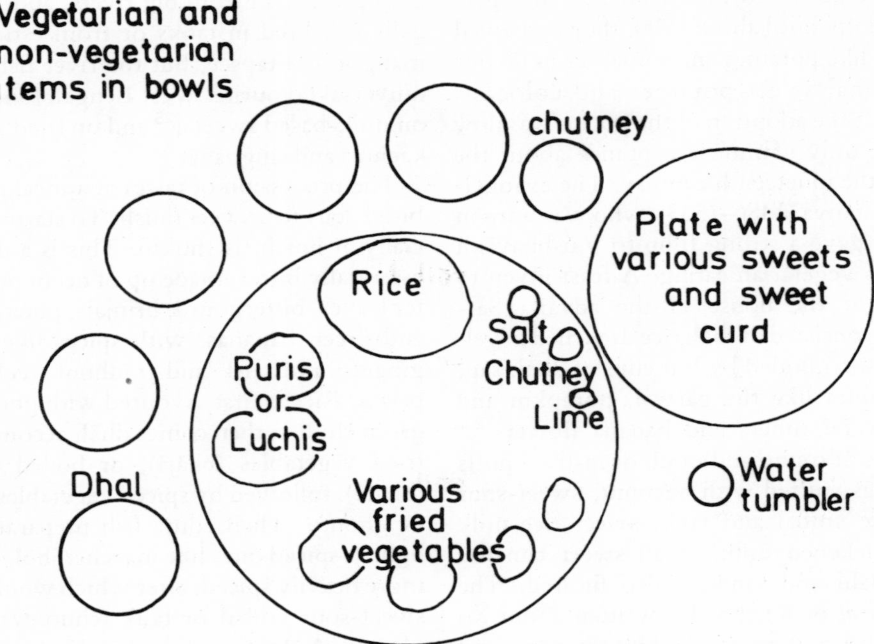

Arrangement of items at a Bengali meal.

the meal, with paan (betel leaves) as a terminal digestive. Traditionally, meals were served on a bell-metal thāla (plate) and in bātis (bowls), except for the sour items. The night meal omits shukto, and could include luchis, a palāo, and a dālnā of various delicately-spiced vegetables.[26]

Historically, food in Bengal has always been strongly seasonal. The 11th century *Khanār Vachana* enjoins arum roots in Kārthik, bael fruits in Agrahāyana, sour rice gruel in Pous, free use of mustard oil in Māgh, ginger in Phālgun, bitter vegetables in Chaitra, the pot herb nālita in Vaishākh, buttermilk in Jyaistha, curds in Āshāda, the popped grain koi in Shrāvana, palm fruit in Bhādra, and cucumber in Āshvin: 'This is the done thing (vāramasē), says Dāk.'[15a] Works of the 11th and 12th centuries, like the *Chikitsā Samgraha* of Chakrapāni Datta, the *Rāmcharita* of Sandhyākaranandi, and the *Vrttaratnākara* of Kedārabhatta, and the Brahmanasarvasva of the smriti writer Halayudha,[76] list the variety of tubers, green leafy vegetables and milk products consumed in Bengal.[27] Even a millennium earlier Sushrutha mentions a dish of the present Bengal area called sūdhaka, which were boiled tender leaves squeezed out and spiced. The range of food materials in moist and fertile Bengal is exceptionally wide: cereals, tubers and rhizomes, vegetables, green pot herbs, a variety of spices, and of course fish.[21,22] A variety of harmonious combinations are employed: pumpkin and shrimps, pumpkin and stems of the climbing spinach (puin), urad dhāl with spices like saunf, ginger and asafoetida, gourd and whole chana, and sponge gourd with poppyseed (posto). Green plantains and ginger are considered an incompatible combination. Many flowers are eaten, like those of the pumpkin and banana; so is the pith of the banana, called thōd; raw jackfruit, water reeds, tender drumsticks, and the peels of potato or pumpkin.[21] Pānchphōron is a spice mixture of five components unique to Bengal. It consists of equal quantities[21] of onion seed, celery seed (rādhuni, *Tachyspermum roxhburghianum*), aniseed, fenugreek and jeera; but mustard seeds can replace rādhuni.[26]

In the Hindu ethos (as described in Chapter 6), food, mood and character are all strongly linked. An excellent illustration of this is provided in the *Chandīmangala* (AD 1589) of Mukundarām Chakravarti, which relates two tales.[28] One is that of the hunter Kālketu and his wife Fullarā, and the other is that of the trader Dhanapati, his good wife Khullānā, and the evil one Lahanā who is childless. There are a series of meals described in considerable detail; these not only illustrate the relationship of food to temperament and situation, but also bring out the very wide range of Bengali cuisine even four hundred years ago.[28] Lord Shiva is of tāmasic temperament, choleric and violent: he gets nothing that has been cooked in ghee (which is a pure and luminous sāttvika product), only food cooked in pungent mustard oil. Among a long list of food items, five may be singled out. These are brinjals mixed with bitter neem leaves; pungent mustard leaves used as a pot herb; lentils seasoned with sour lime juice as soup, pieces of karanja (*Pongamia pinnata*), an astringent fruit, as a relish; and as dessert, sour green mangoes cooked in lime juice. Lord Vishnu, in contrast, is of a serene sāttvika temperament; he does not demand the usual starting sour item, nor pot herbs, but instead is served a tender parwal (gourd) browned in ghee, and a number of milk-

Bengali sweetmeat maker.

based sweet items like mandā, khāndu and nādu; these are all round in shape, and suggestive of the terrestial globe over which he reigns. Two pregnant women get foods which reflect the social class of each. The poor hunter's wife gets nothing cooked in ghee, only roasted foods, while the rich merchant's wife gets food with a tart flavour, rice but no tubers, and a variety of kitchen herbs. Finally the hunter himself, a rājasika even by profession, gets neither rice nor ghee to eat, only tubers, and not even pot herbs.[29] There are numerous other exquisite culinary nuances.

Bengali sweets: The Bengali seems to have always had a sweet tooth. About 1406 the Chinese Māhuan mentions 'white sugar, granulated sugar, candied or preserved fruit', with reference to Bengal.[30] The *Chandimangala* mentions kheer, rābdi (thickened, sweetened milk), mandā, khāndu and nādu, and the *Chandidās Padāvalī*, written about the same period, describes how, when Sri Krishna was born in Nanda's family, the father distributed various kinds of sweets (bibidha-mishta and sakar-mittāi), while the cowherds gave the baby anna (rice), curds, mishta, mittāi, chīnī (sugar) and small bananas (chāpākōlā).[31] Other works of the 16th century mention chhānāborā, khājā, jilēbi, pishtak, mōdak, mālpo, sītamisri and sandesh.[24d, 24e] The *Chaitanya Charitamrit* describes how Shachī, the mother of Chaitanya, gave him sandesh to eat.[23b] All these are sweets based on milk, or partly-thickened milk, or milk solids (khoa).

A new impetus came with the arrival of the Portuguese. By the second half of the 17th century they numbered 20,000 and had settled down mostly near Hughlī, with some at Rājmahal.[32] They baked bread for use of the English or Dutch factories, ships and private homes, and were skilled in the art of preparing preserves of various fruits like the citron, lime, mango, ginger, pineapple and āmla.[18a] The Portuguese also loved cottage cheese, which they made by 'breaking' milk with acidic materials. This routine technique may have lifted the Aryan taboo on deliberate milk curdling,[33] and given the traditional Bengali moirā (sweetmeat maker) a new raw material to work with.[34] Whether the sandesh earlier mentioned in literature was the same as its present namesake remains doubtful: perhaps it was either sweetened curd-solids or khoa, rather than chhānā. Even in recent times the east of Bengal had khoā-based sweets like the leaf-shaped labanga-latikā, glazed in sugar syrup. The simplest sandesh or sweetened chhānā is simply kānchāgollā. Sandesh is also cast in numerous moulds to resemble flowers, fruit, and shells, given various colours, sweetened with palm jaggery, sugar-cane jaggery or sugar, sugar-coated to yield manōharā, and flavoured with orange peel, jackfruit or rose essence. Mild precipitation of milk using whey yields a soft but perishable chhānā product, while the use of lime juice yields a gritty one which sets to a hard, long-lasting product.[34] Sandesh is made from both kinds, and as many as a hundred product variations are believed to be prepared.

Soon chhānā began to be transformed into new sweets by innovative and competing professional moirās. In 1868, the 22-year old Nobīn Chandra Dās of Sutānuti created the spongy rasogollā cooked in sugar syrup and some fifty years later his son Krishna Chandra Dās invented the rasamālāi, flattened chhānā patties floating in thickened milk. In 1930 he also went into mechanized production and canning of milk sweets, notably rasogollā, under the name K. C. Dās.[33] Patties dipped in thickened milk and sprinkled with grated khoa constituted khīrmōhan, and cham-cham were the same in a different shape, soft, oozy and sprinkled with grated khoa. Mouchak was the same product, shaped (as its name indicates) to look like a beehive.[35] Sītābhōg was chhānā with rice powder, shaped to look like rice grains.[36] Frying in ghee yielded yet other confections. Mixing with wheat flour, frying, and immersing in sugar syrup is the basis of sweets like the lāl-mohan, kālō-jām (also called gulāb-jāmūn), and totāpuri (shaped rather like a long mango)[36] Lēdikeni was a similar product of chhānā with ravā created by Bhim Chandra Nag to honour Lady Canning, the Vicereine of India, during an up-country visit, being named after her and finally indigenized. Pantuā is the same but smaller, and chhānār-jilipī and chitrakoot are differently-shaped variations.[26] Nādu, a sweet ball held by the infant Krishna, is mostly a concoction of coconut and thickened milk.

All these sweets were at one time made by moirā families for supply to wealthy landlords on a large scale. Nōbin Chandra Dās first received patronage from the Nawāb of Gaud and Rāni Swarnamoyee,[23] and later others bought his products to serve their guests. For preparation and use in the home, there are desserts like the pāyesh and pithē, using thickened milk and sugar, jaggery or molasses along with rice, coconut and ravā.

Assam

Some early geographical and cultural information about Assam is to be had in the *Yōgini Tantra*. This has been incorporated, along with the *Kālika Purāna* and the *Kulavnava*, in the Sanskrit work entitled *Kāmarupa Yātra* composed in Assam about AD 600–800.[37] The upper classes were permitted no scale-less or serpent-shaped fish. Certain meats (duck, pigeon, tortoise, wild boar) were specially commended, and those of the goat, deer and rhinoceros were permitted. A later work, the *Kumāra-Harana*, recommended pork cooked with the soft roots of the banana. A favourite curry was an alkaline salty extract of banana roots, cooked with certain aquatic green plants, and also with fish. Vegetables mentioned in the *Yōgini Tantra* are mūlaka, rājaka, vāsthuka, pālanga, nālika, sukna, lāphā, kanga and dhēkiya (a kind of fern), showing that both tubers and green leaves were important even in the early Assamese diet. The usual pulses and spices were used. Pāyasa and other sweets were made from milk, curds and ghee, and madhumada may have had a honey base. Rice beer was made domestically, and the tribals brewed a liquor called lāopāni. Bāna records that in the 7th century AD the Emperor Harsha received from King Bhāskara of Assam cups of ullaka, which diffused the fragrance of sweet wine.[37]

Orissa

In the period from AD 600 to 1200, Orissa used rice, wheat and barley,[38] and the fame of the rice of Kalinga finds mention in Someshwara's *Mānasollāsa*. Several bas-relief figures in the temples of Bhagavati and Muktēshwara hold cakes in their hands made perhaps of wheat. In the great tower of the Bhubanēshwara temple, the figure of Ganesha holds a bowl with small round grains, which could perhaps be the sweetmeat now called mōtichūr. A rice preparation filled with milk and ghee offered to the gods was called chāru. Several fruits of the region are referred to by Xuan Zang (7th century AD). Epigraphs describe the rights governing hunting for game and fishing, so both must have been prevalent. The *Dālimba Kumāra Katha* endorses the high food value of the rāghava fish. Frequent references to saundlika, distillers of wine, in the records of the Bhauma-Kara kings point to the prevalence of drinking at least among royalty.[38] Another work, the *Shreerāmbhāgavata*[38] of Shankaraḍēva, refers to the popularity of boiled rice covered with water and kept overnight, to be eaten next morning with brinjal curry or fish as an accompaniment (this was also the practice in Bengal at the time).[24f] The same work refers to the use of the sandesh and the laddu in Orissa.[24f]

Western India

Gujarāt

Prevalence of vegetarianism: Two movements led to a very high degree of vegetarianism in Gujarāt. One was the strong Jain influence in the area even prior to the 6th century BC, when the teachings of Mahāvira had a powerful impact (see Chapter 6). Numerous Jain scholars subsequently exerted a strong influence, like Hemachandra (11th century AD). King Kumārapāla, a meat eater in his youth, was influenced later by Jainism. In the 12th century AD he issued edicts against the slaughter of animals, called amarighōshanās.[39] Vaishnavaism, which also enjoins abstinence from meat, received a strong impetus from the preachings of Vallabhāchārya, who formed the Pushti-Mārga sect in the 15th century AD. His second son Vitthalnātha (1516–86) spent a considerable period in Gujarāt.[40a,41] One of his distinguished disciples was the saint Surdās. Many vaishyas, the trading community, became Vaishnavaites and were active in community service to earn social acclaim. One merchant prince of Sūrat, Vīrji Vōra, and another of Ahmedabād, Sānti Dāsā, gave away large sums in charity to promote vegetarianism. Today two-thirds of Gujarāt is vegetarian, the highest proportion in any Indian state. The proliferation of savoury fried snacks which travel well and thus serve as food on pilgrimages and journeys has much to do with the food regulations of these strict vegetarians.

Historical and current foods: One of the earliest works from Gujarāt, the *Bimalprabhandha* of Lāwanyasamay of about 1200 AD, mentions kūr (boiled rice) and karambho (curd rice), pāpads and vadi (wadian), and a number of sweets like vēdhami, khāja, laddu, sukhadi (from ravā, still a popular favourite), kheer and talwat (fried molasses).[24g] The Jain literature in Sanskrit from the 7th to the early 14th century frequently contains stray references to various food items. These have been sifted and brought together in a doctoral dissertation which quotes the original references.[42] Many food items from among these, which will now be described, clearly originate from Gujarāt.

Ōdana is boiled rice and has numerous variations, karambha is curd rice, and the rice sweet saktu is the sathvo of the present. Several sweet stuffed and fried items derive from wheat, like the mandaka (mándé), pahalika (khāja, phēni), phēnaka (sutar-phēni), murmura (mumra), udumbara (pūran-pūri), sohali or suhālī (wheat breads coated with castor sugar), and ghrtapūra (ghēbar or ghēvara, the juicy sweet characteristic of Sūrat).[43] Roasted jowār cobs yielded hūrada, and jowār rōtis were called didari. Pulses were widely employed to yield the dukkia (first mentioned in AD 1066), which is the well-known steamed dhōkla of today. Ground and cooked pulses constituted avaranna or varan, and veshtika, was a baked product now called vēdhami, based on besan flour. There were several fried vadas, the simple vataka (which was also placed in buttermilk or curd), the ghārika (ghāri), an urad vadā with holes fried to a deep brown, and pūrika, now the well-known mathiyā or chopadā usually made from besan but also from other pulse flours. The vatikā was the vati of the present, a vadā of urad flour that had been allowed to ferment for a few days before shaping into balls that were dried and preserved, to be fried when needed. Among vegetable items appear the kācchrā made of cucumber, today's kachōli, and other relishes include the kosamri (kachumber, a raw salad) and pralēhaka (chatani). Milk was widely used to yield thakra (buttermilk), themanam (kadhi), kshīraprakara (channa), kurchikā (māvā) and the sweet items shikarinī (shrīkhand) and sarkara (dūdhpēda). Another sweet made from sesame seed was shaskulī, perhaps the sānkli of today which is a jaggery chikki.[44,45]

The *Varanaka-Samuchaya* of about AD 1520 is written in the Gujarāthi language but in Devanāgari script. The extensive lists of food items that it carries are shown in Box 20, and most of them are instantly recognizable. Current staple foods of Gujarāt include rice, mung khichdī and several vegetable palāos, thick baked rōtlas of jowār, bājra and maize, thinner khākaras, and deep-fried rōtlis, sometimes stuffed. Spiced parāthās like mēthi-thēplās derive from wheat and are eaten with rāitha. Other wheat-based foods are vegetable-stuffed puffs called gujiyas, karanji or sanyavas, sometimes also sweet-stuffed.[40] Cooked vegetables have the generic name shāk, and the range of raw materials is exceptionally wide. Handva denotes vegetables or even dhāl mixes baked in a handa.[44,46] The well-known ūndhiu is a five-vegetable stew often served with steamed besan balls placed on top.[46] There are a large variety of relishes of various kinds. Pāpads include the kheechara which contains wheat, rice and bājra flours, and is neither fried nor baked, but steamed. Rāithas are made from curd and use many vegetables, nuts and dried fruits, and

Box 20
SIXTEENTH-CENTURY GUJARĀTHI DISHES

The *Varanaka-Samuchaya*[45] of about AD 1520 written by an unknown author (see text) is of considerable interest in that it carries fairly extensive lists of food ingredients and prepared items (unfortunately mixed up together) of the Gujarāt area. These are shown below in their original classification.

Meals: rice, jowāri, bājri made into a palev (palāo) with mirch, ginger, turmeric, pipaliya and vasudiya served along with dhōkla, idāri, khāndvi, rāita and pūran, the meal ending with dahi or chhās

Sweets: laddu made from urad, til, cōpra, rice, broken chana or dallia, maīda, mung, fine boondi, bājra, sattu, simmar-kēsar

Wheat items: mandaka, gari, ghēbar, gōle-pāpadi, gugri, mahisūpa, thin phēni, magaz, shiro (kshīra), shakarpāra

Rice items: kanadu, kamōd, karadiya, karam, kalam, kaumudi, kanwari, karasu, chandrāni, jeeva-sal, dāngiri, dundaniya, tavani, till-vasi, beurijeera, douli, dhanūri, panchashāli, pīlīshāli, mahāshāli, raibhoj, rāj-anna, ratishāli, varadu, vāgadi, vāsaru, thati-shāli. After a marriage was served karambha, a curd-rice blend flavoured with camphor, cardamom, rāi, jeera, green ginger and asafoetida

Dhāls: Apart from the usual common dhāls are listed vāl, vātana (peas) and a pulse-based kadhi flavoured with asafoetida

Vadās: Either vadā varieties, or their spicing, are thus listed; thudi, motia, kānji (in buttermilk), mirī (pepper), haludriya (turmeric), tala, dallia, southalya, khand (sugar), puhādiya, aladhna, magna (mung), bina, gōle, adhrak (green ginger), rāi, thaliya, mirch-ni-vadā, kulatthu (kulthi)

Vegetables: Tindōra, vālōr (cluster beans?), kosamba, chibda (rakdi), chuliphali (chouli), guārphali, mogri, kankōda (a type of karēla), thuraiya, gisola, bangala, chimada, āmla, nīli-marcha, nīli-peepar, nīli-gari, pāpadi, mūla

It is apparent that the variety of raw materials and finished foods was both wide, and that a cuisine which can be recognized as being distinctively Gujarāthi had evolved five centuries ago.

---

chatanis too are varied. Pickles include the distinctive athanu, goondas and chundō, with its sweet-sour flavour, tempered with cardamom and cloves. In fact a touch of sugar goes into most Gujarāthi spicing. Distinctive sweets are the doodhpāk, a kheer, the sweet-stuffed ghāri-pūri made from maīda, thandāi (a cooling, nut-based milk drink), gunder-pāk (which contains the aromatic resin gaund), sheera (of ravā, corn or dhāl) and the mōhanthāl, a halva of besan.

The snacks of Gujarāt, nāsto and farsān, deserve a separate section.

Nāsto and farsān: These are fried items, but they are distinctive and never eaten together.[47] Nāsto are items of many types that can be kept for long in air-tight tins, and even transported. One of them, ganthia, are essentially besan-derived crisps, like the wafer-like pāpri, the solid, cylindrical Bhavnāgri, the flat, long fofda, and the slim and spicy masāla. Sēv is also from besan, fried in long thin strings, or long thicker strings, or as wafers. Chevda consists of beaten rice that has been deep fried to crispness and mixed with salt, spices, groundnuts, almonds and raisins. A mix of all the above, and in fact of anything crunchy, constitutes bhoosoo.

Fārsān items are eaten with a major meal or as a snack. The fluffy dhōkla is based on a flour of chana and curds thereafter fermented and steamed, and the khaman is a coarser version. Yeast and bacteria derived from the bulk components make for both porosity and a range of subtle flavours.[48] Vadās are of course numerous. The tender, rolled-up pancake, khāndvi, sprinkled with mustard and coriander, is a besan product. Bhajiyas denote deep-fried pulse balls, and the delicate muthiyās are rolls of flour and vegetables flavoured with saunf and mēthi, first steamed and then lightly fried.[46] Kachōris are vegetable-stuffed, deep fried puffs, circular or crescent-shaped. Colocasia (arvi) leaves, coated with besan paste, and then steamed and lightly fried, give arvi-nā-pātrā.

Bohri Muslims

These are disciples of Abdullah, a missionary of the 11th century AD, and converts from Hinduism.[7] Even their vegetable items are distinctive. There is the sarka, a hot summer tuvar soup with extracted groundnut and coconut, and for winter, the sarki, a cold tuvar soup with diced cucumber, tomato and onions. The kuddal-pālida is a thick, sour split-pea dish that goes with a special palāo of meat and split peas. Lagania-sheekh is mince meat topped with a beaten egg and baked, and malāi-tikkas are kabābs of beef that have been marinated in cream.[7]

The Pārsis

Though originally from Gujarāt, the Pārsis have now moved all over India. Their food has been considered in Chapter 6.

Gōa

The Portuguese navigator, Vasco da Gama, reached Calicut in 1498 but it was in Gōa, captured by Alfonso de Albuquerque in 1510 from the Sultān of Bijapūr, that the Portuguese consolidated their position and established their maritime empire, the Estado da India. This lasted for about 150 years before yielding first to Dutch and then to British dominance. The cuisine of Gōa is an extraordinary amalgam of Portuguese and local sensibilities, mainly those of the Sāraswath Hindus. Liberal use of vinegar (generally added to finish a cooked dish, since it turns bitter if added earlier), is essentially European, but use of various Indian ingredients, and of the less-spicy whole chillies of Kāshmir and Gōa (called bedigé chillis in Karnātaka) which impart an intense red colour, bespeak the local influence.[49] The name Gōa itself can be traced to the Gubi of Sumerian tablets (2100 BC), the Gouba of Ptolemy, the later Gōvapūri and Gōpapūri, and the Munda word Goen-Bab for an inclined ear of corn.[50]

Let us start with bread, based here on rice. The bolē is a country bread of rice flour with some molasses, leavened with toddy and glazed with an egg yolk before baking, and saanas is a round steamed bread of rice and pulse flours fermented overnight with toddy.[51] Kankōd is a hard, ring-shaped dinner roll, and barki a whorl-shaped pastry, both made of wheat. Pork takes many forms. One is the distinctive Gōa sausage developed by monks. Sorpotel is a curry of pork blood, meat, liver and fat with vinegar and tamarind juice, and vindāloo is a more liquid curry that uses the dried rind of the kokum fruit to impart sourness. Feijoada is pork cooked with beans, and salted pork is also pickled. Fish and prawn also figure. Caladine is a yellow fish curry with turmeric[49] and the roe of the kingfish, lightly salted and fried, is a breakfast delicacy.[51] Prawn balachao has vinegar and lots of chopped onions that give it a sweet-sour flavour, and it keeps well enough to be bottled. A chacuti is a dish of shallow-fried chicken or meat. The desserts are quite distinctive. Bibinca is a concoction of egg yolk, flour and coconut milk which is built up and baked in layers, and turned upside down to cool. Baking together besan, grated coconut and sugar yields Dos de Graō, with a thick firm crust and a chewy centre.[49] Baked yams are coated with melted jaggery, and mangada is a soft, chewy mango cheese. Pastry is frequently decorated with strips of tender coconut dipped in melted sugar, a perfect Indo-European match. Monks were responsible for brewing and distilling distinctive-tasting fēnis from the cashew 'fruit' and the coconut palm, which form the base for cocktails of many kinds.

The East Indians

Portuguese influence is also seen, though less prominently, in the food of the East Indians of Mahārāshtra. This cuisine has a curried chicken moilē, which employs a distinctive masālā which is made in lots and kept in bottles.[52]

North India

Wheat is essentially a northern staple, and a variety of breads have developed which are described in Box 21. The food of certain regions of the north may now be considered.

Kāshmīr

The historical background: An ancient stone-age culture dated about 2400 BC has been excavated at Burzahom in Kāshmīr, with evidence of many tools, animal hunting, and the seeds of many wild plants, but no firm indication of cereals.[53] Rice is now grown on terraces that have been shown to go back to 10,000 BC, so it is probably of ancient provenance.

The name Kāshmīr means the abode (mōr, a Nāgā word) of the descendants of Kashyapa. The Nāgās were later totally absorbed by the Vedic Aryans called Sāraswaths (from the name of the great river), who even now celebrate the Herat festival with mutton, fish, the flesh of forest fowls, and liquor.[54a] The draft animal is the zo, a cross between a yak and a cow, the female of which, the zomo, yields excellent milk.[54b] The *Nilamata Purāna* of AD 550–650 mentions shāli rice as the staple of Kāshmīr; the milk of both cow and buffalo was used, apūpa and pisthaka sweet confections were made, meat and fish were important foods, and the first snowfall was celebrated with drinking.[55] The *Rājatarangini* of Kalhana (*c.* AD 1200) notes the use of rice and barley by the poor.[56] Mung (mudga) was used, but considered an inferior food, perhaps in comparison with meat, fish and pork which were all in use. So was alcohol, the nobility using a light wine flavoured with flowers. Honey and fruits were widely taken, and the spices used were asafoetida, onions and ginger. Both salt and pepper are only rarely mentioned. Products from both cow and buffalo milk are described.

Today's foods: Even Kāshmīri brahmins eat flesh, but the foods of Hindus and Muslims are differently spiced.[7] Hindus use asafoetida, mēthi, ginger and saunf; Muslims employ onions (a variety called praan) and garlic, and both use Kāshmīr chillis which confer an intense red colour and a tart rather than spicy flavour. Appropriate spices are ground and shaped into discs with a hole in the middle, called alasalas or wadis, from which pieces are broken off for use either in cooking, or as a table spice. Lamb dishes abound: yakhni (in curds); aab-gōsht (in milk); rōghan-jōsh (literally red meat, with 'Hindu' spicing and coloured red with dried cockscomb); marzwangan (as a mince); several meat balls, like gōli and rista; and goshtāba, a meat loaf of minced mutton, large and silky in texture. There is even a special mishāni dinner, served say for a wedding, in which exactly seven dishes, all made from lamb, are served.[9] Rib chops are tabakmaaz, fish with radish is gard-mūf, chicken is cooked with brinjals, and shikar is duck cooked with vinegar, garlic and chillis. Before the advent of Islam pork-eating was popular.[71]

Rice is the staple food and is of course cooked in many ways, like the tursh, shụlla and zarda (sweet) palāos. Wheat breads include kulcha,

Box 21
BREADS OF INDIA

But for the fact that they are made of wheat, the term bread is hardly appropriate for the numerous roasted, fried and baked items of India. The text describes some unusual and elaborate historical ones of the Karnataka region. Here current common items from all over the country are described under three heads.

Dry roasted forms of roti include the common chapāti, roasted dry on a hot thavā (griddle), and sometimes puffed out to a phulka by brief contact with live coals.[75] A very thin chapāti of Gujarāt is the rōtlee. The rumāli (literally scarf) is also thin; it is pressed with the fingers and tossed, never rolled, till it achieves an enormous size, after which it is roasted on a large upturned thavā, and then folded over many times to manageable size. Also thavā-roasted are the round, slightly-flattened phefras of Rājasthān which again are finished on live coals and eaten with ghee. The bhātia of the same state is a popular peasant food, and dōpatris, also of Rājasthān, are soft, thin rotis that come apart as two circles because of the style of rolling the dough. Doughs carrying spinach yield distinctive rōtis; the missi-rōti, roasted dry on a tavā and flaky in texture, has, besides spinach, green chillis and onions in the dough. The khākras of Gujarat are kneaded with milk and water, and are crisp products that keep well and are carried by Gujarāthi travellers. Rājasthān has the unusual ball-like bātti, roasted dry in an oven and then on live coals; it is broken open and ghee poured in before consumption. Bāfflās are first cooked in a soup of masūr dhāl and then roasted.[75]

Wheat products after rolling out can be either pan-fried using just a little fat, or deep-fried.[75] Parātās are the commonest form of the first kind, often square or triangular in shape rather than round. The dough can be mixed with seasoned vegetables like potatoes, cauliflower, spinach or mēthi. Or a stuffing of vegetables or chopped eggs may be placed on the parāta which is then folded over and lightly fried. Both types are frequently eaten with curds. Stuffing with besan gives birahi, with an unusual taste and texture. Deep-fried products are exemplified by round, swollen pūris, and the tiny, almost globular gōle-gappās which are a delectable relish when eaten with a fiery pepper-water liquid. The luchis of Bengal are thicker and not as fully puffed as pūris, since some fat has been kneaded into the dough. They can also be stuffed, for example with a mash of cooked urad dhāl placed at the centre of the ball of dough before it is rolled out. The dough of the bhaturā is allowed to ferment using yoghurt, and then rolled out to give a layery fried product. The khjūru or khajūr is made with added sugar and poppy seeds, and deep-fried to crispness, resembling in effect fried slabs of a western bread loaf.[75]

The third class of wheat products are those which are leavened and baked, either in closed and heated ovens, or in Indian-style tandoors, which are open, lined, glowing ovens with live coals placed at the bottom.[75] Naan is made of maida, the white inner flour of wheat, which is leavened before baking to yield a thick elastic product, sometimes sprinkled with tiny black kalōnji (nigella) seeds. Use of more ghee in the batter gives the even more elastic kulcha, which is also sometimes stuffed; use of milk in the dough yields the sweetish and more powdery sheermāl, rather like a round, flat bun. Enriched with butter, and crisper still, is the khastā, a word also used to designate a type

Box 21(*Contd.*)

Pūris, deep-fried puffed-out wheat-meal circles.

of parātā. Naan itself can be dressed in various ways. It can be brushed with saffron water to yield a red surface colour after baking. Or it can be coated with a tomato and garlic paste, or with a sweet mash of dates earlier cooked in jaggery. Almonds, or crumbs of paneer, can also be built into the naan dough.[69]

Western-style oven-baking has yielded leavened breads that are unique to this country. Ordinary loaf bread is called double roti in India, since it was made in jointed sections. Pāo is a Portuguese contribution, rather like an elastic bun, which is baked to form four sections that can be broken apart. The gutlī is a very hard round or rectangular well-risen roll with a brown top, and the crusty pēti-pāo (literally box-bread) looks like an ancient treasure chest. There is a large commercial naan which is vended after cutting into wedges. In fact all these oven-baked items are sold on the street for consumption as on-the-spot snacks, with vegetables (bhāji), boiled eggs, mince meat or chicken as an accompaniment.[75]

sheermāl (see Box 20), the chewy girda, the sesame-encrusted tsachvaru and the soft bakirkhani, all eaten for breakfast with tea.[57] Tea is made in samovārs called kāngri, and is brewed either green, or with cardamoms and almonds to yield the richer kāhwāh, both of which are sipped all day long. Vegetables are grown in summer and dried for winter use in large quantities. The unique floating gardens of Kāshmīr are water weeds bonded with lake mud on which are grown cucumbers, melons, tomatoes, radishes and mint. In the lakes themselves are to be found lotus roots (rhizomes) called nedr which are cooked with meat, fish, and greens, or fried to crispness, or deep fried in a rice batter coating.[7] Chutneys are made from fresh walnuts, sour cherries, yellow pumpkins and white radishes, and for dessert there are fruits like cherries, apples (āmri and maharāji, see Chapter 15), peaches, pears and plums.

The Dōgras are Rājputs who eat wheat, bājra and maize as staple foods. Sri-palāo and mutton-palāo are made from rice.[58] Other popular dishes are the rājmāh, a curd preparation called auria, and the relish ambal. Expert cooks are called sīyān, and community meals called dhaam are served on large lotus leaves, or stitched leaves (pattal) and cups (doona). A Dogra verse has it that a man can never fail in his missions if he takes radish on Tuesdays, sweets on Wednesdays, curd on Thursdays, rāi on Fridays, uses oil on Saturdays, chews betel on Sundays, and looks into a mirror on Mondays.[58]

Rājasthān

Historical: The *Kānhadadé-Prabanda* of Padmanābha written in AD 1455 describes the food served at the table of this ruler. There were 'sēv, suhāli, māndā, pāpads, khājā, sālan, badi, lapsika of the pānchadari variety, kānsār, dhān and many other delicious dishes'. Perhaps these rulers were Vaishnavaites, which would explain the lack of meat dishes, otherwise usual among Rājputs.[59] In ancient Udaipūr, it was customary for a young pig to be roasted whole on a spit called shūla, in a sacrific called the shūlagava. Strips of roasted meat were marinated with spiced curd, placed along with ghee in a wrapper and baked, followed by grilling on a skewer.[60] It was common among Rājputs to drink liquor and take a small pill of opium, and on the eve of battle to double the dose so as to heighten both their own courage, and that of their horses.[61] Of course the bulk of the population are vegetarian through the same historical Jain and Vaishnava influences that operated in neighbouring Gujarāt.

Current cuisine: A speciality of Rājasthan is the bātti, the vātya of Sanskrit, a hard roasted ball of wheat which is cracked open and eaten with plenty of ghee.[62] Crisp rotīs, called bhākri, of bājra and jowār are also made on a griddle, and there is even a besan rōtī with a little wheat flour added to the dough. In fact besan and mung dhāl flour are the base batters for a whole series of crisp-fried savouries like the mangōdi, gātti and pāpdi (sometimes with mēthi incorporated). There are thin and thick pāpads, called khēlada, stuffed kachōri, and vadā and dahī-vadā, besides spicy farsān snacks resembling those of adjacent Gujarāt. Many vegetables are sun-dried for year-round use as gattey-ka-sāg, as are certain berries (like kair and debra), fruits (bījōda), stems and roots (garmār) and even certain aromatic twigs (sanghār). Even many sweets are pulse-based products like besan-barfi, sheera of mung dhāl, and chūrma-laddus.[62]

Uttar Pradesh and Bihār

A 16th century work lists foods of the Gangetic plain as sattu (the flour of roasted pulses), and barley grits eaten with salt or sugar.[24] Pulse preparations included the barā (vadā), mungauri (a mung vadā), pakauri (pakōda), methauri (a pakōda spiced with mēthi), dubaki (identified as a boiled pakōda) and the rolled-up khāndvi pancake now identified with Gujarāt. Precipitated channa from milk is listed. Sweet dishes included the lāpsi, a halvā of wheat flour; kirōra, a rice-flour laddu, and kēsara, a kēsari-bāth of ravā.

A century ago, the everyday foods of Bihār were meticulously recorded in considerable detail by a British official.[63] Rice, barley, wheat and roasted rāgi (ūmi) were all in use. Boiled rice was called bāth by the Hindus and khushka by the Muslims, and it was cooked with linseed to give tīsjauri and with poppy seeds to yield danjauri. Boiled rice flour cakes were termed khiraura, phara meant steamed rice balls, and phulauri was a steam-cooked roll of coarse flour. Lāi was parched rice, chiuri parched barley, lawā parched maize, and parmal denoted any parched grain, but more especially maize. Lāpsi was the flour of any grain boiled in milk and sugar; if salted instead, the product was called ghattha. Wheat was converted into luchuī and pūri. Bread was made from the flour of the mango stone, and called anthi-ki-rōti. Chana flour was termed sattu, boiled to yield pittha. Barā (vadā) were patties of fried pulses, and bari (wadi) balls of them, while phulaura was the present dahi-vadā in curds. The bhāji was termed bhajka. Tilauri were balls of urad or mung with sesame seed, dried in the sun and deep-fried, and kachauri were wheat cakes filled with spiced pulses. Litti and bhabhri signified various cognate kinds of cakes baked on hot ashes, sometimes stuffed with chana flour and spices. From the flowers of the mahua mixed with either cereal flours, besan or linseed came mahaur, and the same flowers with molasses and parched grain yielded latta. Bhartha and taral were both ghee-fried vegetable dishes, and phorān or dhunaur denoted masālā mixes. Numerous sweet delicacies are noted, including the gulāb-jāmūn, jilēbi and rasogollā which is described as being a 'Bengal delicacy'. There were also laddus like the fine-grained mōtichūr, and sesame-seed tilkut. From wheat flour was made the sweet crisp-fried bread khāja, the bālushāhi glazed with sugar, the date-shaped khajūr or khurma, the pua with molasses, and the phēni, described as a 'frothy sweetmeat'. Halvā or kānchi was made from wheat flour, dried fruits and ghee, the Muslims also adding eggs; a superior halvā was mahān-bhōg. The candied gourd delicacy, pētha, is noted. Kheer from rice, milk and sugar was termed bakir, or rasiya in Bihār.[58]

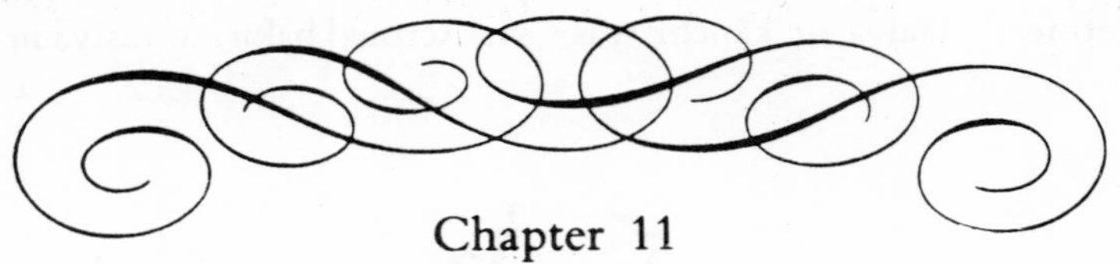

Chapter 11

FOOD TALES OF THE EARLY TRAVELLERS

India has always been a subject of intense curiosity and avarice, and through the writings of its visitors since ancient times we can 'see ourselves as others see us'. For some seven centuries, starting from about 500 BC, and more especially after Alexander's incursion into India in May 327 BC, a number of Greek travellers recorded their impressions. The Chinese travellers, all Buddhist monks drawn to India where their great teacher had lived, took up the tale from about AD 325. Pride of place must go to the account of the indefatigable Xuan Zang, who personally visited '110 of the 138 Indian kingdoms' of the 7th century AD. The Arab travellers, spanning some six centuries commencing about AD 850, were ardent chroniclers and acute observers, with Ibn Battūta, who called himself the Traveller of Islam, easily being the best.

The Greeks and the foods of India

Scylax of Charybanda was sent by Darius, as long ago as 510 BC, to sail down the river Indus from Kaspapyros (Peshāwar) to its mouth, and then home by way of the Red Sea. His account has not survived, but was probably used by Herodotus (484–431 BC) in writing his monumental *Historika*; this mentions an Indian grain the size of a millet that sprang up spontaneously from the earth without cultivation, and was eaten by civilized people, whereas even raw fish was used as food by those inhabiting the river marshes.[1a,2] Ktesias (416-398 BC), court physician and historian, based his *Indika* on his talks with Persian officials who had themselves visited India, and with seven Indians, including two women, whom he had met at the Persian court of Susa.[3] The food of the mountain people, the kyanokephaloi as he called them, consisted of the 'millet of the sheep', and also of what appears to be curd. They also ate the fruit of the sweet siptakhora (?), which was even dried like raisins and packed in hampers, and exchanged their own dried fruit products for flour and loaves of bread with people living in the plains. Both sesame and coconut oils were in use. He distinguished between the male and female reed (sugarcane?), spoke of karpion (Tamil karuppa, Sanskrit dārushila, cinnamon), and noted the existence of palms whose fruits (probably coconuts) were three times as large as those of Babylon (the date?). The cochineal insect was 'about the size of a beetle, red like cinnabar. . . the Indians grind these insects into a powder' which was used to dye clothing.[3]

Of those who accompanied Alexander, Aristobolus of Kassandrelia mentions rice as a strange plant, standing in water and sown in beds; the plant was 4 cubits (1.8 metres) in height, had many ears, and yielded a large produce.[1d] He describes also how the food of two brahmin priests cost them nothing because they simply helped themselves from food stalls to whatever they liked, for example the abundant cakes of sesamum and honey. One of Alexander's right-hand men was Nearchos of Crete, who commanded the return fleet that was built

The rice plant in standing water, a strange phenomenon to the early Greek visitors.

on the river Hydaspes (Jhelum), taking it back to Iraq, and thence to Greece, after a dangerous 5-month journey.[4a] He mentions a reed tree (sugarcane) that 'produced honey without the association of bees', and referred to the abundance of medicinal plants and herbs to be found in India.[1c] There were both a summer and a winter crop, and Nearchos attributed this great 'facility of the soil' not only to the rains, but to the silt which the rivers brought down in great quantities from the mountains. One grain, described as a little smaller than wheat, was first threshed; then, to prevent the seed from being exported, it was roasted in 'a common enterprise', following which each took as much as he required to support him for a year.[1c] This grain was called 'bismoron' by Onesikritos, the pilot of Alexander's return fleet. The visit to Takshasila of Apollonious of Tyana (born *c.*295 BC) was described by Philostratus; though full of inaccuracies, it relates that the king hunted solely for exercise, gave away what he killed, and himself lived on vegetarian food.[5]

Seleukos Nikator had accompanied Alexander to India; after the latter died at Susa in Persia in 323 BC, he returned to win back the territory that had been lost to Chandragupta. He was defeated, came to terms, and appointed Megasthenes as his ambassador in Pātaliputra. Though the latter's own writings are lost except for a few fragments,[6] numerous quotations have been preserved in later compilations by Diodorus, Strabo, Arrian and Pliny among others. Megasthenes writes:

Indians live frugally, especially when in camp. . . they lead happy lives, being simple in their manners and frugal.[7a] They never drink wine except at sacrifices. Their beverage is a liquor composed from rice instead of barley, and their food is principally a rice-pottage. . . they possess good, sober sense: for instance, they eat always alone, and they have no fixed hours when meals are to be taken by all in common, but each one eats when he feels inclined.[1c]

Here he adds that 'the contrary custom would be better for the ends of social and civil life.' Megasthenes noted that agriculturists formed the bulk of the Indian population.[1d] Of them he writes:

They are a most mild and gentle people. They never resort to the cities either to transact business or to take part in public tumults. They are exempted from all military service, and pursue their labours free from all alarm. Indeed it often happens that at the same time, and in the same part of the country, the army is engaged in fighting the enemy, whilst the husbandmen are sowing and ploughing in the utmost security. . . The entire land is the property of the king, to whom they pay one-fourth of the produce as revenue.[1d]

Of the upper classes he writes:

When Indians are at supper, a table is placed before each person, this being like a tripod. There is placed upon it a golden bowl, into which they first put rice, boiled as one would boil barley (the Greek dish *chondros*), and then they add many dainties prepared according to Indian recipes.[6]

Strabo of Ameseia (65 BC–*c.* AD 25) wrote his famous *Geography* based on both his own travels and the writings of others. Between the rivers Jhelum and Chenāb, the land was very fertile. During the rainy season, he wrote, flax and millet, as well as rice ('bismorōn') and sesamum were sown, and in the winter season wheat, barley and other edibles.[1d] Elsewhere there were date palms, and for the first time, salt is mentioned as a product of the territory of King Sopithes (Saubhutu). Strabo relates how from Takshasila Alexander received 3,600 oxen and 10,000 sheep, and how in the country of the Ashvakas he captured 20,000 oxen of a fine breed which he sent back to Macedonia. Our next Greek historian, Diodorus Siculus of Sicily (*c.*85–15 BC), mentions the fleet of ships that Alexander had built from the 'unlimited quantity' of timber fit for the purpose that grew in the mountains.[4d] The *History of Alexander the Great*, written by Quentin Curtius-Rufus (*c.*30 BC–AD 30), has a description of Chandragupta Maurya at dinner: 'His food is prepared by women, who also serve him with wine, which is much used by all the Indians. When the king falls into a drunken sleep his courtesans carry him away to his bedchamber, invoking the gods of the night in

Sugarcane being transported from field to factory.

Alexander of Macedon.

their native hymns.'[7b] Comments by other foreign visitors on Indian kings are featured in Box 22.

Pliny the Elder (AD 23–79) wrote an encyclopaedia in 37 books called *The Natural History*, of which the sixth book on India is based again mainly on the lost writings of Megasthenes.[1d] Pliny describes several Indian trees: the fig (banyan) tree which produced small fruit; the pala (?) tree with wonderfully sweet fruits called ariena, favoured as food by sages; the 'olive' tree, the pepper plant and the grape vine, and, for the first time, the ebony tree, small and lustrous, but scarce to find free from knots. Pliny describes shipbuilding in Trapobane, as Śri Lanka (Tāmraparni) was termed by the Greeks.[1d]

The *Periplus Maris Erythraei* or *Circumnavigation of the Erythrean Sea,* written about AD 50, is posthumous.[4f] It graphically describes from personal knowledge how India's 'seas ebb and flow with tides of extraordinary strength, which increase both at new and full moon, and for three days after each, but fall intermediately.'[4f] The chief exports from south India were listed as spices, perfumes, herbs, precious stones, ivory and textiles, in exchange for which were imported gold, silver, tin and lead, glass vessels, coral, wine and linen cloth.[8b] Aelianus Tacitus, or Aelian (*c.* AD 80–140), whose *Collections of History*[4f] is essentially a compilation from earlier sources, talks of 'the olive tree which was Indian', perhaps the bēr (ziziphus); snakes 'which display to the eye a variety of colours, as if they were painted with pigment,' possibly banded kraits; tame peacocks and tame pheasants; parrots which 'with a clear utterance repeat the words of human speech' (another Greek writer, Kerkion, also mentions talking mainas); and the 'Indian dog . . . of surpassing strength and ferocity (which) despises all other animals but fights with the lion (which is) at times worsted by the Indian dog and killed in the chase.'[4f] From the *Anabasis of Alexander*[4g] written by Arrian, more correctly Flavius Arrianus (*c.* AD 96–160), we learn that Alexander's return fleet 'numbered collectively eighty 30-oared galleys, but the whole fleet, including the horse transports and the small craft and the other river boats ... did not fall short of 2000'. Going down the Indus, 'he came to a large lake formed by the river in widening out... to give it the appearance of a gulf of the sea, for salt-water fish were now seen in it of larger size than anything in our sea.'[4g] Another curious bit of information from Arrian is that elephant wounds were cured in India by the application of roast pork.[6] Writing in the third century AD, Athenaios in his book *Deipnosophists* (which has been translated variously as 'banquet for the learned' or 'contrivers of feasts'), says that among the presents which Chandragupta sent to Seleukos Nikator were certain powerful aphrodisiacs.[4a] This monarch,in the view of Marcus Junianus Justinus (Justin, 3rd century AD) in his *History of Philippae*, after winning back India's freedom from the Greeks, turned into a tyrant and oppressed his own people.

Seekers from China

Hardly had Greek interest in India abated when visitors from the east started to arrive. Of Chi-tao-an, who was here about AD 325, little has

Box 22

FOREIGN SNAPSHOTS OF INDIAN KINGS

Many foreign writers comment in their books on Indian kings with whom they came into contact. Alexander 'entered the dominions of King Sopithes (Saubhutu), whose nation excels in wisdom, and lives under good laws and customs'.[4c] Later he encountered Omphis (possibly Ambhi), son of the sovereign of the territories of which Takshasila was the capital. 'The prince had brought with him (in token of submission) 65 elephants... (along) with a great many sheep of extraordinary size, and 3000 bulls of a valuable breed, highly prized by the rulers of the country...' The ruler of the kingdom lying between the Jhelum and the Chenāb was Poros (probably Pauravā).[4d, 14c] When summoned by Alexander's envoys to meet the conqueror, he proudly replied that he would undoubtedly do so, but at his own frontier and in arms. In the battle Poros fought bravely, and suffered nine wounds on his body. Plutarch continues the story: 'When Poros was taken prisoner, Alexander asked him how he wished to be treated. "Like a king", answered Poros. Alexander further asked if he had anything else to request. "Everything", rejoined Poros, "is comprised in the words, like a king"'.[4e]

Chandragupta Maurya, who defeated Seleukos Nikator, is described by Megasthenes as living in great state.[7b] The royal palace stood in the midst of a walled-in park with ornamental trees, tame peacocks and pheasants, and lakes full of sacred fish. 'The palace is adorned with gilded pillars clasped all round by a vine embossed in gold, while silver images of those birds which most charm the eye diversify the workmanship[7b]... In the Indian palace there are wonders with which neither Memnonian Susa in all its glory, nor the magnificence of Ecbatana can hope to vie.'[15e] We have an interesting anecdote of Chandragupta's son, Bindusāra. Athenaios reports that this king wrote to Antiochus asking for three articles, to which the latter replied: 'We shall send you the figs and the wine (which you requested), but Greek laws forbid a sophist to be sold.'[4a]

A century later the Chinese traveller Xuan Zang came into contact with Emperor Harshavardhana who 'waged incessant warfare until in six years he had fought the five Indias. Then having enlarged his territory, he ... reigned in peace for thirty years without raising a weapon'.[8f] The Chinese pilgrim accompanied the Emperor to Prayāga (Allahabad) for a celebration that took place on a great plain called the Arena of Charitable Offerings.[8g] Here the treasure that he had amassed over the previous five years was bestowed as gifts over 34 days among Buddhists, brahmins, orphans, the destitute and the poor, and indeed to anyone seeking charity. 'All being given away,' Xuan Zang relates, 'the Emperor begged from his sister an ordinary second-hand garment, and having put it on, he paid worship to the Buddhas of the ten regions, and exulted with joy with his hands closed in adoration.'

On his travels Xuan Zang also met King Pulakēsi the Second of Vātāpi (Bādāmi). 'His plans and actions are widespread, and his beneficent actions are felt over a great distance. His subjects obey him with perfect submission... Harshavardhana ... has not yet conquered these troops.'[8h]

There are comments also by Arab visitors on the kings whom they encountered.[23] Sulaiman about 857 AD counted the king of Ballabhrai among the

Box 22 (*contd.*)

four great kings of the world, the others being those of Babylon, China and Constantinople. A century later Al-Ashtari says that 'from Cambay to Chaul is the land of Ballabhrai, and in it there are several subordinate kings.'[22] During the stay of Ibn Battūta the prime ruler was Muhammad-bin-Tughlaq, of whom he writes: 'This king is of all men the most addicted to the making of gifts and the shedding of blood ... There are current among the people many stories of his generosity and courage, and of his cruelty and violence towards criminals. He slew both small and great, and spared not the learned, the pious or the noble ... May God preserve us from such calamities!'[18b]

survived beyond the name. The stay of the next Chinese Buddhist, Fa Xian, was long (AD 399–414), and his writings prolific:

Throughout the country no one kills any living thing, nor drinks wine, nor eats onion or garlic[7c]... In this country they do not keep pigs or fowls, there are no dealings in cattle, no butchers' shops or distilleries in their market-places. As a medium of exchange they use cowries. Only the Chandalas go hunting and deal in flesh. The elders and gentries of these countries have instituted in their capitals free hospitals and hither come all poor or helpless patients, orphans, widowers and cripples. They are well taken care of, a doctor attends them, food and medicine being supplied according to their needs. They are all made quite comfortable, and when they are cured they go away.[7c]

A Buddhist monk.

Buddhist monks had extremely regular and disciplined food habits.

When stranger monks arrive at any monastery, the older residents meet and receive them, carry for them their clothes and alms-bowl, and give them water to wash their feet, oil to anoint themselves, and the liquid food permitted out of the regular hours,[9a]

which lay between sunrise and noon.

A later visitor, I Ching (AD 671–95) states that onions were forbidden because they caused pain, spoilt the eyesight and weakened the body.[10] Guests were offered one of the eight syrups prescribed by the Buddha. At a meal, monks were first served two pieces of ginger with some salt, and then boiled rice, on which was poured a thin extract of beans and hot ghee; these were mixed with the fingers, after which cakes, fruits, ghee and sugar were served. Toothpicks were provided after the meal, and pure water for rinsing the mouth, and sometimes a perfumed paste with which to clean the hands. The beverages that accompanied the meal were cold or warm water, whey, buttermilk or fermented sour gruel.[10] Water could be perfumed with tvāk, elā, patrakā and nāgakēshara.[11] Betel leaves carrying fragrant spices were served at the end to help digestion, remove phlegm, and make the mouth fragrant,[10] other materials for the purpose being bijuparaka (*Citrus medica*) and matsyandika, perhaps granulated sugar.[12] In fact I Ching became a fanatic for oral hygiene, urging his countrymen after a meal to cleanse the hands, wash them with water, chew tooth wood, and clean the tongue and teeth carefully.[13]

By far the most comprehensive account of the India of those times comes through in the accounts of Xuan Zang (the traveller once called Hieun Tsang), who spent 16 years between AD 629 and 645 on his travels away from China, and by his own admission visited '110 of the 138 kingdoms' in every part of the country.[14a] This must surely count as one of the great travel feats of all time, since movement was by no means easy and his own resources were extremely meagre. He writes:

The crownlands are divided into four parts.[15c] The first is for carrying out the affairs of the state; the second, for paying the ministers and officers of the crown; the third, for rewarding men of genius; the fourth for giving arms to religious communities. In this way, the taxes on the people are light and the services required of them are moderate.[15c]

Of the common people Xuan Zang says,

The Kshatriyas and the brahmanas are cleanhanded and unostentatious, pure and simple in life and very frugal.[8d] They are pure of themselves and not from compulsion. With respect to the ordinary people, although they are naturally lightminded, yet they are upright and honourable. In money matters they are without craft, and in administering justice they are considerate. They are not deceitful or treacherous in their conduct, and are faithful to their oaths and promises. In their rules of Government there is remarkable rectitude, while in their behaviour there is much gentleness and sweetness.[8d]

And he goes on:

They are very particular in their personal cleanliness, and allow no remissness in this particular.[15e] All wash themselves before eating; they never use that which has been left over; they do not pass the dishes. Wooden and stone (clay) vessels, when used must be destroyed; vessels of gold, silver, copper, or iron, after each meal must be rubbed and polished. After eating they cleanse their teeth with a willow, and wash their hands and mouth. Until these ablutions are finished they do not touch one another. Every time they perform the functions of nature they wash their bodies and use perfumes of sandal-wood or turmeric.[15e]

What fruits did Xuan Zang find in India?

The fruit of the āmlaka, the madhuka (mahua), bhadra (bēr), kapittha (woodapple, *Limonia acidissima*), mōcha (plantain), nārikela (coconut) and panasa (jack) are common (Sanskrit words are used for these).[15d] It would be difficult to enumerate all the kinds of fruit; we have briefly named those most esteemed by the people. The pear, wild plum, peach, apricot, grape etc. (Chinese terms are employed here) have all been brought from the country of Kashmir, and are found growing on every side. Pomegranates and sweet oranges are grown everywhere. The date, the loquat, the chestnut and persimmon are not known.[14a]

Elsewhere he describes other articles raised for food:

In cultivating the land, those whose duty it is sow and reap, plough and weed, and plant according to the season; and after their labour they rest a while. Among the products of the ground, rice and corn (barley?) are most plentiful. With respect to edible herbs and plants, we may name ginger and mustard, melons and pumpkins, the heun-lo (kandu?) plant, and others. Onions and garlic are little known, and few people eat them; if anyone uses them for food, they are expelled beyond the walls of the town. The most usual food is milk, butter, cream, soft sugar, sugarcandy; the oil of the mustard seed, and all sorts of cakes made of grain are used as food. Fish, mutton, gazelle, and deer they eat mostly fresh, sometimes salted; they are forbidden to eat the flesh of the ox, ass, elephant, horse, pig, dog, fox, wolf, lion, monkey and all the hairy kind. Those who eat them are despised and scorned, and are universally reprobated; they live outside the walls, and are seldom seen among men.[7d]

With respect to the different kinds of wines and liquors, there are various sorts. The juices of the grape and sugarcane are used by the Kshatriyas as drink; the Vaishyas use strong fermented drinks; the Sramans and Brahmans drink a sort of syrup made from the grape or sugar-cane, but not of the nature of fermented wine. The mixed classes and base-born differ in no way (as to food and drink) from the rest, except in respect of the vessels they use, which are very different both as to value and material. There is no lack of suitable things for household use. Although they have saucepans and stewpans, yet they do not know the steamer used for cooking rice. They have many ves-

Box 23

TREES OF THE BUDDHA

The hallowed land of Shākyamuni drew Buddhist monks from China to this country. Places of interest to them were those of the Buddha's birth, enlightenment and death. The indefatigable Xuan Zang visited all three in the 7th century AD and described them with feeling in his monumental account, *Si-yu-ki*.[15h]

Travelling in the Nepal terai, he finally came 'to the Lumbini garden. Here is the bathing tank of the Shākyas, the water of which is bright and clear as a mirror, and the surface covered with a mixture of flowers. To the north of this, 20 or 25 paces, there is an ashoka-flower tree, which is now decayed; this is the place where Bōddhisatva was born,'[15h] almost exactly twelve hundred years earlier. It is noteworthy however that while all accounts agree that the grove at Lumbini consisted of trees of the ashoka (*Saraca indica*), the branch on which Gautama's mother supported herself at the birth is generally held to be that of the shāla (*Shorea robusta*), though the plāksha (pilkhan, *Ficus lucescens*) is sometimes mentioned. All three are beautiful flowering trees, of common occurrence in Nepal even today.

It was under a bōdhi tree or pippali (*Ficus religiosa*) that the Buddha finally received enlightenment after long soul-searching. Of his visit to this tree Xuan Zang says:

In the old days, when Buddha was alive, it was several hundred feet high. Although it has often been injured by cutting, it is still forty or fifty

Birth of the Buddha, his mother holding on to a branch of the shāl tree.

Box 23 (*Contd.*)

feet in height. Sitting under this tree Buddha reached perfect wisdom, and therefore it is called the *Samyak Sambōdhi*, the tree of knowledge ... The leaves wither not either in winter or summer, but they remain shining and glistening all the year round without change.[15h]

About 1890 General Sir Alexander Cunningham visited this tree and wrote: 'It still exists, though very much decayed; one large stem, with three branches to the westward, is still green, but the other branches are barkless and rotten.'[14a] The editor E.B. Cowell adds at this point, 'but of course it has been frequently renewed.' Such scepticism seems gratuitous. A sapling of the original hallowed bodhi tree was taken by Prince Mahindra, son of the Emperor Ashoka, to Sri Lanka about 250 BC, and planted at Anurādhapūra. After 2200 years it still continues to bear shining green leaves and put out fresh aerial roots. It must be the oldest tree in the world of which there is an actual historical record.

Trees figure in the death scene of the Buddha too. Xuan Zang describes how, to the northwest of Kushinagara town, crossing the Ajitavati river, he entered a grove of shāl trees. The trunk of one of these trees, he writes, is 'a greenish blue, and its leaves (are) very white and shining and lustrous; this is the place where the Buddha died. Towers are erected where they burnt his body with sandal wood, and the eight kings divided his bone relics'.[16b] The deep feelings of these Buddhist pilgrims come through in the simple words written two centuries earlier by another: 'I, Fa Xian, was born when I could not meet the Buddha; and now I can only see footprints that he has left and the place where he lived, and nothing more.'[9b]

sels made of dried clay; they seldom use red copper vessels: they eat from one vessel, mixing all sorts of condiments together, which they take up with their fingers. They have no spoons or cups, and in short no sort of chopsticks. When sick, however, they use copper drinking cups.[7d]

Xuan Zang spent about 5 years at the University of Nālandā. Students there were abundantly supplied with the four requisites:

clothes, food, bedding and medicine. Though their family be in affluent circumstances, such men make up their mind (after their studies) to be like vagrants and get their food by begging as they go about. With them there is honour in knowing truth and there is no disgrace in being destitute.[8e]

Xuan Zang's disciple, Shaman Hwui Lūi, has recorded his master's daily diet during his stay at Nālandā:

Every day he received 120 jambīras (citrus fruits), 20 arecanuts, 20 nutmegs, a tael (about 30 grams) of camphor, and a shang measure (perhaps six kg) of mahāshāli rice. This rice is as large as the black bean, and when cooked is aromatic and shining, like no other rice at all. It grows only in Magadha, and nowhere else. It is offered only to the king, or to religious persons of great distinction, and hence its name mahāshāli, or in Chinese kung-ja-tin-mai (rice offered to the great householder). He was also supplied every month with three tou (kg?) of oil, and as regards milk and butter he took as much every day as he needed.[8e]

At the city of Su-yeh, the Khan of the Turks, while himself feasting on wine, mutton and veal, offered his Buddhist guest grape juice and 'pure articles of food such as rice cakes, cream, sugar candy, honey sticks(?), raisins, etc'.[16a]

Two of the Chinese visitors left accounts of trees hallowed by the Buddha that they had visited (Box 23).

Two other Chinese travellers were in India considerably later. Chau Ja-kua, a Chinese commissioner of foreign trade, about AD 1225 mentions both elephant tusks and pearls among the native products of the Chola kingdom of south India, though the great seat of the pearl fisheries was really the Pandya kingdom.[15g,17a] Ma-huan (*c.* AD 1406) was an interpreter in the huge party of 30,000, led by Cheng Ho, which was sent abroad in 62 ships by the Chinese emperor to demonstrate the strength and the wealth of China.[17b,18a] He writes of Bengal that

not having any tea they offer their guests betel nuts in its place ... They have an abundance of rice, wheat, sesamum, all kinds of pulses, millet, ginger, mustard, onions, hemp, squash, brinjals and many kinds of vegetables. Their fruits are plantains, jack-fruits, mangoes and pomegranates. Sugarcane, white sugar, granulated sugar, and various candied and preserved fruits are also common.[18a]

Arab reactions

From about AD 850, a steady stream of Arab travellers began to visit this country. Sulaiman, a merchant who made several voyages from the Persian Gulf to India, and Ibn Rosteh. between AD 850 and 880, were mainly political writers.[15j] Ibn Khordadbah described the exports from various Indian ports, which included nutmeg, coconut and cotton, and Ibn Said the imports of dates into Sindh.[15g] Al-Masudī, a native of Baghdad, visited India in AD 915–16; he wrote: 'The Hindus abstain from drinking wine. . . in the dread of its clouding their reason and depriving them of its powers.'[19a] He noted the prohibitions against eating 'cows, tame poultry and all kinds of eggs among the people'.[10] Trading ships from India, along with those from the middle-east and from south-east Asia, he noted, sailed even to China, often travelling seven days, up river to Khanfu (Canton).[15g] Ibn Haukal (AD 950), an Arab geographer from Baghdad, stated that mangoes, coconuts, lemons, rice and honey were produced in great abundance round Cambay, and pomegranates, grapes and other pleasant fruits in Kasdar, whereas Makrān contained chiefly pasturage and fields, which could not be irrigated on account of the deficiency of water.[18c] Jāts living near the river ate fish and aquatic birds, while another clan, who lived remote from the banks, fed on milk, cheese and millet bread.

Al-Birūnī described the thirteen years that he spent in this country (AD 1017–30) in his monumental *Kitāb-ul-Hind*. His views on why Indians do not eat beef have already been quoted (Chapter 5). On other aspects of food and eating habits in India he writes:

The Hindus eat singly, one by one on a tablecloth of dung. They do not make use of the remnants of a meal, and the plates from which they have eaten are thrown away if they are earthen. They have red teeth on account of chewing areca nuts with betel leaves and lime. They drink wine before having eaten anything, then they take their meal. They sip the stall (urine) of cows, but do not eat their meat'.[10]

Elsewhere Al-Birūnī states that wine 'is allowed to the Shūdra. He may drink it but dare not sell it (just) as he is not allowed to sell meat.' The rule prohibiting the killing of animals

applies in particular only to Brahmins, because they are the guardians of the religion, and because it forbids them to give way to their lusts. . . It is allowed to kill animals only by strangulation, but only certain animals, others being excluded. . . Animals of which the killing is allowed are sheep, goats, gazelles, hares, rhinoceros, the buffalo, fish, water and land-birds such as sparrows, ringdoves, francolins, doves, peacocks, and other animals which are not loathsome to man or noxious.[20]

Five kinds of fasting were noted. Ekanātha was non-eating from one noon to another, upavāsa from noon to the sunset or noon of the third day; kricchra was a sequence of fasting from noon to the following evening, then on the third day eating nothing except what was received by chance without asking; and paraka was eating only once at noon for three days, at sunset for three more days and then fasting uninterruptedly for three whole days. Chandarayana was a fasting sequence of slightly increasing quantities of daily food, starting from nothing, for a fortnight, followed by a diminishing sequence for the next fortnight. Māsavāsa was interrupted fasting for a whole month.[21]

The geographer Al-Idrisī was born in Morocco and travelled all over Europe and India. Speaking of Sindh about the year AD 1080, he says:

The country produces dates and sugarcanes in abundance. There are hardly any other fruits, if we except one, a sort of fruit called laimun, as big as an apple and of a very sour taste, and another which resembles the peach both in shape and taste (mango?). . . Fish is plentiful, meat is cheap, and foreign and native fruits abound. . . The pepper vine grows on (Māli) island. . . each bunch (of pepper) is sheltered over by a leaf which curls over when the fruit is ripe. White pepper is what is gathered as it begins to ripen, or even before. Ibn Khurdadbah states that the leaves curl over the bunches to protect them from the rain, and that they return to their natural position when the rain is over—a surprising fact![18d]

The Moroccan Ibn Battūta, who called himself the Traveller of Islam, was in India for several years around AD 1340, moving over many parts of the country. He writes:

> The wall that surrounds the city of Delhi is unparalleled. The width of the wall itself is eleven cubits (5 metres) and it contains also stores for provisions, which they call granaries. . . Grain keeps in it for a very long time without going bad or becoming damaged. I have seen rice brought out of one of these stores, and although it had gone black in colour, it was still good to the taste. I have also seen kudhrū millet (kōdhra, *Paspalum scrobiculatum*) taken out of them. All these stores had been laid up by the Sultan Balban ninety years before.[18e]

Ibn Battūta mentions that the grains of the rainy autumn season are kudhrū,

> the commonest of grains in their country; qāl, which resembles the type of millet called anlī; and shāmākh, which is smaller in grain than qāl, and often grows without being sown (perhaps this is the shyāmāka, *Echinochloa frumantacea*). It is the food of the devotees and ascetics, and of the poor and needy. They go out to gather what has sprung up of this plant without cultivation, each of them holds a large basket in his left hand and has in his right a whip with which he beats the grain so that it falls into the basket. In this way they collect enough of it to supply them with food for the whole year. The seed of this shāmākh is very small; after gathering, it is put out in the sun, then pounded in wooden mortars; the husk flies off leaving its pith, a white substance, from which they make gruel. They cook this with buffalo's milk and it is pleasanter, prepared in this way, than baked as bread; I used often to eat it in India and enjoyed it.[18f]

The other grains that he mentions are lobia, māsh and mung.[18g] This last was eaten by Hindus along with boiled rice as a khichri for breakfast, but Muslims showed a preference for fried bread and kabab for their morning meal. The tuber called meet (musthaka, *Cyperus rotundus*) was used to feed animals, and other animal foods were chana gram pounded and soaked in water, māsh leaves, and 3 to 4 pounds of ghee every day! The spring cereals were wheat, barley (for use as an animal feed, 'the barley in their country has no strength in it', in his opinion), chana and lentils;[18f] all these crops were 'sown in the same ground where the autumn crops are sown, for their land is generous and of good heart. As for rice they sow it three times a year, and it is one of the principal crops of their country. They sow also sesame and sugarcane along with the autumn grains that we have mentioned'. Among the fruits which the Arab traveller mentions are the 'very sweet' lotē (*Ziziphus lote*, a type of ber) and the mango.[18f] The jack is termed the 'best fruit in India': two types are mentioned: barki from the trunk near the ground and shaki, less sweet and poorer in flavour, higher up; the inner jack nuts, he noted, were stored in red earth and would keep until the next year. He then lists the tandu (tuki, tendu, *Diospyros melanoxylon*); the jāmoon; the mahua; grapes which 'are very rare in India and are to be had only in certain districts, and in the capital Delhi' (elsewhere he notes that grapes were grown in Daulatabād); the kaserū (*Scirpus grossus*, with an edible tuber which is dug out of the ground and 'is very sweet and resembles a chestnut'); pomegranates; sugarcanes (those from Barkur in Kerala were 'unexcelled in the rest of the country'); and the coconut ('which resembles a man's head, for it has marks like eyes

The coconut, resembling a human head.

and a mouth, and the contents, when it is green, are like the brain. It has fibre like hair. . .'). Ibn Battūta describes the preparation of 'coconut honey' by boiling down sweet fresh neera; 'the merchants of India, Yemen and China buy it and take it to their own countries where they manufacture sweetmeats from it.' The Arab visitor describes Bengal as 'a vast country, abounding in rice, and nowhere in the world have I seen any land where prices are lower than there. . .'[18f]

About a hundred years later, in AD 1443, Abdur Razzāk of Herat, an Ambassador from Samarkand at the court of the Zāmorin of Cālicut, wrote of a very different environment, the kingdom of Vijayanagara in the Deccan.[18h] Abdur-Razzāk says that it is 'for the most part well cultivated and fertile, and about three hundred good seaports belong to it'.[18h] The virility of the king he attributed to his habit of chewing the betel leaf:

> it deserves its reputation. . . it lightens up the countenance and excites an intoxication like that caused by wine. It relieves hunger, stimulates the organs of digestion, disinfects the breath, and strengthens the teeth. It is impossible to describe, and delicacy forbids me to expatiate on its invigorating and aphrodisiac qualities .

Ninety years later, in 1533, Fernão Nuniz wrote about a later and greater king, Krishnadēvarāya:

> The king drinks water which they bring from a spring, which is kept enclosed under the hand of a man in whom the king has great confidence, and the vessels in which they draw water come covered and sealed. Thus they deliver it to the women who wait on him, and they take it inside to the other women, the king's wives. . . The king has other women besides. He has ten cooks for his personal service, and has others kept for the times when he has banquets; and these ten prepare the food for no one save for the king alone. He has a eunuch for guard at the gate of the kitchen, who never allows anyone to enter for fear of poison. When the king wishes to eat, every person withdraws, and then come some of the women whose duty it is and they prepare the table for him; they place for him a three-footed stool, round, made of gold, and on it put the messes. These are brought in large vessels of gold, some of which are adorned with precious stones. There is no cloth on the table, but one is brought when the king has finished eating, and he washes his hands and mouth. Women and eunuchs serve him at table.[22]

And of this same king Domingo Paes wrote:

> The king is accustomed to drink three-quarter pint of gingelly (sesame) oil before daylight and anoints himself with the same oil; he covers his loin with a small cloth, and takes in his hand great weights, and then taking his sword he exercises himself till he has sweated out all the oil.'[22]

Vijayanagara was then in its heyday, and the impressions of Portuguese, Italian, Dutch and English visitors to the kingdom will be recorded in Chapter 13.

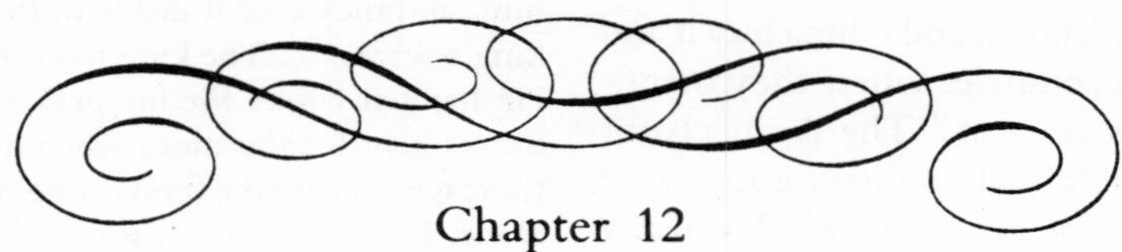

Chapter 12

MUSLIM BONUS

Arab raiders had established their hegemony in Sindh in western India by about AD 712, but the Muslim presence only made itself felt with the raids of Mahmūd of Ghazni from about AD 1000. About AD 1206 the first Sultans, those of the Slave dynasty, set up rule in Delhi. Eleven of them in succession gave place to two from the house of Balban, six Khaljis, three Tughlaks (including Muhammad bin Tughlak from AD 1324–51), four Saiyyids and three Lodis, stretching in all for slightly more than three hundred years. In 1526 the ruler Bābar established the Moghul dynasty in India. He was followed by Humayun, Akbar, Jahāngīr, Shah Jahān and Aurangzeb, with whose death in AD 1707 the empire effectively came to a close.

Two chroniclers of the Sultanate epoch were Amir Khusrau (AD 1253–1325) and the industrious Ibn Battūta who was in India from AD 1325 to 1354.[1, 2, 3] The Moghul period was exceptionally well documented. Both the emperors Bābar and Jahāngīr were themselves superb diarists, and Akbar's affairs were minutely chronicled in the *Ain-i-Akbari* and *Akbar-Nāmā* by his court historian Abul Fazl. From the time of Jahāngīr and thereafter, a series of travellers from Europe left vivid impressionistic accounts of the rulers and the people of India.

To the somewhat austere Hindu dining ambience the Muslims brought a refined and courtly etiquette of both group and individual dining, and of sharing food in fellowship. Food items native to India were enriched with nuts, raisins, spices and ghee. These included meat and rice dishes (palāo), dressed meat (kabāb), stuffed items (samōsas), desserts (halwa, stewed fruit) and sweetened drinks (falooda, sherbet). New dishes enriched the cuisine of the land, like those made of wheat finely ground with meat (halīm, harīsā), or the frozen kulfi, a rich ice-cream of khoa, or the jilēbi (Box 24). Muslims influenced both the style and substance of Indian food.

The Sultān's etiquette

Ibn Battūta has a good deal to say about the dining customs of the Delhi Sultāns, which were perhaps unique to Muslim royalty in India.[2] A certain ritual formality was observed:

> Before the dinner begins, the chamberlain stands at the head of the dinner carpet (simat) and performs the bow (khidmat) in the direction of the Sultān; and all present do the same. The khidmat in India consists of bowing down to the knee as in prayer. After this the people sit down to eat; and then are brought gold, silver and glass cups filled with fine sugar-water perfumed with rose-water which they call sherbet. After they have taken the sherbet, the chamberlain calls out *Bismillah*. Then all begin to eat. At the end of the dinner, jugs of barley-drink (fuqqa) are brought; and when these have been consumed, betel-leaves and nuts are served. After the people

Box 24
THE JILĒBI

According to Hobson-Jobson, the word jilebi is 'apparently a corruption of the Arabic zalābiya or Persian zalibīya'.[21] If so, both the word and the sweet, syrupy article of food that it connotes must have entered India quite early. A Jain work of about AD 1450 by Jināsura has a reference to a feast which includes the jalēbi. A work on the science of cooking which was copied in AD 1678 and was perhaps written earlier in that century describes its preparation in exactly the same way as at present. A poem in Kannada dated AD 1600. the *Soundara Vilāsa* of Annājī, mentions the jil-ābi as an item of food served at an Īshwara pūja.[22a] The *Bhōjana-kutuhala* of Raghunātha, a well-known 17th century work on dietetics, also describes its method of preparation.

Essentially the jilēbi is a flat spiral of fermented batter, about eight centimetres wide, fried, soaked when still hot in sugar syrup of medium consistency, and then withdrawn. The ingredients can be quite varied. To make the batter, which is then piped into hot fat for frying, ground urad with a little rice flour added as a binder, or some besan and wheat flour, are common in south India; the finished product is golden, irregularly wound ('like a creeper', the poet has it), and crisp.[23] The dough is frequently slightly fermented employing curd. In the north, either white flour or besan are used. A similar confection, called imrati or jahāngiri is prepared by piping out a batter of ground urad in regular loops, giving it the appearance of a flower. It is soft and oozy, and a deep orange colour is imparted using saffron. In Bengal either white flour or a mixture of chhānā and khoa is employed; for the latter kind, the spirals are shaped by hand before frying and dipping in syrup.[24,25]

have taken the betel and nut, the chamberlain calls out *Bismillah*, whereupon all stand up and bow in the same way as before. Then they retire.[2]

Two types of dinners were held in the royal palace, says Ibn Battūta:

A private dinner is one that the Sultān attends. It is his way to eat along with those who are present and those whom he calls for the purpose, such as the special amīrs—the head chamberlain (amīrhajīb), the Sultān's paternal cousin, Imad-ul-mulk Sārtēz and master of ceremonies (amīr-i-majlis)—and those out of the a'izza ('The Honourables') and great amīrs whom he wants to honour and revere. Occasionally, when he is inclined to honour any one from among those present, he takes a plate, puts a bread on it and gives it to him. The latter receives it: and placing the plate on his left hand, he bows with his right hand touching the ground. Sometimes the Sultān sends something from that meal to one absent from it, and the latter too bows like the one present and sits down to eat it along with those that be in his company. I attended this special dinner several times; and I noticed that the persons present were about twenty in number.[2]

It has been remarked that such long convivialities in the company of nobles served to throw them into the Sultān s company, and thus keep them out of mischief![2]

About the public dinners of the Sultān, the Moorish traveller has this to say:

The public dinners are brought from the kitchen led by the palace officers, who call out *Bismillah*; and they are headed by the chief palace officer. He holds in his hand a gold mace and is accompanied by his deputy who carries a silver mace. As soon as they enter the fourth gate and those in the council-hall hear the call, all stand up and none remains seated, the Sultan alone excepted. When the dishes are served on the floor, the palace officers stand up in rows, their chief standing right in their front. He makes a discourse in which he praises the Sultan and eulogizes him; then he bows to him and so do his subordinate naqibs and in the same manner bow all those present in the council-hall whether big or small. Their custom is that anyone who hears the utterance of the chief palace officer (naqib-un-nuqaba) stops instantly, if walking; and remains in his place if he happens to be standing and none can move or budge from his place until the said discourse is over. Then his deputy too makes a similar discourse and he bows; and so do the palace officers and all the people a second time. Then all the people take their seats; and the gate secretaries draft a report informing the Sultān that the food has been brought, even though he be aware of it. The report is handed over to a boy from among the mālik's sons appointed for this purpose and he takes the message to the Sultān who, on reading it, appoints whomsoever he likes from among the great amīrs to supervise the seating and feeding of the people.[2]

Ibn Battūta has something to say about the seating arrangements also:

Their custom is that the judges (qāzīs), orators (khatibs), jurists (shorfa), saiyids and dervishes (mashaikh) sit at the head of the dinner carpet (simat): and then come the Sultan's relatives, the great amīrs and the rest of the people. But none sits except at his appointed place; and thus there is absolutely no confusion amongst them. All having taken their respective seats, the cup-bearers (shurbdariya) who give the drink come holding in their hands gold and silver and copper and glass vessels filled with refined sugar dissolved in water, which they drink before the dinner. As they drink it the chamberlains (hujjab) call out *Bismillah*, then they start eating. Every one has before him a set of all the various dishes comprising the dinner, which he eats exclusively; and no one shares his plate with another. When they finish eating, the drink (fuqqa) is served in pewter tankards; and as soon as the people take it the chamberlains call out *Bismillah*. At that time the whole gathering stands up, and the amīr supervising the feast bows, and they bow too; then they retire. Their dinners are held twice a day—one in the forenoon and the other in the afternoon.[2]

The food of the gentry

A graphic account is furnished by Ibn Battūta of the dishes served at a grand dinner given by Sultān Muhammad bin Tughlak (AD 1325–1351) to a distinguished visitor, a qāzi (judge) from a foreign land:

The chamberlain and his companions made the necessary arrangements for feeding (the guest); and they took along with them about twenty cooks from Multān. The chamberlain used to go ahead in the night to a station to secure the eatables and other things; and as soon as the guest arrived, he found his meals ready . . . the order in which the meal is served is this: to begin with, loaves (khubi) are served which are very thin and resemble cakes of bread; then they (the chamberlains) cut the roasted meat into large pieces in such a manner that one sheep yields from four to six pieces. One piece is served before each man. Also they make round cakes of bread soaked in ghee; and in the midst of these they place the sweet called subunia (a mixture of almonds, honey, and sesame oil). On every piece of bread is placed a sweet cake called khishti ('bricklike'), a preparation of flour, sugar and ghee. Then they serve meat cooked in ghee, onion, and green ginger in China dishes. Then is brought a thing called samusak, minced meat cooked with almonds, walnuts, pistachios, onion and spices placed inside a thin bread and fried in ghee. In front of every person is placed from four to five of such samusaks. Then is brought a dish of rice cooked in ghee on the top of which is roasted fowl (dojaj, i.e. palāo with murgmusāllam), next a kind of sweet which is called hāshimi, (and then) al-qahiriya (a kind of pudding borrowed from Qahira).[2]

Elsewhere, the Moorish visitor describes the food served at the tables of the rich: 'Their dinner consists of bread, roasted meat (shiwawoon), round pieces of bread split and filled

The use of almonds enriched Muslim cuisine.

with sweet paste, rice, chicken (dojaj) and samusak.'[2] The description by Amir Khusrau (AD 1253–1325) of the style of food eaten by the Muslim aristocracy further confirms its richness and variety:

Their food consists generally of sharbat-i-labgir (very sweet sherbet), naān-e-tunuk (light bread), naān-e-tanūri (chapātis cooked in tandūrs), samōsa (prepared from meat, ghee, onion etc.), mutton, flesh of various birds such as quail, sparrow (kunjshakka) etc., halwa and sabuni-sakar. They were also accustomed to drink wine. After the meal, they used to take tāmbōl (betel-leaf) for refreshing the palate.

Dishes mentioned elsewhere are branj or rice, surkh-biriyāni, chicken-kabāb, and fish. Eating was done by hand, but spoons (qashaq) and knives (karad) were used for service and for carving.[2]

The aristocracy were lavish in their hospitality. Imad-ul-Mulk, the muster-master of Balban in Sind, was in the habit of feeding his entire secretariat every midday with large trays loaded with fine naan, goat meat, chicken, biriyāni (the modern palāo), fuqqa (a drink of wine or barley), sherbet and tāmbūl (betel leves).[2] Frequently nobles would eat together, and the unconsumed food would be distributed to fakīrs and beggars.

At a more mundane level, Amır Khusrau describes the storage of grain in a khattee or deep pit.[1] Vegetable matter was first burnt in it, and the sides and bottom then lined with wheat or barley straw. The grain was put in, covered with straw, and earth was filled in to raise the top a little above the surface height, followed by tight sealing with clay and cowdung. The grain remained edible for years, except for a change in colour.[1] Ibn Battūta, some fifty years later, describes how he saw rice being brought out from storage in the walls of Delhi fort, where it had been held for 90 years, and 'although it had gone black in colour, it was still good to the taste'.[4a]

Kings' drinks

'Any Muslim who drinks (wine) is punished with 80 stripes, and is shut up in a matamore (cell) for 3 months, which is opened only at the time of meals.' So says Ibn Battūta,[2] and the Qurān itself is explicit on the point (Chapter 6). Nevertheless there is little doubt that drinking was quite common among the Sultāns and their nobility. For the Moghuls, wine had a strong attraction. Bābar had periodic fits of abstinence, when he would break up his flagons and goblets of gold and silver and give away the pieces,[5] only to resume drinking and the use of bhāng after telling himself:[6] 'The new year, the spring, the wine and the beloved are pleasing: enjoy them, Bābar, for the world is not to be had a second time.' He had planned to fill a great tank carved out of a single piece of stone in Dhōlpūr with wine; but when it was finished he had given up wine and it was filled with lemonade instead. Akbar, according to the Jesuit Father Monserrate, rarely drank wine, preferring bhāng.[7] He enforced prohibition in his court, but relaxed rules for the European travellers because 'they are born in the element of wine, as fish are produced in that of water . . . and to prohibit them the use of it is to deprive them of life.'[6] Of his sons, Daniyāl and Murād were both to die young from excessive drinking.[8] His other son Jahāngīr was much addicted, but did not drink on Thursdays and Fridays. However by the end of his reign, he would imbibe 20 cups of double-distilled liquor daily, 14 during the day and the rest at night.[6] Despite this he enforced strict prohibition at court, and at least one European visitor, William Hawkins, was debarred from attendance when he appeared smelling of alcohol. Shahjahān drank, but never beyond the limits of decency, and Aurangzeb was of course a strict teetotaller who in 1668 issued severe prohibition orders to all his subjects, Hindu and Muslim alike.[6] On the other hand his unmarried sister, Jahanāra Begum, was extremely fond of wine: these were either imported from Persia, Kābūl and Kāshmīr, according to Manucci, or distilled in her own home, 'a most delicious spirit, made from wine and rosewater, flavoured with many costly spices and aromatic drugs', of which he was sometimes a recipient.[9a]

Jahāngīr asked Sir Thomas Roe whether he would prefer a natural grape wine or a 'made' wine: he tried the latter, which was strong, and made him sneeze, to the amusement of the

Emperor Akbar was almost a vegetarian and a teetotaller.

court.[10a] To make this liquor, arrack or rice spirit was put into an empty barrel that had contained wine from Europe. The dregs of other wine barrels were added, together with water and sweet sugar. After eight months, the contents had become a clear liquid tasting something like white wine. Another wine was made by steeping raisins in rice spirit for 3 or 4 days, straining, and then holding the liquid in an empty barrel for 6 to 8 months; an extract of dates was sometimes added to this for sweetness and flavour. Jahāngīr in his *Memoirs*, described a strong wine called sīr or achhi, ten years old, made at Pigli, near Attuck, by fermenting together rice and bread.[10a]

The imperial cuisine

Bābar lived for only 4½ years after coming to India. He lamented the fact that this country had 'no grapes, musk-melons or first-rate fruits, no ice or cold water, no bread or cooked food in the bazaars'.[16] He commented most judiciously on the flora and fauna that he first encountered in this new country. The chironji is 'a thing between the almond and the walnut, not bad', he comments. And 'the flesh of Hindustān fishes is very savoury, they have no odour or tiresomeness' (meaning probably a lack of bones). But at heart Bābar remained an alien to India's foods. His son Humayun was more 'Indianized', even giving up animal flesh for some months when he started his campaign to recover his throne, and deciding, after much reflection, that beef was not a food fit for the devout.[6]

Akbar did not like meat and took it only seasonally 'to conform to the spirit of the age,' and because he had 'the burden of the world on his shoulders', according to Abul Fazl.[5] He abstained from meat at first on all Fridays, subsequently on Sundays also, then on the first day of every solar month, then during the whole month of Fawardin (March), and finally during his birth-month of Ābān (November). He started his meal with curds and rice, and preferred simple food. Father Monserrate reports however that:–

> his table is very sumptuous, consisting of more than 40 courses served in great dishes. These are brought into the royal dining-hall covered and wrapped in linen cloths, which are tied up and sealed by the cook, for fear of poison. They are carried by youths to the door of the dining hall, other servants walking ahead and the master-of-the-household following. Here they are taken over by eunuchs, who load them to the serving girls who wait on the royal table. He is accustomed to dine in private, except on the occasion of a public banquet.[7]

The *Ain-i-Akbari* describes three classes of cooked dishes.[12] In the first, called safiyāna, consumed on Akbar's days of abstinence, no meat was used, and the dishes are those made of rice (zard-birinj, khushka, khichrī and sheer-birinj), wheat (chikhi, essentially the gluten of wheat isolated by washing and then seasoned), dhāls, pālaksāg, halwa, sherbets, etc. The second class comprised those in which both meat and rice were employed (like palāo, biriyāni, shulla and shuṛba), or meat and wheat (harīsā, halīm, kashk and qutab 'which the people of Hind call sanbūsa'). The third class was that in which meat was cooked with ghee, spices, curd, eggs, etc. to give such dishes as yakhni, kabāb, dōpiyāza, musammān, dampukht, qaliya and malghuba. Bread was either thick, made from wheat flour and baked in an oven; or thin, and baked on iron plates using a dough of either wheat or khuskha, the latter tasting 'very well when served hot'. Raw materials came from various places: rice from Bharaij, Gwalior, Rajori and Nimlah, ghee from Hissār, ducks, waterfowls and certain vegetables from Kāshmīr, and fruits from across the northwestern borders as well as from all over the country.[12]

Though Jahāngīr, unlike his father, enjoyed eating meat, and especially the animals of the chase, he kept up his father's schedule of abstention, adding Thursday to them, that being the day of Akbar's birth, and banning the slaughter of animals on Thursdays and Sundays.[6] He seems to have given up fish altogether. A rich Gujarāt khichrī called lazizan, made of rice cooked with pulses, ghee, spices and nuts, was one of his favourite foods on his days of abstinence from flesh. Another was fālooda, a jelly made from the strainings of boiled wheat, mixed with fruit juices and cream.[6] A British visitor, William Hawkins, reports that Jahāngīr kept many fasts during the year, but two of them were deserving of special mention: one was that kept on the anniversary of his father's funeral, and the other was the eighteen-day fast marking Nauroz, the Persian new year.[13] For all his hedonism, Jahāngīr was a great naturalist, with an insatiable curiosity about all forms of of plant and animal life. His descriptions of them would do credit to a natural scientist. This judiciousness extended also to matters of gastronomy. 'I found the flesh of the mountain goat more delicious than that of all wild animals, though its skin is exceedingly ill-odoured, so much so that even when tanned the scent is not destroyed,' he says.[4b] 'Though the flesh of the wild ass is lawful food and most men like to eat it, it was in no way suited to my taste.' However he found the milk of the female antelope to be palatable, and adds: 'They say it is of great use in asthma'.

Aurangzeb was a spartan. Tavernier says that no animal food passed his lips; he became 'thin and lean, to which the great fasts that he keeps have contributed . . . he only drank a little water, and ate a small quantity of millet bread . . . besides this he slept on the ground, with only a tiger's skin over him.' Nor did he ever use vessels of silver or gold.[14] Many Muslim kings, including Aurangzeb, insisted on Ganges water for drinking (Box 25).

The fruits of Hindustān

About AD 1300 Amir Khusrau had noted seven varieties of grapes in India,[15a] besides apples, oranges, karna (seville or sour oranges) grapefruit, figs, lemons, jackfruit, coconuts, jāmoon and two fruits of uncertain identity, the jong and the khirnee.[1] He made a special note of the flavour of the pomegranates of Jodhpur which, a couple of centuries later, Sikander Lōdi declared to be superior to those from Irān.[15a] Bābar accurately described the fruits of India, one example being his careful listing, with succint comments, of eight members of the citrus family, the orange, lime, citron, santhra, galgal, jāmbīri lime, amritphal (perhaps the mandarin orange) and the amal-bīd. Another was his description of the jackfruit as being 'like a sheep's stomach stuffed and made into a gipa (haggis) . . . sickeningly sweet'. A melon brought to him made for home-sickness: 'To cut and eat it affected me strongly; I was close to tears.[16] Babar took steps to grow melons and grapes,

Lime.

Sweet orange and lime were mentioned by Babar.

which when they bore fruit 'filled me with content'.[16]

By the time of Akbar, about fifty years later, the *Ain-i-Akbari* is able to remark: 'Melons and grapes have become very plentiful and excellent; and water-melons, peaches, almonds, pistachios, pomegranates etc. are to be found everywhere.'[12] Prices in the Delhi market for a remarkable range of fruits are listed, including items that must only recently have come from America like the pineapple and sītāphal.[12] Many of these fruits came from Kāshmīr, but also from Kābūl, Kandahār and Sāmarkhand.[15a] Jahāngīr noted that the sweet cherry, pear and apricot, so far imported, were now being grown in Kāshmīr through the efforts of his nobleman Muhammad Quli Afshar, and the oranges, citrons and water-melons raised at Kishtwar were all of superior quality.[17] At the royal gardens in Āgra pineapples were raised, and peasants and nobles alike could have all their revenues remitted by raising orchards. The gardens were

The pineapple reached India from South America.

Box 25

ONLY GANGES WATER FOR THE EMPEROR

The Emperor Harshavardhana, as we saw in Chapter 9, lived in Kannauj. It was, therefore, simple for him to get drinking water from the river Ganges., It is, however, surprising that later Muslim rulers should have set such store by it. When Muhammad-bin-Tughlak moved his capital from Delhi to Daulatabād about AD 1340, water was brought to him by runners all the way from the Ganges, some 1500 km away.[19] Akbar termed it the water of immortality, and according to the *Ain-i-Akbari* 'both at home and on his travels he drinks Ganges water.' In Āgra and Fatehpūr-Sikri this water came from Sarūn, and when in Punjāb from Hardwār. 'For the cooking of food, rainwater or water taken from the Jamuna and Chenāb is used, mixed with a little Ganges water . . . His Majesty appoints experienced men as water-tasters.' Jahāngīr continued these practices, and was very particular about drinking only the waters of the Ganges. Even Aurangzeb, according to Francois Bernier 'keeps in Delhi and Āgra kitchen apparatus, Ganges water, and all the other articles necessary for the camp'. His contemporary Tavernier muses that 'considerable sums of money are expended to procure Ganges water' and that 'by many it is constantly drunk in consequence of its reputed medical properties.'[19] Vessels of sealed Ganges water are kept unspoiled for decades in many Hindu homes all over the country to be administered to a dying person as his last ministration. During colonial rule, a British physician noted that water taken from the Hughli at Calcutta would remain fresh all the way to London, but returning ships had to replenish their English water *en route*.[20]

Numerous experimental studies have shown that Ganges water drawn above Hardwār has an unusual capacity for self-purification, and is exceptionally lethal against bacteria and cholera germs. Organic pollutants discharged into the river were removed 10 to 25 times faster than in any other river in India.[20] In the laboratory, river bed samples taken from the Ganges destroyed bacteria completely within a fortnight.

There appear to be three causes for this activity. One is the presence of bacteriophages which are lethal to many organisms; mosquitoes, for example, will simply not breed in Ganges water. The next is the presence of heavy metals with known bactericidal properties, like silver, copper, iron, chromium and nickel. Copper vessels are commonly used in India to store boiled drinking water. The third reason for the prolonged keeping quality of Ganges water is believed to lie in the presence in it of minute quantities of radio-active minerals such as Bismuth-214, one of the radioactive decay products of Uranium-238. Sadly, however, recent studies have shown that below Hardwār the water of the great river has now become so highly polluted that it is even unsafe for human use.[20]

rented out to cultivators and professional fruit-sellers, and the fruits sold for profit.[15a] Mangoes of high quality collected from all over India were grown by Muqqarrab Khan in his garden in Kirana. He was also able to extend their life by nearly two months. On one occasion he served them to Jahāngīr, first on 3 September and then on 17 October.[17] Anything botanical that came to his notice was recorded. Two crops of grapes had been raised in Malwa, though only one, he notes, was really sweet. He tastes a banana, just a finger long (perhaps the poo-bālé of the south): no other banana could compare with it, he declares.[17]

Grafting began to be widely practised in this period, though it had been described as early as the 4th century AD in the *Kāmasūtra* as one of the 64 arts.[15a] The Portuguese in Gōa had employed grafting to produce excellent varieties of mango (see Chapter 13). Grafting had only been permitted at first in the royal gardens, but Shah Jahan lifted this ban, and the technique was applied to cherries and apricots in Kāshmīr, and oranges and mangoes in Bengal. Figs were grafted on mulberry trees, peaches on plum trees, apricots on almond trees, and vines on the apple.[15a]

The common fare

Humbler Muslims appear to have enjoyed their breakfast of naan, frequently with keema or kabāb as accompaniment, rice with plenty of onions, desserts of phirni and sheer-birinj (kheer) prepared from rice, milk and sugar, and halwās and dried fruits.[2] The chewing of betel leaves stuffed with areca nuts and spices, a Hindu practice encountered by the invaders in India, was avidly adopted. Oddly, they did not take to the pūrī and bhathura, also forms of wheat breads deep-fried in oil; these were relished by Hindus, along with various vegetable accompaniments like sāg.[6] Jowār or bājra flour was kneaded with water and jaggery and baked into rōtis. Rice cooked with pulses (khichrī), taken in the evening, was the Hindu meal most often mentioned by visitors. Even poorer folk ate meals of rice, perhaps boiled with some green ginger.[6] Regional variations begin to be noted: rice and fish in Bengal, rice and curds in Gujarāt.[18] The grain staple could be rice, barley or jowār, and the morning nourishment frequently consisted of a handful of parched grain or gram, seasoned perhaps with a little pungent mustard oil.

Stray incidents noted by Ibn Battūta cast light on food habits.[3] In certain tracts adjacent to the Sindh desert, only pumpkins grew in the dry river bed, and the food of the people consisted of a rōti made of jowār and peas. There was a plentiful supply of fish and buffalo meat and a small lizard stuffed with turmeric was a delicacy. Thieves who captured Ibn Battūta gave him 'bread made of peas' to eat, and later he shared 'a handful of chana fried with a little rice' with a Muslim fakīr. Raisins and almonds, he noted, were imported from Khurasān, and he took some as a gift to the governor of Multān.[3]

The Sultāns appeared to have been mindful of the difficulties of their subjects.[3] On returning from a journey, wooden partitions several stories high were built by the ruler, each pavilion with a large tank made of skins; this was filled with sherbet from which everyone, whether native or stranger, could help himself, receiving also betel leaves and areca nuts. When famine broke out, Muhammad bin Tughlak ordered that every resident of Delhi, small or great, free man or slave, should be given six months' provisions from the state granary at the rate of about 675 grams a day.[3] Earlier Alāuddīn Khalji, noting the rampant profiteering by merchants, decided after much deliberation to fix the prices of six basic foodgrains, supported by strong administrative measures.[4c] Prices during the Khalji period were low compared to wages; food for a family of five cost about 5 tankas a month, against a common soldier's salary of 20 to 30 tankas.[1] By Moghul times prices had risen, and food seems to have accounted for some two-thirds of the income of common people.

Chapter 13

THE COMING OF THE EUROPEANS

In Chapter 11 we noted the reactions to Indian food of Greek, Chinese and Arab travellers during the period 500 BC to AD 1200. From the 14th century AD, the European made his appearance as a visitor in India. For four centuries, Italians, Portuguese Jesuit priests and English adverturers, bent (at least at this stage) mostly on trade, appeared in a steady stream to see and wonder, and to record their observations and impressions of the fabulous east, and its strange foods and drinks.

The early comers

John of Monte Corvino, an Italian, whom the Pope afterwards appointed Archbishop of Peking, came to India overland by way of Persia in 1292, and spent 13 months here.[1a] He described southern India as a 'land of great cities and wretched houses', a land of 'perpetual summer' where one might witness sowing and reaping and fruit-gathering at all times. Above all it was to the European a country that produced vast quantities of aromatic spices. He noted ginger, with its enormous roots. Cinnamon spice came from a tree resembling the laurel that grew on an island (Sri Lanka) close to Malabār. There were trees which yielded sugar, honey and a liquor resembling wine, and the wonderful 'Indian nuts' (coconuts), as 'big as melons and as green as gourds', growing on trees that resembled date palms. The people of India were scrupulously clean, feeding on milk and rice, eating no meat, and drinking no wine. The fabled Marco Polo (1294) showed familiarity with both fresh and preserved ginger, and said that the best quality came from Coilum (Quilōn in Malabār);[2a] ginger and cinnamon grew in the Pāndya country, while 'Bengāla' produced spikenard, ginger and sugar.[3a] Odoric of Pordenone, a Franciscan friar, was in Sūrat around 1325, and then sailed round south India to China.[1a] He describes the fire-worship of the Pārsis, the veneration of the ox by the Brāhmins, the climbing pepper plant (which resembled a vine in its growth and its clusters of fruit, and the ivy in its leaves), the ginger of Quilōn, and the preparation in Borneo of sago from palms. Soon after (1328) came Friar Jordanus, a French Dominican monk from Severas, who again described ginger, jackfruit, mango, sugarcane, the coconut and all its products, and the palmyra palm.[1a] 'This land', he declared 'is fairer than any other, its food more savoury, its people more honest and much more moral than the Christians of Europe;' yet the king of France, in his view, without the aid of anyone, possessed sufficient strength in armed men to conquer India! Giovanni di Marignolli, who was sent by Pope Benedict XII with three other envoys overland to China, spent 16 months living in Quilon after his return by sea from that country.

On Palm Sunday AD 1357 I entered Columbum, the most famous city in the whole of India, where all the pepper in the world grows. It grows on creepers, which are planted exactly like vines and first produce wild grapes of a green colour. Thereupon a kind of grape forms containing red wine, which I have

Marco Polo.

squeezed out on to the plate with my own hand as condiment. Thereafter they ripen and dry on the trees. And when the immoderate heat of the sun has dried them hard, they are struck down with staves and collected on linen cloth spread out beneath . . . Pepper is not burnt, as has been erroneously stated, nor does it grow in deserts, but in gardens.[10]

About 1410, a German soldier, Hans Schiltberger, was in India, and on his return detailed, among other things, the three kinds of pepper of south India, and its lemons and limes, fruits then quite new to the whole of Europe except for Italy.[1a] A visitor from Russia, Afanasy Nikhitin (1466–72) remarked of Indians that 'they do not eat with one another or even with their wives. . . . When journeying, each carries a pot to boil food in.' He mentions that horses were fed on pulses, and also on 'khichris, boiled with sugar and oil'.[4a,5] Thereafter, the increasing hostility of the Muslims in India to Christian missionaries and even traders put a damper on such visits. Vasco da Gama arrived in Kērala in 1498. Since the time of the *Periplus*,[5A] Gujarāthi experts had acted as pilots for ships coming to India, and it was one of them, Ibn Majid, who piloted the Portuguese navigator from the ports of Malinithi in Kenya to Kapad, near Kōzhikōde. Vasco da Gama made three trips in all, finally dying in Cochin in 1524. The export of spices was firmly taken over by the Carriera da India, one shipload alone consisting of 14 items, of which the major ones were round pepper 1500 tonnes, ginger 28 tonnes, cinnamon 9 tonnes and cloves 7 tonnes.[6a] Profits on the sale of these in Europe must have been enormous; even the spices that Vasco da Gama carried back on his first voyage

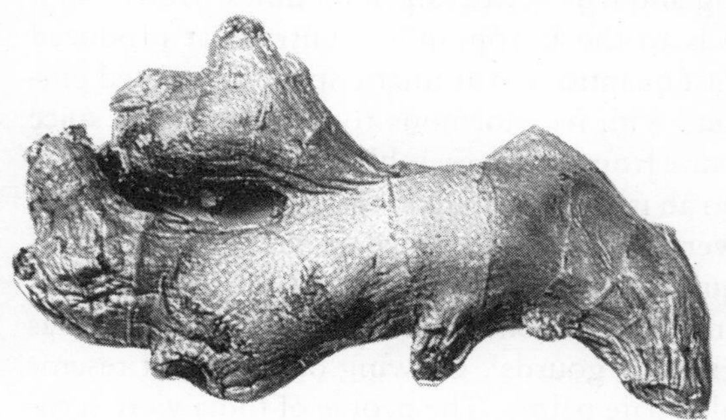

Fresh ginger.

Pepper, shown here on the vine.

paid for the cost of the entire operation six times over.

On the wonders of Vijayanagar

The magnificence of Vijayanagar (see Box 26), situated near the Hampi of today, was a magnet for the European traveller with an eye on a profitable trade deal. Nicolo dei Conti, a Venetian merchant, with his wife and children, touched India at Cambay (see Box 26), then sailed to a port in western Karnātaka, and thence went overland to Vijayanagar.[1b] He called the mango by the Sanskrit-based term āmbāh, and described bamboos so lofty and of such enormous girth that a section between adjacent knots of the stem made a serviceable fishing boat! Later, on the banks of the Ganges, he was fascinated by charming villas and gardens, and plantations of delicious-tasting mūsa, the word for the banana derived from the Sanskrit mōcha. The next visitor to Vijayanagar and south India in 1505–8 was Ludovico di Varthema, who obtained before he left Italy, a sole ten-year copyright from the Pope for an account of his travels in Asia, being well aware of the blatant plagiarism of earlier writers.[1b] In the kingdom of Vijayanagar, one could travel safely anywhere, and Christians were warmly welcomed. He noticed the abundance of domestic cattle, peacocks, parrots and fruits in Kanara, and in Kananoor, the vast quantities of cucumbers, melons, coconut, pepper, ginger, cardamom and other spices, mango fruit, and rice, though no rice grew nearby. In Calicut, none of the brahmins could eat animal food without losing caste, but the Nair or landed gentry were permitted to eat vension, goats, fruits and fish. All the other castes ate any kind of meat, even mice, but not beef, and all classes were very fond of chewing betel leaves. When the Zamorin of Calicut was to eat a meal, four of the principal priests of the town would take the king's food and first offer it to the idol, leaving it exposed for a sufficient time for the god to satisfy his spiritual hunger; it was then placed before the king as he squatted on the ground. When he had finished, the leftover food was taken by the brahmins into the courtyard and placed on the ground; the priests clapped their hands three times, and a number of black crows swooped down and ate up the remains of the king's repast. Varthema describes a number of fruits: the sweet orange, three varieties of bananas (long, short-and-sweet, and bitter), and the jackfruit.[7a] The taste of the latter intrigued him; he declared it to be 'sweet and delicious; when it is eaten it seems as though you were eating musk melons, and it appears to resemble a very ripe Persian quince. It appears also as though you were eating a preparation of honey, and it also has the taste of a

Box. 26

CITIES OF YORE

How did our cities appear to early travellers?

Vijayanagar is 'a great city . . situated near very steep mountains. The circumference of the city is 60 miles; its walls are carried up to the mountains' (Nicolo dei Conti)[3b].

I climbed a hill (from) where the city seemed to me as large as Rome, and very beautiful to the sight; there are many groves of trees within it, in the gardens of the houses, and many conduits of water that flow into the midst of it, and in places there are lakes; and the king has close to his palace a palm-grove and other rich fruit-bearing trees . . . (there are) many orchards and gardens with many fruit trees . . . mangoes and areca palms and jack trees, also many lime and orange trees (and) white grapes. All the water that is in the city comes from two tanks (situated) outside the first enclosing wall. Going forward you have a broad and beautiful street, full of rows of fine houses . . . belonging to men rich enough to afford them. In this street live many merchants (selling) rubies, diamonds, emeralds, seed-pearls, cloths, and every other sort of thing there is on earth that you may wish to buy . . . you have there every evening a fair . . . (and) on every Friday a fair . . . with among other things, the produce of the country (Domingo Paes).[3b]

'There are immense parks for hunting and fowling, with the best of air, great fertility, wealth of merchandise, and abundance of all possible delicacies, a second paradise '(Ludovico di Varthema).[1a] 'There is an infinite trade in this city and strict justice and truth are observed towards all by the governors of the country . . . People come from all parts of the old world to trade and reside in Vijayanagar, and there is complete tolerance for Hindu, Muslim and Christian alike[1c] . . . (So common were lavish costumes) that the more part of this people is very wealthy (and the wealth of this city) is the greatest known to the whole world' (Duarte de Barbosa).[8c] It was the capital city of the kingdom which was even then called Karnāta.[33]

Calicut is eight miles in circumference, a noble emporium for all India, abounding in pepper, lac, ginger, cinnamon, myrobalans and zedoary' (possibly turmeric or some related root) (Nicolo dei Conti).[3d] It was 'a noble city, ruled by the Zamorin . . . The orderly nature of the town and people of Calicut, and the manner in which justice was strictly administered, were admirable' (Ludovico di Varthema).[1d] 'Most of the Muslim merchants are so fabulously wealthy that even one of them could buy the entire freight of the vessels at the port and fit out others like them' (Ibn Battūta).[34]

Āgra has the 'advantage . . . of its mild climate, fertile soil, great river, beautiful gardens, its fame spread to the ends of the earth, and its large size. For it is four miles long and two miles broad. All the necessaries and conveniences of human life can be obtained here, if desired . . . Indeed the city is flooded with vast quantities of every type of commodity . . . and is seldom visited by dearth of food supplies' (Father Monserrate).[13d] 'Its streets are fair and spacious, and there are some of them vaulted, which are above a quarter of a league in length, where the merchants and tradesmen have their shops . . . (there are) eighty caravanserais for foreign merchants, most of them three stories high, with very noble lodgings, storehouses, vaults and stables . . . seventy great mosques . . . and above eight hundred hot-houses (public baths)' (Albert de Mandelslo).[3g] 'You cannot desire anything, but you shall find it in this city' (John Jourdain).[19c]

Sūrat was 'thronged with merchants, and the nearby port is full of ships; it is a safe anchorage, since the river extends deep and broad from the sea right up to the city' (Father Monserrate).[5e] 'It is a great delight to take a seat on the bank of the river and behold the numerous boats which shoot to and fro like arrows . . . a great number of ships (are here) from different parts of Europe, Persia, Arabia, Bengal, Siam, Acheen, Queddah, the Maldives, Malacca, Batavia, Manila, China and many other parts of the world' (Niccolao Manucci).[25] Surat had 'stone and brick houses . . . goodly gardens with pomegranates, lemons, melons, figs continuing all the year.'[31c] It seemed to the priest 'like a terrestial paradise, such is the abundance of all earthy things' (Reverend Patrick Copland).[19c] 'Sūrat (is) of a large extent and very populous, rich in merchandise, as being the mart for the great empire of the Mogol, but ill-contrived into lanes and without any form; and for buildings consists partly of brick (the houses of the richer sort) and partly of wood (bamboo),' the latter being much greater in number. Of the former kind, 'their walls (are) 2 to 2½ feet thick and their roofs flat and covered with plaster . . . which makes them most commodious places to take the evening air in the hotter seasons' (Reverend John L'Escaliot).[35]

Bunches of bananas impressed early European visitors.

sweet orange'.[7a] Two fruits that Varthema mentions are hard to identify. One is the corcopal, which is described as being like a melon growing on a tree, with 3 or 4 large seeds like grapes or sour cherries inside, good for eating and as a medicine. The other fruit he compares to the medlar (loquat), though it has a white pulp like an apple. Varthema says that the scales and weights in use were so small and delicate that even a hair would turn them. Buying and selling was done by a kortor or lella (kārthā or lālā), who negotiated the price under cover of a cloth using finger pressures alternately with the buyer and seller: this practice is still in use in selling foodgrains and oilseeds in Indian markets.

Duarte de Barbosa of Portugal, a cousin of the great sailor Magellan (who may have contributed to the writing of Barbosa's book of 1516), again described the meal of a Rājāh of Calicut.[1c] He first chewed a betel leaf, then bathed in a pool while simultaneously worshipping, after which he donned clean clothes, and proceeding to the eating place, sat on a very low round wooden seat. Attendants then brought in a large silver tray on which were placed empty silver saucers. On another low stool was placed a copper pot of cooked rice. A pile of rice was heaped on the plate, and curried meat, sauces and chutneys placed in the saucers. He ate with his right hand, using the left to pour water from a silver pitcher

Grapes, abundant only at certain times.

into his open mouth without touching it. After finishing, he would return to his dais and chew betel leaves. The ceremonial cleanliness of the Nair women fascinated Barbosa. He felt however that the restricted diet of the brahmins deprived them of the necessary vigour to defend their country against invaders, while their tolerance of poisonous snakes and innumerable harmful insects led to the loss of human life and to the spread of diseases of all kinds. Visiting Vijayanagar, Duarte de Barbosa noted that rice was cultivated both by dry and by wet methods. In ploughing flooded fields, the seeds were sown by a drill contained in the ploughshare.

Domingo Paes, a Portuguese merchant, lived for several years in Vijayanagar around 1520.[7c]

He wrote: 'These dominions are very well cultivated and very fertile and are provided with quantities of cattle, such as cows, buffaloes and sheep; and also of birds, both those belonging to the hills and those reared at home, and this in greater abundance than in our tracts. The land has plenty of rice and jowār, grains, beans, and other kinds of crops that are not grown in our parts; also an infinity of cotton. Of grain there is a great quantity, because, besides being used as food for men, it is also used for horses, since there is no other kind of barley; and the country has also much wheat, and that good'.

Later he says that

Wheat is not so common as the other grains, since no one eats it except the Moors (Muslims) . . . The streets and markets are full of laden oxen without count . . . many loads of limes come each day, such that those of Povos are of no account, and also loads of sweet and sour oranges, and wild brinjals, and other garden stuff in such abundance as to stupefy one. There are many pomegranates also; grapes are sold at three bunches a fanam, and pomegranates at ten a fanam'

Elsewhere Paes describes the birds and poultry: three kinds of partridges, quails, wild fowl, doves of two kinds, large and small, pigeons, lake birds that looked like geese, poultry fowls incredibly cheap, and hares. He says that 'in every street there are men who will sell you mutton, so clean and fat that it looks like pork; and you also have pigs in some streets of butcher's houses so white and clean that you could never see better in any country.'

About fifteen years later there came to Vijayanagar another Portuguese, Fernão Nuniz, who was no less impressed:

Outside these . . . cities are fields and places richly cultivated with wheat and gram and rice and millet, for this last is the grain which is most consumed in this land; and next to it betel, which is a thing that in the greater part of the country they always eat and carry in the mouth. Everything has to be alive so that each one may know what he buys–at least so far as concerns game—and there are fish from the rivers in large quantities. The markets are always overflowing with abundance of fruits, grapes, oranges, limes, pomegranates, jack-fruits and mangoes, all very cheap.[3g]

Scientist travellers

It is a nice change to encounter, among these merchant travellers, some with scientific training and interest. Garcia da Orta was a physician and apothecary who from 1534 spent no less than 35 years in Gōa tending successive Portuguese Viceroys and officials. He was gifted the island of Bombay by the king of Portugal, and built a manor house on it, growing in his own large garden many species of trees and medicinal herbs.[8a, 9] His *Colloquies on the Simples and Drugs of India* is a monumental work of reference. At the court of his friend, Burhān Nizām Shah of Āhmadnagar, he met many Indian doctors.[10] He also travelled extensively in the country, and kept his eyes open. He noticed that flax and elephants were native to Bengal, and claimed to have proved, on himself, the efficacy of Ganges water. Indians, he says, keep the right thumbnail sharp and pointed so as to remove the midrib of the betel leaf. He noted the various varieties of mango, described the two forms of cardamom with their accurate Indian and Sri Lankan vernacular names, showed that the malabathrum of the Arabs was the Indian tējpat leaf, and also verified that the spikenard of the ancient Greeks was *Cymbopogon martini*, rosha grass that grew on the banks of the Ganges. A number of plants were identified: the shāl (sāl, Sanskrit shāla) tree, its resin and wood; the tamarind tree and its many uses; the black myrobalan (*Terminalia chebula*); white and yellow sandal growing in Timor; two varieties of the jāmun tree; the bēr tree; and the coconut, about which Garcia da Orta notes that the name cocos was derived from the resemblance of the nut to a monkey's face (in Spanish *coco*, and in Portuguese *macaco*). His medical bias showed in descriptions of the preparation of drugs from aloes, of kattha from the acacia, and the use of the bilvą fruit (which he calls marmelos) in dysentery. The infamous Spanish Inquisition burnt one of Garcia's sisters at the stake; they failed to get him, but twelve years after his death, his bones were exhumed and burnt, and the ashes cast into the Mandovi river.[11]

John Huygen von Linschoten also lived in Gōa for a few years around 1580.[8b] His *Itinerario* drew heavily on Orta's earlier publication but did contain some interesting original material. Rhubarb root, be noted, really went to Europe not from India but from China, and the material that travelled overland across Asia to Venice was much better than that which went by sea from China to Portugal. As a cure for gout, Charles V of Spain found much relief by using the 'roots of China', the tuber from various types of rhatany which is still listed in modern pharmacopeias. He cynically noted that the native wives of Portuguese officials administered their husbands dhāthura seeds as a narcotic to leave them free to pursue their own amours! Indian melons, Linschoten averred, were less sweet than those of Spain and needed to be eaten with sugar.[12] He had much to say about the manufacture of sugar from 'bamboos', listed many Indian fruit trees, and described at length the growing and manufacture of indigo. Both Orta and Linschoten are frequently quoted as authorities in any historical account of the flora of the time in India, especially in respect of such Portuguese-Spanish introductions as the cashew, pineapple and papaya. A third member of the company is Christophoras Acora, whose *Tract de las Drogas* (1578) describes, *inter alia*, the marking nut (bhilāwan), and many characteristics of the kinds of asafoetida imported into India.[12]

The Jesuits

'It has become a rule in the Society of Jesus that a record should be kept of all events. This rule dates from the blessed memory of our Father Ignatius (Loyola), who first pronounced it.'[13a] So writes Father Monserrate, who was intermittently in India during the period 1581–1600. Even earlier St. Francis Xavier had composed

St. Francis Xavier.

numerous letters: 32 of these, written while he resided in Gōa and Cochin, have survived. This priest learnt Tamil and stressed the importance of doing so for missionary activity. Several other missionaries also learnt Malabār (as they called Tamil); Henrique Henriques wrote a grammar of the language, and between 1576–86 three of his works were printed using Tamil characters at presses in Quilon, Cochin and perhaps Punical. Father Monserrate noted that the diet of the Parsis 'consists of milk, ghī, oil, vegetables, pulses and fruit, they drink no wine'. The Emperor Akbar, he noted, also 'rarely drinks wine, but quenches his thirst with post (see Box 27) or water'. Goncalves Rodrigues says that the land between Belgaum and Bijapūr is 'very black and fertile, and very flat . . . As it is such excellent land, all food grows abundantly with only the dews. The natives make poor use of the land, and many parts lie unused . . . it seems the most fertile soil imaginable, that is if it were in the hands of our Portuguese farmers.' Father Frois observes that the brahmins also claim to have a trinity, the Trimūrthi, but 'that they only speak of three persons because they learnt it from the Christians!' Michael Carneiro says that an indication of royal goodwill is the sending of a bunch of figs (perhaps the small bananas of Kērala are implied), and Michael Pinheiro remarks that the Jain monks 'live in poverty and accept in alms only what is necessary for daily sustenance.' They drink only hot water, because 'water has a soul that will be killed if drunk without being heated' (though this is more likely meant for sterilization of germs). Pedro Texeira (1587), a later visitor, describes two kinds of palm wine:

> Surā (he uses a very old Sanskrit word) is that kind which is got raw, dropping of itself into vessels set to receive it. The other called araca, is distilled by fire from this surā, and is very strong. Into this they throw dried grapes, which takes off its roughness and sweetens it; and it improves with age, which is not the case of that made with dried grapes and water.[7c]

British narratives on Indian food

A British Jesuit, Thomas Stevens, may have been the first from his country to come to India, arriving about 1579, staying 40 years, and learning both Konkani and Marāthi.[3c] Once again it was the pepper and the coconut that attracted his attention, and he says that 'coarse cinnamon grows here in this country (but) the best cinnamon comes from Ceylon and is pilled from the young trees'. Stevens wrote numerous letters home to his father describing the goods of India and died in Gōa in 1619.[1b] The advent of Ralph Fitch in 1583 marks the beginning of British trade thrusts into India, involving bitter rivalry with the dominant Portuguese, and much intrigue in the Moghul court and with trading officials at ports. Fitch described the manufacture of both toddy and arrack (with raisins added) from the palmer (palmyra), 'the profitablest tree in the world', which also yielded 'much sugar from the nut called jagara' (clearly a confusion for palm jaggery from the sap).[14] He noted that camphor, which was much used in India, came from China, but that the best type was from the great island of Borneo. Almonds were eaten and used as small money in Cooch-Behār. The people drove 'handsome two-wheeled carts, carved and gilded, and drawn by miniature bulls, very swift as trotters, but scarcely larger than very big dogs'.[1b] William Finch (1608–11) noted the many betel gardens in Sironj in Mālwa and the abundant wild dates and toddy palms at Variao, near Sūrat; from Āgra to Lahore 'the way is set on both sides with mulberry trees and at Bhalwar, near Sūrat, much wine is made from a sweet fruit called mewa (mahua).' His work is peppered with Indian words like medon (maidān), mohall (mahal, palace), dew (dev, god), cheet (chit), peally (pyali, cup), sikār, punkā and thamāsha.[15a] Thomas Coryat (1612–17) was regarded by his countrymen as somewhat of a wandering Indian fakīr, and died at Sūrat while attempting to walk back from India to England.[1b] He saw antelopes for the first time at the Moghul court, and remarks that Sir Robert Sherley and his lady took back with them to England two elephants and eight antelopes.

Sir Thomas Roe was the British ambassador to the court of Jahāngīr from 1615–19.[1b] It is recorded that he had both an Indian and an English cook, but insisted on eating his meals on tables and chairs, except when dining with easterners.

Box 27

HEADY STUFF

Even the *Atharvaveda* mentions the hemp plant, bhanga, as a sacred grass.[2b] This could however be a case of mistaken identity for the fibrous sann-hemp, since the narcotic property of true bhang, *Cannabis sativa*, only appears to have been realized about the 10th century AD. By the time the Europeans arrived in India the plant was being used in all its three forms. These were bhang, the dried leaves and flowering shoots; gānja, the dried flowering tips of female plants; and charas, the resinous exudate. Of the period 1580–1600 Father Monserrate writes: 'In many places in the neighbourhood of the Indus flax and hemp are sown. The plant which is commonly called bangue, and when used as a drink produces intoxication and stupefaction of the mind and senses, has leaves very similar to that of the hemp plant. It does not however grow on one stalk only, but has a low stem, from which spring a number of other branches, like a bush.'[13b] Linschoten (1580) noted that the poor chewed bhang mixed with nutmeg and mace (which disorder the mind), and the rich with cloves, camphor, amber, musk and opium. Acosta (1578) accurately describes and draws the plant, Mandelslo speaks of the drug as bengi, and Fryer (1672–81) mentions a fakír 'drunk with Bang' whom he encountered in Sūrat.[2b]

Opium in India is of somewhat earlier vintage. The Hindi term afin and the Sanskrit ahiphena are derived from the Arabic afyun.[2c] This knowledge the Arabs brought to India during the 11th and 12th centuries AD, having themselves learnt of it from the Greeks, who called the drug opion. The Uttar Pradesh and Mālwa regions became areas of poppy production, and in 1511 Giovanni da Empoli records that Albuquerque found opium in the cargoes of eight ships from Gujarāt that he had captured. Barbosa in 1516 noted that opium was an export item from India, and both Acosta and Linschoten before the end of that century described Indian indulgence in opium at length.[2c] Bernier in 1668 noted that Rājputs consumed it as a stimulant on the eve of battle.[16]

Father Monserrate describes the preparation of the decoction, using for the poppy capsule not the usual current term khākas (today, khaskhas) but an old term post.[13c] This word is unconnected with Greek or Arabic, and suggests ancient knowledge of the plant, even if not of the nature of its sap. According to the priest,

> the juice, is first drained from the pods, which are split for the purpose; these are then allowed to mature; then the seeds are removed, and the pods thrown into water, in which they are kept immersed until the liquid assumes the colour of wine. It is allowed to stand a little longer, and is then passed off into another vessel through a strainer made of finest linen. After impurities have been removed, the makers of this drink themselves eagerly quaff of it in cupfuls. They eat no meat, garlic, onions or anything of that kind. They even abstain from fruit, and are particularly careful never to take any oil, which is fatal after opium or this drink. They eat only cooked pulse and any sweet food. Then they put their heads between their knees, and sleep as heavily as did Endymion . . . the nature of the drug is such that it numbs and freezes the impure desires of the flesh . . . the drink is commonly known as post.

Jahāngīr regularly sent him meat of the chase, once 'a mighty elk' (perhaps a sāmbhar or nīlgāi) which he described as 'reasonably rank meat', and again wild boar, with a polite request that 'the tusks be returned'. Moghul nobles, Sir Thomas noted, kept luxurious tables: up to twenty dishes were served at a time, sometimes even fifty.[16] The ambassador noted the oppression of the peasantry: 'The people of India live like fishes do in the sea—the great ones eat up the little. For first the farmer robs the peasant, the gentleman robs the farmer, the greater robs the lesser, and the King robs all.'[3b] Many other travellers echo the hard lot of the Indian kisān who grew the country's food.

Roe's chaplain, the Rev. Edward Terry, spent three years in India, and on his return to England presented his first account to the Prince of Wales (later Charles I).[14] An enlarged edition was included later along with the accounts of many other travellers by the Rev. Samuel Purchas in his collected volumes, *Purchas and his Pilgrims*.

They feed not freely on full dishes of mutton and beef, as we, but much on rice boiled with pieces of flesh or dressed many other ways. They have not many roast or baked meats, but stew most of their flesh. Among many dishes of this kind, I will take notice but of one they call *deu pario* (dōpiyāzā), made of venison cut in slices, to which they put onions and herbs, some roots, with a little spice and butter: the most savoury meat I ever tasted, and do almost think it that very dish which Jacob made ready for his father, when he got the blessing.

Buffalo flesh was 'like beef, but not so wholesome . . . Their sheep exceed ours in great bob-tails, which cut off are very ponderous . . . the

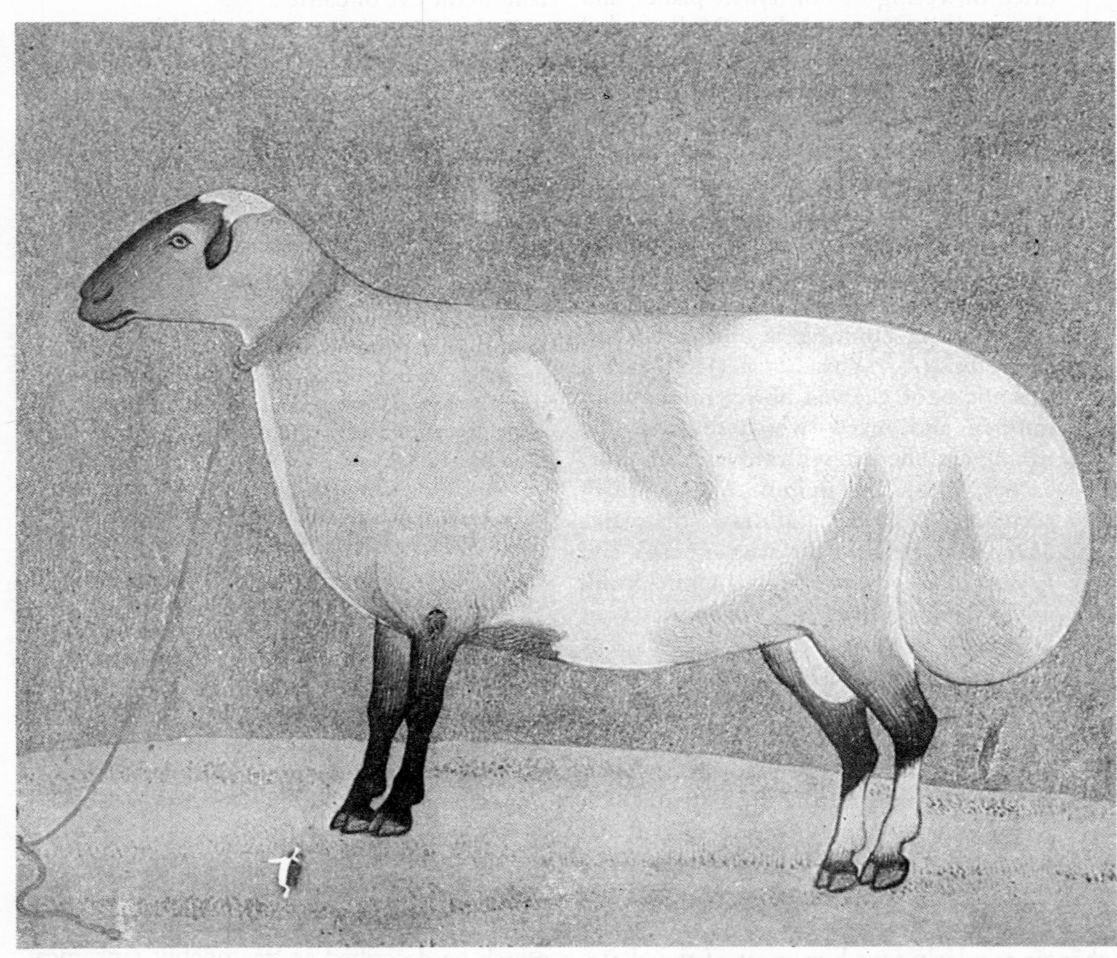

Mughal painting of the fat-tailed sheep praised by Edward Terry.

flesh of them both is altogether as good as ours.' At a dinner given to Sir Thomas Roe by Āsaf Khan (brother of Nūrjahān, and father of Mumtāz Mahal), 'the ambassador', notes Terry, 'had more dishes by ten, and I less by ten than our entertainer had, but for my part I had fifty dishes . . . (all) set at one time'.[17] The poor, he noted, ate rice boiled with green ginger, to which they added a little pepper and butter; it was their principal dish but was seldom eaten. Their 'ordinary food' was not made of flour of wheat but of a coarser grain (possibly jowār, since Terry only visited Gujarāt and Mālwa) baked on small, round iron hearths (doubtless the sigdi of today) to give round, broad and thick cakes that were both 'wholesome and hearty'. Indian wheat, says Terry, 'grows like ours, but the grain of it is somewhat bigger and more white; of which the inhabitants make such pure well-relished bread-(truly a) *panis pane melior*' (super-bread). Water was indeed the common drink, but sometimes it was converted into sherbet with lemon juice and sugar.[17]

> Some small quantity of wine (but not common) is made among them. They call it arrack distilled from sugar and a spicy rind of a tree called jagra (palm sap). It is very wholesome if taken moderately. Many of the people who are strict in their religion drink no wine at all, but instead drink coffee which helped digestion, quickened the spirits and cleansed the blood.[15b]

Hindus observed Thursday as their day of rest.[15b]

There was another side too, the great famine of 1631. Peter Mundy described 'poor people scraping on the dunghills for . . . grain that perchance may come undigested from them . . . the highways strewn with dead people, our noses never free from the stink of them'.[18a]

The diaries of a mixed bouquet of visitors

From about 1620 till the end of the century, the European writers on India constitute a mixed bunch: Dutchmen, Frenchmen, Italians and Britishers, all jockeying for better trade opportunities for their own countries. Francisco Pelsaert, from Holland, was in India for 6 years (1621–7) as the Senior Factor (Manager) of the Dutch East India Company in Āgra.[10c] 'Workmen in India know little of the taste of meat . . . for their monotonous daily food they have nothing but a little kitcherry made of green pulse mixed with rice eaten with butter in the evening; in the daytime they munch a little parched pulse or other grain.' The area around Agra was dry and hard before the rains, and large numbers of wells had to be dug to irrigate the soil.[3d] Fruit trees were scarce, and much fruit came from Kandahār or Kābūl. But

> great and wealthy amateurs have planted in their gardens Persian vines which bear seedless grapes, but the fruit does not ripen properly in one year out of three. Oranges are plentiful in December, January and February, and are obtainable also in June and July; they are very large, especially in the neighbourhood of Bayana. Lemons can be had in large quantities. The supply of meat . . . is ample.

Drawing on the writings of both Terry and Pelsaert, a later Dutch writer, Joannes de Laet says that Indians

> show great cunning in catching water-birds; for they take a skin of a bird of the same kind as they wish to catch and stuff it so skilfully that it seems a real bird; they then immerse themselves in water up to the neck, cover their heads with the sham bird, and then make their way into the flock of wild birds, which they catch by seizing their feet below the water.[20]

Fray (Father) Sebastian Manrique (1628–43) testified to the abundance of food available in Āgra: '. . . entire streets . . . (are) wholly occupied by skilled sweetmeat makers (with) dainties of all sorts in the innumerable bazaars'.[19b] So also Lahore's 'brilliantly lighted bazaars had a great number of occupied tents or cookshops exhaling the aroma of spicy dishes' and displaying 'large spits bearing the flesh of winged creatures . . . Nor did these bazaars lack the simple foods of the native (to meet whose taste) many tents hold different dishes made of rice, herbs and vegetables (besides) the ubiquitous flat bread'. Elsewhere Manrique describes three kinds of bread in Lahore.[21] One was unleavened and paper-thin, baked on a skillet and then on live charcoal, eaten by the poor (the chapāti); the second kind, thick as a finger, was for richer people (perhaps this was naan); and the third kind, a sweet form called khjūru, was made with wheat flour, poppy seed and sugar, with a lot of ghee and a delicate flavour. He noted that in Bengal the flesh of only certain animals was eaten, but not that of 'tame pigs, hens, or eggs or flesh of . . . cows'. Elsewhere he says: 'Wild pigs were considered a great delicacy by Rājputs and Sikhs; pigeons are not generally eaten as being of a blue colour they are held sacred to Shiva, but doves are ordinarily eaten.' The monumental 12-volume *Hortus Malabaricus*, published in Amsterdam between 1680–1700, was compiled by the Dutch governor Henrich van Rheede, with 794 plates. These were sketched for him by an artist from Cochin, while for the textual material he took the help of a Carmelite missionary, Father Matheo, and a traditional Kērala physician, Itty Achyuthan.[3g,22a] The great Linnaeus himself praised the extraordinary accuracy of this work. In 1757 appeared another great botanical work by George Rumphius in six volumes with 696 plates,[3g] also useful to future historians of food plants.

Two Frenchmen wrote extensively and intelligently about India. Jean-Baptiste Tavernier, a French jeweller and merchant, came to India six times during the half century 1640–85, and in fact died at the age of 80 in Moscow on his way once again to India by way of Russia.[1d] His three volumes on the East were written between 1670 and 1684. He mentions that khichrī made with green gram, rice, butter and salt was the popular peasant evening meal;[3e] elsewhere he states that workmen returning from their fields (perhaps at noon) make no supper, but eat some sweetmeats and drink a glass of water. Going from Āgra to Bengal, he came upon a little boy nine or ten years old feeding millet to a rhinoceros which opened its mouth for more. At Dacca the Nawāb sent him 'pomegranates, China oranges, Persian melons and three sorts of pears'.[23] Tavernier also wrote knowledgeably about commercial matters like jute fibres and indigo cultivation.[1d] The other Frenchman, François Bernier, was a doctor who ministered to both prince Dārā Shikoh and his brother the Emperor Aurangzeb, spending in all seven years in India (1659–66).[3f] Kāshmīr charmed him: 'Meadows and vineyards, fields of rice, wheat, hemp, saffron, and many sorts of vegetables, among which are intermingled trenches filled with water rivulets, canals, and several small lakes vary the enchanting scene.' Elsewhere he noted the numerous fruit trees. Even in the city of Delhi he was astonished at the enormous variety of imported fresh fruits all the year round, and their vast consumption.[16] On his travels Bernier took 'a stock of excellent rice for 5 to 6 days' consumption, of sweet biscuits flavoured with anise, of limes and sugar. Nor have I forgotten a linen bag with its small iron hook for the purpose of suspending and draining *days* (dahi); nothing being considered so refreshing in this country as lemonade and *days*'.[1d] He found

Francois Bernier.

the 'bazaar bread of Delhi often badly baked and full of sand and dirt'. As to the water of that city, it contained impurities which, he declared, 'exceeded his powers of description (it being) accessible to all persons and animals, and the receptacle of every kind of filth'. Bernier gives a vivid description of the beauty of Bengal, whose

endless number of channels, cut in bygone ages from that river with endless labour . . . (are) lined on both sides . . . with extensive fields of rice, sugar, corn, three or four sorts of vegetables, mustard, sesame for oil, and small mulberry trees, two or three feet in height, for the food of silk-worms . . . the innumerable islands abounding in fruit-trees and pineapples . . . Meat is salted at a cheap rate by the Dutch and English for the supply of their vessels, fish of every species, whether fresh or salt, is in the same profusion. In a word, Bengal abounds with every necessity of life . . . (all of which) has given rise to a proverb among the Portuguese, English and Dutch, that the kingdom of Bengal has a hundred gates open for entrance, but not one for departure.[3f]

The love of sweets in the area did not miss his eye: 'Bengal likewise is celebrated for its sweetmeats, especially in places inhabited by the Portuguese, who are skilful in the art of preparing them and with whom they are an article of considerable trade.'[24] Preserved fruits seem to be meant because a list of these follows: large citrons, āmbā (mangoes), anānas (pineapple), small myrobalans (probably āmla fruits, which are pronounced 'excellent'), limes and ginger. The observations of Jean de Thevenot (1665–7) have some historic interest.[3c] He noted that in Surat the use of fish manure was well established, and that the brahmins drank nothing but water 'wherein they put coffee and tea', an early reference to these beverages.

Niccolao Manucci was a colourful character, who came to India in 1654 at the age of 15, and died in Madrās after spending six decades in almost every part of the country; though without formal medical training, he got away with a smattering of acquired knowledge, and practised as a doctor.[7c] He noted the prohibitions against meat, and said:

As for shell-fish, they also are classed among the most impure of things, and are not used except by the pariahs. However almost all other castes eat of the other kinds of meats and judge it to be most delicious fare . . . To obtain plenary indulgence for all their sins, they say, it is necessary to obtain a beverage composed of milk, butter, cowdung and cow's urine. With this medicament not only is all sin driven away but all infamy . . . (with their meals) they sup a concoction which is some water boiled with pepper

— an early description of the rasam of the south. He described on the road to Burhānpūr (the seat of Aurangzeb at the time)[25] 'shady and pleasant woods, peopled with many varieties of animals of the chase . . . without hindrance (I) killed whatever I wished, there being no scarcity of things to kill'.[25] His first experience of chewing betel was vividly set down:

. . . my head swam to such an extent that I feared I was dying. It caused me to fall down; I lost my colour, and endured agonies; but (an English acquaintance) poured into my mouth a little salt and brought me to my senses. It happens with the eaters of betel, as to those accustomed to tobacco, that they are unable to refrain from taking it many times a day.

His *Storia di Mogor* was both a personal record, and a history in five parts of the Moghul rulers, including the contemporary ruler Aurangzeb. 'The best mangoes grow in the island of Goa,' he says,[3f] and goes on to name a number of varieties by their Portuguese names, including Niculao Affonso (the Alphonso), Carreira (both white and red) and Babia. 'I have eaten many that had the taste of the peaches, plums, pears and apples of Europe.' He also described three kinds of jackfruit: barca, papa and pacheri. 'Of the seeds (of jackfruit) mixed with rice flour they make a kind of fritters, which in India are called pāniara. These too have their own flavour.' There is a historic interest in his description of 'another fruit found in India called anānas (the pineapple); . . . in no part of India have I seen them in such quantities as in Bengal, where they were large and fine'. Both the coconut and palmyra palm were carefully and accurately described. Manucci tried to pick the brains of a physician visitor, Angelo Legrenzi of Venice, who in his *Travels in Asia* says that Manucci was 'desirous . . . by whatever means he could, to induce me to rest beside him and supply him with a little light in medicine, devoid as he was of letters, and any knowledge of the arts' Obviously the visitor saw through the game.

John Fryer (1672–81) writes in his *New Account of East India and Persia*[19a] that in Bengal, butter 'is in such plenty that although it be a bulky article to export, yet it is sent by sea to numberless places'; probably, clarified butter or ghee is what is meant. Fryer picks out the 'good carrots' of the Deccan for special mention, and was able to discover that while most of the asafoetida of India came from one area in Iran-Afghanistan, the best type was really to be had from elsewhere; this paved the way for our present knowledge that the less-aromatic, water-stable hing is from a different tree species than the more pungent, oil-soluble hingra. Robert Orme came to India in 1743 to serve the East India Company in Bengal.[26] According to him,

> Health is best preserved in this climate by the slightest and simplest diet . . . the preference for vegetables, of which they have various kinds in plenty, is decisively marked among them all (the Hindus) . . . The fruit trees of other countries furnish delicacies to the inhabitants, and scarcely anything more; in India there are many that furnish at once a delicacy and no contemptible nourishment,

probably meaning thereby the coconut, palm, jackfruit ('rich, glewy and nutritive'), banana and papa (probably the papaya) of which he also provides illustrations.

Colonial repast

Early European officials in India laid lavish tables. Mandelslo in 1638 noted '15 or 16 dishes of meat, besides the dessert' in the home of the president of the English merchants at Sūrat who all lived together.[18b] Even in 1780 in Calcutta, Mrs. Eliza Fay, a lawyer's wife and herself a dressmaker, wrote: 'We dine at 2 o'clock in the very heat of the day . . . A soup, a roast fowl, curry and rice, a mutton pie, forequarter of lamb, a rice pudding, tarts, very good cheese, fresh churned butter, excellent Madeira (that is very expensive, but eatables are very cheap).'[27] To prepare and serve these meals a whole array of servants and kedmutgars was in attendance. In 1809 in mofussil Mymensingh, the wine was always claret; 'you buy and fatten your own deer, oxen, sheep, calves, kids, ducks, geese, rabbits, etc.' Bread was made at home; so was butter, from the milk of one's own cows, made by pouring cream into 'very large open-mouthed bottles, which are closely stoppered and gently thumped up and down on the ground'.[18c] Edward Lear, known to posterity for his limericks, had a breakfast while in India in 1874 of 'boiled prawns, prawn curry, cold mutton, bread and butter, and plantains'.[28] A painting of an English family at breakfast shows fried fish, rice, oranges and a baked casserole of some sort.[29]

By the turn of the twentieth century, eating patterns had altered. In the 18th century the main meal, exemplified by the huge spread described by Mrs. Fay, was in the middle of the day,[32] followed by a siesta, evening visits and a light dinner at night. A century later this mid-day meal had become lighter, and a highly-rated book on British cuisine in india, ***Wyvern's Indian Cookery Book*** by Colonel Kenney-Herbert, exults in this change from quantity to quality. About 1910, a suggested lunch consisted of pea soup, roast chicken and tongue, bread sauce, potatoes, cheese macaroni and lemon pudding.[30] The main meal had moved to 7 or 8 in the evening, and in 1909 the writer Maud Divers declares that 'India is the land of dinners, as England is the land of five-o'clock teas . . . all India is in a chronic state of giving and receiving (this) form of hospitality.'[30]

The kind of food served had also clearly changed. The early British travellers had been fascinated with Indian food, and Sir Thomas Roe had both an Indian and an English cook.[31a] With the arrival of the mēmsāhibs, the accent had shifted to English-style soups, roasts, baked pies and puddings. Of course the Indian ambience could not be avoided. A number of hybrid dishes conjured up between the English lady of the house and her Indian cook appeared, like Windsor soup, Patna rice, a broth of doll (dhāl), Burdwan stew, cabobs, fish moley, curry chutney and the renowned Byculla soufflé.[30] Sir John Malcolm, who succeeded Montstuart Elphinstone as Governor of Bombay in 1827, wrote that 'the only difference between Monstuart and me is that I have mulligatawny at tiffin

An English family at breakfast which included fried fish, rice, oranges and a baked casserole.

(lunch), which comes of my experiences at Madrās,' whereas the latter lunched on 'a few sandwiches and figs and a glass of water'.[18d]

The early Europeans saw virtues in toddy brewed from palm juice, and the arrack distilled from it. Then changes set in. Punch was a blend of arrack with spices, sugar, lime-juice and water; it was first noted in 1638 by Mandelslo as palepuntz, and became a popular drink in all the British colonies. The recipe was later varied, even milk being employed as seen in this 1823 recipe from Madrās: 'Soak the rinds of 30 limes in two bottles of arrack for 12 hours; drain off the liquor, add 10 bottles of arrack and 6 of brandy or rum; to this add 2½ bottles of lime juice, 8 nutmegs grated, 12 lbs of moist sugar, 8 quarts of new milk boiling and 14 quarts of boiling water.' This was prepared in a large vessel, cooled, filtered through flannel, and bottled for use.[32]

Once western-style liquors became available, there was a fair amount of drinking. It was usual for a gentleman to have three bottles of claret after dinner each day, besides the Madeira wine that he consumed with his meal; a lady frequently went through a bottle of wine a day.[29] The favourite drink was claret, but one reads also of burnt wine, burnt champagne, brandy and beer. Della Valle (1623) describes 'drinking a little hot wine, boiled with cloves, cinnamon and other spices which the English call burnt wine . . . drinking it frequently in the morning to comfort the stomach, sipping it by little and little for fear of scalding . . . particularly in the winter to warm themselves'.[31b]

Apart from the food items we have noted, some unique Anglo-Indian terms arose in the area of food. Punch was from pānch, and denoted the five components used in making the drink.[4b] Toddy came from the Hindi tari for the fermented sap of the tāla or palmyra palm,[4c] first called by the Portuguese palmeira or the excellent palm. The peg as a measure of liquor got its name, according to British humourists, because each one was a peg in one's coffin.[30] Rice congee, an invalid beverage, was the Tamil kanji, a translucent liquid which was also used by the dhobi as an accessible source of starch for stiffening cotton clothes! Kedgeree for breakfast was the Hindi khichrī, which visitors like Ibn Battūta in 1340, and Abdur Razzāk in 1443, describe as a dish of rice cooked with dhāl, usually that of mung.[4a] Rice cakes, āppa or āppam in Tamil, appeared at an English breakfast as hoppers; this was a word particularly in use in Sri Lanka.[4d] Pepper water (rasam) was literally rendered into English as mulliga-tawny, a fiery soup. The baking of meat in a seal of dough, dumpukht, meaning air-cooled in Persian, and mentioned along with a recipe in the *Ain-i-Akbari*, became dumpoke, frequently applied to a dish of boned and stuffed duck.[4e]

The most widely-used Indian term was curry. This was originally used for any spiced relish employed by south Indians to accompany rice, and is noted as early as 1502 by Correa as caril. Later the word curry was very much enlarged in Anglo-Indian usage to mean a liquid broth, a thicker stew, or even a dry dish, all of which of course appear in a south Indian meal as successive courses, each with various names.[4f] The moley was a corruption of the word Malay perhaps indicative of its origin, and is a wet dish of Tamil Nādu with plenty of coconut, which the British adopted. And what of the ubiquitous tiffin, the present late-afternoon snack meal of south India? Originally the word stood for the Anglo-Indian luncheon, and surprisingly its origin is not Indian at all.[4g] The word derives from both the slang English noun tiffing, for eating or drinking out of meal times, and from the verb to tiff, which was to eat the mid-day meal. When dinner became a heavy evening meal, only a light snack lunch was customary, which explains why the word tiffin appears only as late as 1807 in Anglo-Indian writings.

In 1836 a Lt. Gaisford, revenue survey officer, invented the spoked wheel for the bullock cart in place of solid wooden or stone wheels, which brought about a reduction in weight and far greater manoeuvrability. This was one of the greatest contributions by the British to the Indian food and agriculture system. The first factory for manufacture was set up by a Parsi entrepreneur in Tembhurni in the Satara district of Bombay, and these wheels quickly displaced the old type.[36]

Chapter 14

STAPLES OF YORE

Barley and wheat, we have noted in Chapter 2, were the staples of the northern Harappan settlements. In the south ragi was popular before rice stormed its way in. In central India, jowār and bājra show up in early excavations. A clutch of other grains, such as the various panicums and related species, gavēdhukā (Job's tears), and indrajau all show up from comparatively early times. It is primarily the botanic and the genetic history of these cereals and other food grains that we shall look at in this and subsequent chapters, supplemented with their occurrence in archaeological excavations, or their mention in literature.

The broad outlines of plant evolution are described in Box 28.

Cereals

Barley

Barley is a self-pollinating diploid with $2n = 2x = 14$. Both the wild and the cultivated types are the same species; they hybridize easily to give fully fertile forms, and the botanical names which they were given in the last two centuries, it is now realized, represented only forms or races, and not true species.[1a] All truly wild forms are two-rowed; i.e., of the three spikelets at each node of the ear, the two lateral ones are female-sterile, and only the central one develops a grain. Under domestication six-rowed races appear (by just one recessive mutation) in which all three spikelets produce grains. These cultivated six-rowed forms sometimes yield six-rowed materials with fragile ears, which were earlier mistaken for wild plants. The earliest forms of barley found in archaeological sites in the Middle East are all two-rowed, covered (non-naked) types which do not thresh properly. By 6000 BC, both naked two-rowed and six-rowed types show up. The finds in Syria dated 8000 BC are all wild forms with fragile ears, as are those in Jordan and Iraq, but by 7000–6000 BC cultivated forms appear all over Syria, Iran, Palestine and Turkey.[2] Barley has been found around 6000 BC in Mehrgarh, near Quetta, and in neolithic Chirand in Bihār about 3500 BC.[3a] Later it occurs in many Harappan cities, in huge quantities in Kālibangan in Rājasthan, and in smaller proportions, always mixed with wheat, in Mohenjodaro, Harappā, Chanhudaro and Inamgaon.[4] In Chirand it accompanied wheat and rice, in Daimābād jowār (in finds prior to 1600 BC), and rice in Dangwādā near Ujjain (about 1500 BC). All these finds are of the cultivated six-rowed form, both hulled and naked. Barley was thus an important grain of the vast Indus Valley civilization, except perhaps in the Saurāshtra settlements.[5a] From the *Rigveda* right down to 500 BC, barley is the main staple grain of Sanskrit literature as yava, though the term itself in early Vedic usage may have included wheat as well; even as late as AD 500, two varieties of yava, an inferior and a superior, are mentioned,[6a] though rice was by then the dominant Vedic cereal. Today barley is a minor cereal; in the plains, a six-rowed hulled type is grown, and at upper altitudes, a six-rowed naked variety.[5b]

Box 28
PLANT EVOLUTION

In 1882 Alphonse de Candolle published his pioneering work, *Origin of Cultivated Plants,*[58] and in 1926 Vavilov proposed that there were eight main centres in the world where 'plant evolution was directed by the will of man' in the past, with other secondary centres of plant diversification and differentiation. These propositions were based on careful collection and comparative study of both wild and cultivated plants from all over the world. While the gradual transformation of a wild species in time and place is still broadly valid, it is now known from genetic studies that a sudden single, localized event can yield a new species.[59] For example, this happened not once but twice in the evolution of bread wheat from einkorn grass (see text) by chance crossing with local grasses. Further, the crossing in both instances occurred in the middle East, far to the west of Afghanistan where Vavilov had noted the greatest diversity of wheat forms.

Other interventions can also complicate matters. Some species can be carried for distances by sea without losing viability. A classic example is the coconut, which was dispersed from the Papua New Guinea area all over the southern oceans, so long ago that even an Indian origin was once postulated. Other instances are the sweet potato, which originated in Peru but had spread to the Polynesian islands at an early date, and the bottle gourd, which floated across from Africa to South America even in the wild state to evolve separately in each continent.

To reproduce, plant cells divide into two pieces and then recombine.[58] This happens in flowering plants during the formation of pollen; the contribution of chromosomes, termed X, from both parents is equal, and a 2n diploid is the result. Thus barley has $2n = 2x = 14$. But accidents can occur either during the break-up or the fusion, with various possibilities. These include a doubling of the chromosome complement (4x, 8x) to yield giant plants, or hybridization to polyploids (3x, 6x), or loss of chromosomes ($3x - 1$, $4x - 2$), and so on. In his classic volume *Species Plantarum* (1752), the Swedish botanist Linné classified genus and species by meticulous external morophological observations and the use of a Latin two-word nomenclature. Chromosome mapping has led to considerable re-classification and re-naming, a process which continues constantly. Thus several Indian pulses long classed as *Phaseolus* species are now termed *Vigna*, and the genus *Phaseolus* is now reserved for species that originated in South America, like the rājmāh. The progenitor of thuvar dhāl, for which an African origin had long been postulated, is now believed to be a wild Indian species from a related family, *Atylosia* (see text).

Strategically situated, India received, at various times, plant material from several directions: the Middle East, Africa, south-east Asia, the far East and even South America. This makes it difficult to state categorically that the origin of a particular plant is purely Indian. The sesame (see text) appears to be one of these.

Wheat

Wheat evolved parallel to barley and in the same geographic area, and eventually displaced it in the Middle East, except for saline lands on which only barley could be raised.[1a] The genetic evolution of wheat from wild grasses involved several

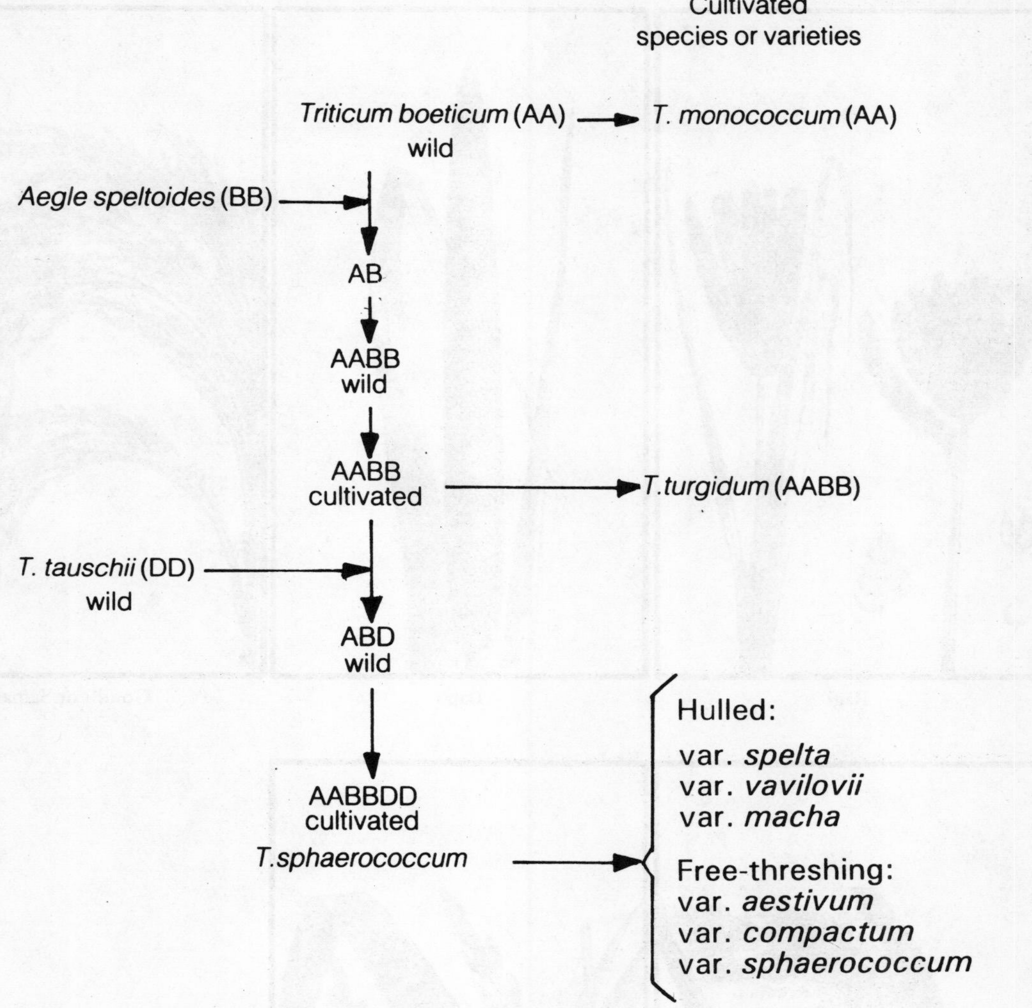

The evolution of wheat, showing chance crossings at two stages.

steps.[1b,7] The wild ancestor, botanically *Triticum boeticum*, is called einkorn since it has one grain to each spikelet. From this the cultivated einkorn was raised by man, which is *T. monoccum* with AA genomes (2n = 14). These early diploid wheats then crossed by chance with a totally useless wild grass that grows alongside, named *Aegle squarrosa* (BB genomes), to give wild *T. dicoccoides* (AABB), and in turn the cultivated tetraploid *T. dicoccum* (also AABB, 4n = 28). This was available in several varieties all carrying large, hard grains, the best-known of which was durum. In course of time, through accumulated mutations, varieties like *T. turgidum* arose which easily yielded the free grains on threshing. The next stage in wheat evolution was a crossing, by chance again, of one of the cultivated tetraploids, *T. turgidum* (AABB), with another local wild grass (once called *Aegilops squarrosa*, but now classified as *T. tauschii*, with DD genomes), followed by the usual chromosome doubling, to yield the cultivated hexaploids, AABBDD (6n = 42). This is the bread wheat so widely-grown today, called *T. aestivum*, of which there are several varieties. The hulled varieties are spelta, vavilovii and macha, which on threshing do not yield their grains freely. The free-threshing varieties within

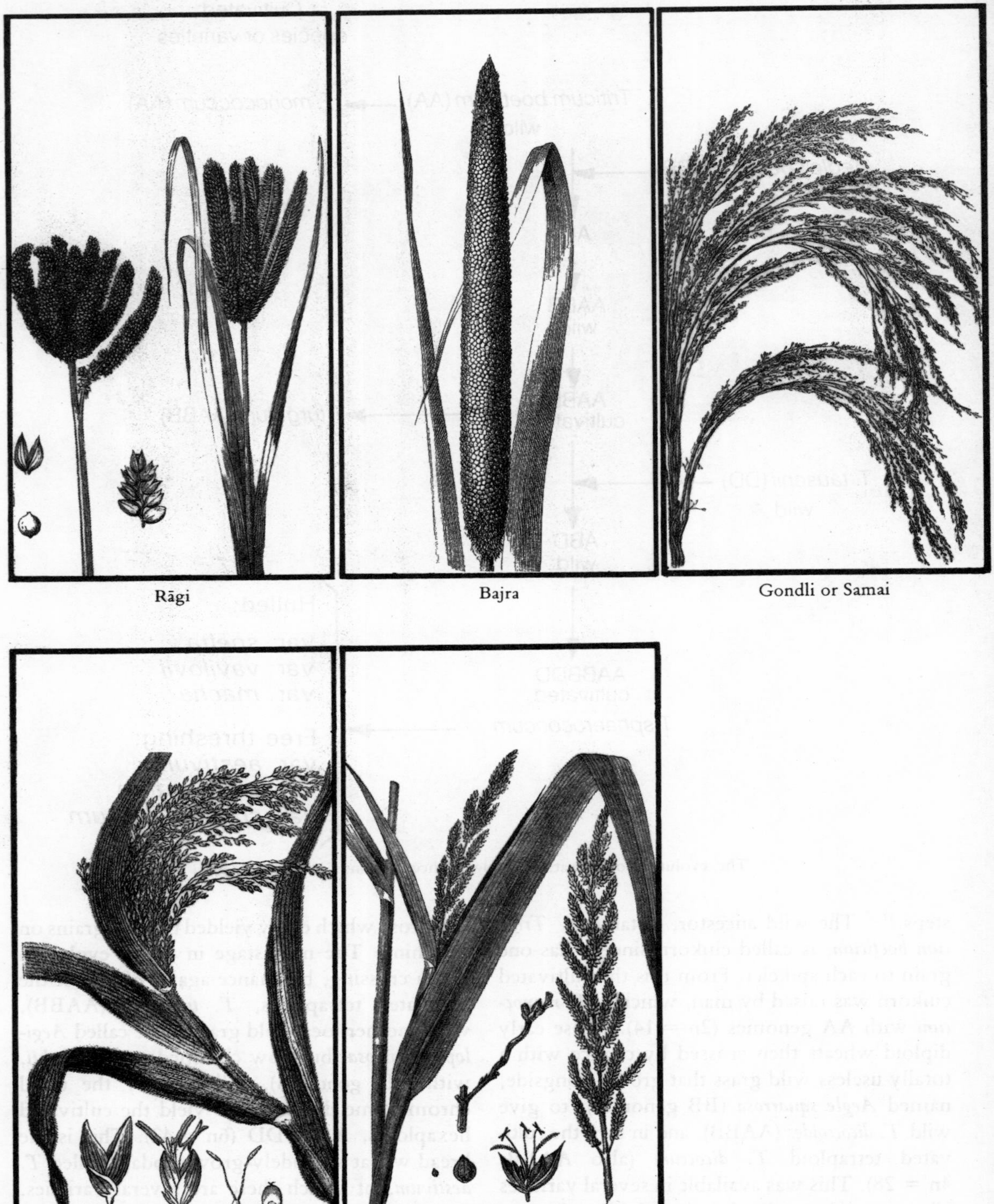

Rāgi Bajra Gondli or Samai

Cheena or Panivaragu Sanwa

Some less-known cereals of India.

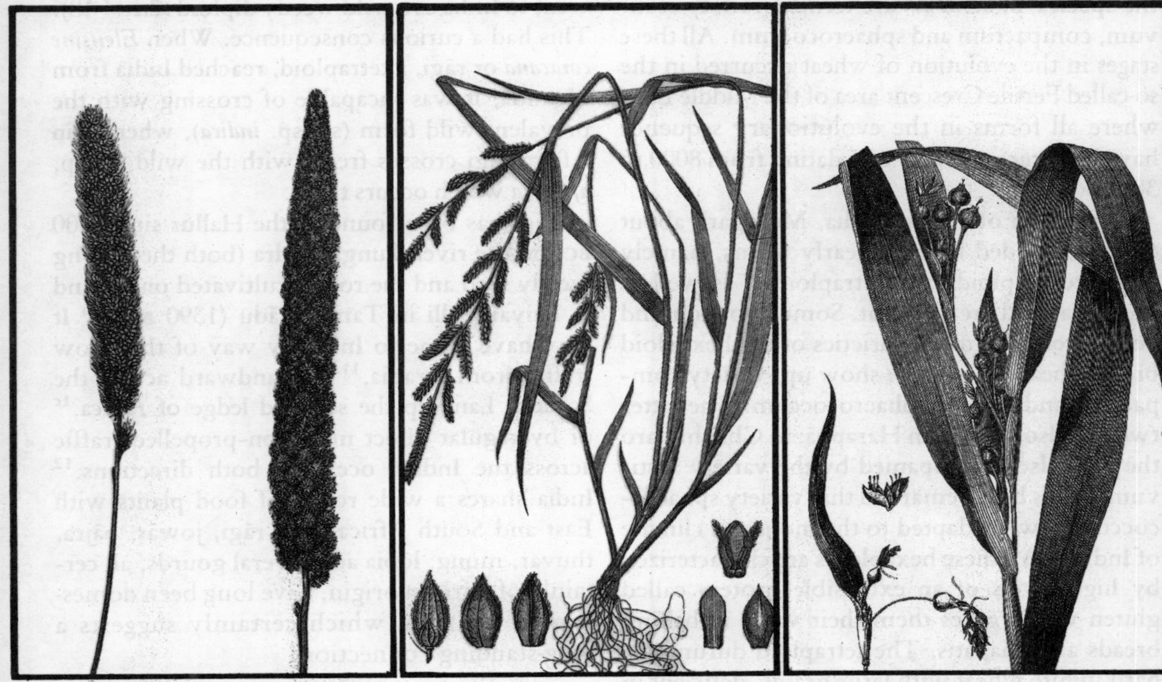
Kangni or Thennai

Sawank

Job's tears

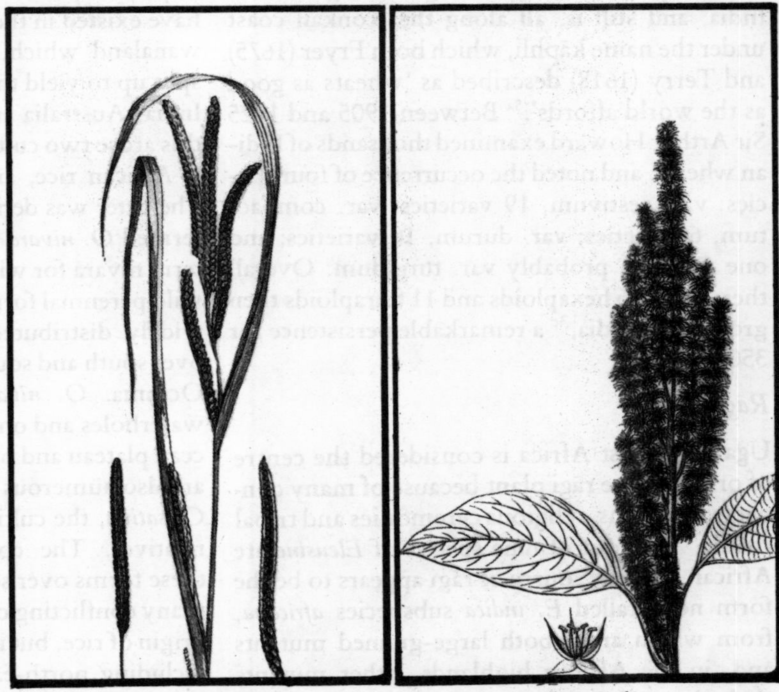
Kodhra or Varagu

Amaranth

Other less-known cereals of India.

the species *T. aestivum* are termed variety aestivum, compactum and sphaerococcum. All these stages in the evolution of wheat occurred in the so-called Fertile Crescent area of the Middle East, where all forms in the evolutionary sequence have been recovered in sites dating from 8000 to 3000 BC.[1b]

In the area of greater India, Mehrgarh about 6000 BC yielded both the early forms, namely cultivated diploids and tetraploids,[2] as well as one hexaploid bread wheat. Some two thousand years later, two more varieties of the hexaploid bread wheat *T. aestivum* show up, variety compactum and variety sphaerococcum. The latter two are also present in Harappā; in Chanhudaro they are also accompanied by the variety aestivum. It has been remarked that variety sphaerococcum is well adapted to the monsoon climate of India.[5a] All these hexaploids are characterized by high levels of an extensible protein called gluten which gives them their value in baking breads and chapātis. The tetraploid durum is a hard, white wheat with large grains, deficient in gluten, but excellent for making macaroni and vermicelli. Durum has long been grown in India, and still is, all along the Konkan coast under the name kāphli, which both Fryer (1675) and Terry (1618) described as 'wheats as good as the world affords'.[8a] Between 1905 and 1925 Sir Arthur Howard examined thousands of Indian wheats, and noted the occurrence of four species: var. aestivum, 19 varieties; var. compactum, 6 varieties; var. durum, 10 varieties; and one *dicoccum*, probably var. turgidum. Overall. there were 36 hexaploids and 11 tetraploids then growing in India,[3c] a remarkable persistence for 3500 years.

Rāgi

Uganda in east Africa is considered the centre of origin of the rāgi plant because of many connected customs, religious ceremonies and tribal rituals.[1c] Six out of nine species of *Eleusine* are African, and the source of rāgi appears to be the form now called *E. indica* subspecies *africana*, from which arose both large-grained mutants and, in the African highlands, other mutants with short glumes and exposed grains. It was this form, called *E. indica* subsp. *indica*, which went to India as a wild weedy diploid (2n = 18). This had a curious consequence. When *Eleusine coracana* or rāgi, a tetraploid, reached India from Uganda, it was incapable of crossing with the prevalent wild form (subsp. *indica*), whereas in Africa rāgi crosses freely with the wild subsp. *africana* which occurs there.

Rāgi has been found at the Hallur site (1800 BC) on the river Tungabhadra (both the oblong weedy seed and the round cultivated one),[9] and at Paiyampalli in Tamil Nādu (1390 BC).[10a] It may have come to India by way of the dhow traffic from Arabia,[11a] or landward across the Sabaean Lane up the seaward ledge of Africa,[1c] or by regular direct monsoon-propelled traffic across the Indian ocean in both directions.[12] India shares a wide roster of food plants with East and South Africa. The rāgi, jowār, bājra, thuvar, mung, lōbia and several gourds, all certainly of African origin, have long been domesticated in India, which certainly suggests a long-standing connection.

Rice

A primitive wild aquatic grass is postualted to have existed in the huge land mass called Gondwanaland which, some 10 million years ago, split up to yield the present land areas of Africa, India, Australia and South America.[1d,13] From this arose two cultigens, *Oryza glaberrima* which is African rice, and *Oryza sativa*, Asiatic rice. The latter was derived from an annual wild form termed *O. nivara* (given to it from the Sanskrit term nīvarā for wild rice); this itself arose from a wild perennial form called *O. rufipogon*, which is widely distributed in deep-water swamps all over south and south-east Asia, south China and Oceania. *O. nivara* is still found in ditches, waterholes and on the edges of ponds in the Deccan plateau and parts of south-East Asia. There are also numerous intergrading hybrids between *O. sativa*, the cultivated form, and its two wild relatives. The continuous distribution of all these forms over so enormous an area had led to many conflicting claims in the past regarding the origin of rice, but it is now believed that 'the area including north-eastern India, northern Bangladesh, and the triangle adjoining Burma, Thailand, Laos, Vietnam and southern China appears to be the primary centre of domestication.' From this region rice flowed out in various directions with the constant and widespread movements of peoples in Asia during prehistoric times, being subject at the same time to conscious human selection to meet cultural needs.

In the event, three ecogeographic races developed, named indica, japonica and javanica. These show morphological differences in the type of plant stems and leaves, resistance to heat and cold, rain and drought, and so on. As food, these rice grains behave differently in the kitchen, and this has been shown to reflect their contents of amylose.[14] Indica varieties high in amylose (25 per cent) cook to fluffy masses with discrete grains that are admirably suited to eating with the fingers as is the practice in India. Low-amylose (15 per cent) japonica varieties cook to sticky masses suitable for eating as lumps using chopsticks, while the javanica varieties are of intermediate amylose content and stickiness. The wild rices of India, termed nīvarā in Sanskrit, being uncultivated grains, have traditionally been permitted for use by hermits. An aquatic floating type of primitive rice plant yields seeds with a high proportion of husk; called nanoi or nāstabha, this grain is eaten by Hindus in the north on ceremonial occasions.[8b] Perennial wild rices still grow in Assam and Nepal.

Archaeological finds of rice date back to 6000–3500 BC in northern Thailand and central China.[13,15] The terraced fields of Kāshmīr, so typical of rice cultivation, have been placed at 10,000 BC.[17] Was rice grown on them then, or something else? Both wild and cultivated rices have been found at 5000 BC levels by radiocarbon dating in Koldiwha, near Allahabād.[16a] Regionwise, the earliest finds of cultivated rice (apart from the very early Koldiwha find) occur in the north and west of India about 2300 to 1900 BC, a couple of centuries later in the Indo-Gangetic plain, and at distinctly later dates of 1400–1000 BC in the Deccan,[3b] suggesting a rather later arrival of rice in south India after its domestication in the fertile Himalayan plains. Thereafter the rice plant spread all over India wherever it encountered a fertile alluvial plain, encouraged in this by the efforts of humans attracted by its prolific grain yields.

Innumerable names turn up in Sanskrit literature after its first mention in the *Yajurveda*,[6a] reflecting the sustained development of rice varieties. Summer rice, of short 60-day duration, is called graishmuka or shāstika,[18] and another summer variety, dark in colour, was called anu.[19] Rainy-season varieties like varshika and vrīhi (also a generic term applied to all rices) were considered of rather ordinary quality. Autumn rices were rare, but one generic name, shāradā, is mentioned. An exceedingly white variety that was not transplanted was called, after its winter season of growth, haimanthika, hayavana or hayana.[19] But the greatest praise was reserved for the winter varieties called shāli, which were all transplanted. There is mention of red-shāli, kalamashāli which was hard, white and flavoured, and mahashāli, the most highly regarded of all rices.[18] This plump rice was grown in Magadha and reserved for royalty or honoured guests. Thus it was served for example to the learned Chinese pilgrim Xuan Zang during his stay at Nalanda University in the 7th century AD (Chapter 11). As early as 1900 BC long-grained rice, a type highly prized even today, was cultivated at Ahār near Jaipūr.[20] There is a legend that fragrant bāsmati rice was brought to the Dehra Dūn valley by Amīr Dost Mohamad of Afghanistan when he was exiled there by the British in 1840.[21] South India has fairly long-established fragrant rices called jeeragasambha, rascadam and chingari.

Jowār

Wild *Sorghum propinquum* is almost certainly the progenitor of sorghum or jowār, either in Ethiopia or elsewhere nearby in west Africa.[1e, 11b] Since sorghum crosspollinates freely, it can diverge by a process of natural selection. Five basic races are recognized, of which it was Red Durra that moved into the Near East and into India, either by land along the Sabaean Lane or by sea with the dhow traffic. Spikelets of jowār have been found in Ahār (Rājasthan) in strata dated 1725 BC, and more profusely in 1550 BC and 1270 BC strata,[5a] and also in Daimabād (Mahārāshtra) about 1700

BC.[16a] A painting resembling sorghum noted on a potsherd from Mohenjodaro could be slightly older.[5a]

The first Sanskrit names for the grain are derived from yava (barley), namely yavanala and yavaprakāra (this actually means resembling barley); other names are akara and jurna, from which the present term jowār originates.[8c] The Sanskrit terms only appear as late as the start of the Christian era, or perhaps a couple of centuries earlier, in the works of Charaka, Bhela and Kashyapa.[6b] Then as now the crop was of importance mainly in western India, which may explain its late identity in Aryan consciousness. The name sorghum is derived from the Italian word sorgho, meaning to rise, and is descriptive of the conspicuous height of the plant in the field.[11b]

Bājra

Despite its current botanical name *Pennisetum americanum* (earlier designations were *P. glaucum, P. typhoideum* and *P. typhoides*), the home of bājra (pearl millet) is tropical western Africa, perhaps in the Sahel zone where many wild forms still exist.[1c] The crop must have come to India at a very early date since it has been found (somewhat doubtfully) at Hallūr, Karnātaka in 1600 BC, and more certainly in Ahār, Rājasthān and in Saurāshtra sites about 1200–1000 BC.[5a] Even today bājra is an important crop in just these areas on the western seaboard closest to Africa. In fact it would seem that rāgi, jowār and bājra, all from West Africa, show up about the same time in India, just before 2000 BC. Did they come in simultaneously, and if so, who were India's unknown benefactors to whom we owe jowār and bājrā rōtis and bhākris that have been relished for four thousand years by vast numbers of people?

The Panicums and other minor grains

While their exact origins are not always certain, the antiquity of this group of cereals is not in doubt. Numerous *Panicum* species are fodder grasses or weeds, and several are cereals that have long been used as human foods. At one time several grains were placed under the genus *Panicum*. Still within the genus are *P. miliare* (now *P. sumatrense*, shavan, gōndli or sāmai) and *P. miliaceum* (akusthaka, cheena or panivaragu). *P. frumantaceum* is now classed as *Echinochloa frumantacea* (shāmā or sānwā); *P. italicum* is now termed *Setaria italica* (kāngni or thennai); *P. glaucum* is now *Setaria glauca* (bāndra); *P. crusgalli*, later *Coix lacryma-jobi* and now termed *Echinochloa crusgalli*, is called Job's tears, and in India sāmāk or sānwāk; and *P. colonum* is now *Echinocloa colona* (sāwank). A related species is *Paspalum scorbiculatum* (kōdo, kōdhra or varagu).

From the time of the Samhitās of the *Yajurveda* the panicums were collectively called shyāmāka[6b] and even given separate appellations: rājāh-, ambhāh- (or toya-) and hastishyāmāka. Āpasthamba (c. 400 BC) describes them as uncultivated grains used by hermits.[6c] The cheenaka or panivaragu (*Panicum miliaceum*) is a very old grain that was cultivated even by the prehistoric Lake Dwellers of Switzerland, and domesticated perhaps in the eastern Mediterranean or even in India.[1f] It originated from several diploid and tetraploid species of Asian *Panicums*, and has one of the lowest water requirements of any cereal.[1f] It has been excavated at Ādichanallur about 1000 BC, and was an important grain of south India during the Sangam period (1st to 7th century AD). Even a century ago *Panicum* grains were widely cultivated in Bengal.[8d]

Setaria italica (Italian millet) again has been found in prehistoric sites in Switzerland and was one of the five sacred plants of China in 2700 BC, so China may be where it was first domesticated.[1f] It has also been excavated very early at Sukōtada in Kutch in 2300 BC layers.[5a]

In the *Yajurveda* (say 1000 BC), both priyangu and kāngni are mentioned.[6c]

Paspalum scrobiculatum (kodo millet) was a sacred grass of the Aryans. Kautilya about 300 BC mentions both the cultivated form kōdhrava and the wild grain dāraka, and the latter also appears to be the grain termed uddālaka by Charaka a century later.[6b] As varagu the grain appears in the Tamil Sangam literature.[22]

Job's tears or coix are small, hard, shiny grains that occur in many shades of black and brown, and indeed are even strung as beads. Related species *Coix aquatica* and *C. gigantea* are also used as food in parts of south-east Asia.[6f] Called giral or kāsi in modern times, this is the grain termed gavēdhukā (modern Hindi, garahēdua) since Vedic times,[6b,23] with ritual significance as an uncultivated foodgrain. It grows abundantly on mountain slopes and even a century ago was an important crop on the north-eastern Assam hills.[8d] The name kāsi and its variations, and the association of the grain with Indians of Mongolian affiliation, suggests an eastern origin.[8d]

Two other cereals find mention in Vedic literature. Upavāka, called indrajau in Hindi, is *Wrightia tinctoria*, which is mentioned as a gruel in the *Yajurveda*.[6b] Bamboo rice is vēnuyava, described by Āpasthamba (*c.* 400 BC) as an uncultivated foodgrain.[6b] This is a curious material. Once every 50 or 60 years, though not everywhere at the same time, the bamboo flowers; a whole clump of trees, whether young or old, flowers and then dies. Normally the seeds fall, and a new progeny establishes itself rapidly. For some reason, famine follows the flowering of bamboo groves, as reflected in the Kodavā couplet:

Aruvatthu warushaké ondhu katté,
Yeppatthu warushaké ondhu yetté.
(Once in sixty years bamboos will decay,
Once in seventy years famine holds sway).

Seeds produced in such abundance naturally constitute an important famine food among the poor in those areas.[25] The seeds resemble small paddy grains which, when husked by pounding, yield the starchy grain; this is eaten either cooked, like rice, or ground and baked into a rōti.

The amaranths

The genus *Amaranthus* yields both a grain and edible leaves, and is of considerable taxonomic complexity. One species has been found in 4000 BC levels in Tehuacan (Pueblo, Mexico), and others at later times, though all before the start of the Christian era.[1g] The early Spaniards who came to South America found that the red colouring matter from the flowers as well as the dark seeds were both used in human blood sacrifices by the Aztecs, and they set about suppressing the cultivation of amaranth crops.[26] Three species are important in Central and South America. *A. hypochondriacus*, originating from *A. hybridus*, is by far the most important: it is grown in northwest and central Mexico, and is believed to have been derived by selection long ago from *A. powelli*. In Guatemala the major crop is *A. cruentus*, while in Peru it is *A. caudatus*.[27a]

The most common grain variety in India is *A. hybridus* subsp. *hybridus*, which is thought to have arisen from the same *A hybridus* that gave rise in the South American continent to *A. hypochondriacus*.[28a] It is the commonest grain amaranth of India, called rāmdhāna, chua, bathua and pungikeerai.[8f] The magnificent golden yellow or purple inflorescence of this plant can be seen between 1000 and 3000 metres in the Himalayan highlands between Kāshmīr and Bhutān, and in Madhya Pradesh, Gujarāt and the Nīlgiri hills of south India.[8f] The grains are popped on hot sand, dehusked, and then either ground into flour or made into a chikkī with jaggery syrup. The flower spikes are long, thick and erect, and the pale seeds show an opaque convex centre and an inconspicuous marginal ring.[29] Another variation in India is *A. hybridus* subsp. *cruentus*; this has green or purple leaves which are eaten as chaulai, māthbhāji or pungikeerai, and slender lax spikes that yield the minor grain rājgeera. The third species that grows in India is *A. caudatus*. This is an ornamental garden plant carrying dark-green, heart-shaped leaves with red veins which is commonly called love-lies-bleeding; it was brought in from South America and does not cross with other Indian species of *Amaranthus*.[8f]

Three other *Amaranthus* species are found in India, with Sanskrit names and probably of Indian origin. In fact some of them have gone as pot herbs in recent times from India and south-east Asia to the western world, under such names as Malabār spinach, Chinese spinach and tampala (a generic Sri Lankan name).[30a] *A. spinosus*, with green to purple leaves, is called in Sanskrit alpamarisha, in Hindi kantachaula and in Tamil mullukeerai. *A. tricolor* is the Sanskrit marisha, makanada or tandūliya, the Hindi chaulai, and the Tamil araikeerai or thandukeerai; its leaves are of many colours, green, pink, brown-red and bright red. *A. viridis* yields excellent edible leaves and has shoots that resemble asparagus; Sanskrit names are tandūliya and vishnaga, and

Tamil ones kuppukeerai and sinnakeerai.[8f] Several other amaranth species of South American provenance are also occasionally encountered in India, and are recent entries.

It is clear that at least some *Amaranthus* species did develop in India, but it is uncertain from present knowledge whether their progenitors were originally indigenous, or New World imports.[31]

Pulses

Urad, mung and masoor

There are a trio of pulses, the three Ms, which occur in Aryan literature. These are māsha (urad, blackgram, *Vigna mungo*), mudga (mung, greengram, *Vigna radiata*) and masūra (masoor, lentil, *Lens culinaris*). The first two are believed to be indigenous, and indeed to have arisen from the same basic form: this gave rise to two forms of *Vigna sublobata*, from one of which came urad, and from the other mung, through adaptive variations.[32a] Urad comes in two types, and is the favoured grain for making pāpads and vadā because of its high content of the phosphorus compound, phytin.[33] Consumption of mung causes the least flatulence among common pulses.[33] Urad and mung grains have been found at Navdatoli (1500 BC), and urad at Daulatapūr.[5a,32a]

Masoor is one of the oldest of cultivated grains, and has been found even in the 7th and 6th millennium BC at many sites from Turkey to Iran, the earliest of these seed finds being much smaller than the present varieties.[1h] India has both a small and a large variety, called māsari and masoor respectively.[33] Masoor has also been found at Navdatoli, Tēr and Chirand dated after 1800 BC.[16a] It is mentioned as masūra and mangālaya in the *Brhad Samhitā*, *Vājasaneyi Samhitā* and *Taittirīya Brahmanā*, about 800BC.[34] It is a food forbidden at a fast, or as a divine offering.[34] Though there are several wild species, *Lens orientalis*, which has the same chromosome number (2n = 24) and shows a series of intermediate types with *L. culinaris*, is believed to be its progenitor.[32b]

Sutari, matki and lobia

Three other pulses of the *Vigna* genus are used in India. One is the sutari (rice bean, *V. umbellata*), whose wild form is still found in India.[35,36] Next is the matki (moth or mat bean, *V. aconitifolia*), the Sanskrit names for which are makustha (in the *Taittirīya Brahmanā*) and vana-mudga, which means forest-mung.[6d] A host of Indian names testify to its antiquity in India,[8g] though it was perhaps domesticated after urad and mung.[32c] It was long taken for granted that the moth bean originated from the wild species *V. trilobata*, but recent studies have shown that they are distinct from each other and have several isolating mechanisms.[37] Wild forms are known in Mexico and Guatemala,[32c] which leaves the origin of the Indian matki open. The third *Vigna*, *V. unguiculata*, the lobia, chowli or cowpea, illustrates some of the complexities of plant diversification. No less than 188 species of the plant are known, of which two-thirds occur in western and central Africa, with the rest in Asia, and just ten species in India.[38] But diversification has occurred in Africa, India, Australia and America, and in each area in a different direction.[39] The common African cowpea *V. unguiculata* var. sinensis, is almost round, medium in size and held in a long pod, and eaten in Africa as a pulse. The variety sesquipedalis grown in India has long pods and large, kidney-shaped seeds which are eaten as a vegetable, lōbia. The third variety, termed catjang or cylindrica, has a short pod and small oblong seeds; it probably came to India from Malaysia and is grown here only as a forage plant for cattle. The cowpea occurs as nishpava from Buddhist canonical literature (400 BC) onwards.[6d] The common term lōbia was once attributed to the Greek word lobos, meaning a projection, but is more probably from the Sanskrit term lōbhya, signifying alluring.[8h] The Tamil term is kārāmani, and the word cowpea was an American corruption of the term cavalance then used for the grain in English.[35]

Kulthi, sem and badā-sem

The apparent resemblance between the lōbia and the kulthi (horsegram) has caused some identity confusion in Sanskrit literature. Until recently even botanists classed the cowpea as a *Dolichos* species; kulthi was once termed *Dolichos biflorus*, before being recently re-designated *Macrotyloma uniflorum*. Kulthi grains have been found in excavations at Daimabād (1800 BC) and at Tekkalakota further south.[5a] The word khalakula occurs in the *Brhadāranyaka Upanishad* (1000 BC), and the even earlier *Yajurveda Samhitā* has the word garmut which has been identified as the horsegram.[6d] Pānini (*c.* 600 BC) is the first to use the word kulattha, and Sushrutha (*c.* AD 200) mentions a wild variety vanyakulattha.[6d] Though an Indian origin was once postulated, this seems unlikely from the fact that two-thirds of the 242 species are native to Africa and only 23 to India, which is therefore probably a secondary centre.[38] The other long-standing *Dolichos, D. lablab*, the hyacinth bean (Hindi sem, Gujarathi vālpāpdi, Tamil avarai) has recently been re-classified as *Lablab purpureus*. It has been known in India for a considerable period, and is thought to be of indigenous origin, though wild forms have never been found.[8i]

Badā-sem (the jackbean or sword bean) looks like a large hyacinth bean with a pronounced white hilum, but is classed as *Canavalia ensiformis*.

Thuvar

An important pulse of the country is the thuvar or arhar (pigeon pea, *Cajanus cajan*), the ādhakī of early Buddhist literature (*c.* 400 BC) and the thuvarika of Charaka. Since no wild form had ever been found in India, it was long held to be of African origin. However careful recent work in India showed that the progenitor of thuvar was one of seventeen species of the genus *Atylosia* which grows wild even today in the Western Ghāts of south India.[5c] Thuvar crosses easily with at least three species of *Atylosia* to give fertile first-generation and later crosses, and no change in the chromosome number of 11 is involved. A southern origin seems likely also from the Dravidian term thuvarai or thuvari which travelled northwards. Even today two distinct varieties are known.[8j] Arhar in north India is a tall shrub that carries yellow flowers streaked with purple, and long, hairy, maroon pods bearing four or five seeds. The southern thuvar are short plants with pure yellow flowers and short green pods carrying three seeds.

Chana

This is *Cicer arietinum* (chickpea), sometimes called the Bengalgram since the British first encountered it there. It has been found in archaeological excavations as early as 2500 BC in Kālibangan, and only slightly later at Atranjikhera.[16a] Finds in the Middle East however go back to Hacilar (5400 BC). The centre of origin is believed to be the Caucasus region and/or Asia Minor[1i], and two types have developed. India developed quick-maturing forms with thin stems and small, wrinkled, dark-coloured seeds, while in the Mediterranean, perhaps by human selection, tall plants evolved that yielded large, oval, smooth, light-coloured seeds.[1i] These latter forms did come quite early to India, but proved poor yielders here, being ill-adapted to the country.[32d] The large Kābūli variety is a very recent introduction into India, perhaps of the 18th century AD, from the Mediterranean region by the overland route.[1i] South India received the chickpea late, perhaps around 500 to 300 BC,[5a] and probably by a different route, since southern names like kadalai are quite different from the Sanskrit chanaka or harimanthaka. The latter grains find mention in Buddhist writings of 400 BC, but the khalva of the much-earlier *Yajurveda* (*c.* 1000 BC) is thought to refer to the same grain.[6d]

Kēsari, bākla and rājmāh

The obnoxious kēsari dhāl, *Lathyrus sativus*, has been found at Jarmo, Turkey (*c.* 6000 BC),[39] and in India at sites dated between 2000 and 1500 BC in Chirand (Bihār), and at Atranjikhera and Navdatoli (Mahārāshtra).[5a] Two forms are distinguished, a small-seeded one called lakhori and

Mung  Masūr  Matki

Lobia Kulthi

Some commonly used pulses of Indi

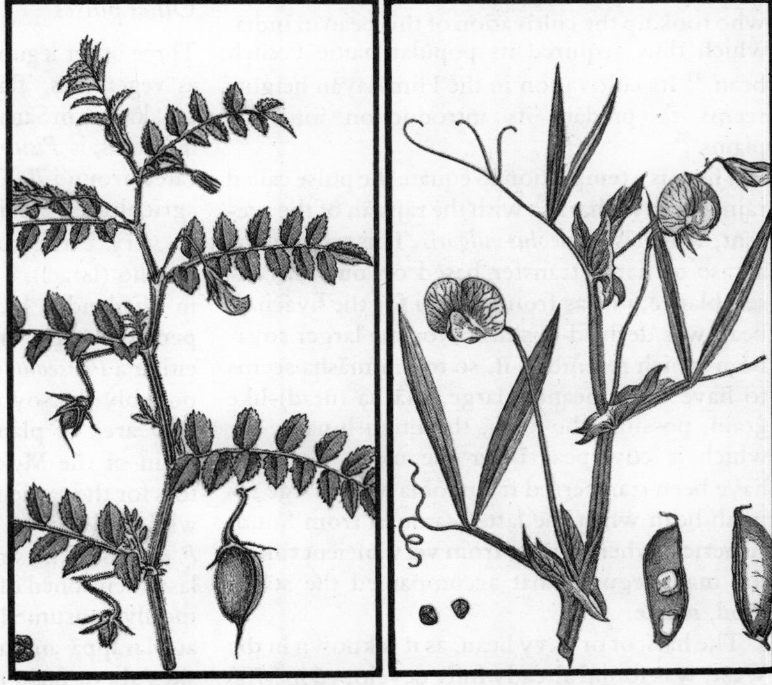

Some less-known pulses of India.

The rājmāh probably came to India from South America.

a large-seeded one called lakh. It is the latter that is believed to cause the distressing crippling disease lathyrism which manifests itself when the pulse is consumed exclusively, or in large quantities, as food. Even in AD 1590, Abul Fazl records the evil effects of consuming kēsari dhāl.[40]

The bākla (broad bean or French bean) is *Vicia faba*, which has been found in Jericho (6250 BC). It probably had its origin in the Mediterranean region, though no wild ancestors are known, and the species does not hybridize with other *Vicia* species.[1j,38] Apparently it was the French who took up the cultivation of this bean in India, which thus acquired its popular name French bean.[41] Its cultivation in the Himālayan heights seems to predate its introduction into the plains.[8k]

There is a temptation to equate the pulse called rājmāsha by Charaka with the rājmāh of the present, which is *Phaseolus vulgaris*. This seems to be a case of name transfer based on outward resemblance; just as from shimbi for the hyacinth bean was derived rājshimbi for the larger soyabean which resembles it, so too rājmāsha seems to have then meant a large, māsha (urad)-like grain, possibly the lōbia, the English name for which is cow pea. Later the name seems to have been transferred from lōbia to the large rājmāh bean when the latter came in from South America, where it was, from very ancient times, the main legume that accompanied the staple food, maize.

The haricot or navy bean, as it is known in the West, was found already fully developed in 5700 to 5000 BC sites in Peru and Mexico, and is perhaps derived from a wild form of which *P. aborigineus* is a modern survivor.[1k] The rājmāh is not even mentioned in 1908 by Watt, and is probably a very recent introduction into the northern hills of India from South America by way of Europe. Again French colonialists are credited with having first grown these beans in Karaikal, Mahé and Pondicherry. The English in India found them an agreeable foodgrain, and the beans were raised first as garden crops till the 19th century, and as commercial crops only thereafter.[41]

Other pulses

Three other legumes are used in India essentially as vegetables. The common cultivated garden pea, kalaya in Sanskrit, mattar in Hindi and patāni in Tamil, is *Pisum sativum*, which was domesticated around 7000 BC at the very dawn of human agriculture.[11] Carbonized peas have been found at very early dates in Hacilar (Turkey) and Jericho (Israel).[39] Recent finds of domestic peas in Thailand in 10,000 BC layers (along with pepper, the areca nut, cucumber, bottle gourd, either a *Phaseolus* or a *Vicia* species, almond, and possibly the soybean) have revealed an entirely new area of plant domestication in the lower basin of the Mekong River.[42] Several progenitors for the garden pea have been suggested: a lost wild field pea, or perhaps *P. humile*, *P. elatius* or *P. arvense*. The small, green, marbled peas of the last-mentioned of these, *P. arvense*, are still commonly consumed in India, and have been found at Harappā and a number of its contemporary sites about 2000 BC.[16a] Literary reference to the pea in India is rather late; early Buddhist literature (*c.* 400 BC) mentions kalāya, while three varieties (satina, khandika and triputaka), come to be mentioned later.[6e]

Guār phali is *Cyamopsis tetragonoloba*, elsewhere called the cluster bean. It has recently found a major non-food use as the source of an important galactomannan gum.[1f] The African species *C. bengalensis* is probably ancestral to guār, which is nowhere found wild. Arab traders may have introduced the plant from Africa to south India. The pods are eaten, and the leaves and stems constitute excellent fodder for cattle and a green manure rich in nitrogen.[81]

The winged bean, *Psophocarpus tetragonolobus*, may have originated in Mauritius or Madagascar.[1f] It is not cultivated in Africa, and seems to be a very recent introduction to India for its high value as food and feed.

Oilseeds

Sesame

A charred lump of sesame seed (*Sesamum indicum*) was found in Harappā (*c.* 2000 BC), along with burnt grains of wheat and peas.[43] The *Rigveda*(*c.* 1500 BC) has the word pala later used in compound forms to refer to the sesame seed, and from the *Atharvaveda* onwards tila is repeatedly mentioned in both religious and secular contexts.[6f] Even a wild sesame seed, jartila, is noted in the *Taittirīya Samhitā*.[6c] Sumerian clay tablets dated about 2300 BC carry references in cuneiform script to an oilseed, se-gis-i, which has been identified as the sesame.[44] This was probably received from India by the early trade contacts between the civilizations of the Indus and Mesopotamian Valleys (Chapter 2).[45] Convincing evidence exists now to show that the progenitor of the sesame is the wild Indian species *Sesame orientale* var. malabaricum which occurs all over India.[44,46] It was probably the jartila of ancient writings, and was again carefully described in the *Hortus Malabaricus* compiled by the Dutch governor, van Rheede (see Chapter 13) in 1689.[44] The names for sesame in many north Indian languages are derived from the Sanskrit tila. The Tamil name gingelli originated about the 8th century AD to describe sesame pods in which the seeds rattle, and which were therefore called juljul or jeljel in Arabic, denoting the jingling of bells. The other Tamil name ellu may derive from older Munda tongues; it is a very old word, and, remarkably, was used in identical form for the oil of sesame in the ancient Akkadian tongue of the 3rd millennium BC, to which area the seed or oil may have been taken from India. Some Indian names derive from the exceptional stability of the oil, like mīttā-thēl, nall-ennāi and acch-ellu, all meaning 'sweet' oil.

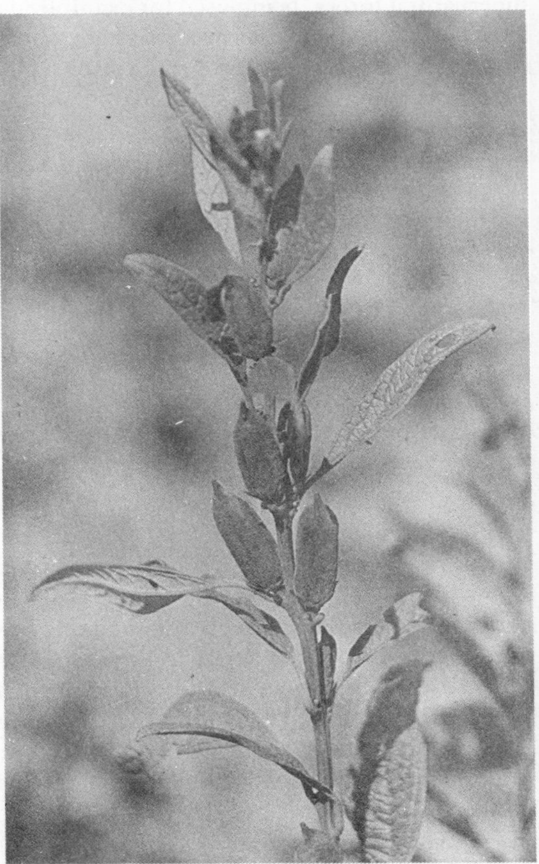

Pods on a sesame plant.

Mustard

The international term for the oil is rape-mustard, since it is derived from seeds of the *Brassica* genus which cover both rape and mustard species. Carbonized seeds of rāi, *Brassica juncea* subsp. *juncea*, have been discovered at the Indus Valley site of Chanhudaro dated about 1500 BC.[5a] Even today this seed, called mustard in India, is the major Indian species.[47] Next in order comes brown sarson, *B. napus* var. glauca, while the reddish-brown toria is *B. napus* var. napus. There is also a minor crop of yellow sarson. All these species are crushed for oil, often in judicious admixture so as to yield a product of distinctive taste and pungent flavour in high yield, to which each type of seed contributes something distinctive.[48] In Indian ritual, mustard seeds have the connotation of warding off supernatural forces, being used for example in a birth chamber, in the new mother's bath water, to sprinkle on a sacrificial fire, or to rub on hands and feet during a shrāddha ancestral ceremony.[49] Use of the oil as food is mentioned much later in Sanskrit literature (*c.* 500 BC) than that of the seed, since the Vedic Aryans and their brahmin descendants despised the oil as only being fit for use by the lower ranks of society.

Two races of rāi are now posited; the oilseed form is important in India, and the other leafy form elsewhere, including China.[47] This species, *Brassica juncea*, was formed by accidental fusion of the nuclei of *B. nigra* (2n = 16, AA) with *B. campestris* (2n = 20, CC) to give rāi with 36 chromosomes, the marriage having probably been effected in the middle East or even the Himalayas. Brown sarson probably originated as one subspecies from *B. campestris*, perhaps in northwestern India, and tōria was a simple human selection from the latter. Yellow sarson is believed to be a human selection from brown sarson, perhaps in northeastern India,[47] for the attractive appearance of the seed or its flavour value in cooking. Yellow sarson is mentioned as siddhārtha in literature as early as 800–1000 BC and is distinguished from both sarshapa (sarson) and rājika (rāi).[44]

Two *Brassica* seeds are only used as condiments in India. *B. nigra* (black mustard, Banārsi rāi, kadugu) finds use in pickles and curries, while *B. alba* (safēd rāi, yellow mustard) is mostly a pretty garden plant with large yellow flowers and a hairy stem.

Two mustard seeds figure in the traditional system of measuring weights in India (Box 29).

Coconut

On several grounds, an origin for the coconut in a land area that is now submerged, northwest of Papua New Guinea, is generally accepted.[50] The plant and nut were fully evolved even 20 million years ago, long before man appeared on the scene, to judge from fossilized remains that have been found. These included one from Rājasthān,[51] which must have got there millions of years ago when the area lay under the sea (see Chapter 1). Coconuts can float in the sea for months and then sprout when they reach a beach, as was dramatically demonstrated when

Hemispheres of coconut being dried.

Box 29

SEEDS AS WEIGHTS

Natural grains formed the basis of early weight systems in India. The Indus Valley (Box 2) seems to have chosen the rati seed, *Abrus precatorius*, as its base in weighing. In later times even smaller seeds like the black mustard, the white mustard, the barley corn, and the māsha or urad grain were brought into the system and related to the rati. Not only were all these grains rather uniform in weight, but could hold their weights for a long period without drying out. Manu lays down the system thus:[60,61]

NATURAL WEIGHTS

1 pepperseed (likya) = 1 black mustard seed
3 black mustard seeds = 1 white mustard seed
6 white mustard seeds = 1 middle-sized barley corn
3 barley corns = 1 krsnala or rati

COPPER WEIGHTS

80 ratis = 1 karshapana

SILVER WEIGHTS

2 ratis = 1 māsha
16 māshas = 1 dharana or pūrana
10 dharanas = 1 shatamāna

GOLD WEIGHTS

5 ratis = 1 māsha
16 māshas = 1 suvarna
4 suvarnas = 1 pala or nishka
10 palas = 1 dharana

In terms of absolute mass, the beautiful orange-red rati seed with a black spot is still used as a weight by goldsmiths and jewellers, each seed averaging 0.109 of a gram (see Box 2). Even the great Koh-i-noor diamond when first mined was weighed against rati seeds.

Measures of length were also based on natural objects like grains. In Manu's period the barley corn or yava was the basic unit of length:

LENGTH

8 yavas = 1 angula (a finger's breadth)
24 angulas = 1 hasta (span of a hand)
4 hastas = 1 danda (pole or rod)
1000 dandas = 1 krōsha, later kōs
4 krōshas = 1 yojana (about 5.2 kilometres)

Natural objects were used all over the world in the early stages of mensuration. The term foot is obvious. The cubit of 18 inches was the length of a man's forearm from elbow to fingertip, the yard was the span from fingertip to chin, and the fathom was the height of water needed to fully cover a drowned sailor!

they were found on a new island created in Krakatoa by volcanic action in 1928–30.[50] Thus the coconut palm spread all over the warm southern seas without the agency of man. The Sanskrit name nārikēla is itself believed to be an earlier Munda word, derived from two words of southeast-Asian origin, niyor for oil and kōlai for nut.[52] The coastline of the Deccan must have known the nut and its oil long before the northern mainland did, and indeed the word used in Tamil for a semi-solid or greasy fat is nāi, from the words ngai and niu used for coconut oil in Polynesia and the Nicobar Islands.[53]

Literary evidence bears this out. The Tamil word for the coconut, thēngāi, means either a sweet fruit, or a fruit from a southerly direction.[52] Tamil literature only goes back to about 100 BC, but the coconut is mentioned regularly. In Sanskrit it received late mention, in the *Rāmāyana*, *Mahābhārata* and *Vishnu Purāna*, all

Coconuts being dehusked on a pointed stake.

The sage Vishwāmitra and a coconut tree.

after around 300 BC. Megasthenes (300 BC) is also believed to have mentioned coconuts in Sri Lanka, to judge from a later reference to his work by Aelian.[51] The late adoption of the coconut into Aryan ritual also argues for late knowledge of the nut in north India. In South India, the water in the unripe nut, fresh coconut meat and copra (obtained by drying coconut hemispheres in the sun), have long been in common use.

Indian mythology attributes the origin of the coconut to the sage Vishwāmitra, who created it long and straight to prop up his friend King Trishanku after the latter had been thrown out of heaven by Indra.[54] The English name for the nut is from the word coquos or hobgoblin, given by Portuguese sailors to the coconut 'face', with two eyes and a mouth.

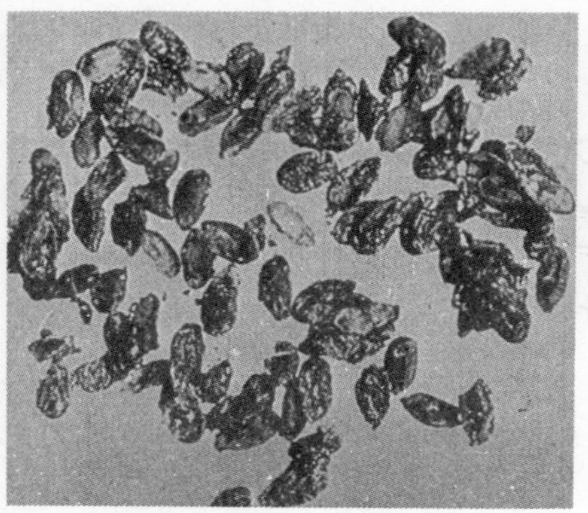

Carbonized linseed excavated from Navdatoli (c. 1500 BC).

Linseed

Two riverside sites, Navdatoli and Daimabād, not far from each other in the west of India, have yielded carbonized linseed grains dated to 1660–1450 BC and 1000 BC, while spun flax fibres in the form of a string of beads have been found in a 1400–1200 BC burial at nearby Chandōli.[5a,55,56a] The name athasī occurs in Buddhist and Jain canonical literature (400 BC) and in the *Arthashāstra* of Kautilya (300 BC), other names being umā, kshumā, haimavati and marsina.[6g] Linseeds have shown up in wesern Iran in excavations dated from 7500 BC.[56] The annual crop *Linum usitatissimum* originated from a wild perennial ancestor, and was developed in Europe into tall, unbranched plants used for production of linen fibre and flax cloth. In India, oil-bearing evolution was stressed. In the north, *L. usitatissimum* crossed with the annual herb *L. strictum* to yield one ecotype with yellow flowers that yielded small seeds rich in oil. In south India, crossing with *L. perenne* (which is favoured over crossing with *L. mysorensis*) yielded another ecotype with blue, lilac or white flowers, and large seeds of low oil content. Linseed oil in south India goes by such names as alshi, agashi and aishi which resemble the Sanskrit athasī.[8m]

Safflower

There are no archaeological finds in India of *Carthamus tinctorius*, but Egyptian mummies of 1600 BC are wrapped with long garlands of cloth or papyrus with florets of the safflower sewn on them.[1m] In India, there are no early records of the use of the dye from the flowers, though a century ago it was a major industry for both internal use and export. Use of the seed as a source of oil occurs from about 400 BC, and the *Arthashāstra* of 300 BC lists the kusumbha seed as one that was crushed in oilmills (ghānās).[8h] The name survives as kusuma in south India, though karadi is the more general term. Two wild plants, *C. lunatus* in Kāshmīr and *C. oxyacantha* in Pākistān and Uttar Pradesh, may have been the ancestors of the safflower, and two distinct types evolved. One was a non-spiny type with orange or yellow flowers tinged scarlet, used as a source of dye. The oily type, with yellow flowers, was grown particularly in western India.[8h]

Niger

Guizotia abyssinica, as its name suggests, seems to have originated in Africa in the region between Ethiopia and Malawi,[1f] the same area from which India received jowār, bājra and rāgi before 2000 BC. This oilseed however probably came to India later, since in many Indian languages the names for the niger resemble those for other older oilseeds. In Sanskrit these are kālā-til and rām-tila (tila being of course the sesame), in Kannada ulishi (castor being alashi), and in Telugu (in which sesame is ellu), the niger seed is termed hucchellu and gurellu.[8n] Cytogenetic work in India has recently shown that the niger probably arose from an ancestral species termed *G. abyssinica* subspecies *schimperi*, which still survives in Ethiopia.[57]

Chapter 15

PLEASING THE PALATE

We have just considered the origins and antiquity of three basic food materials: cereals, pulses and oilseeds. In certain countries, tubers are also used as staple food; in India (apart from the recent example of the tapioca in Kerala) this has hardly ever been so, except perhaps in emergencies like flood or famine. Tubers are thought of as vegetables in India and in now reviewing the origins of Indian vegetables, tubers would represent a convenient starting point. Thereafter we can look into the development or arrival, in India, of more conventional vegetables, of fruits, of spices and of other materials like the sugarcane, all of which may be considered as giving relish to eating.

Tubers

The edible aroids

South America has several species of indigenous edible tubers of the genus *Xanthosoma*, none of which are found in India. India has three families, the *Alocasia* (two species), *Colocasia* (two species) and *Cyrtosperma* (one species), all of very ancient origin (7000–2000 BC) and all essentially denizens of swampy regions.[1a] *Alocasia indica* is a tall plant, called the giant taro (Sanskrit manaka, Hindi manakanda, Bengāli mānkachu); there is also the related boromankachu of Assām, which is *A.macrorrhiza*, a giant of a plant with a high level of bitter crystals of calcium oxalate in the tuber which have to be leached out before cooking the aroid.[2a] This genus originated either in India or Sri Lanka, and then moved eastwards to Oceania. The *Colocasia* genus of aroids includes *C.esculenta*, the well-known arvi, shāmageddē or sēppam-kizhangu; the tubers are of a myriad shapes and sizes, and coloured white, yellow, purple and red. The huge elephant foot, *Amorphophallus campanulatus* (sūran, sēnai-kizhangu) can reach a weight of ten kg; it has two Sanskrit names, sūrana (Charaka) and arsaghna (meaning destroyer of piles),[3a] and dried slices termed madanamast are sold in the bazaar as a remedy for piles and dyspepsia.[2b] This genus also originated in India, and then moved both eastwards and westwards as far as the New World.[1a] The ancient terraces, now used to raise rice, may have originally been set up to raise *Colocasia* tubers as food.[1a] *Cyrtosperma camissonis* is the giant swamp taro of south-east Asia; this may have originated in Indonesia, but does not seem to have reached India.

Yams

The genus *Dioscorea* has as many as 600 species, and about ten of them are edible.[1b,4a] It is an exceedingly ancient plant, and separation of even the Asian from the African ancestral groups is believed to have taken place 26 million years ago. In the Old World species, the basic chromosome number is 10, but most food yams show a high degree of polyploidy, with 2n = 4x = 40, going even up to 100. New World yams have x = 9, and most are tetraploids or hexaploids (2n = 36 or 54). It is clear that domestication was completely separate in Asia, Africa and America, and may have started as early as 10,000 years ago. In India many yams are known.[5a] The greater yam is *D.alata* (khameālu, chupri-ālu, perumvalli-kizhangu) which comes in innumerable variations of shape (globose, lobed, fingered, U-shaped) and colour (white, magenta, red, purple); its origin may lie in the Burma or Thailand area.[4b,6a] The lesser yam, kangar or valli-kizhangu, which appears in sausage-like bunches, is *D.esculenta*; it stems from the same area in south-east Asia as the greater yam, a major centre of diversity for both species being the Papua New Guinea region.[1b] The veunti of Kerala, a hilly form with a delicious flavour, is classed as *D.hamiltonii*, and shares a common ancestry with the *D.alata* species.[4a] The kanta-ālu, bhusa or narunna-kizhangu with brown, yellow or purple tubers is classed as *D. pentaphylla*. The Sanskrit rat-ālu (Hindi pīta-ālu), though bitter and acid, has been known to be eaten after steeping in water as a famine food, and is *D.bulbifera*. The vajrakanda of Kautilya (300 BC), a poisonous tuber even used at one time in India to kill tigers, appears to be *D.daemona*.

The Sanskrit word āluka and Hindi ālu stand for any tuber, with distinctive prefixes. Even the potato was first termed gōle-ālu, but later simply shortened to ālu. The English term yam springs from the Māndē word niam of Africa's west coast, and was brought to Spain by Moorish slaves as a term for the true yams. It was later applied by the Spaniards and Portuguese to the *Dioscorea* yams, and was first used by the English in the forms iniames and yammas.[4b]

Sweet potato

Botanically the sweet potato is *Ipomea batatas*, which is a hexaploid (2n = 90) derived perhaps from *I.trifida* by auto-hexaploidy.[1c] It is definitely of South American origin (Peru, Mexico) and cave remains are dated 10,000 to 8000 BC. Despite this, archaeological sites in Hawaii, New Zealand and Easter Island have yielded tuber remains.[6b] Introduction into India appears to have been more recent. Sushrutha (perhaps about AD 100) mentions the madhvāluka,[3a] later called the mītt-ālu and this must have come to India from these Polynesian islands rather than from South America. At least one other *Ipomoea* tuber is used as a food in India. This was formerly classified as *I.digitata*, but may be simply one of the numerous mutants or hybrids of the sweet potato. It has two Sanskrit names, bhūmikushmānda and vidari,[5b] which would suggest at least some antiquity.

Vegetables

Green leafy vegetables

Vegetables leave no remains, and we have little knowledge of which of them were available to the Harappans, at least perhaps till their script is deciphered. From early Sanskrit writings, green leafy vegetables emerge very clearly as having been important food materials.[3a] Vedic literature describes the patha (which may be a *Coleus, C.amboinicus*, or *Didymocarpus pedicellate* both of which have similar Hindi names), or even the pathua-sāg *Corchorus capsularis* (a variety of jute). The varuna (*Crataeva nurvala*) and the avaka (Hindi shirīsh, *Albizia lebbeck*) are both still in use. Aquatic plants were relished. Four species of the *Nymphaea* or water-lily family exist in India.[5c] The Indian kamal, *N.nouchali*, has flowers of many colours ranging from deep red to white, and its seeds, carpels, fruit and tubers are all edible. The Indian blue water-lily is *N.stellata*, neelkamal or neelpadma, of which again all parts are edible. *N.alba* is the nilofer of Kāshmīr, commonly called the European water-lily, and *N.tetragona* is the pygmy water-lily, which grows only at high altitudes in the Himālayas

The singhādā or water-chestnut, on occasion used as staple food.

and the Khāsi hills of Assām. The old Sanskrit names for these are kumuda, pushkara, andika and shāluka,[3a] but it is difficult to relate these names to specific botanical species. Another water-plant of antiquity, the saphāka or singhātaka (*Trapa natans* var. bispinosa), now called singhāda, has been found as a 70-million-year-old fossil.[7] About 1611, William Finch described the water-chestunt fruit as being 'green and soft and tender, white, of a mealish taste, being exceedingly cold in my judgement; for always after eating it I needed (to drink) *aqua vitae* (water).'[8] It was even cultivated as a food crop; Sleeman writes in 1844 that 'the holdings are staked out and so much paid per acre . . . The nut grows under water after the beautiful white flowers decay, ripening in September and eatable upto November.'[9]

Another lot of green leafy vegetables come to be mentioned during the *Sūtra* period, 800–300 BC.[3d] The water cress was mandakaparni (Hindi brahmi, *Nasturtium officinale*); the vasthuka (*Chenopodium album*) was the Hindi bathua (its wild form was called chilli by Charaka),[10] and the spinach or pālak was the Sanskrit pālankya. Indeed spinach (*Spinacia oleracea*) is a native of south-west Asia,[1e] and has had a long history of use in India before it was even known in the west. Other leaves whose use as food finds mention include the mēthika, in Hindi mēthi (*Trigonella foenum-graecum*), whose seeds constitute the spice fenugreek, and the drumstick tree (*Moringa oleifera*) which in Sanskrit is sigru or shaubhānjana (Hindi sājuna, saonjana); the long pods of this tree are also a popular vegetable. It is notable that green leafy vegetables, used so long ago as food in India, are today recognized as being rich and inexpensive sources of vitamin A, vitamin C, the B-group of vitamins and the minerals, iron and calcium.[12]

Radish and carrot

The radish, mūlaka in Sanskrit, was perhaps developed in the Fertile Crescent area of plant domestication,[1f] and its use is first noted in India by Charaka. There are different wild species in several parts of the Mediterranean, Greece and Europe, and even the *Raphanus sativus* species has four varieties; the type used in India is called the larger radish in Europe, and has little or no fleshy root. Later Europe developed the globular rooted forms, purple, red and white, which are now also grown in India. Indian radishes are conical in shape and white in colour.[5d] Radishes carry the same pungent principles as do mustard (*Brassica*) leaves and seeds. The so-called rat-tailed radish, *R.caudatus*, also found in India and called sungra, singri and mungra, seems to have originated in south-east Asia, where it is called mougri.[1f]

The carrot is *Daucus carota*. In Sanskrit it is called gārjaru and shikamula, and according to George Watt 'seems to have been eaten in India when in Europe it was scarcely more than a wild plant'.[2c] Wild forms of *Daucus* are found all over the world, and are identical in chromosome number (2n = 2x = 18), with polyploidy playing no part in differentiation.[1g] Afghanistān was probably the primary centre of domestication, where the greenish-coloured rounded carrots rich in anthocyanin, now called the dēsi (indigenous) variety in India, were evolved. From this type, the long, orange, carotene-rich root was developed by mutation and human selection. When both types moved westwards to Europe, about the 10th century AD, the Netherlands went on to breed the long, deep-orange and Horn carrots in the 18th century in several sizes. Both the greenish and orange types are now raised in India. As early as 1563 Garcia da Orta wrote of the good carrots of Sūrat and the excellent ones of the Deccan.[2c]

Brinjal, bhendi and ambadi

The vārtāka or vrntāka, today called brinjal, aubergine or eggplant is an old vegetable of India. The Sanskrit names are believed to have a Munda origin (Chapter 1), and there is fair botanical evidence that *Solanum melongena* is descended from a prickly perennial ancestor as a result of human selection for less spininess, less bitterness, large fruit size and an annual habit.[1d] In fact, there are four varieties of the brinjal species whose fruits vary in regard to these attributes, as also in respect to shape (long, round) and colour (green, purple). It has been suggested that a white, oval variety must have been responsible for the early British name, eggplant, while the word brinjal represents an anglicization of the Hindi baingan. Several other *Solanum* species carry Sanskrit names and are edible.[5c] These are *S. nigrum* (kakamachi), *S.surattense* (kantakari, nidigadhika), *S.trilobatum* (alārku), and *S.stramonifolium* (Hindi, rāmbaingan).[11a]

The bhēndi, lady's finger or okra, *Abelmos-*

The bhendi, okra or lady's finger.

chus esculentus, is now a popular vegetable all over India; even if it is the same vegetable as the bhandi mentioned by Charaka, it is not a really old vegetable in India, being probably of African origin. It is a polyploid with 65 chromosomes, made up of 29 from one genome and 36 from another, but even the basic number is uncertain.[1h] Another species, *A.moschatus*, is latakastūrika in Sanskrit, and its seeds, called ambrette in the perfumery trade, have a delicate musk odour.

Both the *Abelmoschus* species just described were classed as *Hibiscus* until recently; two species of the latter are used as food. *Hibiscus cannabinus* is called nālidā, ambādi or gōnkuru in India, and kenaf or mesta elsewhere. It appears to have originated in Angola, Ethiopia or Sudan,[1e,13a] though the fibre that it yields has caused it to be given such names as Deccan Hemp and Bimli Jute. The leaves are used in the Āndhra region to make a popular sour chutney, gōnkura-pacchadi. *Hibiscus sabdariffa*, red roselle or lāl ambādi is a beautiful plant with green leaves and stems; the glossy red calyces are used as a souring agent in curries, as a thickening material in jellies and as the source of a pleasant beverage. It seems to have been domesticated for eating purposes under the Nuclear Māndē culture in Sudān as early as 4000 BC.[1e] Later, two varieties were developed, one a bushy shrub for purposes of eating, termed *var.sabdariffa,* and the other a 5-metre tall, unbranched type, called *var.altissima*, for use as a source of fibre. A Sanskrit work from Kāshmīr of the 8th/9th centuries AD mentions forests of sthalakamalini, 'the red lotus which grows on land';[14] this has been identified as *Hibiscus mutabilis*, called the Chinese rose or cotton rose, the flowers of which are compared in the poem to a woman's red lips and the red-painted soles of her feet.[11b]

Fruits

Melons, gourds and pumpkins

Gourds and pumpkins are largely used as vegetables in India, while the greater melon group serves as both vegetables and fruits. Some species in each can claim considerable antiquity.

The common cucumber, khīra in Hindi, finds mention in the *Rigvēda* and is undoubtedly Indian. Known by the names chirbhita, urvāruka and sukasa in Sanskrit, and botanically *Cucumis sativus*, it may have originated from a bitter wild form *C.hardwickii* which is still found in the Himalayan foothills.[1i] The *Cucumis* family also includes some melons. Of these *C.melo*, the popular kharbūza or musk melon, probably originated in Africa, the wild forms found in India being seen simply as an escape from cultivation. The best known varieties are the Honey Dew of Lucknow, and the Cuddapāh melon, grown in dry river-beds during summer. It has been remarked that the *Cucumis melo* species exploded in terms of variety when it came from Africa to India.[1i] Three varieties are known, all edible.[11c] One is the khākri, which is var. utilissimus, another is the mēki or takmak, var.agrestis, and yet another is var.momordica, the kachra or phūnt.

Other kinds of melons belong to the *Citrullus* family, the best known being the luscious water melon or tarbūz, which is *Citrullus lunatus*, and of Indian-African origin.[15] Its Sanskrit name is kalinda, a term even believed to be of very ancient Munda origin.[3b] *C.lunatus* var.fistulosus is the well-known delicate vegetable tinda or tendu. Another long-known species is *C.colocynthis*, the indrayān or mahēndravaruni, whose spongy, bitter fruit is sold in dried form for use as a rather drastic purgative.

The *Cucurbita* species in America carry such common names as pumpkin, squash, marrow and gourd. All are believed to have originated in the New World, and progenitors up to 10,000 years old have been found by archaeologists in Mexico and Guatemala.[1i,16] Modern forms of squash were probably developed long ago from wild fruits by human selection for lack of bitterness. Even so, many *Cucurbita* species, of which 25 are found in India, have Sanskrit names of

Musk melon variety carrying lacy raised designs.

considerable antiquity.[2c] Long before the intervention of man, the ability of gourds to float in sea water while retaining seed viability must have carried them across the seas from continent to continent. The so-called winter squash or red pumpkin of America is called urubuka in Sanskrit; today it goes by such names as lāl-kumra, kaddhu and kumbalakāyi, and even a wild form still exists. The fruits are round to oval and bluntly-ribbed, with yellow to reddish flesh. There are two other winter squash species, *C.moschata* and *C.maxima*, which are also known as kaddu, kumra, dūdhi and dumbala in India. Some of these are smooth, oblong fruits, while others are fluted and either spherical or flattened. Another winter squash is *C.mixta*, called in America the cushaw, and, in India, the African gourd;[15] it is of large size, has a swollen peduncle at the top, takes a high polish, and is often employed to make the bowls of Indian musical instruments like the thānpura and vichitra veena. *Cucurbita pepo*, called in America summer squash, marrow or pumpkin, carries such Indian names as safēd-kaddhu, kumra and surai-kāyi, and is a green, deeply-ridged, pear-shaped vegetable.

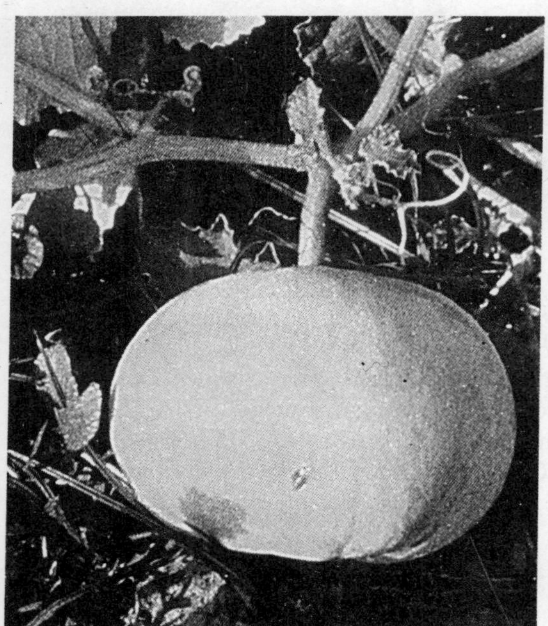

The tender tinda.

Gourd is a general name for vegetables that derive from four plant families, with several species under each genus. Under *Benincasa* falls *B.hispida* (pētha, pushinikāyi, ash gourd), the Sanskrit kushmānda, which may be native to Malaysia;[1e,5e] it is either cooked as a vegetable, or candied in strong sugar solution to give a gritty, firm and brittle confection also called pēthā.

The genus *Luffa* has three species with old Sanskrit names and therefore possibly indigenous.[5f] These are *L.acutangula*, the ridged gourd, *L.acutangula* var amara, and *L.aegyptiaca*. All of them carry slight variations of the Sanskrit name koshātakī (first mentioned by Kautilya), the Hindi thorai and the Tamil pīrkankāyi. The last of them is used as a vegetable, and also yields, on drying, the firm and fibrous loofah sponge.

The two other gourd families apart from *Luffa* are *Trichosanthes* and *Momordica*. *Trichosanthes dioica* is the Hindi parwal, the Bengali pōtōl and the Sanskrit putūlika.[5g] *T.anguina* is the snakegourd, chachinda in Sanskrit and pottalakāya in Telugu, and *T.cucumerina* is the Hindi rāmbel. The first two are probably of Indian origin, the last perhaps Malaysian.[1e] Several species once classed as *Luffa* have now been brought under the genus *Momordica*.[11e] Of several edible species, the best known is *M.charantia*, the bitter gourd or karēlā, in Sanskrit kāravella, which is first mentioned in early Jain literature about 400 BC.[5h] A smaller version of this is *M.dioica*, kāksa or gōlkandra in Hindi, and paluppakāyi or tholoopavai in Tamil; another smaller, knobbly version is *M. tuberosa*, kadavanchi in Hindi and athalaikāyi in Tamil, which is pickled or sundried to chips. The vegetable called kakrōl or bhātkarēla in Hindi is *M. cochinchinensis*. Gourds, pumpkins and melons are thus old and still important dietary items in India.

The aptly-named snakegourd.

Early fruits

Fruits identified at Harappā (*c.* 2000 BC) by way of ornamental clay representations are the date, bēr (*Ziziphus* species) and pomegranate, while Navdatoli (1600 BC) has thrown up carbonized remains both of the bēr and āmlaka (in Tamil nellikāyi, *Emblica officinalis*).[13b] Early literary evidence adds others to this list. Words in Sanskrit believed to be of earlier Munda origin are the āmlika (imlī, tamarind), panasa (jackfruit), dhādima (pomegranate) and jāmoon (*Syzygium cumini*).[3b] The *Rigveda* (*c.* 1500 BC) mentions the akshikiphala or vibhītaka (baheda, *Terminalia bellirica*), the banyan tree nyagrōdha (*Ficus benghalensis*) and the thorny, tart-fruited vikramkata (*Flacourtia indica*), all of which yield fig-like fruits.[3c] Two other *Ficus* species, though undoubtedly of hoary vintage, first find literary mention only in the *Sūtra* literature between 800 and 300 BC.[3d] These are the asvattha or peepal (*F. religiosa*) and the udumbara or gūler (*F.glomerata*). True figs (*F.carica*), are Mediterranean natives which find no mention in early medical literature;[3b] earlier imported from the northwest, they are now grown to a limited extent in India, notably near Punē.[17]

Several varieties of the bēr fruit (*Ziziphus* species) come to be recorded in *Sūtra* works: the large-fruited badara or vadari, the medium-fruited kuvala, and the wild, orange-coloured variety (*Z.nummularia*). Even now at least six varieties of the genus flourish in India.[11f] Other fruits of the earliest literary period[3d] are the bilva (bael, *Aegle marmelos*), which looks like a citrus and has a two-centimetre thick rind and twenty orange-coloured carpels or segments; karīra, the sour caper bud and fruit, *Capparis decidua,* which usually grows on spiny shrubs; madhūka (mahua, *Madhuca indica*) which yields a sweet edible flower from which alcohol is brewed, and a fruit from the seed of which an edible fat is extracted; and plāksha (*Butea monosperma*), the palāsh tree with bright red flowers and leaves that have traditionally been used as plates for eating or to wrap food in. Other fruits mentioned in the period 800–300 BC[3d] are the sleshmātaka (Hindi sebestan, lasora, *Cordia dichotoma*), a sweet mucilaginous fruit mentioned by Kautilya, now eaten raw or pickled, and the samiphala (*Prosopis cineraria*, Hindi chhonkar), whose pods are cooked as a vegetable.

Sour fruits that surface frequently in the literature are the āmlaka (āmlā, *Emblica officinalis*); karumarda (karaunda, *Carissa carandas*), used in making pickles and chutneys;[26] pārusaka (phālsa, *Grewia subinaequalis*), yielding excellent sour beverages; and vrksāmla (kokum, *Garcinia indica*), a popular souring agent.

The thālpatra (toddy palm, *Borassus flabellifer*) yields a soft fruit, sweet when tender, and the kadamba (*Anthocephalus cadamba*), has perfumed yellow flowers that look like woollen badminton balls, and bears edible fruit. The karaunda (*Carissa carandas*) is probably native to India, and the fruit has long been used in pickles and chutneys.[17] The mildly acid star-fruit (*Averrhoa carambola*, kāmarangā in Sanskrit, kāmrākh in Hindi), is a native of the Moluccas; it has long been in India though never highly regarded as a fruit.[5n] The black mulberry, *Morus nigra*, a native of Iran, and the white mulberry, *M.alba*, indigenous to China, have long been grown in India not for their edible fruit but mainly to provide leaves for use as food for silkworms.[1e] Three wild species of strawberries are known in India: *Fragarra indica* in the Himalayas, *F. nilgerrensis* in the south and east of the country, and *F.dattoniana* in the eastern Himalayas. The cultivated strawberry grown in Kashmir, the

The starchy bread fruit.

Doon Valley and Mahabaleshwar are crosses between *F.virginiana* (native to North America) and *F.chiloensis.*[18] The blackberry, *Rubus fruticosus*, a native of Yunan in China, is found in the hills of south India and in the Himālayas between 1000 and 3500 metres.[18]

Of these ancient fruits, a few merit botanical comment. The date palm probably originated in the Middle East, but even if a wild form did exist at one time, it must have crossed with several other compatible *Phoenix* species. Only female trees produce fruit, and when grown artificially only one male is retained for 25 to 50 females, and pollination is effected by human agency.[1j] The pomegranate, *Punica granatum*, is a native of Iran which entered India at a very early date with a Sanskrit name dhādhima or dhālimba that derives from the old Persian dulim.[19] It is a juicy fruit which nevertheless thrives even in arid areas, and there is an ornamental double-flowered orange-red variety which is sterile.[1e] *Tamarindus indica* is native to the tropical savannah of Africā,[1e] but is an example of a species which came into India even in prehistoric times; an Arab writer about AD 1335 refers to it by the term al-tamar-al-Hindi. The English name derives from this, and even in AD 1298 Marco Polo called it tamarind.[20a] The jackfruit belongs to the genus *Artocarpus* which has some 50 species,[1k] from among which one species has found favour in specific regions. In India (and Indonesia) it is *A.heterophyllus*, the jackfruit, in Malaysia and Oceania *A.communis*, the breadfruit, and in south-east Asia *A.integrer*, the champedak, which looks like a small jackfruit and has the same kind of bulbs inside. The jackfruit seems to have originated in India, and other species grow here, like *A.lakoocha* (Sanskrit lakūcha or lakūda, an edible fruit which is poorly rated by Charaka), *A.chaplasha*, and *A.hirsutus*, all three of which yield excellent timber.[11g] The word jack is a corruption of the Malayalam chakka, while the Tamil word sakkei, which means the fruit abounding in rind and refuse, is extremely appropriate.[20b] The first foreigner to describe the tree was Xuan Zang in the 7th century AD. There are two types. One has bulbs that are mushy, with a taste varying from sweet to insipid, while in the other the perianths are crisp and delicious (see Chapter 11). The large, smooth stones have a delicate nutty taste when roasted.

Major cultivated fruits

Banana: In the banana India has a very ancient fruit. Indeed the Sanskrit names kadalī (now

Bananas being vended in Kerala.

Box 30

A BUNCH OF BANANAS

The genome labelled A and that labelled B from two different wild species (see text) have hybridized over the centuries to give ten cultivars that now grow in India. Listed below are the names of these, some common Indian names, and the places where they are found.

Diploid AA			
Sucrier	chingan, matti, kadalī	five-ridged, green or straw-yellow	West coast, Kanya Kumari
Diploid AB			
Ney poovan	safēd-velchi, sōneri, puttubālē, devabālē	small, plump, shining yellow, sweet and cottony, superior table fruit	Bombay, Madras, Kerala
Triploids AAA			
Dwarf Cavendish	basarai, pacchavāzhai, vamankēli, kābūli	large, curved, dull yellow or greenish yellow	Bombay, Madras
Giant Cavendish	harichal, Bombay green, pedda-paccha, avati, Bengal-jahaji	long, big, tapering to apex, green when ripe	Bombay, Madras, Andhra
Red and Green Red	lālkēl, chenkadalī, sevvāzhai, anupan	long, stout, curved, blunt apex	Kerala, Madras, Bombay
Triploids AAB			
Mysore	poovan, lālvelchi, champa, karpūra, chakkara-kēli	medium, plump, slight curve, orange-yellow flesh, red skin	Madras, Andhra Pradesh, Bengal, Bihar.
Silk	rasthāli, marthaban, sōnkel, rasabālē	four-angled, medium size, straw-yellow, fine smell.	Bengal, Mysore, Madras
French plantain	nēndran, rājeli, ethakai, mindoli	three-sided, large, long, yellow when young, blackens on ripening, very sweet core, used for making chips	Coastal Kerala, Bombay
Pome or Hill banana	virupākshi, sirumalai, vannan, malavāzhai, rājapūri, lāden	five-ridged yellow turning black on ripening, good dessert fruit.	Entire west coast, Tamil Nadu.
Triploid ABB			
Bluggoe	monthan, bankēl, khasadia, kānchkalā, madhurangabālē, batheesa	sharply-angular with three to five sides, greenish yellow to straw yellow, primarily a cooking variety.	Kerala, Madras, parts of Bengal, Bombay, Bihar, Assam.

There is a constant search for new banana varieties like dwarf types, early maturing plants and, of course, better eating varieties.

kēla) and mochā (which was eventually incorporated into the Latin botanical name *Musa paradisiaca* for the banana) are both believed to be of pre-Sanskrit, Munda origin. How did the banana originate? It is a rare example of a fruit in which the stimulus to growth of the fruit pulp needs no seeds, being in-built (thanks to three genes present in the wild forms of one of its parents, *Musa acuminata*).[1e] Selection from the thin masses of edible pulp by early man in the Malaysia region led to edible seedless fruits which were diploids (AA) or triploids (AAA). When these small fruits reached India, probably several thousand years ago, they crossed with the wild plant *Musa balbisiana*, the carrier of genome B, to give a diploid AB, and three vigorous and large-fruited triploids AAA, AAB and ABB.[5i] Today the ten banana cultivars that are believed to exist all fall into these diploid and triploid categories, as shown in Box 30. The word banana is of African origin,[21] and may be connected with the Arabic banan, fingers or toes, or banana, a single finger or toe.[20c] This word was carried by slaves to America, where it became established. The word plantain was universally used in British India.[20d] Later it developed the connotation of a cooking as opposed to a table variety, though the distinction is not tenable, since many fruits are of both kinds. The word plantain is an Anglicization of the Spanish plantano, still used in the Philippines, perhaps from the Latin planta for a spreading leaf.

Mango: Whether the saha used in the *Rigveda* is the mango, as in the later term sahakāra, is uncertain. From its very first mention as āmra in the *Brhadāranyaka Upanishad*,[3b] say about 1000 BC, and in the slightly later *Shātapatha Brāhmana*,[22] the virtues of the mango have been extolled for three thousand years. The Buddha is credited with having created a white mango tree which was subsequently revered, while mango blossoms are considered sacred to the moon, have a wish-fulfilling connotation and are also considered the arrows of Manmatha, the Indian Cupid. In later literature it appears as chūtha, rasāla and sahakāra.[23] Wild varieties of *Mangifera indica* still exist in the north-eastern hills of Indo-Burma, where there are several other related species as well, making this the likely point of origin of the mango.[5g] In fact the amrātaka, even now called the wild mango but belonging to the closely-related species *Spondias pinnata*, is also mentioned in the *Brhadāranyaka Samhitā*.[3b] Over a thousand commercial varieties are known, a result of the botanical circumstance that every tree raised from a seedling is potentially of a new type, since seed is formed from the cross-pollination of a female cell of the flowers with the male pollen from other trees.[24]

Vegetative propagation and grafting in the last few centuries have helped to preserve certain types. Grafting was first used on the mango by the Portuguese (see Chapter 13), and yielded such names as Fernandin, and others recorded by Mauncci as 'mangoes of Niculao Affonso, Malaises Carreira branca, Carreira Vermelha, of Conde, of Joani Parreira, Babia (large and round), of Araup, of Porta, of Secreta, of Mainato, of Our Lady, of Agua de Lupe', and by Giovanni Careri (1695) thus: 'Some are called Mangas Carrieras and Mallaias, others of Nicholas Alfanso, others Satias, and others by other names.'[25a] Some modern varieties like the Alphonso, Pairi and perhaps Mulgoa can be discerned in these names. Grafting under Moghul patronage has been described in Chapter 12; this yielded new varieties. Near Chandigarh a giant mango tree with a girth of 10 metres yields 17,000 kg of fruit a year. Trees even 300 years old are not uncommon, but are usually in poor condition, though many orchards have 150-year old fruit-bearing trees.[24] New varieties are constantly being developed. Incidentally grafting is described very clearly in the *Brhatsamhitā* of Varāhamihira dated AD 505 as 'smearing a branch with cowdung and transplanting it on the branch of another; or it may be done by cutting off the branch of a tree and transplanting it like a wedge on the trunk of another tree.'[26] A number of trees amenable to grafting are also mentioned. These include the jack, plantain, lemon, pomegranate, grape, citron, jasmine and others, but not the mango.

Citrus: The citrus family is an enormous one spread all over the world, but it is now accepted

Bharhut sculpture showing veneration of the white mango tree created by the Buddha.

The sweet orange, mosambi or sāthgudi.

that its origins lie in hilly eastern India.[27a] No wild ancestors are known, and no dates are assignable.[1n] New hybrids were constantly arising at one time by natural crossing in south-east Asia, and recently man has played an active role in this process. All citrus species have x = 9, and most of them are diploid. The santhra of India is a very old species which still grows wild in Assam, whereas the grapefruit evolved only in the 17th century, and the blood-red Malta is even more recent. Various authorities place the number of species within the *Citrus* genus at 16, 36, 145, and 157, because of uncertainty about the criteria to be used to justify species ranking.[27b] Box 31 lists one possible classification, and some of the members in each species. Varieties long known in India are the sweet orange or mosambi (*Citrus sinensis*), the lemon (*C.limon*) and the giant citron (*C.medica*). Bābar in 1529 listed and judiciously described eight 'orange-like' fruits of the citrus family that he saw in India,[28a] noting that a single nārangi tree (*C.aurantium*) in Bajaur yielded 7000 fruits. And of the amal-bīd he remarks: 'they say that a needle melts away if put inside it, either from its acidity or some other property. It is as acid perhaps as the citron and lemon.' The word nārangi is from the Sanskrit nāgarangā, itself probably a south Indian term.[20e]

Today there are numerous citrus varieties growing in India.[17] In the acid group, we have the Indian or kāgzhinimbu (*C.aurantifolia*), round or oval and with a very thin skin; the mīttā-nimbu or sweet lime (*C. limettoides*), exemplified by the rather insipid chikna of Sahar-ānpūr; a rough sour lemon, *C.jambhiri*, of great antiquity; and a number of varieties under *C.limon*, like the galgal of Punjab, the pat-nimbu of Assam , the barāmasia of western Uttar Pradesh and the genoa of Cuddapah. A recent introduction from the Mediterranean is the seedless Italian lemon (*C. limetta*), with a thick rind and juicy pulp. The orange group includes such fruits as the nārangi (*C. aurantium*) and members of *C. sinensis* like the mosambi, mālta, sāthgudi, chīnī and batavia, the names of which reflect their foreign origins. Into the mandarin-tangerine group fall the juicy loose-jacketed santhrās of Nagpur and Coorg, and the khāsi, kamalā and dēsi. The word santhrā was once linked to the port called Cintre in Portugal, but is more likely to have originated from the village Santhra-bara (meaning home of the santhra) in the Bhutān hills near the area of origin of the citrus family.[29] Of the large-fruited citrus varieties, both the grapefruit (*C.paradisi*) which is of West Indian origin, and the Malaysian pummelo or

The loose-jacketed orange, santhrā.

Box 31
CITRUS RELATIVES

The sprawling citrus family defies classification (see text); one attempt to do so follows nonetheless. Members marked with an asterisk have representatives growing in India. Some of these are ancient (see text) and others are of recent vintage.

A. THE ACID MEMBERS

*Citrus medica**: citron, native to India (Sanskrit: mātulunga and bījapūraka), now many forms; used to make candied peel

*C.limon**: lemon, native to India, now many forms, like galgal

*C.jambhiri**: rough lemon, native to India

*C.limetta**: lumia and limetta of the Mediterranean; in India, chikna

*C.karna**: native to India, orange skin and orange flesh

*C.aurantifolia**: Indian lime or kāgzhi nimbu; though the word nimbu is of ancient Munda origin, the species is probably native to Malaysia

C. latifolia: South Pacific orange

*C. limettoides**: Indo-Iranian sweet lime, of Indian origin

B. THE ORANGE GROUP

*C.aurantium**: Seville orange, both skin and fruit orange, acidic with bitter after-taste; original species possibly native to north-east India; Sanskrit names nāgarangā and airāvata

C.myrtifolia: myrtle-leaf orange, ornamental, sour, bitter and small; perhaps of Chinese origin

C.bergamia: Bergamot orange, possibly of Italian origin; peel yields Bergamot oil

C.mitsudaidai: Japanese summer grapefruit, of Japanese origin

*C.sinensis**: Common or sweet orange, mosambi type, origin Chinese or Assamese

C. MANDARIN OR TANGERINE GROUP

*C.reticulata**: loose-jacket santhrā, origin probably Chinese

C.unshiu: Satsuma mandarins, origin Japanese

C. deliciosa: Mediterranean mandarin

C.tangerina: Tangerine, colour deep-orange to red

C. reshni: The spice mandarin

C. nobilis: Japanese tangerine

D. PUMMELO-GRAPEFRUIT GROUP

*C.maxima**: Pummelo or shaddock, origin Malayasian, thick, spongy rind, flavour sweet to sour but never bitter

*C.paradisi**: Grapefruit or pomelo, of West Indian origin, commercialized in the United States of America; taste sweet-sour with a trace of bitterness

E. OTHER CITRUS SPECIES

At least eleven other species may be listed here, of which several had their origin in India.

shaddock (*C.decumana*), called chakōtra, are recent types which are grown in India but enjoy only limited popularity.

In many parts of the world, fairly distinctive citrus types have evolved with a local name and appeal, and India is no exception. The Rangpūr lime (*C.limoni*); the gajanimma (*C.pennivesculata*), the Guntūr sour orange (*C.maderasapatana*), which is also called the kichili and vadlapudi, and the calamondin or hazara (*C.madurensis*) are examples of this kind. Species names for these are a matter of opinion. The kinnow or kinna of

Punjāb and Himāchal Pradesh is an orange-tangerine cross which was introduced from California and became popular in the sixties.[3d] It is deep orange in colour, and its abundant acidic juice is relished with added sugar and salt. Karnakhatta (*C.karna*) is an acid fruit native to India, with an orange skin and orange flesh.

Grape: The grape is an ancient species. It originated and was cultivated in the Middle East, probably in Armenia, in the 4th millennium BC. All the 10,000 cultivars now grown are believed to derive as ecospecies rather than as true species from a single wild species, *Vitis vinifera*.[10] Grape seeds have been found in very ancient Tertiary deposits (10 to 15 million years ago); the wild vines of Kāshmīr, once classified within the *Vitis* genus as *V.latifolia*, have now been re-classified as *Ampelocissus latifolia*, whereas a related species, *A.arnottiana*, is now called *Vitis indica*.[5k,11h] The grape is mentioned rather late in Sanskrit as mrdvika or drākshā, first by Pānini (*c.* 600 BC) and then by Kautilya (*c.* 300 BC) and others. Carvings at Sānchi and Bhārhūt, both of the 2nd century BC, show unmistakable vine leaves and grape bunches.[28]

Grape cultivation in India seems to have moved in cycles. Perhaps its use for wine-making led to opposition from puritanical rulers and suppression of its cultivation from time to time. Around AD 1340, Ibn Battūta mentions grapes as being rare, but grown extensively in Daulatābād, but shortly thereafter Firūz Tughlak, the successor of Mohammad bin Tughlak, laid orchards in Delhi to grow seven grape varieties; with abundant production, the price fell to just five times that of the same weight in wheat.[30] In the time of Akbar grapes had become plentiful (*Ain-i-Akbari*),[2d] and Bernier in 1660 rejoiced in the meadows and vineyards of Kāshmīr. Thevenot in 1667 remarked on the passion he noted for the cultivation of the grape, possibly as a result of Portuguese encouragement. Yet by the end of Aurangzeb's long reign of fifty years in 1707, grape cultivation fell into a decline from which it never really recovered till the remarkable resurgence of the 1960s. The dried grape product, raisins, both cream and black, have never been made in India, but imported from the northwest under the name kishmish. This is actually the name of a variety of grape traditionally grown around Quetta and Kandahār. *V. labrusca* is the Bangalore blue grape.

Plums, pears, apples and their like

Prunus: The cherry, plum, peach, apricot and almond belong to the *Prunus* family.[1k] The first diploid member of the species, with $2n = 2x = 16$, probably arose in the way of sweet and sour cherries in Central Asia. The wild form (paddam, phaya, *P.cerasoides*) is still found along the length of the Himālayas; it is not eaten, but the stones are made into rosaries and necklaces,[11i] and the fruit makes an excellent cherry brandy.[51] The sweet cherry is of Chinese origin, and was first extensively grown in Kāshmīr during Akbar's time, according to Jahangīr.[31] The cultivated plum *P.domestica* (ālucha, ālubhukhārā) represents a link between the various fruits of the *Prunus* family and plum varieties developed by human selection at various places in Central Asia, the Middle East, Europe, China and North America.[11i] The peach (*P.persica*) was developed in China as its Sanskrit name, chīnāni, indicates and as Xuan Zang pointed out as early as the 7th century AD. The apricot (*P.armeniaca*) has also been allotted Chinese ancestry, but a wild form, called zardālu, grows in north India. The almond, *P.amygdalus*, is also of Central/West Asian origin and comes in two varieties, sweet and bitter.[16] The Sanskrit names vātāma (for the sweet) and vātāvairi (for the bitter) are derived from the old Persian vādām, and were first employed by Charaka and Sushrutha.[25b]

Pyrus: The *Pyrus* is the pear family, nominally *P.communis*, but with major introgressions from two other *Pyrus* species and minor entries from three others.[1q] The hard country or sand pear, *P.pyrifolia* var.culta, has old Sanskrit names, urumāna and nāshpati,[2f] and a Tamil one, bērikāi, and must have come in long ago from China or Japan.[5m] The soft, sweet European pear *Pyrus communis* made its appearance in India only after British colonization.

Malus: The apple genus, *Malus*, is closely related to that of the pears, and has its primary centre of origin in the mountainous belt running across Asia Minor through Himālayan India and perhaps even up to China.[1q] Wild apple forms like *M.baccata* (called patōl, and used as vegetables) still exist in the northwest Himālayas, and as recently as 1908, Sir Francis Younghusband described wild apple trees in Kāshmīr laden with fruit.[2f] Local Kashmīri apple varieties (*M.pumila*) go by the names āmri (a tiny red variety with a sweet skin) and tarēhli (also tiny and red), while the mahārāji (a sour but juicy and high-yielding variety) appears to be a re-named early import. The fruit sinchitikāphala mentioned by Charaka could well refer to an apple of Chinese origin, and about AD 1100 Dalhana describes 'a bēr as big as a fist and very sweet grown in the northern regions of Kāshmīr,'[3b] which does suggest an apple.

In contrast to the diploids (2n = 2x = 34) of the Old World, most American apples, including the Golden Delicious and the Red Delicious varieties now popular all over the world, are tetraploid (4x = 68).[1q] Both Red Delicious[1q] and Golden Delicious were chance developments in America around 1890, the first as a sport branch in the orchard of Jesse Hiatt in Iowa,[34a] and the second by chance fertilization in a farm of Anderson Mullins in West Virginia.[35b]

Certain earlier imports into India are beginning to disappear. Frederick 'Paharī' Wilson was a colourful British character who married an Indian girl, Gulābi. About 1850 he established a flourishing farm in Gārhwāl growing Wilson apples, described as large, red and juicy, and still offered to travellers on their way to the Gangotri shrine.[32] Around 1920, an American, Stokes, introduced the two Delicious varieties into his orchard in Kotgarh, near Shimla, and played an important role in popularizing apple orchards in the area, as well as the proper grading, packing and marketing of the fruit.[25e] In the early nineteenth century, the British residents of Bangalore experimented with apple cultivation, and Rome Beauty (before it was wiped out by aphis attack)[24] was a smooth, deep-red variety which was popular before the Second World War.[33,34] The two Delicious apples have now replaced almost all other kinds in India.

Spices and Condiments

The use of many spices stretches back so far in time that even in Sanskrit they bear earlier Munda names.[3e] The turmeric is haridrā; the green ginger, srngavēra or ārdraka, with sunthi for the dried form; the coriander is dhānyaka or kastumbīra;[36a] the sacred basil (*Ocimum sanctum*) is tulasi; and the katthā tree, *Acacia catechu*, khadira. The lasuna and the tiny aushad-grnjana, two forms of garlic, appear in early Vedic literature as native foods despised by the Aryans. Spices from India were imported into Egypt even as early as 1700 BC for the embalming of mummies.[36a]

Pungent spices from below the ground

Turmeric: The species *Curcuma longa* is probably native to India, and is a triploid with 42 chromosomes which may have originated from *C.aromatica* (a species found all over India), or from some lost diploid form.[37a] Various polyploids (2n = 32, 62, 64 etc.) have been recorded, and even the basic chromosome number is in doubt.[1e] Its striking yellow colour and dyeing ability soon gave the haridrā an important place in magic and ritual in India.

Ginger: Long cultivation has obscured the sites of original domestication and wild distribution of ārdraka, *Zingiber officinale*; it is certainly native to south-east Asia, but wild forms are found in India and several species are grown in Malaysia.[1e] It figures in the *Atharvaveda* as ādāra.[3e]

Garlic and Onion: The garlic is *Allium sativum* and the onion *Allium cepa*, and both are believed to have been native to the Afghanistān region.[1r] Clay models of the garlic have been found in pre-3000 BC Egyptian tombs, while the onion is described in funerary offerings of that country in 2800 BC and has been noted in mummy stuffings.[38] Long and round, white, yellow and red, and mild and pungent forms of the onion were all described by Greek writers by the 5th century BC.[38] Both the garlic (lasuna) and the onion (palāndu) are not mentioned in Vedic literature even as late as the sixteen *Upanishads*; when they do find mention around the 2nd century BC, it is as despised foods that were relished by the native population (mlecchas) and Europeans (Yavanas),[9] but were forbidden to those seeking an austere life, and in ceremonial.

The pepper family

The betel vine, *Piper betle*, which yields the aromatic leaf for chewing, has been described in Box 7 of Chapter 4, and in Chapter 9. Very early usage in southeast Asia would suggest its origin in that region, while the borrowed Munda words thāmbūla and guvāka for the betel leaf and areca nut would imply early transfer, perhaps to south India, to judge from the name nāgavalli used there for the vine. The first mention of the betel leaf in Sanskrit is in the Buddhist-Jain canonical literature and in the *Āpasthamba Dharma Sūtra*, both dated *c.* 400 BC.[3e] The areca nut, *Areca catechu*, has been found in 10,000 to 7,000 BC layers in the so-called Spirit Cave in Thailand, and skulls dated 3,000 BC with characteristically stained teeth have been found in the Philippines.[40] Central Malaysia, where many other *Areca* species grow, and from where historical evidence also comes, may have been the centre of origin of the areca nut.[1e]

Piper longum is long pepper, pippali in Sanskrit and in Bengali. This was probably indigenous to India, and was an important export item from south India even 4000 years ago. Today it is only a minor commodity derived from shrubby plants growing wild in Kērala and Assām. The name long pepper is from the fruit pods, which, rather strangely, resemble those of the green chillis that came into India in the sixteenth century from Mexico. The root of the plant, pippalimula, is used in Ayurvedic medicine.

Black pepper, *Piper nigrum*, the dried berries of a climbing vine, has all but replaced long pepper. In fact, in many Indian languages black pepper took over the names of the long pepper. Only in Sanskrit does it continue to have a distinct name, maricha as against pippali. This distinction appears only after 400 BC, suggesting a late acquaintance in north India with this form of pepper.[3e]

Wild pepper plants, which occur in Kērala, are perennial and bear both male and female flowers, whereas the cultivated strain is annual and monoecious, with either male or female flowers.[1s] Interestingly enough, since the seeds have a viability of only seven days, the spread of the pepper to south-east Asia must have been brought about through cuttings alone.[1s]

A little known commodity, from *P.retrofactum*, is called chavya in Sanskrit, chavi in Hindi, and Javanese long pepper in English. It is described as being weakly pungent with gingery overtones.

Other spices

The spices that will be considered here derive from many parts of a plant: the pod, seed, bud, stamens, leaves and tree bark.

Cardamom: The elā of Kautilya is the true cardamom, and is the dried fruit of a large-leaved perennial plant, *Elettaria cardamomum*, native to India.[1e] There are three varieties, the inferior Sri Lankan, the pale-green, more delicate Mysore, and the larger and more robust Mysore,[5b] the latter distinction having been known from the start of the Christian era.[40] The distinction was made in Sanskrit long ago between the true cardamom, elā, and the inferior substitute, dāruharidrā. This latter variety is from *Ammomum aromaticum*, now called badi-elaichi or the large Bengal cardamom, and is raised in north Bengal and Assam.[11g] The favoured Alleppey green cardamom of today which makes up the bulk of exports is actually a Mysore variety grown in Kērala.

Cumin: This seed derives from the herb *Cuminum cyminum* native to the Mediterranean region, whose Sanskrit names are ajājī, karavī and kunchikā. Today it is called jeera from the late Sanskrit jeeraka, itself derived from the Persian zīra. It appears rather late in literary usage with Kautilya, Charaka and Sushrutha, around 300 BC.

Mēthi: The fenugreek is a dried seed, that of *Trigonella foenum-graecum*, a herb native to southern Europe, but long cultivated in India, and going by the Sanskrit name mēthika. The word trigonella, meaning little triangle, is from the shape of the flowers, and foenum-graecum means Grecian hay, a name given to it by the Romans because it was a common crop in Greece.[42a]

Clove: This spice originates from the Moluccas in eastern Indonesia, which are also called the Spice Islands. *Syzygium aromaticum* is mentioned as an imported item in Chinese literature in the 3rd century BC,[1t, 42b] and even the word lāvanga first occurs in writing in the *Rāmāyana* and *Charaka Samhitā*.[2g] This suggests knowledge of the clove in India about the start of the Christian era, the word itself being derived, perhaps, from the Malay term bunga-lavanga meaning clove.[2g] The English word derives from the Latin clavus for a nail, which the dried flower-bud that constitutes the clove certainly resembles.

Nutmeg and mace: The Moluccas Islands are also the source of the nutmeg and mace, the first being the nut and the second the scarlet aril which envelops the nut and becomes visible when the fruit is stripped away. The nutmeg is the Sanskrit jaiphal, the mace jatri, and the bushy, evergreen tree is botanically *Myristica fragrans*.[2h]

Cinnamon: The bark of *Cinnamomum zeylanicum* (the coca of Kautilya) constitutes true cinnamon. The true cinnamon tree also goes by the name lāvanga, which could point to a time when these plants were not separately recognized.[2i] The tree grows wild in hilly south India, but the best products still come from Sri Lanka, and the Sanskrit name dār-chīnī means Chinese bark.[2i] Cinnamon bark has a much more delicate flavour than cassia or tējpat (the Sanskrit tvak, mentioned by Vāghbhata and Sushrutha), which comes from the related tree, *C. tamala*, of the Himālayas and Khāsi hills. While the bark of this tree is inferior in quality to cinnamon, tējpat leaves are a popular flavouring agent used in making palāo in north India. The Sanskrit word tamāli occurs in the *Rāja Nirghanta*. Tējpat leaves were exported to Rome under the name malabathrum since before the Christian era.[2i]

Cinnamon, the coca of Kautilya.

Saffron: The gently-dried stigmas of *Crocus sativus* constitute saffron, called kēsara and kumkuma in Sanskrit and zaffrān in Persian and Arabic. It is probably native to Greece, being recorded in the 4th century BC. Saffron first finds mention in Sanskrit in the *Bhava Prakāsha*, a medical dictionary.[2j] Cultivation in Kāshmīr seems to have started about AD 550, and Jahangir records production of '500 maunds by Hindustān weight.'[43] Thereafter cultivation was neglected until revived by Mahārājā Ranbīr Singh.[44] The very dry alluvial plain of Rāmpūr, and to some extent that of Paraspūr, provides excellent conditions for growth of the crocus. The purple blossoms are close to the ground, and are harvested for 3 to 4 weeks in October–November, very early in the morning before the sun comes up.[45]

Asafoetida: Hingu occurs in the early Buddhist *Mahāvagga*, and the word bālhīka in the *Kashyapa Samhitā* reflects its import from Afghanistān.[3e] Hing is the exudate of three species, namely *Ferula asafoetida*, *F. narthex* and *F.galbaniflua*,[2k,11k] each of which shows slight differences in properties.

The Sugarcane

Origin

The likely progenitor of *Saccharum officinarum* is *S.robustum* (2n = 80), which was subject to human selection, starting several thousand years ago, in or near Papua New Guinea, for sweetness and lack of fibre.[1u] These so-called noble

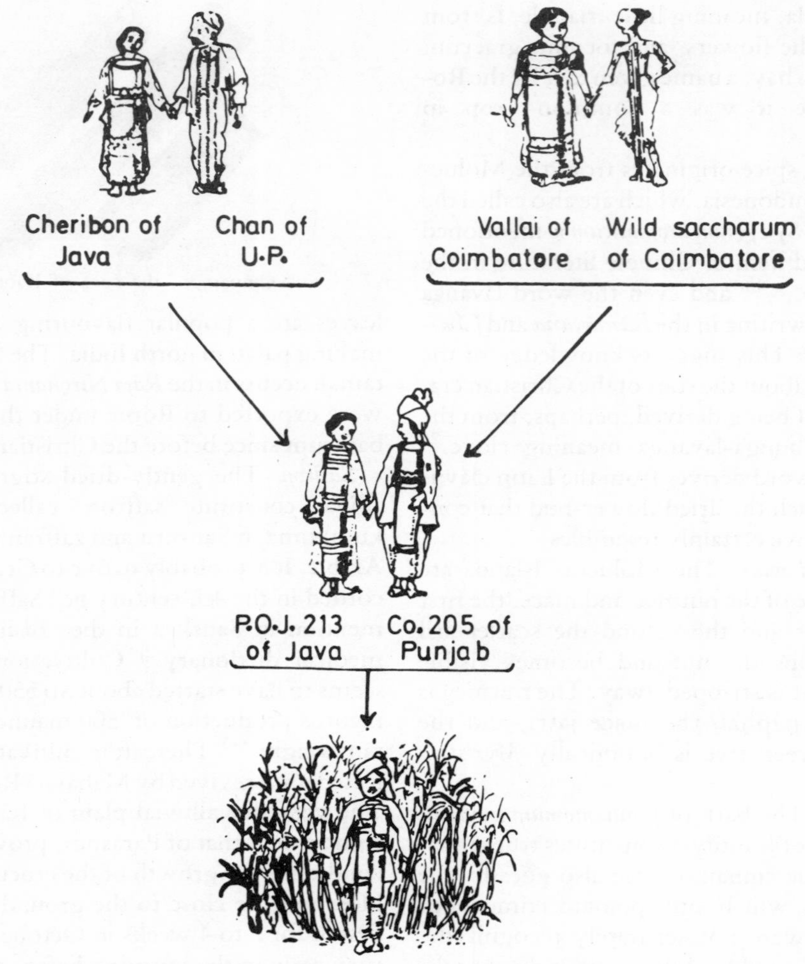

A humorous drawing used by T. S. Venkataraman to popularize his new hybrid sugarcane.

canes then migrated north-west to the Asian continent, and hybridized, probably in India, with wild kasa grass, *S.spontaneum* (2n = 40 to 128) to yield thin canes. These are now called *S.sinense* (2n = 64 in India, and from 80 − 120 elsewhere), and constituted the varieties grown throughout the centuries all over India to form the basis of the sugar juice industry.[1u]

Harappan cities have yielded charcoals derived from some *Saccharum* species, though one cannot be certain whether this was the sugarcane.[13b] The kusara of the *Rigveda* (*c.* 1500 BC) is thought to refer to it, and ikshu, certainly the sugarcane, is thus mentioned in the *Atharvaveda* (*c.* 800 BC): 'I offer you dried sugarcane, white sesamum, reeds and bamboos.'[25f] All the *Samhitās of the Yajurveda* also have references to ikshu.[3f] The *Mahābhāshya* of Patanjali (*c.* 600 BC) mentions sharkarā repeatedly. Charaka derives the word guda (for jaggery) from Gauda (as Bengal was then called), and describes two varieties of sugarcane, the superior paundraka (growing in Pundra, or north Bengal) and the inferior vainsaka. Kautilya (*c.* 300 BC) mentions the whole range of sugar products, namely guda, phanita (thickened juice, now called rāb), khanda (raw sugar crystals, khandsāri), matsyandika (sugar crystals, compared to fish roe) and sharkara.[3g] The emperor Harsha in the seventh century AD received a Chinese delegation which came to India to study the manufacture of crystal sugar.[21]

In 1912 the Sugarcne Breeding Station was founded in Coimbatore as a result of the strenuous efforts of Pandit Madan Mōhan Mālaviya to stop the huge drain of currency in importing sugar into India from Java. In the 1930s, the crossing of sugarcane with the wild species *S.spontaneum* by T.S. Venkatarāman led to a whole family of hybrids that proved to be superior to all existing canes in terms of thickness, sugar content and resistance both to disease and to adverse climate.[27c,28g,46]

Sir T. S. Venkataraman

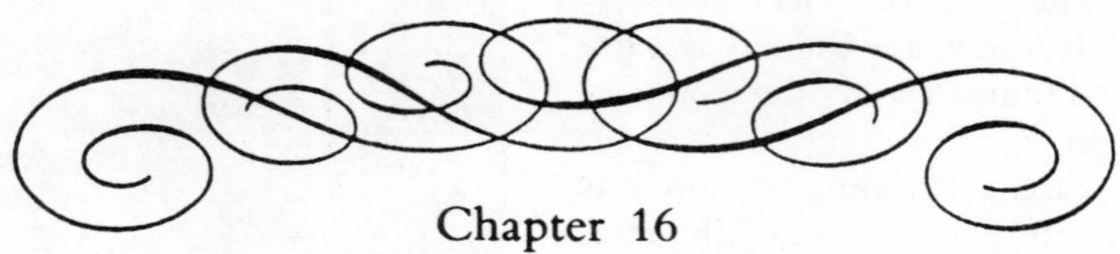

Chapter 16

BOUNTY FROM THE NEW WORLD

Christopher Columbus of Spain set foot in the New World in 1492. Six years later, Vasco da Gama of Portugal reached India. During the next two centuries the Spaniards and the Portuguese were remarkably active in transferring, not only to Europe but to many parts of Asia as well, a number of plant species which they encountered in South and Central America, in expectation of their potential either as food or as medicine.

These plants had been developed to a high degree by the civilizations of the New World. The Maya empire flourished in Central America between the 4th and 16th centuries AD, covering most of the present-day Mexico and parts of Guatemala and Honduras.[1] This civilization cultivated maize, small black beans, red beans, various pumpkins and squashes, sweet potatoes, tomatoes, tapioca; fruits like the chicle (sapota), papaya and avocado; chillis, vanilla, coriander and oregano as flavouring materials, and products like tobacco, rubber, and a lathering nut. The Inca civilization flourished in the Andes of South America from the 12th to the 16th centuries with its capital at Cuzco, and, among other plants, cultivated maize, potatoes, sweet potatoes, squash, tomatoes, groundnuts, chilli varieties, and tapioca. These reached India by several sea routes.

The Portuguese slave trade lay between Brazil and Africa, and thence led to Gōa, with further exchanges between other Portuguese settlements in south-east Asia and China. The Spanish plied between Brazil, Africa and Spain, and from there to Malaysia, China, Burma, Assam, and the east coast of south India. After the conquest of the Philippines by Spain, plant species from Brazil also came to India through the latter islands. Because of this multiplicity of routes, the same plant could enter a land at different places. Thus tobacco seems to have reached both Sūrat on the west coast, and the east coast of Āndhra, from different directions.

This chapter will deal primarily with the plants that came into India from the New World. Also included are a few species which entered the country from elsewhere— the sunflower, the soyabean, the litchi fruit and the tea plant—but were developed here during the same period. Along with the exotic cashewnut from South America, other nuts like the almond, pistachio, walnut, chirōnji and chilgoza, which have been with us longer, will also be reviewed.

Oilseeds

Groundnut

Ancient Peruvian tombs of 3000–2000 BC carry groundnuts (*Arachis hypogaea*). The groundnut plant is, therefore, a very old one, and originated

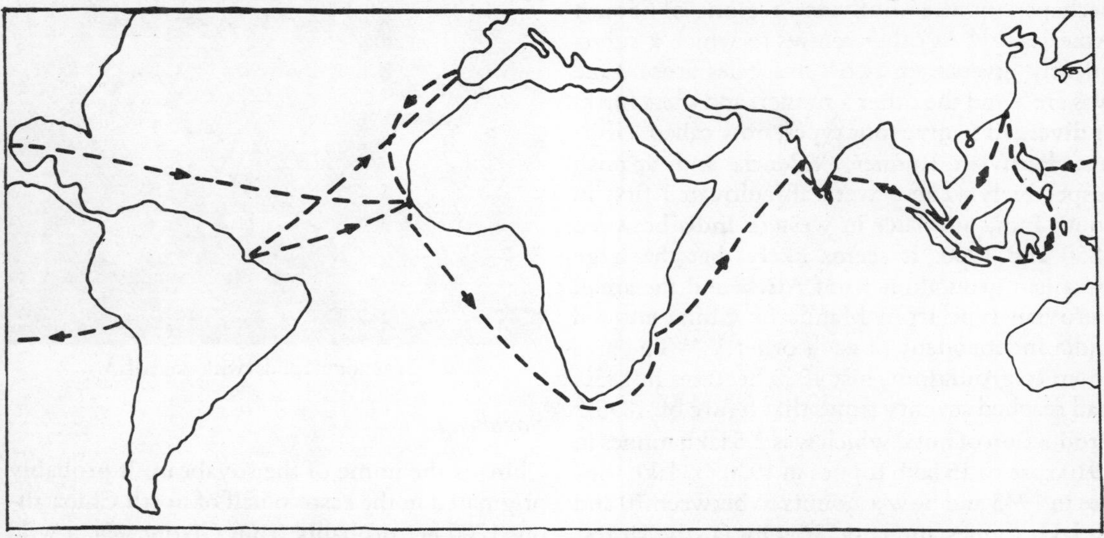

Routes of transfer of food plants from the New World to India.

The tobacco plant reached the eastern and the western coasts via different routes.

perhaps in the Bolivian region of South America.[2a,3,4] At other centres to which it subsequently diversified, two sub-species arose. One was erect and the other a runner, and these further diverged to give four types, now called Virginia, Peruvian Runner, Valencia and Spanish respectively. These were all cultivated first in south India and later in western India between 1850 and 1900. It seems likely that the large Brazilian groundnut from Africa and the small Peruvian type from Manila or China entered India independent of each other.[5a, 6a] The area sown to groundnut, just 1000 hectares in 1850, had reached seventy times that figure by 1895.[7a] Production of nuts, which was 2.5 lakh tonnes in 1910 rose to 15 lakh tonnes in 1930, 33 lakh tonnes in 1945 and now amounts to between 70 and 80 lakh tonnes annually. It is by far the largest oilseed crop in India. Just about a tenth of the crop is used for consumption as nuts and in cooking, the rest being crushed for oil.

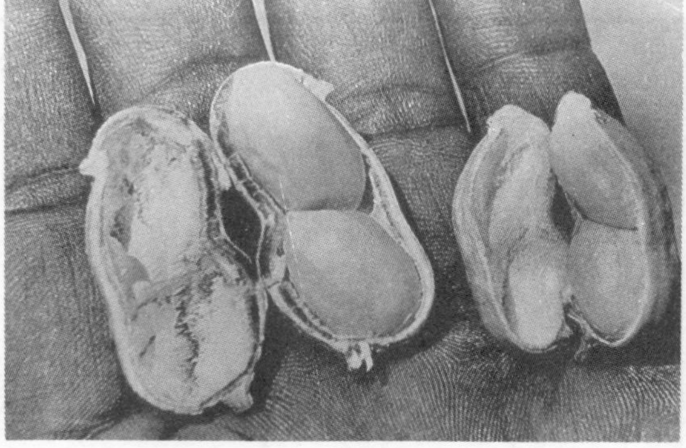

Groundnut pods with kernels.

Soyabean

China is the home of the soyabean. It probably originated in the eastern half of north China about 1200 BC, probably from *Glycine soja*, a wild form related to the cultivated *Glycine max*.[2b] The present name soy may spring from the shu or sou used by Confucius. It spread by 300 BC all

Uprooted groundnut.

over south-east Asia, but even in 1908 was described as 'having only recently been introduced into India', and 'growing as a garden rather than a field crop in hilly eastern India'.[5b] However, a thorough survey in 1911 showed fairly extensive cultivation upto heights of 2000 metres all the way from Punjāb to Manipūr.[8] In the thirties, Mahātmā Gāndhi wrote about the excellent nutritional qualities of the soyabean and of his own experiences of eating it after steam cooking.[8] Alongside, many states in India, notably the princely state of Barōda, looked into the possibilities of growing the soyabean plant both for fodder and for feed,[8] but these made little headway, and even in 1948 soyabean production was estimated at just a thousand tonnes.[9a] The big spurt in soyabean cultivation occurred in the 1970s when agricultural planners were looking for a crop to grow on lands traditionally kept fallow in the rainy season. Varieties brought from America were acculturated at the agricultural universities in Pantnagar and Jabalpūr, and soyabean cultivation increased by leaps and bounds from 25,000 tonnes in 1973 to over a million tonnes in 1988. It is processed to yield an edible oil and a cake of excellent nutritive value.

The soyabean is an ancient Chinese plant.

The oilseed-type sunflower.

Sunflower

Archaeological finds of both wild and cultivated sunflowers dating back to 3000 BC show that the sunflower originated, not in Mexico as earlier believed, but in the southwest of the North American continent.[10a] The seeds of ornamental plants were taken to Spain in 1581, and the huge flowerheads filled with oil-bearing seeds were developed first in Bulgaria and later in Russia. In the 1940s a variety of oil-rich sunflower was introduced into India but did not catch on, and it was Russian varieties brought in during the seventies that became established in India. The states of Karnātaka and Mahārāshtra now raise some 250,000 tonnes of seed which are processed to yield edible sunflower oil.[11a,11b,11c]

Nuts

Both the groundnut, and to a lesser extent the sunflower kernel, are used as edible nuts. But there are others as well, both new and relatively older nuts, which may now be considered together.

Cashew

A native of south-east Brazil, the cashew tree must have been brought into India at a very early date. In 1578 for example, Acosta describes the 'caiu . . . found in the gardens at the city of Santa Cruz in the Kingdom of Cochin'.[12a] The so-called cashew 'fruit' is really the swollen stalk or peduncle; the kidney-shaped nut hangs below it, as aptly denoted by the Tamil word mundiri for the nut. In Kērala the nut is called paranki-māvu or -āndi (foreign mango) and the fruit gō-māngā, perhaps because it came to Kērala from Goa.[13] The name caju which the Portuguese brought to India derives from the term acaju of the Tepi tribe of Brazil.[14] It is remarkable that of the twenty-odd species known to exist in the New World, the colonizers brought *Anacardium occidentale* into India, the only one which would grow well in South Asian conditions.

Almond and peach

Prunus amygdalus, the bādām or vilāyati-bādām, is indigenous to the eastern Mediterranean[15a]. It seems to have come into India at a very late date. Even the Sanskrit name vātāma appears to have been derived from that employed by Charaka for the nut produced by an ancient tree, *Terminalia catappa*;[16] later this came to be called jangli bādām or patee bādām,[15a] perhaps to distinguish it from the by-then more common bādām. Trees yielding sweet and bitter almonds are classified as separate varieties under the species, being called var. dulcis and var. amara.[17a]

The peach also belongs to the *Prunus* family, and evolved from the same ancestral species. This split occurred at an early stage somewhere in western China, the almond then evolving and moving westwards into Central Asia.[2c]

Pishta

Pistachia vera, a small evergreen tree, has been cultivated in the Mediterranean and further east for perhaps 4000 years for its edible drupes, with centres of diversity in Turkey and Kirgistān.[2d] The nuts have always been imported into India from Afghanistān.

Walnut

Juglans regia, akhrot, Sanskrit akshota, is naturalized all along the Himālayan range from

The cashew nut

Afghanistān to Bhutān,[5d] though said to be indigenous to south-eastern Europe and China.[2d] Apart from the delicious nut, walnut wood is of great value. Even North America has an indigenous black walnut, *Juglans nigra*, with a kernel of strong flavour which is difficult to remove from the shell.[2d]

Chirōnji and chilgoza

These are two nuts of long standing in India. Chirōnji kernels from *Buchanania lanzan* were noted by Bābar as having a flavour somewhere between that of an almond and a pistachio; the tree is found in dry forests throughout India, frequently associated with sāl, mahuā and palāsh trees.[5e] The chilgoza is the nut of the neosia pine, *Pinus gerardiana*, a moderate-sized evergreen tree of the inner dry and arid north-west Himālayas that grows at heights between 2000 and 3000 metres.[5f] The cones ripen in October; they are plucked before they open and heated to make the scales expand, when the nuts (abhisukha in Sanskrit) can be removed.[5f]

Fruits

Papaya

Carica papaya is a plant of the lowlands of Central America, evolved by continuous selection by man from small-fruited forms.[2e] Modern papayas grow either on female plants, as in India, or on hermaphrodite plants with flowers of both sexes. In papaya plantations, some 12–15 per cent of male plants are sufficient to effect pollination.[2e] According to Linschoten the plant came to India by way of the Philippines (to which it was carried by the Spanish) and Malaysia,[12b] and according to Delle Valle from Brazil.[18] The name used in Cuba was papaya and in the Caribbean ababai;[12b] the term papīta was in early use in India.[18]

Sapota

Botanically this is the fruit of *Manilkara achras*, called sapodilla in its native areas of Mexico and Central America.[2d] The bark of the medium-sized tree can be tapped every two or three years for its latex, which on boiling with water yields a gum called chicle which was used by the Aztecs for chewing. Flavoured chewing gum was at first made from this latex, and later from other wood exudates,[9b] but is now based on resins synthesized in factories. It is the word chicle that gave rise in India to cheeku. The species was brought either from Mozambique to Goa[19] or from the Philippines to Malaysia and thence to the

Sapota fruits, or cheeku.

east coast, thriving best today in southern and western India.

Guava

Peru in South America may be the centre of domestication of the guava. Remains, dated 800 BC, have been found there in association with a human society, and other remains dated 200 BC in Mexico.[2d] *Psidium guajava*, the botanical name, derives from the original native and Spanish name guajava.[20] Blochmann's English translation of the *Ain-i-Akbari* (1590) suggested that guavas were served at Akbar's table, but this could be an error in translating the word amrud used by Abul Fazl,[12c] which today stands both for the guava and the much older pear. Around 1550 Benzoni correctly describes the fruit in the east of India, but the first unambiguous mention of the fruit is by Fryer in 1673 in India, and by Dampier in 1676 in Kampuchea.[12c] Two other related species, *P. guineense*, the Guinea guava, and *P. cattleyanum*, the strawberry guava, both grow in India and yield small edible fruits.[15b] Pink guavas carry the same pigment, lycopene, which is found in tomatoes.[21a]

Avocado

The butterfruit, *Persea americana*, has been traced back to 6000 BC in Central America,[9c] where the original native name of aguacate or ahuacatl still survives.[12d] Three commercial varieties are known. Variety guatemalensis has fruits with a rougher and thicker skin, and smaller and tighter seed; the drymifolia variety has the smallest fruits and thinnest skin; and the variety americana is of an intermediate kind. The three appear to have been independently domesticated by man from wild forms, all of which still exist. Fossil studies show that *Persea* species grew abundantly in California even 50 million years ago. All three avocado varieties are grown in India, but the plant seems to have entered India not earlier than about 1750.[12d] Even so the avocado has now run wild on the southern hills. The flesh has an excep-

Guavas are a very ancient fruit of Peru.

tionally high content of fat (25 per cent), and a soft creamy texture.

Passion fruit

Passiflora edulis is native to southern Brazil, and is a climbing vine with purple fruit.[2d] The yellow variety of fruit is from a different species, *P. laurifolia*.[15c] The common name derives from the flower, in which the early missionaries in South America saw a representation of the agony of Christ on the cross. The ten petals were seen as representing the apostles who witnessed the crucifixion, the ring of filaments was the crown of thorns, the five stamens the wounds, the three stigmas the nails in the cross, the tendrils the lashes of the persecutors of Jesus, and the spots on the underside the thirty pieces of silver.[22] The loose jelly-like pulp makes a drink with a distinct and pleasant flavour. It is not known when the vine was brought into India but it now grows abundantly in the southern hills.[19]

Litchi

Nephelium litchi is native to southern China, the fruit being really a sweet, pulpy aril surrounding a smooth round seed.[2d] A monograph written in China in 1059 AD on the lītchī may be one of the earliest on a specific fruit.[19] It was introduced into Bengal by the Portuguese at the end of the 18th century, but has rather exacting climatic requirements,[19] and does well almost only in Rāmnagar in north Bihār, and in Dehra Dun. It was earlier termed *Litchi chinensis*.

Vegetables

Tomato

Lycopersicon lycopersicum is believed to have originated in Mexico or in Peru, from a variety now called cerasiforme. This variety still exists wild there, and has even become an aggressive colonizer in the Old World.[2g] It also crosses freely with the ten other species in the family. Consequently, even genetic evidence is not helpful, with Mexican, Central American and coastal Peruvian tomato varieties showing great morphological variation.[2g] There is no native name in the Andean region, but in Mexico it is called tomatl in the Nahua tongue.[23] The tomato was well diversified before the Europeans reached the New World, and from the subspecies *typus* are believed to have sprung the four tomato varieties now known as the common, the cherry, the large-leaved and the pear.[9d]

The tomato reached Europe in 1550, and was first adopted in Italy as an excellent partner to pasta and cheese dishes.[24] Because of its relationship to poisonous plants like the belladonna and mandrake, acceptance in England was slow, while the name love-apple that became attached to it had aphrodisiacal connotations.[24] Unlike many other plants that we have considered, the tomato did not come to India directly from the

Tomatoes came into India via England.

New World but by way of England, perhaps only late in the 18th century. A century ago, Watt states that tomatoes were grown chiefly for the European population; Indians, he added, were beginning to appreciate the tomato and Bengalis and Burmans to use it in their sour curries.[7b] There seems to be no record of where and how the tomato came to India.[26]

Potato

The potato (*Solanum tuberosum*) is believed to have been domesticated on the high plateau of Bolivia-Peru in the general region of Lake Titicaca, sometime between 5000 and 2000 BC. Europeans first saw potatoes in South America in 1537, and around 1570 a Spanish ship brought the first potatoes to Europe. The legends that Raleigh and Drake were the first to do so are now generally believed to be incorrect.[2h] Though termed papa in South America, they were incorrectly called batata (the name for the sweet potato) when John Gerard first described them in English in 1597, and this name stuck. As a result, it is more than likely that the potato mentioned in the well-documented dinner given by Āsaf Khan to Sir Thomas Roe in 1615 (Chapter 13),[25] and again noted by Fryer in 1675 as constituting a garden crop (along with the brinjal) in Karnātaka and Sūrat, is really the sweet potato, which to the foreigner was equally a new product.[27a,28] However, the identity of the 'basket of potatoes', considered worthy enough to be offered as a gift to Sir Warren Hastings around 1780, is not in doubt, since he even invited members of his Council to dine with him and partake of the gift.[27a] About 1830, potatoes came to be grown on terraced slopes on the Dehrā Dūn hills as a result of the efforts of a Captain Youns and Mr. Shore, who simultaneously developed the hill stations of Mussoorie and Landour.[29] An 1860 report states that by 1780, potatoes, peas and beans were in high repute as foods in Calcutta, and that

> the Dutch are said to have been the first to introduce the culture of potatoes, which was received from their settlement of the Cape of Good Hope. From there the British received annually the seeds of every kind of vegetable useful at the table, as well as several plants of which there appears to be much need, especially various kinds of pot herbs.[30]

Tapioca

Though a staple starchy food in Assam and Kērala, elsewhere in India the tapioca is used as a tuberous vegetable like the potato and sweet potato. Outside India, it also goes by such names as *cassava* and *manioc*. *Manihot esculenta* is unknown in the wild state, but maximum diversity has been noted in north-east Brazil and west and south Mexico.[2i] It could have been a descendant from several related *Manihot* species, with much crossing-out at all stages with wild forms. Even as far back as 3000 BC, tapioca flour was an important commodity for trade in the northwest part of South America.[2i]

The crop is stated to have come into India about 1800.[2i] It may have come in much earlier from Africa, to which it went with slaves from Brazil,[31] or from the Philippines to Assam and Bengal. Perhaps there was more than one point of early entry.[32] About a century ago, following widespread distress after a famine, the ruler of Trāvancore, Vaishakam Thirunāl (1880–85), investigated several plants that would provide food and be an insurance against a similar eventuality in the future. The tapioca could be grown in every backyard and kept in the ground until required, and the ruler personally conducted demonstrations of how the bitter principles could be leached out from the tuber before use. All tapioca tubers contain these bitter cyanogenic compounds, but the degree of bitterness seems to be determined by several factors.[9e,21b] Long-duration varieties tend to be bitter; for this very reason they are chosen for production of industrial tapioca starch, since the plants can be left untended in forest areas without danger of animal depredation. Moisture stress, and the location in which raised, also influence the development of bitter compounds. The Second World War gave a great impetus to tapioca production,[9e] but the rice revolution of recent years has caused a distinct decline in its consumption in Kērala. Tapioca tubers, unlike common cereals, are poor in protein; it is therefore fortunate that they are eaten together with fish in Kērala.

Pleasurable Foods

The entry of the chilli added so enormously to Indian culinary practice that it is difficult to believe that it has not always been with us. Tea, coffee and cocoa are also today commonplace items in the diet that add greatly to the joy of living.

Chilli

Writing in 1563, the famous botanist and doctor Garcia da Orta (Chapter 13) does not mention the chilli, and not a single recipe of over fifty given in the *Ain-i-Akbari* of 1590 uses anything except black pepper to impart pungency. In fact once it came in, words for the chilli in many Indian languages were simple extensions of those for black pepper. Hindi has kālimirch and harimirch, Tamil milagu and milagāi (milagu-kāyi), and Kannada harimenasu and mensinkāyi.

The chilli must have entered India very early, because the great south Indian composer Purandaradāsa, who lived between 1480 and 1564, was well aware of its qualities: 'I saw you green, then turning redder as you ripened, nice to look at and tasty in a dish, but too hot if an excess is used. Saviour of the poor, enhancer of good food, fiery when bitten, even to think of (the deity) Pānduranga Vittalā is difficult.'[33] In course of time, the pepper of India and the chilli of Mexico seem to have influenced even the names by which they were called in the land to which they went. In 1604, D' Acosta quotes Grimston on Indian pepper: 'In the language of Cuzco it is called Vchu, and in that of Mexico chili', and Bontius in 1631 refers to it as Piper e Chile.[12e] The name axi for the chilli is mentioned even in 1494 by Chanca, the physician who accompanied Columbus on his second voyage. In 1750 Rumphius notes that it is written 'axi or achi, hence comes the Indian name 'achār' for pickles'.[5g] Commonly however a Persian or Arabic derivation is given for achār.[12h]

The chilli entered India in all its diverse forms. These belong to four or five species of *Capsicum*, each domesticated in various regions of South America, or in Mexico.[2j] Except for *C. pubescens*, the others cross easily, and *Capsicum annuum*, domesticated in Mexico, is the main form.[2j] It has been found wild even in 5000 BC layers in Tehuacan, Mexico, and in domesticated form slightly later. Cultivated *C. baccatum* appears in Peru by 2000 BC, and *C. pubescens* in later dates on the coast, suggesting independent domestication from different wild species, with selection for fruit size and/or pungency. The sweet capsicum types were known early, but only assumed importance as vegetables in recent

Green chillies

Capsicum or bell pepper, one of the forms of *Capsicum annuum*.

times.[2j] Other types of chilli are the tiny and very pungent bird chilli (so called because birds play a large part in seed dispersal), the common bright-red, thin-walled form (ground also to chilli powder), the green chilli, the red pimento and the very pungent Irish chilli used to make Tabasco sauce.

The chilli was avidly received in India. It could be grown all over the country, unlike pepper, and even in every backyard, with a versatility much greater than that of pepper.[32] Perhaps the physical resemblance of the chilli pod to that of long pepper[66] may have hastened its acceptance. Here was a classic case of a new product eminently meeting a felt need.

Tea

Tea is indubitably Chinese, and both the words teh and cha are of Chinese origin. Cultivation has been practised for 2000 years, and at first the wild leaves were probably eaten as a vegetable.[34] Brewing is described in a Chinese book of AD 220–65. The leaves were made into cakes, with rice added as a binder for older leaves; the cakes were then baked to remove the green

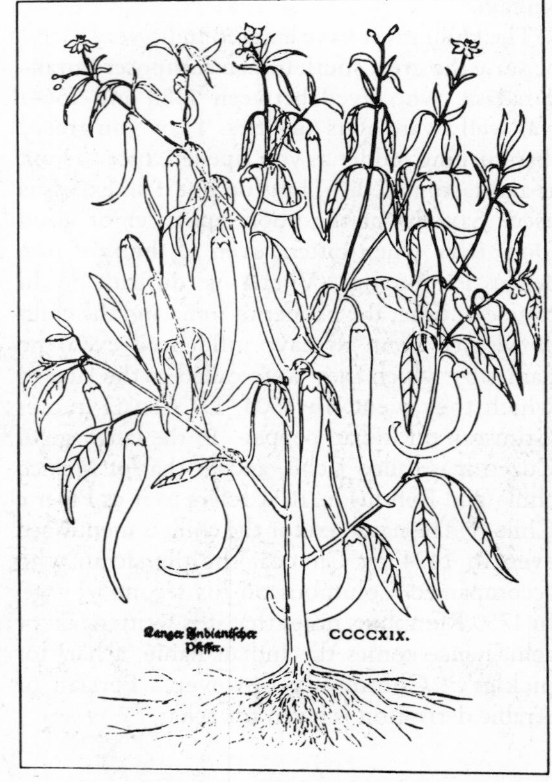

An early woodcut showing long pepper.

odour, and pieces were broken off for brewing. A Chinese book on tea was written in the 7th century,[34] and I-Ching, the Chinese traveller to India, describes the tea brew. In India, the semi-medicinal use of tea brew is noted even in 1662 by Mendelslo:

'At our ordinary meetings every day we took only thay, which is commonly used all over the Indies, not only among those of the country, but also among the Dutch and the English, who take it as a drug that cleanses the stomach, and digests the superfluous humours, by a temperate heat particular thereto.[5h]

In 1689 Ovington records that tea was taken by the baniās in Sūrat without sugar, or mixed with a small quantity of conserved lemons, and that tea with some spices added was used against headache, gravel and gripe.[35] The tea leaves for such use presumably came from China.

There are two major forms of tea, *Camellia sinensis* var. sinensis, a Chinese variety with small leaves, and var. assamica, tree-like and with large leaves.[2k] There are three other minor types. Darjeeling tea may have some introgression of *C.irrawadiensis*, and Sri Lankan tea of *C.assamica* subsp. *lasiocalyx*.

Tea had its origin perhaps in the lower Tibetan mountains. A major secondary centre lay near the source of the river Irrawaddy, from which three routes gave the three important types of tea, those of China, Assam and Cambodia.[2k]

In 1830, when commercial tea-planting in India was proposed by the British, plants were first brought in from China, and did badly. A few years earlier, Major Charles Bruce had reported that he had seen tea plants with thicker leaves growing in Assam, and these, when planted, responded very well. The same plants had long been cultivated by the Singphos tribe of Assam, and chests of tea supplied by the tribal ruler Ningroola, and those grown on British plantations, were enthusiastically received and well-paid-for at a London tea auction. By 1864, £3 million worth of Indian tea was auctioned at London's Mincing Lane and in 1875 £26 million.[36] Tea plantations sprang up all over Assam, the first and largest being the Assam Company of 1840, followed by several estates in Darjeeling (1853). Parallel with these developments, Christie and Crewe experimented with growing tea in Ootacamund at the Ketti Experimental Farm, and 'by 1839, tea was reported as growing luxuriously in the Nīlgiris,' the first plantation being one by Mann near Coonoor.[37] Sri Lanka, where coffee plantations had been wiped out by fungal disease by 1887, was 'saved from absolute bankruptcy by the substitution of tea for coffee'.[5i]

Coffee

The coffee plant may have evolved in Ethiopia, and at first perhaps only the leaves were chewed.[21] From Ethiopia it travelled to Yemen in Saudi Arabia, where the first plantation came up in the 14th or 15th century. The bean seems to have reached India even earlier, because in 1616–19 Terry wrote that

many of the people who are strict in their religion use no wine at all. They use a liquor more healthful than pleasant they call cohha: a black seed boiled in water, which doth little alter the taste of the water. Notwithstanding, it is very good to help digestion, to quicken the spirits and to cleanse the blood.[38]

Coffee berries.

Plucking of coffee berries.

In 1662 Mandelslo wrote: 'The Persians instead of thay (tea) drink their kahwah' (the original Arabic term for the brew).[5h] About 1700 Alexander Hamilton records an invitation from the Nawab of Tattāh (in Sindh) 'to take a dish of coffee with him'.[35]

At first coffee was grown only in Arabia and Ethiopia, and the Arab traders transported seeds from the ports of Hormuz and Bassora. In the 17th century seeds or plants were carried from Saudi Arabia all over southern Asia and even to South America.[21] Arabs had introduced coffee planting in Sri Lanka even before the Dutch invasion in 1665. In that same year a coffee plantation is recorded in south India, though berry quality was stated to be inferior.[39] About 1720, a Muslim divine called Bābā Budān returned from a pilgrimage to Mecca with seven coffee seeds; these he planted outside his cave in the Chikmaglūr hills, where the descendants of the original plants can still be seen. From about 1830, a rapid development of coffee estates occurred, led by Cannon in Chikmaglūr and Cockburn in the Shevaroy Hills, and shortly thereafter also in the Nīlgiris.[40]

The two main species of coffee are *Coffea arabica* (a tetraploid) and *C.camephora*. A mutation induced in the latter (a diploid) using colchicine yielded the tetraploid called *C.robusta*, which is sturdier but yields a brew that has less flavour than *arabica*. Crosses between them, called arabusta, imbibe the best from both parents.

At the start of the twentieth century, tablets of coffee powder were available in Indian villages. These were added to boiling water to give the brew, which was then allowed to settle and drunk with jaggery and sugar.[41]

Cocoa

Both the terms cacao (later smoothened in Europe to cocoa) and chocolate derive from words in the Maya language of South America.[2m] While the equatorial slopes of the

Andes were home to *Theobroma cacao*, the centre of cultivation, about 2000 years ago, was undoubtedly Central America. Three types of beans are recognized in the trade. Criollo are large, plump beans, round in cross-section, with no astringency in the roasted powder; however, the tree is not hardy, and the yields of pods are low. Forestero is now the major variety, the tree being hardy and high-yielding, and the flattened beans providing an astringent roasted product. The third variety of cocoa has a crossed ancestry: tree characteristics are variable, but the beans yield a 'fine' cocoa.[2m] Early in the 20th century, attempts to grow the cocoa tree in India met with failure because the Criollo variety that had been selected was the wrong choice.[9f] In the last two decades, Forestero cocoa has established itself well in Karnātaka, Kērala and Tamil Nādu, encouraged by organizations which buy the beans to produce cocoa products like chocolate.

It was the Spanish conquistador Hernando Cortez who noticed that the Mexican emperor Montezuma drank fifty glasses every day of a drink called xaocatl. Cortes himself liked it so much that he took some of the beans with him to the West Indies, from where they later reached Africa. The Spaniards improved the taste of the drink made from ground cocoa pods by adding sugar and hot water to it. The next step was taken by a Dutch chemist who pressed out some of the fat from the beans, and used the cocoa powder, which is now called drinking chocolate, for beverage-making. Mixing the pressed fat with a paste of ground beans and sugar was found to yield a solid mass of chocolate, and the Swiss added condensed milk to the mix to yield a tasty milk chocolate. Slow grinding of the beans for long periods in special conical pestle-and-mortar machines called conches produces chocolate that is smooth on the tongue and has a full, rich flavour.[42]

Some plant puzzles

There is little doubt regarding the New World origins of the food materials we have just discussed. There are a few instances however, where, despite an indubitable origin in South America or Mexico, there is some evidence that suggests a transfer to the Old World before the contacts of the 16th century were established. In one instance, in fact, that of the domestic chicken (Box 32), a reverse migration from the Old to the New World appears to have occurred.

Maize

The Tehuacan valley caves of Mexico have furnished evidence for the continuous evolution of maize from 6000 BC to 4000 BC from a prehistoric grass to a stage where the plants carried pods two centimetres long, which thereafter increased both in pod size and productivity.[43] The ancestor is now believed to have been a perennial wild grain, teosinte (*Zea mexicana*) which hybridized with *diploperennis*, another perennial teosinte, about 4000 years ago to trigger off an explosive evolution that led to *Zea mays* as a cultivated plant.[44,45] Each of the many forms of corn, sometimes stated to number seven,[17b] was associated with an ancient culture, like the Mayan, Aztec, Inca or Chibehan.[2n]

However there is some puzzling evidence regarding maize in India in pre-Columban times. Very primitive forms of maize have been found in hilly Sikkim,[46] and carefully studied by many experts. They have been classified into 15 races: the question naturally arises as to how so many forms with innumerable local names could have arisen in just 400 years from a single genetic source introduced from the New World.[47] A second finding is that of a potsherd dated 1435 from Kaundinyapūr in Madhya Pradesh which bears an impression on the clay strikingly akin to that of a maize cob with its orderly arrangement of grains. Again, pollen grains from sites in the Kāshmir Valley of a very early date have been identified as those of maize. Finally the temple of Somnathpur, just outside Mysore city, built in the 12th century AD, shows 92 female figures holding, in their right hands, an object that looks remarkably like a corn cob. A European scientist has stated recently that he is quite positive that they represent heads of maize, some even being shown covered with a silky tassel at the apex.[48] On the other hand, it has been argued that the same object is found in a Rājasthān idol of about AD 800, and that it represents a Jain religious item or symbol of which we are unaware.[49] The word markataka of early Sanskrit is not a forerunner of the modern makki, as has sometimes been surmised, but stands for the rāgi grain, while the term makkiyānāh used in a grant of King Indrapālā found in Guwahati has been identified with makhāna or *Euryale ferox*,[50] a prickly aquatic herb of the region, whose seeds are roasted and eaten.[1d]

It has been pointed out that the botanical tribe Maydeae has two branches.[2n] New World species like maize and teosinte have 2n = 20 and a rather similar chromosome morphology, whereas the Old World species like *Coix* (Job's

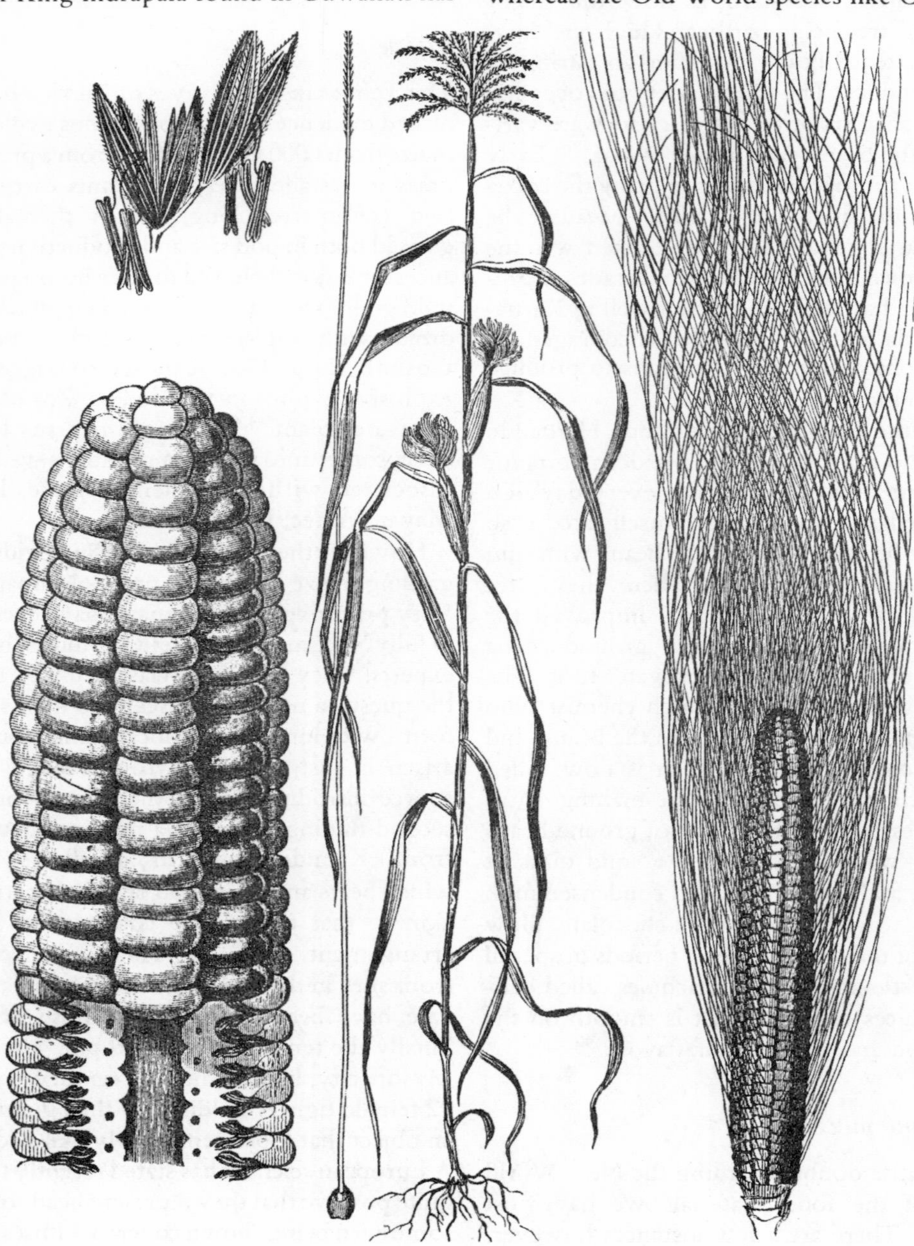

Botanical drawing of a maize plant.

tears) and *Sorghum* which have x = 5 may have given rise to x = 10 plants by amphidiploidy. It is even speculated that both the Old World and the New World tribes arose from more than one very ancient ancestor. In fact, *Coix* species even have knobbed chromosomes that look like those of maize, so an independent evolution of maize in the hilly Himālayan north-east is not a genetic impossibility.

Pineapple

Wild species of *Ananas cosmosus* reported in Brazil, Trinidad and Venezuela may only represent escapes from cultivation, and the development of the pineapple has been variously assigned to the Tupi-Guarani Indians in the Parana-Paraguay basin, or more generally in the lowlands of South America.[20] It was first seen by Columbus on Monday November 4, 1493 on his second voyage, in a West Indian island that he christened Guadeloupe.[51] The Tupi Indian name was nana, and a Huguenot clergyman in Brazil first used the term ananas in print.[51] The word pineapple derives from its remarkable resemblance to the cone of the large stone-pine of southern Europe, and in fact the word pine-apple was in use in English for this pine cone long before the discovery of America.[12f] While called anānas in most Indian languages, it is called poruthi-chakka or the Portuguese jackfruit in Malayalam,[13b] because of a resemblance in size and perhaps flavour between the two fruits.

By 1564 the fruit is described in India, nearly a hundred years before it was seen in England, and in 1616 Edward Terry describes its 'taste to be a pleasing compound, made of strawberries, claret-wine, rose-water and sugar, well-tempered together'.[12f] *The Ain-i-Akbari* of 1590 quotes the price of a pineapple as 4 dams each, an amount that could then buy ten mangoes.[52] A decade later, Jahangīr calls it a fruit of the 'European ports' in India, but adds that 'many thousands' were being grown in the royal plantations in Āgra.[53a]

Despite its undoubted South American origin, there is some evidence of its presence in Europe during the pre-Columban period.[20] In

A goddess holding a maize head (?).

1837 Williamson found numerous products from India in Egyptian tombs; and among them were glazed pottery models of the pineapple.[51] In the Assyrian ruins of Nineveh are to be found carvings of various foods served at a banquet; of one of these Rawlinson says: 'The representation is so exact that I can scarcely doubt the pineapple being intended. Mr. Layard expresses himself

Box 32

EARLY ANIMAL TRANSFERS

The domestic dog attached itself to man fifteen thousand years ago and has followed him all over the world. Terracotta models of dogs found in Indus Valley archaeological finds are of several types: they resemble the terrier, the mastiff and the nondescript pariah dog of present times.

The Indian wild fowl is native to a wide region all the way from Kāshmīr to Kampuchea, with its centre of origin perhaps in the Malaysian land mass.[5j] It has been suggested that this bird was originally domesticated not as a source of meat or eggs, but to increase its availability for purposes of divination. This entailed examination of the entrails or the perforations of the thigh bone, practices that are still prevalent in parts of south-east Asia.[31] The use of cocks for fighting against bets, even now a common sport in Asia, may have been another reason. Perhaps because the fowl is a scavenger (although there must also have been other reasons), its meat frequently found a place on many lists of foods prohibited for Hindus (see Chapters 5 and 6). Even Akbar's inventory of permitted edible animals, which includes the goose, duck, heron and bustard, omits the chicken.[52]

Perhaps as a result of such prohibitions, few definite breeds were evolved in India. The red jungle fowl inhabited the jungles of northern and south-eastern India, and the grey variety those of the west and the south. Only three more or less pure breeds are recognized.[9g] The Aseel, characterized by its valiant fighting qualities, has a scantily-feathered back. The Chittagong, golden in colour, has only scarce plumage at the breast bone. The Ghagus comes in many colours and has a typical baggy neck. All these are notably large birds, which are specially a matter of comment by several early British writers. Hove, in his *Travels in Gujarāt* (1787) says: 'Some of them are so large that they are often mistaken by strangers for turkeys . . . they breed them now about Surat in abundance.[5k] Francois Bernier (1668) also describes 'a small hen, delicate and tender, which I call Ethiopian, the skin being quite black,' and other writers call these Sooty or Nigger Fowls.[5k] While this breed has mostly vanished, it still apparently persists in the Jhabua district of Madhya Pradesh, being called kāli-māsi by the local tribals, and recently renamed kadaknath by a District Collector.[54]

Despite the acknowledged Old World origin of the domestic fowl, it seems to have reached South America long before Columbus. The explorer Magellan, the first European to reach the south coast of Brazil in 1519, describes how he laid in there a supply of chickens on board.[55] Henry Cabot's sailors did the same seven years later. We have here another puzzle of species transfer, though in the opposite direction from several others described in this chapter.

The turkey is a New World domesticate, derived from wild turkeys in Mexico long before the Spaniards reached there.[31] When the bird reached England, the name turkey was given to it in error for the pea fowl, then called the Turkey cock. The present Tamil name for the turkey is vān-kōzhi; yet this word first occurs in the *Mūlūrai* of the 12th century AD. Was an existing word simply transferred to the exotic arrival?

on this point with some hesitation.'[12f] In Pompeii, which was destroyed in AD 70 by volcanic eruption, the reproduction of a fruit on a mural '. . . is most certainly based on a pineapple.' Surprisingly, this is a statement by E. D. Merrill, who has otherwise strong views against the transfer of any food plant from the New to the Old World before 1492 (see Box 33).[56]

Sitāphal and rāmphal

The *Annona* family certainly derive from Peru and Ecuador, but have long been introduced into Mexico.[2d] They are generally understood to have come into India from the West Indies by way of the Cape of Good Hope,[12g] the various fruit forms now being called sharīfā (meaning noble fruit) or sītāphal (*A.squamosa*, the custard apple); rāmphal (*A.reticulata*, which in the West Indies is called the custard apple); hanumānphal or lakshmanphal (*A.cherimola*); and the very large prickly custard apple, *A. muricata*. The first description in India of this fruit type by a westerner is that by P. Vincenzo Maria in 1672: 'The pulp is very white, tender, delicate, and so delicious that it unites to agreeable sweetness a most delightful fragrance like rosewater . . . if presented to one unacquainted with it he would certainly take it for blancmange.'[12g] The word sadāphal of the *Ain-i-Akbari*, which Blochmann translated as custard apple, means only a perennial fruit,[12g] and was employed earlier by Bābar for a citrus fruit.[53c]

The argument for an earlier presence in India of this fruit type, arises from certain facts. Firstly, the sculptures of Bhārhūt (2nd century BC) and the fresco paintings of Ajantā (about the 7th century AD) show a fruit very like the custard apple though Watt is of the opinion that these could be conventionalized representations of the jackfruit or the flowerhead of the kadamba (*Anthocephalus cadamba*). Secondly, it has been

Sitāphal on the tree.

Box 33

REACHING AMERICA BEFORE COLUMBUS

Merrill has stated in the most emphatic terms that 'not a single basic food plant is common to both hemispheres before 1492.'[56] Yet Merrill himself admitted the possibility with regard to the pineapple (see text). Speaking of maize Mangelsdorf states: 'Perhaps there has indeed been a pre-Columban trans-Pacific migration of culture and ... maize has been involved in it;'[57] Yet he maintains categorically that there is no tangible evidence of it whatsoever (see text). Is there any evidence of it outside the area of food plants? After all man himself entered the New World by way of land bridges that once existed at the point where the Bering Strait now separates it from the land mass of the Old World.

Some Indus Valley seals have an animal figure that is remarkably akin to the Peruvian llama, found nowhere else in the world. *Sūrya Siddhānta*, the ancient Sanskrit text on astronomy, describes a land mass Pātaladēsa positioned where South America is. Bhāskarāchārya in the 12th century AD mentions four time zones marked by four equidistant cities on the globe, one of which is Siddāpūra which falls in South America.[58] The Harappan script appears to resemble that of Easter Island (see Chapter 1).[58] The feats of navigation of the Micronesians, who live on islands north of Australia, carried them across the enormous stretch of the Pacific ocean 6000 years ago. They even reached Hawaii and Easter Island,[59] and have been termed the Vikings of the Pacific.[6c] The first European explorers in Melanesia found the inhabitants using sweet potatoes, native to South America, and a number of root and tree cultigens derived from the Indo-Malaysian region, besides, of course, the fowl and the pig.[61a]

Two books have brought together a wealth of material in regard to the India-South America connection.[62,63] Words in common between Sanskrit and the Arya language of Peru were noted in Chapter 1, in respect of food, but there are others. The game of chaupad or pachīsī was played identically and called patolli; the Mexican word for a boat was the Tamil catamarān. The lotus motive interspersed with seated human figures, used for example in the Buddhist structure at Amarāvati in Āndhra Pradesh, is to be seen at Chichan-Itza in Mexico. Indian gods figure in sculpture: Shiva, and Ganesha with his rat, in Inca mythology; a Ganesha figure in the temple of Diego Rivera in Mexico city; a Shiva linga in Vera Cruzi, Mexico; Vishnu's tortoise kūrma in the museum of Quiragua in Guatemala; and the Vāman dwarf incarnation of Vishnu in Mexico. Elephants are not found in the New World, yet two elephant heads with typical Indian ceremonial trappings are to be seen in the ruined Mayan city of Copcan in Honduras, with mahouts wearing wound Indian turbans. A portrait of the last Inca ruler shows him wearing a turban, with a lotus flower crowning his sceptre. The Ayar Inca of Peru (the word itself resembles Ārya) wore a sacred thread as Indian brāhmins do, practised ear-piercing and youth-initiation, and had a caste system. There are traditions of extensive sea voyages and distant ancestral homelands among the Polynesians, Maoris, Incas and Mayas. There is apparently in China a report of a Buddhist monk Harichand (called Hwui Shan in Chinese) who in the fifth century AD went to Mexico and returned to China where he wrote his story, which included sketches of Buddhist and Hindu temples in Mexico.[62, 63]

Box 33 (*contd.*)

Recently Dr. Barry Fell, President of the Epigraphical Society in San Diego, California found, in Tihosuco in the Yucatan Province of Mexico, an inscription written in the Kavi dialect of Java which evolved from the interaction of Sanskrit, Pāli and the local dialect. The inscription records that a merchant Vusaluna, captain of a ship, had made the inscription to record his visit as he explored the coastline in the year AD 923.[64,65] The mercantile town of Camalcalco, which lies across the Mexican isthmus on the other coast, was perhaps his eventual destination. This was 569 years before Columbus crossed the Atlantic from Europe, and even earlier contacts between the South American continent, the Pacific islands and the Indonesian islands do not seem so far-fetched. The transfer of yams, or of maize, or of certain pulses, is therefore less cause for surprise if the inscription is genuine.

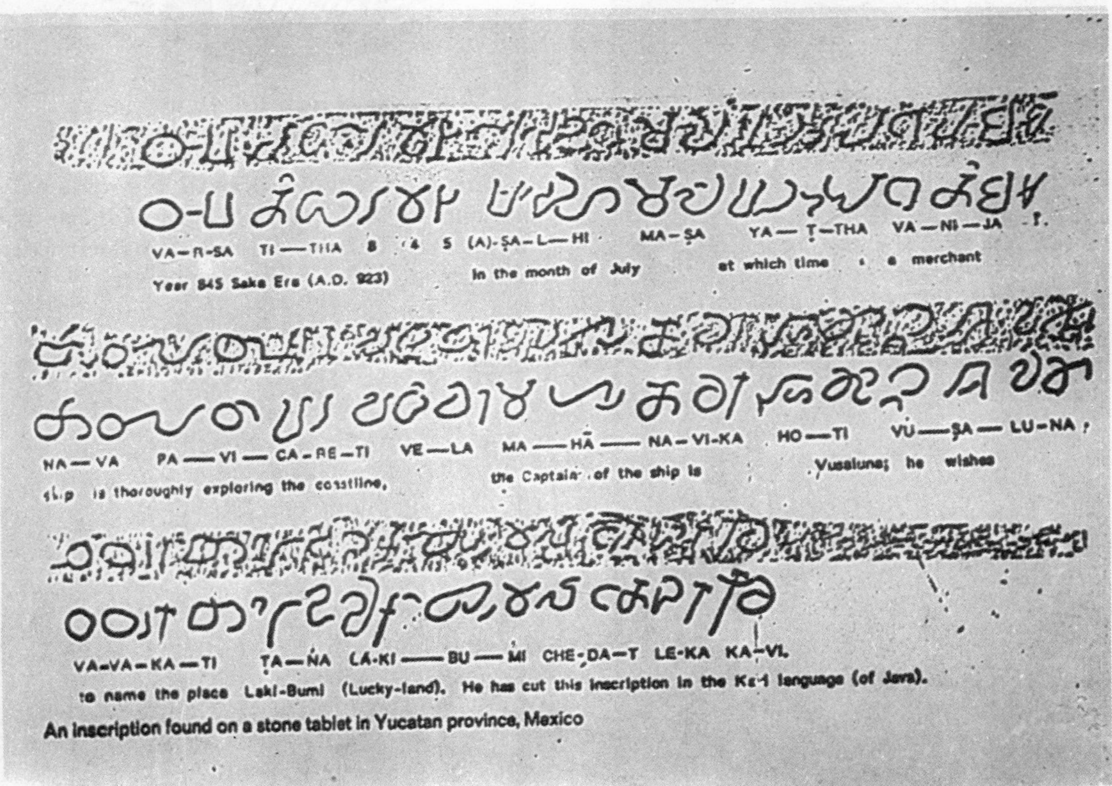

A stone inscription found in Mexico recording the visit of the Indian captain Vusaluna.

argued that the name ātā used for the fruit in certain parts of India has been derived from the Sanskrit ātripriya; however, this argument loses force against the realization that elsewhere in the world, for example in Manila, the sītāphal is called ata or atē, and that there is even a Mexican name até or ahaté.[12g] Sanskrit names are no doubt known for the fruits: the sītāphal is gan-

A sculpture from Bhārhūt showing what appears to be sītāphal fruit.

dagatra and the rāmphal lavali; but these only occur in an 1877 *Materia Medica* of India, and may perhaps be late acquisitions, no reference to earlier usage or derivation being given.[12g]

The rāmphal.

REFERENCES

Chapter 1: Ancestral Legacies

1. Praveen Kumar, *Indian Express*, 16 February 1988, *Science Express*, p. III.
2. *Encyclopaedia Britannica*, 15th edn, vol. 7, p. 1066 and vol. 5, p. 108.
3. V. R. Ramachandra Dikshitar, *Pre-historic South India* (1951), University of Madras, Cosmo Publications, New Delhi, repr. 1981, pp. 6–13.
4. G. H. Pelto and P. J. Pelto, *The Human Adventure: An Introduction to Human Anthropology*, Macmillan Publishing Co., New York, and Collier–Macmillan Publishers, London, 1976, (a) pp. 60–1 (b) p. 84.
5. S. Boyd Eaton and Melvin Konner, 'Palaeolithic nutrition', *The New England Journal of Medicine*, 1985, vol. 312, no. 5, p. 283.
6. S. P. Asthana, *History and Archaeology of India's Contacts with Foreign Countries*, B. R. Publishing Corporation, New Delhi, 1976, pp. 6–12.
7. H. D. Sankalia, 'The early palaeolithic in India and Pakistan', in Fumiko Ikawa-Smith (ed.), *Early Palaeolithic in South and South-East Asia*, Mouton Publishers, The Hague and Paris, 1978.
8. P. T. S. Iyengar, *The Stone Age in India* (1927), Asian Educational Services, New Delhi, repr. 1982, pp. 9, 30.
9. Mortimer Wheeler, *Early India and Pakistan* (1959), Thames and Hudson, London, revised edn 1968, p. 34f.
10. Stuart Piggott, *Prehistoric India* (1950), Penguin Books, Harmondsworth, UK, repr. 1952, p. 36f.
11. John Noble Wilford, 'The tales bones tell', repr. in *Frontline* 1988, vol. 5, no. 1, p. 86.
12. Manohar Malgonkar, 'Catching food', *Sunday Herald*, Bangalore, 1 October 1989, p. 7.
13. L. B. Jensen, *Man's Food*, The Gerrard Press, Champaign, Illinois, USA, 1953, p. 4.
14. H.D. Sankalia, in S. P. Gupta and K. S. Ramachandran (eds), *Aspects of Indian History and Archaeology*, B. R. Publishing Corporation, Delhi, 1977, p. 254.
15. H. D. Sankalia, *Stone Age Tools*, Deccan College, Poona, 1964, p. 86.
16. M. C. Burkitt, *The Old Stone Age*, Rupa and Co., Calcutta, 1963, repr. 1977, p. 65.
17. V. S. Wakankar and R. R. R. Brooks, *Stone Age Painting in India*, D. B. Taraporevala Sons and Co. Ltd., Bombay. 1976.
18. V. S. Wakankar, 'The oldest works of art?' *Science Today*, 1983, vol. 17, no. 3 (April), p. 43.
19. E. Neumayer, *Prehistoric Indian Rock Paintings*, Oxford University Press, Delhi, 1983, pp. 49–134.
20. Indras, 'Lost Saraswati', Registrar, Sardar Patel University, Vallabh Vidyanagar, Gujarat, 1967, p. 10.
21. George Watt, *The Commercial Products of India* (1908), Today and Tomorrow's Printers and Publishers, New Delhi, repr. 1966, (a) p. 518 (b) p. 496.
22. Oroon Kumar Ghosh, *The Changing Indian Civilisation*, South Asia Books in association with Minerva Associates (Publications) Pvt. Ltd., Calcutta, 1976, p. 319.
23. K. P. Chattopadhyaya, *The Ancient Indian Culture Contacts and Migrations*, Firma K. L. Mukhopadhyay, Calcutta, 1970, p. 91.
24. Mark Collins (ed.) (1919 and 1926), *Dravidic Studies*, University of Madras, Madras, repr. 1974, (a) S. Anavartavinayaka Pillai, 'The Sanskritic element in the vocabularies of the Dravidian languages', p. 81 (b) Mark Collins, 'Editorial remarks', p. 165.
25. Sankarananda Mukhopadhaya, *The Austrics of India*, K. P. Bagchi and Co., Calcutta, 1975.
26. Malati J. Shendge, *The Civilized Demons: The Harappans in Rigveda*, Abhinav Publications, New Delhi, 1977, p. 93.
27. L. V. Ramaswami Aiyar, 'Dravidic forms for betel leaf', *Journal of Oriental Research*, Madras, 1932, vol. 5, p. 1.
28. Suniti Kumar Chatterji, *Select Writings*, vol. 1, compiled by A. K. Kanjilal, Vikas Publishing House Pvt. Ltd., New Delhi, 1978, p. 61.
29. P. T. Srinivasa Aiyangar, *Pre-Aryan Tamil Culture*, Madras University, 1930, (a) p. 16 (b) p. 37 (c) p. 29 (d) p. 57 (e) p. 62.
30. G. P. Majumdar, *Some Aspects of Indian Civilization*, published by the author, Calcutta, 1938, p. 30.
31. R. C. Dutt, *A History of Civilization in Ancient India*, Kegan Paul, Trench, Trubner and Co. Ltd., London, 1893, vol. 2, p. 137.
32. K. M. Panikkar, *India and China*, Asia Publishing House, Bombay, 1957, p. 64.
33. Chin Kek-Mu, 'India and China: scientific exchange', in Debiprasad Chattopadhyaya (ed.), *Studies in the History of Science in India*, Editorial Enterprises, New Delhi, 1982, vol. 2, p. 776.
34. C. Gopalan, B. V. Ramasastri and S. C. Balasubrama-

nian. *Nutritive Value of Indian Foods,* National Institute of Nutrition, Hyderabad, 1978, (a) p. 156 (b) p. 151 (c) p. 163.

35. R. Shamasastry, *Kautilya's Arthashāstra,* Mysore Printing and Publishing House, Mysore, 8th edn, 1967, pp. 105, 135, 136 and 138.
36. Om Prakash, *Food and Drinks in Ancient India,* Munshi Ram Manohar Lal, Delhi, 1961, pp. 34–57.
37. Henry Yule and A. C. Burnell, *Hobson-Jobson* (1886), 2nd edn, William Crooke (ed.), 4th edn, repr. 1984, Munshiram Manoharlal Publishers Pvt. Ltd., New Delhi, (a) p. 553 (b) p. 440 (c) p. 448/9 (d) p. 894 (e) p. 89 (f) p. 35 (g) p. 446 (h) p. 281 (i) p. 221 (J) p. 477 (k) p. 595 (l) p. 927 (m) p. 737 (n) p. 36 (o) p. 392.
38. K. A. Nilakanta Sastri, *History and Culture of The Tamils,* Firma K. L. Mukhopadhyay, Calcuttta, 1964, p. 78.
39. Chaman Lal, *India, Cradle of Cultures,* Publisher Chaman Lal, Modern School, New Delhi, 1976.
40. Chaman Lal, *Hindu America,* Vishveshvaranand Vedic Research Institute, Hoshiarpur, 3rd edn, 1956, p. 220.
41. U.P. Upadhyaya and S. P. Upadhyaya, *Dravidian and Negro-African,* Rashtrakavi Govind Pai Research Institute, Udupi, 1983.
42. D. Bedigian and J. R. Harlan, 'Evidence for cultivation of sesame in the ancient world', *Economic Botany,* 1986, vol. 40, p. 137.
43. J. N. Wilford, 'A search for man's earliest lingo', *Science Times,* reproduced in the *Deccan Herald,* Bangalore, 3 March 1988, p. II.
44. R. Swaminatha Aiyar (1975), *Dravidian Theories,* Motilal Banarsidass, Delhi, repr. 1987.
45. E. J. Thomas, 'Buddha's last meal', *Indian Culture,* 1979, vol. 15, p. 1.
46. R. P. Kapleau, *A Buddhist Case for Vegetarians,* Rider and Co., London, 1983, p. 24.
47. D. D. Kosambi, *The Culture and Civilisation of Ancient India in Historical Outline,* Routledge and Kegan Paul, London, 1965, p. 111.

Chapter 2: Harappan Spread

1. Anon, 'Pre-Indus Valley findings at Ladakh', *The Hindustan Times,* Delhi, 31 March 1989.
2. Anon, 'Pakistan: home of the oldest civilization', *The Times of India,* Bangalore, 24 May 1987.
3. J. F. Jarrige and R. H. Meadow, *Scientific American* 1980, vol. 243, no. 2 (August), p. 102.
4. B. B. Lal and S. P. Gupta (eds), *Frontiers of the Indus Civilisation* (Sir Mortimer Wheeler commemoration volume), Books and Books, New Delhi, 1984, (a) K. S. Ramachandran, p. 539 (b) S. P. Gupta, p. 417 (c) E. D. Caspers, p. 363 (d) D. L. Heiskel, p. 333 (c) V. B. Mainkar, p. 121 (f) D. P. Agrawal, p. 163 (g) R. C. Agrawala, p. 157.
5. Mortimer Wheeler, *Early India and Pakistan,* Thames and Hudson, London, revised edn, 1968, p. 102.
6. D. P. Chattopadhyaya, *Religion and Society,* Ma-Le Publishers, Bangalore, 1987; two lectures on 'Science and society in ancient India', Central College, Bangalore, December 1985.
7. K. N. Dikshit, *Prehistoric Civilisation in the Indus Valley* (Sir William Meyer lectures) (1939), University of Madras, Madras, repr. 1973.
8. A. N. Khanna, *The Archaeology of India,* Clarion Books, New Delhi, 1981, pp. 62–9.
9. A. K. Bag, *Science and Civilisation in India: Harappan Period (c. 3000* BC *– c. 500* BC*),* Navrang, New Delhi, 1985, (a) p. 126 (quoting Mitchiner) (b) p. 45 (c) p. 99.
10. D. D. Kosambi, *An Introduction to The Study of Indian History,* Popular Prakashan, Bombay, 1956, 2nd edn. 1975, (a) p. 74 (b) p. 138 (c) p. 54 (d) p. 59 (c) p. 121.
11. B. B. Lal, 'The Harappan fall-out', *Science Age,* September 1985, p. 31.
12. G. L. Possehl, *Harappan Civilization,* Oxford and IBH Publishing Co. Pvt. Ltd., New Delhi, (a) Vishnu-Mittre and R. Savitri, *Food Economy of the Harappans,* p. 205 (b) B. K. Thapar, p. 3.
13. B. S. Padmanabhan, 'Projections of Harappa matrix', *The Hindu,* Madras, 24 July 1983; Anon, The *Indian Express,* Bangalore, 3 July 1983.
14. R. C. Gaur, *Excavations at Atranjikhera,* Motilal Banarsidass, Delhi, 1985; reviewed by H.D. Sankalia, *The Times of India,* 21 December 1986.
15. Archaeological Museum, M. S. University of Baroda, Vadodhara.
16. M. S. Vats, *Excavations at Harappa,* Manager of Publications, Delhi, 1940, vol. 1, p. 466.
17. Vishnu-Mittre, 'Palaeobotanical evidence in India', in J. B. Hutchinson (ed.), *Diversity and Change in the Indian Subcontinent,* Cambridge University Press, 1974, p. 3.
18. O. P. Jaggi, *Technology in Ancient India,* Atma Ram and Sons, Delhi, 1981, vol. 1, p. 89–95
19. M. S. Randhawa, *A History of Agriculture in India,* Indian Council of Agricultural Research, New Delhi, vol. 1, 1980, (a) p. 179 (b) pp. 195f (c) p. 169.
20. F. R. Allchin, in P. J. Ucko and G. W. Dimbleby (eds), *The Domestication and Exploitation of Plants and Animals,* Gerald Duckworth and Co. Pvt. Ltd. London, 1969, p. 323.
21. Indira Chakravarthy, *Saga of Indian Food,* Sterling Publishers Pvt. Ltd., New Delhi, 1972, pp. 8–9.
22. J. N. Kamalapur, 'The Aryan problem and domesticated animals', in *Studies in Indian History and Culture,* P. B. Desai commemoration volume, Karnatak Uni-

versity, Dharwar, 1971, p. 206.

23. A. L. Basham, *The Wonder that was India* (1954), Grove Press Inc., New York, repr. 1959, (a) p. 25 (b) p. 26 (c) p. 27 (d) p. 18.
24. L. B. Jensen, *Man's Food,* The Garrard Press, Champaign, Illinois, USA, 1953, p. 106.
25. R. E. Mortimer Wheeler, 'The civilisation of a subcontinent', in Stuart Piggott (ed.), *The Dawn of Civilisation,* Thames and Hudson, London, 1961, p. 229.
26. B. B. Lal, 'The world's earliest agricultural field', *Science Age,* Bombay, 1983, vol. 1, no. 3/4, October, p. 38
27. H. D. Sankalia, *Some Aspects of Prehistoric Technology in India,* Indian National Science Academy, New Delhi, 1970, (a) pp. 45–51 (b) p. 13.
28. R. J. Forbes, *Studies in Ancient Technology,* E. J. Brill, Leiden, 1965, vol. 2. p. 12.
29. *Prof. K. A. Nilakanta Sastri Felicitation Volume,* Felicitation Committee, Madras, 1971, (a) M. C. Joshi, 'An early inscriptional references to the Persian wheel', p. 214 (b) A. Sundara, 'New discoveries of ash mounds in Karnataka', p. 308.
30. Aniruddha Roy and S. K. Bagchi, *Technology in Ancient and Medieval India,* Sundeep Prakashan, Delhi, 1986, (a) Harbans Mukhia, 'Agricultural technology in medieval India', p. 107 (b) Iqbal Khan Ghani, 'Metallurgy in medieval India (16th to 18th centuries)', p. 71.
31. Lallanji Gopal, 'Agricultural technique in medieval India: its Central Asian contacts', in A. V. Narasimha Murthy and K.V. Ramesh (eds), *The G. S. Dikshit Felicitation Volume,* Agam Kala Prakashan, Delhi, 1987, p. 235.
32. Irfan Habib, 'Technological changes and society (13th and 14th centuries)', in Debiprasad Chattopadhyaya (ed.), *Studies in the History of Sciences in Ancient India,* Editorial Enterprises, New Delhi, 1982, p. 816.
33. M. S. Randhawa, 'Progressive desiccation of northern India in historic times', in J. C. Daniel (ed.), *A Century of Natural History,* Bombay Natural History Society, Bombay, 1983, p. 40.
34. Indras, 'Lost Saraswati', Registrar, Sardar Patel University, Vallabh Vidyanagar, Gujarat, 1967.
35. Dhammanarayana Das, *The Early History of Kalinga,* Punthi Pusthak, Calcutta, 1977.
36. H. K. Kaul, *Traveller's India: An Anthology,* Oxford University Press, India, 1979, p. 319.
37. Vishnu-Mittre, 'Climatic *versus* biotic factor: pollen evidence in the postglacial history of northwest India', in Asok K. Ghosh (ed.), *Perspectives in Palaeoanthropology,* Prof. D. Sen Festschrift, Firma K. L. Mukhopadhyay, 1974, p 25.
38. H. D. Sankalia, *Prehistoric and Historic Technology of Gujarat,* Munshiram Manoharlal Publishers Pvt. Ltd., New Delhi, 1987, pp. 39–54.
39. S. R. Rao, *Lothal: A Harappan Port-town,* Archaeological Survey of India, New Delhi, 1979, vol. 1, pp. 125–34.
40. G. S. Ghurye, *Vedic India,* Popular Prakashan, Bombay, 1979, (a) pp. 372–80 (b) pp. 399–400.
41. Radha Rastogi, 'The nān shops of Kabul', *The Times of India,* New Delhi, 8 December 1988.
42. V. Shankar Charry, ' Mlechas, meluha and the Indus Valley culture', *Sunday Herald,* Bangalore, 1 May 1988.
43. Shereen Ratnagar, *Encounters: The Westerly Trade of the Harappan Civilisation,* Oxford University Press, New Delhi, 1981.
44. Anikhet, 'The neglect of Lothal', *Sunday Herald,* Bangalore, 2 November 1986.
45. Ernst Mackay, 'Excavations at Chanhudaro: Season of 1935–6', Publ. 3473 of the Smithsonian Institute, Washington DC, USA, 1938.
46. G. L. Possehl, *Indus Civilization in Saurāshtra,* B. P. Publishing Corporation, Delhi, 1982, p. 19.
47. P. C. Kashyap, *Surviving Harappan Civilization,* Abhinav Publications, New Delhi. 1984.
48. S. R. Rao, *The Decipherment of the Indus Script,* Asia Publishing House, Bombay, 1982; *Presidential Address,* 7th Annual Congress of the Epigraphical Society of India, Calcutta, January 1981.
49. Saradha Srinivasan, *Mensuration in Ancient India,* Ajanta Publications (India), Delhi, 1979, p. 93.
50. Balaram Srivastava, 'Balances in ancient India', *Vishveshvaranand Indological Journal,* 1964, vol. 2, pt. i. p. 131; Vishveshvaranand Publication Series, no. 108.
51. Moin Qazi, 'The Indus metric system', *Science Express,* Bangalore, 23 May 1989.
52. Swami Shankarananda, *The Indus People Speak,* publisher Nilamoney Maharaj, Calcutta, 1955.
53. I. Mahadevan, 'The Indus scripts: texts, concordance, tables', *Memoirs of the Archaeological Survey of India, New Delhi,* 1977, no. 77.
54. B. V. Subbarayappa, 'Indus script: The womb of numbers', *Quarterly Journal of the Mythic Society,* Bangalore, 1987, vol. 78, 1/2.
55. N. M. Billimoria, *Annals of the Bhandarkar Oriental Research Institute,* 1940, vol. 18, p. 262.
56. A. Metraux, 'Easter Island', *Report of the Smithsonian Institute,* Washington DC, 1944, p. 435; separate reprint, publ. no. 3795, 1944.
57. Gunekar Muley, 'India's gift to the world', *Swagat,* Indian Airlines, May 1987, p. 69.
58. Mark Collins, 'On the octaval system of reckoning in India', in Mark Collins (ed.), *Dravidian Studies* (2 vols, 1919 and 1926), repr. as one volume, University of Madras, 1974, p. 199.
59. Mrinalini Sarpotdar, 'Copper-bronze metallurgy', *Science Express,* Bangalore, 27 December 1988.
60. D. P. Agrawal and A. Ghosh (eds), *Radiocarbon and Indian Archaeology,* Tata Institute of Fundamental Research, Bombay, 1973, (a) K.T. M. Hegde, 'Early stages of metallurgy in India', p. 401 (b) H. C. Bhardwaj, 'Aspects of early iron technology in India', p. 391.
61. F. R. Allchin, *Neolithic Cattle-keepers of South India,*

Cambridge University Press, 1963.

62. Ravindra N. Singh, 'Ancient south Indian metallurgy', *Shraddanjali* (D. C. Sircar commemoration volume), Sundeep Prakashan, Delhi, 1988, p. 189.

63. K. T. M. Hegde, 'How zinc was made in ancient India', *Science Today,* Bombay, 1986, vol. 20, no. 2, February, p. 42.

Chapter 3: Foods for the Gods

1. G. M. Kongard-Levin, *The Origin of the Aryans*, trans. H. C. Gupta, Arnold Heinemann, New Delhi, 1980.
2. A. L. Basham, *The Wonder that was India* (1954), Grove Press, Inc., New York, repr. 1959, p. 29.
3. F. E. Pargiter, *Ancient Indian Historical Tradition* (1922), Motilal Banarsidas, Delhi, repr. 1972, pp. 297–325.
4. G. S. Ghurye, *Vedic India,* Popular Prakashan, Bombay, 1979, (a) p. 368 (b) p. 383.
5. D. D. Kosambi, *An Introduction to the Study of Indian History* (1956), Popular Prakashan, Bombay, 2nd edn, 1975, (a) p. 74 (b) p. 85 (c) p. 71 (d) p. 127.
6. A. N. Chandra, 'Survival of the prehistoric civilisation of the Indus Valley', *Memoirs of the Archaeological Survey of India,* 1929, no. 41.
7. P. T. Srinivasa Iyenagar, *Life in Ancient India* (1912), Asian Educational Services, New Delhi, repr. 1982.
8. P. L. Bhargava, *India in the Vedic Age,* Upper India Publishing House Pvt. Ltd., Lucknow, 2nd edn, 1971, (a) chap 2, p. 80f (b) chap. 3.
9. Harbans Mukhia, 'Agricultural technology in medieval India', in Aniruddha Roy and S. K. Bagchi (eds), *Technology in Ancient and Medieval India,* Sundeep Prakashan, Delhi, 1986, p. 107.
10. S. Paranavitana, 'Ploughing as a ritual of consecration in ancient Ceylon', in Himansu Basu Sarkar (ed.), *R. C. Majumdar Commemoration Volume,* Firma K. L. Mukhopadhyay, Calcutta, 1970, p. 31.
11. Jeannine Auboyer, *Daily Life in Ancient Inda,* Asia Publishing House, Bombay, 1965, (a) p. 63f (b) p. 98.
12. S. P. Raychaudhuri, *Agriculture in Ancient India,* Indian Council of Agricultural Research, New Delhi, 1964, (a) p. 17 (b) p. 59 (c) p. 84 (d) p. 133 (e) p. 44 (f) p. 100 (g) p. 81 (h) p. 79.
13. Lallanji Gopal, *Aspects of the History of Agriculture in Ancient India,* Bharati Prakashan, Varanasi, 1980, (a) p. 90 (b) p. 42.
14. M. Ramakrishna Bhat, *Varāhamihira's Brhat Samhitā, Part 1,* Motilal Banarsidass, Delhi, 1981, repr. 1986, p. 527f.
15. R. Shamasastry, *Kautilya's Arthashāstra,* Mysore Printing and Publishing House, Mysore, 8th edn, 1967, (a) pp. 129–31 (b) p. 104 (c) p. 89.
16. S. P. Raychudhuri, 'A short account of agricultural methods practised in ancient India', *Science and Culture,* Calcutta, vol. 7, no. 1, p. 10.
17. F. Max Mueller, *The Upanishads,* Dover Publications Inc., New York, vol. 1, sixth adhyaya, p. 214f.
18. Debiprasad Chattopadhyaya (ed.), *Studies in the History of Science in India,* Editorial Enterprises, New Delhi, 1982, vol. 1, (a) G. P. Majumdar, 'The history of botany and allied sciences', p. 365 (b) G. N. Mukhopadhyay, 'On the medical authorities', p. 73.
19. Om Prakash, *Food and Drinks in Ancient India,* Munshi Ram Manohar Lal, Delhi, 1961, (a) Vedic period, pp. 7– 33 (b) Sūtra period, pp. 34–57 (c) Early Buddhist and Jain period, pp. 58–86 (d) Maurya-Sunga period, pp. 87–101 (e) Epics and *Manusmriti,* pp. 168–202 (h) Post-Gupta period, pp. 203–39.
20. V. M. Apte, 'Vedic rituals', in *The Culturat Heritage of India,* The Ramakrishna Mission Institute of Culture, Calcutta, 1958, 2nd edn, vol. 1, p. 234.
21. P. K. Gode, 'Indian dietetics : Use of fried grains', Annals of the Bhandarkar Oriental Research Institute, 1948, vol. 29, p. 43.
22. M. A. Buch, *Economic Life in Ancient India,* R. S. Publishing House, Allahabad, 1979, vol. 1, p. 90.
23. Indira Chakravarthy, *Saga of Indian Food,* Sterling Publishers Pvt. Ltd., New Delhi, 1972, p. 13.
24. Doris Srinivasan, *Concept of Cow in the Rigveda,* Motilal Banarsidass, Delhi, 1979, p. 4.
25. D. Bedigian and J. R. Harlan, 'Evidence for cultivation of sesame in the ancient world', *Economic Botany* 1986, vol. 40, p. 137.
26. A. M. Shastri, *India as seen in the Brhat Samhitā of Varāhamihira,* Motilal Banarsidass, Delhi, 1969, pp. 209–16.
27. T. Burrow and M. B. Emeneau, *A Dravidian Etymological Dictionary,* Clarendon Press, Oxford, 1961, p. 161.
28. K. L. Mehra, *Advancing Frontiers of Plant Sicences,* 1968, vol. 19, p. 51.
29. Oroon Kumar Ghosh, *The Changing Indian Civilisation,* South Asia Books in association with Minerva Associates (Publications) Pvt. Ltd., Calcutta, 1976, p. 324.
30. Malini Bisen, *Indian Sweet Delights,* Wilco Publishing House, Bombay, 1981, p. xiii.
31. Padmini Sengupta, *Everyday Life in Ancient India,* Oxford University Press, Indian Branch, 1950, p. 547.
32. V. A. Sanghave, *Jaina Community: A Social Survey,* Popular Prakashan, Bombay, 1980, pp. 258–60.
33. T. J. Shejwalkar, 'The Mahābhārata data for Aryan expansion in India', in V. M. Apte and H. D. Sankalia (eds), the *V. S. Sukhthankar Memorial Volume,* Decan College, Poona, 1944, p. 401.
34. S. B. Roy, *Ancient India,* Institute of Chronology, New Delhi, 1976.
35. John Dowson, *A Classical Dictionary of Hindu Mythology and Religion,* Kegan Paul, Trench, Trubner and Co. Ltd., London, 6th edn, 1928, (a) pp. ix–xv (b) p. 228 (c)

p. 301 and p. 344.
36. K. P. Chattopadhyaya, *The Ancient Indian Culture Contacts and Migrations*, Firma K. L. Mukhopadhyay, Calcutta, 1970.
37. R. C. Majumdar, *Ancient India*, Motilal Banarsidas, Delhi, 8th edn, 1977, pp. 178–82.
38. *The Wealth of India: Raw Materials*, Council of Scientific and Industrial Research, New Delhi, (a) vol. 9, p. 235 (b) vol. 1, p. 131 (c) vol. 3, p. 177.
39. J. C. Ray, 'Soma plant', *Indian Historical Quarterly* 1959, vol. 15, no. 2.
40. R. G. Wasson, *Soma, the Divine Mushroom*, Harcourt Brace and World, New York, 1968.
41. M. H. Ladler, 'Soma and psyche', *British Medical Journal*, 1983, vol. 287, no. 6409, p. 1906.

CHAPTER 4: THE FOODS OF SOUTH INDIA

1 H Kuno *The Times of India*, Bombay, 20 December 1964.
2. Shashi Prabha Asthana, *History and Archaeology of India's Contacts with Foreign Countries*, B. R. Publishing Corporation, Delhi, 1976, (a) pp. 6–14 (b) pp. 71–112.
3. Burton Stein, *Essays on South India*, Vikas Publishing House Pvt. Ltd., India, 1975, (a) Clarence Moloney, 'Archaeology in south India : accomplishments and prospects', p. 1 (b) G. L. Hart, 'Ancient Tamil literature : its scholarly past and future', p. 41.
4. D. D. Kosambi, *The Culture and Civilisation of Ancient India in Historical Outline*, Routledge and Kegan Paul, London, 1965, p. 35.
5. B. K. Gururaja Rao, *The Megalithic Culture in South India*, Prasaranga, University of Mysore, Mysore, 1972.
6. R. J. Forbes, *Studies in Ancient Technology*, E. J. Brill, Leiden, 1965, vol. 2, pp. 12–14.
7. M. S. Nagaraja Rao, 'Significance of pottery headrests from neolithic sites of Karnataka', in S. B. Deo and M. K. Dhavalikar (eds), *Studies in Indian Archaeology* (Prof. H. D. Sankalia felicitation volume), Popular Prakashan, Bombay, 1974, p. 141.
8. S. Rapport and H. Wright (eds), *Archaeology*, Washington Square Press Inc., New York, 1964, (a) S. Casson, 'Finders Petrie and Egyptology', p. 178.
9. U.P. Upadhyaya and S. P. Upadhyaya, *Dravidian and Negro African*, Rashtrakavi Govind Pai Research Institute, Udupi, 1983.
10. M. Srinivasa Aiyangar, *Tamil Studies*, Guardian Press, Madras, 1914.
11. A. A. Abbie, 'India and the Australian aboriginēs', in Asok K. Ghosh (ed.), *Perspectives in Palaeoanthropology* (Prof. D. Sen Festschrift), Firma K. L. Mukhopadhyay, Calcutta, p. 87.
12. F. R. Allchin, *Neolithic Cattle-Keepers of South India*, Cambridge University Press, 1963.
13. M. S. Randhawa, *A History of Agriculture in India*, Indian Council of Agricultural Research, New Delhi, vol. 1, 1980, (a) p. 236 (b) p. 448 (c) p. 331 and pp. 382–4.
14. V. R. Ramachandra Dikshitar, *Prehistoric South India*, University of Madras, 1951.
15. H. D. Sankalia, *Prehistory of India*, Munshiram Manoharlal Publishers Pvt. Ltd., New Delhi, 1977, pp. 100–50.
16. V. Kanakasabhai, *The Tamils Eighteen Hundred Years Ago*, Higginbotham and Co., Madras and Bangalore, 1904, p. 125–35.
17. P. T. Srinivasa Aiyangar, *Pre-Aryan Tamil Culture*, University of Madras, 1930, (a) p. 19 (b) pp. 57–70.
18. K. K. Pillay, *A Social History of the Tamils*, University of Madras, Madras, 1969, 2nd edn, 1975, vol. 1, (a) p. 193 (b) p. 284f.
19. P. T. Srinivasa Iyengar, *History of the Tamils (c. 1932)* Asian Educational Services, New Delhi, repr. 1983, (a) pp. 253–300 (b) p. 236 (c) pp. 303–5.
20. Kalki, *Ponniyinselvan*, Vanathi Pathipakam, Madras, 3rd reprint, 1989, 5 vols, (a) vol. 1, pp. 164–9 (b) vol. 1, p. 5 (c) vol. 3, p. 46.
21. A. Sreedhara Menon, *Social and Cultural History of Kerala*, Sterling Publishers Pvt. Ltd., New Delhi, 1979, pp. 121–6.
22. Mudaliar C. Rasanayagam, *Ancient Jaffna*, Everyman's Publishers Ltd., Madras, 1926, pp. 140–60.
23. X. S. Thani Nayagam (ed.), *Tamil Culture and Civilisation: Readings—The Classical Period*, Asia Publishing House, Bombay, 1970, (a) P. T. Srinivasa Aiyangar, p. 218 (b) Alexander Rea, p. 37 (c) Ralph Linton, p. 4 (d) R. E. Mortimer Wheeler, p. 150.
24. M. R. Kale (ed.) *The Dasakumāracharita of Dandin*, with a commentary, Gopal Narayan and Co., Bombay, 2hd edn, 1925, pp. 104–23.
25. M. Arokiasami, *The Classical Age of the Tamils*, University of Madras, 1972, pp. 82–100.
26. F. Max Mueller, *The Upanishads*, Dover Publications Inc., New York, vol. 1, sixth Adhyaya, p. 214f.
27. K. A. Nilakanta Sastri, *History and Culture of the Tamils*, Firma K. L. Mukhopadhyay, Calcutta, 1964, p. 79.
28. K. T. Achaya, *Ghani: The Historical Oilmill of India*, Olearius Editions, Kemblesville, Pa., USA, 1992, chap. 2.
29. Mu. Varadarajan, *A History of Tamil Literature* (1972), trans. E. Sa. Visswananthan, Sahitya Akademi, New Delhi, 1988, (a) p. 38 (b) p. 57.
30. N. Subrahmaniam, *Sangam Polity*, Asia Publishing House, Bombay, 1966, pp. 306–9.
31. G. U. Pope, 'Extracts from *Purra-Nānnūru* (the 400

lyrics)', *Indian Antiquary*, (a) 1900, vol. 29, p. 57 (b) 1899, vol. 28, p. 29 (c) 1900, vol. 29, p. 281 (d) 1900, vol. 29, p. 250.
32. K. A. Nilakanta Sastri, *The Cholas* (1935), University of Madras, Madras, repr. 1975. p. 46.
33. K. V. Krishna Ayyar, *A Short History of Kerala*, Pani and Co., Ernakulam, 1966, p. 31.
34. K. M. Panikkar, *India and the Indian Ocean* (1945), George Allen and Unwin (India) Pvt. Ltd., Bombay, repr. 1971.
35. Prakash Chandra Prasad, *Foreign Trade and Commerce in Ancient India*, Abhinav Publications, Delhi, 1977, pp. 68–99.
36. S. R. Rao, 'Shipping in ancient India', in Lokesh Chandra (ed.), *India's Contribution to World Thought and Culture* (A Vivekananda commemoration volume), Vivekananda Rock Memorial Committee, Madras, 1970, p. 83.
37. S. R. Rao, 'Marine archaeological excavation', in *Manjusha: Recent Archaeological Researches in India* (Dr. S. R. Rao sixtieth birthday felicitation volume), ed. Satyavrat Shastri and H. G. Ramachandra, Gnanajyoti Kalamandir, Bangalore, 1985, p. 22.
38. B. N. Mukherjee, D. R. Das, S. S. Biswas and S. P. Singh, *Sri Dineshchandrika: Studies in Indology* (D. C. Sircar Festschrift), Sundeep Prakashan, Delhi, 1983, (a) C. Margabandhu, 'Ancient seaports of south India', p. 185 (b) P. V. Parabrahma Sastry, 'Tāmbula, a forgotten Hindu custom', p. 167.
39. Anon, 'Ancient seaport found', *The Times of India*, Bangalore, 26 October 1986.
40. Moti Chandra, *Trade and Trade Routes in Ancient India*, Abhinav Publications, New Delhi, 1977, pp. vi–xviii.
41. E. H. Warmington, *The Commerce between the Roman Empire and India*, Cambridge University, Press, 1928.
42. P. S. Desai, Tulū verses in Greek script', *Sunday Herald*, Bangalore, 16 January 1983.
43. Owen Kail, 'Arikamedu, the mound of ruins', *The India Magazine*, vol. 5, no. 5, April 1985, p. 30.
44. R. E. Mortimer Wheeler, *My Archaeological Mission to India and Pakistan*, Thames and Hudson, London, 1976, p. 43.
45. S. Krishnaswamy Aiyangar, *Ancient India*, Oriental Book Agency, Poona, 1941, vol. 2, pp. 674–82.
46. B. Ch. Chhabra, 'Navy in ancient India', *Vishveshvaranand Indological Journal*, Prof. K. V. Sarma felicitation volume, vol. 18, pts i and ii, 1980, p. 381; also as Vishveshvaranand Indological Paper Series-502, 1980.
47. V. R. Ramachandra Dikshitar, *Prehistoric South India* (Sir William Meyer lectures) (1951), Cosmo Publications, New Delhi, repr. 1981.
48. Chaman Lal, *Hindu America*, Vishveshvaranand Vedic Research Institute, Hoshiarpur, 3rd edn, 1956.
49. 'Evidence of links between ancient India and Mexico', *The Hindu*, Madras, 27 September 1985, p. 20.
50. Madhav N. Katti, 'Karnataka and south-east Asian epigraphy', in Devendra Handa (ed.), *Indological Studies* (Essays in memory of S. P. Singhal), Caxton Publications, Delhi, 1987, p. 205.
51. R. C. Majumdar, *Ancient India*, Motilal Banarsidass, Delhi, 8th edn, 1977, pp. 193 and 448.
52. *The New Encyclopaedia Britannica*, University of Chicago, 15th edn, Micropaedia, vol. 17, p. 138.
53. U. Venkatakrishna Rao, 'Chewing : a peculiar south Indian custom', *Journal of Oriental Research*, vol. 17, pt. 1, Madras, 1949, p. 158.
54. P. K. Gode, 'References to tambula', in J. N. Agrawal and B. D. Shastri (eds), *Sarūda-Bhārati* (The Dr. Lakshman Sarup memorial volume), Vishveshvaranand Vedic Research Institute, Hoshiarpur, 1954; Vishveshvaranand Indological Paper Series-26, 1954.
55. George Lebrun, 'Betel chewing', *Journal of Oriental Research*, vol. 17, pt. 1, Madras, 1949, p. 165.
56. H. Yule and A. C. Burnell, *Hobson-Jobson* (1903), Munshiram Manoharlal Publishers Pvt. Ltd., Delhi, 1903, 4th edn, 1984, p. 35.
57. K. Padmanabha Menon, in T. K. Krishna Menon (ed.), *History of Kerala*, Asian Educational Services, New Delhi, repr. 1984, vol. 4, pp. 412–18.
58. L. V. Ramaswami Aiyar, 'Dravidic forms for the betel leaf', *Journal of Oriental Research*, Madras, 1932, vol. 5, p. 1.
59. Chakresh Jain, 'The culture of paan', *Namaskār*, Air-India, Sept./Oct. 1985, vol. 5, no. 5, p. 59.
60. Peter T. White, 'Coca', *National Geographic*, Washington, January 1989, p. 3.
61. S. S. Baglodi, 'Sacred leaf', *Deccan Herald*, Bangalore, 21 December 1989.

Chapter 5: Meat and Drinks

1. Jeannine Auboyer, *Daily Life in Ancient India*, Asia Publishing House, Bombay, 1965, (a) p. 98f (b) p. 259.
2. S. P. Raychaudhuri, *Agriculture in Ancient India*, Indian Council of Agricultural Research, New Delhi, 1964, (a) p. 116f (b) p. 133f.
3. P. T. S. Iyengar, *Life in Ancient India*, Srinivasa Varadachari and Co., Madras, 1912, pp. 86–91.
4. D. D. Kosambi, *An Introduction to the Study of Indian History*, Popular Prakashan, Bombay, 1975, (a) pp. 136–8 (b) p. 361.
5. G. S. Ghurye, *Vedic India*, Popular Prakashan, Bombay, 1979, p. 52.
6. D. R. Bhandarkar, *Some Aspects of Ancient Indian Culture* (Sir William Meyer lectures), University of Madras, 1940, pp. 70–84.
7. C. Kunhan Raja, 'Vedic culture', in *The Cultural Heritage of India*, The Ramakrishna Mission Institute of Culture, Calcutta, 2nd edn., 1958, vol. 1, ch. 12,

p. 199.
8. A. M. Shastri, *India as seen in the Kuttanī-Mata of Damōdara Gupta*, Motilal Banarsidass, Delhi 1975, (a) p. 88 (b) pp. 130–2.
9. A. M. Shastri, *India as seen in the Brhat Samhitā of Varāhamihira*, Motilal Banarsidass, Delhi, 1969, pp. 229–16.
10. Thakur Harendra Dayal, *The Visnu Purāna*, Sundeep Prakashan, Delhi, 1983, pp. 96–104.
11. Shyamasunder Nigam, *Economic Organisation in Ancient India*, Munshiram Manoharlal Publishers Pvt. Ltd., New Delhi, 1975, p. 103f.
12. I. B. Horner 'Early Buddhism and the taking of life', in D. R. Bhandarkar, K. A. Nilakanta Sastri, B.M. Barua and P. K. Gode (eds), *The B. C. Law Volume*, The Indian Research Institute, Calcutta, 1945, vol. 1, p. 436.
13. Copy of the Girnar Edict of Ashoka, National Museum, New Delhi.
14. Rosanne Rocher (ed.), *India and Indology: Selected Articles of W. Norman Brown*, Motilal Banarsidass, Delhi, 1978.
15. James Legge, *The Travels of Fa-Hsien* (1886), Oriental Publishers, Delhi, repr. 1972, p. 43.
15a. R. K. Mookherji, *Harsha* (1926), Motilal Banarsidass, Delhi, repr. 1959, p. 147.
16. E. C. Sachau, *Alberuni's India*, Kegan Paul, Trench, Trubner and Co. Ltd., London, 1910, col. 2, p. 151.
17. A. A. Macdonell, *Vedic Mythology*, Indological Book House, Varanasi/Delhi, 1971, pp. 104–15.
18. Om Prakash, *Food and Drinks in Ancient India*, Munshi Ram Manohar Lal, Delhi, 1961, (a) p. 34–57 (b). p. 87–101.
19. Ramshraya Sharma, *A Socio-Political Study of the Vālmiki Ramāyana*, Motilal Banarsidass, Delhi, 1971, pp. 232–2.
20. Jyotsna K. Kamat, in M. S. Nagaraja Rao (ed.), *The Chālukyas of Bādāmi*, The Mythic Society, Bangalore, 1978, p. 170.
21. H. C. Chalakdar, *Social Life in Ancient India: Studies in Vatsayana's Kāmasūtra*, Bharatiya Publishing House, Delhi, 1976, p. 159.
22. H. Pathak, *Cultural Life in the Gupta Period*, Bharatiya Publishing House, Delhi, 1978, p. 58.
23. R. S. Mugali, *The Heritage of Karnataka*, Satyasodhana Publishing House, Bangalore, 1946, p. 140.
24. J. Jolly, 'Physicians and therapy', in Debiprasad Chattopadhyaya (ed.), *Studies in the History of Science in India*, Editorial Enterprises, New Delhi, 1982, vol. 1, p. 175.
25. Claus Vogel, *Vāghbhata's Astāngahrdayasamhitā*, Kommissionsverlag Franz Steiner Gmbh, Wiesbaden, 1965, p. 138.
26. Arjun Dev, 'India in the eyes of early Muslim scholars', in Lokesh Chandra (ed.), *India's Contribution to World Thought and Culture* (A Vivekananda commemoration volume), Vivekananda Rock Memorial Committee, Madras, 1970, p. 589.
27. G. P. Majumdar, *Some Aspects of Indian Civilisation*, published by the author, Calcutta, 1938, pp. 30–1.
28. Oroon Kumar Ghosh, *The Changing Indian Civilization*, South Asia Books - Minerva Associates (publications) Pvt. Ltd., Calcutta, 1976, vol. 2, p. 322.
29. Indira Chakravarthy, *Saga of Indian Food*, Sterling Publishers Pvt. Ltd., New Delhi, 1972, p. 25.
30. Jaya Goswami, *Cultural History of Ancient India*, Agam Kala Prakashan, Delhi, 1976, p. 27.
31. Padmini Sengupta, *Everyday Life in Ancient India*, Oxford University Press, Indian Branch, 1950, pp. 547–58.

Chapter 6: Indian Food Ethos

1. R. S. Khare, *The Hindu Hearth and Home*, Vikas Publishing House Ltd., India 1976.
2. R. S. Khare, *Culture and Reality*, Indian Institute of Advanced Study, Simla, 1976.
3. T. R. Anandalwar, 'Contribution of Ayurveda to food science', in *Symposium on the Impact of Pollution in and from Food Industries and its Management*, Association of Food Scientists and Technologists (India), Mysore, May 1989, Paper BAS 22.
4. G. S. Ghurye, *Caste and Race in India* (1932), Popular Prakashan, Bombay, 5th edn. 1979, repr. 1986, p. 312.
5. Doris Srinivasan, *Concept of Cow in the Rigveda*, Motilal Banarsidass, Delhi, 1979, p. 51.
6. *India International Centre Quarterly*, New Delhi, 1985, vol. 12, no. 2, (a) Dina Simoes Guha, 'Food in the Vedic tradition', p. 141 (b) Meera Chatterjee, 'The food of healing', p. 129.
7. Jeannine Auboyer, *Daily Life in Ancient India*, Asia Publishing House, Bombay, 1965, pp. 161–99.
8. V. M. Apte, 'Vedic rituals', in *The Cultural Heritage of India*, The Ramakrishna Mission Institute of Culture, Calcutta, 2nd edn, 1958, vol. 1, 14, pp. 234–63.
9. Nilakshi Sengupta, 'Symbolism in ancient Indian marriage rituals', in the J. N. Banerjea volume, The Alumni Association, Department of Ancient Indian History and Culture, University of Calcutta, Calcutta, 1960, p. 313.
10. B. N. Banerjee, *Hindu Culture, Custom and Ceremony*, Agam Kala Prakashan, Delhi, 1979, p. 152.
11. Mary Louise Skelton and G. Gopal Rao, *South Indian Cookery*, Orient Paperbacks, New Delhi, 1975.
12. G. P. Majumdar, *Some Aspects of Indian Civilisation*, published by the author, Calcutta, 1938, p. 22.
13. B. N. Puri, *India in the Time of Patanjali*, Bharatiya

Vidya Bhavan, Bombay, 1957, pp. 89–115.
14. R. Nagasami, *Art and Culture of Tamil Nadu*, Sundeep Prakashan, Delhi, 1980, p. 61.
15. Central Food Technological Research Institute, Mysore, personal communication, December 1989.
16. Sarat Chandra, 'A kitchen of the gods', *The India Magazine* 1987, vol. 7, no. 12, November, p. 30.
17. Sarat Chandra, 'Food of the Gods', *The India Magazine* 1989; vol. 9 no. 3, February, p. 29.
18. B. N. Sharma, *Social and Cultural History of Northern India about 1000–1200* AD, Abhinav Publications, New Delhi, 1972, ch. 5.
19. P. C. Divanji, '*Lankāvatārasūtra* on non-vegetarian diets', *Annals of the Bhandarkar Oriental Research Institute*, 1940, vol. 18, p. 317.
20. S. Tachibana, *The Ethics of Buddhism*, Oxford University Press, London, 1926, pp. 114–20.
21. Chandra Sekhar Prasad, 'Meat eating and the rule of Tikotiparisuddha', in A.K. Narain (ed.), *Studies in Pāli and Buddhism*, B. R. Publishing Corporation, Delhi, 1979, p. 285.
22. R. P. Kapleau, *A Buddhist Case for Vegetarianism*, Rider, London, 1983, p. 39f.
23. *Aspects of Jainism*, Jain Mission Society, Bangalore, 1955, (a) Prithvi Raj Jain, 'The fundamentals of Jainism—I', Article 3 (b) Prithvi Raj Jain, 'The fundamentals of Jainism-II', Article 4.
24. T. G. Kalghatgi (ed.), *Jainism: A Study*, Department of Jainology and Prakrits, University of Mysore, Mysore, 1976, (a) T. G. Kalghatgi, 'Buddha and Mahāvīra : A philosophical perspective', p. 8 (b) P. B. Badiger, 'A critical study of Pralambakalpa from *Brhatkalpabhāsya*', p. 70.
25. V. A. Sanghave, *Jaina Community: A Social Survey*, Popular Prakashan, Bombay, 1980, (a) p. 46 (b) pp. 258–60.
26. M. A. Kannoomal, *The Study of Jainism*, Atmanand Jain Pustak Pracarak Mandal, Agra, 1916, (a) pp. 52–77 (b) p. 78f.
27. Jogendra Singh, *Sikh Ceremonies*, International Book House, Bombay, 1941, pp. 3–10, p. 95.
28. Surendra Singh Kohli, *A Critical Study of the* Ādi Granth, Motilal Banarsidass, Delhi, 1961, p. 1 and p. 116
29. Minakshi Raja, 'India's children of Israel', The *Sunday Observer*, 27 September 1987.
30. A. V. Varghese, 'Am Israeli hai', *Sunday Herald*, Bangalore, 6 September 1987.
31. Anand Parthasarathy, 'The Jews of Cochin', *Frontline*, Madras, 1988, vol. 5, no. 1, p. 70.
32. Corinne H. Robinson, *Normal and Therapeutic Nutrition*, Macmillian Publishing Co., New York, 14th edn, 1972, p. 219.
33. S. G. Pothan, *The Syrian Christians of Kerala*, Asia Publishing House, Bombay, 1963, pp. 5, 31.
34. Mme. Lourdes Louis, 'Food of Pondicherry', personal communication, November 1989.
35. Roxana S. Irani, 'The Parsees', *The Indian Magazine*, vol. 8, no. 7, June 1988, p. 70.
36. Irach J. S. Taraporewala, 'The exact date of the arrival of the Parsis in India', S. M. Katre and P. K. Gode (eds), in *A Volume of Studies in Indology* (presented to Prof. P. V. Kane), Oriental Book Agency, Poona, 1941, p. 506.
37. Bhickoo J. Manekshaw, 'Parsi bhonu: a traditional mix', *Saturday Times of India*, 19 July 1986.
38. Santha Rama Rao, *The Cooking of India*, Time-Life Books, New York, 1969, p. 152.
39. Saud Twaigery and Diana Spillman, 'An Introduction to Moslem dietary laws', *Food Technology*, vol. 43, February 1989, no. 2, p. 88.
40. *The Holy Qurān*, (a) verse 2 : 22 (b) verse 5.91.
41. W. H. Siddiqui, 'India's contribution to Arab civilisation', in Lokesh Chandra (ed.), *India's Contribution to World Thought and Culture* (A Vivekananda commemoration volume), Vivekanada Rock Memorial Committee, Madras, 1970, p. 573.
42. Imtiaz Ahmad (ed.), *Caste and Social Stratification among Muslims in India*, Manohar Publications, New Delhi, 2nd edn, 1978. p. 1.
43. H. A. Rose, *Rites and Ceremonies of Hindus and Muslims* (1908), Amar Prakashan, New Delhi, repr. 1983.
44. Lina M. Fruzetti, 'Muslim rituals: The household rites versus the public rituals in rural India', in Imtiaz Ahmad (ed.), *Ritual and Religion Among Muslims in India*, Manohar Publications, New Delhi, 1984, p. 91.
45. Jaffur Shurreef, *Qanoon-e-Islam, or the Customs of the Mussulmans of India* (1832), transl. G. A. Herklots, Higginbotham and Co., Madras, 1895.
46. Abbē J. A. Dubois, *Hindu Manners, Customs and Ceremonies* (1817), transl. H. K. Beauchamp, Oxford University Press, Delhi, 3rd edn, 1906, repr. 1983, p. 152.

Chapter 7: Food and the Indian Doctors

1. P. Spratt, *Hindu Culture and Personality*, Manaktalas, Bombay, 1966, p. 12.
2. Pratapa Chandra Roy trans., *The Mahābhārata of Krishna-Dwaipāyana Vyāsa*, Bharata Press, Calcutta, 1887, vol. 6 : Bhīsma Parva, p. 87.
3. Meera Chatterjee, 'The food of healing', *India International Centre Quarterly*, New Delhi, 1985, vol. 12, no. 2, p. 129.
4. Priyadaranjan Ray and Hirendra Nath Gupta, *Caraka Samhitā: A Scientific Synopsis*, Indian National Science

Academy, New Delhi, 2nd edn, 1980, pp. 15–20.
5. Debiprasad Chattopadhyaya (ed.), Studies in the History of Science in India, Editorial Enterprises, New Delhi, 1982, (a) J. Jolly, 'On the medical authorities', vol. 1, p. 73 (b) A. F. Hoernle, 'The Bower manuscript', vol. 1, p. 117.
6. Om Prakash, *Food and Drinks in Ancient India*, Munshi Ram Manohar Lal, Delhi, 1961, (a) pp. 87–101 (b) pp. 132–67 (c) 168–202 (d) p. 253 (e) pp. 284–95.
7. Priyadaranjan Ray, Hirendra Nath Gupta and M. Roy, *Suśruta Samhitā: A Scientific Synopsis*, Indian National Science Academy, New Delhi, 1980.
8. S. C. Banerjee, *Flora and Fauna in Sanskrit Literature*, Naya Prakash, Calcutta, 1960, p. 19.
9. Claus Vogel, *Vaghbhata's Astāngahrdayasamhitā*, Kommissionsverlag Franz Steiner Gmbh, Wiesbaden, 1965.
10. G. U. Thite, 'Prophylactics in Indian medicine', in S. S. Janaki (ed.), *Prof. Kuppuswami Sastri Birth Centenary Commemorative Volume*, Kuppuswami Research Institute, Madras, 1985, vol. 1, p. 139.
11. L. B. Jensen, *Man's Foods*, The Garrard Press, Champaign, Illinois, USA, 1953, p. 237.
12. Nagendra Nath Sengupta, *The Ayurvedic System of Medicine* (1919), Logos Press, New Delhi, 3rd edn, repr. 1984, vol. 1, p. 6.
13. R. Shamasastry, *Kautilya's Arthashāstra*, Mysore Printing and Publishing House, Mysore, 8th edn, 1967, p. 104.
14. Oroon Kumar Ghosh, *The Changing Indian Civilisation*, South Asia Books-Minerva Associates (Publications) Pvt. Ltd., Calcutta, 1976, vol. 2, ch. 29, p. 319.
15. Bhagwan Dash and Manfred M. Junius, *A Handbook of Ayurveda*, Concept Publishing Co., New Delhi, 1983, p. 6.
16. P. N. Bose, *Epochs of Civilisation* (1912), Asian Educational Services, New Delhi, repr. 1978, p. 195.
17. G. H. Pelto and P. J. Pelto, *The Human Adventure:* An Introduction to Anthropology, Macmillan Publishing Co., New York and Collier-Macmillan Publishers, London, 1976, p. 439.
18. Paul Fieldhouse, *Food and Nutrition : Constraints and Culture*, Croom Helm Ltd., London, 1986, p. 50f.
19. B. N. Sharma, *Social and Cultural History of North India about 1000–1200 AD*, Abhinav Publications, New Delhi, 1972, ch. 5.
20. Anon, 'Foods', *Eve's Weekly*, Bombay 11-17 May 1985, p. 17.
21. Jenny Storer, 'Hot and cold food beliefs in an Indian community and their significance', *Journal of Human Nutrition*, vol. 31, 1977, p. 33.
22. P. S. V. Ramanamurthy, 'Physiological effects of "Hot" and "cold" foods in Human subjects', *Indian Journal of Nutrition and Dietetics*, vol. 6, 1969, p. 187.
23. R. P. Shastri, 'The acid test', *The Times of Inda*, Bombay, 22 June 1986.
24. B. V. Subbarayappa, 'Treasure trove of Indian medicine', *Indian Express*, Bangalore, 29 December 1987.
25. Moin Qazi, 'Magical cures from Unāni', *Indian Express*, Bangalore, 23 August 1988.
26. Debiprasad Chattopadhyaya, 'Science and society in ancient India', in Debiprasad Chattopadhyaya (ed.), *Marxism and Indology*, K. P. Bagchi and Co., Calcutta, 1981, p. 231.
27. S. K. Ramachandra Rao, *Encyclopaedia of Indian Medicine, vol. 1: Historical Prespective*, Popular Prakashan, Bombay, 1985, p. 41.
28. Thiruvāchakkan's *Thiruvalluvar* trans, A. A. Manavalan 95, lines 941–50.

Chapter 8: Royal Fare

1. R. C. Majumdar, *Ancient India*, Motilal Banarsidass, Delhi, 8th edn, 1977, p. 373.
2. Krishna Murari, *The Chālukyas of Kalyāni* Concept Publishing Co., Delhi, 1977, pp. 154–8 and pp. 281–2.
3. Radha Krishnamurthy, 'History of Keladi based on *Shivatattva Ratnākara*', *The Quarterly Journal of the Mythic Society*, Bangalore, July/September 1988, vol. 79, no. 3, p. 235.
4. Om Prakash, *Food and Drinks in Ancient India*, Munshi Ram Manohar Lal, Delhi, 1961, (a) pp. 203–39 (b) p. 284.
5. G. K. Shrigondekar, Mānasollāsa *of King Someshwara*, Gaekwad's Oriental Series, Baroda, 1939, vol. 84, pt. 2, Vimsati 3, Annabhoga, pp. 21–3.
6. Saradha S. Srinivasan, 'The relation between Karnataka and Gujarat from the 7th to the early 14th century AD', Ph.D. thesis, M. S. University of Baroda, Baroda, March 1974, 2 vols., vol. 1, 1–5.
7. Saradha S. Srinivasan, 'An appraisal on *annabhōga* of *Mānasollāsa*', personal communication, February 1988.
8. Shalini Holkar, 'The gourmets of the desert', *Indian Express Magazine*, 5 December 1982.
9. M. N. Srinivas, 'Some thoughts on the sociological aspects of food in India', in Mahipal Bhuriya and S. M. Michael (eds), *Anthropology as a Historical Science* (Essays in honour of Stephen Fuchs), Satprakashan, Indore, 1984, p. 105.
10. B. N. Sharma, *Social and Cultural History of Northern India about 1000–1200 AD* , Abhinav Publications, New Delhi, 1972, pp. 95–104.
11. B. A. Saletore, *Social and Political Life in the Vijayanagara Empire, AD 1346–1646*, B. G. Paul and Co., Madras, 1934, vol. 2, pp. 312–16.
12. S. N. Krishna Jois (ed.), *Sūpa Śāstra of Mangarasa (1516 AD)*, University of Mysore, Mysore, 1969, Appendix, pp. 255–91.

13. Radha Krishnamurthy, '*Shivatattvaratnākara*: A cultural study', Ph. D. thesis, University of Poona, Poona, 1983, ch. 9, pp. 799–830.
14. Sudha V. Desai, *Social Life in Maharashtra Under the Peshwas*, Popular Prakashan, Bombay, 1980, pp. 169–73.

Chapter 9: Utensils and Food Preparation

1. H. D. Sankalia, in S. P. Gupta and K. S. Ramachandran (eds), *Aspects of Indian History and Archaeology*, B. R. Publishing Corporation, Delhi, 1977, p. 254.
2. H. D. Sankalia, *Stone Age Tools*, Deccan College, Poona, 1964, p. 86.
3. H. P. Ray, *Monastery and Guild*, Oxford Univesity Press, Delhi, 1986, (a) p. 137 (b) p. 134 (c) p. 137.
4. H. D. Sankalia, *Prehistoric and Historic Archaeology of Gujarat*, Munshiram Manoharlal Publishers Pvt. Ltd., New Delhi, 1987, pp. 39–54.
5. K. N. Dikshit, *Prehistoric Civilisation in the Indus Valley*, University of Madras, Madras, 1939.
6. E. J. H. Mackay, *Further Excavations at Mohenjodaro*, Government of India, Delhi, 1938, vol. 2, (a) plate 54, item 20 (b) plate 64, item 13.
7. A. K. Bag, *Science and Civilisation in India: Harappan Period*, Navrang, New Delhi, 1985, p. 43.
8. M. K. Dhawalikar, *Sanchi : A Cultural Study*, Deccan College, Poona, 1965; plate showing domestic life in the village of Urvila.
9. M. R. Kale (ed) *The Dasakumāracharita of Dandin*, with a commentary, Gopal Narayan and Co., Bombay, 2nd edn, 1925, pp. 111–15.
10. Mudaliar C. Rasanāyagam, *Ancient Jaffna*, Everyman's Publishers Ltd., Madras, 1926, pp. 130–611.
11. Malati J. Shendge, *The Civilized Demons: The Harappans in the Rigveda*, Abhinav Publications, New Delhi, 1977, p. 241.
12. M. K. Dhawalikar, *Studies in Indian Archaeology*, 1970, vol 4, nos. 1–4, p. 32.
13. W. J. Wilkins, *Hindu Mythlogy* (2nd edn, 1890), Rupa and Co., Calcutta, repr. 1983, p. 479.
14. C. D. Deshmukh, *Amarakōsha : Gems from the Treasure House of Sanskrit Words*, Uppal Publishing House, New Delhi, 1981, pp. 99–110.
15. G. S. Ghurye, *Vedic India*, Popular Prakashan, Bombay, 1979, (a) pp. 372–80 (b) p. 400 (c) p. 383.
16. H. D. Sankalia, *Prehistory of India*, Munshiram Manoharlal Publishers Pvt. Ltd., New Delhi, 1977, pp. 100–24.
17. Ghulam Yazdani, *Ajanta* (1952), Swati Publications, Delhi, repr. 1983, part 4, pp. 58, 104.
18. H. D. Sankalia, *Some Aspects of Prehistoric Technology in India*, Indian National Science Academy, New Delhi, 1970, (a) p. 13 (b) p. 45.
19. Om Prakash, *Food and Drinks in Ancient India*, Munshi Ram Manohar Lal, Delhi, 1961, (a) pp. 7–33 (b) pp. 34–57 (c) pp. 58–86 (d) pp. 87–101 (c) pp. 102–31 (f) pp. 132–67 (g) pp. 251–2.
20. Ernest Mackay, in Dorothy Mackay (ed.) *Early Indus Civilisation*, Indological Book Corporation, Delhi, repr. 1976, (a) p. 106 (b) plate 19.
21. V. M. Apte. *Social and Religious Life in the Grihy Sūtras* (1939), The Popular Book Depot, Bombay, reset 1954, pp. 95–102.
22. S. N. Krishna Jois (ed.), *Sūpa Śāstra of Mangarasa (1516 AD)*, University of Mysore, Mysore, 1969, appendix, (a) Yelandu Harīswara's '*Prabhudeva Purāna* (AD1606)', p. 268 (b) Sivakotyācharya's 'Vaddarādané (AD1920)', p. 255.
23. A. M. Shastri, *India as seen in the Brhat Samhitā of Varāhamihira*, Motilal Banarsidass, Delhi, 1969, pp. 209–16.
24. B. N. Pandey, A Book of India 1977, Rupa and Co., India, by arrangement with Collins, London, repr. 1982, p. 38.
25. J. Inder Singh Kalra, 'From the frying pan to the tandoor', *The Times of India*, Bombay, 3 May 1987.
26. P. T. Srinivasa Aiyengar, *Pre-Aryan Tamil Culture*, University of Madras, Madras, 1930, pp. 57–70.
27. F. R. Allchin, *Neolithic Cattle-keepers of South India*, Cambridge University Press, 1963.
28. Ernest Mackay, *Excavations at Chanhudaro: Season of 1935–36*, Publication 3473, Smithsonian Institute, Washington DC, USA, 1938.
29. R. C. Agrawala, in B. B. Lal and S. P. Gupta (eds), *Frontiers of the Indus Civilisation* (Sir Mortimer Wheeler commemoration volume), Books and Books, New Delhi, 1984, p. 157.
30. P. T. S. Iyengar, *Life in Ancient India*, 1932, Asian Educational Services, New Delhi, repr. 1982, p. 28f and p. 47f.
31. K. K. Chaudhuri, in *Sraddānjali* (D. C. Sircar commemoration volume), K. K. Das Gupta, P. K. Bhattacharya and R. D. Choudhury (eds), Sundeep Prakashan, Delhi, 1988, p. 321.
32. Chitrabhanu Sen, *Dictionary of Vedic Rituals* (1978), Concept Publishing Co., Delhi, repr. 1982, Three plates.
33. Uma Maria Vesci, *Heat and Sacrifice in the Vedas*, Motilal Banarsidass, Delhi, 1985, pp. 32, p. 69, 315.
34. Saradha S. Srinivasan, *Mensuration in Ancient India*, Ajanta Publications (India), Delhi, 1979, pp. 71–9.
35. Ramachandra Sagar (ed.), *Concise Hindi Shabdh-Sagar*, Banaras, 1933, p. 184.
36. M. Monier-Williams, *A Sanskrit-English Dictionary*, 1899, Motilal Banarsidass, Delhi, 1983, p. 243/4.
37. B. N. Puri, *India in the Time of Patanjali*, Bharatiya Vidya Bhavan, Bombay, 1957, pp. 89–115.
38. E. B. Cowell and F. W. Thomas, *The Harśacharita of*

Bāna, Motilal Banarsidass, Delhi, repr. 1961, (a) p. 200 (b) p. 208 (c) p. 206 (d) p. 139.

39. V. S. Agrawala, *The Deeds of Harśa,* Prithvi Prakashan, Varanasi, 1969, pp. 119, 174, 195, 215.
40. A. Sreedhara Menon, *Social and Cultural History of Kerala*, Sterling Publishers Pvt. Ltd., New Delhi, 1979, pp. 121–6.
41. P. T. Srinivasa Iyengar, *History of the Tamils*, 1932, Asian Educational Services, New Delhi, repr. 1982 and 1983, pp. 253–300.
42. N. Subrahmaniam, *Sangam Polity*, Asia Publishing House, Bombay, 1966, pp. 306–9.
43. K. K. Pillay, *A Social History of the Tamils*, University of Madras, Madras, 2nd edn, 1975, vol. 1, (a) p. 284 (b) p. 224.
44. Radha Krishnamurthy, 'Cooking in ancient India', *Bhavan's Journal*, Bombay, 1 August 1984, p. 227.
45. M. S. Randhawa, *A History of Agriculture in India*, Indian Council of Agricultural Research, New Delhi, vol. 2, 1982, (a) p. 31 (b) p. 51.
46. Jeannine Auboyer,*Daily Life in Ancient India*, trans. S. W. Taylor, Asia Publishing House, Bombay, 1965, (a) p. 265 (b) p. 259 (c) p. 121.
47. D. Schlingloff, Studies in the Ajanta Paintings, Ajanta Publications, Delhi, 1987, p. 104.
48. Thakur Harendra Dayal, *The Viśnu-Purāna*, Sundeep Publication, Delhi, 1983, p. 157.
49. K. A. Nilakanta Sastri, *The Cholas*, University of Madras, Madras, 1955, p. 74.
50. Vijay Kumar Thakur, *Urbanisation in Ancient India*, Abhinav Publications, New Delhi, 1981, p. 202.
51. V. Kanakasabhai,*The Tamils Eighteen Hundred Years Ago,* Higginbotham and Co., Madras, 1904, pp. 125–35.
52. *Silappaddikāram*, Chapter 5; *Perumpānūru*, line 377; *Mathuraikkānchi*, lines 624/7.
53. S. Mahdi Hassan, 'Distillation assembly of pottery in ancient India with a single item of special construction', *Vishveshvaranand Indological Journal,* 1979, vol. 17, p. 264; Vishveshvaranand Indogoical Paper Series-457.
54. Ramshraya Sharma, *A Socio-Political Study of the Vālmiki Ramāyana*, Motilal Banarsidass, Delhi, 1971, p. 232–42.
55. Sten Konow, *Kautalya Studies* (1945), Oriental Publishers and Distributors, Delhi, 1975, pp. 60–3.
56. R. P. Kangle, *The Kautilya Arthaśāstra*, 2nd edn. 1972, Motilal banarsidass, Delhi, repr. 1986, vol. 2, pp. 154–6.
57. V. S. Agrawala, in B. C. Law (ed.), *D.R. Bhandarkar Memorial Volume*, Indian Research Institute, Calcutta, 1940, p. 291.
58. K. V. Krishna Ayyar, *A Short History of Kerela*, Pai and Co., Ernakulam, 1966, p. 31.
59. P. K. Code, 'Indian dietetics : Use of fried grains', *Annals of the Bhandarkar Oriental Research Institute*, 1948, vol. 29, p. 43.
60. Dasharatha Sharma, 'Life in Rajasthan in the fourteenth and fifteenth centuries', *Journal of Indian History*, April 1960, p. 101.
61. K. T. Achaya, *Oilseeds and Oilmilling in India*, Oxford and IBH Publishing Co. Pvt. Ltd., New Delhi, 1990, p. 208, *Indian Journal of the History of Science*, 1992, vol. 27, no. 1, p. 5.
62. S. R. Rao, Bangalore, personal communication, October 1988.
63. J. T. Platt, *A Dictionary of Urdu, Classical Hindi and English*, Sampson Low, Marston and Co., London, 2nd edn, 1899, p. 106.
64. George Watt, *Dictionary of the Economic Products of India (1885–94),* Cosmo Publications, Delhi, repr. 1972, vol. 6, pt. 2, p. 502.
65. J. Daniels and C. Daniels, 'The origin of the sugarcane roller mill', *Technology and Culture*, 1988, vol. 29, no. 3, p. 493.
66. Vishnu-Mittre, in J. B. Hutchinson (ed.), *Diversity and Change in the Indian Subcontinent*, Cambridge University Press, 1974, p. 3.

66a. K. C. Das, 'Calcutta: History of the rosogolla', *Indian Express*, Bangalore, Supplement, 14 April 1990, p. xii.

67. K. N. Dave, *Indian Bee Journal*, 1954, pp. 92, 149, 169 and 196; *Indian Bee Journal* 1955, pp. 11, 49, 87, 115, 169 and 202; cited in M. A. Joshi, V. V. Divan and M. C. Suryanarayanan, *Khadigramodyog*, May 1980, p. 384.
68. Lallanji Gopal, 'Honey industry in ancient India', in *Dr. Satkari Mookherji Felicitation Volume*, The Chowkhamba Sanskrit Series Office, Varanasi, 1969, p. 255.
69. J. J. H., *Pickings From Old Indian Books*, Higginbotham and Co., Madras, 1872; 'Management of bees in Kashmir', p. 123 (reprinted from the *Asiatic Journal* 1832, vol. 9).
70. F. J. Monahan, *The Early History of Bengal* (1924), Bharatiya Publishing House, Varanasi, repr. 1974, p. 54.
71. Dharampal, *Indian Science and Technology in the Eighteenth Century*, 1971, Academy of Gandhian Studies, Hyderabad, repr. 1983, p. 219.
72. Margaret MacMillan, *Women of the Raj*, Thames and Hudson, New York, 1988, p. 82.
73. Abul Fazl, *The Ain-i-Akbari*, trans. H. Blochmann, 1871, repr. 1965, Aadiesh Book Depot, Delhi, pp. 57–78.
74. Baljit Malik, 'Kasauli', *The India Magazine*, 1989, vol. 9, no. 11, October, p. 44.
75. Harry Johnston, *Pioneers in India*, Blackie and Sons Ltd., London, 1913, p. 223.
76. Geoffrey Moorhouse, *India Britannica*, Paladin Books, Granada Publishing Ltd., London, 1983, p. 91.
77. S. Muthiiah, 'Ice: from Walden Pond to Madras beach', *Swagat*, Indian Airlines, January 1987, p. 50.
78. H. A. Cahill, *The Sunday Times*, 22 September 1985.
79. J. B. Khot, 'Ice cream', *Science Age*, Bombay, May 1984, Illustration on p. 33.
80. Chetna Misra, 'It froze its way into the menu card', *The Times of India,* Bombay, 25 August 1985, p. III.

Chapter 10: Regional Cuisine

1. S. N. Krishna Jois, (ed.), *Sūpa Śāstra of Mangarasā (1516 AD)*, University of Mysore, 1969.
2. Ibid, Appendix, pp. 225–91, containing works of the following authors:
(a) Shivakōtyācharya, *Vaddarādané* (AD 920) (b) Shāntināthа, *Sukumāracharité (AD* 1068) (c) Hariharā, *Basavaragalé (AD* 1165) (d) Rāghavānka, *Siddarāmacharitra (AD* 1200) (e) Parshva Panditā, *Parshvanātha Purāna (AD* 1222) (f) Kamalabhavā, *Shāntīswara Purāna (AD* 1235) (g) Chāmarasā, *Prabhulingaleelé (AD* 1430) (h) Tērekanambi Bommarasā, *Sanatkumāracharité (AD* 1485) (i) Ratnākarā, *Bharatesha Vaibhava (AD* 1557) (j) Vīrakata Thonda Dārya, *Siddeshwara Purana (AD* 1560) (k) Vīrupāksha Panditā, *Channabasava Purāna, Khanda I (AD* 1584) (l) Gurulinga Dēsik, *Lingapurāna, Sandhi 8 (c.* AD 1594) (m) Annājī, 'Soundara Vilāsa' (second part of *Kavicharité*) (AD 1600) (n) Yēlanduru Harīshwara, *Prabhudēva Purāna* (AD 1606) (o) Pancha Bāna, 'Bhujjabal Charité' (second part of *Kavicharité) (AD* 1614) (p) Gōvinda Vaidya, *Kanteerava Narsa Rajendra Vijayé (AD* 1648) (q) Lakshmeesha, *Jaimini Bhāratā* (AD 1700) (r) Ayyappā, *Mauneshwara Bāla Leelé (AD* 1700) (s) Kōneyyā, *Krishna-Arjunara Sanghara (AD* 1750) (t) Shankara Kavi, *Nava Mōhana Taringini (AD* 1763) (u) Anon, *Ūtadha Ragalé (c.* 19th century AD) (v) Anon, *Durvasa Bhōjana* (modern) (w) Anon, *Shukrawāra Hādu* (modern)
3. H. Sesha Iyengar (ed.), *Lokōpakāra of Chāvundarāya*, Oriental Manuscripts Library, Madras, 1950, chap. 8: Sūpaśāstram, pp. 120–34.
4. Kandhi Subha Rao, *Pāka Śāstra* (AD 1890), Vāvila Ramaswami Sastrulu and Sons, Madras, 4th edn, 1926, pp. 7–8.
5. P. V. Jagadisa Ayyar, *South Indian Customs*, Asian Educational Services, repr. 1982.
6. H. Y. Sharada Prasad, in *Exploring Karnataka*, Department of Information and Publicity, Government of Karnataka, Bangalore, 1981.
7. Madhur Jaffrey, *A Taste of India* (1985), Pavilion Books Ltd., London, 2nd impression 1986.
8. Bilkees Latif, 'The subtle opulence of Hyderabad', *Sunday Express*, 8 February 1987.
9. Santha Rama Rao, *The Cookery of India*, Time Life Books, New York, 1969.
10. Personal information from Mrs. Anna Cheria, Mrs Naomi Meadows, Dr. A. G. Mathew and Mr. P. M. Joseph.
11. Ummi Abdulla, *Malabar Muslim Cookery*, Sangam Books, Orient Longman Ltd., New Delhi, 1981.
12. A. Sreedhara Menon, *Social and Cultural History of Kerala*, Sterling Publishers Pvt. Ltd., New Delhi, 1979, p. 124.
13. K. M. Panikkar, *A History of Kerala 1498–1801*, Annamalai University, Annamalainagar, 1959, p. 2.
14. Foods and flavours of India', *Eve's Weekly*, Bombay (special issue), 1983, vol. 27. no. 51, 17/23 December.
15. D. C. Sen, *History of Bengali Language and Literature*, University of Calcutta, 1911 (a) pp. 1–24 (b) p. 408.
16. Harbans Mukhia, 'Agricultural technology in medieval India', in Aniruddha Roy and S. K. Bagchi (eds), *Technology in Ancient and Medieval India*, Sundeep Prakashan, Delhi, 1986, p. 107.
17. J. N. Das Gupta, *Bengal in the Sixteenth Century AD*, University of Calcutta, Calcutta, 1917, pp. 98–120.
18. B. N. Pandey, *A Book of India* (1965), Rupa and Co., Calcutta, repr. 1982, (a) p. 53/4 (b) p. 38/9.
19. S. N. Sen, 'The Portuguese in Bengal', in D. R. Bhandarkar, K. A. Nilakanta Sastri, B. M. Barua and P. K. Gode, (eds.) the *B. C. Law Volume*, The Indian Research Institute, Calcutta, vol. 1, 1945, p. 92.
20. R. C. Majumdar, *History of Bengal, Vol. I: Hindu Period*, University of Dacca, Dacca, 1943, p. 611f.
21. R. P. Gupta, 'Curry and rice and Bengali spice', *The Time of India*, 10 June 1984.
22. R. P. Gupta, 'The marinated centuries', *The Times of India*, 3 June 1984.
23. *Chaitanya Charit-amrit of Krishnadas Kaviraj Gosvami*, Bhakti Grantha Prachar Bhandar, Calcutta, 3rd edn, 1948, (a) Canto 15, trans. Sachin Chaudhuri (b) p. 675.
24. K. P. Sahu, *Some Aspects of North Indian Social Life 1000–1526 AD*, Punthi Pusthak, Calcutta, 1973, ch. 2: Food and housing, pp. 29–44, quoting the following sources. (a) Kavi Narāyan Dēvā, *Mansamangal;* (b) Vijaya Gupta, *Padmapūran;* (c) Vrindābandas, *Chaitanya Bhagavata*; (d) Krittivāsa, *Suchitra Saptakānda Rāmāyana:* (e) Raghunāth Bhagavatāchārya, *Sreee Krishna Prema Tarangini;* (f) Shankaradēva, *Shreerāmbhagavata*; (g) Lāwanyasamay, *Bimalprabhanda*; (h) Maulāna Dāud Dalmai, *Chandayan*.
25. J. Inder Singh Kalra, 'Pass the mustard', *The Times of India*, 27 September 1989.
26. Minakshie Dasgupta, *Bangla Ranna*, published by Jaya Chaliha, Calcutta, 1982.
27. Ratikanta Tripathi, *Social and Religious Aspects in Bengali Inscriptions*, Firma K. L. Mukhopadhyay, Calcutta, 1987, ch. IV: Food and drink, p. 71.
28. France Bhattacharya, *Food Rituals in the Chandi Mangala*, trans. Radha Sharma, *India International Centre Quarterly*, 1985, vol. 12, no. 2, p. 169.
29. R. C. Dutt, *Cultural Heritage of Bengal* (1877), Punthi Pusthak, Calcutta, 3rd revised edn, 1962, p. 67f.
30. P. K. Gode, *Studies in Indian Cultural History*, Bhadarkar Oriental Research Institute, Poona, 1969, vol. III, pt. II, p. 61.
31. *Chandidāsa Padavali*, ed. Monindra Mohan Basu, Calcutta University Press, Calcutta, 1934, vol. 1, pp. 47, 50.
32. Ahsan Jan Quaiser, *The Indian Response to European Technology and Culture (AD 1498– 1707)*, Oxford University Press, New Delhi, 1982, p. 117.
33. Arindam Nag, 'A milk-curdling tale', *Society*, Bombay, February 1989, p. 33.

34. Bunny Gupta and Jaya Chaliha, 'The babu culture and the evolution fo the sandesh: descovery of the resogolla', *The Times of India*, Bombay, 6 February 1988.
35. Sumitra Banerjea, 'Any time is mishti time', *Swagat*, Indian Airlines, May 1989, p. 36.
36. 'K. C. Das's Rossogolla and Other Sweets', K. C. Das Pvt. Ltd., Calcutta and Bangalore.
37. P. C. Choudhury, *The History and Civilisation of the People of Assam to the 12th Century AD*, Department of Historical and Antiquarian Studies in Assam, University of Gauhati, Gauhati, 1959, p. 350.
38. Ayodhya Prasad Sah, *Life in Mediaeval Orissa (c. AD 600–1200)*, Chaukhamba Orientalia, Varanasi, 1976, p. 140.
39. Oroon Kumar Ghosh, *The Changing Indian Civilisation*, South Asia Books - Minerva Associates (Publications) Ltd., Calcutta, 1976, vol. 2, p. 326.
40. Surendra Gopal, 'Merchants in western India in the 16th and 17th centuries', in R. S. Sharma and Vivekanand Jha (eds), *Indian Society: Historical Probings*, 1974 (D. D. Kosambi memorial volume), Peoples Publishing House, New Delhi, 3rd edn., 1984, p. 235.
41. Esther David, 'The blue god school of art', *The Times of India*, Bombay, 5 November 1989.
42. Saradha Srinivasan Sankaran, 'The relation between Karnataka and Gujarat from the 7th to the early 14th century AD' (in two volumes), Ph.D. thesis, M.S. University of Baroda, Baroda, 1974, vol. 1, ch. IV; some major references are: (a) Laksmanagani, *Supasanahacariu* (b) Harisena, *Brhat katha kosa* (c) Jinendra Suri, *Katha kosa prakarana* (d) Dhanapāla, *Bhavisayattakaha* e) Hemachandra, *Abhidana-Chintāmani* (f) Someshwara, *Mānasollāsa* g) Chavundarāya, *Lōkopakāram*.
43. Malini Bisen, *Indian Sweet Delights*, Wilco Publishing House, Bombay, 1981, pp. x-xxvi.
44. Veena Shroff and Vanmala Desai, *Hundred Easy-to-make Gujarati Dishes*, 1979, Tarang Paperbacks, Vikas Publishing House Pvt. Ltd., New Delhi, 6th edn, 1989.
45. Bhogilal J. Sandaresa and R. N. Mehta (ed), *Varanaka-Samuchaya*, M. S. University of Baroda, Baroda, 1959, ch. 1, p. 9.
46. Aroona Reejsinghani, *Vegetarian Wonders from Gujarat*, Jaico Publishing House, Bombay, 1975
47. Bachi Karkaria, 'Fare play', *The Taj Magazine*, The Taj group of hotels, Bombay, vol. 17, no. 3, December 1988, p. 11.
48. Neeta Joshi, S. H. Godbole and Pradnya Kamekar, *Journal of Food Science and Technology*, 1989, vol. 26, p. 113.
49. Jennifer Fernandes, *Hundred Easy-to-make Goan Dishes*, Vikas Publishing House Pvt. Ltd., New Delhi, 1977.
50. H. D. Sankalia, 'Once upon a Goa', *The Times of India*, 15 November 1987.
51. Frank Simoes, 'Gourmet Goa', *Swagat*, Indian Airlines, January 1983, p. 76.
52. J. Inder Singh Kalra, 'Don't foregt the bottle masala!' *The Times of India*, 24 January 1988.
53. M. S. Randhawa, A History of India Agriculture in India, Indian Council of Agricultural Research, New Delhi, vol. 1, 1980, p. 216.
54. F. M. Hassnain (ed.), *Heritage of Kashmir*, Gulshan Publishers, Srinagar, 1980, (a) J. L. K. Jalali, 'Kashmir, its people and their languages', p. 12 (b) K. I. Khan, 'Culture heritage of Kargil', p. 156.
55. Sukla Das, *Socio-economic Life of Northern India (AD 550–650)*, Abhinav Publications, New Delhi, 1980, ch. 6, p 134.
56. Ashwini Agrawal, 'Social picture of Kashmir in the 11th and 12th centuries AD as depicted in the Rājatarangini of Kalhana', Vishveshvaranand Indological Paper Series 552, *Vishveshvaranand Indological Journal*, 1981, vol. 19, pts. i and ii, p. 199.
57. M. L. Kapur, *The History of Medieval Kashmir*, Oriental Publishers and Distributors, Delhi, 1975, p. 218.
58. Jyoteshwar Patik, *Cultural History of the Dogras*, Light and Life Publishers, New Delhi/Jammu, 1980, pp. 129, 137.
59. Dasharatha Sharma, 'Life in Rajasthan in the fourteenth and fifeenth centuries', Joural of Indian History, April 1960, p. 101.
60. Shivaji Rao Holkar and Shalini Devi Holkar, *Cooking of the Maharajas*, The Viking Press, New York, 1975, p. 89.
61. A. K. Shrivastava, *Hindu Society in the 16th Century* (with special reference to northern India), Milind Publications Pvt. Ltd. New Delhi, 1981, ch. v, p. 42.
62. Mumtaz Currim, 'Desert delights', *The Times of India*, 23 October 1988.
63. G. A. Grierson, *Bihar Peasant Life* (2nd edn, 1885), Government Printing, Bihar and Orissa, Patna, 1926, p. 345.
64. K. L. Shrigondekar (ed.), *Mānasollāsa of King Someswara*, Gaekwad's Oriental Series, 1939, vol. 84, pt. 2, Vimsati 3, Annabhoga, pp. 21–3.
65. *Maccapurānam*, Racakayāna: 16.
66. K. H. Steinkraus, Nestlé Research News, 1980–1, p. 23.
67. C. R. Krishna Murti, personal communication, March 1985.
68. S. K. Soni, D. K. Sandhu, K. S. Vilkhu and N. Kanra, *Food Microbiology*, 1986, vol. 3, no. 1, p. 45.
69. Jaroslav Formanek, 'Something out of the ordinary', *The Hindu*, Madras, 28 August 1987.
70. P. T. Srinivasa Aiyangar, *Pre-Aryan Tamil Culture* University of Madras, Madras, 1930, pp. 57–70,
71. Ka. Naa. Subrahmanyam, 'Food for thought', *The City Tab*, Bangalore, 25 Sept. –1 Oct. 1988, p. 19.
72. Om Prakash, *Food and Drinks in Ancient India*, Munshi Ram Manohar Lal, 1961, (a) pp. 34–57 (b) p. 249.
73. B. V. Nagaraju, 'Crisp and tasty Maddur vada', *Deccan Herald*, Bangalore, 10 October 1987.
74. Donald Richie, *A Taste of Japan*, Kodansha, Tokyo, 1985; review, *Time Magazine* 25 November 1985, p. 58.
75. Purobi Babbar, 'Breads of India', *Namaskar*, Air-India, 1986, vol. 6, no. 1, p. 19.
76. Taponath Chakravarty, *Food and Drink in Ancient Bengal*, Firma K. L. Mukhopadhyay, 1959, pp. 4, 18.

Chapter 11: Food Tales of the Early Travellers

1. B. N. Puri, *India as Described by Greek Writers*, The India Press Ltd., Allahabad, 1939, (a) pp. 1–22 (b) pp. 89–92; pp. 96–106 (d) pp. 78–88.
2. H. G. Rawlinson, 'Early contacts between India and Europe', in A.L. Basham (ed.), *A Cultural History of India*, Oxford University Press, Delhi, 1975, p. 425.
3. J. W. McCrindle, *Ancient India as Described by Ktesias the Kuidian* (1882), Manohar Reprints, Delhi, repr. 1976, pp. 16, 21,23, 30 and 70.
4. J. W. McCrindle, *The Invasion of India by Alexander the Great*, Metheun and Co. Ltd., London, 2nd edn, 1896, repr. 1969, (a) pp. 375–413 (b) pp. 267–301 (c) pp. 343–74 (d) pp. 57–180 (e) pp. 321–30 (f) pp. 181–266 (g) pp. 306–17.
5. Osmond de Beavoir Priaulx, *The Indian Travels of Apollonius of Tyana*, Quartich, London, 1873, pp. 15–44.
6. J. W. McCrindle, 'Ancient India as Described by Megasthenes and Arrian', Thacker Spink and Co., Calcutta, 1877; reprinted from the *Indian Antiquarian* 1876–7.
7. B. N. Pandey, *A Book of India*, Rupa and Co., India, by arrangements with Collins, London, 1977, repr. 1982 (a) p. 204 (b) p. 36 (c) p. 37 (d) p. 38.
8. R. C. Majumdar, *Ancient India*, Motilal Banarsidass, Delhi, 8th edn, 1977 (a) p. 213 (b) p. 454 (c) p. 453 (d) p. 252 (e) p. 255 (f) p. 276.
9. James Legge, *A Record of Buddhistic Kingdoms: Being an Account by the Chinese Monk Fa-Hien of his Travels in India and Ceylon (AD 399–414)*, The Clarendon Press, Oxford, 1886, (a) p. 44 (b) p. 93
10. Om Prakash, *Food and Drinks in Ancient India*, Munshi Ram Manohar Lal, Delhi, 1961; references to the Gupta period under each category of food.
11. Sukla Das, *Socio-economic Life of Northern India (AD 550–650)*, Abhinav Publications, New Delhi, 1980, chap. 6, p. 134.
12. R. N. Saletore, *Life in the Gupta Age*, The Popular Book Depot, Bombay, 1943, p. 121.
13. K. M. Panikkar, *India and China*, Asia Publishing House, Bombay, 1957, p. 95.
14. M. Elphinstone, E. B. Cowell, W. W. Hunter and J. Talboys Wheeler (eds), *Ancient India*, Sunil Gupta (India) Ltd., Calcutta, 1953, (a) E. B. Cowell. 'The Chinese Buddhist pilgrims in India', pp. 68–85 (b) J. Talboys Wheeler, 'Greek and Roman India', p. 97 (c) W. W. Hunter, 'the Greeks in India', p. 86.
15. M. S. Randhawa, *A History of Agriculture in India*, Indian Council of Agricultural Research New Delhi, vol. 1, 1980, (a) p. 423 (b) p. 426 (c) p. 427 (d) pp. 478–80 (e) pp. 480–1 (f) p. 325.
16. Rajendra Ram (ed.), *The Life of Hieun Tsang by Shaman Hwui Lüi*, Academica Asiatica, Delhi, 1973, (a) p. 43 (b) p. 97.
17. Tapan Raychaudhuri and Irfan Habib (eds), *The Cambridge Economic History of India*, Orient Longman Ltd., India, vol. 1, 1982, (a) p. 41 (b) p. 54.
18. M. S. Randhawa, *A History of Agriculture in India*, Indian Council of Agricultural Research, New Delhi, vol. 2, 1982, (a) p. 70 (b) pp. 10–11 (c) p. 12 (d) p. 51 (e) pp. 65–70 (f) p. 54 (g) pp. 100–5 (h) p. 38.
19. Arjun Dev, 'India in the eyes of early Muslim scholars', in Lokesh Chandra (ed.), *India's Contribution to World Thought and Culture* (a Vivekananda commemoration volume), Vivekananda Rock Memoral Committee, Madras, 1970, p. 589.
20. E. V. Sachau, *Alberuni's India*, Kegan Paul, Trench, Trubner and Co. Ltd., London, 1910, vol. 2, pp. 151–3.
21. Qeyammudin Ahmad (ed.), *India: Al-Biruni*, abridged edition of Sachau's English translation, National Book Trust, India, New Delhi, 1983, p. 253.
22. Robert Seull, *A Forgotten Empire*, Asian Education Services, New Delhi, repr. 1982, pp. 274, 375, 382.
23. C. V. Vaidya. *History of Medieval Hindu India: Early History of the Rajputs (750–1000 AD)*. Oriental Book Supply Agency, Poona, 1924, pp. 162–6.

Chapter 12: Muslim Bonus

1. K. M. Ashraf, *Life and Conditions of the People of Hindustan* (1935), Munshiram Manoharlal, New Delhi, repr 2nd, 1970, pp. 118–19 and pp. 158–63.
2. K. P. Sahu, *Some Aspects of North Indian Social Life 1000–1526 AD*, Punthi Pusthak, Calcutta, 1973, ch. 2, pp. 29–44.
3. H. A. R. Gibb (trans.), *Ibn Battūta, Travels in Asia and Africa 1325–1354*, Routledge and Kegan Paul Ltd., London, 4th impression, 1957, pp. 185–217.
4. M. S. Randhawa, *A History of Agriculture in India*, Indian council of Agricultural Research, New Delhi, vol. 2, 1982, (a) p. 51 (b) p. 257 (c) p. 30.
5. S. Lane-Poole, *Medieval India from Contemporary Sources*, K. and J. Cooper, Bombay, undated, pp. 47, 76. 99.
6. P. N. Chopra, *Society and Culture in Mughal India*, Shiv Lal Agarwala and Co. (Pvt.) Ltd., Agra, 2nd edn, 1963.
7. J. S. Hoyland and S. N. Banerjee, *The Commentary of Father Monserrate*, S. J. Humphrey Milford, Oxford

University Press, India, 1922, p. 199.

8. Rumer Godden, *Gulbadan: Portrait of a Rose Princess at the Mughal Court*, Macmillan, London, 1980, pp. 60, 146.
9. Niccalao Manucci, *Storio de Mogor 1653–1708*, trans. William Irvine, John Murrary, London, 1906, vol. 1, p. 219.
10. A. Rahman, 'Science and technology in medieval India', in A. Rahman (ed.), *Science and Technology in Indian Culture: A Historical Perspective*, National Institute for Science, Technology and Development, New Delhi, 1984, p. 123.
11. Shalini Holkar, 'The wonders of yoghurt', *Express Magazine*, 8 May 1983, p. 3.
12. Abul Fazl, *The Ain-i-Akbari*, trans. H. Blochmann (1871), Aadiesh Book Depot, Delhi, repr. 1965, pp. 57–78.
13. William Foster, *Early Travels in India 1583–1619*, S. Chand and Co., New Delhi, repr. 1968, pp. 60–121.
14. S. Lane-Poole, *Aurangzib*, Clarendon Press, Oxford, 1908, pp. 65–7.
15. Lallanji Gopal, 'Agricultural technique in medieval India: its Central Asian contacts', in *Giridharashrī: Essays in Indology* (Dr. G. S. Dikshit felicitation volume), Agam Kala Prakashan, Delhi, 1987, p. 235
16. A. S. Beveridge (trans.), *Bābur-nāma*, 1922, Oriental Books Reprint Corporation, New Delhi, 1970, pp. 645, 687.
17. M. A. Alvi and A. Rahman, *Jahangir, The Natvralist*, National Institute of Sciences, New Delhi, 1968, pp. 92–127.
18. A. K. Shrivastava, *Hindu Society in the 16th Century* (with special reference to northern India), Milind Publications Pvt. Ltd., New Delhi, 1981. pp. 42–9.
19. P. K. Gode, 'Use of Ganges water by Muslim rulers (1300–1800AD)', *Studies in Indian Cultural history* , vol. III, Bhandarkar Oriental Research Institute, Poona, 1969, pt. 1, p. 139.
20. G. V. Joshi, 'Ganges water baffles researchers', *Deccan Herald*, Bangalore, 7 December 1989.
21. Henry Yule and A. C. Burnell, *Hobson-Jobson* (1886), ed. William Crooke, Munshiram Manoharlal Publishers Pvt Ltd., New Delhi, 4th edn, 1984, p. 458.
22. S. N. Krishna Jois (ed.), *Sūpa Sāstra of Mangarasa (1516 AD)*, University of Mysore, Mysore, 1969, (a) Annājī, *Soundara Vilāsa* (Second part of *Kavicharité* AD 1600), p. 267.
23. Shanti Rangarao, *Good Food from India* (1968), Jaico Publishing House, Bombay, 3rd impression, 1977, p. 240.
24. Sipra Das Gupta, *The Home Book of Indian Cookery*, 1976, Rupa and Co., Calcutta, 1978, p. 138.
25. Minakshie Dasgupta, *Bangla Ranna*, published by Jaya Chaliha, Calcutta, 1982, p. 198.

Chapter 13: The coming of the Europeans

1. Harry Johnston, *Pioneers in India*, Blackie and Son Ltd., London, 1913, (a) pp. 33–55 (b) pp. 149–209 (c) pp. 126–48 (d) pp. 210–40.
2. George Watt, *The Commercial Products of India* (1908), Today and Tomorrow's Printers and Publishers, New Delhi, repr. 1966, (a) p. 1140 (b) p. 249 (c) p. 845.
3. M. S. Randhawa, *A History of Agriculture in India*, Indian Council of Agricultural Research, New Delhi; vol. 1, 1980 (a) p. 479 (b) pp. 100–15 (c) pp. 216–17 (d) p. 282 (e) p. 313 (f) pp. 286–93; (g) vol. 2, 1982, p. 113.
4. Henry Yule and A.C. Burnell, *Hobson-Jobson* (1886), ed. William Crooke, Munshiram Manoharlal Publishers Pvt. Ltd., New Delhi 4th edn, 1984, (a) p. 475 (b) p. 737 (c) p. 927 (d) p. 425 (e) p. 330 (f) p. 281 (g) p. 919 (h) p. 664.
5. Afanasy Nikitin, *Voyage Beyond the Three Seas (1466–1472)*, trans. Stepan Apresyan, Raduga Publishers, Moscow, 1985, pp. 31–2.

5A. Amba Prasad, 'India's contaets with Africa from ancient times', in Lokesh Chandra (ed.), *India's Contribution to World Thought and Culture* (a Vivekananda commemoration volume), Vivekananda Rock Memorial Committee, Madras, 1970, p. 601.

6. Genevieve Bouchon, 'Glimpses of the beginning of the Carriera da India (1500–1518)', in *Third International Seminar on Indo-Portuguese History*, Xavier Centre of Historical Research, Goa, January 1983, paper 3.
7. H. K. Kaul, *Traveller's India: An Anthology*, Oxford University Press, 1979, (a) p. 310 (b) p. 288 (c) p. 351.
8. Donald F. Lach, *India in the Eyes of Europe: The Sixteenth Century*, Phoenix Books, University of Chicago Press, Chicago/London, 1968, (a) p. 410 (b) p. 388 (c) p. 370.
9. K. Sridharan (Admiral, retd), 'Log book of I.N.S Angre', personal communication, October 1986.
10. Ethel M. Pope, *India in Portuguese History*, Tipografia Rangel, Bastora, Portuguese India, 1937, p. 116.
11. P. D. Gaitonde, *Portuguese Prisoners in India: Spotlight on Medicine*, Popular Prakashan, Bombay, 1983.
12. George Watt, *The Commerical Products of India*, ref. 2 above, entries under several products mentioned in the text.
13. J. S. Hoyland and S. N. Banerjee, *The Commentary of Father Monserrate*, S. J., Humphrey Milford, Oxford University Press, India, 1922, (a) p. xv (b) p. 213 (c) p. 25 (d) p. 35 (e) p. 11.
14. William Foster, *Early Travels in India 1583–1619*, S. Chand and Co., New Delhi, repr. 1968.
15. R. C. Prasad, *Early English Travellers in India*, 1965, Motilal Banarsidass, Delhi, 2nd edn. 1980, (a) p. 202

(b) p. 267.
16. P. N. Chopra, *Society and Culture in Mughal India*, Shiv Lal Agrawala and Co. (Pvt.) Ltd., Agra, 2nd edn, 1963 pp. 32–54.
17. Mohommad Azhar Ansari, *European Travellers under the Mughals (1580–1627)*, Idarah-i-Adabiyat-i Delhi, Delhi, 1975, pp. 76–103.
18: Philip Woodruff, *Men Who Ruled India*, Jonathan Cape, London, 1963, (a) p. 46 (b) p. 53 (c) p. 175 (d) p. 244 and p. 219.
19. Tapan Raychaudhuri and Irfan Habib (eds), *The Cambridge Economic History of India, vol. 1: c. 1200–1750*, Orient Longman Ltd., India, 1982, (a) p. 330 (b) p. 263 (c) p. 326.
20. J. S. Hoyland and S. N. Banerjee, *The Empire of the Great Mogol*, A translation of De Laet's 'Description of India' and 'Fragment of Indian History', D. B. Taraporewala Sons and Co., Bombay, 1928, p. 82.
21. Indira Chakravarthy, *Saga of Indian Food*, Sterling Publishers Pvt. Ltd., New Delhi, 1972, pp. 73–4.
22. P. J. Thomas, 'Kerala culture : its distinctive features', in *K. V. Rangaswami Ayyangar Commemoration Volume*, Published by P. S. Sivaswamy Aiyar, Madras, 1940, p. 275.
23. J. Talboys Wheeler, *Early Records of British India*, Vishal Publishers, Delhi, 2nd edn. 1972, pp. 154, 159.
24. B. N. Pandey, *A Book of India*, Rupa and Co., India, 1982, p. 53.
25. Niccolao Manucci, *Storio di Mogor* 1653–1708, trans. William Irvine, John Murray, London, 1906, vol. 1, pp. 62–8.
26. Robert Orme, *Of the Government and People of Indostan*, Pustak Kendra, Lucknow, repr. 1971.
27. Eliza Fay, *Original Letters from India*, ed. E. M. Foster, The Hogarth Press, London, 1986, p. 181.
28. N. J. Nanporia, *Sunday Herald, Bangalore*, 19 November 1989, p. 6; review of a book by Vidya Dehejia, 'Impossible picturesqueness'.
29. Shalini Holkar, 'Eating habits of the British in India', *MARG*, bombay, 1989, vol. 41, no. 1, p. 35.
30. Margaret Macmillan, *Women of the Raj*, Thames and Hudson, New York, 1988, pp. 161–4.
31. J. N. Das Gupta, *India in the 17th Century (as described by European travellers)*, University of Calcutta, Calcutta, 1916 (a) p. 170 (b) p. 163 (c) p. 75.
32. N. S. Ramaswamy (ed.), *The Chief Secretary*, New Era Publications, Madras, 1983, p. 79.
33. Vasundara Filliozat, *Aliluda Hampi*, Manasallosana Prakashana, Bangalore, 1983; review in *the Hindu*, Madras, 3 January 1984.
34. K. L. Bernard, *Flashes of Kerala History*, published by the author, 2nd edn, Cochin, 1980, p. 17.
35. R. P. Patwardhan and H. G. Rawlinson, *Source Book of Maratha History, vol. 1: To the Death of Shivaji*, Government Central Press, Bombay, 1929, pp. 185–93.
36. V. D. Divekar, in Dharma Kumar (ed.), *The Cambridge Economic History of India, Part 2: c. 1757 - c. 1920*, Orient Longman/Cambridge University Press, 1982, Hyderabad, repr. 1984, pp. 332–52.

Chapter 14: Staples of Yore

1. N. W. Simmonds (ed.), *Evolution of Crop Plants*, Longman, London and New York, 1976, (a) J. R. Harlan, p. 93 (b) Moshe Feldman, p. 120 (c) J. W. Purseglove, p. 91 (d) T. T. Chang, p. 98 (e) H. Doggett, p. 112 (f) P. M. Smith, p. 302 (g) J. D. Sauer, p. 4 (h) D. Zohary, p. 163 (i) S. Ramanujam, p. 157 (j) D. A. Bond, p. 179 (k) A. E. Evans, p. 168 (I) Roy Davis, p. 172 (m) P. F. Knowles, p. 31.
2. J. F. Jarrige and R. H. Meadow, 'The antecedents of civilisation in the Indus valley', *Scientific American*, vol. 243, no. 2, August 1980, p. 102.
3. M. S. Randhawa, *Agriculture in India*, Indian Council of Agricultural Research, New Delhi, vol. 1, 1980, (a) p. 104 (b) p. 271; vol. 2, 1982 (c) p. 343.
4. A. N. Khanna, *The Archaeology of India*, Clarion Books, New Delhi 1981.
5. J. B. Hutchinson (ed.), *Diversity and Change in the Indian Subcontinent*, Cambridge University Press, 1974, (a) Vishnu-Mittre, 'Palaeobotanical evidence in India', p. 3 (b) S. D. Sharma and S. V. S. Shastry, 'Rice', p. 60 (c) D. N. De, 'Pigeon pea', p. 79.
6. Om Prakash, *Food and Drinks in Ancient India*, Munshi Ram Manohar Lal, Delhi, 1961, (a) Sections on cereals in various historical periods (b) pp. 260–3 (c) pp. 7-33 (d) pp. 263–5 (e) pp. 272-9 (f) sections on oilseeds in various historical periods (g) pp. 265–6.
7. H. G. Baker, *Plants and Civilisation* Macmillan and Co. Ltd., London, 1964, p. 68.
8. George Watt, *The Commercial Products of India* (1908), Today and Tomarrow's Printers and Publishers, New Delhi, repr. 1966 (a) p. 1082 (b) p. 823 (c) p. 1021 (d) p. 845 (c) p. 393 (f) p. 62 (g) p. 879 (h) p. 1107 (i) p. 508 (j) p. 196 (k) pp. 1106–7 (I) p. 449 (m) p. 174 (n) p. 625.
9. M. S. Nagaraja Rao, *Protohistoric Cultures of the Tungabhadara valley*, Karnatak Univerisity, Dharwar, 1971.
10. F. R. Allchin, 'Early cultivated plants', in P. J. Ucko and G. W. Dimbleby (eds), *The Domestication and Exploitation of Plants and Animals*, Gerald Duckworth and Co., London, 1969, p. 323.
11. J. H. Hulse, E. M. Laing and O. E. Pearson, *Sorghum and the Millets*, Academic Press, 1980, (a) p. 177 (b) p. 33f.
12. G. P. Murdoch, *Africa, its People and their culture and History*, McGraw Hill, New York, 1959.
13. T. T. Chang, 'The origin, evolution, cultivation, dissemination and diversification of Asian and African rices', *Euphytica*, 1976, vol. 25, p. 425.
14. K. R. Bhattacharya, C. M. Sowbhagya and Y. M. Indudhara Swamy, *Journal of food Science*, 1982, vol. 47,

p. 562
15. Ruth D. Whitehouse (ed.), *The Macmillan Dictionary of Archaeology*, Macmillan Press, London, 1983, p. 429.
16. Vishnu-Mittre and R. Savitri, in G. L. Possehl (ed.), *Food Economy of the Harappans*, Oxford and IBH Publishing Co., India, 1982, p. 205.
17. D. H. Grist, *Rice*, Longman, 5th edn, 1975, repr. 1978, p. 3.
18. S. P. Raychaudhuri, *Agriculture in Ancient India*, Indian Council of Agricultural Research, New Delhi, 1964, p. 16.
19. A. C. Das, *Rigvedic Culture*, Bharatiya Publishing House, Varanasi, 1979, pp. 200, 279.
20. H. D. Sankalia, *Prehistory of India*, Munshiram Manoharlal Publishers Pvt. Ltd., New Delhi, 1987, pp. 39–54.
21. S. Mohamed Osman, 'The royal refugees', *The Times of India, Sunday Review*, 20 August 1982.
22. Mudaliar C. Rasanayagam, *Ancient Jaffna*, Everyman's Publishers Ltd., Madras, 1926, pp. 140–60.
23. J. Venkateswarulu and R. S. K. Chaganti, 'Job's tears', Tech. Bull. no. 44, Indian Council of Agricultural Research, New Delhi, 1973, pp. 1. 45 and 46.
24. G. Richter, *Gazetteer of Coorg (1870)*, B. R. Publishing Corporation, Delhi, repr. 1984, p. 22.
25. Anon, 'The bamboo blooms', *The Hindu*, Madras, 24 June 1984, p. 26.
26. Lee Durrell, *State of The Ark*, The Bodley Head, London, 1986.
27. O. L. Oke, 'Amaranth', in Harvey T. Chan (ed.), *Handbook of Tropical Foods*, Marcel Dekker Inc., New York and Basel, 1983, p. 1.
28. *The Wealth of India: Raw Materials*, Council of Scientific and Industrial Research, New Delhi, 1948, vol. 1, p. 66 and 1985, vol. 1–A, p. 213.
29. Harbhajan Singh, *Grain Amaranths, Buckwheat and Chenopods*, Indian Council of Agricultural Research, New Delhi, 1961.
30. Anon, *Amaranth Round-up*, Rodale Press Inc., Emmaus, Pennsylvania, 1977 (a) note by J. D. Sauer, p. 13.
31. A. S. Marroquin and N. Subramaniam, *Agro-industrial Potential of Amaranths*, Centre for Economic and Social Studies of the Third World, Mexico, 1980, p. 22.
32. B. Baldev, S. Ramanujam and H. K. Jain, *Pulse Crops*, Oxford and IBH Publishing Co. Pvt. Ltd., New Delhi, 1988, (a) J. L. Tickoo and H. K. Jain, p. 161 (b) L. M. Jeswani, p. 199 (c) Laxman Singh and S. P. Misra, p. 215 (d) P. N. Bahl, p. 95.
33. Ashok Bendre and Ashok Kumar, *Economic Botany*, Rastogi Publications, Meerut, 4th edn, 1980, pp. 21–5.
34. K. L. Mehra, 'History of masura pulse in India and its cultural significance', *Vishveshwaranand Indological Journal*, 1972, vol. 10, p. 131; *Vishveshvaranand Indological Paper Series*-320.
35. P. Kachroo (ed.), *Pulse Crops of India*, Indian Council of Agricultural Research, New Delhi, 1970, p. 158.
36. Umrao Singh, A. M. Wadhwani and B. M. Johri, *Dictionary of Economic Plants in India*, Indian Council of Agricultural Research, New Delhi, p. 241.
37. Majibar S. Biswas and S. Dana, 'Phaseolus aconitifolius x Phaseolus trilobus', *Indian Journal of Genetics and Plant Breeding* 1976, vol. 36, no. 1, p. 125.
38. S. Dana, 'Origin, evolution and distribution of some grain legumes', *Indian Journal of Genetics and Plant Breeding*, 1976, vol. 36, no. 1, p. 143.
39. J. Smartt, *Tropical Pulses*, Longman, 1976, pp. 3–22.
40. Tapan Raychaudhuri and Irfan Habib, *The Cambridge Economic History of India*, 1982, Orient Longman/Cambridge University Press, Hyderabad, repr. 1984, vol. 1, p. 462.
41. B. G. L. Swamy, *Namma Hoteyalli Dakshina America*, Prasaranga, Bangalore University, Bangalore, 1978, pp. 613.
42 W. G. Solheim, 'An earlier agricultural revolution', *Scientific American* 1972, vol. 226, no. 4, p. 34.
43. M. S. Vats, *Excavations at Harappa*, Manager of Publications, Delhi, 1970, vol. 1, p. 466.
44. D. R. Bedigian and J. R. Harlan, 'Evidence for the cultivation of sesame in the ancient world', *Economic Botany*, 1986, vol. 40, p. 137.
45. Shireen Ratnagar, *Encounters: The Westerly Trade of the Harappan Civilisation*, Oxford University Press, New Delhi, 1981.
46. D. R. Bedigian, C. R. Smyth and J. R. Harlan, 'Pattern of morphological varration in *Sesamum Indicum*', *Economic Botany*, 1986, vol. 40, p. 353.
47. K. Hinata and Shyam Prakash, 'Ethnobotany and evolutionary origin of oleiferous Brassicae', *Indian Journal of Genetics*, 1984, vol. 44, p. 102.
48. J. Adhikari, S. Adhikari and K. T. Achaya, 'Glucosinolates in the seeds of Indian brassicas and *Eruca sativa*', *Journal of the Oil Technologists' Association of India*, 1989, vol. 21, no. 1, p. 13.
49. K. T. Achaya, *Oilseeds and Oilmilling in India*, Oxford and IBH Publishing Co. Pvt. Ltd., New Delhi, 1990, p. 144.
50. R. Child, *Coconuts*, Longman, 2nd edn, 1974, pp. 1–14.
51. K. P. V. Menon and K. M. Pandalai, *The Coconut Palm*, Indian Central Coconut Committee, Ernakulam, 1958, pp. 7–19.
52. M. Srinivasa Aiyangar, *Tamil Studies*, 1913, Asian Educational Services, New Delhi, repr. 1982, p. 426.
53. K. P. Chattopadhyaya, *The Ancient Indian Culture Contacts and Migrations*, Firma K. L. Mukhopadhyaya, Calcutta, 1970, p. 91f.
54. S. M. Gupta, *Plant Myths and Traditions in India*, E. J. Brill, Leiden, 1971, p. 34.
55. M. D. Kajale, 'On the botanical findings from excavations at Daimabad', *Current Science*, 1977, vol. 46. p. 818.
56. David Wilson, *Atoms from Time Past*, The Scientific Book Club, London, 1976, p. 150.
57. S. C. Hiremath and H. N. Murthy, 'Domestication of niger (*Guizotia abyssinica*)', *Euphytica*, 1988, vol. 37, p. 225.
58. Alphonse de Candolle, *Origin of Cultivated Plants*

(1882), Hafner Publishing Co., New York and London, 2nd edn, 3rd printing, 1967.
59. C. D. Darlington, *Chromosome Botany and the Origins of Cultivated Plants*, George Allen and Unwin Ltd., London, 2nd ed., 1964, pp. 2–16 and p. 95.
60. R. S. Vaidyanatha Iyer, *Manu's Land and Trade Laws*, Higginbotham, Madras, 1927, p. 85.
61. R. Shamasastry, *Kautilya's Arthashāstra*, Weslyan Mission Press, Musore, 2nd edn, 1923, p. 123.
62. A. H. Church, *Food Grains of India*, South Kensington Museum Science Handbooks, London, 1886.

Chapter 15: Pleasing the Palate

1. N W. Simmonds (ed.), *Evolution of Crop Plants*, Longman, London and New York, 1976, (a) D. L. Plunkett, p. 10 (b) D. G. Coursey, p. 70 (c) D. E. Yen, p. 42 (d) B. Chowdhary, p. 278 (e) P. M. Smith, p. 301 (f) O. Banga, p. 60 (g) O. Banga, p. 291 (h) A. B. Joshi and M. W. Hardas, p. 194 (i) T. W. Whitaker and W. P. Bemis, p. 64 (j) J. H. M. Oudejans, p. 229 (k) Jaques Barrau, p. 201 (l) N. W. Simmonds, p. 211 (m) L. B. Singh, p. 7 (n) J. W. Cameron and R. K. Soost, p. 261 (o) H. P. Olmo, p. 294 (p) Ray Watkins, p. 242 (q) Ray Watkins, p. 247 (r) G. D. McCollum, p. 186 (s) A. C. Zeven, p. 234 (t) F. Wit, p. 216 (u) N. W. Simmonds, p. 104.
2. George Watt, *The Commercial Products of India*, 1908, Today and Tomorrow's Printers and Publishers, New Delhi, repr. 1966, (a) p. 398 (b) p. 65 (c) p. 490 (d) p. 1112 (e) p. 1118 (f) p. 910 (g) p. 527 (h) p. 791 (i) pp. 311–16 (j) p. 429 (k) p. 533 (l) p. 931.
3. Om Prakash, *Food and Drinks in Ancient India*, Munshi Ram Manohar Lal, Delhi, 1961, (a) pp. 272–9 (b) pp. 266–72 (c) pp. 34–57 (e) pp. 279–83 (f) pp. 251–2 (g) Sections on honey and sugar in various historical epochs.
4. D. G. Coursey, *Yams*, Longman, London and New York, 1967, (a) pp. 1–4 (b) pp. 5–27.
5. *The Wealth of India: Raw Materials*, Council of Scientific and Industrial Research, New Delhi (a) 1959, vol. 5, p. 75 (b) 1959, vol. 5, p. 237 (e) 1966, vol. 7, p. 70 (d) 1976, vol. 10, p. 19 (e) 1948, vol. 1, p. 173 (f) 1962, vol. 6, p. 177 (g) 1976, vol. 10, p. 286 (h) 1962, vol. 6, p. 448 (i) 1962, vol. 6, p. 448 (j) 1962, vol. 6 p. 265 (k) 1976, vol. 10, p. 526 (l) 1969, vol. 8, p. 250 (m) 1969, vol. 8, p. 327 (n) 1985, vol. 1–A, p. 500.
6. I. C. Onwueme, *The Tropical Tuber Crops*, John Wiley and Sons Ltd., 1978, (a) p. 3 (b) p. 167.
7. Anon *The Indian Express*, Bangalore, 26 November 1985.
8. J. N. Das Gupta, *India in the 17th Century (as depicted by European travellers)*, University of Calcutta, 1916, p. 102.
9. W. M. Sleeman, *Rambles and Recollections of an Indian Official*, 1844, 2 vols, ed. V. A. Smith, Archibald Constable and Co., London, 1903 p. 74.
10. P. R. Ray and H. N. Gupta, *Charaka Samhitā : A Scientific Synopsis*, 1965, Indian National Science Academy, New Delhi, 2nd edn, 1980, Table 3, pp. 54–77.
11. Umrao Singh, A. M. Wadhwani and B. M. Johri, *Dictionary of Economic Plants in Idnia*, Indian Council of Agricultural Research, New Delhi, 1983, (a) p. 212 (b) p. 100 (c) p. 61 (d) p. 51 (e) p. 144 (f) p. 249 (g) p. 22 (h) p. 242 and p. 15 (i) pp. 184–8 (j) p. 14 (k) pp. 85–6.
12. K. T. Achaya, *Your Food and You*, National Book Trust, India, New Delhi, 5th edn, repr. 1988, p. 18.
13. J. B. Hutchinson (ed.), *Diversity and Change in the Indian Subcontinent*, Cambridge University Press, 1974, (a) A. B. Joshi, V. R. Gadwal and M. W. Hardas, p. 101 (b) Vishnu-Mittre, p. 3.
14. A. M. Shasti, *India as seen in the Kuttāni-Mata of Damodaragupta*, Motilal Banarsidass, Delhi, 1975, p. 200.
15. T. W. Whitaker and G. N. Davis, *Cucurbits*, Leonard Hill (Books) Ltd., London, 1962.
16. B. Brouk, *Plants Consumed by Man*, Academic Press, London, 1975, pp. 132–5.
17. Sham Singh, S. Krishnamurthy and S. L. Katyal, *Fruit Culture in India*, Indian Council of Agricultural Research, New Delhi, 1963.
18. Ashok Bendre and Ashok Kumar, *Economic Botany*, Rastogi Publications, Meerut, 4th edn, 1980, p. 67.
19. P. K. Gode, 'References to tāmbula', Vishveshvaranand Indological Paper Series-26, Vishveshwaranand Vedic Research Institute, Hoshiarpur, 1954.
20. Henry Yule and A. C. Burnell, *Hobson-Jobson, 1886*, ed. William Crooke, Munshiram Manoharlal Publishers Pvt. Ltd., New Delhi, 4th edn, repr. 1984 (a) p. 894 (b) p. 440 f (c) p. 56 (d) p. 715 (e) p. 642.
21. *Shorter Oxford English Dictionary*, 1964, vol. 2, p. 1515.
22. S. R. Gangolly, Ranjit Singh, S. L. Katyal and Daljit Singh, *The Mango*, Indian Council of Agricultural Research, new Delhi, 1957.
23. P. L. Bhargava, *India in the Vedic age*, 1956, Upper India Publishing House Pvt. Ltd.,Lucknow, 2nd edn, 1971, p. 80f.
24. Ranjit Singh, *Fruits*, National Book Trust, India, New Delhi, 1979, pp. 16–96 and pp. 152–70.
25. P. K. Gode, *Studies in Indan Cultural History*, Vishveshvaranand Vedic Research Institute, Hoshiarpur, vol. 1, 1961, (a) p. 452 (b) p. 357.
26. M. Ramakrishna Bhat, *Varāhamihira's Brhat Samhitā*, vol. 1 (1981), Motilal Banarsidass, Delhi, repr, 1986, ch. 55, p. 527.

27. S. Krishnamurthy (ed.), *Advances in Agricultural Sciences*, publisheed by the *Madras Agricultural Journal*, Agricultural College and Research Instutite, Coimbatore, 1965, (a) T. Tanaka, 'Achievements in the improvement of citrus', p. 332 (b) R. W. Hodgson, 'Taxonomy and nomenclature of the citrus fruits', p. 317 (c) N. R. Bhat, 'Sugarcane breeding in India', p. 34.
28. M. S. Randhawa, *A history of Agriculture in India*, Indian Council of Agricultural Research, New Delhi, (a) 1982, vol. 2, p. 150 (b) 1980, vol. 1, p. 382 (c) 1982, vol. 2, p. 66 (d) 1986, vol. 4, p. 457 (e) 1986, vol. 4, p. 458 (f) 1980, vol. 1, p. 299 (g) 1983, vol. 3, pp. 332–7.
29. M. S. Randhawa, Asok Mitra and Giselle Mehta, *Farmers of India*, Idian Council of Agricultural Research, New Delhi, 1964, vol. 3, p. 37.
30. Dharma Kumar (ed.), *The Cambridge Economic History of India*, 1982, Orient Longman/Cambridge University Press, 1st edn., repr. March 1984, vol. 2, p. 53.
31. A. S. Beveridge (trans.), *Bābur-Nāma* (1922), Orient Books Reprint Corporation, new Delhi, 1970.
32. Ruskin Bond, 'Along the Bhagirathi', *Sunday Herald*, Bangalore, 31 January 1988; 'The Ganga descends', *Swagat*, Indian Airlines, February 1988, p. 46.
33. Anon, 'Apple season', *The Times of India*, Bangalore, 8 September 1986.
34. 'Apples', *Science Today*, Bombay, August 1986, p. 9.
35. Fred Lape, *Apples and Man*, Van Nostrand Reinhold Co., New York, 1979, (a) pp. 45, 80 (b) p. 50.
36. H. N. Ridley, *Spices* (1912), International Book distributors, Dehra Dun, repr. 1983, (a) p. 205 (b) p. 324.
37. J. W. Purseglove, E. G. Brown, C. L. Green and S. R. J. Robbins, *Spices*, Longman, 1981, vol. 1, p. 532.
38. H. A. Jones and L. K. Mann, *Onion and its Allies*, Leonard Hill (Books) Ltd., London, 1963, pp. 18, 36.
39. Ramesh Bedi, 'Garlic', in H. L. Hariyappa and M. M. Patkar (eds.), *Prof. P. K. Gode Commemoration Volume*, Oriental Book Agency, Poona, 1960, pt. II, p. 9.
40. V. S. Govindarajan, Shanti Narasimhan, K. G. Raghuveer and Y. S. Lewis, 'Cardamom: Production, technology, chemistry and quality', *CRC Critical Reviews*, 1982, vol. 16, issue 3, pp. 229–326.
41. Ruth D. Whitehouse (ed.), *The Macmillan Dictionary of Archaeology*, Macmillan Press, London, 1983, p. 62.
42. F. Rosengarten, *The Book of Spices*, Livingstone Publishing Co., Philadelphia, 1969, (a) p. 248 (b) p. 202.
43. S. Muktar, 'Saffron: losing out to Spain', *Sunday Express*, Bangalore, 4 January 1987.
44. M. L. Kapur, *The History of Medieval Kashmir*, Oriental Publishers and Distributors, Delhi, 1975, p. 228.
45. Shalini Holkar, 'A spice for sovereigns', *Express Magazine*, Bangalore, 19 June 1983, p. 3.
46. John and Cherry Ojha, 'Sweet exchanges', *SPAN*, June 1986, p. 36.

Chapter 16: Bounty from the New World

1. Sylvanus G. Morley, revised by George W. Brainerd, *The Ancient Maya* (1947), Stanford University Press, Stanford, California, 3rd edn, 1956, p. 128.
2. N. W. Simmonds (ed.), *Evolution of Crop Plants*, Longman, London and New York, 1976, (a) W. C. Gregory and M. P. Gregory, p. 151 (b) T. Hymowitz, p. 159 (c) Ray Watkins, p. 242 (d) P. M. Smith, p. 302 (e) W. B. Storey, p. 21 (f) B. O. Bergh, p. 148 (g) Charles M. Rick, p. 268 (h) N. W. Simmonds, p. 279 (i) D. L. Jennings, p. 81 (j) C. B. Heiser, p. 265 (k) T. Visser, p. 18 (l) F. P. Ferwerda, p. 257 (m) F. W. Cope, p. 285 (n) M.M. Goodman, p. 128 (o) Barbara Pickersgill, p. 14.
3. H. G. Baker, *Plants and Civilisation*, Macmillan and Co. Ltd., London, 1964, p. 180.
4. E. A. Weiss, *Oilseed Crops*, Longman, London and New York, 1983, p. 100.
5. George Watt, *The Commercial Products of India* (1908), Today and Tomorrow's Printers and Publishers, New Delhi, repr. 1966, (a) p. 75 (b) p. 565 (c) p. 902 (d) p. 700 (c) p. 188 (f) p. 888 (g) p. 265 (h) p. 209 (i) p. 218 and p. 367 (j) p. 316 (k) p. 75.
6. A. Krapovickas, in P. J. Ucko and G. W. Dimbleby (eds), *The Domestication and Exploitation of Plants and Animals*, Gerald Duckworth and Co. Pvt. Ltd., London, 1969, p. 427.
7. George Watt, *Dictionary of the Economic Products of India (1888–1893)*, Cosmo Publications, Delhi, repr. 1972, (a) vol. 1, p. 282 (b) vol. 5, p. 101.
8. F. S. Kale, *Soyabean: its Dietetics, Cultivation and Uses*, 1936, F. Doctor and Co., Baroda, 2nd edn, 1937.
9. *The Wealth of India: Raw Materials*, Council of Scientific and Industrial Research, New Delhi, (a) 1956, vol. 4, p. 142 (b) 1948, vol. 1, p. 23 (c0 1966, vol. 7, p. 315 (d) 1962, vol. 6, p. 187 (e) 1962, vol. 6, p. 286 (f) 1976, vol. 10, p. 210 (f) 1956, vol. 4, p. 142.
10. E. D. Putt, 'History and present world status', in J.E. Carter (ed.), *Sunflower Science and Technology*, American Soceity of Agronomy, Crop Science Society of America and Soil Science Society of America, Inc., Madison, Wisconsin, 1978, p. 1.
11. H. C. Srivastava, S. Bhaskaran, B. Vatsya and K. K. G. Menon, *Oilseed Production: Opportunities and Constraints*, Oxford and IBH Publishing Co. Pvt. Ltd., New Delhi, (a) L. M. Jeswani, p. 233 (b) T. P. Yadava, p. 41 (c) S. S. Sindagi, p. 141.
12. Henry Yule and A.C. Burnell, *Hobson-Jobson* (1886), ed. William Crooke, Munshiram Manoharlal Publishers Pvt. Ltd., New Delhi, 4th edn, repr. 1984, (a) p. 168 (b) p. 670 (c) p. 399 (d) p. 14 (e) p. 196 (f) pp. 26–7 (g) p. 284 (h) p. 3.
13. K. Padmanaba Menon, in T. K. Krishna Menon (ed.),

History of Kerala, Asian Educational Services, New Delhi, repr. 1986, (a) p. 445 (b) p. 437.
14. Anon, *Cashew*, Central Plantation Crops Research Institute, Kasargod, Kerala, March 1979, ch. 1.
15. Umrao Singh, A. M. Wadhwani and B. M. Johri, *Dictionary of Economic Plants in India*, Indian Council of Agricultural Research, New Delhi, 1983, (a) p. 227 (b) p. 185 (c) p. 165 (d) p. 85 (e) p. 17.
16. P. R. Ray and H. N. Gupta, *Caraka Samhitā: A Scientific Synopsis* (1965), Indian National Science Academy, New Delhi, 2nd edn, 1980, table 3, pp. 54–77.
17. Ashok Bendre and Ashok Kumar, *Economic Botany*, Rastogi Publications, Meerut, 4th edn, 1980, (a) p. 34 (b) p. 11.
18. K. L. Mehra, 'Portuguese introduction of fruit plants into India-pt. II', *Indian Horticulture*, 1965–6, vol. 10, no. 3, p. 9.
19. Sham Singh, S. Krishnamurthy and S. L. Katyal, *Fruit Culture in India*, Indian Council of Agricultural Research, New Delhi, 1963.
20. B. Brouk, *Plants Consumed by Man*, Academic Press, London, 1975, p. 180.
21. Harvey T. Chan (ed.), *Handbook of Tropical Fruits*, Marcel Dekker Inc., New York and Basel, 1983, (a) H. T. Chan, p. 351 (b) E. U. Odigboh, p. 145.
22. Anon, 'A flower on the cross', *Sunday Times*, Bangalore, 21 July 1985.
23. Charles M. Rick, 'The tomato', *Scientific American*, 1978, vol. 239, no. 2, p. 66.
24. Sheena Davis, *Food through the Ages*, Readers Digest Association, London, 1977.
25. Mohommad Azhar Ansari, *European Travellers under the Mughals (1580–1627)*, Idrah-i Adabiyat-i Delhi, Delhi, 1975, pp. 76–103.
26. Bishwajit Choudhury, *Vegetables* (1967), National Book Trust, India, New Delhi, 8th rev. edn, 1987, p. 39.
27. M. N. Upadhya, 'Potato', in J. B. Hutchinson (ed.), *Diversity and Change in the Indian Subcontinent*, Cambridge University Press, 1974, p. 139.
28. Pushkarnath, *The Potato in India*, Indian Council of Agricultural Research, New Delhi, 1964.
29. Ruskin Bond, 'How potato spawned a hill station', *Sunday Herald*, Bangalore, 18 January 1987.
30. James Long (ed.), 'The Adventures', *Calcutta Review*, 1860, vol. 35; reproduced in S. Das Gupta (ed.), *Echoes of old Calcutta*, Naya Prakash, Calcutta, 1981, p. 68.
31. C.B. Heiser, *Seed to Civilisation*, W. H. Freeman and Co., San Francisco, 1973.
32. A. K. Yegna Narayan Aiyer, *Field Crops of India*, Bangalore Printing and Publishing Co. Ltd., Bangalore City, 6th edn., 1966, p. 264.
33. B. G. L. Swamy, *Namma Hoteyalli Dakshina America*, Prasaranga, Bangalore University, Bangalore, 1978, p. 16.
34. *Ancient China's Technology and Science*. Institute of Natural Sciences, Chinese Academy of Science, Foreign Language Press, Beijing, 1983, p. 329.
35. P. N. Chopra, *Life and Letters under the Mughals*, Ashajanak Publications, New Delhi, 1975, pp. 32–54.
36. Shoba Puri, 'Tea's me', *Swagat*, Indian Airlines, December 1987, p. 40.
37. Kalyani Devidar, 'Ooty's English edge', *Sunday Herald*, Bangalore, 13 March 1988.
38. William Foster, *Early Travels in India 1583–1619*, S. Chand and Co., New Delhi, repr. 1968, pp. 268–332.
39. D. M. Bose, S. N. Sen and B. V. Subbarayappa (eds), *A Concise History of Science in India*, Indian National Science Academy, New Delhi, 1971, p. 400.
40. Geeta Doctor, 'King coffee', *Swāgat*, Indian Airlines 1985, October, p. 23.
41. Anon, 'Coffee, coffee', *Indian Express*, Bangalore, 19 August 1986.
42. K. T. Achaya, *Everyday Indian Processed Foods*, 1984, National Book Trust, India, New Delhi, revised edn. 1986, p. 153.
43. David Wilson, *Atoms of Time Past*, The Scientific Book Club, London, 1976, p. 170.
44. Paul C. Mangelsdorf, 'The origin of corn', *Scientific American*, 1986, vol. 255, no. 2, September, p. 72.
45. G. W. Beadle, 'The ancestry of corn', *Scientific American*, 1980, vol. 242, no. 1, p. 96.
46. J. K. Thapa, 'Primitive grain with the Lepchas', *Tibetology*, 1966, vol. 3, p. 29.
47. Bhag Singh, *Races of Maize in India*, Indian Council of Agricultural Research, New Delhi, 1977.
48. C. L. Johannesen, 'Indian maize in the twelfth century', *Nature*, London 1988, vol. 332, p. 587.
49. Nandana Sigamani, 'Somnathpur sculptures puzzle historians', *Sunday Herald*, Bangalore, 30 July 1989, p. 8.
50. Abhay Kant Choudhary, *Early Medieval Village in North-eastern India (AD 600–1200)*, Punthi Pustak, Calcutta, 1971, p. 170.
51. J. L. Collins, *The Pineapple*, Leonard Hill (Books) Ltd., London, 1960.
52. Abul Fazl, *The Ain-i-Akbari*, trans. H. Blochmann, 1871, Aadiesh Book Depot, Delhi, repr. 1965, pp. 57–78.
53. M. S. Randhawa, *A History of Agriculture in India*, Indian Council of Agricultural Research, New Delhi, (a) 1982, vol. 2, p. 261 (b) 1980, vol. 1, p. 81 (c) 1982, vol. 2, p. 151.
54. Press Trust of India, 'Rare variety of fowl', *Deccan Herald*, Bangalore, 10 December 1985.
55. G. H. Pelto and P. J. Pelto, *The Human Adventure: An Introduction to Anthropology*, Macmillan Publishing Co., New York and Collier-Macmillan Publishers, London, 1976, p. 218.
56. E. D. Merrill, 'Observations on cultivated plants with reference to certain American problems', *Ceiba*, vol. 1, pp. 3–36; 'The botany of Cook's voyages', 1954, *Chronica Botanica*, Waltham, Massachussetts; both quoted in ref. 57 below.
57. Paul C. Mangelsdorf, *Corn: Its Origin, Evolution and*

Improvement, Harvard University Press, Cambridge , Massachussetts, 1974, p. 203.

58. Abu Abraham, '"Kala pani" of the mind', *Sunday Herald*, Bangalore, 12 June 1988.
59. Stephen D. Thomas, *The Last Navigator*, Hutchinson, London; review by Theodore S. Bhaskaran, 'Sailor's quest,' *The Hindu*, Madras, 1 December 1987.
60. Peter Buck, *Vikings of the Pacific*, The University of Chicago Press, Chicago, 1962.
61. Mary Elizabeth Shutler and Richard Shutler, 'Origin of the Melanesians', *in Cultures of the Pacific (Selected readings)*, The Free Press/Collier Macmillan Ltd., New York/London, 1970, p. 39.
62. Chaman Lal, *Hindu America*, Vishveshvaranand Vedic Research Institute, Hoshiarpur, 3rd edn, 1956.
63. Chaman Lal, *India, Cradle of Cultures*, published by the author, Modern School, New Delhi, 1976.
64. Anon, 'Evidence of links between ancient India and Mexico', *The Hindu*, Madras, 27 September 1985, p. 20.
65. Madhav N. Katti, 'Karnataka in S. E. Asian epigraphy', in Devendra Handa (ed.), *Indological Studies* (Essays in memory of S. P. Singhal), Caxton Publications, Delhi, 1987, p. 205.
66. Leonard Fuchs, *Neue Kreuterbuch*, Basel, AD 1543; reproduced in *MARG*, Bombay, vol. 40, no. 4, p. 22.

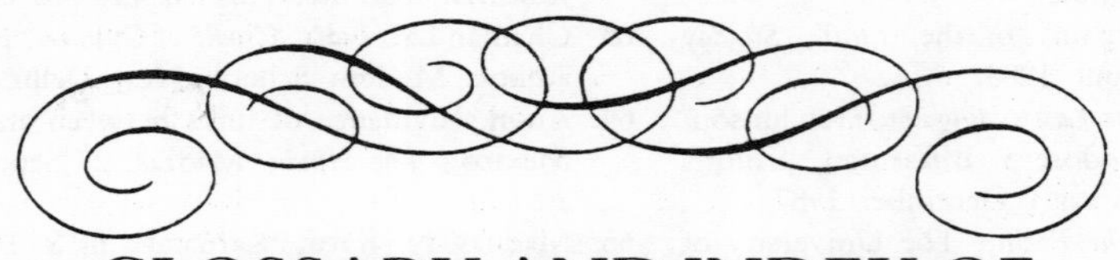

GLOSSARY AND INDEX OF NON-ENGLISH WORDS

Definitions have been kept brief. The different languages are indicated thus:

Afr: African	Jap: Japanese	Pal: Pali
Akk: Akkadian	Kan: Kannada	Per: Persian
Ara: Arabic	Kas: Kashmiri	Por: Portuguese
Ass: Assamese	Kod: Kodava	Raj: Rajasthani
Ben: Bengali	Kon: Konkani	S: Sanskrit
Chi: Chinese	Lat: Latin	S.Am: South American
Dra: Dravidian	Mal: Malayalam	Sin: Sinhalese
Gre: Greek	Mar: Marathi	Spa: Spanish
Guj: Gujarathi	Mex: Mexican	Sum: Sumerian
Heb: Hebrew	Msn: Malaysian	T: Tamil
Hin: Hindi	Mun: Munda	Tel: Telugu
Ita: Italian	Ori: Oriya	Urd: Urdu

aab-gosht (Kas): lamb dish 137
ababi (S. Am): papaya 223
Ābān (Per): November 158
abdār (Urd): colonial servant 115
abhisukha (S): edible pine nut 223
abhyūsa (S): sweet barley flour dish 38
abanam (T): a ladle 105
accha (Mal): metal frame 124
acch-āppam (Mal): a fried cookie 125
acchi (Per): a strong wine 158
achār (Hin): pickle 227
achechana (S): storage vessel 103
achi (Spa): chilli 227
adai (T): fried pulse snack 11, 46, 108
adai (T): a cluster 48
ādara (S): soma (q.v.) substitute 58
adārā (S): ginger 213
addaka (Mal): areca nut 11, 48
ādhaka (S): a weight measure 109
ādhakī (S): thuvar, *Cajanus cajan* 10, 34
adhrak (Guj, Hin): green ginger 135
adhrastam (S): not seen 70
adhri (S): grinding stone 103
adhsvamātrakah (S): irrigated land 29
adhvaita (S): system of non-dualistic philosophy 129
afin (Hin): opium 171
afyun (Ara): opium 171
agappai (T): spoons 105
agashi (Kan): linseed 197
aghnya (S): inviolable (masc.) 55
aghnyā (S): inviolable (fem.) 55
aghil (T): dark, aromatic wood 52
agrahāyana (S): January-February 130
agrāyanasthāli (S): soma (q.v.) vessel 104
aguacate (S. Am.): avocado 224
āhāra (S): food 65
ahāra (S): storage vessel 103
āhāratattva (S): science of dietetics 78
āhārayōgi-varga (S): class of ascetic foods, vegetable oils 82
ahate (Mex): *Annona squamosa* 237
ahichattaka (Pal): snake umbrella 65
ahimsā (S): non-injury 70
ahiphena (S): opium 171

airāvata: *Citrus aurantium* 211
aishi (?): linseed 197
āivanam (T): mountain rice 45
a'izza (Ara): honourable persons 155
ajājī (S): cumin 214
ajamedha (S): goat sacrifice 103
ājyasthāl (S): iron griddle 103
akara (S): *Sorghum vulgare* 186
akaraphālika (S): wooden board 104
akeedar (Guj): egg-based dish 75
akhrōt (Hin): walnut 83, 222
akki-otti (Kod): rice bread 122
akshikiphala (S): *Terminalia bellirica* 204
akshota (S): walnut 83, 222
akuri (Guj): egg-based dish 75
akusthaka (S): *Panicum miliaceum* 186
alābu (S): *Lagenaria siceraria,* the bottle gourd or pumpkin 7, 35
aladhna (Guj): vada (q.v.) 135
alarika (S): a cook 108
alarku (S): *Solanum trilobatum* 201
aleesa (Mal): wheat-meat porridge 124
alisandaga (S): perhaps *Cicer arietinum* 34
alkkar (T): salt bed 114
alpamarishā (S): *Amaranthus spinosus* 187
al-qahiriya (Ara): sweet confection 156
ālu-bukhārā (Per): plum 212
ālucha (Hin): plum 212
aluhi (S): iron pan 105
ām (Hin): mango 10
amal-bid (Per): a citrus 159, 210
amarighōshanā (S): edict 134
amatra (S): storage vessel 103
ambādi (Hin): *Hibiscus cannabinus* 42, 208
ām-bada (Kan): a vadā (q.v.) 137
ambāh (S): unidentified grain 34
āmbāh (S): mango 165, 175
ambal (T): lotus 106
ambal (Kas): a relish 139
ambah-shyāmāka (S): a *Panicum* grain 186
ambar (S, Ara): edible resin 76
amber (S): wild fig 205
ambodē (Kan): a vadā (q.v.) 121
amīr (Ara): head, chief 155
amīr-hajib (Ara): head chamberlain 155
amīr-i-majlis (Ara): master of ceremonies 155
amīr-qāzi (Ara): chief judge 156
amishka (S): curd-milk solids 35
āmlā (Hin): *Emblica officianalis* 35, 39, 132, 135, 175, 205
āmlaka (S): *Emblica officinalis* 35, 81, 86, 148, 204, 205
amlīkā (S): tamarind 204
aṃmi (T): grinding stone 105
āmra (S): mango 10, 208
āmrataka (S): *Spondias pinnata,* the wild mango 208
āmri (Hin): Kāshmīr apple 139, 213
amritphal (Hin): a citrus 159
amrud (Per, Hin): once pear, now also guava 224
amrul (Hin): *Oxalis corniculata* 86
amshala (S): tender 55
āmvadē (S): a vadā (q.v.) 121
anānas (S. Am, Hin): pineapple 175
anda (T): pot 12
andon-ki-peosi (Guj): baked egg dish 123
andika (S): water lily 35, 200
angarapōlika (S): sweet stuffed parāta (q.v.) 88
angula (S): small linear measure 15, 195
anjan (Hin): *Memecylon umbellatum* 78
anlī (Ara): an Indian grain 152
anna (S): cultivated grains 61, 62, 65
annaprāsana (S): ceremony introducing solid food to the infant 67, 76
antardhāna (S): a ladle 104
anthi-ki-rōti (Hin): rōti (q.v.) from mango-stone flour 140
anupa (S): watery land 94
anuvaka (S): section 32
anvahāryasthāli (S): cylinder 104
ap (S): aqueous state of matter 77
apakva (S): frying 101
aparivīrtikam (S): not suspected 70
āppā (Kan): the āppam (q.v.) 178
āppam (T): a rice pancake 11, 45, 108, 123, 127
apūpa (S): sweet fried confection 11, 33, 34, 37, 68
apūpika (S): a cook 108
aqua vitae (Lat): water 200
arabika (S): vendor of sheep meat 53
araca (Mal): arrack (q.v.) 170
araghatta (S): water wheel 20
arāk (Ara): distilled palm wine 11
aral (T): the Malabar sole, *Cyanoglossus semifasciatus* 49
arani (S): fire-raising spindle 105
ardhraka (S): green ginger 213
arec (Sunda Islands): the arecanut 48
arghya (S): type of honey 114
arhar (Hin): pulse *Cajanus cajan* 10, 34, 189
ariena (Gre): unidentified Indian fruit 145
ari-patthiri (Mal): rice roti (q.v.) 124
arishta (S): medicated alcoholic liquor 59, 77
arisī (T): rice 11
arivar (T): wise men 43
arjuna (S): a soma (q.v.) substitute 58
arjuna (S): *Terminalia arjuna* 101
arpana (S): a tree 30
arrack (Hin): distilled palm toddy 158, 170, 173, 177

aruvatthu (Kan): sixty 187, 236
arvi (Hin): *Colocasia esculentum* 47, 129, 136, 198
āsara-dadhi (S): diluted curd 84
āsava (S): alcoholic liquor 59, 77, 82, 109
Āshāda (S): June-July 130
ashmanchakra (S): a water wheel 20, 29
ashōka (S): *Saraca indica* 149
ashtaka (S): octave 32
ashvabala (S): fenugreek 35
ashvamēdha (S): horse sacrifice 103
ashvatta (S): *Ficus religiosa* 36, 83, 204
Ashwin· (S): September-October 130
ashwins (S): twin Vedic dieties 78
asrutam (S): not heard 70
asuras (S): foes of the Aryans 10, 58
āsuta (S): vinegar preserve 86
ata (Spa): *Annona squamosa* 237
atē (Mex, Spa): (S): *Annona squamosa* 237
athasī (S): linseed 31, 37, 83, 197
athirasā (Kan): fried sweet patty 119, 122
athirasam (T): fried sweet patty 46
atisauhitya (S): over-eating 79
ato-sang (Mun): *Dioscorea* tuber 7
atripriya (S): a fruit 237
attukal (T): grinding stone 105
audbhida (S): type of salt 114
auddhalika (S): type of honey 114
auria (Kas): curd preparation 139
aushad-grnjana (S): garlic 213
avadatika (S): alcoholic liquor 59
avaka (S): aquatic plant 35
avaka (S): *Albizia lebbeck* 199
aval (T): flattened rice 45
avālika (S): a cook 108
avalōse (Mal): sweet rice preparation 124
avalōse-unda (Mal): sweet rice ball 124
avarai (T): *Lablab purpureus* 53, 166, 189
avaranna (Kan): pulse dish 134
aviyal (Mal): mixed vegetable dish 69, 123, 125
axi (Spa): chilli 227
ayas (S): iron 103
ayir (T): coarse crystal sugar 49, 114

bādām (Hin): almond 222
bādām-ki-jali (Urd): almond confection 123
badara (S): *Ziziphus* species 205
badari (S): *Ziziphus* species 83
badi (Guj): fried pulse snack 134, 140
badi-elaichi (Hin): *Ammomum aromaticum* 214
bael (Hin): *Aegle marmelos* 35, 83, 205
bafflas (Hin): type of bread 138
baghaar (Hin): frying of spices 102
baghāra-baingan (Hin): spicy brinjal dish 123
baghārna (Hin): frying of spices 67
baheda (S): *Terminalia bellirica* 204
baingan (Hin): brinjal 123, 201
baja (S): mustard 37
bāji (Hin): brinjal mash 92, 119; also a vegetable dish
bajji (Hin): mashed vegetable dish 120; also deep-fried snack
bājra (Hin): *Pennisetum americanum* 42, 140, 162, 184, 186
bājri (Guj): bajra (q.v.) 135
bakīr (Hin): rice-milk sweet 141
bakirkhani (Kas): wheat bread 139
bākla (Hin): *Vicia faba* 189, 192
balachao (Kon): prawn relish 136
balaka (Kan): fried vegetable crisps 119, 120
balhīka (S): asafoetida 215
bālu (Mun): betel leaf 48
bālushāhi (Hin): glazed wheat patty 141
banan (Afr): fingers or toes 208
banana (Afr): a finger or toe 208
Banārsi-rāi (Hin): *Brassica nigra* 194
bāndra (Hin): *Setaria glauca* 186
bang (phonetic): bhang (q.v.) 171
bangala (Guj): a vegetable dish 135
bangue (phonetic): bhang (q.v.) 171
bania (Hin): trader 229
bankel (Hin): a banana 207
bara (Guj, Hin): vadā (q.v.) 140
baramasia (Hin): *Citrus limon* 210
barca (phonetic): jackfruit 175
barfi (Guj, Hin): khoa (q.v.) sweetmeat 140
barhal (Hin): *Artocarpus lakoocha* 83
bāri (Hin): wādi (q.v.) 140
barki (Kon): whorl pastry 136
bāsi (S): stale, left-over food 62
bastūk (Ben): a leafy vegetable 129
bāsmati (Hin): a fragrant rice 185
batata (Spa): correctly, sweet potato 226
batavia (Hin): *Citrus sinensis* 210
bāth (Hin): rice dish 67, 120, 122, 140
battala (Kan): concave grill-plate 102; also a dish
batheesa (Hin): a banana 207
bātti (Raj): a hard wheat ball 138, 140
bavto (Mun): *Eleusine coracana* 7
bedavi (Guj): stuffed wheat cake 90
bengi (phonetic): bhang 171
bengo-nari (Mun): *Dioscorea* tuber 7
ber (Hin): *Ziziphus* spp. 35, 36, 39, 47, 83, 85, 97, 109, 145, 148, 169, 204, 205, 213
bērikāi (T): country pear 212
besan (Hin): chickpea flour 67, 110, 121, 135, 136, 140, 145
bethua (Ben, Hin): *Chenopodium album* 129

beurijeera (Guj): a rice dish 135
bhabri (Hin): baked cakes 140
bhaditraka (S): skewer-roasted meat 90
Bhādra (S): August-September 130
bhadra (Hin): *Ziziphus* spp. 148
bhājā (Guj): pulse-vegetable dish 129
bhāji (Hin): cooked vegetable 35, 129
bhajka (Hin): deep-fried snack 140
bhākri (Raj): crisp rōti (q.v.) 140
bhakshya (S): chewed foods 64, 94
bhallātaka (S): *Semecarpus anacardium* 35
bhandi (S): perhaps *Abelmoschus esculentus* 202
bhang (Hin): opium 38, 157
bhanga (Hin): opium 171
bharjanam (S): roasting 101
bhartha (Hin): mashed vegetable dish 119, 129, 140
Bharuchi-akuri (Guj): egg-based dish 75
bhatē (Guj): pulse-vegetable dish 129
bhāt-karēla (Hin): *Momordica cochinchinensis* 204
bhatia (Hin): type of bread 138
bhatura (Hin): deep-fried bread 138
bhavita (S): seasoning 101
bhavya (S): *Atropa carambola* 83
bhendi (Hin); *Abelmoschus esculentus* 10, 201
bhilāwan (Hin): *Semecarpus anacardium* 35
bhōga-mandapa (S): dining hall 68
bhōjana-pīta (S): eating platform 94
bhojandika-rōti (S): baked wheat circlet 97, 118
bhōjya (S): non-chewed foods 64
bhoosoo (Guj): crisp snack 136
bhrngāra (S): water goblet 105
bhrsta (S): griddle 105
bhrstadhānya (S): parched grains 110
bhūlōkamalla (S): wrestler of the earth 89
bhūmikushmānda (S): *Ipomoea* spp. 199
bibinca (Por): layered sweet 136
bījapūraka (S): *Citrus medica* 148, 186
bijoda (Raj): a fruit 140
bilva (Hin): *Aegle marmelos* 35, 83, 85, 109, 169, 205
bimba (S): *Momordica balsamina* 36
bimbi (S): *Cephalandra indica* 97
bīna (Guj): deep-fried pulse patty 135
birahi (Hin): stuffed wheat circlet 138
birinj (Per): rice 162
biriyāni (Per, Urd): meat-rice dish 123, 124, 157, 158
bir-sang (Mun): *Dioscorea* tuber 7
bisibēlē-huli-anna (Kan): spiced rice 121, 122
bismoron (Gre): an Indian grain 143, 144
bisumborigē (Kan): unidentified dish 119
boda (Ben): deep-fried pulse patty 129
bōdhi (S): *Ficus religiosa* 149
bolē (Kon): rice bread 136
bonda (Hin): globular stuffed fried snack 121
boondhi (Hin): deep-fried droplets of pulse flour 121, 135
boorani (Hin): onion-curd relish 123
brahma (S): *Centella asiatica* 83
brahmāchāri (S): celibate 125
brāhmana (S): priestly class 148
brāhmara (S): type of honey 85, 114
brahmi (S): *Nasturtium officinale* 200
branj (Per): rice 157
bungē-lavanga (Msn): clove 215
burudē (Kan): globular confection 119
burudegallu (Kan): globular sweets 93

cabob (phonetic): kabāb (q.v.) 176
cacao (Maya): cocoa 230
cāju (Por): cashew 222
caladine (Por): fish curry 136
calamondin (phonetic): a *Citrus* 211
catamaran (T, phonetic): sea-going country craft 263
cha (Chi): tea 228
chachinda (S): *Trichosanthes anguina* 204
chacuti (Por): fried meat 136
Chaitra (S): March-April 89, 130
chakka (Pal): wheel 111
chakka (Mal): jackfruit 206
chakkali (Kan): crisp fried snack 93, 119, 120
chakkalika (S): spiced roast pork 96
chakkara (Mal): brown crystal sugar 11
chakki (Hin): pulley, wheel 24, 111
chakna (S): dish of offal 123
chakota (Kan): grapefruit 119, 120
chakotra (S): grapefruit 211
chakra (S): wheel 111
chalani (S): sieve 101
chamasa (S): a vessel 104
chamu (S): storage vessel 103
chana (S): *Cicer arietinum* 31, 34, 119, 120, 121, 122, 127, 130, 135, 136, 140, 152, 155, 162, 189
chanaka (S): *Cicer arietinum* 34, 189
chanchu (Hin): *Nasturtium officinale* 83
chandala (S): a low caste 9, 147
chandrani (Guj); a rice dish 135
chandrasūr (S): *Nasturtium officinale* 83
chandrāyana (S): type of fast 151
changeri (S): *Oxalis corniculata* 86
channa (Hin): acid-precipitated milk solids 91, 132, 155
chhānār-jlipī (Ben): fried confection 132
chapal (Ben): small, sweet banana 129
chapāti (Hin): flat griddle-roasted wheat circlet 24, 138, 173
charaka (S): a wanderer 78
charas (S): opium 171

chāru (S): a saucepan 105
chāru (Ori): a rice dish 77
chasuka (S): wine goblet 58
chatani (S): chutney 134, 135
chatti (T): clay cooking pot 127
chātra (S): type of honey 114
Chatūrdasi (S): the fourteenth day 128
chaupad (S): game of dice 263
chaulai (Hin): an *Amaranthus* 187
chāval (Hin): rice 7
chavi (Hin): *Piper retrofactum* 214
chavya (S): *Piper retrofactum* 214
cheeku (Hin): sapota 223
cheena (S): *Panicum miliaceum* 186
cheenaka (S): a *Panicum* 186
cheet (Hin): a note 170
chekka (Mal): jackfruit 11, 111
chembu (T): *Colocasia esculenta* 47
chennel (T): red rice 45
chevdo (Guj): beaten-rice snack 135
chhas (Guj, Hin): buttermilk 135
chibda (Guj): vegetable dish 135
chicle (Spa): *Manilkara achras* 218
chidbhita (S): cucumber 36
chidva (Hin): parched rice snack 110
chikhi (Per): wheat dish 158
chikki (Hin): chewy jaggery confection 187
chakna (Hin): a *Citrus* 210, 211
chilgoza (Hin); *Pinus gerardiana* 218, 223
chili (Mex): the chilli 227
chilli (S): wild *Chenopodium album* 200
chilumuri (Kan): rope-like sweet 120
chimada (Guj): vegetable dish 135
chīna (S): a *Panicum* 11
chīnakaon (S): *Panicum miliaceum* 128
chīnāni (S): the peach 212
chīnakarpūra (S): camphor 11
chīnapistha (S): vermilion 11
chīnarājaputra (S): cultivated pear 11
chīnasālit (S): *Pisonia alba* 11
chincha (Mun): tamarind 9
chingari (Kod): a fragrant rice 185
chīnī (S): sugar 11, 132
chīnī (S): a *Citrus* 210
chīnībādām (Hin): groundnut 11
chipita (S): parched rice 34, 110
chirbhita (S): cucumber 202
chirōnji (Hin): *Buchanania lanzan* 90, 109, 158, 218, 223
chirotti (Kan): layery wheat sweet 96, 121
chitrakoot (Beng): fried confection 132
chitranna (S): mixed cereal dish 34, 122
chitrannam (T): flavoured rice 45
chiuri (S): parched barley 140
chivda (Hin): parched rice snack 34, 110
chōlam (T): *Sorghum vulgare* 44
chōm-la (Mun): to eat 7
chondros (Gre): barley gruel 144
chowka (Hin): sitting mat 93
chouli (Guj): a green pulse preparation 135
chowli (Hin): *Vigna unguiculata* 188
chucchu-roti (Kan): type of rōti (q.v.) 118
chūlāh (S, Hin): cooking hearth 24, 25, 68, 101
chuliphali (Guj): green pulse preparation 135
chūlli (S): chūlāh (q.v.) 103, 104
chunadāni (S): container for lime paste 48
chunām (S, T): slaked lime 81
chundo (Guj): type of pickle 135
chupriālu (S); *Dioscorea alata* 199
chura (S): parched rice 110
chūrnādīvāsin (S): flavoured drinking water 87, 94
churuttu (Mal): cigar, cigar-like confection 124
clavus (Lat): a nail 215
coca (S): cinnamon 215
coco (Spa): monkey's face 169
cocos (Spa): coconut 169
cohha (phonetic): coffee 229
conjee (phonetic): boiled rice-water 178
coquos (Spa): hobgoblin 196
copra (Hin): dried coconut meat 135
corcopal (phonetic): unidentified fruit 167
cushya (S): foods to be sucked 64

dadhanwat (S): perhaps cheese 35
dadhi (S): curds 35
dahi (Hin): curds 39, 129, 135, 174
dahi-vadā (Hin): fried pulse patty in curds 87, 127, 140
dāla (S): type of honey 114
dālcha (Urd): stewed lamb 123
dāllia (Hin): wheat grits, or a vadā (q.v.) of the same 135
dalna (Ben): vegetable-pulse dish 130
dandā (S): measure of length 195
dāngiri (Guj): a rice dish 135
danjauri (Hin): rice with poppyseed 140
daraka (S): *Paspalum scorbiculatum* 186
dār-chīnī (Hin): cinnamon 215
daruharidra (S): *Ammomum aromaticum* 214
dārushila (S): cinnamon 142
darvi (S): small ladle or scraper 93, 104
days (phonetic): curds (dahi) 174
debra (Raj): a berry 140
Deepavali (Hin): a festival of lights 69
desi (Hin): indigenous 201
deu-pario (Lat): heavenly dish 172
dev (Hin): god 170

dew (Hin): god 170
dhaam (Kas): community meal 139
dhādima (S): pomegranate 204, 206
dhaitya (S): non-Aryan 28, 83
dhāl (Hin): literally split pulse, also used loosely for the whole pulse 30, 90, 118, 119, 124, 125, 126, 129, 140, 158
dhālimba (S): pomegranate 206
dhāmmapattana (S): term for pepper 52
dhān (Raj): unspecified cereal dish 140
dhana (S): food 34
dhānāh (S): parched barley 110
dhanidhaka (S): perhaps puffed grains 110
dhansākh (Guj): Pārsi meat/veg-pulse dish 75
dhanuri (Guj): rice dish 135
dhānya (S): grain 110
dhanyaka (S): coridander 213
dhanyāmla (S): soured gruel 39
dhātaki (S): *Woodfordia fruticosa* 58, 109
dhātu (S): one of three body conditions expressing attributes of matter 77
dhāthura (S): *Datura stramonium* 169
dharana (S): a gold weight 195
dhenki (Hin): cereal foot-pounder 101
dhishana (S): nested vessels 103
dhmātr (S): bellows 103
dhoklā (Guj): steamed pulse preparation 134, 135, 136
dhōsakā (S): fried rice-pulse pancake 90
dhrsti (S): fire tongs 105
dhruva (S): large ladle 104
dhruvanka (S): astrological chart 89
dhunaur (Hin): mixed spices 140
didari (Guj): sorghum rōtī (q.v.) 134
divya (S): a flavoured alcoholic liquor 59
dōhaka (S); commercial milking 35
dojaj (Per): chicken, chicken palāo 156, 157
doll (phonetic): dhāl (q.v.) 176
doodhpāk (Hin): milk sweet 135
doodhpeda (Hin): milk sweet 134
dōpatri (Hin): twin-style bread 138
dōpiyaza (Per): meat dish cooked with a lot of onions 159, 172
dosa(i) (T): rice-pulse shallow-fried pancake 46, 68, 89, 90, 96, 125, 126, 127
dosha (S): bodily defect 77, 128
double-ka-meeta (Urd): sweet based on slices of bread 123
double-rōti (Urd): loaf of bread 123
douli (Guj): rice dish 135
drākshā (S): grapes 212
drōna (S): storage vessel 103; volume measure 103
drōnakalasha (S): covered bucket 104
drshad (S): grinding stone 103, 105
drshadputra (S): upper milling stone 105
drti (S): storage bag 103
dru (S): storage vessel 103
dubaki (Hin): type of pakoda (q.v.) 140
dukkia (Guj): steamed pulse preparation 134
dulim (Per): pomegranate 206
dum (Urd): cooking in a seal of dough 123
dumpoke (phonetic): corruption of dumpukht (q.v.) 178
dumpukht (Urd): cooking in a seal of dough 102, 178
dundaniya (Guj): a rice dish 135
Durgāshtami (S): birthday of Durga 69

edu (T): curds 47
ekādashi (S): eleventh day 70
ela (S): cardamom 214
elaichi (Hin): cardamom 214
ell (T, Akk): sesame seed or oil 8, 12
ellu (T): sesame 8
ellu-ennai (T): sesame oil 8
enn (T, Akk): sesame seed or oil 8, 12
ennai (T): oil 8
en-patthu (T): nine 15
eracchi-olaithiya (Mal): fried meat 124
eranda (S): castor 37
erisseri (Mal): pumpkin dish 125
etāluka (S): a *Convolvulus* species 36
ethakāi (Mal): a banana 207

falooda (Per): sweet milk drink 154, 159
fanam (Dra): a coin 168
feijoada (Kon): pork with beans 136
fēni (Kon): distilled cashew liquor 137
fuqqa (Per): a sweet barley drink 154, 156, 157

gadōdhaka (S): syrup of molasses 39
gajanimma (Hin): a lime 211
galantika (S): strainer 105
galgal (Per): *Citrus limon* 159, 210, 211
gandagatra (S): *Annona squamosa* 237, 238
gandharva (S): celestial goblin 31
gandum (Per): wheat 34
gānjā (Hin): marijuana 38
garagē (Mar): fried pulse ball 90
garaghatanam (S): beef abattoir 53
garahedua (Hin): *Coix lacryma-jobi* 186
gārhyapatya (S): potsherd for baking 104
gari (Guj): wheat dish 135
gārjaru (S): carrot 200
garmar (Raj): a stem 140
garmut (S): *Macrotyloma uniflorum*, kulthi (q.v.) 189
gattey-ka-sāg (Raj): dried vegetables 140

gatti (Raj): crisp savoury 140
gau (S): cow 55
gaurashārshapa (S): yellow *Brassica* seed 36
gavēdhukā (S): *Coix lacryma-jobi* 186
gāyal (Hin): cattle, (S): *Bos frontalis* 55
gēbar (Guj): sweet wheat dish 134, 135
genasu (Mun): a *Dioscorea* tuber 7
genoa (Hin): *Citrus limon* 210
gēvara (Guj): sweet wheat dish 37, 91, 134
ghānā (S): oil mill 111, 197
ghānchi (S): oil crusher 110
ghāni (Hin): oil mill 111, 112
gharatta (S): grinding stone 107
ghāri(ka) (Guj): fried pulse preparation 90, 134
ghārial (Hin): alligator 18
ghari-puri (Guj): sweet stuffed wheat concoction 135
gharma (S): large milk-boiling cauldron 103, 104
ghatani (Guj): mill 111
ghatanika (S): heavy club 111
ghatayantra (S): water wheel 20
ghatta (Hin): salted wheat-milk dish 140
ghavan (Mar): stone mortar 111
ghayapunna (S): perhaps the sweet dish gēvara (q.v.) 37
ghee (Hin): clarified butterfat 28, 47, 64, 68, 131, 159, 179
ghī (phonetic): ghee (q.v.), clarified butterfat 170
ghrtapūra (S): ghee-fried wheat flour confection 91, 97, 134
ghrtapūran (Kan): ghee-fried wheat flour confection 119
ghola (S): diluted whole-milk curd 84
ghutika (S): toothpick 94
ghutipāka (S): partly boiled-down milk 94
gidhabaddaka (S): vendor of flesh of aquatic animals 53
gima (Ben): a green leafy vegetable 129
gingelli (Dra): sesame 153, 193
gipa (Per): a haggis 159
giral (Hin): Job's tears 186
girda (Kas): wheat bread 139
gisola (Guj): a vegetable dish 135
gōdha (S): iguana 85
godhūma (S): wheat 34, 82
godhūma-ramba-kusuma (Kan): a dish of wheat and banana flowers 118
gogataka (S): vendor of cattle meat 53
go-hatya (S): slaying of bovines 55
gojju (T): mixed vegetable dish 122
gōle (Guj): round pulse patty 135
gōle-ālu (Hin): potato 199
gōle-gappa (Hin): tiny pūris (q.v.) 138
gōle-pāpadi (Hin): tiny, blown-up puris (q.v.) 39, 135
gōli (Kas): meat balls 137
gōlkandra (Hin): *Momordica dioica* 204
gōmānga (Mal): cashew 'fruit' 222
gondli (Mun): *Panicum sumatrense* 186
gonkuru (Tel): *Hibiscus cannabinus* 202
gonkura-pacchadi (Tel): spicy relish of *Hibiscus cannabinus* 202
goonda (Guj): a pickle 135
gosht (Kas): mutton 137
goshtaba (Kas): a meat loaf 137
grahani (S): a spoon 104
graishmuka (S): summer rice 185
grão (Por): literally grain, later pulse 12
grāvan (S): grinding stone 103, 111
grīshma (S): period from mid-May to mid-July 81
grnjana (S): garlic 213, 214
guajava (Spa): guava 224
guār (Hin): *Cyamopsis tetragonalobus* 193
guārphali (Guj): green pods of above 135
guda (S): coarse brown sugar 11, 85, 89, 109, 113, 216
gugri (Guj): wheat dish 135
gujiya (Guj): vegetable puffs 134
gulāb-jāmūn (Urd): fried globe in sugar syrup 132, 140
gulalalāvaniya (S): a small pūri (q.v.) 39
guler (S): wild *Ficus carica* 205
gun (Mun): *Dioscorea* spp. 7
guna (S): attribute of matter 77
gunder-pāk (Guj): aromatic confection 135
gunji (Hin): *Abrus precatorius* 14
gūr (Hin): coarse brown sugar 11
gutika (S): medicated pills 77
gutli (Hin): hard crusty bun 139
guvāka (S): the arecanut 10, 48, 214

haimantha (S): winter rice 185
haimāvati (S): linseed 197
halāl (Ara): ritual animal slaughter 75
hāla-ugu (Kan): a milk junket 121
haldi (Hin): turmeric 9, 109
haleem, halīm (Urd): ground wheat-meat dish 76, 154, 159
hālubhai (Kan): a milk junket 121
haludriya (Guj): turmeric 135
hālugharigē (Kan): sweet rice balls 97
hāl-undē (Kan): balls of sweetened milk solids 119, 121
hālundigē (Kan): rice patties in sweet milk 93
halwa (Per): class of semi-solid sweet confections 73, 76, 80, 135, 141, 154, 157, 162
handa (Hin): a clay cooking pot 134; or a vegetable

dish cooked in it 123
handva (Guj): clay pot-cooked vegetables or pulses 134
hanumānphal (Hin): *Annona cherimola* 235
happala (Kan): crisp pulse criclets 119, 120
hārahūraka (S): wine from Afghanistān 59
hareesh (Urd): ground wheat-meat dish 154
harichal (Hin): a banana 207
harid (S): underground spices 82
haridrā (S): turmeric 9, 37, 82, 105, 213
harimanthaka (S): *Cicer arietinum* 189
harimenasu (Kan): green chilli 227
harimirch (Hin): green chilli 227
harīsā (Per): ground wheat-meat dish 154, 158
harītakī (S): *Terminalia chebula* 83, 94
hāshimi (Per): a sweet confection 156
hasta (S): measure of length 195
hastaka (S): a spit 105
hasti (S): a *Panicum* grain 186
havani (S): a priest's spoon 104
havispura (S): fried wheat flour confection 91
hayana (S): winter rice 185
hayanga (S): milk or curd dish 119
hayavana (S): winter rice 185
hemantha (S): mid-November to mid-January 81
hesaru (Kan): *Vigna radiata* 12
heun-lo (Chi): the kandu plant (?) 148
hilsa (Ben): *Clupea ilisha* 129
hing (Hin): asafoetida 176
hingra (Hin): asafoetida 176
hingu (S): asafoetida 37, 87, 215
holigē (Kan): sweet stuffed wheat circlet 119, 120, 122
hoppers (phonetic): corruption of āppā(s) (q.v.) 178
hucchelu (Kan): nigerseed 197
hulī (Kan): liquid pulse preparation 118, 119, 122
hurada (Guj): roasted sorghum cobs 134
hūrigē (Kan): sweet stuffed wheat circlet 119
husseni-kabāb (Urd): skewered roast meat 76

idanam (T): a loft 106
idapātra (S): container for ghee 104
idari (Guj): the idli (q.v.) 135
iddaligē (Kan): the idli (q.v.) 126
iddarikā (S): the idli (q.v.) 90, 126
idi-āppam (T): steamed rice noodles 46, 108, 122, 124, 127
idli (T): steamed patties of a fermented batter of rice and *Vigna mungo* 68, 89, 90, 93, 119, 125, 126
ikh (S): the sugarcane 112
ikshu (S): the sugarcane 82, 112, 216
imli (Hin): tamarind 204
indalam (T); censer 106
indrajau (S): *Coix lacryma-jobi* 179
indrayan (S): *Citrullus colocynthis* 202
ingudi (S): *Balanites aegyptiaca* 37

jahāngiri (Kan): jilēbi (q.v.) 155
jaiphal (S): nutmeg 37, 215
jalebi (Kan): jilēbi (q.v.) 155
jambīla (S): *Citrus jambhiri* 37
jambīra (S): *Citrus jambhiri* 150
jambīrī (Per): *Citrus jambhiri* 159
jāmbu (S): the rose-apple, *Syzygium jambos* 109
jāmbu-āsava (S): wine flavoured with jambu (q.v.) 59, 109
jāmbūla (S): the jamoon (q.v.) 8
jāmoon (S): the purple or Java plum, *Syzygium cumini* 35, 37, 39, 47, 86, 109, 152, 204
jāmūn (Urd): fried delicacy in sugar syrup 132, 140
jangli-bādām (Hin): nut of *Terminalia catappa* 222
jartila (S): wild sesame *Sesamum orientale* var. malabaricum 193
jatamanshi (S): *Nardostachys jatamansi* 37
jāthi (S): jasmine; or jasmine flavoured wine 59, 109
jatri (S): mace 215
jeera (Hin): cumin seed 135
jeera-sāl (Guj): flavoured rice dish 135
jeljel (Ara): sesame 193
jhalar (Guj): liquid pulse dish 92
jibba (Hin): stitched upper garment 64
jilabi (Kan): jilēbi (q.v.) 119, 121
jil-ābi (Kan): jilēbi (q.v.) 119
jilēbi (Hin): coiled tubular fried pastry soaked in sugar syrup 119, 121, 122, 132, 140, 154, 155
jom (Mun): to eat 7
jowār (Hin): sorghum 43, 179, 185, 186, 197
jowari (Guj): sorghum 135
jūhū (S): wooden ladle 104
juljul (Ara): sesame 193
jurna (Mun): sorghum 186
jūtha (S): left-over food 62
Jyaistha (T): May-June 130

kaazhiyar (T): snack vendor 108
kabāb (Per): spit-roasted meat 76, 90, 102, 136, 152, 154, 157, 159, 162
kabūli-chana (Hin): large-sized *Cicer arietinum* 123
kaccha (S): class of ritually-cooked foods 62
kacchadi (Kan): curd-based relish 119
kacchi-biriyāni (Urd): meat-rice dish 123
kacchia-mooru (Mal): spiced buttermilk 124
kacchra (Guj): cucumber relish 134
kacchumber (Guj): raw vegetable dish 134
kāchampuli (Kod): extract of *Garcinia indica* 123
kacchauri (Hin): stuffed wheat patty 140

karappa-pattai (T): cinnamon 11
karasu (Guj): a rice dish 135
karaunda (S): *Carissa carandas* 35, 205
karavella (S): *Momordica charantia* 35, 97, 204
karavi (S): cumin 214
karēlā (Hin): the bitter-gourd *Momordica charantia* 35, 97, 135, 204
kari (T): pepper 11, 49
karivrnta (S): *Mormodica charantia* 35
karīra (S): *Capparis decidua* 36, 97, 205
karkari (S): strainer 105
karna (Ara): unidentified fruit 159
karnakhatta (Hin): an acid citrus fruit 212
karōtara (S): a strainer 105
karphea (Gre): cinnamon 11
karpion (Gre): cinnamon 142
karpūra (S): camphor 11, 76
karsha (S): a volume measure 109
karshapana (S): a copper coin 195
kārthā (Hin): trade functionary 167
Kārthik (S): October-November 130
karugu (T): fowl 49
karuppa (T): cinnamon 142
karuva (T): cinnamon 11
kāsā (S): *Saccharum spontaneum* 216
kasāra (S): sweet wheat-flour confection 91
kaserū (S): *Scirpus grossus* 152
kashāya (S): a rice wine 59
kashya (S): a strong liquor 59
kashk (Per): wheat-meat dish 158
kāsi (Mun): *Coix lacryma-jobi* 187
kasmarya (S): perhaps *Berberis* spp. 36
kastumbīra (S): coriander 213
kataha (Prakrit): deep frying pan 103
katakarna (S): snack based on peas 90
kathinya (S): receptacle 31
katōri (Hin): bowl 102
katta-yōgara (Kan): dressed rice dish 119
kattē (Kan): perish 187
kattha (Hin): *Acacia catechu* heartwood extract 48
kattōgara (Kan): dressed rice dish 93, 118, 121
kauki (Hin): *Manilkara kauki* 36
kaula (S): wine from *Ziziphus* fruit 59, 109
kaumudi (Guj): a rice dish 135
kavachandi (S): fried mutton 90
kavali (Kan): iron griddle 118
kaval-prasād (Hin): Sikh sacred food 73
kayur (Mun): *Eleusine coracana* 7
kazhi (T): salt bed 114
kedgeree (phonetic): Anglicization of khichdi (q.v.) 178
kedli (Indonesia): steamed rice-pulse patty 126
kedmutgar (phonetic): table-boy 176
kēlvaragu (T): (red) rāgi 46
kenāf (Afr): *Hibiscus cannabinus* 202
kenchu (Kan): baking tile 102
kēnē (Kan): cream 97
kesar (Hin): stamens of *Crocus sativus* 116, 155
kēsara (S): stamens of *Crocus sativus* 215
kēsari (Hin): *Lathyrus sativus* 43
kēsari-bāth (Hin): confection of wheat grits flavoured with kēsar (q.v.) 120, 122, 140
kevar (Mun): *Eleusine coracana* 7
khada (S): leafy soup 83
khada (S): spiced curd-based dish 86
khadga (S): rhinoceros 55
khadi (Hin): fried pulse balls in a spiced curd base 86, 134, 135
khadira (S): *Acacia catechu* 101, 213
khāja (Hin): sweet fried rusk 91, 132, 134, 140, 141
khājakka (S): sweet fried rusk 91
khajūr (Per): sweet crisp bread 76
khajūr (Hin): date-shaped sweet 138, 141
khajūra (S): the date 35
khajūrāsava (S): date wine 59
khakas (S): poppy capsule and seed 171
khākra (Guj): thin baked wheat circlet 134, 171
khākri (S): *Cucumis melo* var. utilissimus 188
khalada (Raj): a papad (q.v.) 140
khalakula (S): *Dolichos uniflorus* 31, 189 189
khali (Hin): solid residues from crushing an oilseed 111, 113
khalli (Hin): solid residues from crushing sugarcane or an oilseed 113
khalva (S): *Lens culinaris* 31
khaman (Guj): steamed pulse dish 136
khamar (Ara): to cover up 76
khamē-ālu (Hin): *Dioscorea alata* 199
khand (S): sugar candy 11, 37, 113, 135, 217
khanda (Ben): round milk sweet 132
khanda (S): section of a literary work 32
khanda-mandigē (Kan): stuffed wheat circlet 118
khandakari (Kan): samovar 107
khandika (S): green peas 193
khandsāri (Hin): raw sugar 217
khāndu (Ben): round milk sweet 132
khāndvi (Guj, Raj): a pulse pancake 134, 135, 140
khara (S): sugar syrup 94
kharbūza (Hin): musk melon 202
kharpava (S): griddle 107
khaskhas (Hin): poppy capsule and seeds 171
khāsi (Hin): *Citrus reticulata* 210
khasta (Hin): type of bread 138
khatīb (Urd): orator 156
khattee (Ara): grain storage pit 157
kheechara (Guj): steamed papad (q.v.) 134

kunjshakka (Ara): the sparrow 157
kuplū (S): clay oven 104
kuppu-keerai (T): *Amaranthus viridis* 187
kupra (Mun): *Eleusine coracana* 7
kūr (Guj): boiled rice 134
kura (Tel): mixed vegetable dish 122
kurakan (Mun): *Eleusine coracana* 7
kurchikā (S): milk solids 35, 134
kurfi (S): knife 156
kurinji (T): mountainous land 45
kurma (S): the tortoise 263
kusāmra (S): unidentified oil-bearing material 37, 83
kusara (S): perhaps the sugarcane 113, 216
kushmānda (S): *Benincasa hispida* 203
kusuma (Hin): the safflower 197
kusuma (Kan): a dish of mixed ingredients 118
kusumbha (S): the safflower 31, 36, 197
kutuh (S): leather storage bottle 105
kutup (S): leather storage bottle 105
kuuviyar (T): vendor of snacks 108
kuzhal-āppam (Mal): baked rice snack 102
kuzhi-āppam (Mal): baked rice snack 102
kvāthanam (S): parboiling 101

labanga-latika (Ben): a sugar-glazed confection 132
laddu (Hin): fried globules of ground pulses, or sesame seeds, or rava (q.v.) moulded into balls with sugar or jaggery syrup 68, 80, 89, 97, 129, 133, 134, 135, 140
laddugē (Kan): the laddu (q.v.) 120, 121
ladduka (S): the laddu (q.v.) 36, 91
laimun (Per): a sour fruit 151
lājāh (S): parched rice 33, 67
lākh (Hin): large *Lathyrus sativus* 192
lākhori (Hin): small *Lathyrus sativus* 189
lakucha (S): *Artocarpus lakucha* 206
lakuda (S): *Artocarpus lakucha* 206
lakshmanphal (Hin): *Annona cherimola* 235
lālā (Hin): trade functionary 167
lāl-ambadi (Hin): *Hibiscus sabdariffa* 202
lāl-kumra (Hin): *Cucurbita maxima* 203
lāl-mohan (Ben): confection in sugar syrup 132
lāphā (Ass): a vegetable 133
lāpsi (Hin): wheat flour halwa 140
lāpsika (S): perhaps a dish of mixed cereal flours 140
lasora (Hin): *Cordia sebestana* 36
lāsuna (S): garlic 78, 213
latakastūrika (S): *Abelmoschus moschatus* 202
lāvali (S): *Annona reticulata* 238
Lavaṇadhyāksha (S): Superintendent of Salt 114
lavanga (S): clove 215
lavanga (S): cinnamon tree 215
lāvangē (Kan): perhaps a wheat dish 119
lawā (Hin): parched maize 140
lazizan (Per): a rich rice-pulse dish 159
lēdi-keni (Ben): a sweet confection 132
lēhya (S): a food to be licked 64
lēhyapāka (S): boiled-down milk 94
lella (phonetic): lālā, trade functionary 167
likya (S): peppercorn 195
limetta (Ita): *Citrus karna* 211
litchi (Chi): *Nephelium litchi* 218, 225
litti (S): baked cakes 140
lobhya (S): alluring 188
lobos (Gre): a projection 188
lōbia (Hin): *Vigna unguiculata* 34, 184, 188, 192
loquat (Chi): *Eriobotrya japonica* 167
lōta (Hin): waisted metal vessel 103
lote (Hin): *Ziziphus* spp. 152
lucchahi (Guj): deep-fried wheat circlet 92
lucchi (Ben): deep-fried flour circlet 130, 138
lumia (Hin): *Citrus karna* 211

mā (T): mango 10
macaco (Por): monkey face 169
macchar-jhol (Ben): liquid fish curry 128, 129
madakangalu (Kan): milk-based dish 119
mādala (Kan): *Citrus medica* 118
madanamast (S): slices of tubers of *Amorphallus campanulatus* 198
madanaphala (S): *Minusops elengi* 85, 109
madhu (S): honey, sweet 9
madhuchhista (S): literally honey-residue, viz., bees-wax 114
madhugōlaka (S): fig-shaped confection 38
madhuka (S): *Madhuca indica* 35, 37, 109, 148, 205
madhukrōda (S): sweet confections 85
madhulika (S): variety of wheat 82
madhumada (Ass): a sweet confection 133
madhumestaka (S): sweet confections 88
madhunālā (Kan): tubular sweet confection 97, 121
madhuparka (S): honey-based ritual nectar 64, 65, 66, 67
madhusarika (S): sweet cake 39
madhushirsaka (S): sweet confections 85
madhvāluka (S): *Ipomoea batata* 199
madhyama (S): sugar syrup 94
madhyavarga (Ben): liquors as a class 61
madhya (Ben): any strong liquor 59
madīrā (S): high-quality wine 59
madugu (S): perhaps *Majorana hortensis* 35
magaz (Guj): a wheat dish 135
Māgh (Ben): January-February 130
magna (Guj): *Vigna radiata* 135
mahāja (S): a large goat 53
mahāghrta (Ben): century-old ghee 84

mattar (Hin): green peas 31, 34, 110, 192
matthi-meen (Kod): sardine 123
mātulunga (Kan): *Citrus indica* 97, 211
maulsari (Hin): *Mimusops elengi* 109
meda (S): animal fat, tallow 83
meddhu-vada (Kan): deep-fried pulse snack 127
medhaka (S): rice wine 59, 109
medon (phonetic): maidān, open grassy land 170
meen (T): fish 10, 49, 123
meenam (S): fish 11
meenavar (T): fishermen 43, 49
meen-patticchadu (Mal): fish preparation 124
meen-vevicchadu (Mal): fish preparation 124
meet (Hin): *Cyperus rotundus* 152
meki (Hin): *Cucumis melo* var. agrestis 202
meksana (S): square wooden scraper 104
melōgara (Kan): vegetable savouries 120
mensinkāyi (Kan): chilli 227
mesashringi (S): *Gymnema sylvestre* 37, 109
mesta (Spa): *Hibiscus cannabinus* 202
methauri (Hin): deep-fried pulse savoury 140
mēthi (Hin): fenugreek 33, 134, 136, 137
mēthika (S): fenugreek 200, 215
mēva (S): mixed fruit drink 69
mēwa (phonetic): mahua (q.v.) 170
milagāi (T): chilli 227
milagu (T): pepper 10, 227
milagu-kāyi (T): chilli 227
mirchi (Hin): green chilli 10, 135
mirchi-ka-sālan (Urd): dish of chillis 123
mirchi-ni-vadā (Guj): spiced deep-fried pulse snack 135
miri (Guj): pepper 135
miriyam (S): pepper 10
mishāni (Kas): all-lamb dinner 137
mishti-doi (Ben): sweet curd 129
missi-roṭi (Hin): spiced bread 138
missita (S): perhaps puffed rice 110
misti (Ben): sweets 132
mittai (Hin): sweets 132
mītt-ālu (Hin): *Ipomoea batatas* 199
mītta-nimu (Hin): *Citrus limettoides* 210
mītta-thēl (Hin): sesame oil 193
mleccha (S): barbarian 26, 34, 214
ṁlu (Mun): betel leaf 48
mochā (S): banana 83, 148, 165
mōdagam (T): stuffed confection 46, 108
mōdak (Hin): stuffed confection 46, 132
mōdaka (S): stuffed confection 38, 69, 77, 91, 97
mogri (Guj): vegetable dish 135
mohall (phonetic): mahal, palace 170
moilē (phonetic): curried dish 137
moira (Ben): sweetmeat maker 133
Moitra (Ben): a Bengali surname 132
moley (phonetic): a liquid curry 178
moolee-ka-sāg (Hin): dish of radish leaves 83
mor (S): abode 137
mora (S): peacock 39, 91
morabba (Urd): sweet fruit preserve 76
moranda (S): egg-shaped sweets 92
morata (S): *Alangium salviifolium* 109
morendaka (S): egg-shaped sweets 38, 91
mōrkozhambu (T): curd-based vegetable dish 122
mosambi (Hin): *Citrus sinensis* 210, 211
motia (Guj): deep-fried pulse snack 135
motichūr (Hin): a laddu (q.v.) with fine grains 121, 133, 140
mouchak (Ben): beehive-shaped sweet 132
mougri (Hin): rat-tailed radish 200
mrdu (S): sugar syrup 94
mrdvika (S): the grape 212
mucchalā (Kan): a lid 118
mudga (S): *Vigna radiata* 7, 33, 70, 82, 137, 140, 188
mudhira (T): *Dolichos uniflorus* 46
mukta (S): pearl 11
mūla (S): roots 62
mūla (Guj): a vegetable dish 135
mulaka (S): radish 133, 200
mulāli (S): *Trapa natans,* var. bispinosa 35
mūlam (T): a gourd 47
mullai (T): forest tracts 45, 46
mulligatawny (phonetic): pepper-water, a soup 178
mullu-keerai (T): *Amaranthus spinosus* 187
mumra (Guj): sweet-stuffed wheat item 134
mundiri (T): cashewnut 222
mung (Hin): *Vigna radiata* 17, 42, 43, 83, 89, 110, 118, 120, 134, 135, 137, 140, 187, 188
mungilarisi (T): bamboo grains 45
mungra (Hin): rat-tailed radish 200
munnai (T): *Meyna laxiflora* 47
munnīr (T): a three-component drink 49, 110
murg-massālam (Per): spiced chicken dish 156
murmura (Hin): puffed rice 89
murmura (S): sweet wheat confection 91
murram (T): winnowing pan 106
murrul (T): plate 106
murukku (T): rice-based crisp relish 120
musa (S): banana 165
musāla (S): wooden pestle 101, 105
musamman (per): spiced meat dish 159
mushk (Ara): musk 76
musthaka (S): *Cyperus rotundus* 152
mut (S): to pound 12
muthiyas (Guj): flour-vegetable rolls 136
muthu (T): pear 10
muttai (T): ladle 105

pāī (T): mat 106
pajji (Kan): ground relish 122
pāk (S): type of sweet confection 121, 124
pāk (T): betel quid 48
pakku-vadā (Guj): a pakōda (q.v.) 124
pakōda (Hin): deep-fried batter-coated snack 124, 140
palā (S): a weight 55, 195
pala (S): perhaps the sesame 36
pala (phonetic) a tree 145
pālada-prathamān (Mal): milk-rice confection 125
pālai (T): desert land 45
pālak (Hin): spinach 200
pālaka (S): spinach 36
palāla (S): sesame-jaggery confection 37
palandu (S): onion 214
pālang (Hin): bed 48
pālanga (S): spinach 133
pālankya (S): spinach 36, 200
palāo (Per, S): meat-rice dish 11, 54, 76, 98, 122, 134, 136, 137, 154, 156, 157, 158, 215
palāsh (Hin): *Butea monosperma* 63
palāsha (S): *Butea monosperma* 35
palepuntz (phonetic): a five-component drink 177
palev (Guj): palao (q.v.) 135
palevat (Hin): kind of apple 83
pālidhya (Kan): curd-based relish 93, 97, 119, 120, 121, 122
pallao-mevach (S): serving of palāo (q.v.) 54
palmer, palmeira (phonetic): the palmyra (q.v.) palm 50, 170, 178
palmyra (Por): *Borassus flabellifer* 214
pālundē (Kan): milk-based confection 119
palva (S): winnowing basket 105
paṇa (S): coin 195
pāna (S): fruit drink 85
pānabhūmi (S): drinking area 58
pāṇaka (S): a spiced fruit drink 68, 85
pānapāka (S): boiled-down milk 94
panasa (S): jackfruit 8, 35, 148
paṇavai (T): loft 106
pānch (Hin): five 178
pancha (S): five 178
panchabhōjaniyas (S): wet or soft foods 64
panchagavya (S): concoction of five cow-derived products 64, 65, 66
panchkhādaniyas (S): hard or solid foods 64
panchamrita, panchamruta (S): ceremonial confection 65, 69, 86
panchanam (S): cooking in water 101
panchānga (S): astrological chart 96
panchashāli (S): rice dish 135
panchasevapanaka (S): spiced barley water 86
panchasugandhika-tāmbula (S): flavoured betel quid 91
panchphoron (Ben): five-component spice mixture 130
paneer (Hin): precipitated pressed milk solids 119, 129
pāṇi (Mal): thickened palmyra juice 124
paniara (Mal): banana fritters 175
panis-panē-melior (Latin): superior bread 173
panivaragu (T): *Setaria italica* 42, 186
pankti (S): ten 15
panra (S): a leaf 48
pāntua (Ben): a confection 132
pāo (Hin): type of bread 139
pāpa (S. Am): potato 226
pāpa (S. Am): papaya 176
pāpa (Mal): jackfruit 175
pāpad (Hin): crisp wafers 27, 83, 92, 110, 140
pāpadi (Guj): vegetable dish 118, 134, 135
pāpdi, papri (Hin): crisp wheat wafers 90, 135, 140
papeeta (S. Am): papaya 223
pappu (Tel): pulse 122
paraka (S): a fast 151
parakki-naan (Per): type of naan (q.v.) 24
paramana (Kan): rice-milk confection 119, 120
paramānna (S): ritual rice-milk confection 67
paran (T): loft 106
paranki-āndi (Mal): cashewnut 222
paranki-māvu (Mal): cashewnut 222
parāta (Hin): pan-fried wheat circlet 38, 119, 134, 138
pāravata (S): kind of apple 83
pariah (Hin): outcast 175
pārika (S): batter-coated deep-fried snack 90
pariplava (S): spoon 104
pariplupātra (S): a ladle 104
parishasa (S): tongs 104
parishrāvana (S): water-strainer 70
parisrūta (S): drink of fermented flowers 59, 109
parisuka-māmsam (S): roasted dried meat 54
parmal (Hin): parched grains 140
parna (S): leaf 10
parpata (S): crisp wafers, pāpad (q.v.) 34, 83
parshva (S): stirrer-spoon 104
parūsaka (S): *Grewia subinaequalis* 36, 86, 205
parva (S): book 33
parvan (S): new or full moon days 128
parwal (Hin): *Trichosanthes dioica* 83, 87, 128, 129, 131
pata (Ben): kind of moss 113
pātala (S): *Stereospermum sauveolens* 87, 109
patāni (T): peas 192
patec-bādām (Hin): nut of *Terminalia catappa* 222
patha (Hin): green vegetable 199
pathua (Ben): *Corchorus capsularis* 199

pātia (Guj): baked fish preparation 75
pat-nimbu (Hin): *Citrus limon* 210
patōl (Hin): wild apple, *Malus baccata* 213
patōl (Hin): *Trichosanthes dioica* 128, 129
patōla (Mun): *Trichosanthes dioica* 7
patolli (S. Ame): game of dice 263
pattadai (T): stand for pots 105
pattal (Hin): leaf plate 139
patthu (T): ten 15
patra (S): leaves 62, 136
patra (Guj): fish baked in a leaf 75
pātra (S): bowl or vessel 103, 104
pātra (S): begging bowl 70
patrakā (S): perhaps *Cinnamomum tamala* 147
patravali (S): leaf plate or cup 105
patrikā (S): pile of wheat circlets 96
paundraka (S): sugarcane of Bengal 85, 113, 216
Paurnamāsi (S): an auspicious full moon day 68
pauttika (S): kind of honey 114
pavitra (S): pure 85
pavitra (S): strainer 104
pāyas (S): milk-rice confection 79
pāyasa (Kan): milk-rice confection 39, 97, 119, 121, 122, 125, 133
pāyasam (T): milk-rice confection 68, 119, 120, 125
pāyasarpis (S): ghee from fresh milk butter 102
pāyasya (S): sweet from curd solids 35
pāyesh (Ben): milk-rice confection 129, 130, 133
pāyovarga (S): milk products 61
peally (phonetic, Hin): cup 170
peepal (Hin): *Ficus religiosa* 83
peperi (Gre): pepper 11
pērana-hūrigē (Kan): stuffed wheat circlet 118
perugu (T): cream 47, 103
perumavalli-kizhangu (T): *Dioscorea alata* 199
peshanī (S): pair of grinding stones 105
pesarattu (Tel): fried mixed-pulse snack 90
pesaru (Tel): *Vigna radiata* (12)
pēthā (Hin): candied gourd 141, 203
pēti-pāo (Hin): crusty box-like bread 139
peya (S): drinks 64
peyara (phonetic): the guava 128
phalā (S): non-cultivated grains 65
phalā (S): fruit 61, 62, 67, 82
phalāhar (S): phala (q.v.) prepared for eating 65
Phālgun (ben): February-March 128, 130
phālsa (Hin): *Grewia subinaequalis* 36, 39, 86, 205
phānita (S): molasses 37, 109
phānita (S): buttermilk relish 91
phānita-shāli (S): molasses pot 105
phanta (S): butter from fresh milk 102
phara (Hin): steamed rice balls 140
phaya (Hin): *Prunus cerasoides* 212
phefras (Hin): type of bread 138
phenaka (S): vermicelli 91, 97, 134
pheni (Hin): vermicelli 89, 93, 120, 121, 134, 135, 141
phirni (Hin): vermicelli 76, 162
phoron (Ben): whole spice seasoning 140
phulaura (Hin): fried pulse patty in curds 140
phulauri (Hin): steamed roll 11
phulka (Hin): dry, puffed wheat circlet 138
phunt (Hin): *Cucumis melo* var. momordica 202
pilāu (Ara): meat-rice dish 11, 130
pilāv (Per): meat-rice dish 11
pīlī-shāli (Hin): white radish 135
pilkhan (Hin): *Ficus lucescens* 149
pīlu (S): nutrition 55
pīlu (Hin): *Salvadora* species 36
pinda (Hin): ball-type confection 121
pindāluka (S): perhaps the sweet potato 36
pindavāsa (S): perfumed drinking water 94
pinnanthāppam (Mal): egg-white sweet confection 124
pinvana (S): pair of milk vessels 104
pipaliya (Guj): cereal dish 135
pippala (S): *Ficus religiosa* 149
pippali (S): *Piper longum* 11, 31, 37, 82, 85, 214
pippali-mūla (S): root of *Piper longum* 214
pīs (S): to grind 12
pishtha (S): ground, shaped meat 54
pishthaka (S): ground rice cakes 34
pishthaudana (S): rice-mince meat dish 54
pishthak (Ben): a confection 132
piska (Mun): a tuber 7
pīstha (Hin): nut of *Pistacia vera* 222
pītaka (Pal): repository 33
pittha (S): one of the three dhātus (q.v.) 77, 82
pitha (Ben): a dessert 133
pitha-ālu (Hin): *Dioscorea bulbifera* 199
pittha (S): boiled pulse flour 140
plāksha (S): *Ficus lucescens* 36, 149
planta (Lat): spreading leaf 208
plantano (Spa): banana 208
podi-patthiri (Mal): rice bread 124
pōli (Hin): sweet stuffed wheat circlet 83, 89
pōlika (S): sweet stuffed wheat circlet 88
pongal (T): a rice-pulse dish 45, 68
poo-balē (Kan): small sweet banana 162
pori (T): puffed rice 45, 110
pori-kari (T): fried spiced meat 49
poruthi-chakka (Mal): pineapple 233
post (Hin): opium drink 171
Pous (Ben): December-January 130
praan (Kas): an onion 83
pracharani (S): large ladle 104

pralēhaka (S): acidic relish 91
prānitapranāyana (S): oblong container 104
prasād (S): food offered to a deity 68, 73
prasādam (T): food offered to a deity 68
prasādjya (S): liquid from curd churning 35, 102
prasaka (S): a decanting vessel 104
prasannā (S): rice wine 59, 109
prastha (S): volume measure 79, 109
pratāpta (S): roasted and basted meat 54
prathaman (Mal): sweet milk confection with fruit or pulses 125
pratima (S): a Jain feast 72
pratipana (S): flavoured beverages 87
pravan (S): devotional 128
pravani (S): frying pan 107
priyangu (S): *Panicum miliaceum* 31, 34, 186
prthuka (S): beaten rice 34
prthvi (S): earth 77
pua (S): sweet confection 33
pucca (Hin): ghee-cooked ritual food 62
pūdē (Kan): fried mixed vegetables 97
pudunel (T): refined rice 45
pūgapatta (S): bark of *Areca catechu* 94
puhādiya (Guj): fried pulse patty 135
puin (Ben): type of spinach 130
pulāo (Per): meat-rice dish 11
pulayar (T): fishermen 44
puḷi (T): tamarind or sour 9
puḷi-inji (T): fried ginger dish 125
puḷi-kari (T): sour meat dish 45
puḷingari (T): spiced meat 49
puḷi-sādam (T): sour rice dish 45
pulisseri (Mal): mango curry 125
puḷiyodarē (Kan): sour rice dish 121
puḷungalarisi (T): parboiled rice 45
pulusu (Tel): pulse preparation 122
punch (phonetic): five-component drink 178
pundarika (Mun, S): lotus flower 7
pungikeerai (T): *Amaranthus hybridus* subsp. *hybridus* 187
pungikeerai (T): *Amaranthus hybridus* subsp. *cruentus* 187
punjistha (S): fowler 9
pụnkā (phonetic): overhead fan of cloth 170
pūpalika (S): omelette 85
pūra (S): granary 12; also town
pūrabhattaka (S): meat-stuffed brinjals 90
pūran (Hin): sweet stuffed wheat confection 135
pūrana (S): sweet stuffed wheat circlets 89
pūrana (S): silver weight 195
purāna (S): work embodying dynastic records 32
puranpōli (S): sweet stuffed wheat confection 135
pūri (Hin): puffed, deep-fried wheat circlet 90, 105, 138, 162
pūrigē (Kan): sweet stuffed wheat circlet 119, 120
purikā (S): pulse flour relish 133
pūrika (S): crisp wheat snack 90
pūri-vilangāyi (Kan): crisp fried relish 96
purnaputa (S): funnel fashioned from a leaf 105
purodāsha (S): sacrificial baked cake 104
puryala (S): sourish meat dish 90
pushakara (S): water lily 200
pushkara-kēshavu (Kan): advanced devotees 122
pushpā (S): flowers 62, 82
pushpavāsa (S): perfumed drinking water 94
puta (S): shell 12
pūtabhrt (S): clay trough 104
putapāka (S): unidentified plant 35, 58
putikā (S): unidentified plant 38
putrika (S): dolls 91
puttika (S): type of bee 114
puttil (T): stone muller 105
puttū (Mal): class of rice-based steamed dishes 122, 123, 124, 125
pyali (Hin): cup 170

qabooli (Urd): rice-pulse dish 123
qāl (Ara): an Indian grain 88
qaliya (Ara): spiced meat dish 159
qashak (Ara): spoon 157
qutab (Ara): meat-wheat dish 159

rabbri (Hin): clotted cream flakes 97, 132
rādhuni (Ben): celery seeds 129, 131
rāga (S): fruit juice 39, 86
rāgā (S): red 7
rāgasādhava (S): thickened mango juice 86
rāghava (S): a fish 133
rāgi (Kan): *Eleusine coracana* 7, 17, 41, 184, 186, 197
rāi (Hin): *Brassica juncea* subsp. *juncea* 36, 85, 91, 135, 139, 194
raibhoj (Guj): a rice dish 135
raitha (Hin): curd-based relish 36, 119, 134, 135
rājādana (S): *Manilkara kauki* 36, 85
rājāh (S): a king 167
rājanna (Guj): rice dish 135
rājanna-akki (Kan): bamboo grains 96
rājannan (T): type of rice 45
rajas (S): excited action 77
rāja-shyamaka (S): *Panicum* grain 186
rājasika (S): an excitable temperament 132
rājika (S): *Brassica juncea* subsp. *juncea* 36, 194
rājikaraddha (S): buttermilk flavoured with mustard seed 91
rājmāh (Hin): *Phaseolus vulgaris* 34, 80, 82, 90, 192
rājmāsha (S): now *Phaseolus vulgaris*, earlier perhaps

sapodilla (Mex): the sapota 223
sappa (S): foot of a tree 12
saptapadi (S): seven steps in a marriage ceremony 67
sāranga (S): deer 55
saravaligeya-pāyasa (Kan): a vermicelli-milk confection 119
sarika (S): sugar syrup 94
sarishaka (S): cowdung 29
sarka (Guj): a soup 136
sarki (Guj): a soup 136
sarpirdhana (S): butter bowl 104
sarpōsh (Kas): metal tray-cover 107
sarshapa (S): *Brassica napus* var. glauca 7, 36, 83, 194
sarson (Hin): *Brassica napus* var. glauca 7, 36, 83, 194
sarson-ka-saag (Hin): leaves of sarson (q.v.) 36
sarvajna (S): omniscient 89
sāsa (S): kitchen knife 105
sata (S): carrier for embers 105
sāthkudi (T): *Citrus sinensis* 210
satina (S): kind of peas 83, 194
sattaka (S): spiced curd 84
sattu (Hin): grits from parched grains 110, 135, 140
sattuvam (T): ladle 105
sāttvika (S): a serene temperament 70, 77, 122
saundhika (S): a distiller 133
saunf (Hin): fennel, *Foeniculum vulgare* 80, 130, 136, 137
sauvarchala (S): type of salt 114
savastika (S): leafy vegetables 36
sāwank (Hin): *Echinochloa colona* 186
sebestan (Hin): *Cordia dichotoma* 205
seekharanē (Kan): fruit pulp relish 97
seer (phonetic) weight measure, sēr (Hin): 115
se-gis-i (Sum): the sesame 193
sem (Hin): *Lablab purpureus* 189
sēmiya (Kan): vermicelli 122
sēnai-kizhangu (T): *Amorphophallus campanulatus* 198
sēppam-kizhangu (T): *Colocasia esculenta* 198
sēv (Hin): deep-fried strands of pulse flour 75, 89, 135, 140
sēvagē (Kan): vermicelli 122
sēvigē-dosai (Kan): shallow-fried pancake of vermicelli 119
sēvika (S): sēv (q.v.) 89
sēviyān (Urd): sweet vermicelli dish 76
shadai (T) a gourd 47
shahakārasura (S): mango wine 59, 109
shāhi-tukda (Urd): bread-based confection 123
shāk (Guj): cooked vegetables 134
shāka (S): vegetables 35, 82
shakara (S): milk solids confection 134
shakarapāka (Hin): milk solids confection 92
shakarkand (Hin): sweet potato 199
shakarpūra (Guj): sweet wheat dish 135
shaki (Ara): jackfruit 152
shākna (S): vegetables 61
shakula (S): a fish, 128
shakuntika (S): vendor of fowl 53
shāl (Hin): *Shorea robusta* 169
shālā (S): *Shorea robusta* 149, 169
shāli (S): fine winter rice 34, 81, 82, 94, 129, 137, 188
shāli-anna (Kan): sweet rice dish 119
shāluka (S): lotus roots 35, 200
shāma (Hin): *Echinochloa frumantacea* 186
shāmagaddē (Kan): *Colocasia esculenta* 198
shāmākh (Ara): *Echinochloa frumantacea* 152
shammi-kabāb (Urd): type of spit-roasted meat 176
shankli (Guj): sesame seed confection 134
sharad (S): mid-September to mid-November 81
shārada (S): autumn rice 185
sharāva (S): sacrificial wooden vessel 104
sharāva (S): volume measure 130
sharbat-i-labgīr (Ara): sweet drink, 157
sharīfā (Urd): *Annona squamosa* 235
sharkara (S): sugar 11, 114, 217
sharkarapāka (S): isolated milk solids 94
sharkari-putrikā (S): sugar dolls 69, 91
shaskuli (S): sweet confection with sesame seed or its oilcake 34, 134
shastika (S): summer rice 81, 82, 185
shastika (S): barley confection 38
shāstra (S): learning; one of the sixty-four arts 88
shatamana (S): silver weight 195
shaubhanjana (S): *Moringa oleifera* 200
shaundika (S): drinking area 58
sheekh-kabāb (Per): roasted meat 76, 136
sheera (Hin): sweet confection of grain grits 135, 140
sheer-birinj (Per): rice-milk confection 158, 162
sheermāl (Hin): type of bread 76, 123, 138, 139
sherbet (Per): a sweet drink 76, 154, 158, 162
shīdhu (S): distilled liquor 59, 109
shikarinī (S): sweet dewatered curds 35, 84, 91, 119, 121, 134
shimbi (S): *Lablab purpureus* 82, 192
shimili (T): rope sling to hold pots 105
shirai (T): a gourd 47
shirīsh (Hin): *Albizia lebbeck* 199
shirka (S): vinegar 86
shirra-agappai (T): spoon 105
shishira (S): mid-January to mid-March 81
shishira-kriya (S): kept cold with ice 115
Shivarāthri (S): festival of Shiva 70
shiwawoon (Ara): roast meat 156
shola (Urd): meat-rice dish 76
shoojan (Guj): barbecued mutton 75
shorfa (Ara): jurist 156

surali-hōligē (Kan): sweet-stuffed wheat confection 121
sūran (Hin): *Amorphophallus campanulatus* 91, 198
sūrana (S): the sūran (q.v.) 36, 198
surkh-biriyāni (Per): meat-rice dish 157
sutari (Hin): *Vigna umbellata* 188
sūtar-pheni (S): vermicelli dish 134
suvarna (S): gold weight 195
svadhiti (S): dissecting knife 105
svānin (S): dog-keepers 9
svastika (S): barley confection 82
svedanam (S): steaming, or steamed food 101, 102
sveta-sarshapa (S): white mustard seed 36
svetasurā (S): a clear, perhaps distilled, liquor 59, 109
svinnabhakshya (S): steamed food 102

tadavu (T): censer 106
tai (Hin): simmering pan 105
tala (Guj): deep-fried pulse-lump 135
taindulu (Mun): *Eleusine coracana* 7
tamāli (S): *Cinnamomum tamala,* tejpat 215
tāmasic (S): an excitable temperament 131
tāmbōl (Per): betel leaf 157
tamidelu (Mun): *Eleusine coracana* 7
tampala (Sin): leafy *Amaranthus* 187
tandoor (Hin): open baking oven 24, 102, 138
tandoori (Hin): food baked in a tandoor (q.v.) 107
tanduliya (Mun): *Amaranthus viridis* 187
tandūram (S): grilling 101
tapsee (Ben): a kind of fish 129
tār (Mun): edible *Dioscorea* tuber 7
taral (Hin): fried vegetable dish 140
tarār (Mun): edible *Dioscorea* tuber 7
tari (Hin): fermented palm exudate 11, 178
tarbuz (Per): water melon 202
tauk (Ben): sour relish 129, 130
teh (Chi): tea 228
tejas (S): fire, a state of matter 77
tejpat (Hin): *Cinnamomum tamala* 215
tendu (Hin): *Diospyros melanoxylon* 35
tempura (Jap): snacks deep-fried in batter 127
teri (T): sand dunes 41
thaduppu (T): ladle 105
thaila (S): oil 8, 36
thaila (S): medicated oil 77
thaila-pēshana-yantra (S): oil press 112
thaila-varga (S): oils as a class 82
thailika (S): oil miller 112
thakra (S): buttermilk 134
thāla (S): palmyra palm 178
thālā (Ben): metal dinner plate 130
thalaka (S): baking trays 105
thālakka (S): palm wine 59, 109
thalanam (S): baking with dry heat 101
thālapatra (S): palmyra palm 205
thālē (Kan): aromatic flower 118
thāli (Hin): round metal dinner plate 103, 105
thaliya (Kan): metal plate 123
thāliya (Guj): spiced pulse lumps 135
thaliya-puttu (Kod): steamed rice slab 123
thallita-kari (T): spiced meat dish 49
thamāsha (Hin): group fun 170
thambālu (Kan): colostrum 119
thambittu (Kan): wheat flour preparation 119
thāmbūla (S): betel leaf 10, 48, 81, 91, 214
thambuli (Kan): curd-based relish 120
thambuttu (Kod): banana dessert 123
thandai (Guj): cooling drink 135
thānpura (Han): Indian string instrument 203
thapaka (S): iron griddle 105
thapika (S): simmering pan 105
thari (Kan): rice grits 123
tharkāri (Hin): vegetables 35
tharkāri (Guj): egg-vegetable dish 75
thati-shāli (Guj): rice dish 135
thattai (T): plate 105
thattai-agappu (T): spoon 105
thattu (T): plate 106
thavā (Hin): metal griddle for roasting circlets of wheat or other cereals 24, 103, 105, 118, 138
thavani (Guj): rice dish 135
thay (phonetic): tea 229, 230
thayir-sādham (T): rice-curd dish 122
thayirum-pazham-pāni (Mal): banana-curd confection 124
thayir-vadai (T): fried pulse patties in curd 127
thayiru (T): curds 47
thēlika (S): oil miller 112
themanam (Guj): fried pulse balls in a curd base 134
thenga-ennāi (T): coconut oil 8
thennai (T): *Setaria italica* 43, 45, 46, 186
thithau (S): sieve 101
thōd (Ben): banana stem pith 130
thogai (T): peacock 11
thogay (Kan): unspiced relish 93
tholoopāvai (T): *Momordica dioica* 204
thōran (Mal): vegetable dish 124, 125
thoppi (T): rice liquor 110
thorai (Hin): a *Luffa* gourd 204
thorai (T): mountain rice 45
thotti (T): ladle 105
thovvē (Kan): bland dhāl dish 122
thudi (Guj): spiced pulse lumps 135
thulasi (S): *Ocimum sanctum* 170, 213
thumbē (Kan): aromatic flower 96
thuraiya (Guj): vegetable dish 135

varan (Guj): pulse dish 134
varga (S): class or kind 32, 82
varselapāka (S): flavoured thickened milk 94
varshā (S): mid-July to mid-September 81
varshika (S): the monsoon 185
varsopālagōlaka (S): sweet rice-flour dainty 91
vārtāka (S): brinjal 7
vartika (S): sweet rice roli 85
varuna (S): *Crataeva nurvala* 199
vārunī (S): distilled liquor 59, 109
vasā (S): animal body fat 83
vasantha (S): mid-March to mid-May 81
vāsaru (Guj): a rice dish 135
vasthuka (S): *Chenopodium album* 83, 133, 200
vasudiya (Guj): cereal dish 135
vatai (T): vadā (q.v.) 10
vataka (S): vadā (q.v.) 10, 34, 37, 68, 90, 97, 134
vātāma (S): almond 83, 212, 222
vatāna (S, Guj): green peas 135
vātāvairi (S): bitter almond 212
vatha (S): wind 77, 94
vati (S): vadi (q.v.) 96, 134
vati (S): toothpick 94
vatigai (T): stone muller 105
vatikā (S): a pill 77
vatikā (S): vadi (q.v.) 90, 96, 134
vatingana (S): brinjal 7
vatya (S): parched barley gruel 34
vatya (S): baked wheat ball 140
vāyavya (S): cylinder for offerings 104
vāyu (S): air, mind 77
vāyuputa-mandigē (Kan): stuffed wheat circlet 118
vāzhana (Mal): kind of leaf 124
vchu (S.Am): chilli 227
vedduvar (T): shepherds or huntsmen 43
vedhami (Guj): sweet, baked, pulse circlet 96, 134
vellai (T): *Cleome viscosa* 47
vellam (T): jaggery 114
velli-āppam (T): rice pancake 123, 125
vendekāyi (T): brinjal 10
vennai (T): butter 8, 47
venuyava (S): bamboo grains 31
vẹr (T): root 9
vēr (T): a gourd 47
veru-ila (Mal): 'simply-a-leaf' 11
vesavāra (S): gound meat for stuffing 54, 85
veshta (S): to surround 96
veshtika (S): sweet stuffed wheat circlet 90, 96, 134
vetr (T): a stem word, meaning only 48
vetrilai (T): 'simply-a-leaf' 48
vetthalai (T): betel leaf 11
vetthilē (T): betel leaf 48
veunti (Mal): *Dioscorea hamiltonii* 199
vibhītaka (S): *Terminalia bellirica* 83
vicchitra-veena (S): stringed instrument 203
vida (S): black salt 37, 85, 86
vīda (S): betel quid 95
vidala (S): cooking 96
vidalapāka (S): dish of five pulses 90, 96
vịdari (S): an *Ipomoea* tuber 197
vikramkata (S): *Flacourtia indica* 204
vilāyati-bādām (Hin): almond 222
villavar (T): bowmen or landed gentry 43
Vināyaka Chathurthi (S): festival of Lord Ganesha 68
vindāloo (Kon): sourish pork curry 136
vīra (S): stalk 12
virūdhaka (S): sprouted grains 82
visa (S): lotus stem 35
vishnaga (S): *Amaranthus viridis* 187
visyanda (S): milk and fried-cereal concoction 97
vitasti (S): small ladle 104
vrata (S): fast 68
vrīhi (S): monsoon rice 34, 82, 178
vrksāmla (S): *Garcinia indica* 205
vrntāka (S): brinjal 7, 201
vrsya-pūpalika (S): large omelette 85
vyanjana (S): beverage of buttermilk and rice water 91

wadi (Kas): spice mixture 137
wadi (Hin): fermented pulse lumps 140
wadian (Hin): wadi (q.v.) 90, 109
warri (Hin): wadi (q.v.) 109
wazwan (Kas): professionally-cooked meal 107

xaocatl (Mex): cocoa 231

yāgu (S): gruel 34
yakhni (Kas): fried lamb 137, 159
yava (S): barley 31, 82, 179, 186, 195
yava (S): a weight 195
yavāgu (S): barley gruel 77
yavaka (S): barley-milk porridge 34
Yavana (S, T): literally Greek, but used for other Europeans 10, 51
yavanala (S): sorghum 186
yavaprakāra (S): sorghum 186
yavasu (S): barley gruel 34
yavodaka (S): barley water 86
yeppatthu (Kan): seventy 187
yettē (Kan): famine 187
yusa (S): thickened fruit juice 86
yusa (S): pulse soup 34, 83

zaffrān (Per): stamens of *Crocus sativus* 215
zakat (Ara): food sharing 76

INDEX OF LATIN NAMES

The English equivalents of Latin names have been denoted by '(E)'. Some Indian names have also been given.

AUTHOR INDEX

The decimal numbers following the authors' names denote the chapter and reference numbers (e.g. 4.11 is chapter 4, reference 11)

GENERAL INDEX

Occasional cross-references are made to the Index of Non-English words, denoted by INEW